Costs & Funding following
Reforms: Questions & Ans\

D0537582

005585

Costs & Funding following the Civil Justice Reforms: Questions & Answers

3rd Edition

SWEET & MAXWELL

Practical Law

First Edition 2015 by Peter Hurst, Simon Middleton and Roger Mallalieu
Second Edition 2016 by Peter Hurst, Simon Middleton and Roger Mallalieu
Third Edition 2017 by Peter Hurst, Simon Middleton and Roger Mallalieu

Published in 2017
by Thomson Reuters (Professional) UK Limited,
trading as Sweet & Maxwell, 5 Canada Square, Canary Wharf, London, E14 5AQ
(Registered in England & Wales, Company No.1679046. Registered Office and address for
service: 5 Canada Square, Canary Wharf, London, E14 5AQ).

For further information on our products and services, visit
www.sweetandmaxwell.co.uk
Printed in Great Britain by CPI Grp Ltd, Croydon
Typeset by Servis Filmsetting, Stockport, SK2 5AJ

No natural forests were destroyed to make this product; only farmed
timber was used and re-planted.

A CIP catalogue record for this book is available from the British Library.

ISBN 978-0-41406-262-7

Contributors

Peter Hurst LLB MPhil FCIArb, General Editor. Peter was the Senior Costs Judge of England & Wales, at the Royal Courts of Justice, from 1992 to 2014. During a judicial career which has spanned thirty years, he was also Judicial Taxing Officer of the House of Lords from 2002 to 2009 and of the United Kingdom Supreme Court from 2009 to 2014 and also of the Judicial Committee of the Privy Council from 2002 to 2014. He sat not only as a costs judge in the SCCO but also as a recorder in civil and criminal matters, including costs appeals from District Judges. He sat as an assessor with High Court Judges dealing with numerous costs appeals. He was invited to sit with the Court of Appeal as an assessor when that Court was dealing with difficult or complex costs appeals. He joined 39 Essex Chambers as a door tenant in December 2014.

He is the author of *Civil Costs* (Sweet & Maxwell Litigation Library), now in its fifth edition, and *Criminal Costs* (OUP). He was, until retirement, a member of the Senior Editorial Board of *Civil Procedure* (the *White Book*, Sweet & Maxwell) as well as being an editor contributing the commentary on all the costs rules and practice directions. He is now an advisory editor of the *White Book*.

Simon Middleton was appointed a District Judge in 2004 and a Regional Costs Judge at the inception of the scheme in 2005. He has sat in both the Midlands and the Western regions. Before his appointment he was a solicitor with Higher Court (Civil Advocacy) qualification.

Simon was a member of the Judicial College tutor team for six years. In that capacity he was a member of the team charged with delivering education on the April 2013 reforms. He is currently one of the Course Directors appointed for civil education. In that role he is responsible for, amongst other things, the current training on case and costs management.

Simon has written and lectured extensively on the subject of costs and case and costs management.

Roger Mallalieu is a barrister at 4 New Square specialising in matters relating to costs, litigation funding and civil procedure. He routinely ranks as one of the leading juniors in the field of costs law of all types and has appeared in a considerable number of the leading cases in the area. He is regularly instructed on important test issues and appears regularly in the Court of Appeal and other higher courts on such matters.

Publisher's Note

Costs & Funding following the Civil Justice Reforms: Questions & Answers is a unique book. Produced in conjunction with **Practical Law**, it tackles common practitioner questions on the effects of the 2013 Jackson reforms on costs and funding. The authors answer questions on topics ranging from funding of litigation, case and costs management and proportionality to settlement offers, QOCS and summary assessment. As well as updating the existing questions and answers, the third edition adds a significant number of new questions and answers, and much of the commentary is revised in light of new and ongoing case law and legislation in the fast-evolving costs and funding landscape post-Jackson.

Subscribers to the *White Book Service* 2017 will receive this book gratis as part of their subscription. It is up-to-date to 17 February, 2017. The authors have had sight of the Civil Procedure (Amendment) Rules 2017 (SI 2017/95) and the CPR 88th Update, the provisions of which come into force generally by 6 April 2017 but at the time of press the corresponding court form amendments had not been published. In addition, please note that two first instance decisions of importance were being appealed at the time of going to press: *Merrix v Heart of England NHS Foundation Trust* (QBD (Birmingham)) (DJ Lumb 13 October 2016), and *May v Wavell Group plc* [2016] EWHC (B16) Costs.

This book would not have been possible without the time, help and expertise of Peter Hurst, Simon Middleton and Roger Mallalieu. The publisher wishes to thank them for the impressive speed with which they wrote, updated and edited the book. This project was the result of collaboration between the Dispute Resolution team at Practical Law and the author team; it would not have got off the ground without either of them.

We welcome any feedback—please email *whitebook@sweetandmaxwell.co.uk*

Contents

		Page
Chapter 1	**Introduction** *Peter Hurst*	1
Chapter 2	**Funding Litigation** *Roger Mallalieu*	000
Chapter 3	**Proportionality** *Simon Middleton*	000
Chapter 4	**Case and Costs Management** *Simon Middleton*	000
Chapter 5	**Part 36 and Other Settlement Offers including ADR and Costs Consequences** *Peter Hurst*	000
Chapter 6	**Qualified One-Way Costs Shifting** *Roger Mallalieu*	000
Chapter 7	**Fixed Costs; Indemnity Costs; Litigants in Person** *Peter Hurst*	000
Chapter 8	**Assessments of Costs and Payment on Account of Costs** *Simon Middleton*	000
Chapter 9	**The Effect of the Jackson Civil Justice Reforms on Solicitor-Client Costs** *Roger Mallalieu*	000

List of Questions

Page

Chapter 1 **Introduction**

Chapter 2 **Funding Litigation**

A. Transfer and variation of funding
Q1. Is it possible to assign pre LASPO Conditional Fee Agreement
and to retain between the parties recoverability of success fees?   31
Q2. What is the effect on recoverability of the success fee of
assigning a pre-April 2013 CFA post-April 2013?   32
Q3. Do you think the exceptional circumstances which applied
in *Jenkins v Young Brothers Transport* to allow the assignment of a
CFA might apply in the following circumstances: One part of an
LLP was trading under the name of SS until the LLP demerged, at
which point the SS business and trading name was transferred to
SL Ltd. The LLP continued to trade as a separate entity, but the
SRA has treated SL Ltd as a successor practice rather than a new
practice. Can we or should we:
  • Enter into new CFAs with all our clients (in which case how
    will costs incurred prior to the transfer be dealt with and, in
    particular, what will happen to any recoverable success fees
    under pre-April 2013 CFAs)?
  • Novate or assign the existing CFAs?
  • Rely on having told our clients of the change of legal entity?   33
Q4. My client instructed me prior to 1 April 2013, but I was not able
to offer a CFA until later. Is it possible to backdate the CFA to the
date of first instruction?   33
Q5. Can you amend a CFA in advance of detailed assessment? If so,
what is the risk of doing so?   34
Q6. Is it possible to vary a pre-April 2013 CFA and still recover the
success fee?   34
Q7. In a number of recent cases a claimant moved from legal aid
funding to a pre-Jackson conditional fee agreement, the court has
disallowed the recovery of success fees and additional liabilities
where in principle they were recoverable, but allowed other costs
to be recovered. The result seems fair enough, but on what legal
basis did the court specifically disallow some costs but not others?
Wasn't the CFA either valid or invalid?   35

Q8. In the light of the *Surrey* appeal decision, do you think challenges by paying parties to additional liabilities in cases where there has been a change of funding are likely to increase or are they going away? 36

Q9. Is a pre-April 2013 ATE policy premium still recoverable if the policy holder changes solicitors post–April 2013? Should the policy be 'assigned' to the new firm? 37

B. Conditional Fee Agreement terms

Q10. Do you need to name all defendants in a CFA? 37

Q11. My client entered into a CFA prior to 1 April 2013, but has now died. I wish to offer the personal representatives a CFA to continue the claim. Will I be able to recover the success fee? 38

Q12. We wish to enter into a CFA with our client whereby in addition to the success fee being capped as required by s.58 of the Courts & Legal Services Act 1990 and the CFA Order 2013, the total costs payable under the agreement will also be capped as a percentage of the damages. We have been told that this means our agreement is a contingency fee agreement, or DBA, and must comply with the DBA Regulations 2013. Is this correct? 38

C. After the Event Insurance

Q13. If a staged premium ATE policy was incepted prior to 1 April 2013, but the further staged premiums are only incurred after that date, will the further premiums be recoverable? 39

Q14. Would an increased premium on a pre-1 April 2013 ATE policy be payable by a losing defendant? I.e. is the increased premium payable or only the original premium amount? 39

Q15. In a clinical negligence case, where a claimant obtains a breach and causation report and the defendant then admits liability, could the claimant recover the cost of the premium if it then obtained ATE insurance in relation to obtaining a quantum report? 40

Q16. We act for two claimants, one of whom is insolvent. We have entered into an ATE policy and are planning to rely on the insolvency exemption to LASPO 2012 if we are successful, so that we can recover the ATE premium from the defendant. Will the fact that only one of the claimants is insolvent prevent us from relying on the insolvency exemption to LASPO 2012? If we are allowed to recover the ATE premium from the defendant, will it be reduced to 50% to reflect the fact that only one of the claimants is insolvent? 40

Q17. If a claimant with a pre-1 April 2013 ATE insurance policy is successful at first instance, an appeal is granted and a top-up of the ATE premium (after 1 April 2013) is required to cover the appeal, is the post-1 April 2013 ATE top-up premium recoverable from the other side if the appeal is successful? 41

D. Issue and notification

Q18. Our client entered into a CFA and ATE insurance policy before April 2013 in relation to insolvency proceedings. Since then, another party has been added as a party to the CFA and ATE insurance policy. Are we required to notify the defendants of this variation to the CFA and ATE insurance? If so, how do we notify them and do we need to file the notice? 41

Q19. Is there a long stop date whereby a party who has entered into a pre-April 2013 funding arrangement in relation to a claim must issue proceedings? 42

Q20. Is a notice of funding required for a Damages Based Agreement? 42

Q21. We are acting for the claimant in a litigation matter. The defendant's solicitors have asked us to confirm how the litigation is being funded. Is there any obligation on our client to provide this information? 42

Q22. Where a claimant entered into a CFA prior to 1 April 2013 and provided written notice (a letter) to the defendant of such CFA, but then failed to file/serve form N251 upon issue of the Claim, what are the consequences? 43

Q23. Where a CFA in one of the excepted cases (where the success fee is still recoverable) is entered into and the proceedings are issued on the same day but only served four months later and we realise that we haven't served a Notice of Funding some weeks after service, what advice would you give? For example, should a formal application seeking relief be made? 44

Q24. Is a claimant entitled to recover the success fee under his "pre-1 April 2013" CFA from the defendant, where the claim was only commenced and the funding was only notified after 1 April 2013? Please explain why the amendment to s.58A(6) does not apply to CFAs entered into prior to 1 April 2013, in circumstances where the funding is notified after 1 April 2013? 45

Q25. In the excepted cases, where a success fee is still recoverable:
- Do you have to provide a notice of funding when issuing proceedings, even if it will be allocated to the small claims track?
- What date do you give in the N251 Notice of Funding when the matter is funded by a CCFA. Is it the date of the CCFA with the insurer or the date of the subsequent signed retainer with the insured client? 45

Q26. Where two CFAs (one with solicitor and one with counsel) were entered into pre-1 April 2013 and notice of funding was only served in relation to the first one (solicitor) is that ok because Costs Practice Direction para.19.3(2)(a) says further notification is not required where notice has already been given that the party has entered into a CFA with a legal representative and during the currency of that agreement either of them enters into another such agreement with an additional legal representative? Will the success fee on the second CFA still be recoverable?   45

E. Third Party Funding
Q27. Are parties required to notify an opponent that they are being funded by a third party litigation funder?   46

Q28. When third party funding is used in an arbitration, under what circumstances could costs be awarded against third party funders and how could the tribunal cost orders against the funders be made enforceable against the funders (given that funders are not a party to the arbitration).   46

F. Conditional Fee Agreements and Success Fees
Q29. How should the success fee be calculated in a post-April 2013 CFA?   47

Q30. A CFA was entered pre-April 2013 and therefore falls under the old rules. An interim hearing was won by the applicant and the applicant would therefore like to apply for a detailed cost assessment against the losing party for their costs in the application. However, the success in the interim hearing, has not triggered 'success' under the terms of the CFA (and the CFA itself does not include a clause relating to interim hearings). Could you advise whether it is therefore possible to still seek base costs from the losing party (not the additional liability) or whether this would fall foul of the indemnity principle? Research so far points to CPR r.32.3 which states that if a party is seeking detailed assessment without any additional liability they do not need to provide information about CFAs etc.   48

Q31. If the solicitor has entered into a pre-April 2013 CFA, but counsel's CFA with the solicitor postdates April 2013, is counsel's success fee -recoverable between the parties?   49

Q32. What is the effect on the success fee where a CFA relating to a group claim was entered into before 1 April 2013, but some of the claimants were added after that date?   49

Q33. We have an insolvency case on a CFA with a success fee and have ATE insurance in place. We have not yet issued. Now that the Government has removed the exemption from LASPO for insolvency related cases, presumably the success fee and premium will still be recoverable from the other side if the claim is successful even though we hadn't issued before the exemption was removed?   50

Q34. I understand that for an ATE insurance premium to be recoverable from the other side in insolvency proceedings it must have been put in place before 6 April 2016. Is it also necessary to have given notice of funding to the other side before 6 April 2016?   50

Q35. We note that insolvency proceedings were excluded from ss.44 and 46 of LASPO 2012 where proceedings in England and Wales were brought by:

- A person acting in the capacity of a liquidator of a company in -creditors' voluntary liquidation (CVL) or compulsory liquidation; a trustee in bankruptcy; or an administrator.
- A company that is in: CVL; compulsory liquidation; or administration.

What is the situation if you acted for an insolvency practitioner outside the jurisdiction (the insolvent company also being outside the jurisdiction) who brought a claim in England and Wales against a company based in England and Wales for monies owed? If you entered into a CFA with the client in these circumstances, would the success fee be recoverable from the other side if your client is successful?   51

Q36. What are the rules on recoverability of success fees in a defamation matter and, assuming that recoverability is allowed, does the success fee have to be capped in any way?   51

Q37. Given that success fees in CFAs entered into from 1 April 2013 are not recoverable in English civil litigation (apart from in the excepted cases), are they recoverable in arbitrations? Nothing in the Arbitration Act or LCIA Rules appears to preclude an arbitrator awarding a success fee under a CFA.   51

Q38. What is the current position with regard to the question of whether the recoverability of pre-April 2013 additional liabilities is compatible with the European Convention on Human Rights?   52

G. Damages Based Agreements

Q39. What exactly is a hybrid DBA, and what is the difference between a concurrent hybrid DBA and a sequential hybrid DBA?   52

Q40. We have a client for whom we currently act on a pre-April 2013 hybrid-CFA in ongoing litigation. Our client's circumstances have changed and he has asked whether we would be willing to change our funding arrangement with him to a Damages Based Agreement. Is there any guidance on whether this is possible and, if so, what the implications would be? (As DBA's do not currently allow the solicitor to charge anything until the client receives a financial benefit, would we have to repay any fees he has paid under the hybrid-CFA?)   53

Q41. What is the authority or rule which specifies that if a DBA in a non-employment matter does not comply with the Damages-Based Agreements Regulations 2013, it will not be enforceable?   54

Q42. Under the DBA Regulations 2013, a party can recover costs from the other side based on normal costs recovery principles, but subject to the indemnity principle. Given then that the lawyer may not be entitled to any costs until actual recoveries are made at the end of a case, does this not cause a problem with seeking costs from the other side at interim hearings as the case progresses? Appropriate drafting of the DBA might seek to get around this but it would seem that such drafting would be a highly complex task with various pitfalls. For example, if the DBA provided that sums would immediately become due to the solicitor as and when costs are recovered from the other side, are those costs considered part of the ultimate recovery from the client and to be deducted and as a kind of payment on account, or would the solicitor be entitled to those costs plus the agreed success percentage? Wouldn't that breach the DBA Regulations?   55

H. Consumer Regulations
Q43. Do the doorstep selling regulations, which aim to protect consumers when they sign contracts in certain circumstances, apply to CFAs? If so, in what kind of circumstances would they apply?   55

I. Proportionality
Q44. Given that the pre-April 2013 rules on recoverability of additional liabilities continue to apply to pre-commencement funding arrangements, does the old test of proportionality also continue to apply when assessing those additional liabilities?   56

J. Funding costs
Q45. Can you charge your client for the costs of: (i) negotiating and drafting a conditional fee agreement (the case of *Motto v Trafigura Ltd* [2011] EWCA Civ 1150, suggests not? However, the case is pre-Jackson and suggests that you cannot because the client is not yet your client. In this case the client is an existing client and we are at the pre-action stage of proceedings); (ii) Negotiating and entering into an ATE policy and keeping the insurers updated during the proceedings; (iii) Negotiating and entering into a third party funding agreement and keeping the funders updated during the proceedings.   57

Chapter 3   **Proportionality**

A. The proportionality test
Q1. How do the transitional provisions relate to proportionality at assessment?   65
Q2. Does the court look at the sums reasonably claimed or the sums recovered when determining 'the sums in issue in the proceedings' under CPR r.44.3(5)(a)?   66

B. At the case/costs management stage

C. At the assessment stage

Q3. Why is only the conduct of the paying party included in the
definition?   67

*D. The relationship between proportionality, reasonableness and
necessity*

Q4. Is there any distinction between proportionality and
reasonableness in reality?   69

Q5. Is the effect of proportionality to prescribe that in a case about
money, the costs cannot exceed the sums in dispute?   70

Q6. Is the case of *Kazakhstan Kagazy Plc v Zhunuss* the touchstone
regarding proportionality—namely that it defines what is
'reasonable and proportionate' as ". . . the lowest amount (of costs)
which it (a party) could reasonably have been expected to spend in
order to have its case conducted and presented proficiently, having
regard to all the circumstances"?   71

Q7. In the case of *Stocker v Stocker* Mr Justice Warby observed: "I
readily acknowledge the importance of ensuring that the costs
budgeting process does not result in a party being unable to recover
the costs necessary to assert their rights." Does this mean that
proportionate costs can never be less than those that are necessary?   71

E. The extent of proportionality considerations

Q8. Is proportionality to be applied in all cases, or, as some wish to
suggest, is it really for the small to medium value claims, where
disproportionate costs are more likely?   72

Q9. What relevance, if any, does proportionality have in cases where
an order for costs is made on the indemnity basis?   73

Q10. Is proportionality a 'fixed sum' throughout the life of a claim?   74

F. The practical implications of CPR r.44.3(2)(a) at assessment

Q11. If there is no 'good reason' to depart from the budgeted costs
on assessment, how does the court apply the proportionality 'cross
check' under CPR r.44.3(2)(a) at the end of the assessment?   76

Q12. If the effect of CPR r.44.3(2)(a) is that the sum to be allowed on
an assessment is that which is proportionate, why does the court
trouble first with undertaking an assessment of what is reasonably
incurred and reasonable in amount?   76

G. Proportionality, outcomes and the solicitor/client relationship

Q13. Is there not a risk that similar claims will have different
outcomes because of the determination by separate case managing
judges of what is proportionate in a particular case?   77

Q14. How useful are the comments in cases such as *CIP Properties*

(AIPT) Limited v Galliford Try Infrastructure Limited, GSK Project Management Limited v QPR Holdings Limited and Stocker v Stocker [2015] EWHC 1634 (QB) in setting benchmarks for proportionality?   78

Q15. Can legal representatives look to the sums budgeted as proportionate at costs management or allowed as proportionate at assessment of costs in previous cases as evidence of what will be deemed proportionate in another case?   78

Q16. Given the fact that only general guidance is emerging from the courts, how can a solicitor best offer advice to a client on what is likely to be deemed the proportionate cost of any specific case?   78

Chapter 4   **Case and Costs Management**

A. The scope of the costs management scheme

Q1. How prescriptive is the wording of CPR r.3.12(1) and (1A)? In particular can the court costs manage cases that fall within the definition of those outside the scheme and when may the court exclude cases from the regime under CPR r.3.12(1)(e)?   107

Q2. Can the court order a litigant in person to file and serve a Precedent H?   109

Q3. Do the costs management provisions at CPR r.3.12-3.18 apply to cases in the Chancery Division?   111

Q4. Can parties agree to dispense with costs management?   114

Q5. Does costs management apply to the disposal stage of a claim after the entry of a default judgment for damages to be decided by the court?   114

Q6. Do the provisions apply to a claim brought under CPR r.8, where the court has expressly listed a case management conference?   115

Q7. Do Landlord and Tenant Act 1954 lease renewal claims automatically fall within the costs management regime?   115

Q8. Must parties file and exchange Precedents H in possession claims under CPR r.55 which the court concludes are genuinely disputed on grounds which appear substantial, which the court then allocates to the multi-track and lists for a CMC?   116

Q9. Are claims where the claimant has a limited or severely impaired life expectation (defined as five years or less of life remaining) excluded from the costs management regime without the need for any court order to that effect?   116

Q10. What should parties do when the notice of provisional allocation under CPR r.26.3 is to the multi-track, but one or more parties believe that the appropriate allocation is to the fast track?   117

Q11. Does the fact that a party has a contractual right to indemnity costs against the other party mean costs management is not applicable or pointless because the claimant has a contractual right to claim costs under *Gomba Holdings (UK) Ltd v Minories Finance Ltd (No.2)*?   118

Q12. Can the court costs manage detailed assessment proceedings?   118

Q13. The Shorter Trial Pilot Scheme available for certain claims issued after 1 October 2015 under CPR r.51 PD N disapplies CPR r.3.12 and the costs management regime unless the parties agree otherwise (CPR r.51 PD N 2.58). Why might parties wish to opt in?   119

B. The time for filing and exchanging Precedent H

Q14. In respect of those cases where the value of the claim is less than £50,000 and a party fails to file and exchange Precedent H by the date set out in the CPR r.26.3(1) notice, but does file and exchange it by the extended date given in the further notice under CPR r.26.3(7A), does CPR r.3.14 apply?   120

Q15. Can the parties agree to extend the times prescribed in CPR r.3.13 for the filing and exchange of Precedents H by using CPR r.3.8(4)?   120

Q16. Does filing by e-mail satisfy the requirement in CPR r.3.13 to file a budget?   121

Q17. Does CPR r.3.14 apply to any failure to file a costs budget?   122

C. The content of Precedent H

Q18. Does the budget have to be on Precedent H or can parties produce their own forms provided that they recognisably contain the same information?   123

Q19. Which version of Precedent H should be used and is a budget discussion report required in a claim with a statement of value that exceeds £50,000 and which falls within the costs management regime, which was issued before 6 April 2016, but, following various extensions of time for filing and serving statements of case and subsequent stays, has only just been listed for a CCMC?   124

Q20. Given that the format of Precedent H was amended substantially in April 2016 why was it altered again in the 86th CPR amendment in October 2016?   124

Q21. Should a party file its Precedent H on the basis of the way in which it thinks the claim should progress, e.g. if it thinks a split trial is appropriate should the budget be completed on that basis?   125

Q22. Will the introduction of 'J-Codes' or other forms of time recording all work against the discrete phases lead to Precedent H being completed to include all costs – including those of a solicitor/client nature?   126

Q23. Do the costs allocated to contingencies count when determining whether or not a budget exceeds £25,000 and, in consequence, in determining whether only page 1 of the Precedent H needs to be completed?   127

Q24. Should applications to enforce compliance with case management decisions be included in the contingency section of Precedent H?   127

Q25. How detailed should be the assumptions upon which the budget is based? 127

Q26. Do parties who are required to file and exchange budgets using only page 1 of Precedent H (i.e. claims where the costs do not exceed £25,000 or the value of the claim as stated on the claim form is less than £50,000) need to provide assumptions upon which the budget is based? If assumptions are required in these cases where should they be inserted in Precedent H? If not required, how will the court know the basis upon which the budget is predicated? 128

Q27. If work has already been undertaken on an interim application at the time that Precedent H must be prepared, should this work be reflected in the budget, and, if so, where? 129

Q28. The guidance notes for completion of Precedent H are brief and it is not always clear where certain items of work should be included. Is there any sanction for inserting items in what the court may regard as the wrong phase of the budget? 130

Q29. Is it better for a party to over-estimate costs in the budget filed and exchanged, on the basis that it is then likely to see a higher budget set and less likely to need to go back to the court asking for the budget to be varied under CPR r.3 PD E 7.6? Conversely, if a party recognises that it is likely to be the paying party is underestimation better, trying to persuade the court to reduce the budgets of all parties to that level to limit the potential liability for costs or limit the work that can be undertaken, making the outcome of the claim less certain as a result? 131

Q30. If a defendant brings an additional claim against a party other than the claimant, does the defendant need to produce two budgets—one for the defence of the claim and one for the pursuit of the additional claim—or will one total budget suffice? 131

Q31. If a number of defendants are represented by the same solicitors, should separate budgets be prepared for each such defendant? 132

Q32. Should the costs of surveillance evidence be included in a budget? If not, if surveillance evidence is subsequently obtained, should applications be made under CPR r.3 PD E 7.6 to amend the budgets? 132

D. Preparation for the CCMC

Q33. Some courts are asking parties to produce a composite summary enabling comparison of the parties' budgets. Is there a specified precedent form for this? If not, what format should be used for that summary? 134

Q34. A number of courts are issuing detailed directions when listing a CCMC. Are these necessary and should they be standardised? 135

Q35. How detailed should be the summary in Precedent R of the
reasons why a phase of the budget is not agreed?   135

Q36. Should the discussions that the parties have when attempting
to agree the costs budgets be without prejudice?   136

Q37. Is there a sanction if a party fails to agree a budget discussion
report (Precedent R) or fails to file this?   136

E. Approval and agreement of budgets

Q38. If one party puts in an absurdly low budget is it advisable for
the other party to agree it or will this suggest an acceptance that
any costs above that level are not reasonable and proportionate
and so prejudice its own budget which is significantly higher?   137

Q39. The Precedent H guidance notes have been amended to include
a specific reference to CPR rules 44.3 (5) and 44.4(3) and state that
when deciding the reasonable and proportionate costs the court
will include in its consideration "'where and the circumstances in
which the work was done as opposed to where the case is heard'".
What is the significance of these amendments?   138

Q40. Does the introduction of costs management mean that the
court is rarely likely to dispense with a case/costs management
conference and deal with directions and budgets as a paper exercise? 139

Q41. Does the court give the directions first and subsequently costs
manage?   139

Q42. Should costs lawyers attend CCMCs?   140

Q43. The Court of Appeal has suggested that costs already incurred
at the time of the costs management order can be the subject of a
costs management order by agreement. Is this correct?   141

Q44. The court seems to have adopted a number of approaches to
dealing with incurred costs. Is it possible to discern clear guidance
on the treatment of these costs in the budgeting exercise?   141

Q45. Are incurred costs relevant to the overall costs at the budgeting
stage or only relevant on a phase by phase basis?   142

Q46. What happens if the total incurred costs means that even with
the most proportionate case management possible it is not possible
to budget costs 'to be incurred' at a level that, when added to
those 'incurred costs', comes within the court's overall assessment
of reasonableness and proportionality?   144

Q47. If there has been a significant front loading of the costs so that
by the time of the costs management hearing the costs already spent
exceed what the court regards as the proportionate expenditure on
the claim, can the court set a budget going forward of nil?   145

Q48. What can be done to avoid the potential injustice of the court
setting a phase budget by basing this on an overall view of the
reasonable and proportionate sum for that phase, deducting the
incurred costs and budgeting the difference, only for the assessing

judge then to reduce the incurred costs undermining the basis
upon which the budget was set? 146

Q49. Should parties coming to the first CCMC to debate their
respective budgets do so on the basis that it is the appropriate
occasion on which to contest the costs in the budgets (both
incurred and estimated) as per para.44 of *SARPD Oil International
Ltd v Addax Energy SA* ? 146

Q50. Should the court set hourly rates as part of the budgeting
exercise? 147

Q51. If the court does not set the budget by reference to hourly rates
and time, then why does Precedent H require this information
and, linked to this, what does "the underlying detail in the budget
for each phase used by the party to calculate the totals claimed is
provided for reference purposes only to assist the court in fixing a
budget" in CPR r.3 PD E 7.10 mean? 148

Q52. How can the court set the budget without assessing
prospectively the work that is required and the appropriate hourly
rate(s) at which that work should be done? 149

Q53. If the court is budgeting only be reference to a global sum and
not taking account of the respective hourly rates, surely this means
that a party who has agreed a lower hourly rate retainer will be
able to do more work than one with a higher hourly rate? If so this
appears unfair. 149

Q54. If the court does set the hourly rate in the budget what
happens if, at assessment, the assessing court sets a different
hourly rate for the non budgeted work? 150

Q55. What, if anything, can the court do when the parties agree
budgets or phases of the budgets in sums that the court thinks are
disproportionate? 150

Q56. How important is the breakdown between disbursements and
solicitors' fees in an approved/agreed budget? 151

Q57. Should parties re-file budgets after the CCMC when a costs
management order has been made under CPR r.3.15? 152

F. Post costs management order general issues

Q58. Can the parties agree to vary their budgets from that recorded
by the court in a costs management order, where there has
been no 'significant development' in the litigation, but both are
unhappy with the amount budgeted by the court? 152

Q59. Once a budget has been set, should solicitors be monitoring
the budgets? 152

Q60. Upon taking over instructions for a client from another firm
it is clear that the 'incurred costs' for the pre-action phase in the
Precedent H filed and exchanged by that firm are considerably
lower than the amount of costs that the client paid that firm for

work done during that period. Whilst estimating future costs may
be somewhat speculative, is there any explanation for why the
incurred costs in Precedent H differ from 'actual costs' incurred?   153

Q61. To which sum do the percentages in CPR r.3 PD E 7.2 apply—
the total sum in the Precedent H after the budget has been set or
just those parts of the Precedent H that the court has budgeted?   153

Q62. What if a client still wants the legal representatives to incur
costs that the court has not allowed within the budget?   155

Q63. Does the statement of truth on the budget prevent a solicitor
recovering more than the budget from the client?   155

Q64. What is the position if a Part 7 claim commences as a fast track
claim, but subsequently it becomes apparent that the claim is undervalued and needs to be re-tracked to the multi-track, but it is not
within one of the costs management exceptions in CPR r.3.12(1)?   156

Q65. Is a party who was acting in person at the costs management
conference (and so has no budget), but who subsequently instructs
solicitors, required to exchange and file a Precedent H?   157

Q66. Is a further Precedent H required with a pre-trial checklist
("PTCL") as CPR r.29 imposes no such requirement and yet the
wording of the Precedent H guidance still suggests this is work
included at the PTR stage?   157

Q67. What is the purpose of the reference in CPR r.36.23 to CPR
r.36.17(4)(b)?   158

G. Variation of budgets and freestanding costs orders

Q68. What is a significant development for the purposes of CPR r.3
PD E 7.6?   159

Q69. Is there a potential tension between CPR r.3.15(3) and CPR r.3
PD E 7.6?   160

Q70. Can a party make repeated agreed variations or, in default of
agreement, applications to the court to vary a budget?   161

Q71. If an appeal is launched against a decision on an interim
application that falls within a discrete phase (e.g. against an order
in respect of permission for expert evidence) does CPR r.3 PD E 7.6
apply and should budgets be revised with a view to agreement or
an application to vary?   161

Q72. It seems that some parties are not applying to vary budgets,
but instead prefer to wait to argue 'good reason' to depart from the
budget at any subsequent assessment. Is this because it is easier to
depart from a budget retrospectively when the work may be easier
to justify than to vary prospectively when the work may be seen to
be speculative?   162

Q73. If a costs management order has been made in a case but
not long afterwards a party makes a potentially determinative
application for summary judgment ("SJ"), should the parties apply

promptly for the budgets to be revised? Suppose that they do, but the hearing for SJ is likely to come on before the application to revise costs budgets can be heard, what should they do? Could the potential respondent to the SJ application not justifiably seek, in such circumstances, an order that the costs thrown away by this change of tack by the applicant be paid by it in any event?   163

Q74. If a costs management order was made based on the Precedent H in use before 6 April 2016 and a party seeks variation of the budget set, which version of Precedent H should be completed and submitted to the other parties and the court?   164

Q75. What sort of applications fall within the provisions of CPR r.3 PD E 7.9? How does this link with the provisions for contingencies in the budget and budget variation?   164

H. The relevance of a budget at a subsequent assessment

Q76. What is the effect of a costs management order at an assessment of costs on the standard basis?   165

Q77. Is the budget 'without prejudice' to any subsequent assessment?   170

Q78. Can you explain how an award of costs on the standard basis differs from an award of costs on the indemnity basis in circumstances where a costs budget is in place?   171

Q79. If an award of indemnity costs is made and CPR r.3.18 does not apply, does the budget still form the starting point for the assessment of costs?   171

Q80. What effect will a 'costs sanction' for unreasonable conduct, as suggested by the Court of Appeal in *Denton v T H White*, have on a costs budget?   172

Q81. What guidance is there on what may constitute 'good reason' under CPR r.3.18 to enable a departure from a budget at assessment?   173

Q82. Can a trial judge ordering a detailed assessment of the costs of a party subject to a costs management order, give guidance to the assessing judge on what may be 'good reason' to depart from the budget set.?   173

Q83. Does CPR r.3.18(b) prescribe an automatic sanction where the receiving party has failed to amend its budget prospectively and can show no 'good reason' for this failure or, as is suggested in *Simpson v MGN Ltd* (see **4.20** and **Q81** above), is it for the court, applying the overriding objective, to determine what the just and proportionate sanction should be?   174

Q84. Can the budgeted sum exceed the sum due from that party to the solicitor under the contractual retainer, and, if so, is this a permitted breach of the indemnity principle?   175

I. Case management

Q85. Does the decision of the Court of Appeal in *Denton v T H White* mean that relief from sanction will be granted provided that there is no prejudice to any other party that cannot be compensated by a costs order and that a trial date can still be met?   175

Q86. Does the decision in *British Gas Trading Ltd v Oak Cash and Carry Ltd* impact on the likelihood of relief from sanction being granted under CPR r.3.9?   176

Q87. Does the emphasis on proportionality impact on the situation where a claim falls within fast track financial limits, but the number of witnesses is such that the time needed for trial exceeds one day?   177

Q88. Do the case management rules apply as much to litigants in person as to represented parties?   178

Q89. Will cost capping under CPR 3 Section III be ordered more rarely?   178

Chapter 5   **Part 36 and Other Settlement Offers including ADR and Costs Consequences**

A. Section 1 Part 36—Circumstances in which Part 36 offers can be made (CPR r.36.2).

Q1. Is there anything in CPR Part 36 or the Privy Council Rules which prevents a Part 36 offer being made in costs proceedings before the Privy Council? (Rule 2.1).   217

B. Content requirements for Part 36 offers (CPR r.36.5).

Q2. Can a valid Part 36 offer include settlement terms which (if accepted), impose conditions; require a defendant to do something other than pay money; or provide for interest to run after the end of the relevant period? (CPR r.2.1; CPR r.36.2(2), (CPR r.36.5(4)).   218

Q3. There are numerous questions on the effect of Part 36.5:
i) Must a valid defendant's Part 36 offer include an offer to pay the claimant's costs?
ii) Can an offeror now legitimately state in his Part 36 offer that the offer is only open for a limited period of time? Does a Part 36 offer automatically expire after the 21 day period or does it only expire if it is withdrawn or if explicitly states it expires after a certain amount of time?
iii) Is a Part 36 offer valid if it includes non-monetary terms e.g. the defendant will provide an indemnity to the claimant in respect of any direct claim by a third party which arises out of current proceedings?
iv) Can a Part 36 offer be made in relation to liability rather than an offer to pay a settlement sum? For example, offering to agree that liability is a 50/50 basis in relation to motor claims?

v) Is it possible to make two offers in a single Part 36 offer? E.g., the defendant pays £8500 immediately, or £10,000 in instalments?

vi) Can a valid Part 36 offer be made in a small claim?   218

Q4. If a defendant makes a Part 36 offer which does not take into account its counterclaim and the offer is then accepted, what happens to the counterclaim? (CPR r.36.5).   219

Q5. Where there's more than one claimant, in his Part 36 offer must the defendant apportion the settlement sum he offers between each claimant?   220

Q6. In a case where there is no counterclaim and the claimant makes a Part 36 offer, does that offer need to state whether it takes into account any counterclaim given that there is no counterclaim in existence? (CPR r.36.5(1)(e)).   220

Q7. If one of two defendants with joint and several liability makes a Part 36 offer, what are that defendant's costs implication assuming that before the offer he would have been jointly and severally liable for all of the plaintiff's costs? (CPR r.36.5).   220

C. Time when a Part 36 offer may be made (CPR r.36.7).

Q8. What is the position when a Part 36 offer is made pre-action and accepted after the issue of proceedings, but before the proceedings have been served on the defendant, where service has been reserved for up to four months? (CPR r.36.7).   221

Q9. Will a Part 36 offer still have effect if it is made during a stay of proceedings which were for reasons other than to allow for settlement of the case? (CPR r.36.7).   221

D. Part 36 and asking for clarification (CPR r.36.8).

Q10. Where there is a Part 36 offer, what is the position where the offeree seeks clarification of the offer? Should I ask my opponent to clarify his badly drafted unclear Part 36 offer? (CPR r.36.8.)   221

E. Withdrawing or changing terms of Part 36 offers (CPR rules 36.9, 36.10).

Q11. If an offeree serves a notice of acceptance during the relevant period, when does that acceptance take effect, given that the offeror may apply for permission to withdraw or vary its offer within seven days of the notice of acceptance (or, if earlier, before the first day of trial)?   223

Q12. Where a claimant made a pre-action Part 36 offer which was rejected and now that proceedings have been issued wishes to make a Part 36 offer that is more advantageous to the defendant, what is the position with regard to the original offer? If the claimant equals or beats the offer at trial when are indemnity costs

likely to be awarded from: the earlier offer date or the one which
supersedes it? (CPR r.36.9(5)).   223

Q13. What is the position where a Part 36 Offer is withdrawn at the
same time as the claimant purports to accept it? (CPR rules 36.9
and 36.10).   224

F. Part 36 offer acceptance requirements (CPR rules 36.11, 36.12)/
Disclosure of Part 36 offer (CPR r.36.16).

Q14. Where there has been a split trial or a trial of preliminary
issues, what is the position with regard to Part 36 Offers which
may have been made? (CPR r.36.12).   225

G. Costs consequences of acceptance of a Part 36 offer (CPR r.36.13)

Q15. What is the procedure for recovering costs in an action that
settles without proceedings as a result of the acceptance of a pre-
action Part 36 offer? (CPR r.36.13).   226

Q16. I act for a proposed claimant in a dispute where legal
proceedings have yet to be issued. The proposed defendant
has served a Part 36 offer by form N242A which states that the
defendant will be liable for the claimant's costs in accordance with
Part 36.13. Part 36.13 states the claimant will be entitled to the
Costs of proceedings including their recoverable pre-action costs.
Does this mean my client can only recover pre action costs as part
of the costs of any proceedings? If this is so, can we agree that the
pre-action costs are recoverable and if so, if the amount cannot be
agreed can we issue costs only proceedings pursuant to Part 8A to
have the court adjudicate upon costs? (CPR r.36.13).   227

Q17. If a defendant accepts a claimant's Part 36 offer after
proceedings have been issued, is a consent order to dispose of the
proceedings necessary?
I understand that generally speaking, there is no need for there
to be a consent order if a settlement results from acceptance of a
Part 36 offer. Am I right? If so, are there any significant exceptions
from this general proposition? (CPR r.36.13(1)).   228

Q18. CPR r.36.2 provides that a Part 36 offer may be made in a
counterclaim or additional claim, and it includes a reminder that
CPR r.20.2 and CPR r.20.3 provide that counterclaims and other
additional claims are treated as claims. With that in mind, if a
defendant makes a Part 36 offer in relation to its counterclaim,
which is accepted within the relevant period ("RP"), does that
mean that the defendant is automatically "entitled to the
costs of the proceedings" (that is, the costs relating to both the
original claim and the counterclaim) under CPR r.36.13(1)? (CPR
r.36.13(7)).   228

Q19. Are costs recoverable if a claimant's Part 36 offer is accepted in

circumstances where the claimant's costs budget has not been filed
on time? (CPR r.36.13).   231

H .Other effects of acceptance of a Part 36 offer (CPR r.36.14).
Q20. In a claim by a claimant (C) against two separate defendants
(D1 and D2), where separate allegations are advanced against
each defendant, if C makes a Part 36 offer to settle the whole of
his claim which is addressed to both D1 and D2 as "the offeree",
and only D1 accepts the offer, is the claim against D2 stayed, even
though D2 did not accept the offer? (CPR r.36.14).   232
Q21. Where a defendant has failed to comply with a Part 36 offer
that has been accepted, is it possible for the claimant to disclose
the Part 36 offer to the court when seeking judgment on the Part
36? (CPR r.36.14).   232
Q22. May a defendant who is a protected party acting by her
litigation friend make a joint Part 36 offer with three other
defendants? Is it possible to avoid the obligation under CPR
r.36.14(6) to pay out within 14 days? (CPR r.36.14(6)).   233

I. Part 36 offers in multi-party disputes (CPR r.36.15).
Q23. Can a Part 20 defendant make a Part 36 offer? We have a case
where the claimant is suing the first defendant (D1), the claimant
is also suing the second defendant (D2), and D1 is suing D2, who
they brought in as a Part 20 defendant. D2 wishes to make a Part
36 offer, but is it possible for one Part 36 offer to encompass both
claims?

How can you best use Part 36 in multi-party disputes? We act
for Party A in an action against Party B. Party B has issued Part 20
proceedings against Party C. Our client wishes to resolve the claim
by making a Part 36 offer to settle the entire action, including the
Part 20 proceedings, on terms that my client will accept a small
sum in settlement from Party B, and that Party B will discontinue
against the Part 20 defendant (who is a LiP, and therefore has no
costs consequences). There is a connection between Party A and
Party B. (CPR r.36.2(1), (CPR r.36.5, 36.15).   233

*J. Calculating whether judgment more advantageous than Part 36
offer (CPR r.36.17).*
Q24. Can an admissions payment improve the value of Part 36
offer? (CPR r.36.17).   234
Q25. When considering whether a claimant has failed to obtain
a judgment more advantageous than a defendant's Part 36 offer
how do you deal with any interest element that the judge awards
the claimant at trial? Assuming that the defendant's offer was
inclusive of interest until the expiry of the relevant period do you

compare that figure with the principal sum that the judge awards at trial plus any interest awarded too up to the date of judgment? Or can you argue that for the purposes of working out whether the judgment is more advantageous you should only take into account the principal sum awarded and interest up to the date of expiry of the Part 36 offer? (CPR r.36.17). 234

K. Part 36 and costs consequences (CRP rules 36.17, 36.20 and 36.21).

Q26. Where a defendant has made a Part 36 offer for settlement of the claimant's costs, and the claimant has rejected that offer but fails to beat/meet it at trial: a) is there a cap on how much the claimant has to pay to the defendant? b) is the cost consequence awarded as a percentage of the settlement offer or as a percentage of the value of the claim? 235

Q27. In a case where the claimant makes a Part 36 offer less than 21 days before trial, would the claimant still recover the additional 10% damages if he/she obtains a judgment at least as advantageous as the offer? (CPR r.36.17). 235

Q28. Can you explain how an award of costs on the standard basis (e.g. under CPR r.36.17(3)(a)) differs from an award of costs on the indemnity basis (e.g. under CPR r.36.17(4)(b)) in circumstances where a costs budget is in place? The definition of 'standard basis' and 'indemnity basis' appear to be hard to reconcile with the concept of costs budgets, because there should be no doubts about reasonableness to resolve in anyone's favour if the costs are within the court-approved costs budget. (CPR r.36.17(4). 236

Q29. Is it appropriate to award a lower additional amount under CPR r.36.17(4)(d) than the prescribed amount because the proceedings were determined early, for example, as a result of summary judgment being given, rather than going to full trial? 236

Q30. How do the Court of Appeal decision in *AJ Insurance v Sugar Hut, Hammersmatch Properties (Welwyn) Ltd v Saint Gobain Ceramics and Plastics Ltd*, tie together with the Court of Appeal decision in *Coward v Phaestos*? It's not clear to me why a party who makes a Part 36 offer should be deprived of the benefits of CPR r.44.2, as interpreted by the *Court of Appeal in Coward v Phaestos*. 236

Q31. Do you agree that it may be difficult to decide who has obtained the more advantageous result in a detailed assessment? Also, does CPR r.36.17(4)) about enhancing claimants' recovery by 10% apply in detailed assessments? (CPR r.36.17). 237

L. Part 36 and IPEC, Part 45, Section IV

Q32. How does the cap on damages in the IPEC apply where there is also a claim for costs? (CPR r.36.17(4)). 237

M. Genuine attempt to settle (CPR r.36.17(5)).

Q33. We represent a client in a case where we feel that the client is bound to succeed. We are considering making a claimant Part 36 offer to settle at 100% liability plus costs. This would save the defendant the time and cost of preparing for trial and the trial itself. Will this succeed? What is a genuine effort to settle under Part 36? (CPR r.36.17).   238

N. Part 36 and set off (CPR r.36.22).

Q34. Where a claimant accepts a defendant's Part 36 offer after the expiry of the relevant period, can the defendant's costs for the period after the end of the RP to the date of acceptance be offset against the amount of the Part 36 offer? (CPR r.36.22).   239

O. Relief from sanctions where Part 36 offer may be affected (CRP r.3.9).

Q35. My firm needs to serve an expert's report out of time. The defendants are objecting to relief from sanctions. How does this affect potential Part 36 Offers? (CPR r.3.9).   239

P. Part 36 and detailed assessments (CPR rules 44.2 and 47.20).

Q36. If we make a successful Part 36 offer will we recover all our costs? (CPR r.44.2). Please explain the decision in *Webb v Liverpool Womens' NHS Foundation Trust* [2015] EWHC 449 (QB).   240

Q37. When the question of costs is being decided is it possible for a party to refer to without prejudice correspondence in order to establish that the other party did not respond to Part 36 Offers? (CPR r.44.2).   240

Q38. Where a Part 36 offer is accepted in a small claim that has not yet been allocated to the small claims track, is it the case that the fixed costs regime will generally apply?

Is the claimant entitled to its costs if it accepts a pre-action Part 36 offer where the case would be allocated to the small claims track if it went to court? (CPR r.46.13).   241

Q. Part 36 offers made after issue but before service

Q39. We have a matter which settled following acceptance of a Part 36 offer after the issue of proceedings but prior to service. Proceedings were never served, and the time for service has now expired. We take the view that we can commence detailed assessment proceedings without Part 8 proceedings, despite the fact that proceedings were never served. We refer to CPR r.46.14(1)(c) which says that Part 8 proceedings are required if no proceedings have been "started". Do you agree, or do you believe that we would need to issue Part 8 proceedings for an Order for costs before commencing assessment? (CPR r.46.14).   241

Q40. What is the requirement for open offers in detailed assessment proceedings meant to achieve and how they will co-exist with Part 36 Offers? (PD47 para.8.3).   242

Section 2 Settlement other than under Part 36

R. Calderbank offers
Q41. How are Calderbank offers treated in relation to costs? (CPR r.44.2(4)).   243

S. ADR and Mediation
Q42. Does anyone/any kind of company (for example) have to use ADR because the law says so? If so we would be grateful if you would direct us to that law or illuminate what kind of people MUST use ADR.   243

T. Mediation and unreasonable refusal
Q43. Can you give examples when it is reasonable to refuse to mediate? Are parties using the court's sanctioning of parties for unreasonable refusal to mediate tactically particularly in detailed assessments? To avoid such costs orders and keep the idea and costs of mediation sensible, is it sensible to agree to mediate but make it clear that both sides should bear their own costs.   246

Q44. When we suggest mediation on behalf of clients we are often met with a variety of reasons why there should be no mediation. Have you any suggestions?   246

Q45. There must be drawbacks to mediation – what are they?   248

U. Options when all issues resolved except costs
Q46. Can you please advise on the available options where the parties to an ongoing case have essentially agreed on every issue other than costs. It is at an early stage (just post CCMC). Both sides are saying that the other should pay their costs. Both parties are alleging that the other's conduct has been in breach of the pre-action protocol. Because of the circumstances it is uncertain which party (if any) will be deemed to have "won" the case. What are the options available to the parties? It doesn't seem correct that the main case should proceed as everything other than costs is essentially agreed. I see from the practice note that costs only proceedings are not available where it is not decided as to who is paying who's costs. So, for example, could the parties make an application to end the current proceedings and just deal with costs, or go straight to assessment?   248

Q47. We have a matter in which our client has successfully sued for professional negligence. The opponent made a Part 36 offer

which was accepted and the damages settled. The issue remaining
is our costs. The Part 36 offer included an offer to pay reasonable
expenses. Having assessed our costs schedule the opponent has
made a Part 36 offer significantly less than our costs. How does
one challenge the offer made by the opponent for costs? This
is a matter in which we do not want this to go to court for a
detailed assessment but would certainly want a better offer than is
currently being made.   249

Q48. Are you aware of any cases where a refusal to mediate a small
claims track claim has resulted in the court making an adverse
costs award against the refusing party? It is settled that refusal to
accept an offer which is not beaten at trial is not "unreasonable
behaviour" for the purposes of CPR Part 27 and will not lead to
adverse costs consequences, but it is unclear what effect, if any,
refusal to mediate might have on the usual "no costs" rule.   249

V. Assessing costs in arbitration

Q49. What is the proper approach to assessing costs in an
Arbitration?   249

Chapter 6   **Qualified One-Way Costs Shifting**

A. The circumstances in which QOCS applies

Q1. How will QOCS apply where a claim comprises both a personal
injury and a non-personal injury element?   246

Q2. Is QOCS excluded where the claimant has Before The Event
Insurance?   265

Q3. Does QOCS apply to costs incurred prior to 1 April 2013?   265

Q4. Is QOCS excluded where the claimant has entered into a pre-
commencement funding arrangement, even if the claimant then is
advised not to pursue the claim by the initially instructed solicitor
but later does so under a post April 2013 funding arrangement
with a different firm?   265

Q5. Can a personal injury claimant who had a pre-action CFA
(entered into before 1 April 2013) with a 100% success fee, and
who wishes to proceed with the claim with the benefits of QOCS
protection, terminate the existing CFA, on the basis that the law
firm will waive its success fee, and enter into a new post-Jackson
CFA? Would the claimant then be able to benefit from QOCS,
even though the pre-action base costs are covered under a CFA
entered into before 1 April 2013? Alternatively, could the client
and or the solicitor agree to end the existing CFA, but enter into a
new, post LASPO CFA, with any success fee payable by the client
only, but with the CFA expressly covering all work done since first
instruction and thereby benefit from QOCS?   266

Q6. Will qualified one way costs shifting apply where a personal
injury claimant entered into a CFA pre Jackson reforms but did
not enter into an after the event insurance policy until after the
introduction of QOCS? 267

Q7. Does QOCS apply to just personal injury? We have a commercial
litigation matter for breach of contract so nothing to do with
personal injury. 267

Q8. Does QOCS apply to claims for damages for clinical negligence? 267

Q9. Where a claimant is currently subject to an 'old style' CFA (pre-
April 2013 where QOCS would not apply) but the client seeks the
protection of QOCS, would the previous presence of the old style
CFA prevent the claimant ever obtaining the benefit of QOCS
under the workings of CPR r.44.17 If the claimant was to continue
as a litigant in person would she then obtain the benefit of QOCS? 267

Q10. In *Howe v Motor Insurers' Bureau* [2016] EWHC 884 (QB), the
High Court concluded that a claim for compensation from the MIB
(motor insurers' bureau) under the untraced drivers agreement was
not a "claim for damages for personal injury" as required for QOCS
to be applicable. The court acknowledged that this was an unusual
situation because claims before a court in respect of the untraced
drivers agreement are rare because it contains its own internal
procedure. Will the position be the same if C sues an RTA insurer
direct? 268

B. QOCS and discontinuance

Q11. The claimant has incurred costs unnecessarily in an unmeritous
claim. They have now served a notice of discontinuance and, as
QOCS applies, they are not liable for the defendant's costs (unless
an exception applies). In the above circumstances, is it possible
for the defendant to apply for a wasted costs order even though a
notice of discontinuance has been filed by the claimant? 268

Q12. I need to discontinue proceedings against a number of
defendants in an action. Obviously, when I file a notice of
discontinuance, there will be a deemed order for costs against
the claimant unless the court orders—otherwise (CPR r.38.6(1)).
However, my understandings of QOCS (from CPR rules 44.14,
44.15 and 44.16) is that an order for costs may only be enforced
if the claim has been struck out (no court permission needed) or
if it is fundamentally dishonest (court permission needed). We
do not have sufficient time to obtain written consent from each
and every defendant in a consent order but in any event consider
that we would be QOCS protected even by serving a Notice of
Discontinuance. 270

C. QOCS and settlement offers

Q13. In respect of CPR r.44.14 (1) relating to QOCS, can an order for costs be made up to the extent of any damages when a Calderbank offer has been made, or does this rule only apply when a Part 36 offer has been made (i.e. this rule does not apply to Calderbank offers)? 270

D. QOCS and set off

Q14. A claimant loses a personal injury claim and a costs order is made in the usual way but the judge also finds fundamental dishonesty and thus allows enforcement of the costs order totalling £7,210.00. The claimant appeals against the finding of fundamental dishonesty, but not the loss of the claim, and wins and so the finding of fundamental dishonesty is quashed and the claimant is awarded costs of the appeal of £12,500.00.The original order against the claimant in respect of the costs of losing the personal injury claim remains in place but is now unenforceable. Could the defendant, successful in the primary claim, set-off the £7,210.00 owed to it, under the common law doctrine of set-off? 271

E. QOCS and costs management

Q15. Do parties still have to costs budget where QOCS applies and, if so, is the agreeing of budgets in such cases likely to be more difficult? 272

F. QOCS—the future

Q16. Will QOCS be extended to other areas in due course? 272

Chapter 7 Fixed Costs; Indemnity Costs; Litigants in Person

A. Fixed Costs

Q1. What indications are there about fixed costs for the future? Are there any arguments for fixed fees? 302

Q2. What guidance can be given about retainer arrangements to emphasise the importance of the advice to a client about these and ensuring that retainer arrangements are still clear and enforceable where a legal representative is asked to represent a client in litigation which will inevitably involve the application of fixed costs? 303

B. Fixed costs and multi-party situations (where fixed costs may not apply equally)

Q3. Where a claim is made against more than one defendant, one of whom admits the debt and judgment is obtained under CPR r.14.4(3), while the other defendant does not respond and judgment in default is obtained under CPR r.12.4(1), is the

claimant entitled to two sets of fixed costs given that there are
two defendants and judgment has been obtained on two different
bases? (CPR r.45.1).   304

C. Getting the court to order more than fixed costs
Q4. Can you/how do you get more than fixed costs? Can you give
some guidance/authorities regarding when the court will order
otherwise than fixed costs under CPR r.45 in a case where the fixed
costs provisions should otherwise apply? Is it possible for costs be
assessed when requesting default judgment or are only fixed costs
allowed pursuant to CPR r.45?   305

D. Relationship between fixed costs and assessed costs and between fixed costs and Part 36 costs
Q5. What is the relationship between fixed costs and assessed costs
and fixed costs and Part 36? IE what happens if they overlap?   305
Q6. In proceedings in the Intellectual Property Enterprise Court
where costs are awarded against a party for unreasonable
behaviour does the stage costs cap in Part 45 apply?   306
Q7. Does CPR r.46.5 apply to Litigants in person on the small claims
track? What costs can a Litigant in person recover in the small
claims court?   307
Q8. Following the decision in *Chaplair v Kumari*, it is clear that
a landlord can recover costs of proceedings under a leasehold
indemnity in its favour irrespective of whether the claim would fall
within the fixed costs regimes of the small and fast tracks. What is
the position in relation to residential possession claims under CPR
Part 55, to which the fixed costs regime under CPR Part 45 applies?   308

E. Costs on the Indemnity Basis
Q9. Is the indemnity basis applicable in cases where there is an abuse
of process or where a party has been guilty of unreasonable
conduct?   309
Q10. What is the position of litigation funders in relation to orders
for costs, particularly orders for costs on the indemnity basis?   310
Q11. The rules suggest that costs management does not affect
indemnity costs. However there is now a confusion about this
since Coulson J's decision in *Elvanite Full Circle Ltd v Amec Earth
and Environmental UK Ltd* suggests otherwise.   311
Q12. What is the position if the losing party has won on certain
issues and lost on others?   312

F. Litigants in Person
Q13. What is the position of a solicitor or barrister acting on his or
her own behalf?   313

Q14. If a litigant in person instructs a barrister under the Direct Access scheme can the litigant recover any costs? Are there any rules relating to recovery of costs, where the party is a litigant in person, but uses a barrister through direct access? Has a barrister been used throughout whole claim, not just for hearings?   314

Q15. Is it possible for the court to make an order for costs on the indemnity basis against a litigant in person?   315

Q16. Is it possible for a firm of solicitors which is an LLP to be regarded as a litigant in person for the purpose of a costs assessment? 316

Q17. To what extent will the court grant some leeway to a litigant in person who fails to comply with a rule practice direction or court order?   316

Q18. Is it possible for a company to be represented by a McKenzie friend?   319

Q19. Will the court order interim payments to enable litigants in person to obtain legal representation?   319

Chapter 8   **Assessments of Costs and Payment on Account of Costs**

A. Summary and detailed assessment

Q1. What is the position when form N260 is either served/filed late or not at all?   329

Q2. Does the introduction of the breakdown of time spent on documents on the Form N260 mean that the court will deal with challenges to this on an item by item basis or will the court make one overall assessment of time spent on documents?   331

Q3. How does the proportionality cross check at CPR r.44.3(2)(a) work in the summary assessment process that is already one undertaken with a broad brush?   332

Q4. How can the court use the costs budgets at a summary assessment of the costs of the claim when the N260 is, inevitably, not divided into the same phases as the Precedent H to enable easy comparison?   332

Q5. Albeit in a family context, does not the case of *SB v MB* (Costs) suggest that summary assessment is confined to fast track trials and other hearings lasting a day or less?   334

Q6. Does the decision in *Transformers and Rectifiers Limited v Needs Limited* mean that summary assessments of the costs a) of applications, whether disposed of either at a hearing or on the papers and, b) after trials, may be conducted by a judge other than the one who dealt with the application/trial?   335

Q7. In the light of the voluntary 'new bill' pilot introduced in the SCCO what, if anything, should practitioners be doing in anticipation of the new bill format becoming compulsory?   335

Q8. Who is responsible for the costs of providing the breakdown
  required in a model form like Precedent Q?   336
Q9. Does qualified one-way costs shifting ("QOCS") apply to the
  detailed assessment procedure?   337
Q10. Is there any sanction if a paying party fails to make an open
  offer under CPR r.47 PD 8.3?   338

B. Provisional Assessment
Q11. Does the £75,000 limit for provisional assessment include or
  exclude VAT?   339
Q12. Does the £75,000 limit for provisional assessment include
  'additional liabilities' (where the transitional provisions still permit
  recovery of these between the parties)?   339
Q13. There seems to be a feeling that a paying party who does not
  serve Replies to the Points of Dispute is at a disadvantage at a
  provisional assessment. Should receiving parties serve Replies in
  this situation as a matter of course?   339
Q14. What papers should a receiving party file in support of a bill for
  a provisional assessment?   339
Q15. Is there a sanction if the receiving party fails to file the required
  documents with the request for provisional assessment and can
  this be rectified? If so how?   341
Q16 How does the court deal with the proportionality cross check
  after a provisional assessment where the assessed bill is returned to
  the parties to do the arithmetic?   343
Q17. Does the costs cap include or exclude success fees (where the
  transitional provisions still permit recovery of success fees between
  the parties)?   344
Q18. Can the court make an award of indemnity costs under CPR
  r.36.17(4)(b) in provisional assessment proceedings and, if so,
  what, if any effect does this have on the costs cap of £1,500. 345

C. The costs or oral hearing
Q19. What happens in respect of the costs where at an oral hearing a
  party does not achieve an adjustment in its favour of 20% or more,
  but the adjustment made does make a CPR r.47.20 offer relevant? 346
Q20 Does the costs cap at CPR r.47.15(5) include the additional
  amount under CPR r.36.17(4)(d) as applied by CPR r.47.20?   348
Q21. How does the £1,500 cap operate in respect of cases that are
  dealt with under the provisional assessment provisions, but where
  there are interim applications, e.g. to set aside a default costs
  certificate, for an interim costs certificate or for relief from
  sanction?   348
Q22. Is the amount of the bill or the sum in which it is assessed in a
  provisional assessment likely to inform how much of the capped

fee is awarded, e.g. does a bill of £70,000 justify an award of a
higher proportion of the £1,500 than a bill of £20,000? 349

Q23. Can the court make more than one award of costs for the
provisional assessment and, if so, is the total amount apportioned
between the parties limited to £1,500 or may there be separate
awards to each party, each with a cap of £1,500? 349

Q24. Does the £1,500 cap on costs under CPR r.47.14 include costs
incurred in 'Costs Only Proceedings' under CPR r.46.14? 350

Q25. Under CPR r.36.17(4)(d) can a party recover the additional
sum on a detailed assessment by operation of CPR r.47.20 if it has
already received an additional amount in respect of the substantive
award in the claim? 351

Q26. Is the determination of disbursements under the procedure set
out at CPR r.47 PD 5.7 a provisional assessment? 352

D. Payments on account

Q27. Is there any rule of thumb as to what proportion of the
costs claimed the court will order as a reasonable sum by way of
payment on account? 352

Q28. Does the court consider the proportionality of costs sought
when ordering a payment on account? 354

Q29 Must a party have filed a Form N260 (or equivalent statement
of costs) if it wishes to seek a payment on account of costs? 354

Q30. When may a departure from the general rule at CPR r.44.2(8)
be justified? 354

Q31. Can a payment on account of costs be ordered under CPR
r.44.2(8) other than at the hearing awarding the costs? 355

**Chapter 9   The Effect of the Jackson Civil Justice Reforms
on Solicitor–Client Costs**

Q1. Have the 'Jackson' reforms changed the basis on which I, as a
solicitor, can charge my client? 374

Q2. Can you advise the client of the full range of funding options
but then say but we as a firm do not offer X, or Y or only offer X or
Y on this basis? 375

Q3. My case is subject to costs management. Am I required to seek
my client's approval to the budget and does the budget, if agreed
or approved, limit the costs I can charge my client? 376

Q4. Do the revised rules on Part 36 apply in a solicitor-client
assessment? 376

Q5. Can we charge/recover for preparing the solicitor-client estimate? 377

Q6. It is still not clear how solicitors should go about doing estimates
of costs for their clients and the extent to which Precedent H is
sufficient/useful for this purpose. Can you express a view? 377

Table of Cases

A&M v Royal Mail Group unreported 27 August 2015 and 1 October 2015 CC
  (Birmingham) 9–19
AB v CD [2011] EWHC 602 (Ch) 5–57
ABCI (formerly Arab Business Consortium International Finance & Investment Co)
  v Banque Franco-Tunisienne (Costs) [2002] EWHC 567 (Comm)...........................7–16
AF v BG [2009] EWCA Civ 757; [2010] 2 Costs L.R. 164........................... 5–06, 5–40, 5–49
Agassi v Robinson (Inspector of Taxes) [2005] EWCA Civ 1507; [2006] 1 W.L.R.
  2126; [2006] 1 All E.R. 900; [2006] S.T.C. 580, CA; [2006] 2 Costs L.R. 283; [2006]
  B.T.C. 3; [2005] S.T.I. 1994; (2005) 155 N.L.J. 1885; (2006) 150 S.J.L.B. 28; [2005]
  N.P.C. 140 ....7–21, 7–25
Agents' Mutual Ltd v Gascoigne Halman Ltd (t/a Gascoigne Halman) [2016] CAT
  20 ....3–15, 4–27
AH v Lewisham Healthcare NHS Trust. *See* Surrey (A Child) v Barnet and Chase Farm
  Hospitals NHS Trust
Ahmud & Co Solicitors v MacPherson [2015] EWHC 2240 (QB) 9–06, 9–23
Akhtar v Bhopal Productions (UK) Ltd [2015] EWHC 154 (IPEC); [2015] F.S.R. 30 7–14
Akhtar & Khan v Ball unreported 10 July 2015...6–25
Allen v Colman Coyle LLP [2007] EWHC 90075 (Costs) 9–23
Alpha Rocks Solicitors v Alade [2016] 4 Costs L.R. 657 Ch D.............................9–05
Altomart v Salford Estates (No.2) Ltd [2014] EWCA Civ 1408; [2015] C.P. Rep. 8;
  [2014] 6 Costs L.R. 1013..5–61, 8–26
Amber Construction Services Ltd v London Interspace HG Ltd [2007] EWHC 3042
  (TCC); [2008] B.L.R. 74; [2008] 5 Costs L.R. 715; [2008] 1 E.G.L.R. 1; [2008] 9 E.G.
  202; [2008] Bus. L.R. D46 7–01
Americhem Europe Ltd v Rakem Ltd [2014] EWHC 1881 (TCC); 155 Con. L.R. 80;
  [2014] 4 Costs L.R. 682..4–51, 4–16
Angel Airlines v Dean & Dean [2008] EWHC 1513 (QB); [2009] 2 Costs L.R. 159........9–08
Arkin v Borchard Lines Ltd (Costs Order) [2005] EWCA Civ 655; [2005] 1 W.L.R.
  3055; [2005] 3 All E.R. 613; [2005] 2 Lloyd's Rep. 187; [2005] C.P. Rep. 39; [2005]
  4 Costs L.R. 643; (2005) 155 N.L.J. 902................................... 1–11, 2–19, 2–49
Art & Antiques Ltd v Magwell Solicitors [2015] EWHC 2143 (Ch)................................5–38
Ashman v Thomas [2016] EWHC 1810 (Ch) 8–57
Astonleigh Residential Care Home Ltd v Goldfarb [2014] EWHC 4100 (Ch)...............8–55
Attorney General v Carruthers unreported 26 April 2016 DC......................................7–12
Axelrod v University Hospitals of Leicester NHS Trust unreported 28 January 2016
  CC (Liverpool) 2–11
Azim v Tradewise Insurance Services Ltd unreported 22 August 2016 CC (Bow)
Bailes v Bloom unreported 23 November 2015 QBD...5–48
Bank of Ireland v Philip Pank Partnership [2014] EWHC 284 (TCC); [2014] 2 Costs
  L.R. 301..4–51, 4–16
Bank St Petersburg PJSC v Arkhangelsky [2015] EWHC 2997 (Ch) 7–25, 7–26
Bataillon v Shone [2015] EWHC 3177 (QB) 5–16, 5–53
Beasley v Alexander [2012] EWHC 2715 (QB); [2013] 1 W.L.R. 762; [2012] 6 Costs
  L.R. 1137; [2013] R.T.R. 7 5–14
Benaim (UK) Ltd v Davies Middleton & Davies Ltd (No.1) [2004] EWHC 737 (TCC);
  (2004) 154 N.L.J. 617..2–56

Bent v Highways and Utilities Construction & Allianz Insurance [2011] EWCA Civ 1539; [2012] 2 Costs L.O. 127 5–18

Bird v Acorn Group Ltd [2016] EWCA Civ 1096; [2016] 6 Costs L.O. 959.........1–12, 7–04

Birmingham City Council v Forde; sub nom. Forde v Birmingham City Council [2009] EWHC 12 (QB); [2009] 1 W.L.R. 2732; [2010] 1 All E.R. 802; [2009] 2 Costs L.R. 206; [2009] N.P.C. 7...2–20

Blackmore v Cummins [2009] EWCA Civ 1276; [2012] 2 Costs L.O. 127..................8–13

Blankley v Central Manchester and Manchester Children's University Hospitals NHS Trust [2015] EWCA Civ 18; [2015] 1 W.L.R. 4307; [2015] 1 Costs L.R. 119.......2–09

Bloomsbury Law Solicitors v Macpherson unreported 27 October 2016 9–05

Bolt Burdon Solicitors v Tariq [2016] EWHC 1507 (QB); [2016] 4 W.L.R. 112; [2016] 4 Costs L.O. 617 2–13

BNM v MGN Ltd [2016] 3 Costs L.O. 441 SCCO 1–04

BNM v MGN Ltd [2016] EWHC B13 (Costs) 3–03, 9–14

BNM v MGN Ltd unreported 11 January 2016 SCCO..2–63

Bolt Burdon Solicitors v Tariq [2016] EWHC 811 (QB); [2016] 2 Costs L.R. 359.........9–03, 9–19

Brahilika v Allianz Insurance Plc unreported 30 July 2015 CC (Romford)...................6–09

Brand v Berki [2015] EWHC 3373 (QB)..7–24

Brighton & Hove Bus v Brooks [2011] EWHC 2504...6–10

Bristol and West Building Society v Evans Bullock & Co unreported 5 February 1996 CA...5–07

British Gas Trading Ltd v Oak Cash and Carry Ltd; sub nom. Oak Cash & Carry Ltd v British Gas Trading Ltd [2016] EWCA Civ 153; [2016] 1 W.L.R. 4530; [2016] 4 All E.R. 129; [2016] 2 All E.R. (Comm) 840; [2016] C.P. Rep. 27; [2016] 2 Costs L.O. 289 4–109

Broadhurst v Tan; sub nom. Smith v Taylor [2016] EWCA Civ 94; [2016] 1 W.L.R. 1928; [2016] C.P. Rep. 22; [2016] 2 Costs L.O. 155; [2017] R.T.R. 1; [2016] P.I.Q.R. P12...1–09, 8–39

Buckland v Watts [1970] 1 Q.B. 27; [1969] 3 W.L.R. 92; [1969] 2 All E.R. 985; (1969) 113 S.J. 384 ....7–08, 7–09

Budana v Leeds Teaching Hospitals NHS Trust unreported 4 February 2016 CC (Hull)... 1–04, 2–08, 2–09, 2–20

Butt v Nizami [2006] EWHC 159 (QB); [2006] 1 W.L.R. 3307; [2006] 2 All E.R. 140; [2006] 3 Costs L.R. 483; [2006] R.T.R. 25; (2006) 103(9) L.S.G. 30; (2006) 156 N.L.J. 272...2–02, 9–16

C v D [2011] EWCA Civ 646; [2012] 1 W.L.R. 1962; [2012] 1 All E.R. 302; [2011] C.P. Rep. 38; 136 Con. L.R. 109; [2011] 5 Costs L.R. 773; [2011] 2 E.G.L.R. 95; [2011] 23 E.G. 86 (C.S.); (2011) 161 N.L.J. 780 ....5–07, 5–25

Caliendo v Mischon De Reya LLP [2015] EWCA Civ 1029; [2016] C.P. Rep. 3; [2015] 5 Costs L.R. 849 2–07

Campbell v Campbell [2016] EWHC 1828 (Ch)...7–25

Campbell v Campbell [2016] EWHC 2237 (Ch)...4–25

Campbell v Mirror Group Newspapers Ltd (Costs); sub nom. Campbell v MGN Ltd (Costs); Campbell v MGN Ltd (No.2) [2005] UKHL 61; [2005] 1 W.L.R. 3394; [2005] 4 All E.R. 793; [2006] 1 Costs L.R. 120; [2006] E.M.L.R. 1; [2006] H.R.L.R. 2; 21 B.H.R.C. 516; (2005) 102(42) L.S.G. 23; (2005) 155 N.L.J. 1633 2–03

Capital For Enterprise Fund A LP v Bibby Financial Services Ltd [2015] 6 Costs L.R. 1059 4–105

Carillion J M Ltd v PHI Group Ltd [2012] EWCA Civ 588; [2012] C.P. Rep. 37; [2012] B.L.R. 329; [2012] T.C.L.R. 5; 142 Con. L.R. 96; [2012] 4 Costs L.O. 523; [2012] C.I.L.L. 3180 ....5–07, 5–18

Carleton (Earl of Malmesbury) v Strutt & Parker (A Partnership) [2008] EWHC 424

Lotus Cars Ltd v Mechanica Solutions Inc [2014] EWHC 76 (QB) 4–52
Lowin v W Portsmouth & Co Ltd [2016] EWHC 2301 (QB); [2017] C.P. Rep. 1;
  [2016] 5 Costs L.O. 719 ....8–10, 8–39, 8–41, 8–42, 8–43
Lownds v Home Office [2002] EWCA Civ 365; [2002] 1 W.L.R. 2450; [2002] 4 All
  E.R. 775; [2002] C.P. Rep. 43; [2002] C.P.L.R. 328; [2002] 2 Costs L.R. 279; (2002)
  99(19) L.S.G. 28; (2002) 146 S.J.L.B. 86.............................3–02, 3–03, 3–06, 8–35, 9–14
MacDonald v Taree Holdings Ltd [2001] C.P.L.R. 439; [2001] 1 Costs L.R. 147; (2001)
  98(6) L.S.G. 45 ....8–14, 8–15
MacLennan v Morgan Sindall (Infrastructure) Plc [2013] EWHC 4044 (QB); [2014] 1
  W.L.R. 2462; (2014) 158(2) S.J.L.B. 37..4–10
Magon v Royal Sun Alliance unreported 26 February 2016 CC (Central London) 6–11,
                                                                                  6–25
Malloch v Aberdeen Corp [1973] 1 W.L.R. 71; [1973] 1 All E.R. 304; 1973 S.L.T.
  (Notes) 5; (1972) 117 S.J. 72...7–09
Mars UK Ltd v Teknowledge Ltd (Costs) [1999] 2 Costs L.R. 44; [2000] F.S.R. 138;
  (1999) 22(10) I.P.D. 22097...8–53
May v Wavell Group Plc [2016] EWHC B16 (Costs), [2016] 3 Costs L.O. 455
  SCCO 1–04, 3–03, 3–23
McDaniel & Co v Clarke [2014] EWHC 3826 (QB); [2014] 6 Costs L.R. 963.......9–01, 9–19
McGraddie v McGraddie [2015] UKSC 1; [2015] 1 W.L.R. 560; [2015] 3 All E.R. 61;
  2015 S.C. (U.K.S.C.) 45; 2015 S.L.T. 69; [2015] 2 Costs L.O. 235; 2015 G.W.D.
  4-83 2–19
Meadows v La Tasca Restaurants Ltd unreported 16 June 2016 CC (Manchester) 6–11
Mehmi v Pincher unreported hearing 20 July 2015 CC (Liverpool)...................8–32, 8–33,
Merck KGAA v Merck Sharp & Dohme Corp [2014] EWHC 3920 (Ch).........................5–45
Merrix v Heart of England NHS Foundation Trust [2016] EWHC B28 (QB).................4–99
MGN Ltd v United Kingdom (39401/04); sub nom. Mirror Group Newspapers Ltd v
  United Kingdom (39401/04) [2011] 1 Costs L.O. 84; [2011] E.M.L.R. 20; (2011) 53
  E.H.R.R. 5 ECHR 2–03
Mid-East Sales Ltd v United Engineering and Trading Co (PVT) Ltd [2014] EWHC
  1457 (Comm); [2014] 2 All E.R. (Comm) 623; [2014] 4 Costs L.O. 605.....................8–34
Milton Keynes NHS Foundation Trust v Hyde. *See* Hyde v Milton Keynes NHS Trust
Minotaur Data Systems Ltd, Re; sub nom. Official Receiver v Brunt [1999] 1 W.L.R.
  1129; [1999] 3 All E.R. 122; [1999] B.C.C. 571; [1999] 2 B.C.L.C. 766; [1999] 2
  Costs L.R. 97; [1999] B.P.I.R. 560; (1999) 96(12) L.S.G. 33; (1999) 149 N.L.J. 415;
  (1999) 143 S.J.L.B. 98; [1999] N.P.C. 27 7–09
Mitchell v News Group Newspapers Ltd [2013] EWCA Civ 1537; [2014] 1 W.L.R.
  795; [2014] 2 All E.R. 430; [2014] B.L.R. 89; [2013] 6 Costs L.R. 1008; [2014]
  E.M.L.R. 13; [2014] C.I.L.L. 3452; (2013) 163(7587) N.L.J. 20 .... 1–04, 1–05, 2–07,
                                                             4–04, 4–05, 4–19, 4–108, 5–36, 5–50
Mole v Hunter [2014] EWHC 658 (QB) 7–09
Montgomery v Lanarkshire Health Board; sub nom. NM v Lanarkshire Health Board
  [2015] UKSC 11; [2015] A.C. 1430; [2015] 2 W.L.R. 768; [2015] 2 All E.R. 1031;
  2015 S.C. (U.K.S.C.) 63; 2015 S.L.T. 189; 2015 S.C.L.R. 315; [2015] P.I.Q.R. P13;
  [2015] Med. L.R. 149; (2015) 143 B.M.L.R. 47; 2015 G.W.D. 10-179 9–01
Morgan v Spirit Group Ltd [2011] EWCA Civ 68; [2011] C.P. Rep. 22; [2011] 3 Costs
  L.R. 449; [2011] P.I.Q.R. P9..8–18
Motto v Trafigura Ltd [2011] EWCA Civ 1150; [2012] 1 W.L.R. 657; [2012] 2 All E.R.
  181; [2011] 6 Costs L.R. 1028...2–64, 9–13
Multiplex Construction (UK) Ltd v Cleveland Bridge UK Ltd [2010] EWCA Civ 449;
  [2010] C.I.L.L. 2863 5–17
Murray v Bernard [2015] EWHC 2395 (Ch); [2015] 5 Costs L.O. 567 5–31
N J Rickard Ltd v Holloway unreported 3 November 2015 CA (Civ Div).....................5–49

Nader (t/a Try Us) v Customs and Excise Commissioners [1993] S.T.C. 806 CA 7–09
NAP Anglia Ltd v Sun-Land Development Co Ltd (Costs) [2012] EWHC 51 (TCC);
 [2012] B.L.R. 195; 141 Con. L.R. 247; [2012] 4 Costs L.O. 485 QBD (TCC) 7–25
Nokes v Heart of England NHS Foundation Trust [2015] EWHC B6 2–11
Northrop Grumman Mission Systems Europe Ltd v BAE Systems (AL Diriyah C41)
 Ltd [2014] EWHC 3148 (TCC); [2014] TCLR 8; 156 Con. L.R. 141; [2014] 6 Costs
 L.O. 879; [2014] C.I.L.L. 3572 5–31
Northstar Systems Ltd v Fielding (Costs); Ultraframe (UK) Ltd v Fielding (Costs); sub
 nom. Ultraframe (UK) Ltd v Fielding (No.2) [2006] EWCA Civ 1660; [2007] 2 All
 E.R. 983; [2007] C.P. Rep. 12; [2007] 2 Costs L.R. 264 4–105
O'Beirne v Hudson [2010] EWCA Civ 52; [2010] 1 W.L.R. 1717; [2010] C.P. Rep. 23;
 [2010] 2 Costs L.R. 204; [2010] P.I.Q.R. P10...5–60
O'Brien v Shorrock; sub nom. Motor Insurers Bureau v O'Brien [2015] EWHC 1630
 (QB); [2015] 4 Costs L.O. 439...2–23
Oak Cash & Carry Ltd v British Gas Trading Ltd. *See* British Gas Trading Ltd v Oak
 Cash and Carry Ltd
Obrascon Huarte Lain SA v Gibraltar [2014] EWHC 2291 (TCC) 7–07
Octoesse LLP v Trak Special Projects Ltd [2016] EWHC 3180 (TCC); [2016] 6 Costs
 L.R. 1187 QBD (TCC) 7–25
Onay v Brown [2009] EWCA Civ 775; [2010] 1 Costs LR 29 CA 5–04
Ontulmus v Collett [2014] EWHC 4117 (QB) 5–20
OOO Abbott v Design & Display Ltd [2014] EWHC 3234 (IPEC).....................5–56, 8–32
Owners and/or Bareboat Charterers of the Ship Samco Europe v Owners of the Ship
 MSC Prestige; sub nom. Samco Europe, The (Costs); MSC Prestige, The (Costs)
 [2011] EWHC 1656 (Admlty); [2011] 2 C.L.C. 679; [2012] B.L.R. 267; (2011) 161
 N.L.J. 988 5–07
Parker v Butler [2016] EWHC 1251 (QB); [2016] 3 Costs L.R. 435... 2–36, 6–04, 6–06, 8–25
Pentecost v John [2015] EWHC 1970 (QB); [2015] 4 Costs L.O. 497............................2–23
PGF II SA v OMFS Co 1 Ltd [2013] EWCA Civ 1288; [2014] 1 W.L.R. 1386; [2014] 1
 All E.R. 970; [2014] C.P. Rep. 6; [2014] B.L.R. 1; 152 Con. L.R. 72; [2013] 6 Costs
 L.R. 973; [2013] 3 E.G.L.R. 16; [2013] 44 E.G. 98 (C.S.); (2013) 157(42) S.J.L.B.
 37 .... 1–09, 5–26, 5–49
Price v Egbert H Taylor & Co Ltd unreported 16 January 2016 CC (Birmingham) 6–05,
 6–06
Prince Abdulaziz v Apex Global Management Ltd; sub nom. Apex Global
 Management Ltd v Fi Call Ltd [2014] UKSC 64; [2014] 1 W.L.R. 4495; [2015] 2 All
 E.R. 206; [2015] 1 All E.R. (Comm) 1183; [2015] 1 Costs L.O. 79 4–05
Proctor v Raleys Solicitors (A Firm) [2015] EWCA Civ 300...9–01
Psari Holdings Ltd v Association of Litigation Funders of England and Wales. *See*
 Excalibur Ventures LLC v Texas Keystone Inc (Defendants and Costs Claimants)
 and Psari Holdings Ltd (Costs Defendants); Texas Keystone Inc v Psari Holdings Ltd
Purser v Hibbs [2015] EWHC 1792 (QB) 4–55, 5–13
Qader v Esure Services Ltd; Khan v McGee [2016] EWCA Civ 1109; [2016] 6 Costs
 L.O. 973 .... 1–12, 7–04, 9–19
R. (Bar Standards Board) v Disciplinary Tribunal of the Council of the Inns of Court
 and Sivanandan (Interested Party) [2014] EWHC 1570 (Admin); [2014] 4 All E.R.
 759 7–20
R. (Burkett) v London Borough of Hammersmith & Fulham [2004] EWCA Civ 1342;
 [2005] C.P. Rep. 11; [2005] 1 Costs L.R. 104; [2005] J.P.L. 525; [2005] A.C.D. 73;
 (2004) 101(42) L.S.G. 30; (2004) 148 S.J.L.B. 1245 6–09
R. (CJ) v Cardiff City Council [2011] EWCA Civ 1590; [2012] 2 All E.R. 836; [2012]
 P.T.S.R. 1235; [2012] C.P. Rep. 15; [2012] 1 F.C.R. 461; [2012] H.L.R. 20; [2012]
 B.L.G.R. 157; [2012] A.C.D. 44...5–57

R. (Idira) v Secretary of State for the Home Department [2015] EWCA Civ 1187........4–05, 4–108

R. (MVN) v Greenwich LBC (Costs) [2015] EWHC 2663 (Admin)...............................5–57

R. (Whitston) v Secretary of State for Justice [2014] EWHC 3044 (Admin); [2015] A.C.D. 5 2–03

R. (Wulfsohn) v Legal Services Commission; sub nom. R. (on the application of Wulfsohn) v Legal Service Commission [2002] EWCA Civ 250; [2002] C.P. Rep. 34; [2002] 3 Costs L.R. 341..7–08

Radford v Frade [2016] EWHC 1600 (QB); [2016] 4 Costs L.O. 653 ....2–24, 2–25

Rahimian & Scandia Care Ltd v Allan Janes LLP [2016] EWHC B18 (Costs)................9–05

Rallison v North West London Hospitals NHS Trust [2015] EWHC 3255 (QB); [2015] 6 Costs L.O. 771 ....8–53, 8–54

Ralph Hume Garry (A Firm) v Gwillim [2002] EWCA Civ 1500; [2003] 1 W.L.R. 510; [2003] 1 All E.R. 1038; [2003] C.P. Rep. 16; [2003] 1 Costs L.R. 77; (2002) 99(45) L.S.G. 35; (2002) 152 N.L.J. 1653; (2002) 146 S.J.L.B. 237..9–05

Rawlinson & Hunter Trustees SA v ITG Ltd [2015] EWHC 1924 (Ch).........................8–56

Redwing Construction Ltd v Wishart [2011] EWHC 19 (TCC); [2011] B.L.R. 186; [2011] T.C.L.R. 5; [2011] 2 Costs L.O. 212; [2011] Lloyd's Rep. I.R. 331; [2011] 1 E.G.L.R. 13; [2011] 15 E.G. 94; [2011] C.I.L.L. 2997; (2011) 161 N.L.J. 137 2–11

Rees v Gateley Wareing (a firm) [2014] EWCA Civ 1351; [2014] 6 Costs L.O. 953 9–04

Reid v Buckinghamshire Healthcare NHS Trust [2015] EWHC B21..............................5–31

Revenue and Customs Commissioners v GKN Group; sub nom. GKN Group v Revenue and Customs Commissioners; Test Claimants in the FII Group Litigation v Revenue and Customs Commissioners [2012] EWCA Civ 57; [2012] 1 W.L.R. 2375; [2012] 3 All E.R. 111; [2012] S.T.C. 953; [2012] C.P. Rep. 20; [2012] B.T.C. 35; [2012] S.T.I. 217 7–26

Raiffeisen Zentralbank Osterreich AG v Crossseas Shipping Ltd [2003] EWHC 1381 (Comm) (QB)..2–40

Rogers v Merthyr Tydfil CBC [2006] EWCA Civ 1134; [2007] 1 W.L.R. 808; [2007] 1 All E.R. 354; [2007] 1 Costs L.R. 77; [2006] Lloyd's Rep. I.R. 759; (2006) 150 S.J.L.B. 1053 ....2–11, 2–32

Rolf v De Guerin [2011] EWCA Civ 78; [2011] C.P. Rep. 24; [2011] B.L.R. 221; [2011] 5 Costs L.R. 892; [2011] 7 E.G. 97 (C.S.); (2011) 108(8) L.S.G. 20; [2011] N.P.C. 17..5–31

Romer & Haslam, Re [1893] 2 Q.B. 286...9–06

Rouse v Aviva Insurance Ltd unreported 15 January 2016 CC (Bradford) 6–11

Rowles-Davies v Call 24-7 Ltd [2010] EWHC 1695 (Ch); (2010) 160 N.L.J. 1043.........5–18

RTS Flexible Systems Ltd v Molkerei Alois Muller GmbH & Co AG [2010] UKSC 14; [2010] 1 W.L.R. 753; [2010] Bus. L.R. 776; [2010] 3 All E.R. 1; [2010] 2 All E.R. (Comm) 97; [2010] 1 C.L.C. 388; [2010] B.L.R. 337; 129 Con. L.R. 1; [2010] C.I.L.L. 2868; (2010) 107(12) L.S.G. 20; (2010) 160 N.L.J. 421; (2010) 154(11) S.J.L.B. 28...5–05

RXDX v Northampton BC [2015] EWHC 2938 (QB); [2015] 5 Costs L.R. 897..............5–16

Sargeant v UK Insurance Ltd [2015] EWHC 3304 (QB)..7–24

Sarpd Oil International Ltd v Addax Energy SA [2016] EWCA Civ 120; [2016] C.P. Rep. 24; [2016] B.L.R. 301; [2016] 2 Costs L.O. 227 ..1–04, 4–18, 4–50, 4–66, 4–72, 9–22

Sarwar v Alam; sub nom. Sawar v Alam [2001] EWCA Civ 1401; [2002] 1 W.L.R. 125; [2001] 4 All E.R. 541; [2002] 1 Costs L.R. 37; [2002] R.T.R. 12; [2002] Lloyd's Rep. I.R. 126; [2002] P.I.Q.R. P15; (2001) 151 N.L.J. 1492 ....2–08, 9–01

Savoye v Spicers Ltd [2015] EWHC 33 (TCC); [2015] 1 Costs L.R. 99; [2015] C.I.L.L. 3629 3–04

SB v MB (Costs) [2014] EWHC 3721 (Fam) 8–20, 8–21

Seals v Williams [2015] EWHC 1829 (Ch); [2015] 4 Costs L.O. 423; [2015] W.T.L.R. 1265 5–33

SG (a child) v Hewitt (Costs) [2012] EWCA Civ 1053; [2013] 1 All E.R. 1118; [2012]
  5 Costs L.R. 937 ....5–19, 5–45
Sharland v Sharland; sub nom. S v S [2015] UKSC 60; [2015] 3 W.L.R. 1070; [2015]
  2 F.L.R. 1367; [2015] 3 F.C.R. 481; [2015] Fam. Law 1461 5–29
Sharp v Blank [2015] EWHC 2685 (Ch) 4–24
Sharp v Leeds City Council [2017] EWCA Civ 33 1–12
Sibthorpe v Southwark LBC; sub nom. Morris v Southwark LBC [2011] EWCA Civ
  25; [2011] 1 W.L.R. 2111; [2011] 2 All E.R. 240; [2011] C.P. Rep. 21; [2011] 3 Costs
  L.R. 427; [2011] H.L.R. 19; (2011) 108(6) L.S.G. 18; (2011) 161 N.L.J. 173; [2011]
  N.P.C. 11 9–04
Siegel v Pummell [2015] EWHC 195 (QB); [2015] 3 Costs L.O. 357 7–07
Simmons v Castle [2012] EWCA Civ 1288; [2013] 1 W.L.R. 1239; [2013] 1 All E.R.
  334; [2013] C.P. Rep. 3; [2012] 6 Costs L.R. 1150; [2013] E.M.L.R. 4; [2013] P.I.Q.R.
  P2; [2013] Med. L.R. 4; (2012) 162 N.L.J. 1324; (2012) 156(39) S.J.L.B. 31......2–08, 6–02
Simpkin Marshall Ltd, Re [1959] Ch 229; [1958] 3 W.L.R. 693; [1958] 3 All E.R. 611;
  (1958) 102 S.J. 878...9–03
Simpson v MGN Ltd [2015] EWHC 126 (QB); [2015] 1 Costs L.R. 139 ....3–17, 4–20,
                                                                                                    4–104, 4–106, 4–107
Sinclair v Dorsey & Whitney (Europe) LLP [2015] EWHC 3888 (Comm) 4–05, 4–108
Slick Seating Systems v Adams [2013] EWHC 1642 (QB); [2013] 4 Costs LR 576 4–20,
                                                                                                                            8–20
Smith v Taylor. *See* Broadhurst v Tan
Smith v Trafford Housing Trust (Costs) [2012] EWHC 3320 (Ch); (2012) 156(46)
  S.J.L.B. 31...5–19
Solomon v Cromwell Group Plc [2011] EWCA Civ 1584; [2012] 1 W.L.R. 1048;
  [2012] 2 All E.R. 825; [2012] C.P. Rep. 14; [2012] 2 Costs L.R. 314; [2012] R.T.R.
  24; [2012] P.I.Q.R. P9..5–46
Sony Communications International v SSH Communications Security Corp; sub
  nom. SSH Communications Security Corp v Sony Mobile Communications AB
  [2016] EWHC 2985 (Pat); [2016] 4 W.L.R. 186 Ch D (Pat) 4–20, 4–99, 4–106, 8–20
Stocker v Stocker [2015] EWHC 1634 (QB); [2015] 4 Costs L.R. 651; [2015] E.M.L.R.
  24 ....3–14, 3–21
Stocznia Gdanska SA v Latreefers Inc; Stocznia Gdanska SA v Latvian Shipping Co
  (Abuse of Process); sub nom. Latreefers Inc, Re [2000] C.P.L.R. 65; [2001] B.C.C.
  174; [2001] 2 B.C.L.C. 116; [2001] C.L.C. 1267 CA (Civ)...2–17
Sugar Hut Group Ltd v A J Insurance [2014] EWHC 3775 (Comm); [2015] 2 Costs
  L.R. 179.. 5–18, 5–53, 5–54
Summit Navigation Ltd v Generali Romania Asigurare Reasigurare SA [2014] EWHC
  398 (Comm); [2014] 1 W.L.R. 3472; [2015] 1 All E.R. (Comm) 360; [2014] 2 Costs
  L.R. 367...4–16
Surrey (A Child) v Barnet and Chase Farm Hospitals NHS Trust; sub nom. AH v
  Lewisham Healthcare NHS Trust; Yesil (A Child) v Doncaster and Bassetlaw
  Hospitals NHS Foundation Trust [2016] EWHC 1598 (QB); [2016] 4 Costs L.O.
  571 ....2–08, 2–11, 2–26, 2–27, 9–01
Sutherland v Turnball [2010] EWHC 2699 (QB) 5–45
Symphony Group PLC v Hodgson [1994] Q.B. 179; [1993] 3 W.L.R. 830; [1993] 4
  All E.R. 143; [1997] Costs L.R. (Core Vol.) 319; (1993) 143 N.L.J. 725; (1993) 137
  S.J.L.B. 134...6–25
Tasleem v Beverley; sub nom. Bartkauskaute v Bartkauskiene [2013] EWCA Civ
  1805; [2014] 1 W.L.R. 3567; [2014] C.P. Rep. 25; [2014] 4 Costs L.O. 551.......8–49, 8–50
Tchenguiz v Serious Fraud Office [2014] EWCA Civ 1471 7–07
Ted Baker Plc v Axa Insurance UK Plc [2012] EWHC 1779 (Comm); [2012] 6 Costs
  L.R. 1023...5–14, 5–45

Tel-Ka Talk Ltd v Revenue & Customs Commissioners [2010] EWHC 90175 (Costs);
  [2011] S.T.C. 497; [2011] S.T.I. 267..2–02, 9–03
Texas Keystone Inc v Psari Holdings Ltd. *See* Excalibur Ventures LLC v Texas
  Keystone Inc (Defendants and Costs Claimants) and Psari Holdings Ltd (Costs
  Defendants)
TGA Chapman v Christopher [1998] 1 W.L.R. 12; [1998] 2 All E.R. 873; [1997]
  C.L.C. 1306; [1998] Lloyd's Rep. I.R. 1...6–13
Thai Airways International Public Co Ltd v KI Holdings Co Ltd (formerly Koito
  Industries Ltd) [2015] EWHC 1476 (Comm); [2015] 3 Costs L.R. 545......................5–16
Thevarajah v Riordan [2015] UKSC 78; [2016] 1 W.L.R. 76; [2015] 6 Costs L.R. 1119....4–05
Thewlis v Groupama Insurance Co Ltd [2012] EWHC 3 (TCC); [2012] BLR 259;
  [2012] T.C.L.R. 3; 142 Con. L.R. 85; [2012] 5 Costs L.O. 560....................................5–04
Thomas Pink Ltd v Victoria's Secret UK Ltd [2014] EWHC 3258 (Ch); [2015] 3 Costs
  L.R. 463..8–53
Thompson v Bruce [2011] EWHC 2228 (QB)...5–45
Tibbles v SIG Plc (t/a Asphaltic Roofing Supplies) [2012] EWCA Civ 518; [2012] 1
  W.L.R. 2591; [2012] 4 All E.R. 259; [2012] C.P. Rep. 32; [2013] 1 Costs L.O. 41........4–05
Transformers and Rectifiers Ltd v Needs Ltd [2015] EWHC 1687 (TCC); [2015] 3
  Costs L.R. 611; [2015] C.I.L.L. 3702...8–02, 8–21, 8–22
Troy Foods v Manton [2013] EWCA Civ 615; [2013] 4 Costs L.R. 546................3–17, 4–99
Trustees of Stokes Pension Fund v Western Power Distribution (South West) Plc
  [2005] EWCA Civ 854; [2005] 1 W.L.R. 3595; [2005] 3 All E.R. 775; [2005] C.P.
  Rep. 40; [2005] B.L.R. 497; [2006] 2 Costs L.R. 226; (2005) 102(30) L.S.G. 28...........5–01
Turner & Co v O Palomo SA [2000] 1 W.L.R. 37; [1999] 4 All E.R. 353; [1999] 2 Costs
  L.R. 184; [1999] N.P.C. 114..9–06
United Building and Plumbing Contractors v Kajla [2002] EWCA Civ 628; [2002]
  C.P. Rep. 53..7–09
Van Oord UK Ltd v Allseas UK Ltd [2015] EWHC 3385 (TCC)..........................5–06, 5–49
Vava v Anglo American South Africa Ltd [2013] EWHC 2326 (QB); [2013] 5 Costs LR
  805...6–09
Venn v Secretary of State for Communities & Local Government [2014] EWCA Civ
  1539...7–05
Vestergaard Frandsen A/S v Bestnet Europe Ltd [2014] EWHC 4047 (Ch)................5–59
Viridor Waste Management Ltd v Veolia ES Ltd [2015] EWHC 2321 (Comm)..............4–05
Vlamaki v Sookias & Sookias (A Firm) [2015] EWHC 3334 (QB); [2015] 6 Costs L.O.
  827...9–05
Wagenaar v Weekend Travel Ltd (t/a Ski Weekend) [2014] EWCA Civ 1105; [2014]
  C.P. Rep. 46; [2014] 5 Costs L.O. 803; [2014] P.I.Q.R. P23............ 6–04, 6–17, 6–18, 8–25
Wall v Royal Bank of Scotland Plc [2016] EWHC 2460 (Comm); [2017] 4 W.L.R. 2;
  [2016] 5 Costs L.R. 943 (QB) 2–40
Watchorn v Jupiter Industries Ltd; sub nom. Husky Group Ltd, Re [2014] EWHC
  3003 (Ch); [2015] 3 Costs L.O. 337; [2015] B.P.I.R. 184 5–16
Webb v Bromley LBC unreported 18 February 2016 (SCCO)....................................2–20
Webb v Liverpool Women's NHS Foundation Trust [2015] EWHC 449 (QB); [2015]
  3 Costs L.O. 367 5–58
Webb Resolutions Ltd v E-Serv Ltd [2014] EWHC 49 (QB); [2014] 1 Costs L.R.
  182..8–15, 8–34
Wheeler v Chief Constable of Gloucestershire [2013] EWCA Civ 1791......................8–15
Williams v Jervis [2009] EWHC 1838 (QB)...5–19
Willis v MRJ Rundell & Associates Ltd [2013] EWHC 2923 (TCC); [2013] 6 Costs L.R.
  924; [2013] 3 E.G.L.R. 13; [2013] C.I.L.L. 3428...4–69
Wilsons Solicitors LLP v Bentine; Stone Rowe Brewer LLP v Just Costs Ltd [2015]
  EWCA Civ 1168; [2015] 6 Costs L.O. 779..9–08, 9–23

Worthington v 03918424 Ltd unreported 16 June 2015 CC (Manchester)....................7–19
Wright v Rowland [2016] EWHC 2206 (Comm); [2016] 5 Costs L.O. 713....................4–15
Yampolskaya v AB Bankas Snoras (In Bankruptcy); sub nom. Akcine Bendore Bankas
    Snoras (In Bankruptcy) v Antonov [2015] EWHC 2136 (QB).....................................7–24
Yentob v MGN Ltd [2015] EWCA Civ 1292; [2015] 6 Costs L.R. 1103 5–15
Yeo v Times Newspapers Ltd [2015] EWHC 209 (QB); [2015] 1 W.L.R. 3031; [2015]
    2 Costs L.O. 243; [2015] E.M.L.R. 18... 4–18, 4–19, 4–67, 4–69
Yesil (A Child) v Doncaster and Bassetlaw Hospitals NHS Foundation Trust. *See*
    Surrey (A Child) v Barnet and Chase Farm Hospitals NHS Trust

Table of Statutes

1934 Law Reform (Miscellaneous
      Provisions) Act (c.41) 5–10,
                                     6–04
1954 Landlord and Tenant Act
      (c.56) 4–30
      s.24 4–30
      s.29 4–30
1974 Solicitors Act (c.47) 9–03, 9–04,
                                     9–05, 9–08, 9–10
      Pt III....................................7–13
      ss.56–75 9–01
      s.57 .... 2–02, 2–13, 9–03
          (2) 9–03
      s.59 ....9–03, 9–04
      s.64 9–06
      s.68 9–05
      s.69 9–05
      s.70 .... 2–59, 9–05, 9–06,
                                     9–07, 9–23
          (1) 9–06, 9–23
          (2) 9–06
          (3) 9–06
          (5) 9–08
          (9) 9–06, 9–08, 9–23
      s.74(3)..................................4–86
      s.87 9–03
1975 Litigants in Person (Costs
      and Expenses) Act
      (c.47) 7–08, 7–09
      s.1 7–08
          (1) 7–08
1976 Fatal Accidents Act (c.30).........5–10,
                                     6–04, 6–08
1978 Civil Liability (Contribution)
      Act (c.47) 5–07, 6–04
1981 Senior Courts Act (c.54)
      s.51 .... 2–19, 2–40, 2–47,
                                     2–51, 5–19,
                                     7–22, 9–02
1986 Insolvency Act (c.45) 2–03
1990 Town & Country Planning
      Act
      (c.8)
      s.288 7–05
1990 Courts & Legal Services Act
      (c.41) 7–25

      s.57 ....9–03, 9–04
      s.58 .... 2–02, 2–04, 2–06, 2–17,
                   2–24, 2–50, 2–310, 2–56,
                          9–03, 9–04, 9–16
          (1) 2–02
          (2) 9–16
          (4) 2–20
          (c) 2–04, 2–55
          (4A) 2–02
          (b)....................................2–02
          (4B) 2–02, 2–04, 2–06
          (b)....................................2–04
          (5) 2–02, 9–04
          (6) 2–19, 2–56
      s.58A..........................2–04, 9–04
          (4) 2–19, 2–56
          (6) 2–02, 2–19, 2–37, 2–43
      s.58AA..... 2–02, 2–13, 2–17, 2–31,
                   2–59, 9–03, 9–04
          (2) 2–60
          (3) 2–17
          (a) 2–17
          (4) 2–13, 2–60
          (b)....................................2–60
          (7) 1–11
          (9) 9–04
      s.58C........ 2–10, 2–11, 2–32, 2–33
      s.61 9–04
1996 Arbitration Act (c.23) 2–19, 2–46,
                                     5–36, 5–69
      s.1 5–36
      s.4 5–36
      s.7 5–36
      s.9 5–36
      s.59(1)(c)..............................2–19
      ss.59–65 2–47
      s.61 ....5–36, 5–69
      s.63 5–36
          (5) 5–69
      s.68(4)..................................2–19
1996 Housing Grants,
      Construction and
      Regeneration Act
      (c.53) 5–35
1999 Access to Justice Act (c.22)........1–01
      s.11 6–02

s.29   2–10, 2–19, 2–36
      s.30 2–10
2006 Compensation Act 2006
      (c.29) 1–11, 2–17
      Pt 2 .... 1–11, 2–17
      s.4(2)(b) 1–11, 2–17
2007 Legal Services Act (c.29)
      Sch.3 7–25
2009 Local Democracy, Economic
      Development and
      Construction Act (c.20)
      Pt 8 5–35
2012 Legal Aid, Sentencing &
      Punishment of Offenders
      Act (c.10) 1–07, 2–01, 2–08,
            2–17, 2–35, 2–51, 9–01
      s.26 6–02

Pt 2   1–07
      s.44 .... 2–02, 2–03, 2–04,
            2–19, 2–51, 2–54
      (6) 2–03, 2–08, 2–09, 2–20,
          2–23, 2–37, 2–43, 2–50,
          2–51, 2–52,
      ss.44–46 1–06
      s.45 2–13
      s.46 .... 2–10, 2–19, 2–54, 6–01
      (3) 2–36, 2–52
      s.47 2–10
      s.48 .... 1–07, 2–03
2015 Criminal Justice and Courts
      Act (c.2)
      s.57 .... 6–08, 6–10, 6–11
      (3) 6–11

Table of Statutory Instruments

1965 Rules of the Supreme Court
        (SI 1965/1776)...................5–69
      Ord.62 r.3(3).........................5–69
        r.12.................................5–69
        r.18.................................7–20
          (6)................................7–20
        Appendix 2 5–69
        para.1 5–69
1980 Litigants in Person (Costs
      and Expenses) Order (SI
      1980/1159).........................7–08
1998 Civil Procedure Rules (SI
      1998/3132).... 3–01, 3–11, 4–01,
            4–03, 4–05, 4–23, 4–30,
            5–07, 5–49, 5–64, 7–05,
            7–20, 8–02, 8–26, 8–55,
            9–01, 9–16, 9–20, 9–23
      Pt 1 4–27
      r.1.1 .... 3–02, 4–02, 4–07,
                              4–55, 4–95,
          (1) 3–03
          (2)(e) 3–03, 4–60, 4–110
            (f)......................4–02, 4–03
      r.1.2(f).................................8–03
      Pt 2 8–51
      r.2.1 ....5–37, 5–38
      r.2.3 6–04
          (1) 6–22
      r.2.11 4–38
      PD 2B para.11.1(a).................4–30
      Pt 3 .... 3–17, 4–32, 4–49,
                              4–112, 6–25
      Pt 3 II......................................9–12
      r.3.1(2)(ll) 4–49
            (m)......... 4–02, 4–49, 5–33
          (7) 4–05
          (ll)......................................4–89
      r.3.1A............... 4–111, 7–09, 7–24
          (1) 4–111
      r.3.3(5)...................................4–26
      r.3.4(2)(a)..................... 6–09, 7–01
          (b) 6–09
      r.3.8 4–05
          (3) 4–38
          (4) 4–05, 4–38
      r.3.9 .... 2–07, 3–03, 4–02, 4–03,
            4–04, 4–05, 4–103, 4–104,
            4–108, 4–109, 5–37, 5–61,
                7–24, 8–26, 8–32
          (1) 4–03
      r.3.12 ...... 3–04, 3–15, 4–16, 4–18,
            4–23, 4–25, 4–28, 4–30,
            4–36, 4–40, 4–67, 4–73,
                6–29, 9–15
          (1) 4–23, 4–25, 4–29, 4–32,
                4–87
          (a) 4–15
          (b).....................4–15, 4–30
          (c) 4–87, 4–96
          (e) 4–15, 4–23, 4–24,
                4–112
          (1A) 4–15, 4–23, 4–25,
            4–29, 4–35, 4–94, 4–112
          (2) 4–01, 4–25, 4–60
      rr.3.12–3.18 ...... 4–02, 4–14, 4–25,
                4–84, 4–89
      r.3.12(2).....................4–18, 4–78
      r.3.13 ...... 4–23, 4–24, 4–25, 4–28,
            4–33, 4–37, 4–38, 4–39,
            4–40, 4–63, 4–80, 4–89,
                4–90, 9–13
          (1) 4–25, 4–32, 4–42
          (a) 4–28
          (b)....................4–18, 4–28
          (2) 4–16, 4–25, 4–38,
            4–42, 4–59, 4–60, 4–63
      r.3.14 ...... 4–05, 4–13, 4–16, 4–24,
            4–27, 4–33, 4–30, 4–37,
            4–39, 4–40, 4–44, 4–50,
                4–90, 5–50
      r.3.15 ...... 1–03, 1–05, 4–15, 4–16,
            4–18, 4–22, 4–40, 4–67,
            4–73, 4–78, 4–84, 4–87,
          (1) ... 4–18, 4–25, 4–60, 4–112
          (2) 4–24, 4–26, 4–27, 4–84
          (3) 4–19, 4–55, 4–81,
                4–92, 4–95
      r.3.16 4–88
      r.3.17 ...... 3–03, 3–15, 4–01, 4–22,
            4–24, 4–26, 4–27, 4–55,
            4–60, 4–78, 4–87, 4–92,
                4–95

r.3.18   1–09, 2–19, 3–16, 3–17,
          3–18, 4–15, 4–20, 4–21,
          4–25, 4–55, 4–62, 4–68,
          4–71, 4–84, 4–90, 4–95,
          4–99, 4–100, 4–101, 4–102,
          4–103, 4–104, 4–105,
          4–107, 6–29, 8–19, 8–53,
          9–22
          (a) 4–20
          (b) 4–20, 4–99, 4–106
          r.3.19(5)(b) 4–112
          rr.3.19–3.21 1–10
          r.3.20...................4–89, 4–112
          (3)(a) 4–112
PD 3E...... 1–03, 3–17, 4–02, 4–14,
          4–16, 4–20, 4–25, 4–26,
          4–41, 4–73, 4–89, 4–112
          para.2......... 1–03, 4–23, 4–25,
          4–29
          (a) 4–31, 4–112
          (b).....................4–15, 4–32
          paras 2–5..........................4–15
          para.5...............................4–23
          (a)–(f).........................4–15
          para.6....................4–41, 4–50
          (a) 4–26, 4–30, 4–44
          (b).....................................4–48
          (c) 4–26, 4–49
          para.6.3(a).......................4–50
          (b)...............................4–50
          para.6A..............................4–16
          (c) 4–58
          para.7.2........ 4–60, 4–84, 9–24
          para.7.3...... 3–03, 3–11, 4–18,
          4–58, 4–62, 4–68, 4–70,
          4–73, 4–74, 4–79, 4–99,
          4–101, 4–102, 4–112, 8–19
          para.7.4...... 3–09, 4–18, 4–50,
          4–51, 4–67, 4–68, 4–70,
          4–72, 9–22
          para.7.6...... 3–09, 3–17, 4–11,
          4–15, 4–17, 4–19, 4–50,
          4–51, 4–55, 4–88, 4–89,
          4–91, 4–92, 4–93, 4–94,
          4–95, 4–98, 4–104
          para.7.7.................4–16, 4–80
          para.7.8..... 4–15, 4–25, 4–111
          para.7.9...... 3–09, 4–17, 4–19,
          4–45, 4–47, 4–50, 4–96,
          4–98,
          para.7.10.... 4–18, 4–58, 4–99,
          4–73, 4–74, 4–77
PD 3F 4–89, 4–112

para.2   4–112
          para.4.1 4–112
Pt 4 PD..............................4–31
r.5.5 4–39
PD 5B....................................4–39
          para.1.2(a).......................4–39
          para.2.2...........................4–39
          para.2.3...........................4–39
          para.3...............................4–39
          para.4...............................4–39
          para.5...............................4–39
r.6.2(a).................................4–50
          (b) 4–50
Pt 7 .... 1–03, 4–15, 4–24, 4–28,
          4–30, 4–31, 4–87, 5–46,
          8–49, 8–55
r.7.2(1)................................5–42
r.7.3 4–58
r.7.6 4–17
r.7.10 4–58
Pt 8 .... 4–26, 4–29, 4–30, 5–04,
          5–22, 5–46, 7–04, 8–49,
          8–50, 9–07
PD 8A....................................5–45
          para.6.4 4–29
PD 8B........................5–04, 5–22
r.12.4(1)..............................7–01
PD 12 para 2(1)(a) 7–04
r.13.3(2)..............................8–33
r.14.1 5–35
r.14.4(3)..............................7–01
r.14.5(6)..............................7–01
r.16.3 4–24
          (2)(b) 4–24
          (7) 4–87
r.20.2 5–04
r.20.3 ....5–04, 5–40
Pt 21 ....4–15, 9–19
r.21.1(2)..............................7–03
r.21.10 7–05
          (2) 6–04
          (b)..............................6–04
r.21.12 9–19
          (1A) 9–19
          (7) 9–19
PD 21 9–19
PD 22 para.2.2A..........3–16, 3–21,
          4–52, 4–83, 4–86,
          para.5.............................4–52
Pt 23 5–08
r.23.8 8–22
PD 23A para.6.2(c) 4–63
Pt 24 ....4–96, 7–01

r.25.13(2)(c)...........................5–31
r.25.14 2–40
r.26.3 ...... 4–02, 4–06, 4–28, 4–33,
4–38
(1) 4–16, 4–37, 4–38
(6A) 4–30, 4–38
(7A) 4–37, 4–38
r.26.6(3)...................... 4–02, 4–07
r.26.7(3)...................... 4–02, 4–07
r.26.8(2)................................7–01
PD 26 para.12.3(2)................4–28
para.12.4.........................4–28
Pt 27 .... 5–67, 7–15
r.27.2 7–15
r.27.14 .... 2–44, 7–15
(5) 4–02, 4–07
(6) 4–02, 4–07
Pt 29 4–89
r.29.1(2)...................... 4–02, 4–08,
4–09, 4–111
r.29.4 4–63
r.29.5 4–38
(1)(a) 4–38
PD 29 para.2.6A....................4–62
para.8.1(1) 4–89
para.10.5............... 8–02, 8–21
r.31.5 .... 4–09, 9–15
(1) 4–09
(2) 4–09
(3)–(8) 4–02, 4–09
(7) 4–09, 4–17, 4–22
(b)..............................4–17
r.31.6 4–09
r.31.22 7–07
r.32.1 4–10
r.32.2 9–15
(3) ... 4–02, 4–10, 4–22, 4–110
r.32.3 2–49
r.32.14 4–52
r.35.4 .... 4–02, 4–11, 4–49, 9–15
(2) 4–11
PD 11...................................4–12
PD 35 para.11 .... 4–02, 4–12
Pt 36 .... 2–01, 4–13, 4–55, 4–90,
4–21, 5–01, 5–02, 5–03,
5–04, 5–06, 5–07, 5–16,
5–17, 5–18, 5–20, 5–25,
5–26, 5–28, 5–37, 5–42,
5–45, 5–46, 5–49, 5–61,
5–62, 6–27, 8–06, 8–08,
8–11, 8–25, 8–39, 8–40,
8–41, 8–42, 8–44, 8–48,
9–06, 9–22, 9–23

s.I 5–04, 5–06, 5–42, 5–49
r.36.1 5–04
r.36.2 .... 5–04, 5–48, 5–49
(2) 5–38, 5–39, 5–49
(c) 5–49
(d)............................5–18
(3) 5–04, 5–40, 5–49
(5) 5–04
r.36.3 .... 5–03, 5–04, 5–12, 5–45
(e).......................5–12, 5–45
(g).......................4–21, 5–06
r.36.4(1)...............................5–05
(2) 5–05
r.36.5 ...... 5–04, 5–18, 5–39, 5–42,
5–48, 5–49
(1) 5–06, 5–40, 5–49
(c) 5–49
(d)............................5–18
(2) 5–06
(4) 5–38, 5–41
r.36.7 .... 5–06, 5–40, 5–41, 5–42
r.36.9 .... 5–42, 5–43, 5–44
(1) 5–07, 5–43
(2) 5–07
(3) 5–07
(4) 5–07
(b)............................5–07
(5) 5–07
r.36.10 .... 5–07, 5–08, 5–15, 5–42,
5–43, 5–44, 9–23
(1) 5–04, 5–25
(3) 5–44
(4) 5–25, 5–48
(5) 5–13, 5–25, 7–19
r.36.11 .... 5–03, 5–15
(1) 5–09
(2) 5–09
(3) 5–10
(4) 5–10
r.36.12 .... 5–03, 5–12, 5–44,
5–45
r.36.13 .... 5–04, 5–06, 5–10,
5–15, 5–45, 5–49
(1) 5–13, 5–25, 5–46, 5–47,
5–48, 5–49, 5–50
(2) 5–13, 5–47
(4) 4–55, 5–13, 5–25,
5–48, 5–50
(5) 4–55, 5–13, 5–25,
5–45, 7–19
(b)..................... 4–90, 5–21
(5)–(7) 5–13, 5–45
(7) 5–48, 5–49

r.36.14 .... 5–15, 5–16, 5–17, 5–19,
5–45, 5–50, 5–51, 5–56,
9–23
(1) 5–47
(1A) 5–17
(2) 5–45
(3) 5–16, 5–40, 5–51
(a) 5–16
(b) 5–18
(c) 5–18
(d) 5–16
(4) 5–19
r.36.15 5–51
(1)–(4) 5–11
r.36.16 .... 5–03, 5–45
(1)–(4) 5–14
r.36.17 .... 1–09, 5–15, 5–16, 5–17,
5–19, 5–45, 5–53, 5–54,
5–56, 8–39, 8–41, 8–45,
8–51
(1) 4–90
(a) 8–41, 8–44
(b) 8–38, 8–39, 8–41,
8–44
(1)–(3) 5–15
(2) 5–17, 5–62
(3) 5–15, 5–45, 8–41,
8–44
(a) 4–90, 5–21, 5–51
(4) 5–15, 5–16, 5–49, 5–51,
5–54, 5–55, 5–56, 5–57,
8–38, 8–39, 8–41, 8–44
(b).......... 1–09, 4–21, 4–90,
5–18, 5–21, 5–51,
8–37, 8–39
(c) 5–18
(d).......... 4–02, 4–13, 5–16,
5–23, 5–52, 5–53, 5–55,
8–38, 8–45, 8–51
(5) 5–13, 5–16, 5–19, 5–45
(e) 5–57
(6) 5–16
(7) 5–07, 5–15
(8) 5–15
r.36.20 .... 5–06, 5–49
r.36.21 5–15
r.36.23 ..... 4–13, 4–90, 5–21, 5–50
s.II................. 5–04, 5–22
r.36.24 5–22
r.36.25 5–22
r.36.26 .... 5–22, 5–23
r.36.27 5–22
r.36.28 5–22

r.36.29 5–23
(1)–(4) 5–23
r.36.30 5–24
PD 36A................................5–01
para.1.2............................5–06
para.2...............................5–08
para.3.1............................5–47
r.38.4 .... 6–11, 6–25
r.38.6 .... 6–25, 6–26
(1) 6–25
r.39.2(3) 9–10
r.39.4 4–110
r.39.6 7–25
r.41.3A 5–10
r.43.2(1)(a)............................8–28
PD 43 para.11.7 2–48
para.11.8 2–48
Pts 43–48 .... 2–07, 2–41, 2–53
Pt 44 .... 2–39, 4–99, 5–16, 5–62
r.44.1 ...... 4–66, 8–02, 8–22, 8–25,
8–27, 8–45, 8–50
r.44.2 ..... 2–19, 4–105, 5–17, 5–26,
5–42, 5–49, 5–57, 5–58,
6–07
(4) 5–17, 5–28, 5–54, 5–61
(a) 3–10, 5–17, 5–54
(b)....................3–07, 5–17
(c) 5–17, 5–54, 9–23
(6) 3–07, 8–48
(7) 8–48
(8) 7–04, 8–13, 8–56, 8–57
r.44.3 ..... 2–16, 2–19, 4–68, 4–101
(1) 4–68
(1)–(3) 7–06
(2) 3–03, 3–05, 3–19, 8–17
(a) 1–08, 3–03, 3–04,
3–11, 3–12, 3–13, 3–14,
3–15, 3–18, 3–19, 3–23,
4–20, 4–21, 4–36, 4–64,
4–68, 4–69, 4–75, 4–95,
4–99, 8–10, 8–35, 8–36,
8–54
(4) 7–06
(5) 1–07, 1–08, 3–03, 3–04,
3–05, 3–11, 3–12, 3–13,
3–14, 3–21, 3–22, 3–23,
4–07, 4–15, 4–18, 4–19,
4–25, 4–36, 4–55, 4–62,
4–75, 4–95, 4–99, 4–110,
8–18, 8–47, 8–35, 8–36,
9–14
(a) 3–07,
(c) 3–07, 4–55

(d)........... 3–09, 3–10, 8–36
(e) 4–55
(6)(g) 5–19
(7) 2–63, 3–06, 8–02, 8–06
(b)..................................2–63
r.44.3B 2–07
(1)(c) 2–41
(d) 2–07, 2–41
r.44.4 ....3–07, 4–105
(1)(a) 3–19
(b)....................3–16, 8–39
(2) 4–99, 8–18, 9–07
(3) 3–06, 3–16, 4–25, 4–62, 4–99, 8–47, 9–07
(g) 4–62
(h)................................4–99
r.44.5 ....7–15, 9–02
(3) 3–02, 3–06
r.44.6 8–02
(a)...................................2–51
(b) 7–04
r.44.7 6–07
r.44.9(1)(b) 5–46, 5–47
Pt 44 Pt II....................6–03, 6–07
r.44.11 4–103
(1)(b) 4–103
(2)(a) 4–103
r.44.12 6–28
(2)(a) 6–12
(b)....................6–01, 6–12
r.44.13 .... 6–04, 6–12, 6–17, 6–26, 8–25
(1) 6–01, 6–04, 6–21, 8–25
(3) 6–15
r.44.14 .... 6–08, 6–09, 6–15, 6–16, 6–25
(1) 6–08, 6–27
(2) 6–07, 8–25
r.44.15 .... 2–07, 6–08, 6–09, 6–25, 6–26, 8–39
(1) 6–08
(a) 6–11
r.44.16 .... 6–08, 6–10, 6–12, 6–15, 6–25
(1) 6–08, 6–11
(2) 6–11, 6–12, 6–13
(a) 6–12
(b)................................6–12
(3) 6–13
r.44.17 .... 6–05, 6–06, 6–18, 6–19, 6–20, 6–23

Pt III............................6–16, 6–30
r.44.18 2–16
(2)(b) 2–16
PD 44 6–15
para.3 .... 4–26, 4–27, 4–69, 4–89, 4–112
para.3.1 4–112
para.3.6.............................3–15
para.3.7.............................3–15
paras 4.1–4.2..................5–28
para.4.2.............................5–20
para.9 8–02
para.9.1 8–21
para.9.2 ....2–49, 8–21
(a) 8–21
(b)................................8–21
para.9.5 8–15
(3)....................4–41, 8–03
(4)....................8–04, 8–15
para.9.6 8–14
para.9.7 8–22
para.12 6–11
para.12.1 6–03
para.12.2 6–12
para.12.4(a)....................6–11
(b)................................6–11
(c) 6–11, 6–25
para.12.5 6–13
para.19 2–07
(2)....................................2–41
(3)....................................2–39
Pts 44–48 2–07
Pt 45 .... 1–09, 7–01, 7–05, 7–13, 7–14
s.I 7–01
r.45.1 7–15
(1) 7–01
(2)(a) 7–01
(b)................................7–01
r.45.2 7–01
r.45.3 ....7–01, 8–04
r.45.4 7–01
r.45.5 7–15
r.45.6 7–15
s.II....................................5–46, 7–01
r.45.9(2)............................7–01
(4) 7–01
r.45.15(7)............................8–36
s.III....................................7–01
r.45.18 ....5–22, 7–03
r.45.20 5–23
r.45.24 7–04
r.45.26 5–23

s.IIIA 5–06, 5–15, 5–49,
            7–01, 7–04
r.45.29A 7–04
r.45.29E(4)(c) 7–04
r.45.29J 7–04
s.IV 7–01, 7–04
r.45.30(1) 7–04
    (2) 7–04
    (3) 7–04
s.V 7–01, 7–04
r.45.33 7–04
    (3)–(6) 7–04
r.45.34 7–04
r.45.35 7–04
r.45.36 7–04
s.VI 7–01, 7–05
r.45.37(1) 7–05
    (2) 7–05
s.VII 7–01, 7–05
r.45.41 7–05
    (2) 7–05
r.45.42 7–05
r.45.43 7–05
r.45.44 7–05
PD 45 paras 1.1–1.3 7–01
    paras 4.1–4.3 7–05
    para.5.1 7–05
    para.5.2 7–05
Pt 46 4–112
r.46.2 6–13
r.46.4 9–18
r.46.5 .... 4–25, 7–08, 7–09
    (3)(b) 7–25
    (c) 7–09
    (4)(a) 7–20
    (6) 7–20, 7–23
    (a) 7–23
    (b) 7–23
r.46.9 .... 9–10, 9–12, 9–17,
            9–20
    (3) 9–12
    (a) 9–12
    (b) 9–12
    (c) 4–85, 4–86, 9–10
    (4) 9–17
r.46.10 9–10
r.46.13 5–59
    (2) 5–60
    (3) 5–60
r.46.14 ..... 5–46, 8–48, 8–49, 8–50
    (5) 5–46
    (6) 5–46
PD 46 para.3 7–20

para.3.2 7–20
para.8.2 5–60
Pt 47 .... 4–99, 5–47, 7–04, 8–06,
        8–08, 8–30, 8–39, 8–46,
            8–50
r.47.1 ....4–35, 8–51
r.47.6 4–35
    (1) 8–496
r.47.11 8–46
r.47.14 .... 4–35, 8–48, 8–49
    (1) 8–46
    (7) 8–06
r.47.15 .... 4–35, 8–07, 8–27, 8–30,
        8–39, 8–41, 8–43, 8–50,
            8–52
    (3) 8–08, 8–30, 8–31
    (4) 8–08, 8–09, 8–30
    (5) 8–10, 8–38, 8–39, 8–41,
            8–46, 8–48, 8–52
    (6) 8–07
    (10) 8–41, 8–42,
    (a) 8–41
    (b) 8–41
r.47.16(1) 8–46
r.47.20 .... 8–06, 8–10, 8–11, 8–38,
        8–39, 8–40, 8–41, 8–44,
            8–45, 8–48,
    (1)(a) 8–48
    (b) 8–48
    (3) 4–19, 8–48
    (a) 5–61, 8–26
    (4) 5–25, 8–10, 8–48
    (7) 8–25, 8–51
PD 47 8–27
    para.1.1 8–51
    para.5.1A 8–06
    para.5.2(f) 8–06, 8–23
    para.5.7 .... 8–06, 8–48, 8–52
    (7) 3–06
    para.8.2 8–06
    para.8.3 ...... 5–60, 5–61, 8–06,
            8–25, 8–26, 8–30
    para.12.1 8–06
    para.13.2 ....8–30, 8–33,
    (i) 8–32, 8–33, 8–41,
    (m) 8–06
    para.13.13 ....8–32, 8–33
    para.13.4 8–09
    para.13.6 8–09
    para.13.9 8–12
    para.13.11 ... 8–08, 8–09, 8–30
    para.13.12 ... 8–08, 8–09, 8–30
    para.13.13 8–08

para.14..................8–07, 8–52
para.14.2...............8–38, 8–46
  (1)...............................8–39
  (2)...........8–08, 8–12, 8–30
para.14.3.........................8–30
  (b)–(e).........................8–08
para.14.4(1).........8–30, 8–31,
                   8–46
  (2).....................8–10, 8–35
para.14.5...............8–11, 8–41
para.19..........................5–25
  (3)...............................2–45
para.32.................2–07, 2–39
  (3)...............................2–49
  (5)...............................2–37
Sch. 8–06
r.48.1 ...... 2–07, 2–37, 2–39, 2–41,
                   2–45
  (1) 2–42
r.48.2 ...... 2–09, 2–19, 2–50, 6–02,
      6–05, 6–17, 6–18, 6–20,
  (1)(b)...............................2–41
    (i)(aa)...........................6–06
r.48.6(6)................................7–20
r.48.8 ....9–07, 9–08, 9–10
  (2) 9–07
r.48.9 9–08
  (5) 9–19
r.48.10 ....9–08, 9–10
  para.54.1 9–08
PD 51G 3–16, 3–17, 4–99
  para.1.3.................3–17, 4–99
  para.4.2.................3–17, 4–99
  para.6...........................9–12
PD 51L.... 1–13, 4–39, 8–06, 8–19,
                   8–23
PD 51M................................4–26
PD 51N 4–26, 4–36
  para.2.56..........................4–26
  para.2.57..........................4–36
  para.2.58..........................4–36
  para.2.59..........................8–05
Pt 52 4–93
r.52.3(5)................................8–33
r.52.9A 7–09
  (4) 7–09
Pt 55 .... 4–31, 7–14, 7–15
r.55.3(5)................................4–31
PD 55 para.1.5.......................4–31
r.56.3(2)(b) 4–30
  (c) 4–30
  (3) 4–30
  (4) 4–30

PD 56 para.3.16.....................4–30
s.II...7–15
r.61.4(10)–(12).......................5–07
r.63.26 .... 7–04, 7–14
2000 Conditional Fee Agreements
      Regulations (SI
      2000/692)....... 1–01, 2–14, 2–26
      reg.4....................................2–26
2000 Conditional Fee Agreements
      Order (SI 2000/823)
      art.4 2–55
2001 Litigants in Person
      (Costs and Expenses)
      (Magistrates' Courts)
      Order (SI 2001/3438) 7–08,
                   7–09
2005 Conditional Fee Agreements
      (Revocation) Regulations
      (SI 2005/2305)...................1–01
2006 Civil Procedure (Amendment
      No.3) Rules (SI 2006/
      3435) 5–01
2008 Cancellation of Contracts
      made in a Consumer's
      Home or Place of Work
      etc. Regulations (SI
      2008/1816).........................2–62
2009 Judicial Committee
      (Appellate Jurisdiction)
      Rules Order (SI 2009/224)..5–37
      r.43(1)....................................5–37
2013 Legal Aid, Sentencing
      and Punishment of
      Offenders Act 2012
      (Commencement No.5
      and Saving Provision)
      Order (SI 2013/77) 2–03
      art.4 ....2–35, 2–54
      (b) 2–55
2013 Recovery of Costs Insurance
      Premiums in Clinical
      Negligence Proceedings
      Regulations (SI 2013/92)....6–05
2013 Civil Procedure
      (Amendment) Rules (SI
      2013/262)
      r.16 2–07
2013 Damages–Based Agreements
      Regulations (SI
      2013/609)...... 1–11, 2–13, 2–17,
             2–50, 2–31, 2–58, 2–60,
                  2–61, 9–19
      reg.1............................2–14, 2–17

reg.4 .... 2–14, 2–17, 2–58,
2–59, 2–61
(1)(b) 2–14
(2) 2–15
(3) 2–14
reg.5 2–14

2013 Conditional Fee Agreements
Order (SI 2013/689) 2–04,
2–06, 2–19, 2–24, 2–50,
2–31
art.2 2–02
art.4 2–04
art.5 .... 2–04, 2–06
(1)(b) 2–05
(2) 2–04
art.6 2–04

2013 Recovery of Costs Insurance
Premiums in Clinical
Negligence Proceedings
(No.2) Regulations (SI
2013/739) 2–11, 2–34

2013 Consumer Contracts
(Information,
Cancellation and
Additional Charges)
Regulations (SI 2013/
3134) 2–62

2014 Civil Procedure (Amendment
No.8) Rules (SI
2014/3299) 5–01, 9–19
r.18(1) 5–03
(2) 5–03
Sch.1 5–01

2015 Alternative Dispute
Resolution for Consumer
Disputes (Competent
Authorities and
Information) Regulations
(SI 2015/542) 5–63
Pts 1–3 5–63
reg.3 5–63
Pt.4 5–63
reg.19 5–63
reg.19A 5–63
Pt.5 5–63
Sch.1 5–63

2015 Alternative Dispute
Resolution for Consumer
Disputes (Amendment)
Regulations (SI 2015/
1392) 5–63
reg.2(3) 5–63

2016 Civil Procedure
(Amendment) Rules (SI
2016/234) 4–42

2016 Legal Aid, Sentencing
and Punishment of
Offenders Act 2012
(Commencement No.12)
Order (SI 2016/345) 2–03
art.2 2–52

2017 Civil Procedure
(Amendment) Rules (SI
2017/95) 1–04, 7–04

CHAPTER 1

Introduction

By the time this book is published, Lord Justice Jackson's reforms will have been in force for four years. When Lord Woolf's reforms were introduced in 1998, it took five years for those reforms to bed in. This ignores the costs wars which came about as a result of the introduction, by Lord Irvine, the Lord Chancellor, of recoverable success fees and ATE premiums which were not part of Lord Woolf's Reforms. The difficulties brought about by the Access to Justice Act 1999 led to the Conditional Fee Agreements Regulations 2000 being revoked by the Conditional Fee Agreements (Revocation) Regulations 2005. The purpose of the revocation of the Regulations was to put an end to the technical challenges which had grown up and which, if successful, meant that the CFA would be unenforceable and therefore no costs at all would be recoverable. **1–01**

Recoverable success fees and ATE premiums remained as part of the litigation funding scene to such an extent that the liability insurers and ABI mounted a powerful lobbying campaign calling for the abolition of recovery. When Lord Justice Jackson undertook his Civil Justice Review, one of the first decisions he reached was to recommend the abolition of recoverable success fees and ATE premiums. This recommendation, along with the majority of his other recommendations, was accepted by the Government and, with certain exceptions, his reforms were introduced with effect from the 1 April 2013.

Legal representatives throughout the jurisdiction, knowing of the change that was to take place, signed up many thousands of claimants to Conditional Fee Agreements prior to the 1 April 2013. Those claims have a very long tail and are still making their way through the court system. At a recent meeting of the White Book Editorial Board, the Senior Costs Judge indicated that in his view the end of the pre-April 2013 cases was not yet in sight. **1–02**

Because of this situation, and also because of the radical changes in respect of case and costs management and costs budgeting, introduced following Lord Justice Jackson's Review, it seems unlikely that the reforms will be fully bedded in for several more years.

There are many aspects of the new regime which have yet to be definitively decided by the Court of Appeal. Perhaps foremost among these is the question of proportionality.

Lord Neuberger MR (as he then was) gave the fifteenth lecture in the Implementation Programme on 29 May 2012. He stated: **1–03**

"8. This Rule [44.4(5)] reflects, and is intended to introduce into the conduct of civil litigation, the fundamental element of both the Woolf Reforms and the Jackson Reforms. As was explained in Sir Rupert's Final Costs Report:

'The policy which underlies the proposed new rule is that cost benefit analysis has a part to play, even in the realm of civil justice. If the parties wish to pursue claims or defences at disproportionate costs, they must do so, at least in part, at their own expense.'

The point is simple, and it was made by Lord Devlin in 1970. It was cited by Lord Woolf in 1995 and it underpins the Jackson Report and its recommendations: it is a fallacy to think that time and money are no object where the operation of the Civil Justice System is concerned. Parties and their lawyers must keep firmly in mind that they ought to expend no more than a proportionate amount of money in pursuit of justice. If they wish to spend more, they must appreciate that such sums will not be recoverable from their opponent. That is proportionality, proportionate costs, as between the parties."

Lord Neuberger continued:

"14. While the change in culture should reduce the scope of costs assessments at the conclusion of proceedings, it will not obviate the need for a robust approach to such assessments. Again the decision as to whether an item was proportionately incurred is case-sensitive, and there may be a period of slight uncertainty as the case law is developed.

15. That is why I have not dealt with what precisely constitutes proportionality and how it is to be assessed. It would be positively dangerous for me to seek to give any sort of specific or detailed guidance in a lecture before the new rule has come into force and been applied. Any question relating to proportionality and any question relating to costs is each very case sensitive and when the two questions come together, that is all the more true. The law on proportionate costs will have to be developed on a case by case basis. This may mean a degree of satellite litigation while the Courts work out the law, but we should be ready for that, and I hope it will involve relatively few cases."

1–04 In fact, it has taken until the latter end of 2016 for any cases[1] to come to the fore which will be dealt with on appeal, either in the High Court or the Court of Appeal. One of the cases mentioned (*BNM*) has been leap-frogged to the Court of Appeal. *May* is to be heard at Cicuit Judge level. At the time of writing, however, the judgments following the hearing of these appeals are likely to be some time after this book will be published. There will, therefore, continue to be uncertainty in respect of proportionality for some time to come.

Another area of difficulty that arises out of a decision of the Court of Appeal concerns the extent to which a costs management order reflecting agreed or approved budgets affects incurred costs[2]. This issue has been the subject of discussion in the CPRC and rule amendments have been put in place to rectify the situation.[3] The latest position is given in **Chapter 4**.

---

[1] Namely, *BNM v MGN Limited* [2016] 3 Costs LO 441, Chief Master Gordon-Saker; and *May v Wavell Group Plc* [2016] 3 Costs LO 455, Master Rowley.

[2] *SARPD Oil International Limited v Addax Energy SA* 2016] EWCA Civ 120.

[3] Civil Procedure (Amendment) Rules 2017.

It is worth mentioning one further issue which is giving rise to a great deal of uncertainty, and that is the position surrounding assignment of CFAs. This may happen where a client changes firms of solicitors (possibly following the legal representative who has left one firm and joined another); or where a firm is taken over by another firm or changes its character by becoming a limited company, a limited liability partnership or an ABS. Another case awaiting hearing in the Court of Appeal is again unlikely to be heard until after the publication of this book[4]. There are numerous conflicting decisions at first instance, prompting the heartfelt comment by a District Judge in a recent case:

> "*A judgment is needed at a higher level – it makes no sense for District Judges around the Country to be hearing these cases in the absence of clear binding authority.*"

In the meantime, Lord Justice Jackson has continued to work tirelessly to bring to the attention of the Government, the Judiciary and the Professions those areas of his proposed reforms which have either not been implemented or are being under-used. Prominent among these is the topic of fixed costs. In a lecture to the Westminster Legal Policy Forum, "*The Future for Civil Litigation and the Fixed Costs Regime*"[5], he said at 2.6 to 2.11:   **1–05**

> "*2.6 Fast track cases. In the Final Report I recommended that, as a first step, fixed recoverable costs should be introduced for all cases in the fast track before we tackle the multi-track. The Final Report set out detailed figures and proposals for how this should be achieved. The MoJ and the Rule Committee in late 2012 accepted this recommendation in respect of personal injury cases, but not in respect of non-personal injury cases. Fixing recoverable costs for all remaining fast track cases is unfinished business, which needs to be addressed as soon as possible.*
>
> . . .
>
> *2.8 The multi-track. I have previously proposed that we should develop a fixed costs regime for the lower regions of the multi-track and I stand by that proposal. There is room for debate about precisely what constitutes the 'lower regions of the multi-track' . . . the new rules on proportionate costs pave the way for, creating a fixed costs recoverable costs regime. Furthermore, we have gained three years' experience of costs budgeting by reference to the Precedent H phases. Against that background, we are now in a position to establish a scheme for the lower reaches of the multi-track.*
>
> *2.9 Benefits of fixed recoverable costs. . .The benefits include certainty, the saving of process costs and an adverse costs risk which is always proportionate.*
>
> . . .

---

[4] *Budana v Leeds Teaching Hospitals NHS Trust* Kingston Upon Hull County Court, 4 February 2016, DJ Besford.
[5] 23 May 2016.

2.11 I understand that the Government is taking a close interest in fixed recoverable costs. I look forward to any future announcement on this issue with great interest."

The Lord Chief Justice has lent his support to the concept of fixed recoverable costs in his Report to Parliament (November 2016):

"One area that the judiciary has consistently pressed to see implemented is the widespread adoption of fixed recoverable costs across the range of fast-track cases, and, potentially, to the lower reaches of the multi-track. This would help to ensure that litigation costs are reasonable and proportionate, enabling parties to proceed with greater certainty. However, the costs must be fair, and information gathering will be required before recoverable costs are fixed. The Government has signalled its intention for further reforms, and, in particular, extending the application of fixed recoverable costs to further areas of civil litigation. The judiciary has indicated that it will assist with a review that will help to develop proposals."

1–06   For reasons which are not apparent, the Government, whilst paying lip service to the concept, failed to do anything about it for some time. On 11 November 2016, however, it was announced that Lord Justice Jackson had been commissioned by the Lord Chief Justice, and the Master of the Rolls, to undertake a review of fixed recoverable costs, to be completed by 31 July 2017. The Review will be undertaken by Lord Justice Jackson as a logical extension of his wider review of civil litigation procedures and costs (published in 2010), in which he first recommended the application of fixed recoverable costs.

The terms of reference for his review are as follows:

1. To develop proposals for extending the present civil fixed recoverable costs regime in England and Wales so as to make the costs of going to court more certain, transparent and proportionate for litigants.
2. To consider the types and areas of litigation in which such costs should be extended, and the value of claims to which such a regime should apply.
3. To report to the Lord Chief Justice and the Master of the Rolls by the 31 July 2017.

Lord Justice Jackson said:

"I have set out my present views on the principles of fixed recoverable costs in the final report of my review and in recent lectures and publications.

I have been commissioned to undertake this review because it is integral to the overall package of reforms which I originally proposed. Chapter 16 of my final report recommended that serious consideration should be given to extending fixed recoverable costs to the lower reaches of the multi-track after the other reforms had bedded in.

Although the momentum is heavily for reform, the review will provide ample opportunity for comments and submissions on the form and scope that reform should take. I am inviting the views of practitioners, users of the civil courts and any other interested parties on these points. Seminars will be held in London and elsewhere to discuss the issues. There is a great deal to be done on the detail of the review, which will inform the Government as it prepares proposals for formal consultation in due course."[6].

If evidence is being submitted of actual recoverable costs, this should identify the type of case (e.g. clinical negligence, property, judicial review etc.), and the source of evidence (e.g. detailed assessments under the post-April 2013 rules, approved budgets, agreed budgets etc.).   **1–07**

Material submitted should take account of the Civil Procedure Rules on proportionality, in particular the factors set out in CPR r.44.3 (5).

Views are also sought on the level of claim at which fixed recoverable costs should stop and costs budgeting should apply instead.

Other issues that the review will need to consider, and on which views are welcomed, are how to accommodate counsel's fees, experts' fees and other disbursements within a fixed recoverable costs regime. Another issue for consideration is the difference which frequently arises between claimant and defendant costs.[7]

In addition to giving numerous speeches and lectures, Lord Justice Jackson has also found time to write a book, *"The Reform of Civil Litigation"*[8]. The book covers numerous topics, some of which are highlighted below. The aim of the book is stated to be "a simple and clear explanation of the principal reforms". The target audience is law students and young practitioners. "These are the people who hold the future of civil justice in their hands."

Proportionality

The purpose of the amendments to the overriding objective is to ensure that litigation proceeds, efficiently and at proportionate cost, towards resolution in accordance with the substantive law and that there is a general culture of compliance with Rules, Practice Directions and Orders. CPR r.44.3(5) contains the new definition of proportionality. There was some debate about whether a Practice Direction should supplement the definition of proportionate costs. The Senior Costs Judge was asked to draft a proposed Direction. The draft Direction was very short and stated: **1–08**

"Costs which are disproportionate in amount may be disallowed or reduced even if they were reasonably or necessarily incurred."

---

[6] Lord Justice Jackson has invited written evidence or submissions to assist the review by 30 January 2017, to be sent to: fixed.costs@judiciary.gsi.gov.uk.

[7] The assessors to the review are: Sara Ashby, Nicholas Bacon QC, Professor Richard Disney, Professor Paul Fenn;Senior Master Barbara Fontaine, Senior Costs Judge Andrew Gordon-Saker, Richard Lander, David Marshall, HH Judge Martin McKenna, District Judge Simon Middleton, Andrew Parker, Vikram Sachdeva QC, Ian Stark and Nicole Sandells.

[8] Sweet & Maxwell, 2016.

The draft was not accepted, but the wording now appears in CPR r.44.3(2)(a).

Alternative Dispute Resolution

1–09   Under this head, reference is made to the decision in *PGF II SA v OMFS Co. 1 Limited*[9], where the Court of Appeal held that the defendant's silence in the face of two offers to mediate amounted to an unreasonable refusal to mediate, meriting a costs sanction. The court endorsed the *Jackson ADR Handbook* (now in its second edition).

Part 36

The book points out that CPR r.36.17 (Costs Consequences Following Judgment) is assuming increasing importance in relation to fixed costs. If the claimant obtains an Order for Indemnity Costs under CPR r.36.17(4)(b), that is a means of escaping from the fixed costs regime for fast track PI cases from the date when the offer expires[10]. Similarly, if a claimant obtains an Order for Indemnity Costs under CPR r.36.17(4)(b), he escapes from the operation of CPR r.3.18 (assessing costs on the standard basis where a Costs Management Order has been made)[11].

Costs Management

1–10   **Chapter 4** of this book deals with costs management in detail. It is, however, worth repeating the conclusions of Lord Justice Jackson under this heading:

- *"Costs management may not be popular, but it is slowly bedding down. As it does so, the benefits of the process are becoming more apparent;*
- *It is quite likely that there will be fixed recoverable costs for cases in the lower reaches of the multi-track. When that happens, the volume of cases requiring costs management will diminish;*
- *Once the next round of reforms is complete, it will be appropriate to look again at pre-action costs management."*

QOCS

The final report suggested that QOCS might be considered in other areas of litigation, *"where there is an asymmetrical relationship between the parties"*[12]. A Civil Justice Council Working Group, set up to consider the question, concluded in its report that there were strong grounds for extending QOCS to actions against the police, although arguments in respect of claims against solicitors for mishandling PI claims was more finely balanced. Another working group under the chairmanship of Professor Rachael Mulheron is considering

---

[9] [2013] EWCA Civ 1288; [2014] 1 WLR 1386.
[10] See *Broadhurst v Tan* [2016] EWCA Civ 94; [2016] 1 WLR 1928.
[11] See *Denton v TH White Limited* [2014] EWCA Civ 906; [2014] 1 WLR 3926 at [43].
[12] See Section 5(4), Final Report Chapter 9.

whether QOCS should apply in any other fields of litigation. **Chapter 2** deals with the topic of Litigation Funding which covers both QOCS and DBAs.

DBAs

At a meeting of the Civil Justice Council in October 2016 MoJ officials stated that Professor Rachael Mulheron's report and the reform proposals "remain under review". There is presently no sign of any progress being made in respect of DBAs which remain largely un-used. Lord Justice Jackson states in his book:

1–11

> *"It is not surprising that the MoJ is still considering the CJC report. The drafting issues are complex and it is vital that the MoJ gets it right next time. When the amended DBA Regulations are published, it is very much hoped (and expected) that these will create a workable regime. There is a very substantial need for such a regime."*

Third Party Litigation Funding

Litigation Funding by third parties is on the increase, many of whom are members of the Association of Litigation Funders, whose members abide by their voluntary Code of Conduct. Those who are not members of the Association are to some extent unregulated but, depending upon their activities, may be caught as claims management companies providing litigation services and so regulated in that way. This is a situation which makes DBAs unattractive to litigation funders.[13]

Lord Justice Jackson recommended the removal of the so called *Arkin* cap (limiting a funder's liability for adverse costs to the extent of the funding). To date this has not happened. In *Excalibur Ventures LLC v Texas Keystone Inc and between Texas Keystone Inc v Psari Holdings Ltd*[14] it was held that it was appropriate that nine commercial funders, who had funded a hopeless action, should pay the successful defendants' costs on the indemnity basis even though they themselves were not guilty of any discreditable conduct or conduct which could be criticised. The court specifically declined to revisit or comment upon the *Arkin* cap.

Another question which needs to be addressed is whether there should be a requirement to give some sort of notice of funding. There are obvious issues of privilege involved. This is a topic which is relevant in arbitration proceedings as well: in the case of *ESSAR Oilfields Services Limited v Norscot Rig*

---

[13] The preamble to the Compensation Act 2006 states: "*An Act to specify certain factors that may be taken into account by a court determining a claim in negligence or breach of statutory duty; to make provision about damages for mesothelioma; and to make provision for the regulation of claims management services.*" Part 2 of the Act deals with claims management companies, and it is that part of the Act which causes the problem.

In the DBA Regulations the definition of "claims management services" comes from s.58AA(7) of the Courts and Legal Services Act 1990 and is stated to have "the same meaning as in Pt 2 of the Compensation Act 2006 (see s.4(2) of that Act". Section 4(2) of the Compensation Act 2006 provides at subparagraph (b):

"*Claims management services means advice or other services in relation to the making of a claim.*"

It is that definition which causes problems for litigation funders. There is no doubt that the funders are providing "*other services in relation to the making of a claim*". Unless or until that definition is amended to exclude e.g. third party litigation funders, the problem will persist.

[14] [2016] EWCA Civ 1144.

Management PVT Limited[15] the losing claimant (*ESSAR*) was faced with a bill of £1.94 million, being the original funding obtained by *Norscot* plus the 300% uplift payable on success. This is a decision on its own facts in a situation in which the CPR did not apply. It may be, however, that had the claimant had notice of the funding it might have moderated its conduct (for which it was criticised) and saved itself a large amount of money.

Fixed Recoverable Costs

1–12   The Court of Appeal has dealt with three important cases, Lord Justice Briggs giving the lead judgment in each case: *Bird v Acorn Group Limited* [16]which decided that a disposal hearing is a listing for trial; *Qader v ESure Services Ltd*[17]where the court held that the intended purpose of the fixed costs regime for cases which had started under the RTA Protocol was that it should not apply to cases where there had been a judicial determination that they should continue in the multi-track: and, *Sharp v Leeds City Council*[18] which decided that the fixed costs regime applies to the costs of a Pre Action Disclosure (PAD) application made by a claimant who is pursuing a claim for damages for personal injuries which began with the issue of a CNF in the portal pursuant to the EL/PL Protocol but which at the time of the PAD application, is no longer continuing under that protocol. **Chapter 7** of this book deals with fixed costs and will set out any developments which have taken place before the book goes to press.

New Bill of Costs Pilot Scheme

1–13   Practice Direction 51L, as amended, came into effect on 3 October 2016 with a view to establishing a mandatory form of bill of costs to apply to all work done after 1 October 2017. The pilot scheme is running in the Senior Courts Costs Office. The new form of bill should be in the form of new precedent AB. Strict adherence to the J codes is not mandatory.

It will be seen from this brief overview that developments are taking place on all aspects of the Jackson Reforms. As Lord Justice Jackson never tires of reminding us, in his final report he proposed "a coherent package of interlocking reforms, designed to control costs and promote access to justice". That process is well underway, but the end is not yet in sight.

---

[15] [2016] EWHC 2361 (Comm) HHJ Waksman QC.
[16] [2016] EWCA Civ 1096.
[17] [2016] EWCA Civ 1109.
[18] [2017] EWCA Civ. 33.

CHAPTER 2

Funding Litigation

Introduction

The Legal Aid, Sentencing & Punishment of Offenders Act 2012 and associ-   **2–01**
ated secondary legislation had a significant impact on the funding of litigation. Some aspects, in particular the greater restrictions on availability of
public funding, are beyond the scope of this section.

This section will instead focus on the changes to funding arrangements
available to litigants, in particular Conditional Fee Agreements (CFAs),
Damages Based Agreements (DBAs) and After the Event Insurance (ATE).

Lord Justice Jackson's Final Report contained detailed and inter-related proposals for the means of Funding Litigation. These included:

- emphasising the benefits of public funding and stressing the 'vital-
  necessity' to avoid any further cutbacks in its availability or eligibility[1];
- recommendations for the encouragement of take up of Before the Event
  Insurance in certain circumstances[2]; and
- perhaps most notably, a recommendation for the abolition of between
  the parties recovery of ATE premiums,[3] allied to the introduction of qualified one way costs shifting for certain litigants and the abolition of the
  between the parties recoverability of success fees in CFAs,[4] in turn allied
  to a 10% increase in awards for general damages, the -enhancement of
  Part 36 benefits for claimants and the capping of success fees-chargeable
  by solicitors in personal injury claims.

Whilst broadly Jackson LJ's package of reforms in relation to CFAs, ATE, and
QOCS were adopted, his call for public funding not to be further restricted
was not, and the reforms of funding introduced did not always follow his
precise recommendations.

This can be seen in particular in relation to QOCS, where Jackson LJ's proposal for a means-tested model based on that applicable to public funding
costs protection was not adopted,[5] but also in relation to DBAs, where the
reforms introduced have not had the desired effect in practice of making a
new form of funding widely available to litigants.

The transitional provisions in relation to the abolition of between the
parties' recovery of success fees and ATE premiums have given rise to problems

---

[1] Final Report, p.70.
[2] Final Report, p.79.
[3] Final Report, p.89.
[4] Final Report, p.112.
[5] For further details, see Ch.6 on QOCS.

of their own. These have become particularly apparent in circumstances where, for one reason or another, there is some need to vary or change the funding arrangement after 1 April 2013 in circumstances where that arrangement was first entered into prior to that date. These issues will be considered further below.

Conditional Fee Agreements

2–02   Section 44 of LASPO amended s.58A(6) of the Courts & Legal Services Act 1990 to provide that a costs order may no longer include provision requiring another party to pay part of the successful party's success fee. This was a simple reversal of the position prior to 1 April 2013.

Whilst certain changes were made to s.58 in relation to the specific requirements for a CFA in personal injury claims[6], the basic circumstances in which a CFA could be entered into, its basic requirements and the type of cases where such an agreement was lawful were not amended.

Accordingly, the effect of the amendment to s.58A(6) was simple—where success fees had formerly been recoverable in principle between the parties, they are now no longer recoverable – save in relation to a limited, and diminishing, category of excepted cases – and, where a CFA with a success fee is entered into, such success fees will have to be paid by the client, with no prospect of any between the parties' recovery.

It is important to note that the fundamental principle in s.58(1) of the Act, that a CFA which does not satisfy all of the conditions applicable to it by virtue of s.58 shall be unenforceable, remains unchanged.

Equally, Lord Justice Jackson's clear recommendation that the indemnity principle should be abrogated[7], at least in part to limit the scope for satellite litigation in relation to issues of enforceability of retainers, was rejected. The call was repeated in early 2015,[8] and in September 2015 the Civil Justice Council Working Group on DBA Reform made a reasoned recommendation for its abolition, at least in the context of DBAs, but recognised that this was closely tied to the question of the abolition of the principle more generally, which was 'a thorny policy issue' and one where the Government has shown a marked disinclination to intervene[9]. At present, there is no particular reason to anticipate that any of these calls will be heeded. However, in some areas, at least, its relevance will be diminished in light of the proposed expansion of the scheme of fixed costs (addressed in **Chapter 7**). It is now trite law that the indemnity principle does not apply to a between the parties claim for profit costs which are themselves fixed by the CPR[10].

---

[6] These are the 'specified claims' under s.58(4A)(b) by virtue of art.2 of the Conditional Fee Agreements Order 2013 (SI 2013 No.689).

[7] Final Report, Chapter 5, paragraph 4.1

[8] http://www.judiciary.gov.uk/wp-content/uploads/2014/10/litigation-post-jackson-world.pdf [Accessed 29 January, 2015].

[9] Civil Justice Council, The Damages-Based Agreements Reform Project – 'Drafting and Policy Issues', 2 September 2015, Chapter 23.

[10] See *Butt v Nizami* [2006] EWHC 159 (QB), [2006] 1 WLR 3307, as approved in *Kilby v Gawith* [2009] 1 WLR 853 (amongst others).

Such fixed costs regimes aside, a failure to comply with the requirements of s.58, including the post-April 2013 requirements imposed by the new s.58(4A) and (4B) in relation to personal injury CFAs, will leave the litigant, and their solicitor, exposed to the well-rehearsed arguments that the agreement is unenforceable and that accordingly no costs under the CFA may be recovered between the parties. Whether the removal of the between the parties recovery of success fees will result directly or indirectly in a reduction in the appetite or ability of paying parties to take such points still remains to be seen.

The final point to note in relation to issues of general application is that s.58(5) of the 1990 Act remains untrammelled. This is the section that provides that where the CFA is a non-contentious business agreement under s.57 of the Solicitors Act 1974, s.58(1) does not render it unenforceable. The scope of this was considered in detail by the then Senior Costs Judge in 2010 in an authoritative judgment[11] and the ability to use CFAs (and now DBAs) which are not subject to the restrictions of ss.58 and 58AA for what might be termed non-contentious business is an option which is potentially a valuable one, particularly in the commercial sphere, though one which needs to be approached carefully.

Transitional provisions

The transitional provision provided for by s.44(6) states that: 2–03

> *"The amendment made by [the subsection] does not prevent a costs order including provision in relation to a success fee payable by a person ("P") under a conditional fee agreement entered into before [1 April 2013] if—*
>
> *(a) the agreement was entered into specifically for the purposes of the provision to P of advocacy or litigation services in connection with the matter that is the subject of the proceedings in which the costs order is made, or*
>
> *(b) advocacy or litigation services were provided to P under the agreement in connection with that matter before the commencement day."*

This ensured that the court retains its discretion to allow a between the parties success fee where the CFA was entered into before 1 April 2013. The one proviso is that the CFA relates to a specific matter which is the subject of the proceedings before the court **or** advocacy or litigation services were in fact provided under the CFA before 1 April 2013.[12]

In addition, s.48 of the Act contained saving provisions allowing for the continued between the parties recovery of success fees in diffuse mesothelioma claims. On 4 December 2013 the Government announced that this

---

[11] *Tel-Ka Talk Ltd v Revenue & Customs Commissioners* [2010] EWHC 90175 (Costs).

[12] The latter part of this provision appears primarily directed to the position in relation to Collective Conditional Fee Agreements (CCFAs). Such an agreement may have been entered into prior to 1 April 2013, but may cover all claims of a particular type a solicitor is undertaking for a particular client or funder. The agreement may therefore cover claims in respect of matters which had not even arisen prior to 1 April 2013. If the transitional provision simply focused on the date of the funding arrangement, the CCFA could be used to ensure the ongoing recovery of additional liabilities even in respect of post-April 2013 instructions. Accordingly, in such circumstances, it is not the date of the CCFA which is relevant (because the CCFA did not relate to a specific matter which is the subject of proceedings) but rather whether the legal representative had started to provide services in respect of that specific matter before 1 April 2013.

exception was to be removed and success fees would cease to be recoverable between the parties in such claims. However, in October 2014 the High Court[13] ruled that the consultation process leading to that decision had been flawed and that the decision had to be quashed, leading to the Government announcing that there would be a further review of whether or not to remove the exception. Accordingly, if and when the mesothelioma exception will be lifted remains to be seen.

Implementation of s.44 was also 'suspended' in relation to publication and privacy proceedings and insolvency proceedings. In respect of publication and privacy proceedings, this was intended to be only until further, related, reforms, including the possible extension of QOCS to such claims, initially anticipated in October 2013 and then April 2014, were introduced. However, the position remains under review by the Government and no further date has been set for implementation.

There is a certain irony in the continued exception for publication and privacy proceedings given that it was in precisely such a claim that the European Court of Human Rights held that the exposure on the part of a media defendant to such additional liabilities constituted a breach of Article 10 of the Convention[14].

Although the Supreme Court, in *Coventry v Lawrence*[15] rejected a challenge in a non-media claim that additional liabilities incurred under pre-April 2013 CFAs and ATE breached Article 6 or Article 1 of the First Protocol to the Convention, the continued recoverability of such additional liabilities in media claims has provoked fresh challenge on the basis of Article 10. The Supreme Court has granted permission to appeal in the case of *Frost v MGN* against the decision of Mann J[16] that he was bound by the House of Lords decision in the earlier *MGN* case[17] to hold that such arrangements did not breach Article 10.

Article 10 was not in issue in *Coventry* and accordingly this will be the first occasion since 2005 that the Supreme Court will be asked to consider whether such funding arrangements constitute a disproportionate interference with a party's rights to freedom of expression. See also Lord Justice Jackson's comments in the 2015 Mustill lecture[18], above, as to the potential arguments as to the legality of the continued between the parties recoverability of additional liabilities in the excepted cases. In light of the *Coventry* decision, the Supreme Court's decision in *Frost* is unlikely to have any wider ramifications beyond the field of publication and privacy proceedings. In particular, it seems doubtful, in light of *Coventry*, whether a decision against the principle of recoverability

---

[13] *R (Ex parte Whitston) v Secretary of State for Justice* [2014] EWHC 3044 (Admin).
[14] *MGN Ltd v United Kingdom* [2011] ECHR 66.
[15] [2015] UKSC 50, [2015] 1 WLR 3485.
[16] Sub nom *Eight Representative Claimants v MGN Ltd* at first instance [2016] EWHC 855 (Ch).
[17] Sub nom *Campbell v MGN Ltd* [2005] 1 WLR 3394 – the decision which was then referred to the ECHR as set out above.
[18] "The Civil Justice Reforms And Whether Insolvency Litigation Should Be Exempt": https://www.judiciary.gov.uk/wp-content/uploads/2015/10/mustill-jackson-lj.pdf

in *Frost* would cast any doubt on the lawfulness of continued recoverability in the main other remaining exception, namely mesothelioma claims.

Article 10 aside, whilst *Coventry* appears to have largely disposed of the Article 6 point, there may be issues, in particular in relation to those instances where between the parties recoverability has been preserved post-April 2013, where arguments in this regard remain. Moreover, whether the European Court of Human Rights would agree with the Supreme Court's analysis, particularly given its decision in the *Naomi Campbell* case[19], if given the opportunity, must be in at least some doubt and therefore, whilst parties are likely to be very wary of further challenges on this ground, they cannot be entirely ruled out.

In respect of insolvency proceedings, the implementation was originally intended to be postponed until April 2015 only. However, in a written ministerial statement on the 26 February 2015, the Government announced that the implementation in respect of insolvency proceedings was to be further suspended pending further consideration of the 'appropriate way forward'.

On 17 December 2015 the Government announced that the insolvency exemption would end with effect from 1 April 2016 and, by virtue of the Legal Aid, Sentencing & Punishment of Offenders Act 2012 (Commencement No. 12) Order 2016 the exemption was finally brought to an end and s.44 and 46 of the 2012 Act were brought into effect in relation to insolvency proceedings, albeit that there was a slight slippage in the start date, the provisions not coming into force until 6 April 2016.

Where a CFA is entered into or an ATE policy is taken out in relation to insolvency proceedings on or after that date, the additional liability is not recoverable between the parties.

It should in any event be noted that the insolvency exception was a narrow one and only applied to office holders or companies in administration bringing proceedings under the Insolvency Act 1986 – see the Legal Aid, Sentencing & Punishment of Offenders Act 2012 (Commencement No.5 & Saving Provisions) Order 2013. Other cases, which might fall within a general description of 'insolvency' claims did not benefit from the exception and were subject to the general removal of between the parties recoverability of additional liabilities – see *Re Hartmann Capital* [2015] EWHC 1514 (Ch).

Such specific types of cases aside, therefore, the key point remains that where the CFA was entered into before 1 April 2013 the success fee continues to be recoverable in principle. If entered into on or after 1 April 2013 the success fee is irrecoverable from the paying party.

Personal injury claims—additional requirements

2–04

Section 44 of LASPO amended s.58 and s.58A of the Courts & Legal Services Act 1990 to impose additional conditions on CFAs, including the requirement that in certain classes of case, primarily personal injury claims (but for the

---

[19] *MGN Ltd v United Kingdom* [(2011]) 53 EHRR 195.

time being excluding mesothelioma claims), the success fee does not exceed a maximum limit expressed as a percentage of certain types of damages.[20]

There is a strange circularity in the 2013 Order in that the types of cases in respect of which the cap on the success fee imposed by s.58(4)(c) applies (personal injury claims – see art.4) are expressly specified in the Order. However, art.6 provides that art.4[21] does not apply to publication, privacy and insolvency proceedings. Given that they are not specified in art.4, art.4 could not apply to them in any event, so this part of art.6 serves no purpose. It is assumed that art.6 was phrased in this way in anticipation of the success fee cap possibly being extended to cover other proceedings (in particular mesothelioma proceedings) if and when success fees in such claims are no longer recoverable between the parties, though given that such claims could then simply be specified under art.4, the wording of art.6(2) remains something of a mystery.

The insolvency 'exception' was lifted with effect from the 6 April 2016, as noted above. However, insolvency proceedings have not been added to the list under art.4 and therefore, as with all other claims which may be the subject of a CFA other than personal injury claims, the only statutory limitation on the success fee that may be specified as payable by the client under a CFA in such proceedings is that the percentage of the success fee cannot exceed the 100% maximum. There is no other 'cap' on the success fee that may be charged.

The key restriction in relation to a post-April 2013 CFA for a claim involving personal injury is contained in art.5 of the Order, which must be read in conjunction with s.58(4B) of the 1990 Act.

The success fee in any such agreement must be limited to a maximum of 25% of specified classes of damages awarded in the proceedings, in respect of proceedings at first instance. Note, the express reference in s.58(4B)(b) is to damages 'awarded' and not to damages actually recovered.

The specified classes of damages are general damages for pain, suffering and loss of amenity and damages for pecuniary loss, other than future pecuniary loss, in both cases net of any sums recoverable as CRU (Compensation Recovery) (art.5(2)).

Accordingly, under such a CFA, the success fee, which cannot be recovered between the parties, cannot exceed 25% of the damages for general damages and past pecuniary loss (net of CRU).

2–05   It is important not to confuse the cap on the quantum of the success fee with the percentage of the success fee itself. The maximum percentage success fee, that is to say the maximum percentage by which the solicitors' base fees may be multiplied, remains at 100%, in all claims where a CFA is permissible, including personal injury claims. The 25% cap operates as a financial limit on how much of the success fee the client may be charged and is an additional limitation which applies in personal injury claims only.

---

[20] As set out in the Conditional Fee Agreements Order 2013.
[21] And art.5, which sets the maximum percentage success fee in cases covered by art.5.

If the amount of damages for general damages and past loss awarded is sufficiently high, or the amount of base fees to which the success fee is to be applied, or the percentage success fee itself is sufficiently low, then the full success fee may be payable, because it is less than the cap. Where, however, the success fee calculated at the applicable percentage on the base fees payable under the agreement exceeds 25% of the prescribed damages, then the amount of the success fee is limited accordingly.

The interaction of the maximum limit on the percentage success fee (100%) with the newly introduced cap on the maximum fee chargeable caused some confusion initially in some quarters and some errors of drafting, particularly in relation to CFAs which covered appeal proceedings.

This is because, under art.5(1)(b) of the 2013 Order, the cap on the maximum success fee is lifted from 25% to 100% in relation to proceedings other than at first instance. It is important to note that this is still a cap. It is merely that the effect of the cap in this situation is that the maximum success fee is limited to the full amount of the net damages for general damages and past loss, rather than only 25% of that sum. This 100% (of specified damages) cap is separate and distinct from the 100% (of base fees) limit on the success fee itself.

As a matter of practice, it would appear that many practitioners have chosen 2–06 to ignore the ability to include a higher cap on the success fee where the CFA covers matters other than first instance proceedings. This is no doubt because of the concerns about ensuring that the agreement is fully compliant with both limitations where it covers both first instance and appellate proceedings and because of the danger of a simple error leading to the entire CFA being deemed unenforceable. Undoubtedly, the simpler and safer, if potentially less remunerative, course is to apply the 25% cap alone.

The cap is intended to be inclusive of VAT – that is to say that the maximum success fee chargeable, including VAT, should not exceed the 25% limit. Peculiarly, this is not specified within art.5, but rather is explained in the Explanatory Note to the Order which, as it states, is not part of the Order itself.

It is generally accepted that the cap should include any success fee payable to counsel (including VAT) under any CFA in relation to the same matter between the solicitor and counsel. However, neither the 2013 Order nor s.58 of the 1990 Act, as amended, specify this. As a result, it is open to argument that reference to 'the success fee' specified under s.58(4B) of the 1990 Act, which must be subject to a maximum limit, is to the success fee (that is to say the solicitor's success fee) chargeable under the CFA, and that any success fee chargeable under any separate CFA (for example with counsel) is subject to a separate, but identical maximum limit. That does not appear to have been the intention, but appears to be an argument left open by the drafting.

Notification and advice requirements

2–07   Prior to April 2013, the between the parties notification requirements in relation to additional liabilities were contained in CPR r.44.15, CPR r.44 PD 19 and CPR r.47 PD 32. These were replaced by substitution as part of the general substitution of CPR r.44–48[22] and have no effect in relation to retainers entered into on or after 1 April 2013, save in relation to insolvency, publication and privacy and mesothelioma claims, where they continue to apply for as long as such claims are exempt from the general prohibition on recovery of additional liabilities[23]. However, they have continued effect in relation to pre-commencement funding arrangements[24] (as do the former provisions of CPR r.43–48 generally, for example in relation to the between the parties assessment of success fees) by virtue of CPR r.48.1.

Accordingly, care must be taken in the unlikely event, for example, of a claimant who entered into a pre-April 2013 CFA where a letter before claim has not yet been sent[25], or, perhaps more likely, where proceedings have not yet been issued, to ensure that the proper notification has been given as required by the 'old' rules. Similarly, in the more common situation of assessment of costs where the funding arrangement is a pre-April 2013 CFA (or there is a pre-April 2013 ATE premium) the requirements of old CPR r.47 PD 32 must be observed if the between the parties recoverability of the additional liabilities is not to be jeopardised.

The confusion which surrounded the correct interpretation of the 'new' CPR r.3.9 following the Court of Appeal's decision in *Mitchell*[26] pending clarification in *Denton*[27] led to a much stricter approach being taken towards any breaches of these notification requirements and the application of old CPR 44.3B.

That strict approach has now been moderated in light of *Denton*, as seen, for example, in *Caliendo*[28]. The existence of the strict approach did result in some clarification of the scope of the sanctions under CPR r.44.3B being provided in *Long v Value Properties Ltd*,[29] which may be material in cases of such breaches in relation to pre-April 2013 funding arrangements.[30]

---

[22] Effected by r.16 of the Civil Procedure (Amendment Rules) 2013 (SI 2013/262).

[23] See CPR r.48.2(i)(b). This is achieved by classifying CFAs in such proceedings as 'pre-commencement funding arrangements'. The insolvency exception ended with effect from the 6 April. 2016 and accordingly a CFA in such a claim entered into on or after 6 April 2016 is no longer a pre-commencement funding arrangement and the notification provisions under CPR r.43 to 48 no longer apply.

[24] As defined in CPR r.48.2, which broadly means a CFA or ATE policy entered into prior to 1 April 2013 (or a CCFA where, in the individual case in which costs are being considered, work was begun in relation to that case under the CCFA prior to 1 April 2013).

[25] There is a second appeal pending to the Court of Appeal, to be heard in 2017, in relation to the precise operation of the notice requirements and, in particular, whether the obligation to provide notice where a CFA has been entered into is triggered by the service of the Letter of Claim or whether the obligation arises earlier if the CFA is entered into before the letter of claim – *Springer v University Hospitals Leicester NHS Trust* [2016] EWCA Civ 769.

[26] *Mitchell v News Group Newspapers Ltd* [2013] EWCA Civ 1537; [2014] 1 WLR 795.

[27] *Denton v T H White Ltd* [2014] EWCA Civ 906; [2014] 1 WLR 3926.

[28] *Caliendo v Mischon De Reya LLP* [2014] EWHC 3414.

[29] *Long v Value Properties Ltd* [2014] EWHC 2981.

[30] In that case, it was made clear that the sanction of disallowance of the success fee under CPR r.44.3B(1)(d) for late service of the relevant information in relation to the CFA in detailed assessment proceedings was limited to the loss of the success fee for the period of the default, rather than there being a disallowance of the entire success fee for the whole case, as had previously generally been thought to be the case.

Implementation issues

There have only been a limited number of reported cases in relation to the   2–08
implementation of the changes to the structure of CFAs, though that may
largely be because it will take some time for any post LASPO CFA cases involving any substantial amounts of costs to come before the court.

However, there are a number of latent issues. Key amongst those are issues
relating to changes of funding around the time of the introduction of LASPO
and in relation to the transfer and assignment of CFAs.

In relation to the former, the core issue relates to the reasonableness of
claimants incurring additional liabilities—and seeking to recover the same
from an unsuccessful opponent – where those claimants had available to
them an alternative form of funding which would not have involved any
additional liability.

Anecdotally, there were a substantial number of claims, particularly clinical negligence claims, where there was a change of funding – commonly from
public funding to a CFA/ATE arrangement – shortly prior to 1 April 2013.

In principle, such cases should not involve any new issue of principle. The
issue of the choice of funding is one of reasonableness and the broad principles have been relatively well established since *Sarwar*[31]. However, LASPO
and the number of cases involving a change of funding in early 2013 appear
to have thrown the issue into sharp focus. Three cases in which different
first instance courts had held that the change in funding was unreasonable
were heard together on appeal by Foskett J sitting with the Senior Costs Judge
sub nom *Surrey v Barnet & Chase Farm Hospitals NHS Trust*[32]. All three cases
involved changes from public funding to CFAs in circumstances where the
client had not been fully advised that by doing so the client would lose the
right to the 10% general damages uplift[33] as a result of the change, if the claim
was successful.

The judge allowed all three appeals, reaffirming that the test to be applied
was the *Sarwar* test of whether the choice of funding made by the claimant
was an objectively reasonable one having regard to the individual circumstances of the particular claimant and that, in the context of the cases before
him, the choice was objectively reasonable and additional advice about the
10% uplift on general damages would have been unlikely to make any difference to the reasonableness of the choice. The defendant has sought permission to appeal from the Court of Appeal for a second appeal in all three cases
and a final conclusion on this issue appears to be some time away.

In relation to the transfer and assignment of CFAs, the common scenario
where this occurs is where a personal injury claimant has entered into a pre-
commencement funding arrangement, as defined in s.44(6) of LASPO, but
wishes to change firms after that date. By virtue of the strict wording of the

---

[31] *Sarwar v Alam* [2002] 1 WLR 125.
[32] [2016] EWHC 1598 (QB).
[33] *Simmons v Castle* [2012] EWCA Civ 1039, [2013] 1 WLR 1239.

transitional provision, the claimant will probably not be entitled to QOCS protection if he enters into a new, post-LASPO agreement with the new firm of solicitors[34]. Equally, if he enters into such a new agreement, the success fee under the new agreement will be irrecoverable and the claimant may be exposed to a deduction from any damages in respect of that success fee.

The decision of a regional costs judge in the case of *Casseldine*[35] suggests that there may be some scope for a more purposive interpretation, whereby, provided the court can be satisfied that, despite having entered into a pre-commencement funding arrangement, there were no circumstances whereby the claimant, if successful, would have been able to seek recovery of an additional liability from the opponent, the court will allow the claimant the benefit of QOCS protection despite the earlier CFA. However, the correctness of the reasoning in *Casseldine* is open to some doubt until such matters are the subject of higher judicial consideration. Moreover, the ratio in *Casseldine* itself appears to be limited to the relatively unusual situation where the first firm of solicitors 'walked away' from the case, rather than some of the more common scenarios where clients change firms.

An equally common scenario, capable of causing difficulties with the transitional provisions, is where a firm of solicitors is changing status (for example from a partnership to LLP or ABS), or wishes to transfer a number of clients to another firm.

Perhaps the most common questions in this scenario are whether the CFAs (or indeed other retainers) may lawfully be assigned and, if so, whether they should be.

2–09   It is beyond the scope of this chapter to describe in detail the fundamental legal principles relating to assignment and novation. It suffices to note that the key argument usually concerns the difference between novation and assignment. Novation results in the original agreement coming to an end, as a matter of law, and a new contract on the same terms and relating to the same subject matters, coming into being between one of the original parties and the new party, with the other original contracting party being released from the contract. Whereas assignment merely transfers the existing rights under a contract from one party (the assignor) to another (the assignee).

Accordingly, it has been argued that if a CFA is capable of assignment, then the effect of that assignment is that the CFA continues. It would follow, therefore, that the assignment of a pre-April 2013 CFA from, say, one solicitor to another post-April 2013 would result in the CFA still being regarded as a 'pre-commencement funding arrangement' for the purposes of s.44(6) of LASPO, CPR r.48.2 and all other related provisions. Accordingly, the recoverability of the success fee would be preserved.

---

[34] One of the claimant's arguments on the cross appeal in *Budana v Leeds Teaching Hospitals NHS Trust*, listed to be heard by the Court of Appeal in 2017, is to the effect that a purposive construction should be taken of the transitional provisions which would allow for such a new agreement to be treated as a pre- commencement funding arrangement in circumstances where it was, in practice, intended to be a mere continuation of an earlier, pre April 2013, CFA the claimant had with his or her previous solicitor.

[35] *Casseldine v Diocese of Llandaff Board for Social Responsibility* (unreported, Cardiff County Court, 3 July 2015).

The correctness of that argument has been the subject to detailed critique. At the time of writing, there is some authority, principally Rafferty J's decision in *Jenkins*[36], which supports the principle that a CFA is capable of assignment and does not offend the usual principle that only the benefit (in general under a CFA, the solicitor's right to payment) and not the burden (in general under a CFA, the solicitor's obligation to perform) can be assigned.

Whilst the weight of that authority is open to question, particularly since Rafferty J expressly stated that she was not laying down any issue of general principle, but was merely deciding the case on its particular facts, it has been followed by judges in some first instance and County Court appellate level cases, most notably by HHJ Wood QC in *Jones v Spire Healthcare Ltd*[37] *and by Master Leonard in Azim v Tradewise Insurance Services Ltd*[38], though in both of these cases the judges considered that they were bound by the ratio of *Jenkins* whether they disagreed with it or not. In addition, it is open to argument whether the principle of conditional benefit and burden was properly analysed in that case (particularly in light of the Court of Appeal's comments in *Davies v Jones*[39]) and whether all issues in relation to the law of assignment were fully raised or argued – a point also considered in *Jones* which the judge did not consider to be sufficiently made out to prevent him concluding that he was bound by *Jenkins*.

In *Budana v Leeds Teaching Hospitals NHS Trust*[40], Regional Costs Judge Besford found for the paying party on a prior point, itself of interest, namely that the circumstances in which the CFA came to be 'transferred' amounted to a termination of the retainer by the first firm of solicitors. However, he also went on to hold that but for such a finding, he too would have considered himself to be bound by *Jenkins*, though he expressed some doubts as to the reasoning in that case. Whilst the Regional Costs Judge's judgment is of interest in its own right, its key interest lies in the fact that the judgment is the subject of a leapfrog appeal to the Court of Appeal, to be heard in 2017, at which it is anticipated that both the termination point and, more importantly, the assignment issue will be argued. It is likely to lead to the first authoritative higher appellate decision on the point from a court not fettered by the decision in *Jenkins*.

Similar difficulties with the 'transfer' of retainers may arise in the context of the need to appoint a Litigation Friend in cases where the claimant has entered into a pre-April 2013 CFA but has subsequently been found to lack capacity, or where the claimant was a child when a pre-April 2013 CFA was entered into with a Litigation Friend, but the claimant has subsequently attained the age of 18.

It was hoped that some general guidance on these latter issues might be

---

[36] *Jenkins v Young Brothers Transport Ltd* [2006] EWHC 151 (QB).
[37] Liverpool County Court, 27 April 2016, unreported.
[38] Bow County Court, 22 August 2016, unreported.
[39] *Davies v Jones* [2009] EWCA Civ 1164.
[40] Hull County Court, 4 February 2016, unreported.

forthcoming in the Court of Appeal's decision in *Blankley*, but in the end it focused on the narrow issue of whether the claimant's supervening incapacity had caused the CFA in question to be terminated by reason of frustration because the claimant could not give instructions to the solicitor.[41]

Among the issues to be looked at by the Civil Justice Council working group on the impact of the Jackson reforms is the question of problems arising out of changes in the client's or the lawyer's status or basis of instruction in cases which straddle April 2013. No recommendations in this regard have yet been made and considerable uncertainty remains in this area.

After the Event Insurance

2–10 Section 46 of LASPO introduced s.58C of the Courts & Legal Services Act 1990 with the effect of repealing s.29 of the Access to Justice Act 1999 (and s.47 LASPO repealed the similar s.30 of the 1999 Act in relation to the 'notional' premiums charged by bodies such as trade unions). These legislative changes had the effect of preventing the between the parties recovery of ATE premiums where such policies were taken out on or after 1 April 2013.

Again, this ties in (in personal injury claims) with the introduction of QOCS, in that the existence of a pre-LASPO ATE policy prevents the claimant being eligible for QOCS protection.

As with success fees, an exception exists allowing for continued between the parties recoverability in mesothelioma, publication and privacy and insolvency proceedings, such exceptions being subject to the same process of review and possible revocation in due course (with the insolvency exception having ended with effect from the 6 April 2016).

The wording of the general transitional provision, however, is different from that in relation to CFAs, in that pursuant to s.58C of the 1990 Act, the amendments (i.e. the revocation of between the parties recoverability) do not apply "in relation to a costs order made in favour of a party who took out a costs insurance policy in relation to the proceedings before [1 April 2013[42]]".

Accordingly, the test is whether 'a' costs insurance policy was taken out in relation to the proceedings prior to 1 April 2013. The apparent effect is that the amendments (that is to say, the revocation of recoverability) do not apply at all where this is the case. It seems open to argument, therefore, that provided the claimant has taken out a single pre-April 2013 ATE policy, the claimant is entitled to seek to recover between the parties any (reasonably incurred) ATE premiums for any subsequent policies. This was probably not the intention and places too great a stress on the reference to 'a' costs insurance policy.

However, the precise limits of the section and whether, for example, it is possible to recover the costs of post-April 2013 'top up' or further staged

---

[41] *Blankley v Central Manchester Children's University Hospital NHS Trust* [2015] EWHC 18.

[42] Or 6 April 2016 in the context of insolvency proceedings. References in this section to April 2013 should be read as referring to April 2016 where the claim in question is an insolvency proceeding within the meaning of the Act.

premiums in respect of a pre-April 2013 policy – or indeed of an entirely discrete further policy provided 'a' policy of some type was taken out prior to April 2013 – will no doubt be considered in detail in forthcoming cases. Judgment is awaited from the Supreme Court in the case of *Plevin v Paragon Personal Finance Limited*[43] in relation to the issue of whether a premium for a top up to a pre-April 2013 policy is recoverable where the top up was taken out after April 2013 in relation to an appeal to the Supreme Court.

A saving provision relating to the continued between the parties recoverability of ATE premiums in very limited circumstances in Clinical Negligence claims was provided by s.58C of the 1990 Act and the Recovery of Costs Insurance Premiums in Clinical Negligence Proceedings (No.2) Regulations 2013 (finally laid before Parliament four days before the implementation date after a flawed earlier provision).   **2–11**

These allow for the continued recovery between the parties of ATE premiums in clinical negligence claims in certain circumstances, namely where:

- the claim has a value in excess of £1,000; and
- the insured risk relates to liability for the cost of an expert's report on issues of liability or causation.

The recoverable premium is limited to the cost of such a limited policy or, if the policy is wider, to the part of the premium that can be identified as relating to that part of the risk identified above.

The process of implementation of the clinical negligence exception was not a smooth one, with the original statutory instrument being found to be unhelpfully drafted, and possibly ultra vires. The second version does not appear to have addressed all of these problems and, in particular, there appears to be a tension between the authority delegated to the Lord Chancellor to make provision for continued recoverability, under s.58C of the 1990 Act, and the precise provision he has made under the 2013 Regulations. Some of these issues were addressed by the court in *Nokes*[44] and have been further addressed in an appeal in a County Court appellate case named *Axelrod*[45], heard in December 2015. Further cases seeking to resolve some of the ambiguities created by the implementation provisions are likely.

The legacy of recoverable ATE premiums in the clinical negligence context has led to a continuation of the additional liability costs wars. This has been particularly fuelled by the combination of this continued element of recoverability with the introduction of the new, and more robust, post-April 2013 test on proportionality, which has led to arguments as to whether the arguably generous approach to the between the parties recoverability of ATE premiums established by the Court of Appeal in *Rogers v Merthyr Tydfil CBC*[46] no longer   **2–12**

---

[43] UKSC 2014/0037.
[44] *Nokes v Heart of England Foundation NHS Trust* [2015] EWHC B6.
[45] *Axelrod v University Hospitals of Leicester NHS Trust* (Liverpool County Court, 28 January 2016).
[46] [2006] EWCA Civ 1134, [2007] 1 WLR 808.

applies and, in particular, whether a court is entitled, or bound, to have regard to 'the needs of the insurance market' when deciding whether a premium is proportionate. There have been a number of interesting first instance and county court appellate judgments, which are not recited here. More fundamentally, the Court of Appeal is to consider some of these issues in a number of cases, under the name of the lead case *McMenemy v Peterborough & Stamford Hospitals NHS Foundation Trust* in 2017.

Issues of proportionality and reasonableness are beyond the scope of this chapter. It suffices to note that the April 2013 changes have encouraged paying parties to adopt a more robust approach to challenging ATE premiums even where those premiums are subject to the pre-April 2013 rules. As the appellate judgment in *Surrey*, above, illustrates, the courts appear to be increasingly willing to rely on their greater experience since the time of *Rogers* to reduce premiums where appropriate – an approach that was arguably starting to become evident even before April 2013 – see cases such as *Redwing*[47], *Black Horse*[48] and *Hahn*[49].

More generally, the changes in relation to between the parties recoverability of ATE premiums were on a more limited basis and, unlike the CFA and DBA provisions, related only to the removal of the between the parties recoverability issue and not to a fundamental change to the nature and terms of such arrangements.

General implementation issues are most likely to relate to matters such as whether a further premium paid after 1 April 2013 to 'top up' an existing policy should be regarded as part of the same pre-commencement funding arrangement (thereby being recoverable) or whether it should be regarded as a new policy and to the technical points identified above.

Damages-Based Agreements (DBAs)

2–13   The introduction of DBAs was long awaited. They had, of course, been in existence for some time in relation to employment tribunal matters and the use of a contingency fee arrangement was permissible under s.57 of the Solicitors Act 1974 in relation to non-contentious business matters. The proposed introduction of a regulated form of arrangement whereby the solicitor's payment would be directly proportionate to the client's recovery, in general litigation, was seen by many, if not all, as a positive step in widening the available forms of funding.

Unfortunately, the precise method of their introduction has been widely criticised as being too narrow and restrictive, with the result that to date there appears to have been very limited use of DBAs in circumstances where they were prohibited prior to April 2013.

The widening of the permissibility of DBAs in contentious business was

---

[47] *Redwing Construction Ltd v Wishart* [2011] EWHC 19 (TCC).
[48] *Kelly v Black Horse Ltd* [2013] EWHC B17 (Costs).
[49] *Hahn v NHS England* (unreported, Liverpool County Court, 3 August 2015).

achieved by virtue of s.45 of LASPO, amending the existing s.58AA of the 1990 Act, with effect from 1 April 2013. By virtue of s.58AA(4), a DBA is now permissible in all matters save those which cannot presently be subject of an enforceable CFA (primarily criminal and family matters).

As with CFAs, a DBA must comply with the conditions imposed by the permitting statute. If it fails to do so, it is unenforceable. Again, as with CFAs, an exception exists for agreements which fall under s.57 of the Solicitors Act 1974, that is to say non contentious business agreements[50].

Beyond the basic requirements of the agreement being in writing and not relating to prohibited classes of proceedings, the amended s.58AA provides that for such a DBA to be enforceable it must comply with the requirements of the DBA Regulations 2013. It is therein that the problems are said to lie.

Jackson LJ had proposed that in order for a DBA to be 'valid', there should be a requirement for a client to receive specific and independent advice before it was signed.[51] The recommendation was not implemented – primarily it would appear out of concerns that it might lead to a return to the sort of between the parties arguments over enforceability and adequacy of advice which had been a feature of the Conditional Fee Agreement Regulations 2000. However, there are certain requirements for the provision of information in relation to DBAs in employment matters (set out in reg.5 of the DBA Regulations 2013). Presumably, such advice is thought to be more desirable and, perhaps more importantly, less likely to lead to indemnity principle arguments of the type which were notoriously prevalent in relation to CFAs generally as a result, in particular, of the specific advice requirements under the (now revoked) CFA Regulations 2000, given the limited scope for between the parties costs recovery before the Employment Tribunal. **2–14**

The basic provisions in relation to DBAs in employment matters have not changed and the remainder of this section will focus on the requirements in non-employment matters.

The effect of the 2013 Regulations is that a solicitor is entitled to agree with his client that he shall be paid by way of a percentage of the damages ultimately recovered by the client. Such 'payment', as defined by reg.1 of the 2013 Regulations, must be net of any between the parties costs recovered or recoverable by way of profit costs or counsel's fees (reg.4)—the so called 'Ontario' model. In other words, the solicitor cannot enjoy the benefit of both the 'payment' from the client and the between the parties costs recovery, but must allow such between the parties costs recovery to reduce the client's liability to pay the 'payment'.

In addition, the agreement can allow for the solicitor to charge disbursements to the client (other than counsel's fees) on top of the percentage fee

---

[50] 2016 saw a rare and significant decision in relation to the use of 'contingency fee arrangements' in the form of non-contentious business agreements and therefore used outside the context of proceedings. In *Bolt Burdon Solicitors v Tariq* [2016] EWHC 1507 (QB), [2016] 4 WLR 112 the High Court upheld the validity of a 50% contingency fee and gave some useful guidance on how the court would approach challenges to such fees. The Court of Appeal refused permission for an appeal against that decision [2016] EWCA Civ 845.

[51] Final Report, p.133.

(with credit being given against that charge for any between the parties costs recovered or recoverable in respect of such disbursements) (reg.4(1)(b)).

The 2013 Regulations include a requirement for any DBA (other than one in relation to employment proceedings) to contain a cap on the amount of the client's recovered damages which may be used to pay the solicitor's fee under the DBA. In proceedings generally the sum is 50% (inclusive of VAT) (reg.4(3) – and unlike the CFA Order, the Regulation does expressly mention VAT).

2–15   In personal injury claims there is a stricter limit, with the cap being restricted to 25% of the same classes of damages as apply in relation to the cap on a success fee under a CFA, namely general damages and damages for pecuniary loss other than future pecuniary loss (reg.4(2)).

This latter restriction immediately illustrates a potential, though not necessarily insuperable, obstacle to the use of a DBA in personal injury litigation. With a post-April 2013 CFA, the success fee is capped at 25% of the prescribed classes of damages. However, there is no cap on base fees (other than their reasonableness) and counsel's fee can be charged in addition to the base fees and success fee (though counsel's success fee is probably included in the cap).

With a DBA, however, the total fee, including counsel's fee, is capped at 25% of the same classes of damages. Whilst there will be cases where the figures are such that a DBA is still attractive, the most valuable heads of loss in a large personal injury case are usually future losses (care, loss of earnings, etc.) and not past losses or general damages and the limitation of the total fee under a DBA to a fraction of those heads of loss will limit their attractiveness and suitability in all but a small minority of cases.

This is before any more general obstacles to the use of a DBA are considered, as to which see below.

Between the parties costs recovery

2–16   CPR r.44.18 provides that the fact of a DBA will not affect between the parties costs recovery and that between the parties costs shall be assessed in accordance with CPR r.44.3. The rule itself is somewhat vague in this regard, and the limited use of DBAs to date means that its scope has yet to be properly tested.

However, it is generally understood that it is intended to result in between the parties costs being assessed on a 'conventional' basis, that is to say on the basis of an hourly rate and time spent basis.

What is clear is that the between the parties costs will not be assessed by reference to the 'payment' the client is liable to pay the solicitor under the DBA save that, as noted below, such payment may act as an indemnity principle 'cap' on the opponent's total liability. Accordingly, clients entering into a DBA must be made expressly aware that there is likely to be a fundamental difference (and often a shortfall) between the payment due under the DBA and the equivalent sum in profit costs an opponent is likely to be ordered to pay if the claim succeeds.

The between the parties assessment will involve the court identifying a 'notional' hourly rate where none has been contractually agreed, much as occurs in between the parties assessments in publicly funded cases.

It also means that a solicitor who believed that acting on a DBA would allow the firm to avoid having to conduct detailed time recording would be wrong. Not only would a lack of detailed time recording hamper any between the parties costs recovery, it could be very unfortunate were the DBA to be challenged on a solicitor–client basis.

As noted previously, the indemnity principle has not been disapplied, despite Jackson LJ's recommendation. This is expressly reflected in CPR r.44.18(2)(b) which recites that a party may not recover more by way of costs than the total amount payable under the DBA.

Accordingly, if the 'notional/conventional' between the parties costs in a case exceed the sum payable under a DBA, then the between the parties costs recovery will be limited to the DBA sum. However, if the 'notional/conventional' between the parties costs are less than the DBA sum, then because the assessment is conducted on that 'notional' basis, the between the parties costs recovery will be limited to that conventional sum.

Problems with DBAs

Some issues have already been highlighted above. Specific problems include: 2–17

- The wording of para.4 of the DBA Regulations 2013, and in particular the definition of 'payment' appears to prevent the use of hybrid DBAs. That is to say, it appears to prevent the agreement allowing the legal representative to be paid anything by way of profit costs other than the percentage share of damages if the case is won or nothing if the case is lost. Hybrid or discounted DBAs would allow for the solicitor to charge a low hourly rate win or lose, with a percentage share of damages on success. Discounted CFAs have been popular in commercial litigation, where a client is able and prepared to pay something win or lose, but wishes to share the risk with the solicitor. Hybrid DBAs would potentially be popular for offering the same opportunity whilst tying the reward directly to the amount of recovery. The present drafting appears to prevent such agreements and the wording of the regulations appears to mean that such agreements would be unenforceable. It is a moot point whether this is a deliberate decision, but it would appear to be so. That impression was emphasised by the fact that when asking the Civil Justice Council to consider some technical revisions to the DBA Regulations in November 2014 the Ministry of Justice appeared to rule out revising them to permit (or to make clear that they already permitted) hybrid DBAs. The then Master of the Rolls referred to the Government having decided to 'not permit hybrid DBAs'.[52] Lord Justice Jackson called for

---

[52] http://www.judiciary.gov.uk/related-offices-and-bodies/advisory-bodies/cjc/working-parties/civil-justice-council-cjc-to-look-at-damages-based-agreements-revisions/ [Accessed 29 January, 2015].

the Government to rethink its position in this regard and gave cogent reasons why the position should be reconsidered.[53] That reconsideration has yet to take place.

- This also appears to create a problem with using a DBA in a form similar to a CFA 'lite'. That is to say a DBA which includes a provision allowing for the solicitor to retain between the parties costs in full in the event that the between the parties costs payable on the hypothetical hourly rate/time spent basis (the 'Ontario model') exceed the sum which would otherwise be payable under the agreement on a simple percentage of damages basis. There seems no particular reason why such an agreement should not be permissible if CFA lites are to remain permissible. It would not require an opponent to pay more than a reasonable and proportionate sum. At the same time, the prospect of enhanced between the parties recovery would facilitate the greater use of DBAs on a solicitor–client basis. However, such agreements do not presently appear to be permissible under the 2013 Regulations.

- The Regulations appear to require the legal representative's fee to be calculated only by reference to damages 'ultimately recovered' by the client (reg.1), whilst at the same time requiring the solicitor to give credit for any between the parties costs (profit costs or counsel's fees) which are 'paid or payable' to the client (reg.4). In other words, the legal representative bears the risk of the opponent's solvency, having to give credit for between the parties costs payable, even if not received, whilst only being able to charge the client his percentage fee where damages are actually received. The same applies to disbursements.

- The Regulations do not contain any provisions for payment on termination of the agreement. There appears to be nothing preventing the agreement providing that, if the client instructs another firm and subsequently wins the claim, the 'payment' under the agreement will be payable in full (or indeed in part). However, the restriction on permitting any other form of 'payment' appears to prevent the rendering of a different form of charge, for example on an hourly rate basis or otherwise, if the client simply 'walks away' or if the firm feels obliged to cease acting and in particular appears to prevent the solicitor from providing for some non-contingent charge (that is to say one not dependent on the client's ultimate success in the case) being made. This would be particularly problematic in cases where the risk is not of the client switching to a different firm of solicitors, but of the client abandoning the claim other than on the firm's advice for any reason.

The limiting effect of these matters is enhanced by the continuing treatment of DBAs and CFAs in litigation as islands of legality in a sea of legality

---

[53] http://www.litigationfutures.com/news/jackson-outlines-two-pronged-strategy-promote-dbas [Accessed 29 January, 2015].

whereby, if the requirements of s.58AA and s.58 respectively are not fully complied with, the agreement is unenforceable. In conjunction with the continued application of the indemnity principle this exposes the solicitor to a risk that if the DBA departs in any material fashion from the strictures of the Regulations, the agreement will be unenforceable and no payment at all will be permitted.

It is not clear to what extent these restrictions were intended (though it now seems clear that the continued non-permissibility of hybrid DBAs, at least, is intentional). However, the combined effect of all of these factors has resulted in very limited use of DBAs.

In addition to these problems, a peculiar problem arguably arises with commercial third party funding. Section 58AA(3) of the 1990 Act, as amended by LASPO, provides that a DBA includes an agreement of that type entered into between a person providing claims management services and the recipient of those services. 'Claims management services' are given the same definition as in Pt.2 of the Compensation Act 2006. The definition in s.4(2)(b) of the 2006 Act provides that 'claims management services' means 'advice or <u>other services</u> in relation to the making of a claim'. This is a very wide definition and on its face it would appear that, for example, the provision of third party funding for a claim would be the provision of an 'other service' in respect of the claim.

Since the funder is then being rewarded for that funding by a payment which (usually) is determined by reference to the amount of the financial benefit obtained (s.58AA(3)(a)(ii) of the 1990 Act), such a funding arrangement is prima facie a DBA and must comply with the Regulations or be unenforceable. Not only would a non-compliant agreement mean that the funder could not rely on the agreement to recover its reward in the event of a successful claim, but the use of an agreement which was contrary to statute in order to bring a claim would possibly give rise to arguments as to whether the claim should be stayed[54].

If this analysis of the effect of s.58AA(3)(a) is correct, then all third party funding arrangements which rely on a share of the proceeds for the funder's reward must comply with the DBA Regulations 2013 or be unenforceable. Given that this is the common form of such arrangements, and given that the DBA Regulations were introduced as part of the package of 2013 reforms, which included a review of third party funding and the conclusion that statutory regulation of that market was not presently required, a recommendation which the Government accepted, it would be a very surprising outcome if such regulation had been introduced in this 'back door' fashion. It would appear that either third party funding is far more tightly regulated than has been appreciated or there has been a failure to appreciate the potential effect

---

[54] Though note that the Court of Appeal has been reluctant to hold that the use of an unlawful or champertous funding arrangement should prevent the claim itself proceedings – see for example *Faryab v Smyth* (Court of Appeal, 28 August 1998 unreported) and *Stocznia Gdanska SA v Latreefers Inc* [2000] CPLR 65.

of using the wide definition of claims management services from the 2006 Act when introducing the amendments at s.58AA of the 1990 Act.

Future Amendment

2–18   As mentioned above, the Civil Justice Council Working Group was asked to look at a number of technical issues. These were:

- dividing into two sets the existing regulations with employment tribunal regulations (as per the 2010 regime) separated from regulations for civil litigation proceedings;
- changing the regulations so that defendants will be able to use DBAs, by widening the application of the regulations where the party receives a specified financial benefit (rather than restricting them to receiving a payment);
- reviewing whether the regulations should contain provisions on terminating the DBA;
- clarifying that different forms of litigation funding cannot be used during a case when a DBA is being used to fund litigation; and
- clarifying that the lawyer's payment can only come from damages, and the payment should be a percentage of the sum ultimately received (not awarded or agreed).

The CJC's report was published in September 2015[55] and focused primarily on the issue of hybrid DBAs.

The report contains 45 recommendations, which are not repeated here. It noted that the inability to enter into what it describes as 'concurrent hybrid DBAs'- that is to say a hybrid DBA as described above, as opposed to the ability to have separate, consecutive retainers (perhaps first a conventional retainer and then a DBA) has had an 'incredibly chilling effect' on the take up of DBAs, but ultimately concluded that the introduction of such arrangements, whether generally or only in relation to certain practice areas, remained a policy decision for the Government.

Other recommendations included changes to make DBAs more available for use by defendants, an increase in the 25% DBA cap for personal injury claims to 50% for defendants, and greater freedom as to the 'trigger points' for payment of the DBA fee and for the effect of early termination of DBAs. The CJC's call for further modifications to try and improve the use of DBAs has been supported by the Master of the Rolls. Whether the call and recommendations will be heeded remains to be seen and more than 12 months on no timetable has yet been set for any revision. Absent such revision DBAs are likely to remain little used.

---

[55] The Damages-Based Agreements Reform Project Drafting And Policy Issues – https://www.judiciary.gov.uk/wp-content/uploads/2015/09/dba-reform-project-cjc-aug-2015.pdf

Third Party Funding / Litigation Funding

The general operation of third party funding arrangements and matters   2–19
such as the voluntary Code of Conduct for Litigation Funders published by
the Civil Justice Council in its most recent form in November 2011 and the
potential liability of third party funders to adverse costs orders is beyond the
scope of this text. A summary of the relevant background to the operation
of third party funding may be found in Chapter 11 of Lord Justice Jackson's
Final Report.

However, two decisions in 2016 are of particular note.

In *Excalibur Ventures LLC v Texas Keystone Inc*[56], the Court of Appeal upheld
the judgment of Sir Christopher Clarke by which he had held that the professional funders of the failed litigation were liable on a joint and several liability
basis to pay the other party's costs on an indemnity basis.

The case breaks no new ground on the core approach to the making of a
non party costs order against commercial funders, set out by the Court of
Appeal in 2005 in *Arkin v Borchard Lines Ltd*[57]. However, in addition to reaffirming those principles, it did also provide clarity on two important points.
Firstly, whilst a commercial funder (in the absence of impropriety or the
funding arrangement being champertous) will not normally be held liable
for adverse costs in a sum greater than the amount of funding that particular
funder provided (the so called 'Arkin cap'), when considering how to calculate
that cap, the court will not only take into account the level of funding the
funder provided for the litigant's own costs and disbursements, but will also
take into account any money the funder advanced to allow the litigant to
provide security for costs. Both are to be regarded as 'funding' for the purposes
of the cap. This potentially widens the scope of a funder's exposure.

Secondly, the court made clear that a funder can be ordered to pay adverse
costs under a non-party costs order on the indemnity basis where the circumstances of the case generally warrant such an order, even where the funder's
own conduct, in isolation, would not. The fact that costs are awarded on the
indemnity basis does not lift the Arkin cap. The funder's maximum exposure
is still limited by the cap, but the fact that it may be liable for costs on the
indemnity basis means that its exposure within that cap is likely to be higher.
This is likely to be particularly important given the increased impact of the
proportionality test post-April 2013. Put simply, the gap between costs on the
standard basis and on the indemnity basis (where the proportionality test
does not apply – see CPR r.44.3) is likely to widen. It is also important, in the
context of the funding of larger cases, in light of the greater use of costs budgeting. The relative certainty that a funder would have been able to take from
the fact that an opponent party's costs were budgeted is removed if the funder

---

[56] [2016] EWCA Civ 1144.
[57] [2005] EWCA Civ 655, [2005] 1 WLR 3055. It is notable, in passing, that Lord Justice Jackson's recommendation in
Chapter 11 of the Final Report that the Arkin cap should be lifted such that commercial funders are generally liability
for all (reasonable and proportionate) adverse costs if the case is lost was not adopted.

is potentially exposes to a non-party costs order on the indemnity basis, since the limitation in CPR r.3.18 only applies to costs awards on the standard basis.

Both aspects of the judgment are likely to increase the care with which sensible litigation funders consider whether a case is suitable for funding and are also likely to increase the cost of such funding. The former point seems to have been an outcome that the judges at both first instance and on appeal considered not merely an acceptable, but a desirable consequence of their judgments.

In *Essar Oilfield Services Ltd v Norscot Rig Management PVT Ltd*[58], HHJ Waksman QC held that an arbitrator's general powers under s.59(1)(c) of the Arbitration Act 1996 included the power to award to the successful party the costs that party had incurred in obtaining third party funding – in effect, the 'reward' that the party had paid to the funder in return for the provision of that funding.

That award was on the basis that s.59(1)(c) allows an award of 'legal or other costs'[59]. It was accepted that third party funding costs were not a 'legal' cost and that such costs were not traditionally capable of being the subject of an award of costs in litigation, pursuant to s.51 of the Senior Courts Act 1981, CPR r.44.2 or any of the conventional routes to an award of 'costs' within proceedings. However, the judge accepted the submission that 'other' costs under s.59(1)(c) was wide enough to include such costs and that it was therefore within the tribunal's discretion to allow such costs if it considered it appropriate to do so.

The decision makes no inroads on the well-established principle that funding costs are not recoverable in litigation. However, it does create a radical difference between the potential costs recovery in an arbitration under the 1996 Act in comparison with those in litigation.

The decision in *Essar* has been the subject of much interest and some criticism. It would appear ripe for consideration at higher appellate level. However, the High Court refused permission and as a result s.68(4) of the 1996 Act operates as a bar on any further appeal. This is unfortunate, particularly since the use of third party funding has been allowed to develop incrementally, though the common law rather than by legislative intervention, and it would be useful to have as much clarity and authority as possible on its operation.

In principle, the logic of the decision could also be used to argue that success fees – now expressly irrecoverable in litigation by virtue of s.44 of the Legal Aid, Sentencing and Punishment of Offenders Act 2012 – are nevertheless recoverable in principle in proceedings under the 1996 Act. However, this would appear to run into the barrier that s.58A(4) of the Courts & Legal Services Act 1990 contains a very wide definition of 'proceedings' which is wide enough to encompass proceedings under the 1996 Act and s.58(6) (as amended by the 2012 Act) then prohibits an award of costs in any such proceedings from including payment of the success fee.

---

[58] [2016] EWHC 2361 (Comm).
[59] As to 'legal' costs, see inter alia *London Scottish Benefit Society v Chorley* [1884] XIII QB 872.

The position in relation to ATE premiums is less clear. The revocation of s.29 Access to Justice Act 1999 by s.46 of the 2012 Act does not appear to lead to the same sort of positive prohibition on recovery as part of a costs order under the 1996 Act as s.58A(6) of the 1990 Act does with success fees. *McGraddie v McGraddie*[60] makes clear that an ATE premium cannot be recovered between the parties absent the receiving party being able to identify express statutory provision permitting the same. It remains to be seen, however, whether the provision in s.59(1)(c) of the 1996 Act allowing the tribunal to award 'other costs' will be considered to be wide enough to allow the award of an ATE premium.

The use of third party funding in England & Wales has developed incrementally through precedent rather than having been the subject of specific statutory approval or regulation. As a result, and as the use of such funding grows, there are likely to be further cases in the near future exploring the boundaries of its use.

Questions and answers

A. Transfer and variation of funding

Q1. Is it possible to assign a pre-LASPO Conditional Fee Agreement and to retain between the parties recoverability of success fees?
This is a complex question and the answer is uncertain. The case of *Jenkins*[61] offers some support for the argument that a CFA is capable of assignment, but is High Court appellate authority only, was decided on its own peculiar facts and may not be followed or might be capable of being distinguished in future cases. If *Jenkins* is correct, then the assignment of a CFA is at least possible in principle.

    2–20

If an assignment of a CFA can validly take place then following the principle of the effect of an assignment, the existing agreement continues and accordingly there would appear to be a good argument that the assigned agreement should be regarded as being the same CFA and therefore the same 'pre-commencement funding arrangement' for the purposes of CPR r.48.2 and/or s.44(6) of LASPO. However, even if the assignment is valid, there are public policy arguments which might lead a court to conclude that the agreement should not be so regarded.

These are complex issues and there will be no certainty unless and until they are resolved in an authoritative judgment.

Care needs to be taken when considering such assignments. In particular, with personal injury CFAs, if a pre-LASPO CFA 'assignment' was held not to be valid, there would be an argument that there were two CFAs, a pre-LASPO CFA and a post-LASPO CFA, on the same terms – namely the terms of the

---

[60] [2015] UKSC 1, [2015] 1 WLR 560.
[61] *Jenkins v Young Brothers Transport Ltd* [2006] EWHC 151 (QB).

original agreement. However, standard pre-LASPO CFA terms for a personal injury CFA would not comply with the requirements for the capping of a success fee under s.58(4) of the 1990 Act and the CFA Order 2013 and it might be argued that the 'new' CFA on the 'old' terms was therefore unenforceable. This could result in all costs (and not just the success fee) under the new CFA being irrecoverable both against the client and, by virtue of the indemnity principle, between the parties.

In *Jones*, above, the court held that it was bound by *Jenkins*, but the tenor of the judgment also approves the reasoning in *Jenkins*. In *Budana*, above. the regional costs judge appeared to express greater scepticism as to the correctness of *Jenkins*, but nevertheless considered himself bound by it. In *Webb*[62] Master Rowley distinguished *Jenkins* and held the 'novated' CFA to be unenforceable in consequence. There have been a number of other decisions to contrasting effects and no certainty is likely to be provided until higher appellate authority is available, which may come when *Budana* is heard by the Court of Appeal in 2017.

For solicitors, the position therefore is one of a state of uncertainty, though given that the main (but not only) issue appears to relate to post-April 2013 assignment of pre-April 2013 CFAs (particularly in the personal injury field) the number of technical challenges should hopefully diminish over time.

One final point to note is that there may be steps which can be taken to mitigate the risks of an adverse judicial decision on the point, such as by the use of -'fallback' retainers which only operate, for example, in the event of an assignment failing or a CFA being declared unenforceable as a result. There does not appear to have been such an arrangement in *Jones*. Such arrangements are not, themselves, entirely beyond the scope of argument, though they have been used in other areas and the use of them was supported by Sir Christopher Clarke in the High Court decision of *Forde*[63]. Such arrangements would probably need to be entered into before the case concluded[64].

Q2. What is the effect on recoverability of the success fee of assigning a pre-April 2013 CFA post-April 2013?

2–21 The general question of assignment is addressed in the previous question. Subject to that answer, if the assignment is effective there would appear to be a strong argument that the CFA remains a pre-commencement funding arrangement and the success fee remains recoverable in principle between the parties, subject to assessment of reasonableness of the percentage in the usual way.

---

[62] *Webb v Bromley London Borough Council* (SCCO, 18 February 2016).
[63] *Birmingham City Council v Forde* [2009] EWHC 12 (QB).
[64] See *Kellar Carib West Ltd v Williams* [2004] UKPC 30.

Q3. Do you think the exceptional circumstances which applied in *Jenkins v Young Brothers Transport* to allow the assignment of a CFA might apply in the following circumstances: One part of an LLP was trading under the name of SS until the LLP demerged, at which point the SS business and trading name was transferred to SL Ltd. The LLP continued to trade as a separate entity, but the SRA has treated SL Ltd as a successor practice rather than a new practice. Can we or should we:

- Enter into new CFAs with all our clients (in which case how will costs incurred prior to the transfer be dealt with and, in particular, what will happen to any recoverable success fees under pre-April 2013 CFAs)?
- Novate or assign the existing CFAs?
- Rely on having told our clients of the change of legal entity?

The issue of *Jenkins* is covered in some detail in the main text. In the instant case, there would appear to be a transfer of retainers from one legal entity (the old LLP, trading in part as SS) to another (SL Ltd). If the retainers were assigned, then whether such assignment is effective will depend on the outcome of the arguments identified in the main text. Which of the identified courses of action would be best on the facts of the individual case is a matter of detailed advice which is beyond the scope of this text.

2–22

Q4. My client instructed me prior to 1 April 2013, but I was not able to offer a CFA until later. Is it possible to backdate the CFA to the date of first instruction?

The first point is that the use of the term 'backdating' is dangerous and has been the subject of judicial criticism. It suggests some form of deception and that the date on the written document does not reflect the date on which it was entered into. This should never happen. If an agreement is intended to have retrospective effect, it should expressly state the date on which it was entered into and expressly state the earlier date from which it is said to apply. Note also the High Court's comments in this regard in the decision of *O'Brien*[65].

2–23

As to applying a CFA retrospectively so that it can benefit from pre-LASPO principles of recoverability, this would not seem possible. Section 44(6) of LASPO provides that the amendments do not apply if the relevant CFA was 'entered into' prior to 1 April 2013. Here, the agreement would be entered into after that date, but with retrospective effect. There seems no contractual reason why the agreement would not have retrospective effect, but it would not turn the CFA into a pre-LASPO CFA and the success fee would be irrecoverable.

---

[65] *O'Brien v Shorrock & MIB* [2015] EWHC 1630 (QB) and see also the decision in *Pentecost v John* [2015] EWHC 1970 (QB).

Q5. Can you amend a CFA in advance of detailed assessment? If so, what is the risk of doing so?

2–24   It is assumed that by referring to '*In advance of detailed assessment*' the question is referring to the 'window' between the conclusion of the substantive action/making of the costs order in the successful receiving party's favour and the hearing of the detailed assessment of the costs so awarded.

If so, the position is that there is no contractual or legislative bar to amending a CFA, though any amendment would have to comply with usual contractual principles as well as ensuring that the amended agreement satisfied the requirements of s.58 of the Courts & Legal Services Act 1990, the Conditional Fee Agreements Order 2013, and any applicable consumer legislation. However, the practical effect is that any such amendment is highly unlikely to have any effect on the between the parties costs.

In *Kellar v Williams*[66], the Privy Council confirmed that, whilst such an agreement could be amended by agreement between the parties to the agreement after the costs order had been made, the paying party opponent would be entitled to disregard the amendment to the extent that it resulted in any increase in the paying party's liability over and above what that liability would have been but for the amendment.

Although *Kellar* is 'only' a Privy Council decision and is therefore not binding on courts in England & Wales, it has been regularly cited and followed by those Courts – see, for example, *Radford v Frade*[67] and the answer to Q6 below.

The key risk of such an amendment, therefore, is that it is simply unlikely to achieve its intended aim, assuming that aim is to cure some defect which was not perceived prior to the completion of the substantive claim.

Q6. Is it possible to vary a pre-April 2013 CFA and still recover the success fee?

2–25   In principle, this seems possible. A variation does not change the date of the original agreement. However, in practice it may depend on the variation. If the variation was seen in some way to offend the broad principle against the inter partes recoverability of additional liabilities incurred after 1 April 2013 then there would be a substantial risk of it being disallowed. To take an extreme example, if the pre-April CFA had provided for a 5% success fee, but was varied after the 1 April 2013 to include a 100% success fee on a retrospective basis, the court might well disallow the success fee, though it could probably do so (subject to the facts) on the simple basis that even if the success fee was recoverable in principle, the increase was unreasonable on a between the parties basis.

Variation is sometimes confused with issues of construction or rectification of CFAs. Where there is some doubt as to the precise meaning of terms in a

---

[66] [2004] UKPC 30, [2005] 4 Costs LR 559.
[67] [2016] EWHC 1600 (QB).

CFA, these may be resolved by reference to standard principles of construction and this simply involves identifying the true terms of the original agreement. This would have no effect on the recoverability of any success fee under the CFA. Similarly, where it can be established that the written terms do not properly record the true intention of the parties, it may be possible for the CFA to be rectified. Again, rectification is not variation – it is simply ensuring that the written document properly records the true terms as originally agreed but imperfectly recorded, and this would probably not affect the recoverability of any success fee. Variation may not always be the only, or best, solution to perceived problems with a pre-April 2013 CFA.

Radford v Frade[68] is a good example of the difficulties that can be faced where the CFA, as originally drafted, later turns out to be less than ideally drafted for the particular case. As well as providing a good illustration of the sort of approach the court will take to the construction of a CFA in such circumstances, it also provides a sound illustration of the *Kellar v Carib West* point mentioned in the answer to **Q5** above, namely that an attempt to correct the CFA after the conclusion of the case is likely to fail on a between the parties basis. In *Radford*, as in the *Oyston* case referred to therein, it is arguable that where the court is referring to rectification, it is in fact referring to poorly or mis described attempts to vary the agreement, since rectification does not involve making any change to the original agreement.

Q7. In a number of recent cases a claimant moved from legal aid funding to a pre-Jackson conditional fee agreement, the court has disallowed the recovery of success fees and additional liabilities where in principle they were recoverable, but allowed other costs to be recovered. The result seems fair enough, but on what legal basis did the court specifically disallow some costs but not others? Wasn't the CFA either valid or invalid?
No. The leading case on this issue at the moment is the decision of Foskett J in *Surrey v Barnet & Chase Farm Hospitals NHS Trust*[69], in respect of which an application for permission to appeal to the Court of Appeal is pending. However, regardless of the eventual outcome in *Surrey*, the issue in these cases is not one of enforceability (or validity) of the CFA. Rather, the issue is one of reasonableness. Put simply, the paying party accepts (broadly) that the claimant would have incurred some costs in pursuing his or her successful case, but contends that it was unreasonable to choose a CFA in place of public funding and therefore the additional cost involved – the success fee and any ATE premium – were unreasonably incurred. If the paying party is correct, reasonable base costs remain payable (subject to assessment and any other arguments).

2–26

The basis of the argument is commonly that the advice provided by the solicitor to the client as to the choice of funding methods was objectively unreasonable, having regard to the subjective characteristics and particular

---

[68] [2016] EWHC 1600 (QB).
[69] [2016] EWHC 1598 (QB).

circumstances of the individual concerned at the time the particular funding arrangement was entered into. However, the effect would be the same if the argument was that the client made an unreasonable choice despite receiving appropriate advice from his solicitors.

These situations – where, if the argument is correct, the base costs are still recoverable but the additional liabilities are lost – may be contrasted to the sort of arguments that were run in respect of CFAs which had to comply with the Conditional Fee Agreement Regulations 2000 (revoked with effect from November 2005) where a failure to give proper advice as to alternative forms of funding could be held to be a breach of Reg.4 of the Regulations, with the effect that the CFA would be held to be unenforceable in its entirety, with consequent non-recoverability of base costs as well as additional liabilities.

Whilst most such arguments as to enforceability (as opposed to reasonableness) ceased following the revocation of the 2000 Regulations, they do still arise occasionally in specific narrow contexts, as seen in cases such as *Hyde v Milton Keynes NHS Foundation Trust*[70].

Q8. In the light of the *Surrey* appeal decision, do you think challenges by paying parties to additional liabilities in cases where there has been a change of funding are likely to increase or are they going away?

2–27 There are three points to note in response. Firstly, an application has been made to the Court of Appeal for permission to appeal the *Surrey* decision. If permission is granted, then it will be necessary to await the outcome of that appeal before any certainty may be ascertained in relation to the correctness of the paying party's challenges. Secondly, the *Surrey* case (and related cases) relate to a particular phenomenon, namely changes of funding from a form of funding which did not give rise to any additional liability (commonly public funding) to one with additional liabilities (a CFA supported by ATE). That phenomenon is limited in time in light of the fundamental changes introduced in April 2013 which mean that, in the majority of cases, additional liabilities are no longer recoverable between the parties where the funding arrangement was entered into on or after 1 April 2013. Accordingly, such challenges are likely to reduce in number by virtue of the passage of time regardless of the outcome in *Surrey*.

Lastly, even if *Surrey* is upheld, there remains the scope for challenges (in relation to the diminishing number of claims where the funding arrangements include additional liabilities which are recoverable in principle) in circumstances which fall outsider the precise factual ambit of the *Surrey* case – and in particular in cases where, for example, the 10% general damages uplift would have been potentially more significant to the particular claimant by reference to the facts of their particular case or where the terms of the CFA

---

[70] [2016] EWHC 72 (QB) – on appeal to the Court of Appeal – in which the Defendant's reasonableness challenge (of the type mentioned above) failed, but where the defendant also pursued an enforceability challenge to the CFA on the basis that an alleged overlap in time between the CFA and a public funding certificate rendered the CFA unenforceable. That challenge also failed at first instance and on appeal, but is the subject of the second appeal noted above.

offered to the claimant were materially more disadvantageous than the available alternatives.

Q9. Is a pre-April 2013 ATE policy premium still recoverable if the policy holder changes solicitors post–April 2013? Should the policy be 'assigned' to the new firm?

An ATE policy is a contract between the claimant and the insurer. Provided   2–28
the policy is not voided or terminated by virtue of the change of solicitor (and this is often the case, particularly with policies issues by the solicitor under delegated authority) then the policy remains in place and, as a pre-April 2013, the premium charged for it remains recoverable in principle between the parties.

There should be no question of 'assignment' of the policy to the new firm. Neither the new firm nor the old are likely to be parties to the contract of insurance.

B. Conditional Fee Agreement terms

Q10. Do you need to name all defendants in a CFA?

No. What is necessary is to ensure that the CFA adequately identifies what   2–29
claim or claims the CFA covers so that the parties to the agreement can be sufficiently certain as to its scope. That may be achieved, for example, by Identifying the underlying matter which gives rise to the claim (for example an accident in which the claimant was involved on a particular date) and that the agreement covers the claimant's claim for damages arising out of that accident against any opponent who might be identified.

There have been a large number of reported cases where parties have encountered difficulties as a result of a CFA identifying the potential defendants to a claim too narrowly in a CFA and failing to notice during the lifetime of the claim that the CFA may need to be amended to reflect additional defendants who have subsequently been identified, perhaps the best known example of which is *Engeham v London & Quadrant Housing Trust Ltd*[71], where the claimant managed to recover her costs despite such a problem. Parties should be wary of undue reliance on *Engeham*. If anything, it emphasises the point that errors in the naming of defendants to a CFA may be fatal to a claim for costs – the claimant in *Engeham* was only successful in recovering her costs by way of a secondary argument having decided not to appeal before the Court of Appeal the decision of the judges below that the CFA, properly construed, did not name the relevant defendant.

Such experience suggests that adopting an approach of limiting the CFA to a single, specifically identified, defendant at the outset may be an unwise practice. However, there will be cases where it is helpful or advisable to specifically name the potential defendants, in particular where the intention is

---

[71] [2015] EWCA Civ 1530.

to ensure that the solicitor is only bound to act in relation to certain specific matters and is not bound to pursue a claim against other potential defendants unless the solicitor later expressly agreed to do so. In such circumstances, the solicitor needs to make sure that it has robust processes in place to ensure that any necessary variation to the CFA is agreed with the client, in writing, before any work on the additional aspect of the claim is undertaken.

Q11. My client entered into a CFA prior to 1 April 2013, but has now died. I wish to offer the personal representatives a CFA to continue the claim. Will I be able to recover the success fee?

2–30 It is a moot point whether the original CFA is automatically assigned to the personal representatives on the death of the client. Certain contracts are so assigned by operation of law on death (unless the contract provides otherwise). However, personal contracts are generally an exception to this and it is arguable whether a CFA falls into this category.

Equally, there is no reason in principle why the CFA should not expressly provide for the consequences on death of the client, including for its continuation. There is nothing preventing the (now) deceased making contractual provision to bind his personal representatives on his death, though such provision is rare in CFAs.

In addition, it was very common in CFAs, particularly personal injury CFAs, for the CFA to expressly provide that the agreement ended on the death of the client. The Law Society standard model prior to April 2013, expressly so provided. If such a CFA was used, then there is no need to consider whether it is arguable in law that the CFA persists, because the issue has been expressly addressed in the CFA. It does not.

In summary, therefore, there are certain circumstances, depending on the terms of the original CFA and how it is categorised by a court, where there may be arguments that the original CFA may continue in some way, though this could only be determined by reference to the specific terms of the CFA. If the CFA is a standard Law Society model (or one of the many variants based thereon) or if these specific circumstances do not apply, then any new CFA is likely to be seen to be a post-LASPO CFA and accordingly the success fee will be irrecoverable. The success fee under the original CFA will probably be recoverable for work done before the death of the claimant.

Q12. We wish to enter into a CFA with our client whereby in addition to the success fee being capped as required by s.58 of the Courts & Legal Services Act 1990 and the CFA Order 2013, the total costs payable under the agreement will also be capped as a percentage of the damages. We have been told that this means our agreement is a contingency fee agreement, or DBA, and must comply with the DBA Regulations 2013. Is this correct?

2–31 No, it would appear not. As a matter of pure terminology, any agreement where the right to or amount of payment depends on the outcome of the case

is probably a form of contingency fee agreement. However, that loose terminology has been replaced by the specific terminology used in s.58 and s.58AA.

A CFA whereby the fees payable under the CFA are not calculated by reference to the damages awarded, but whereby there is an overall cap on the
amount that can be paid by reference to the damages is a CFA. It is not a DBA.
The key distinction is that the cap is precisely that. If the fees payable are
less than the cap, then the fees payable are those fees, as calculated. The cap
merely operates as an overall limit, rather than as the method of calculation
of the fees.

A DBA, by contrast, is an agreement where the fee payable is determined as
a percentage of the damages recovered. It is not a cap, but rather the primary
method of determination of the applicable fee.

Prior to the introduction of recoverable success fees, the Law Society model
CFA used to provide for a cap on the success fee payable under the CFA. The
new provisions for personal injury CFAs operate on a similar model. The
agreements remain CFAs and this principle applies even if the capping effect
is extended beyond the success fee to the fees generally.

C. After the Event Insurance

**Q13. If a staged premium ATE policy was incepted prior to 1 April 2013,
but the further staged premiums are only incurred after that date, will the
further premiums be recoverable?**
Probably. Staged premiums were a common feature of litigation and their use   2–32
had been expressly approved by the courts in cases such as *Rogers v Merthyr
Tydfil CBC*.[72] Their existence and use was well known at the time of the
amendment of the rules and it would have been simple for the rule to provide
that only the stages incurred prior to 1 April, 2013 would be recoverable, if
that had been the intention. Instead, s.58C of the 1990 Act refers to 'a policy
of insurance' having been 'taken out' prior to 1 April 2013 and the taking out
of a staged policy would appear to satisfy that requirement, with the effect
that subsequent premiums under the policy remain recoverable in principle.

The point may be tested, however, if there has been abuse of the system
with polices being incepted on a wide scale basis for nominal premiums
merely to get them 'on the books' prior to 1 April 2013 and then substantial
premiums being later charged when the case is properly evaluated. Whether
this has occurred and how the courts will approach claims for premiums in
such cases remains to be seen.

**Q14. Would an increased premium on a pre-1 April 2013 ATE policy be
payable by a losing defendant? I.e. is the increased premium payable or
only the original premium amount?**
See the preceding answer. On the plain wording of s.58C of the 1990 Act, a   2–33

---

[72] *Rogers v Merthyr Tydfil CBC* [2006] EWCA Civ 1134; [2007] 1 W.L.R. 808.

further (part) premium payable under a policy incepted prior to the 1 April 2013 would appear to be recoverable in principle. As noted, the point is likely to be tested and perceived abuse of the transitional provisions may encourage the court to adopt a purposive approach which may lead to a different result.

Q15. In a clinical negligence case, where a claimant obtains a breach and causation report and the defendant then admits liability, could the claimant recover the cost of the premium if it then obtained ATE insurance in relation to obtaining a quantum report?

2–34   Yes, in principle. The recoverability of a premium under the Recovery of Costs Insurance Premiums in Clinical Negligence Proceedings (No.2) Regulations 2013 is not contingent on whether or not the claimant takes out some other ATE in respect of other aspects of the case. However, the premium (or part of the premium) that is recoverable is only that premium (or part thereof) that relates to the cost of obtaining reports on liability and causation. The premium or part premium for the ATE insurance in respect of the other aspects of the case would not be recoverable.

Q16. We act for two claimants, one of whom is insolvent. We have entered into an ATE policy and are planning to rely on the insolvency exemption to LASPO 2012 if we are successful, so that we can recover the ATE premium from the defendant. Will the fact that only one of the claimants is insolvent prevent us from relying on the insolvency exemption to LASPO 2012? If we are allowed to recover the ATE premium from the defendant, will it be reduced to 50% to reflect the fact that only one of the claimants is insolvent?

2–35   This point is open to argument. The saving provision in art.4 of the Legal Aid, Sentencing and Punishment of Offenders Act 2012 (Commencement No.5 and Saving Provision) Order 2013 provides that the amendments removing recoverability of additional liabilities '*do not apply to. . .proceedings*' of various types. The Order does not provide that the amendments do not apply to particular claimants.

This suggests that, provided the proceedings themselves are within the exception, any of the parties to the proceedings may rely on that exception, regardless of whether they are one of the identified classes of legal persons referred to in the Order.

However, the underlying premise in the exception appears to have been to allow particular office holders and companies being wound up or entering into administration to benefit from the continued availability of funding arrangements with recoverable additional liabilities. Accordingly, a purposive construction of the Order may exclude parties other than those identified within the Order from its operation.

If one party is excluded from the operation of the exemption, it will not necessarily follow that only 50% (or indeed as much as 50%) of the premium will be recoverable. It may be that the remaining party is able to show that the all or the majority of the cost of the premium would have been incurred by it in any event and that it is liable for that premium in full (whether jointly and severally with the other party or otherwise). The precise outcome is likely to be fact dependent.

Q17. If a claimant with a pre-1 April 2013 ATE insurance policy is success-ful at first instance, an appeal is granted and a top-up of the ATE premium (after 1 April 2013) is required to cover the appeal, is the post-1 April 2013 ATE top-up premium recoverable from the other side if the appeal is successful?

This is open to argument. However, in light of the terms of s.46(3) LASPO and   2–36
the Court of Appeal's decision in *Hawksford Trustees*[73] which held that appeals were to be regarded as separate proceedings for the purposes of s.29 Access to Justice Act 1999, it seems highly likely that the appeal would be regarded as separate proceedings. If that is correct, a post-April 2013 premium in respect of an ATE policy for that appeal would not fall within the transitional provi-sions under s.46(3) and therefore would be irrecoverable.

The *Hawksford* point, however, remains arguable. The Court of Appeal's judgment on the point is only binding in the specific context in which context in which it was made and a different conclusion may be arrived at in different contexts – see *Parker v Butler*[74] dealing with the question of whether an appeal was to be regarded as separate proceedings for the purpose of Qualified One Way Costs Shifting and see also the point in the context of detailed assessment in *Khaira v Shergill*[75], currently on appeal to the Court of Appeal. The Hawksford principle would appear to be the one most likely to apply in the present situa-tion, given that the core issue relates to whether an appeal is separate proceed-ings for the purpose of recoverability of an ATE premium. However, the point has not yet been authoritatively decided in the context of s.46 of the 2012 Act.

D. Issue and notification

Q18. Our client entered into a CFA and ATE insurance policy before April 2013 in relation to insolvency proceedings. Since then, another party has been added as a party to the CFA and ATE insurance policy. Are we required to notify the defendants of this variation to the CFA and ATE insurance? If so, how do we notify them and do we need to file the notice?

Assuming this case falls within the insolvency exception (which some, but   2–37
not all, insolvency cases will do) then the April 2013 date is a red herring. The correct question is whether the funding arrangements were entered into on or before 5 April 2016.

---

[73] *Hawksford Trustees Jersey Ltd v Stella Global UK Ltd* [2012] EWCA Civ 987.
[74] [2016] EWHC 1251 (QB).
[75] [2016] EWHC 628 (Ch).

In relation to the addition of parties to an existing CFA, the notification requirements under the former CPR r.47 PD 32.5, as preserved in operation by CPR r.48.1, require notification to be given where '*a claimant [or defendant] has entered into a [relevant] funding arrangement*'. Accordingly, the matter should be looked at from the perspective of each individual party. The additional party here has now entered into a relevant funding arrangement by joining the existing CFA and notice should be given by way of a fresh N251 in respect of that particular party. It may be appropriate, depending on the facts, to provide additional information to make clear, for example, the date from which the client's liability under that arrangement runs it if is otherwise unclear.

If the case is not within the insolvency exception, or if the later joining party was added to the CFA on or after the 1 April 2016, then the later joining party will (probably) fall foul of s.58A(6) of the Courts & Legal Services Act 1990 and s.44(6) LASPO and will not be able to recover any additional liabilities, despite the CFA having been entered into earlier by the other party.

Q19. Is there a long stop date whereby a party who has entered into a pre-April 2013 funding arrangement in relation to a claim must issue proceedings?

2–38 No (save, of course, for the general law of limitation in respect of that party's claim). However, the funding arrangement must relate to the '*matter that is the subject matter of the proceedings in which the costs order is made*'. Accordingly, if the claim subsequently brought is seen to relate to a different matter, then any additional liabilities will not be recoverable (and indeed there may be an issue as to what retainer in fact covers the proceedings that have been issued, with potential consequences between the parties as a result of the application of the indemnity principle and on a solicitor–client basis).

Q20. Is a notice of funding required for a Damages Based Agreement?

2–39 No. The requirements for notices of funding in (old) CPR r.44 were revoked with effect from 1 April 2013. They continue to apply in relation to pre-April 2013 funding arrangements and in the excepted cases where additional liabilities remain recoverable, as referred to in the main text (as do the requirements relating to provision of information about additional liabilities on detailed assessments in CPR r.47 PD 32) and should be complied with fully in respect of such arrangements (see CPR r.48.1). This includes the provision under the 'old' CPR r.44 PD 19.3 whereby there is a requirement to provide notice of change if the information previously provided is no longer accurate. Accordingly, if there is a change in relation to a pre-April 2013 CFA or ATE which means information provided in respect of those arrangements is no longer accurate, the opposing party should be notified accordingly.

Q21. We are acting for the claimant in a litigation matter. The defendant's solicitors have asked us to confirm how the litigation is being funded. Is there any obligation on our client to provide this information?

There is no procedural obligation to provide this information. However, it is **2–40** well established that the court may order a party to provide information in relation to its funding arrangements where the court accepts that to do so would serve a proper purpose. For example, the court has ordered a party to provide details of the identity of third party funders where to do so would serve the purpose of allowing a party to consider whether to bring an application for security for costs pursuant to CPR r.25.14[76]. it might take a similar approach for the purposes of an application for third party costs pursuant to s.51 of the Senior Courts Act 1981.

Accordingly, where there is a legitimate purpose to be served by the request and the information or documentation requested is not privileged (a question, in relation to funding arrangements, which is still not satisfactorily resolved), there is at least some risk that a court would order that the information be provided.

The court is likely to scrutinise closely whether such a legitimate purpose exists at the time the application is made. See, for example, the judgment of HHJ Keyser QC in *Dawnus Sierra Leone Limited v Timis Mining Corporation Limited*[77] where the court concluded that an application for disclosure of the identity of the third party funder was premature – on the evidence available the funder did not appear to be operating for commercial gain, and therefore the disclosure was not needed for the purpose of considering any CPR r.25.14 application and it was premature. It was also premature in relation to any potential application under s.51 of the Senior Courts Act 1981 since such matters would only usually arise at the end of the case.

However, even in that case the application was only refused because the defendant (who was bringing a counterclaim) had disclosed both that it had third party funding and the basic nature of that funding.

Q22. Where a claimant entered into a CFA prior to 1 April 2013 and provided written notice (a letter) to the defendant of such CFA, but then failed to file/serve form N251 upon issue of the Claim, what are the consequences?

Where a CFA is a pre-April 2013 CFA. the full rigour of the pre-April 2013 CPR **2–41** r.43 to 48 apply, as expressly provided for by CPR r.48.1.

To provide a full recitation of all of the applicable provisions and caselaw In relation to the giving of notifications of funding and related information before, during and after proceedings (for example, within the context of detailed assessments) would result in an unduly lengthy answer. However, in short, the failure referred to in the question would mean that the claimant was in breach of the pre-April 2013 CPR r.44 PD 19.2, as a consequence of which, pursuant to the pre-April 2013 CPR r.44.3B(1)(c) and (d) (if the failure

---

[76] *Wall v Royal Bank of Scotland PLC* [2016] EWHC 2460 (Comm) and *Riaffesien Zentralbank Osterreich Ag v Crossseas Shipping Limited* [2003] EWHC 1381 (Comm).
[77] *[2016] EWHC B19 (TCC).*

to give notice also related to an ATE premium), the claimant's success fee would be disallowed for the period of any default (i.e. from when the notice should have been given until it was, in fact, given) and any ATE premium would be disallowed. This would all be subject to any application for relief from sanction.

Given the fact that notice appears to have been given, but not in the proper form, there would appear to be a reasonable argument that relief should be granted, but it is not possible to say without consideration of the precise facts. See, for example, *Forstater v Python (Monty) Pictures Ltd*[78].

These principles also apply to any of the 'excepted' cases such as insolvency related proceedings, publication and privacy proceedings or mesothelioma claims were success fees remained recoverable after the 1 April 2013. Per CPR r.48.2(1)(b), such agreements are 'pre-commencement funding arrangements', even where entered into on or after the 1 April 2013 and are therefore subject to the rigours of the pre-April 2013 notice provisions and consequent sanctions for non-compliance.

Q23. Where a CFA in one of the excepted cases (where the success fee is still recoverable) is entered into and the proceedings are issued on the same day but only served four months later and we realise that we haven't served a Notice of Funding some weeks after service, what advice would you give? For example, should a formal application seeking relief be made?

2–42   The first point to note is that the problem may be greater than indicated. Although the provisions on providing Notices of Funding, as continued in force in such cases by virtue of CPR r.48.1(1), relate to the date of issue and service, it is open to argument whether it is still a requirement to provide such notice at an earlier date. The requirement to do so, contained in the previous version of the Practice Direction on Pre-Action Conduct, has not been replicated in the current version of the Practice Direction and CPR r.48.1(1) does not continue the application of the old version for these purposes. Accordingly, it is not clear whether the requirement to provide notification of a relevant funding arrangement 'as soon as possible and in any event either within seven days of entering into the funding -arrangement concerned or, where a claimant entered into a funding arrangement before sending a letter before claim, in the letter before claim' still applies.

Best practice would be to follow that course in any event. In the event of non-compliance with a relevant provision, best practice would be to remedy the provision as soon as the error is noted. This could be done by providing the necessary notice, inviting the opponent to agree that relief from sanction should be granted in respect of any breach, where appropriate by inviting the opponent to agree that it will not take the point on assessment and that a formal application need not be made. In the event that the opponent does

---

[78] [2013] EWHC 3759, [2014] 1 Costs LR 36.

not agree, a prompt application for relief should be issued, even if it is then agreed that the hearing of the application may be adjourned pending the outcome of the claim or any detailed assessment proceedings. In some cases, where the sums at risk are substantial, it may be appropriate to proceed to determination of the application without delay.

Q24. Is a claimant entitled to recover the success fee under his "pre-1 April 2013" CFA from the defendant, where the claim was only commenced and the funding was only notified after 1 April 2013? Please explain why the amendment to s.58A(6) does not apply to CFAs entered into prior to 1 April 2013, in circumstances where the funding is notified after 1 April 2013?

Yes. The amendment to s.58(A)(6) of the Courts & Legal Services Act 1990   2–43
does not apply to CFAs entered into prior to the 1 April 2013 by virtue of the express provision at s.44(6) LASPO – subject to satisfying the precise terms of that section.

Q25. In the excepted cases, where a success fee is still recoverable:

- **Do you have to provide a notice of funding when issuing proceedings, even if it will be allocated to the small claims track?**
- **What date do you give in the N251 Notice of Funding when the matter is funded by a CCFA. Is it the date of the CCFA with the insurer or the date of the subsequent signed retainer with the insured client?**

The answer to the first question is 'yes' unless you are willing to accept that   2–44
any additional liabilities potentially claimable from the opponent if the case succeeds are to be surrendered. Whilst, in a case likely to be allocated to the Small Claims Track, this might seem to be an inevitable consequence of the general costs limitations, there is no certainty at the time of issue that a claim will be allocated to or will remain in that track, or that there may not be circumstances under CPR r.27.14 where costs might be sought despite such allocation. Accordingly, not serving an N251 may be shutting out a potential claim for additional liabilities.

In relation to the second question, the N251 requires the date of the agreement. That is the date of the CCFA.

Q26. Where two CFAs (one with solicitor and one with counsel) were entered into pre-1 April 2013 and notice of funding was only served in relation to the first one (solicitor) is that ok because Costs Practice Direction para 19.3(2)(a) says further notification is not required where notice has already been given that the party has entered into a CFA with a legal representative and during the currency of that agreement either of them enters into another such agreement with an additional legal representative? Will the success fee on the second CFA still be recoverable?

2–45   Yes. Assuming all other notice requirements have been complied with, counsel's success fee will remain recoverable in principle. As the question notes, CPR r.47 PD 19.3 (pre-April 2013 and with continuing effect for CFAs entered into before that date by virtue of CPR r.48.1) expressly provides that where proper notification has been given of a CFA between solicitor and client, notification is not required of a subsequent CFA between the solicitor and an additional legal representative – in this case counsel. It should be noted that this only applies where counsel's CFA follows that of the solicitor. If, for example, the solicitor was on a conventional, non CFA, retainer but counsel entered into a CFA, then notice would have to be given of the CFA with counsel.

E. Third Party Funding

Q27. Are parties required to notify an opponent that they are being funded by a third party litigation funder?

2–46   See the answer to **Q21** above. There is no rule based obligation to provide such information, but it would be open to the court to order disclosure of the fact and any relevant and appropriate details of such funding if a legitimate purpose was served by doing so.

   Although beyond the scope of this text, it is certainly arguable that a general obligation to disclose the presence of such funding may be established in the context of proceedings under the Arbitration Act 1996. Not only have arbitration tribunals shown a willingness to order such disclosure, but if the decision in *Essar Oilfield Services Ltd v Norscot Rig Management PVT Ltd*[79] is correct, and the costs of obtaining third party funding are recoverable as a 'non-legal' cost in the arbitration, then it seems highly likely that the tribunal will expect the fact of such funding – and therefore the risk of liability for such additional adverse costs – to have been notified in advance and may consider a failure to provide such advance notification as a reason to refuse to award such costs under its broad discretion.

   Such an issue does not arise outside the context of arbitrations since (at present at least) it is settled law that the costs of third party funding are not a recoverable cost between the parties.

Q28. When third party funding is used in an arbitration, under what circumstances could costs be awarded against third party funders and how could the tribunal cost orders against the funders be made enforceable against the funders (given that funders are not a party to the arbitration).

2–47   Due to the consent based nature of an arbitration, a tribunal will not usually have any power to regulate the conduct of a third party which is providing funding for that arbitration or to make any order for costs against it. The costs provisions of the Arbitration Act 1996 (ss.59 to 65) do not contain any provision for the making of a costs order against a third party akin to that to be

---

[79] [2016] EWHC 2361 (Comm).

found in s.51 Senior Courts Act 1981 and, as the Court of Appeal has recently made clear in a very different context[80,] it is necessary to identify a specific statutory power or alternatively, in the context of arbitrations, a specific contractually binding provision giving a tribunal power to bind a third party to such an order before such an order may be made.

It therefore appears that, absent the third party becoming 'bound' in some way to the arbitration, there is no scope for a third party funder in an arbitration to be made subject of a direct order for costs against it. There is, therefore, something of an irony in the fact that it is in the arbitration context that it has been held that the cost of obtaining third party funding is a recoverable cost – see *Essar Oilfield Services Ltd* above. It appears arguable that the apparent inability to make a direct order against such a funder would not merely be a reason to reach a contrary view, but also would potentially support an argument that third party funding should either not be permitted or should be subject of greater restrictions within the arbitration context than in the general litigation context.

At the very least there would appear to be an argument that if a party is to seek to recover third party funding costs if successful, on the *Essar* principle, then:

- either it and/or the funder should be prepared to submit to some earlier order or agreement providing some security to the opposing party that, in the event of their succeeding, they would either have some greater security for their costs recovery than would otherwise have been the case; or
- or the funder should submit to an order or agreement that the opposing party would have some direct right against the funder for at least some of their costs, if awarded in that party's favour.

The tribunal's scope for seeking to 'encourage' such an agreement would appear to lie in its discretionary ability to refuse to award the third party funding costs at the conclusion of the claim in the absence of such agreement. Whether this is the approach that will be taken or, if not, what alternative approach might be adopted remains to be seen.

F. Conditional Fee Agreements and Success Fees

Q29. How should the success fee be calculated in a post-April 2013 CFA?
The maximum success fee remains at 100%. In setting the success fee, the   2–48
solicitor is entitled to have regard to those matters set out at the revoked CPR r.43 PD 11.7 and 11.8. In addition, the solicitor is entitled to take into account matters such as the delay in payment under a CFA (a matter which could be used to justify the success fee on a solicitor-client basis prior to April 2013 but

---

[80] See *Darroch v Football Association Premier League Limited* [2016] EWCA Civ 1220.

not on a between the parties basis). The main component of the success fee is likely to remain the risk of losing and not being paid, and in that regard the traditional 'ready reckoner' remains useful.

Ultimately, however, the issue is one of agreeing a reasonable success fee with the client in light of the terms and conditions of the CFA, the risks to which it exposes the solicitor of not being paid their base fees in whole or part, any additional financial burden placed on the solicitor, such as the arrangements for paying disbursements and the likely delay in payment overall, and the application of these matters to the facts of the case.

It is important to explain the success fee clearly and properly to the client and to ensure their informed agreement. It is vital that the client is informed that the success fee is not recoverable between the parties in any circumstances, even if the claim is won, and will remain payable by the client.

Q30. A CFA was entered pre-April 2013 and therefore falls under the old rules. An interim hearing was won by the applicant and the applicant would therefore like to apply for a detailed cost assessment against the losing party for their costs in the application. However, the success in the interim hearing, has not triggered 'success' under the terms of the CFA (and the CFA itself does not include a clause relating to interim hearings). Could you advise whether it is therefore possible to still seek base costs from the losing party (not the additional liability) or whether this would fall foul of the indemnity principle? Research so far points to CPR r.32.3 which states that if a party is seeking detailed assessment without any additional liability they do not need to provide information about CFAs etc.

2–49   The reference to CPR r.47 PD 32.3 misses the point. In order to recover any costs between the parties (save where those costs are fixed) the receiving party must be able to satisfy the court that the indemnity principle is not breached. The standard N260 Statement of Costs for Summary Assessment contains a statement, which the receiving party's solicitor is required to sign, confirming that the costs claimed in the statement do not exceed the costs which the receiving party is liable to pay in respect of the work which the statement covers.

In the unusual situation envisaged above (it being more common that CFAs generally provide for the client to be liable for interim costs where such an award is made), the solicitor would be unable to sign the statement and would be unable to claim the costs at that stage. This would probably be a 'good reason'[81] for the court not to undertake summary assessment. A summary assessment at that point would not be able to include these costs which might, in fact, be payable and recoverable if the client ultimately succeeds on the claim. See further *Arkin v Borchard Lines Ltd*[82].

---

[81] See CPR r.44 PD 9.2.
[82] [2001] CP Rep 108.

As the question notes, even if costs recovery was allowed at the interim stage, this would be of base costs only and the success fee would have to be subject of detailed assessment or agreement at the end of the case. There have been reports of astute judges on detailed assessments checking the CFA to see if the claimant had indeed been entitled, under the CFA, to seek recovery of base costs in relation to interim awards and where it has been discovered that they were not, of the success fee on those base costs being disallowed as a sanction. Whether this is a common practice or whether such a sanction is an appropriate sanction in the circumstances is beyond the scope of this supplement. More fundamentally, as noted above, such recovery should not be sought unless the solicitor can sign the certificate to confirm the claimant is entitled to the same at that time and, as is now trite law, the signature of such a statement by a solicitor, as an officer of the court, is an important matter which should not be undertaken lightly.

Q31. If the solicitor has entered into a pre-April 2013 CFA, but counsel's CFA with the solicitor postdates April 2013, is counsel's success fee -recoverable between the parties?
It has been suggested in some quarters that this is the case. The point is proba-   **2–50**
bly arguable. However, the wording of s.44(6) refers to the between the parties recovery of a success fee under a CFA not being prevented if the agreement was entered into before 1 April, 2013. It would seem to fit with the spirit and intent of the changes and the wording of the statute (and CPR r.48.2) that each agreement is looked at individually. The solicitor's success fee would be recoverable in principle, but counsel's would (probably) not be.

Q32. What is the effect on the success fee where a CFA relating to a group claim was entered into before 1 April 2013, but some of the claimants were added after that date?
The answer to this is unclear. The transitional provisions in relation to the   **2–51**
recoverability of success fees in s.44 of LASPO are statutory provisions and do not admit of a discretion (indeed, their express effect is to remove any discretion to allow a success fee in respect of cases covered by s.44).

Accordingly, and despite the possible temptation to do so, a court managing a GLO probably cannot simply exercise a discretion to decide how to treat such a situation (for example by reference to s.51 of the Senior Courts Act 1981) but is limited to considering the particular CFA and how it interacts with the provisions of s.44(6).

Section 44(6) appears to require the court to look not merely at the date of the CFA but at whether the CFA was entered into for the purposes of providing services to a specific person in relation to the subject matter of the claim or, if not entered into for a specific person (for example, a CCFA), whether services were provided, before 1 April 2013, to the specific person in whose favour the costs order has been made.

The CCFA analogy appears the most apt here and there must be a substantial likelihood that the later joining claimants will be held not to be able to recover the success fee in respect of their claims. This may involve some question of a pro rata division of any success fee payable on common costs. The quid pro quo would be that the later joining claimants would benefit from QOCS (if it is a personal injury claim).

However, alternative approaches are possible and it is conceivable, given that the potential claimants in a GLO could be seen as being a limited and identifiable class of persons, that a court might conclude that the test under CPR r.44.6(a) was satisfied in respect of all claimants when the CFA was first entered into and accordingly a success fee is recoverable in respect of all claimants.

The precise outcome will be heavily affected by the terms of the CFA, the precise circumstances of the case, the terms of any related documentation, such as costs sharing agreements, and the court's approach to the interpretation of s.44(6), which at present is uncertain.

Q33. We have an insolvency case on a CFA with a success fee and have ATE insurance in place. We have not yet issued. Now that the Government has removed the exemption from LASPO for insolvency related cases, presumably the success fee and premium will still be recoverable from the other side if the claim is successful even though we hadn't issued before the exemption was removed?

2–52   The answer to this is largely covered by **Q23**. The key date is the date on which the funding arrangement was entered into, provided it properly relates to the claim that was issued. The insolvency exception ended with effect from the 6 April 2016. The same transitional provisions as applied to the core changes in 2013 (namely s.44(6) and 46(3) of the 2012 Act in respect of success fees and ATE premiums respectively) expressly apply to these changes[83]. Accordingly, provided the CFA and ATE are incepted before the date fixed for the ending of recoverability (6 April 2016, therefore on or before 5 April 2016), the additional liabilities will continue to be recoverable.

As noted in the commentary above, in any insolvency case care should be taken to ensure that the case falls within the narrow scope of the exemption. Not all 'insolvency' cases will.

Q34. I understand that for an ATE insurance premium to be recoverable from the other side in insolvency proceedings it must have been put in place before 6 April 2016. Is it also necessary to have given notice of funding to the other side before 6 April 2016?

2–53   See the answer to the preceding question and **Q23**. Provided the funding arrangement was entered into on or before the 5 April 2016, the insolvency 'exemption' will apply. However, as noted, the pre-April 2013 provisions of CPR rules 43 to 48 will apply to such an arrangement and the obligation to

---

[83] See art.2 of the Legal Aid, Sentencing & Punishment of Offenders Act 2012 (Commencement No. 12) Order 2016.

provide notice of funding in relation to it. Those provisions do not require notice to be given before 6 April 2016. Provided notice is given in accordance with the requirements of those sections – for example by giving of a notice of funding when filing or serving the claim form, even if that is not due until after the 6 April 2016 – then the additional liabilities will be recoverable in principle, subject to any assessment as to quantum.

Q35. We note that insolvency proceedings were excluded from ss.44 and 46 of LASPO 2012 where proceedings in England and Wales were brought by:

- **A person acting in the capacity of a liquidator of a company in -creditors' voluntary liquidation (CVL) or compulsory liquidation; a trustee in bankruptcy; or an administrator.**
- **A company that is in: CVL; compulsory liquidation; or administration.**

What is the situation if you acted for an insolvency practitioner outside the jurisdiction (the insolvent company also being outside the jurisdiction) who brought a claim in England and Wales against a company based in England and Wales for monies owed? If you entered into a CFA with the client in these circumstances, would the success fee be recoverable from the other side if your client is successful?

The situation described appears to fall outside the scope of art.4 of the Legal   2–54
Aid, Sentencing and Punishment of Offenders Act 2012 (Commencement No.5 and Saving Provision) Order 2013. Accordingly, any additional liabilities are unlikely to be recoverable. This will therefore be unaffected by the ending of the insolvency exception with effect from 6 April 2016.

Q36. What are the rules on recoverability of success fees in a defamation matter and, assuming that recoverability is allowed, does the success fee have to be capped in any way?

By virtue of art.4(b) of the Legal Aid, Sentencing and Punishment of Offenders   2–55
Act 2012 (Commencement No. 5 and Saving Provision) Order 2013 the commencement of the provisions removing the recoverability of additional liabilities is suspended in respect of publication and privacy proceedings. Accordingly, success fees are recoverable in principle in such cases in the same way as before April 2013.

There is no statutory provision imposing a cap on the success fee other than the 100% maximum percentage set by Lord Chancellor pursuant to s.58(4)(c) and art.4 of the Conditional Fee Agreements Order 2000 (SI 2000/823).

Q37. Given that success fees in CFAs entered into from 1 April 2013 are not recoverable in English civil litigation (apart from in the excepted cases), are they recoverable in arbitrations? Nothing in the Arbitration Act or LCIA Rules appears to preclude an arbitrator awarding a success fee under a CFA.

2–56   It is entirely correct that neither the Arbitration Act 1996 nor the rules of any of the main institutions deal directly with the issue of the recoverability of success fees.

The lawfulness of such arrangements will be determined by reference to the law of the country in which the arrangement is entered into, the law of the place of arbitration and the law of the country where any award (including costs) would be enforced.

Assuming the question relates to whether a success fee would be awarded in principle in what might loosely be termed an 'English' arbitration, following *Benaim UK Ltd v Davies Middleton & Davies Ltd* [2004] EWHC 737 (TCC) it was generally accepted that such additional liabilities may be awarded in principle. However, whether such an award would be made in practice and, if so, whether the amount awarded would be at the level sought is very much within the discretion of the tribunal and in practice tends to be far less certain than would be the position in court proceedings.

Following the LASPO changes it is strongly arguable that success fees are no longer recoverable in arbitrations. Section 58A(4) of the Courts & Legal Services Act 1990 makes clear that the reference to proceedings under s.58 is wide enough to include an arbitration. Pursuant to the amended s.58(6) of the Act, 'a costs order made in proceedings [which appears to include an arbitration] may not include provision requiring the payment by one party of all or part of a success fee'. Accordingly, and subject to the transitional provisions, there would appear to be a strong case for contending that success fees are no longer recoverable within arbitrations within the English and Welsh jurisdictions.

This throws into stark light the effect of the decision in *Essar* (see main text and Q27 above) to allow the recoverability of third party funding costs.

Q38. What is the current position with regard to the question of whether the recoverability of pre-April 2013 additional liabilities is compatible with the European Convention on Human Rights?

2–57   This is addressed in the main text above. In *Coventry*, the Supreme Court rejected the argument that additional liabilities permitted by primary and secondary legislation and subject to the test of reasonableness and, where applicable, proportionality on assessment amounted to an unwarranted interference with a party's rights under Article 6 or Article 1 of the First Protocol to the European Convention on Human Rights. That issue now appears to be conclusively determined. However, the Supreme Court will revisit the related issue of whether such arrangements breach a media defendant's rights under Article 10 of the Convention in 2017.

G. Damages Based Agreements

Q39. What exactly is a hybrid DBA, and what is the difference between a concurrent hybrid DBA and a sequential hybrid DBA?

There is no statutory definition of a hybrid DBA. It is a term that has developed amongst practitioners and is discussed in the Civil Justice Council Working Committee Report. It is broadly understood to refer to a DBA which provides for some element of payment to the solicitor other than the pure, all or nothing, contingent payment anticipated by reg.4 of the DBA Regulations 2013. Perhaps the closest comparator is with a discounted CFA, where the solicitor receives an element of payment, whether or not the case is won or lost, but with a higher payment in the event of success. Whilst the issue is not totally closed to argument, the DBA Regulations appear to prevent a DBA from operating in this way.

2–58

A sequential hybrid DBA is generally understood to refer to the situation where the solicitor initially agrees some form of non DBA retainer, but then agrees at a later stage to switch to a DBA arrangement, but more widely refers to any situation where there is a DBA for one or more stages of a case and a different form of funding for other stages. In the most common, chronologically sequential, arrangement, the DBA when applied might retrospectively cover all work done, or may be limited only to future work. In either case, because the DBA itself does not provide for any payment to the solicitor other than the contingent payment in respect of the work it covers, it is not thought to fall foul of the apparent prohibition on hybrid arrangements under the Regulations and the MOJ's terms of reference to the CJC Working Part appear to support this conclusion[84].

A concurrent hybrid DBA is the sort of DBA described at the start of this answer – that is to say one that provides for both the contingent DBA payment and some other form of payment under a single agreement in relation to the same work or stage. For the reasons given, it is generally understood that such arrangements are not permitted. The inability to enter into such arrangements is believed to be one of the major reasons for the limited use of DBAs since April 2013.

Q40. We have a client for whom we currently act on a pre-April 2013 hybrid-CFA in ongoing litigation. Our client's circumstances have changed and he has asked whether we would be willing to change our funding arrangement with him to a Damages Based Agreement. Is there any guidance on whether this is possible and, if so, what the implications would be? (As DBA's do not currently allow the solicitor to charge anything until the client receives a financial benefit, would we have to repay any fees he has paid under the hybrid-CFA?)

It is assumed that the reference to a hybrid-CFA is to a form of discounted CFA of the type mentioned in the previous answer. As explained in the previous answer, on a literal interpretation, s.58AA of the 1990 Act and reg.4 of the 2013 Regulations do not seek to restrict anything other than the terms

2–59

---

[84] See the Working Party's summary of the position at page 26 of its report – https://www.judiciary.gov.uk/wp-content/uploads/2015/09/dba-reform-project-cjc-aug-2015.pdf.

of payment under the DBA itself. Prima facie, therefore, they do not prevent what was described in the previous answer as a 'sequential hybrid DBA' and this would include an arrangement whereby the solicitor initially agreed a CFA and then subsequently entered into a DBA in circumstances where the client remained liable, on success, for payments under both agreements, provided the two agreements (and in particular the DBA) did not cover the same work.

The potential for abuse is obvious and there is clearly scope for an argument that such an approach would be contrary to the statutory purpose inherent in s.58AA of the 1990 and the 2013 Regulations, namely that a client who enters into a DBA should not be at risk of paying, in total, more than 50% of any damages recovered in base costs and counsel's fees.

Whether, in an appropriate case, the court would consider that this risk is one to be addressed by virtue of the client's rights under s.70 of the Solicitors Act 1974 to seek assessment of the solicitor's charges and therefore conclude that, provided both the CFA and the DBA individually and separately complied with their respective statutory regimes they were enforceable, or whether the court would instead adopt a purposive approach and conclude that any combination of retainers in relation to a single transaction which exposed the client to a total liability which could potentially exceed that provided for by the 2013 Regulations breach the purpose of s.58AA and was therefore unenforceable is a matter for argument and is undecided.

Sensible application of the precautionary principle suggests that the safer course in such a situation would be to replace the previous arrangement with a DBA which covered the entirety of the work undertaken or at least to make some attempt, whether by revising the structure of any payment due under the earlier retainer or by limiting the scope of the DBA, to ensure that the total payment under the two agreements taken together could not breach the statutory cap for a DBA, though this would not address all potential arguments. Such an approach would potentially limit the commercial attractiveness of the switch and may be an unnecessary fetter of the solicitor's ability to seek remuneration for the case. However, until some of these points are argued and authoratively decided there is a significant element of uncertainty.

Q41. What is the authority or rule which specifies that if a DBA in a non-employment matter does not comply with the Damages-Based Agreements Regulations 2013, it will not be enforceable?

2–60 Section 58AA(2) of the Courts & Legal Services Act, which provides that a DBA relating to any matter (employment or non-employment) and which does not satisfy the conditions specified in subsection (4) shall be unenforceable. The conditions in subsection (4) include 'such other requirements as to [the DBA's] terms and conditions as are prescribed. Amongst the prescribed conditions are the relevant sections of the DBA Regulations 2013. In addition, subsection 4(b) prescribes that, if regulations so provide,' the agreement must not provide for a payment about the prescribed amount or for a payment about an amount calculated in a prescribed manner. The DBA Regulations 2013 contains prescriptions of this kind which must therefore be complied with if the agreement is not to be unenforceable by force of clear and unambiguous primary statutory legislation.

Q42. Under the DBA Regulations 2013, a party can recover costs from the other side based on normal costs recovery principles, but subject to the indemnity principle. Given then that the lawyer may not be entitled to any costs until actual recoveries are made at the end of a case, does this not cause a problem with seeking costs from the other side at interim hearings as the case progresses? Appropriate drafting of the DBA might seek to get around this but it would seem that such drafting would be a highly complex task with various pitfalls. For example, if the DBA provided that sums would immediately become due to the solicitor as and when costs are recovered from the other side, are those costs considered part of the ultimate recovery from the client and to be deducted and as a kind of payment on account, or would the solicitor be entitled to those costs plus the agreed success percentage? Wouldn't that breach the DBA Regulations?

Yes, this does cause a problem. It is one of the issues addressed by the CJC Working Group's report. For the reasons given in the question, the inclusion within the DBA of some sort of immediate right to payment may well breach the prohibition under Reg.4 (which does not apply in employment matters) on any payment other than the specified contingency payment under the Regulations and expenses. It is one of the matters that may be addressed in any future amendment to the Regulations.   2–61

H. *Consumer Regulations*

Q43. Do the doorstep selling regulations, which aim to protect consumers when they sign contracts in certain circumstances, apply to CFAs? If so, in what kind of circumstances would they apply?

Such regulations apply to contracts entered into between consumers and traders. Solicitors are traders for these purposes – see the Court of Appeal's decision in *Cox v Woodlands Manor Care Homes Ltd*[85] for an example of the application of the point and the potentially draconian effects of non-compliance.   2–62

Fortunately, the most draconian version of these regulations (the Cancellation of Contracts made in a Consumer's Home or Place of Work etc Regulations 2008) were replaced with effect from June 2014 with the apparently less draconian, but far more complex Consumer Contract (information, Cancellation and Additional Charges) Regulations 2013, so contracts entered into from that date are less vulnerable to being found unenforceable for non-compliance.

---

[85] [2015] EWCA Civ 415, [2015] 3 Costs LO 327.

The precise circumstances in which the Regulations apply are set out in the Regulations themselves and their precise operation and implications will have to be the subject of caselaw. However, once again, they apply to contracts entered into by traders, including solicitors, with consumers. Different requirements apply depending on where the contract was entered into, but it should be noted that at least some regulation applies even where the contract was entered into at the solicitor's offices (contrast the 2008 Regulations). There is a helpful practice note provided by the Law Society[86], but the effect on non-compliance can potentially be severe and any solicitor regularly dealing with consumers as defined should consider the regulations closely and seek advice where necessary.

I. Proportionality

Q44. Given that the pre-April 2013 rules on recoverability of additional liabilities continue to apply to pre-commencement funding arrangements, does the old test of proportionality also continue to apply when assessing those additional liabilities?

2–63   Probably. See the recent decision of Master Rowley in *King v Basildon & Thurrock University Hospitals NHS Foundation Trust*[87]. There would appear to be considerable logic in relation to this where the additional liability is relating to a funding arrangement entered into on or before 1 April 2013, since the application to the 'old' proportionality test to such liabilities would appear prima facie consistent with CPR r.44.3(7) and the disapplication of the new proportionality test to costs incurred in respect of work done prior to 1 April 2013.

However, even that is arguable, since CPR r.44.3(7)(b) refers to costs incurred 'in respect of work done' prior to 1 April 2013 and it must be arguable that where a success fee is claimed, then in so far as the success fee is claimed on work done (in part) on or after 1 April 2013, then the new test of proportionality applies to that part.

The arguments grow when consideration is given to the legacy claims, where additional liabilities remain recoverable in respect of funding arrangements entered into after April 2013 (and up to April 2016 in the context of insolvency proceedings). Master Gordon Saker, in *BNM v Mirror Group Newspapers Ltd*[88] concluded that in such circumstances the additional liabilities were subject to the new test of proportionality, the old rules as to recoverability of additional liabilities were preserved, but not the old test of proportionality, for reasons he cogently set out in paragraphs 25 to 32. *BNM* is on appeal to the Court of Appeal, which may provide some further clarity on some of these issues.

---

[86] At http://www.lawsociety.org.uk/support-services/advice/practice-notes/consumer-contracts-regulations-2013/.
[87] SCCO, unreported, 30 November 2016.
[88] SCCO, 11 January 2016.

J. Funding costs

Q45. Can you charge your client for the costs of: (i) negotiating and drafting a conditional fee agreement (the case of *Motto v Trafigura Ltd* [2011] EWCA Civ 1150, suggests not? However, the case is pre-Jackson and suggests that you cannot because the client is not yet your client. In this case the client is an existing client and we are at the pre-action stage of proceedings); (ii) Negotiating and entering into an ATE policy and keeping the insurers updated during the proceedings; (iii) Negotiating and entering into a third party funding agreement and keeping the funders updated during the proceedings.

The ratio in *Motto* is not entirely clear and the questioner is correct to identify   2–64
that, at least as far as setting up a CFA is concerned, the core of the ratio relates to the fact that the 'client' is only a potential client until terms of business are agreed. However, at paragraphs 113 and 114 Lord Neuberger went on to deal with reporting to insurers. He accepted that the dividing line was blurred, but regarded such costs, incurred after the client was indeed a client, as the wrong side of the blurred line and as being costs which were collateral to the litigation (and therefore not recoverable) rather than costs of (and incidental to) the litigation.

There is clearly some scope for further argument. However, on the basis of *Motto* it would appear likely that all three categories of costs identified in the question fall the wrong side of the blurred line of recoverability.

CHAPTER 3

Proportionality

Introduction

The terms of reference for the costs review conducted by Jackson LJ[1] were   **3–01**
"to make recommendations in order to promote access to justice at proportionate cost". The need for change was acknowledged in the foreword to the
final report, which stated:

> *"In some areas of civil litigation costs are disproportionate and impede access to
> justice. I therefore propose a coherent package of interlocking reforms, designed to
> control costs and promote access to justice."*

Inevitably, therefore, proportionality lies at the core of the package of reforms –
it permeates into every aspect of the civil litigation process. The overriding
objective has been amended to include specific reference to proportionality,
costs and case management are determined by it and any assessment of costs
is subject to it. Almost four years on from the April 2013 amendments to the
Civil Procedure Rules, proportionality still provokes more debate, more controversy and more concern than any other aspect of the reforms. What does it
mean, when does it arise, and what impact does it have on litigation?

Proportionality – the concept

Proportionality is not a new concept. Whilst the amended overriding   **3–02**
objective[2] refers to "dealing with a case at proportionate cost", the previous
version, from introduction in 1999, defined "dealing with a case justly" by reference, amongst other things, to proportionate cost. However, in reality, prior
to April 2013, proportionality only had a retrospective role at the conclusion
of a case, at the time of the assessment of costs. Where it was suggested that
the costs claimed were disproportionate, the Court of Appeal required the
assessing judge to determine that issue at the outset of the assessment adopting the *Home Office v Lownds*[3] two-stage approach:

> *"In other words what is required is a two-stage approach. There has to be a
> global approach and an item by item approach. The global approach will indi-
> cate whether the total sum claimed is or appears to be disproportionate having
> particular regard to the considerations which Pt. 44.5(3) states are relevant. If the
> costs as a whole are not disproportionate according to that test then all that is
> normally required is that each item should have been reasonably incurred and the*

---

[1] *Review of Civil Litigation Costs: Final Report*, December 2009.
[2] CPR r.1.1: "These Rules are a new procedural code with the overriding objective of enabling the court to deal with
cases justly and at proportionate cost.".
[3] *Home Office v Lownds* [2002] EWCA Civ 365.

cost for that item should be reasonable. If on the other hand the costs as a whole appear disproportionate then the court will want to be satisfied that the work in relation to each item was necessary and, if necessary, that the cost of the item is reasonable."

Immediately it is apparent that this approach does not genuinely meet the requirement of dealing with a case at proportionate cost. Even if the first stage of *Lownds* resulted in a finding that the costs were disproportionate, the court could not change the way it had dealt with the case procedurally. Instead all it could do was to reduce the amount of costs recoverable between the parties. Even this retrospective ability to reduce the recoverable costs did not lead to proportionality in its purest sense, as there was no certainty that necessarily incurred costs were proportionate – in essence the imposition of the 'necessarily incurred' test seemed more a sanction for incurring disproportionate costs than any genuine attempt to reduce the costs to a level that was proportionate. Indeed, in giving his judgment in *Lownds*, Lord Woolf had hinted at the purists' position on proportionality when commenting:

"If, because of lack of planning or due to other causes, the global costs are disproportionately high, then the requirement that the costs should be proportionate means that no more should be payable than would have been payable if the litigation had been conducted in a proportionate manner."

Something more was needed to ensure that cases are managed so that no more is spent as the case progresses than is proportionate.

Proportionality – what does it mean and when does it arise?

3–03   The 2013 reforms seek to provide that 'something more' by requiring the court to:

- deal with each case "at proportionate cost" (CPR r.1.1(1)) – which includes allotting to it an appropriate share of the court's resources, while taking into account the need to allot resources to other cases (CPR r.1.1(2)(e));
- ensure that every case management decision is made taking account of the costs involved in each procedural step (CPR r.3.17);
- set costs budgets that are proportionate (CPR r.3 PD E 7.3);
- determine whether or not to grant relief from sanction by giving particular weight to the need for litigation to be conducted at proportionate cost (CPR r.3.9); and
- undertake assessments of costs on the basis that only proportionate costs will be awarded, even if that means reasonably or necessarily incurred costs are disallowed. CPR r.44.3(2)(a) signals the demise of the *Lownds* test at assessment, reversing the timetable for consideration of proportionality. The court will assess those costs that are reasonably incurred and reasonable in amount and, having done so, step back and determine if the resultant figure is proportionate. If it is not, then the court will

reduce the costs to the sum it determines is the proportionate figure. Examples of this arise in *BNM v MGN Ltd*[4] and *May v Wavell Group Plc*[5]. In both cases the court reduced the costs assessed as reasonable on the basis that they remained disproportionate. However, in the former the proportionality cross-check was made more by reference to specific items, whereas in the latter, having determined that the reasonable costs were disproportionate and identified the relevant CPR r.44.3(5) factors, the court simply applied CPR r.44.3(2)(a) to reach an overall proportionate figure. It is right to say that the court in *BNM* expressly concluded that it did not have to consider additional liabilities separately, it simply chose so to do. Whilst neither decision is binding and both are subject to appeal, the *May* approach appears to be in line with the comments of Jackson LJ in the final report:

> "The court should first make an assessment of reasonable costs, having regard to the individual items in the bill. . .The court should then stand back and consider whether the total figure is proportionate. If the total figure is not proportionate, the court should make an appropriate reduction."[6] para.5.13

Of course, the court can only fulfil the functions set out above by reference to the proportionate costs for a claim. How does it determine that sum? The simple answer is by reference to CPR r.44.3(5), which contains the definition of proportionate costs as follows:

> "Costs incurred are proportionate if they bear a reasonable relationship to:
> (a) the sums in issue in the proceedings;
> (b) the value of any non monetary relief in issue in the proceedings;
> (c) the complexity of the litigation;
> (d) any additional work generated by the conduct of the paying party; and
> (e) any wider factors involved in the proceedings, such as reputation or public importance."

Accordingly, the court must identify which of the factors listed in CPR r.44.3(5) are relevant to any case and, having done so, relate that to a costs figure. It is this step that many critics of the new approach see as unsatisfactory. They view the process as an entirely unscientific one – as the factors do not readily equal a sum in pounds and pence. The simple answer from those proponents of the process is that there is no 'absolute' answer, but, as with many exercises of judicial discretion, there are a range of answers and, provided the discretion has been exercised properly, none within that range are wrong. This is nothing new. Indeed, if different judges were asked to assess the same bill of costs at the conclusion of a claim, the likelihood is that there would be as many different figures as there were judges assessing the bill, but, again on the

---

[4] *BNM v MGN Ltd* [2016] EWHC B13 (Costs).
[5] *May v Wavell Group Plc* [2016] EWHC B16 (Costs).
[6] *Review of Civil Litigation Costs: Final Report*, December 2009.

proviso that those judges had properly exercised their discretion, none of the assessments would be 'wrong'.

3–04   It is for this reason that in the 15th Implementation Lecture on 29 May 2012 the then Master of the Rolls, Lord Neuberger, stressed the case-sensitive nature of proportionality and anticipated little case law on the topic:

> *"While the change in culture should reduce the scope of costs assessments at the conclusion of proceedings, it will not obviate the need for a robust approach to such assessments. Again the decision as to whether an item was proportionately incurred is case-sensitive, and there may be a period of slight uncertainty as the case law is developed.*
>
> *`That is why I have not dealt with what precisely constitutes proportionality and how it is to be assessed. It would be positively dangerous for me to seek to give any sort of specific or detailed guidance in a lecture before the new rule has come into force and been applied. Any question relating to proportionality and any question relating to costs is each very case-sensitive, and when the two questions come together, that is all the more true. The law on proportionate costs will have to be developed on a case by case basis. This may mean a degree of satellite litigation while the courts work out the law, but we should be ready for that, and I hope it will involve relatively few cases."*

It is hard to see what further guidance is either necessary or likely other than in extremely general terms. Unnecessary because the very flexibility of the definition makes it hard to think of any case where relevant features impacting on costs do not fall to be taken into account within one of the five factors. Unlikely because each case is fact sensitive, the ambit of judicial discretion is wide and any decision falling outside the parameters would only define proportionality in a very broad sense in that specific case. This view was confirmed by Jackson LJ in his May 2016 lecture 'The Future for Civil Litigation and the Fixed Costs Regime'[7], in which he stated:

> *"There has been much debate about whether a PD should provide supplementary guidance. . .Unfortunately any attempt to draft a PD which supplements those five general rules (44.3(5)) with another set of general rules, albeit more specifically focused, is doomed to fail. If a PD were to give more detailed guidance it would inevitably be lengthy. The PD would be helpful in some cases and confusing in others. There would be arguments about its interrelationship with rule 44.3(5). No legislator can foresee all the vagaries of litigation. Any detailed PD would generate satellite litigation. Then we would have rule 44.3(5) + a lengthy PD + an encrustation of case law, followed up inevitably by much learned commentary by the academic community. Surely we are better off without all that?"* para.2.2

Accordingly, beyond defining proportionality within discretionary parameters in any given case, any comments will be of a general nature, e.g. in *CIP*

---

[7] Westminster Legal Policy Forum *'The future for civil litigation and the fixed costs regime'* May 2016.

Properties (AIPT) Ltd v Galliford Try Infrastructure Ltd[8] where Coulson J commented that:

> *"Costs budgets are generally regarded as a good idea and a useful case management tool. The pilot schemes (including the one here in the TCC) have worked well. They are not automatically required in cases worth over £2 million or £10 million, principally because the higher the value of the claim, the less likely it is that issues of proportionality will be important or even relevant. A claimant's budget of £5 million might well be disproportionate to a claim valued at £9 million, but such a level of costs is probably not disproportionate to a claim worth £50 million."*[9]

and in *Savoye and Savoye Limited v Spicers Limited*[10], a case concerning enforcement of an adjudication, Akenhead J concluded that:

> *"...for the purposes of costs assessment, the Court should have regard when assessing proportionality and the reasonableness of costs, in the context of the current case or type of case to the following:*
>
> (a) *The relationship between the amount of costs claimed for and said to have been incurred and the amount in issue. Thus, for example, if the amount in issue in the claim was £100,000 but the costs claimed for are £1 million, absent other explanations the costs may be said to be disproportionate."*

Whilst the court in *Kazakhstan Kagazy Plc v Zhunus*[11] purported to define what is 'reasonable and proportionate' as "...the lowest amount (of costs) which it (a party) could reasonably have been expected to spend in order to have its case conducted and presented proficiently, having regard to all the circumstances", this appears to overlook the provisions of CPR r.44.3(2)(a), which is not considered in the judgment and which could not be clearer, that proportionality trumps reasonableness. Accordingly any attempt to define proportionality by equating it to, or by any measurable reference to, reasonableness appears to overlook this procedural provision. In any event this decision was concerned with payments on account of costs and not the assessment of recoverable costs. (See **Q4** below for more detailed consideration of the link between reasonableness and proportionality and **Q7** below).

Those seeking certainty are, in effect, wishing for something akin to a form of fixed fee regime for all cases. Given the variety of claims it is almost inevitable that any regime of fixed fees would be set with a very broad brush. As stated in previous editions, be careful for what you wish, for it leads in only one direction. Indeed, Jackson LJ concluded his consideration of the concerns expressed about CPR r.44.3(5) in his May 2016 lecture as follows:

---

[8] *Properties (AIPT) Ltd v Galliford Try Infrastructure Ltd* [2014] EWHC 3546 (TCC).
[9] The reference to £2 million and £10 million being to the respective versions of CPR r.3.12 in place from 1 April 2013 and 22 April 2014.
[10] *Savoye and Savoye Limited v Spicers Limited* [2015] EWHC 33 (TCC).
[11] *Kazakhstan Kagazy Plc v Zhunus* [2015] EWHC 404 (Comm).

"*The best way to satisfy the requests for clarification is to convert the five identi-fied factors into hard figures: In other words a fixed costs regime.*" para.2.3

It is, perhaps, unsurprising, that this edition will be published whilst Jackson LJ undertakes a review of fixed recoverable costs.

Proportionality—the effect on litigation

3–05   For a more detailed consideration of the effect on litigation see **Chapter 4** – Case and Costs Management. In essence, though, proportionality will arise at all stages of a case, as any case management decision engages the overriding objective, which now includes the obligation to deal with a case at propor-tionate cost, regardless of any additional burdens imposed by specific provi-sions. This applies to all claims, regardless of track and regardless of value, where there is no fixed cost regime in place. The court, and the parties, should have proportionality in mind whether they are dealing with the lowest value small claim or the highest value multi-track. It follows that any party seeking any specific case management direction must be prepared to justify it in the context of a consideration of the factors at CPR r.44.3(5).

The discretion offered by the flexible definition of proportionality means that it can be adapted to meet the diverse considerations of all claims, which is just as well as, despite Jackson LJ's recommendation and the current review, fixed fees have yet to be introduced for non personal injury fast track claims and for any multi-track claims. Jackson LJ regards this as a serious omission because CPR r.44.3(5) was not designed as a mechanism to control costs in the fast track. Both he, and Dyson MR returned to this theme, encourag-ing the implementation of further fixed fee schemes to all fast track claims and some lower value multi-track claims, in their respective *Confronting Costs Management* lectures in May 2015[12] and, as referred to above, Jackson LJ revis-ited the theme in 2016[13] and is now charged with undertaking a further review "*To develop proposals for extending the present civil fixed recoverable costs regime in England and Wales so as to make the costs of going to court more certain, transparent and proportionate for litigants*".[14] Without fixed fees and costs man-agement in fast track a significant emphasis in fast track claims remains on proportionality after the costs have been spent under CPR r.44.3(2)(a) at assessment.

This discretion means that provided that the court has considered the factors in CPR r.44.3(5) when reaching any decision on proportionality, it will have made no error of principle and so appealing any decision will be extremely difficult.

---

[12] Harbour Lecture '*Confronting Costs Management*' May 2015.
[13] IPA Annual Lecture '*Fixed Costs – The time has come*' January 2016 and Westminster Legal Policy Forum '*The future for civil litigation and the fixed costs regime*' May 2016.
[14] Terms of reference for the review of fixed recoverable costs.

Questions and answers

A. The proportionality test

Q1. How do the transitional provisions relate to proportionality at assessment?
Three possible scenarios arise – two of which are straightforward and the other   3–06
presents some practical difficulties.

CPR r.44.3(7) makes it clear that the 'new' proportionality provisions – namely the new definition of proportionality at CPR r.44.3(5) and the cross-check at CPR r.44.3(2)(a) do not apply:

- at all to a case which was issued before 1 April 1 2013; and
- to those bits of work done on a case prior to 1 April 2013, where the case was issued after 31 March 2013.

This transitional provision leads to three scenarios as follows:

1. In cases issued before 1 April 2013, *Lownds* still applies and if proportionality is challenged at assessment it must be dealt with at the outset, by reference to what were the 'seven pillars of wisdom' at CPR r.44.5(3) and which are now the first seven of eight 'pillars' at CPR r.44.4(3). The outcome will be that the costs are either assessed against a necessarily or reasonably incurred test.
2. In cases which are issued after 31 March 2013 and no work is done on that case prior to that date, then the new provisions apply to all the costs.
3. In cases where the claim is issued after 31 March 2013 but some work is done before that date, the *Lownds* approach must be adopted in respect of the work done prior to 1 April 2013 and the new test to all the work after 31 March 2013.

It is the last of the three scenarios above that presents challenges. Parties seeking assessment of costs, whether by summary or detailed assessment, will need to ensure that the costs pre and post 1 April 2013 are clearly separated. From 6 April 2016 there is a requirement under CPR r.47 PD 5.8(7) to divide a bill for detailed assessment into parts matching the relevant proportionality test where the transitional arrangements provide that both the 'old' and 'new' provisions apply under 3)) above. However, there is no procedural requirement for separate Forms N260 that would similarly divide between the costs under the 'old' and the 'new' test in a summary assessment. As the court will require this information, it seems sensible that practitioners should produce two Forms N260. Experience to date suggests that this approach has not routinely been adopted. The risks that remain if there are not separate N260s for the relevant periods are that:

- It is not proportionate to adjourn off the summary assessment to another date or for written submissions and the court may be forced to do the best it can on the information available. This may result in the court concluding that if a party has not troubled to separate out the two periods, the sanction (and proportionate way forward) is to assess all the costs under the new test.
- The court does adjourn and demands a re-drawn Form N260, but does not permit any recovery of costs for so doing.

If there are separate Forms N260 or separate parts of the bill, (and, as stated above, under CPR r.47 PD 5.8(7) the bill must be divided into the relevant 'proportionality test' period), the court's function is invidious. It must do one proportionality determination at the beginning (for the pre-1 April 2013 costs) and one at the end (for the post-31 March 2013 costs). However, both exercises are artificial, because the court cannot aggregate the costs of both parts to do the exercise under each discrete test. To do so would be to ignore the clear language of CPR r.44.3(7). Instead the court will have to identify the work undertaken in each period and apply the relevant test to determine the proportionality of that work.

Q2. Does the court look at the sums reasonably claimed or the sums recovered when determining 'the sums in issue in the proceedings' under CPR r.44.3(5)(a)?

3–07 Obviously at the time that proportionality is considered for the purposes of budget setting and case management, the court does not know what sums will ultimately be recovered. At that stage the determination must be based on what is claimed less what is admitted – which emphasises the importance of realistic valuation (how often does the statement of value on a claim form limit to a particular sum, but the subsequent schedule of loss attached to later served Particulars of Claim reveal that the alleged losses are significantly higher than that sum, but there is no application to increase the statement of value?). If there is an argument, namely that the claim is exaggerated, then all that does is confirm that the sums claimed are in issue (and remember the wording of CPR r.44.3(5)(a) is *'the sums in issue in the proceedings'*). It might seem attractive to the court, if it considers a claim to be inflated, to adopt what if considers to be a more realistic value under CPR r.44.3(5)(a) when budgeting. However, unless the court strikes out part of the claim, if it adopts this course, then it ignores the fact that the defendant must still meet the larger claim and its proportionate budget should recognise this. This may explain why the wording of this provision does not refer to sums claimed, but to sums in issue. Of course, if the court thinks that part of the claim will be easily defeated, it can reflect this in its proportionality determination under CPR r.44.3(5)(c) in any event.

At the conclusion of the claim the court will know what sum was recovered. The fact that the sum may be less than was claimed does not, of itself, necessarily alter the determination of proportionality. The fact that one sum was claimed and one was recovered does not mean that the original sum was not in issue. However, this does assume that it was reasonable to pursue the claim as stated if the claimant's costs are being considered. Again, though, the court must be astute to the position of a defendant who has successfully defeated a claim and has been awarded costs. To approach CPR r.44.3(5)(a) at the assessment stage on any basis other than that the entire sum claimed was in issue would be to approach the question of the defendant's proportionate costs incorrectly. As stated above, the fact that part of the claim was seen off easily can be reflected when the court considers CPR r.44.3(5)(c).

If, for example, it emerges that the claim was exaggerated, but the claimant still obtains an award of some costs, then in cases costs managed, this may well be a 'good reason' to depart from the budget as that will have been set on a basis that the claimant knew was wrong. In non-budgeted cases conduct can be considered when assessing the reasonable costs under CPR r.44.4 and the 'real' value is likely to apply on the proportionality 'cross check'. If, as a result of the exaggeration, the defendant secures some form of costs award, it is right that the defendant's budget reflected the proportionate work that it did as the 'exaggerated' element of the claim was plainly in issue.

In contrast, if the claimant recovers a lower sum than that claimed, but it was reasonable to pursue the higher sum, e.g. if there was a complicated causation argument where the defendant's expert evidence was preferred or where the case turned on a factual dispute and the court preferred the evidence of the defendant's witnesses, then it is likely that will not alter 'the sums in issue' for the purpose of proportionality and so will not represent a 'good reason' to depart from the budget in costs managed cases and will not influence proportionality in non-budgeted cases.

In practice, in these scenarios the limited recovery is likely to sound in the award of costs itself, with something less than a full costs order being made under CPR r.44.2(4)(b) and 44.2(6) or a partial costs award to the defendant. The court must be astute to avoid 'double jeopardy', although as is clear from *Drew v Whitbread*[15] conduct may be considered both on the award and the assessment of costs.

Q3. Why is only the conduct of the paying party included in the definition?

This question really arises at two stages – at case/costs management and at assessment. It is important, though, when considering the question to remember the full wording of this factor. It is not conduct generally, which falls to be considered, but only conduct of the paying party which generates additional work.

3–08

---

[15] *Drew v Whitbread* [2010] EWCA Civ 53.

B. At the case/costs management stage

3–09   At the costs management stage the rationale is that the past conduct of the parties (for at this stage it is not clear who will be the receiving and who the paying party) is not relevant. This is because the court can only budget the costs "to be incurred". As such, the court can control conduct going forward by proportionate costs and case management. In other words, the court's directions should preclude the possibility of conduct generating additional work. The court sets and manages the progression of the case. If a party persists in conduct that is likely to generate additional work, then the other party may always apply under CPR r.3 PD E 7.6 to vary the budget as a result of that conduct or seek discrete costs sanctions on any applications that arise outside the budget under CPR r.3 PD E 7.9, relying on the stark warnings given by the Court of Appeal about non co-operation in *Denton v T H White*,[16] which resonate beyond the specific scenario which was under consideration:

> "The court will be more ready in the future to penalise opportunism. The duty of care owed by a legal representative to his client takes account of the fact that litigants are required to help the court to further the overriding objective."[17]

In any event, CPR r.3 PD E 7.4 requires the court to take incurred costs into account when considering the reasonableness and proportionality of the costs to be budgeted. So, if unreasonable and/or disproportionate costs have been incurred by a party as a result of its conduct up to costs management, it may find its budget going forward suffers as a result. In *Group Seven Ltd v Nasir*[18] the court took this a step further. It concluded that at the costs management stage the court should assume that each party will be the receiving party when its budgeted costs are set. It also found that the conduct of some of the defendants up to the costs case management conference suggested some future procedural difficulties for other parties. As a result of these conclusions the court indicated that it would consider allowing the costs of future applications to ensure compliance by those defendants as contingent budgeted costs of the other parties finding that:

> "Rule 44.3(5)(d) refers to the relationship of the costs to any additional work generated by the paying party. That rule applies where an order for costs has been made and one knows who the paying party is. At the costs budget stage, there is not yet an order that anyone pay the budgeted costs but I consider that the question of proportionality should be judged on the hypothetical basis that the party who has prepared the budget turns out to be the receiving party. . . as to future costs, I would be prepared to allow Group Seven and ETS sums for contingencies to reflect the possibility that there will be future procedural difficulties which might be attributable to a lack of cooperation from some of the Defendants."

---

[16] *Denton v T H White* [2014] EWCA Civ 906.
[17] para.43.
[18] *Group Seven v Nasir* [2016] EWHC 620 (Ch).

C. At the assessment stage

The reason that the conduct of the receiving party does not form part of **3–10** the definition at assessment seems more complicated. Whilst it is likely that such conduct will already have been taken into account by the court when making the award of costs – see CPR r.44.2(4)(a) – that is by no means certain as it may not always be obvious at that stage whether certain conduct has generated additional costs. However, conduct is also taken into account at the assessment – see CPR r.44.4(3). Both these provisions, though, relate to the conduct of the parties. So if the argument is that conduct has already been considered, then that ought also to apply to the conduct of the paying party.

The explanation may be that it is difficult to imagine a situation where any additional costs of the receiving party generated by the conduct of that party survive the test of whether they are reasonably incurred or reasonable in amount and, as such, have already been disallowed by the time that the court does the proportionality cross check. In contrast, the receiving party's additional costs caused by the paying party's conduct will survive the test of whether they were reasonably incurred and reasonable. If the court does not remind itself under CPR r.44.3(5)(d) when undertaking the CPR r.44.3(2)(a) cross check, that these reasonably incurred and reasonable in amount costs include those extra costs caused by the conduct of the paying party, there is a danger that the overall sum is deemed disproportionate and the paying party escapes the consequences of its actions.

D. The relationship between proportionality, reasonableness and necessity

Q4. Is there any distinction between proportionality and reasonableness in reality?

The answer, as an exercise of semantic interpretation of the CPR, is yes, because **3–11** throughout the CPR the two are referred to separately – see for example CPR r.3 PD E 7.3 which requires the court to approve budgets for phases that are "reasonable and proportionate" and CPR r.44.3(2)(a) which clearly draws a distinction between the two. Indeed it is the latter provision that makes it clear that some costs may be reasonable, but not proportionate. As the court said in *Group Seven Ltd v Nasir*[19]:

> "...*proportionality can result in the non-recovery of costs even where they are otherwise reasonable costs and even where they are necessary costs*".

In practice, there will be cases where the court, having assessed the reasonable costs, then applies the CPR r.44.3(5) factors to the proportionality cross check under CPR r.44.3(2)(a) and determines that those costs are also proportionate

---

[19] *Group Seven v Nasir* [2016] EWHC 620 (Ch).

– indeed the court's assessment of proportionality might be at a higher figure than the reasonable costs for a variety of reasons (e.g. because of limits imposed by the contractual retainer). There will also be cases where the same cross-check reveals the reasonable costs are still disproportionate. Perhaps the better answer, therefore, is, not necessarily so.

Q5. Is the effect of proportionality to prescribe that in a case about money, the costs cannot exceed the sums in dispute?

3–12 Before 1 April 2013, there was an acceptance within the CPR that there were cases where the proportionate cost would exceed the sum in issue. Section 11 of the then Costs Practice Direction expressed it in these terms:

> *"11.1 In applying the test of proportionality the court will have regard to rule 1.1(2)(c). The relationship between the total of the costs incurred and the financial value of the claim may not be a reliable guide. A fixed percentage cannot be applied in all cases to the value of the claim in order to ascertain whether or not the costs are proportionate.*
>
> *11.2 In any proceedings there will be costs which will inevitably be incurred and which are necessary for the successful conduct of the case. Solicitors are not required to conduct litigation at rates which are uneconomic. Thus in a modest claim the proportion of costs is likely to be higher than in a large claim and may even equal or possibly exceed the amount in dispute."*

What is immediately clear is that 11.2 accords precedence to 'necessary' costs. Work that was necessary informed the assessment of proportionality. This is no longer the situation, for CPR r.44.3(2)(a) expressly gives primacy to proportionality, even if that means that necessary costs (and by implication necessary work) are not recoverable. This does no more than codify the comments at Ch.3 para.5.10 of Jackson LJ's Final Report[20] under the bold heading 'Costs do not become proportionate because they were necessary'.

Does this mean that costs can never exceed the amount in dispute? The answer must surely be no, but not because a certain amount of work is necessary in any given claim, but, instead, because CPR r.44.3(5) does not limit the relationship between proportionality and costs solely to the amount in issue. If there are other relevant factors then those inform the determination of the proportionate sum. This, again, illustrates the flexibility of the definition that enables it to apply to all circumstances. The Final Report concluded, when making the recommendation for the new definition of proportionality, that:

> *"Proportionality of costs is not simply a matter of comparing the sum in issue with the amount of costs incurred, important though that comparison is. It is also necessary to evaluate any non-monetary remedies sought and any rights which are in issue, in order to compare the overall value of what is at stake in the action with the costs of resolution."*[21]

---

[20] *Review of Civil Litigation Costs: Final Report*, December 2009.
[21] Ch.3 para.5.5.

Notwithstanding this, it is likely to be rare indeed for costs to exceed the sums in dispute. As Stuart-Smith J observed in *GSK Project Management Ltd v QPR Holdings Ltd*[22]:

> "*My starting point is that a case would have to be wholly exceptional to render a costs budget of £824,000 proportionate for the recovery of £805,000 plus interest.*"

This confirms that where the only relevant factor under CPR r.44.3(5) is the sum in issue, it is difficult to envisage a court determining that it is proportionate for the parties to spend more than this sum in determining the dispute.

Q6. Is the case of *Kazakhstan Kagazy Plc v Zhunuss*[23] the touchstone regarding proportionality – namely that it defines what is 'reasonable and proportionate' as "...the lowest amount (of costs) which it (a party) could reasonably have been expected to spend in order to have its case conducted and presented proficiently, having regard to all the circumstances"?

No. See the commentary at para.3–04 above. CPR r.44.3(2)(a) is clear that rea- 3–13
sonable costs may be disallowed if they are disproportionate. It matters not that these costs may be at the very bottom of the bracket that the court deems reasonable. What matters is that the costs must bear a reasonable relationship to the factors at CPR r.44.3(5). If they do not then they are disproportionate even if a party could not reasonably have spent less to have a case conducted and presented proficiently.

It is important to note that this was a short decision in which the court was concerned only with determining the extent of a payment on account of costs. It was not assessing the costs, which would have required detailed consideration of CPR r.44.3(5) and CPR r.44.3(2)(a) (of pertinence is that neither of these provisions is mentioned). Indeed Leggatt J. expressly concluded in general terms that the costs claimed were neither reasonable nor proportionate and that the reasonable and proportionate costs could only properly be determined by a detailed assessment.

Q7. In the case of *Stocker v Stocker*[24] Mr Justice Warby observed: "I readily acknowledge the importance of ensuring that the costs budgeting process does not result in a party being unable to recover the costs necessary to assert their rights." Does this mean that proportionate costs can never be less than those that are necessary?

No. CPR r.44.3(2)(a) makes this quite clear: 3–14

> "*Costs which are disproportionate in amount may be disallowed or reduced even if they were reasonably or necessarily incurred.*"

---

[22] *GSK Project Management Ltd v QPR Holdings Ltd* [2015] EWHC 2274 (TCC).
[23] *Kazakhstan Kagazy Plc v Zhunus* [2015] EWHC 404 (Comm).
[24] *Stocker v Stocker* [2015] EWHC 1634 (QB).

In fact the extract quoted in the question needs to be put in context. It comes at the conclusion of a paragraph considering 'purely financial proportionality'. Of course costs are proportionate if they bear a reasonable relationship to the five factors at CPR r.44.3(5) and not simply the sums in issue in the proceedings. However, Warby J did acknowledge the difficulty 'to cut radically, at a stroke, the costs of this class of litigation' (libel claims), suggesting overtly that this would need to be a gradual process. However, that said, he had no hesitation in concluding that "the Defendant's global costs figure is clearly considerably out of proportion to what is at stake and the nature of the issues, and should be substantially reduced for that reason".

E. The extent of proportionality considerations

Q8. Is proportionality to be applied in all cases, or, as some wish to suggest, is it really for the small to medium value claims, where disproportionate costs are more likely?

3–15   Whilst costs management is limited to those claims specifically referred to in CPR r.3.12, and any other claims where the court orders it, this does not limit the all-encompassing relevance of proportionality. It is part of the overriding objective and, as such, all case management decisions must be made against the obligation on the court to deal with cases at proportionate cost whatever the value of a claim. This is reinforced by CPR r.3.17, which provides that:

> *"When making any case management decision, the court . . . will take into account the costs in each procedural step."*

Chapter 4 considers the effect of proportionality on obvious case management decisions, but the effect is more wide ranging than that. By way of example, in *Agents Mutual Ltd v Gasgoine Halman Ltd*[25] the court considered proportionality in the context of an application for security for costs, describing some of the costs as 'seriously disproportionate'.

Even in those cases where the filing of Precedent H is required and the court chooses not to make a costs management order, the rules on the relevance of that budget at assessment have been strengthened. CPR rules 44 PD 3.6 and 3.7 reiterate and expand previous provisions. They enable the assessing court, where there is a difference of 20% or more between the costs claimed and those shown in a budget, to:

- Restrict the recoverable costs where reliance has been placed on the budget by the paying party to what is reasonable even if that results in a sum less than that which would otherwise be proportionate and reasonable.
- Regard the difference between the costs claimed and those in the budget as evidence that the costs claimed are unreasonable or disproportionate, even where no reliance on the budget is established.

---

[25] *Agents Mutual Ltd v Gasgoine Halman Ltd* [2016] EWHC 2315 (Ch).

Expect the court to be more robust in applying these provisions, than it was before 1 April, 2013.

Proportionality also has a role to play in non-fixed fee fast track and small claims track cases. Indeed, cases that might previously have been allocated to multi-track (e.g. because the time estimate for trial exceeded one day) may now be allocated to fast-track with directions targeted to reduce the time estimate to one day and cases that are over the small claim track limit may now be allocated to that track as the consent of the parties to this is no longer required. In both these tracks, directions will be targeted to ensure that the cases are dealt with proportionately (and that includes the amount of court time that they occupy).

So far as assessments of costs are concerned, in respect of those that fall under the new proportionality regime (see **Q1** above), then the court must apply the proportionality cross-check under CPR r.44.3(2)(a) as the 'court will only allow costs which are proportionate'. It is no longer a case of proportionality only arising if raised by the paying party.

Q9. What relevance, if any, does proportionality have in cases where an order for costs is made on the indemnity basis?

Proportionality is still relevant before the costs order is made, as the court will have case managed on a proportionate basis. Where the order for indemnity costs has significance is on the assessment of the amount of recoverable costs. When conducting an assessment on the indemnity basis under CPR r.44.4(1)(b), the court must decide whether costs were unreasonably incurred or unreasonable in amount – it is not required to consider proportionality. Albeit that the rule number may have changed (from CPR r.44.4(3)) this does not alter the provision in place before April 2013. However, where the change in outcome is marked is in cases where a costs management order has been made. This is because CPR r.3.18, which provides that the court will not depart from the last approved or agreed budget at assessment unless there is 'good reason', expressly only applies to cases where the court is assessing costs on the 'standard basis'.

3–16

Whilst Coulson J in *Elvanite Full Circle Ltd v AMEC Earth & Environment*[26] suggested that even where there was an order for indemnity costs, the budget should be the starting point, it must be remembered that he was considering a budget prepared under CPR r.51 PD G. The budget form (Form HB) did not require any certification suggesting that the budget was constrained in any way by proportionality – in other words it was probably a fair reflection of all the costs that the client was likely to incur and so represented an approximation of indemnity costs. Now the budget does require a certification linking the sums included to those that are proportionate as is set out in CPR r.22 PD 2.2A:

---

[26] *Elvanite Full Circle Ltd v AMEC Earth & Environment* [2013] EWHC 1643.

"This budget is a fair and accurate statement of incurred and estimated costs which it would be reasonable and proportionate for my client to incur in this litigation."[27]

As a result the link between the budget sum and indemnity costs relied upon by Coulson J is no more. If there was still any vestige of doubt, that has been dispelled by the Court of Appeal in the judgment of Dyson MR and Vos LJ in *Denton v T H White*.[28] The relevant section of the judgment was considering sanctions in costs for non co-operation between the parties. It dealt with indemnity costs as a possibility and said this:

"If the offending party ultimately loses, then its conduct may be a good reason to order it to pay indemnity costs. Such an order would free the winning party from the operation of CPR rule 3.18 in relation to its costs budget."

It is clear from this that there is a greater benefit to a receiving party of an order for indemnity costs than was the case before the 2013 reforms. However, the test for whether or not an order for indemnity costs is merited has not altered. However, as Akenhead J observed in *Courtwell Properties Limited v Greencore PF (UK) Limited*,[29] where a party entitled to an automatic standard basis costs order under Part 36 sought an order for indemnity costs instead:

". . . parties must act in a proportionate way .. Where the indemnity costs application depends on evidence which is likely to involve material conflicts of evidence, the applicant party needs to think long and hard about whether it is appropriate to pursue the application."

Q10. Is proportionality a 'fixed sum' throughout the life of a claim?

3–17   This depends entirely on the specific features of any claim, e.g. an assessment of proportionality is made at the costs management stage in a claim where two heads of loss are pursued, each with a considerable value. After disclosure it becomes apparent that one head of loss is unsustainable and the claimant discontinues that part of the claim. At that stage plainly the sum in issue has altered. In those circumstances there has been a significant development for the purposes of CPR r.3 PD E 7.6 and we would expect the parties either to agree revised budgets or, in the absence of agreement, to seek the approval of the court to revised budgets on the basis that what was proportionate for the claim as originally presented is not for the claim that then remains (remember that revision where there is a significant development is expressly referred to as *'upwards or downwards'* in CPR r.3 PD E 7.6). In other words, the proportionality of a claim may alter throughout its course.

However, this does not mean that as a matter of routine the court will revisit earlier decisions on proportionality. Many saw the decision to grant

---

[27] para.43.
[28] *Denton v T H White* [2014] EWCA Civ 906.
[29] *Courtwell Properties Limited v Greencore PF (UK) Limited* [2014] EWHC 184 (TCC).

permission to appeal in *Troy Foods v Manton*[30] as opening the door to revisiting proportionality in costs managed cases at subsequent assessment. This interpretation overlooks some important points as follows:

- This was simply a decision on whether or not to permit an appeal. As such it is not a binding authority.
- The case was under the pilot scheme at what was CPR r.51 PD G. At para.4.2 of the practice direction, the objective of costs management was said to be "to control the costs of litigation in accordance with the overriding objective". The overriding objective was in its pre-April 2013 form without specific reference to dealing with a case at proportionate costs. Whilst para.1.3 of the Practice Direction makes a reference to proportionate costs it does so in the context of the relevance of costs already incurred. Nowhere in the Practice Direction does it state that the court is expressly charged with setting the budget by reference to proportionality.
- The costs managing judge appeared to have applied a test of approving the budget "provided it was not so unreasonable as to render it obviously excessive or, as he put it, 'grossly disproportionate'". Accordingly, permission was given on the basis that it was arguable the judge had applied the wrong test and been overgenerous as a result.
- When setting a budget under the costs management provisions of CPR r.3 and 3 PD E, the court is required to budget phases by reference to what is 'reasonable and proportionate'. In other words, the court has assessed the proportionality of any phases budgeted already.
- As a matter of semantics it seems CPR r.3.18 could not be clearer – on a standard basis assessment the court will not depart from the last approved or agreed budget for each phase of the proceedings unless it is satisfied that there is 'good reason' to do so. To do otherwise would be to adopt no more than an inappropriate appellate function. However, there does seem to be a concerted attempt by some parties to argue against this view, in part relying upon *Simpson v MGN*[30] (which is considered in **Chapter 4**), to treat the sum set in a budget as a cap only or an approved fund from which departure may take place under a standard basis costs order by an item by item assessment. Higher Court authority is both expected, desirable, and imminent.[31] This is dealt with in more detail in **Chapter 4** at **4–20** and at **Q76**.

Subject to any Higher Court authority to the contrary, we remain of the view that unless there is 'good reason' to depart from the last budget, the court will not revisit the proportionality determination of any phase of the claim that

---

[30] *Troy Foods v Manton* [2013] EWCA Civ 546.
[31] At the time of writing the appeal decision in the case of *Merrix v Heart of England NHS Foundation Trust* [2016] EWHC B28, QB is awaited. The first instance decision is considered at Chapter 4 Q76 below.

has been budgeted (see **Chapter 4** for consideration of 'good reason' in this context). Pre-empting, in part, what is said in **Chapter 4 Q76**, were the reverse to be correct, then the purpose of costs management would be defeated.

F. The practical implications of CPR r.44.3(2)(a) at assessment

Q11. If there is no 'good reason' to depart from the budgeted costs on assessment, how does the court apply the proportionality 'cross-check' under CPR r.44.3(2)(a) at the end of the assessment?

3–18　At the end of the assessment the court will have determined the reasonably incurred and reasonable in amount sum of the non budgeted costs (i.e. those incurred before the costs management order which were not agreed) and these must then be added to the budgeted costs. The proportionality cross check is then applied, but on the basis that this cannot reduce the overall costs to less than the budgeted costs, for, as is set out above, those costs were subject to a determination of proportionality at the time the budget was set and the wording of CPR r.3.18 precludes departure from this sum. Accordingly, if the total of the assessed costs is not proportionate, then the court must reduce the costs to a level that is proportionate, but that cannot be less than the budgeted costs. For example, if the total of the budgeted costs for the 'to be incurred' part of the phases budgeted, whether by agreement between the parties, approval of the court or a combination of both, is £50,000 (and there is no 'good reason' to depart from this) and the total for the assessed non budgeted costs is £30,000, but the court determines that the combined sum of £80,000 is disproportionate, then the proportionate figure that the court assesses under CPR r.44.3(2)(a) is somewhere between £50,000 to £80,000. It cannot be less than £50,000.

Q12. If the effect of CPR r.44.3(2)(a) is that the sum to be allowed on an assessment is that which is proportionate, why does the court trouble first with undertaking an assessment of what is reasonably incurred and reasonable in amount?

3–19　There are a number of reasons why the court must first assess the reasonable sum. These are:

- Because that is what the combined effect of CPR rules 44.4(1)(a) and 44.3(2) require of the court (this sits happily with the approach referred to by Jackson LJ in his final report – see **3–03** above).
- The effect of the indemnity principle. The increasing use of fixed fee solicitor and client retainers and pressure on hourly rates means that there may well be cases where the proportionate sum exceeds the reasonable sum. However, to proceed straight to the proportionality assessment would lead to the assessment of a sum that exceeds the permitted recovery under the retainer. Linked to the point above is that it is also not sufficient in such a situation to say that as the costs claimed are less than the proportionate

sum, they then should be allowed in full. This is because, as said above, proportionality does not necessarily equal reasonableness (**Q4**). The court must be satisfied under CPR r.44.4(1)(a) that the costs are both proportionate and reasonable. There may still be items of costs that were unreasonably incurred or unreasonable in amount even if the overall sum is proportionate. Those items should not be allowed, even if that means the eventual sum assessed is reduced still further from what may be the proportionate sum. In these cases proportionality acts as a cap and not as fixed costs.

• That, as seen under **Q3** above, the question of the conduct of the parties demands an assessment of what is reasonable by looking at items where it is said that this has generated additional costs. It is only the assessment of reasonableness that introduces the conduct of the receiving party and informs the court as to whether the conduct of the paying party sounds in the proportionality determination.

G. Proportionality, outcomes and the solicitor/client relationship

Q13. Is there not a risk that similar claims will have different outcomes because of the determination by separate case managing judges of what is proportionate in a particular case?

Yes – there is such a risk and this is something that advisors should stress to their clients when giving them the best view they can as to the likely reasonable and proportionate costs (see **Q16** below). It is also why evidence of what was budgeted in any given case is of no more than general guidance at best of what might be budgeted in a similar case. The determination of proportionality will dictate what case management directions are given. Different determinations will lead to different directions, e.g. permission for an expert in one case and not in another. However, that does not mean that the judges are necessarily 'wrong', simply that one has exercised discretion in another way from the other. Of course, that happens, and legitimately so, regardless of proportionality, on a daily basis in all courts—not just on procedural matters, but on factual disputes of a similar nature. Whilst there is judicial discretion there will be instances where there are a number of outcomes – none of which are 'wrong'. This question ought to be linked, however, with consideration of whether the risk is justified as an attempt to curb disproportionate costs and to promote access to justice. It is too early to say whether the drive to introduce proportionality will achieve this aim.

3–20

However, it is surely unarguable that a system that provides transparency of the 'recoverable costs' at large at an early stage will focus the attention of the parties and enable them to make decisions and give their legal representatives instructions on a more informed basis as to how they wish a claim pursued or defended, than a system where they find out the exact extent of the other party/parties' costs only when they are ordered to pay them and find out the shortfall between their legal fees and the exact amount of those that they may recover from the other party at assessment, after the costs have been spent.

Q14. How useful are the comments in cases such as *CIP Properties (AIPT) Limited v Galliford Try Infrastructure Limited*[32], *GSK Project Management Limited v QPR Holdings Limited*[33] and *Stocker v Stocker*[34] [2015] EWHC 1634 (QB) in setting benchmarks for proportionality?

3–21   As set out at **3–04** above, proportionality, other than in terms of very general (and relatively obvious) observations, is case and fact specific. Accordingly, whilst some general guidance may emerge from authorities – such as those set out in **3–04** and **Q5** above – proportionality in each individual case will depend upon the outcome of the consideration of the CPR r.44.3(5) factors in that specific case.

What does emerge, by way of reinforcement, is that when preparing budgets parties should remember the wording of the statement of truth on Precedent H and the requirement at CPR r.22 PD 2.2A (see **Q9** above) for the costs set out in the budget to be a statement of the proportionate incurred and estimated costs. Failure to do so is likely to result in unfavourable comment and possible costs sanctions, as occurred in *GSK Project Management Limited* where Stuart-Smith J imposed a costs order upon the claimant for producing a *'grossly excessive'* costs budget.

Q15. Can legal representatives look to the sums budgeted as proportionate at costs management or allowed as proportionate at assessment of costs in previous cases as evidence of what will be deemed proportionate in another case?

3–22   There is no doubt that previous determinations of what is proportionate in a particular type of case will be informative. However, they will neither be determinative nor definitive. This is for the reasons set out in the answers to **Qs 13** and **Q 14** above. Each case will be fact specific and subject to a discretionary proportionality assessment. Even in cases based on the same factual matrix judges may legitimately reach different assessments of the proportionate costs by a reasoned and principled application of CPR r.44.3(5). As the court said in *Group Seven v Nasir*[35], when considering the relationship between costs and the sums in issue *'the decided cases do not give much direct help when considering this relationship.'* At best, as the court did in that case, previous decisions might be useful for general guidance purposes only (perhaps setting likely brackets).

Q16. Given the fact that only general guidance is emerging from the courts, how can a solicitor best offer advice to a client on what is likely to be deemed the proportionate cost of any specific case?

3–23   The solicitor-client relationship is considered in more detail in **Chapter 9**. However, what is clear is that solicitors must tailor their advice on costs to

---

[32] *CIP Properties (AIPT) Limited v Galliford Try Infrastructure Limited* [2015] EWHC 481 (TCC).
[33] *GSK Project Management Limited v QPR Holdings Limited* [2015] EWHC 2274 (TCC).
[34] *Stocker v Stocker* [2015] EWHC 1634 (QB).
[35] *Group Seven v Nasir* [2016] EWHC 620 (Ch).

clients at the outset to the key provisions of the CPR relating to recoverability of costs, stressing that:

- the court emphasis on proportionality means that they will only recover reasonable and proportionate costs if awarded costs (but equally will only be liable for reasonable and proportionate costs if an award of costs is made against them);
- CPR r.44.3(2)(a) means that clients may not recover costs that are reasonable and/or necessary to pursue/defend claims if the court decides that these are not proportionate;
- they (the solicitors) may have to sign a statement of truth on a budget certifying that, because of CPR r.44.3(5) and 44.3(2)(a), the reasonable and proportionate costs may be for a lesser sum than they think clients may need to spend to have the best chance of achieving the desired outcome;.
- the best advice they can give applying the relevant test in respect of proportionality under CPR r.44.3(5), rather than by reference to what they think the clients reasonably and/or necessarily need to spend, is in the region of £x to £y;.
- the best advice they can give on solicitor/client costs is £z (or £x to £y if they think the two are the same) so that an informed decision may be made as to any shortfall (reinforcing the distinction between the two at the outset);.
- the proportionality assessment may change as the claim evolves (e.g complexities perceived at the outset may fall away or unexpected ones may arise) and clients will be informed if such a situation occurs when further advice will be given.

The key is to be realistic when considering proportionality. Already it is clear from authorities emerging that there are a number of cases where budgets have been deemed disproportionate (and significantly so). This suggests that there remains a difference in the way in which some solicitors and the courts are approaching CPR r.44.3(5) and CPR r.44.3(2)(a). Whilst solicitors may not be able to identify precisely the figure that the court will decide is proportionate, it should be possible, by analysis of these procedural provisions, to give a bracket within which the court figure will fall. At the very least, as Master Rowley suggested in *May v Wavell Group Plc*[36] clients should be informed that *"even if successful, they will receive no more than a contribution to the costs that will be incurred".*

---

[36] *May v Wavell Group Plc* [2016] EWHC B16 (Costs).

CHAPTER 4

Case and Costs Management

Introduction

Although the title of this chapter suggests that case and costs management   **4–01**
are two separate exercises, in reality they are two sides of the same coin. As
Jackson LJ commented in his Final Report:

> "First, case management and costs management go hand in hand. It does not
> make sense for the court to manage a case without regard to the costs which it
> is ordering the parties to incur. The Rubicon was crossed on 26th April 1999,
> when the court assumed under the CPR wide powers and responsibilities for case
> management."[1]

This link is something to which Jackson LJ returned in May 2015[2], when
acknowledging that the court was adopting various approaches to case and
costs management in practice, and concluding that:

> "The objective of the 2013 civil justice reforms is to enable the court to manage
> each case so that it proceeds at proportionate cost" para.7.2.

and

> "In my view the norm shall be for the court to do both case management and costs
> management at a single hearing" para.7.5.

He confirmed this view formally in *Jamadar v Bradford Teaching Hospitals NHS
Foundation Trust*[3].

The April 2013 amendments to the CPR inextricably linked both in CPR
r.3.12(2), when defining the purpose of costs management as being "that the
court should manage both the steps to be taken and the costs to be incurred
by the parties to any proceedings" and in CPR r.3.17 which strengthens the
link between the two by requiring the court to have regard to any available
budgets and to take account of costs when making any case management
decision. In fact, it may be artificial to talk of both case and costs management
as, in those cases where costs management orders are standard (see below),
the latter is simply part of the former.

In this chapter we shall consider the procedural changes made to the existing case management provisions of the CPR and the costs management rules
that were introduced in April 2013 separately, and then illustrate how they
combine in a seamless practical application.

---

[1] Review of *Civil Litigation Costs*: Final Report, December 2009, Ch.40 para.7.1.
[2] "Confronting costs management" 13 May 2015.
[3] *Jamadar v Bradford Teaching Hospitals NHS Foundation Trust* [2016] EWCA Civ 1001.

In his Final Report Jackson LJ asked if costs management was worth the candle. He answered the question in the affirmative giving two reasons in support of that answer. The first is set out above. The other reason was:

> "*Secondly, I am in full agreement with the Law Society's view that costs management, if done properly, will save substantially more costs than it generates.*"[4]

Presented with the same question two years after the introduction of the April 2013 amendments, Jackson LJ remained as emphatic, stating unequivocally[5]:

> "*The first and most important conclusion to be drawn from the experience of the last two years is the same as that which was drawn from the pilots. Costs management works*" para. 2.1.

It is clear that the changes made to case management cannot work in isolation and 'proper' costs management is essential to the success of the reforms.

The changes made to the existing CPR case management provisions

4–02 The principal procedural change that affects and informs all case management decisions (and informs costs management decisions) is the change to the overriding objective at

CPR r.1.1 to introduce the obligation to deal with a case "at proportionate cost". All the other changes are designed to achieve this objective. These are:

1. Enforcing stricter compliance with court orders, rules and practice directions (both in CPR r.1.1(2)(f) and 3.9).
2. Replacing allocation questionnaires with directions questionnaires designed to provide more relevant case information (CPR r.26.3).
3. A greater discretion to the court when determining the track to which to allocate claims and an increase to the small claims limit (CPR r.26.6(3) and the removal of what was CPR Pts 26.7(3), 27.14(5) and (6)).
4. The encouragement to use standardised directions to ensure consistency and facilitate the production of orders (CPR r.29.1(2)).
5. More targeted disclosure provisions (CPR r.31.5(3–8)).
6. More prescriptive powers in respect of witness statements (CPR r.32.2(3)).
7. The provision of more information about any expert evidence proposed (CPR r.35.4).
8. The option to hear the oral evidence of experts concurrently (CPR r.35 PD 11).
9. Increasing the incentive for claimants to make realistic settlement proposals (r.36.17(4)(d)).
10. The introduction of costs management (CPR r.3.12–3.18 and CPR r.3 PD E).

---

[4] Review of Civil Litigation Costs: Final Report, December 2009, Ch.40 para.7.1.
[5] "Confronting costs management" 13 May 2015.

From 1 October 2015 the court has also expressly been given the power to hear an Early Neutral Evaluation with the express aim of helping the parties to settle a case (by an extension of the broad jurisdiction under CPR r.3.1(2)(m)) – recognising that this may result in earlier and more proportionate resolution.

1. Enforcing stricter compliance with court orders, rules and practice directions (both in CPR r.1.1(2)(f) and 3.9)

In the Final Report, Jackson LJ identified the change of culture that was required, commenting:

4–03

> *"First, the courts should set realistic timetables for cases and not impossibly tough timetables in order to give an impression of firmness. Secondly, courts at all levels have become too tolerant of delays and non-compliance with orders. In so doing they have lost sight of the damage which the culture of delay and non-compliance is inflicting upon the civil justice system. The balance therefore needs to be redressed."*[6]

In the pre-April 2013 case of *Fred Perry (Holdings) Ltd v Brands Plaza Trading Ltd*,[7] the Court of Appeal gave an indication of the imminent alteration of emphasis, leaving no doubt that a wind of change was blowing:

> *"The Rule Committee has recently approved a proposal that the present rule 3.9(1) be deleted . . . It is currently anticipated that this revised rule will come into force on 1st April 2013. After that date litigants who substantially disregard court orders or the requirements of the Civil Procedure Rules will receive significantly less indulgence than hitherto."*[8]

Whether the warnings went unheeded or whether some practitioners failed to appreciate quite how much less indulgence was to be afforded by the court is unclear, but from November 2013, and the decision in *Mitchell v News Group Newspapers Ltd*,[9] until July 2014, and the clarification provided in *Denton v T H White*[10] the court reverberated to the sounds of applications for relief from sanctions and the disappointed cries of those whose applications were dismissed. *Denton* has clarified that the court should approach these applications in three stages:

4–04

- Stage 1 requires an evaluation of the breach. The Court of Appeal made it clear that this must be looked at in isolation – concentrate solely on the seriousness and significance of this breach. If there have been other failures/misconduct by the defaulting party, those must be ignored at this stage, but may merit consideration at stage 3. The court then moves on to stages 2 and 3. If it has concluded that there is not a serious or significant

---

[6] Review of Civil Litigation Costs: Final Report, December 2009, Ch.39 para.6.5.
[7] *Fred Perry (Holdings) Ltd v Brands Plaza Trading Ltd* [2012] EWCA Civ 224.
[8] Jackson LJ, para.4.
[9] *Mitchell v News Group Newspapers Ltd* [2013] EWCA Civ 1537.
[10] *Denton v T H White* [2014] EWCA Civ 906.

breach, then stages 2 and 3 may not occupy much court time, but if there has been a serious or significant breach then the final 2 stages take on a greater importance.

- Stage 2 involves consideration of whether there was good reason for the breach. The Court of Appeal declined to produce an 'encyclopaedia' of what might constitute 'good reason'. This will be fact specific. However, *Mitchell* at para.41 sets out some examples.

- Stage 3 At this stage the court considers "all the circumstances of the case", but, remembering that the two factors specifically mentioned in CPR r.3.9 carry 'particular weight' (although Jackson LJ dissented, on the basis that the two factors were mentioned to draw attention to them, but that they carried no weight above any others). It is worth noting that the Court of Appeal specifically drew attention to the fact that the importance of complying with rules, practice directions and orders had received insufficient emphasis in the past stating:

"The court must always bear in mind the need for compliance with rules, practice directions and orders, because the old lax culture of non-compliance is no longer tolerated."

4–05 It is clear from the extract above that those who think that the position has reverted to what it was on 31 March 2013 remain due for an unpleasant shock. For those who pointed to the dissenting judgment of Jackson LJ in *Denton* to counter this, his comments in the Preface to the *White Book* 2015[11] leave no room for uncertainty. He accepted the majority judgment as the correct construction of CPR r.3.9 and added:

"It is very important that in the euphoria with which some have greeted Denton, we do not slip back into the 'old culture of non-compliance. . ."

The decision of the Court of Appeal in *Jamadar v Bradford Teaching Hospitals NHS Foundations Trust*[12] reinforces this message as, with echoes of the decision in *Mitchell*, the Court of Appeal upheld a refusal to grant relief from the sanction of CPR r.3.14.

If evidence from an even higher authority of a shift towards compliance is required, it was provided in *HRH Prince Abdulaziz Bin Mishal Bin Abdulaziz Al Saud v Apex Global Management Ltd*,[13] where the Supreme Court, whilst at pains to reiterate that generally case management and CPR was the domain of the Court of Appeal, confirmed that:

"The importance of litigants obeying orders of court is self-evident. Once a court order is disobeyed, the imposition of a sanction is almost always inevitable if court orders are to continue to enjoy the respect which they ought to have . . . One of the important aims of the changes embodied in the Civil Procedure Rules and,

---

[11] *White Book* 2015 Preface page xvi.
[12] *Jamadar v Bradford Teaching Hospitals NHS Foundation Trust* [2016] EWCA Civ 1001.
[13] *HRH Prince Abdulaziz Bin Mishal Bin Abdulaziz Al Saud v Apex Global Management Ltd* [2014] UKSC 64.

more recently, following Sir Rupert Jackson's report on costs, was to ensure that procedural orders reflected not only the interests of the litigation concerned, but also the interests of the efficient administration of justice more generally."[14]

So, whilst the change may not be as dramatic as *Mitchell* suggested, relief will still be granted more sparingly than previously.

Hand in hand in *Denton* with guidance on relief was:

i) an entreaty by the Court of Appeal (coupled with costs threats if ignored) for parties to co-operate and not use court rules as technical trip wires. This links to the amendment made to CPR r.3.8 in April 2014 to add a provision at 3.8(4) enabling parties to agree extensions to the period for compliance with orders, rules and practice directions that specify the consequences of a failure to comply, provided that this does not jeopardise any hearing. This costs threat was carried out in *Viridor Waste Management v Veolia Environmental Services*[15]. The court concluded that the defendant had taken an opportunistic and unreasonable advantage of late service of Particulars of Claim in opposing the application for relief from sanction. As a consequence the defendant was subjected to an indemnity costs order; and

ii) a reminder to members of the judiciary to ensure that "the directions that they give are realistic and achievable". The Court of Appeal acknowledged that it was of no use to set a timescale so tight that it was obvious that it could not be met, stressing that "the court must have regard to the realities of litigation in making orders in the first place". This harks back to the extract from Jackson LJ's Final Report quoted above, in which he stressed that the court should set realistic timetables for cases and not impossibly tough timetables in order to give an impression of firmness (see above and the Final Report Ch.39 para.6.5).

The then Master of the Rolls had cause to re-visit his comments in i) above in *R (on the application of Idira) v The Secretary of State for the Home Department*[16] and left no doubt in so doing that *Denton* did not represent a return to the pre-*Mitchell* regime, stressing that absence of prejudice did not inevitably lead to relief being granted, saying:

"At para.43 in Denton, this court said that parties should not "adopt an uncooperative attitude in unreasonably refusing to agree extensions of time and in unreasonably opposing applications for relief from sanctions". It added: "it is unacceptable for a party to try to take advantage of a minor inadvertent error. . .". I would emphasise the words "unreasonably" and "minor inadvertent". A party is not required to agree to an extension of time in every case where the extension will not disrupt the time-table for the appeal or will not cause him to suffer prejudice.

---

[14] paras 23–25.
[15] *Viridor Waste Management v Veolia Environmental Services* [2015] EWHC 2321 (Comm).
[16] *R (on the application of Idira v The Secretary of State for the Home Office* [2015] EWCA Civ 1187.

> *If the position were otherwise, the court would lose control of the management of the litigation."*

Similarly the fact that refusal to grant relief will cause significant prejudice to the party in default does not mean that relief should be granted. In *Sinclair v Dorsey & Whitney*[17] a professional negligence claim said to be valued at £30 million was struck out for breach of an unless order to provide security for costs. An application for relief was dismissed on application of the *Denton* 3 stage test. The fact of prejudice was insufficient when considered in all the circumstances and giving particular weight to the two factors in CPR r.3.9.

The latest decision in the ill-fated case of *Thevarajah v Riordan*[18] (two visits to the Court of Appeal and this one to the Supreme Court), confirmed, if confirmation was needed, that compliance with the terms of an unless order after the date set for compliance does not amount to a material change in circumstance as required pursuant to *Tibbles v SIG Plc*[19] (one of the factors necessary to support an application under CPR r.3.1(7) for the court to vary or revoke an order).

2. Replacing allocation questionnaires with directions questionnaires designed to provide more relevant case information (CPR r.26.3)

4–06   Directions questionnaires should assist the court with determining proportionate case management decisions. More information is required about proposed expert evidence and, unless there is a valid explanation for being unable to do so, expect the court to police the requirement to provide details of witnesses and the issue(s) to which their evidence will be addressed. Questionnaires that suggest that this information is 'to be advised' or 'to be confirmed' are likely to receive short shrift and their authors may find themselves the recipients of orders, including 'unless orders' to provide the information or a satisfactory explanation of why it cannot be provided or face the consequences (e.g. being unable to rely upon any witness evidence without permission of the court).

3. A greater discretion to the court when determining the track to which to allocate claims and an increase to the small claims limit (CPR rules 1.1 and 26.6(3) and the removal of what was CPR Parts 26.7(3), 27.14(5) and (6))

4–07   The court must take account of proportionality when allocating. Accordingly those claims that might previously have been allocated to the multi-track simply because of time estimate (e.g. where the value is within fast track limits and none of the other CPR r.44.3(5) proportionality factors justifies allocation to the multi-track, but there are a number of witnesses) are now likely to be allocated to fast track with a restriction on the evidence that may be adduced to ensure the claim is disposed of within a day. Similarly the omission of CPR

---

[17] *Sinclair v Dorsey Whitney* unreported QBD 20 November 2015.
[18] *Thevarajah v Riordan* [2015] UKSC 78.
[19] *Tibbles v SIG Plc* [2012] EWCA Civ 518.

Part 26.7(3), which prevented a court allocating a claim to the small claims track if the value exceeded the limit for that track without the agreement of all parties, seems designed to enable the court to allocate more claims to the limited 'fixed fee on issue' regime of that track.

This aim is bolstered by the removal of previous provisions (CPR r.27.14(5) and (6)), which enabled parties agreeing to allocation to the small claims track to include an agreement that fast track costs would still apply and that any appeal would carry the costs consequences as if it had been a fast track claim. These provisions are no more and so whether a claim with a fast track value is allocated to the small claims track with or without the consent of the parties, the limited small claims track costs allowances prevail.

At the same time the proportion of claims proceeding in the small claims track has been increased as the financial scope of that track has been doubled to £10,000 (save for personal injury and housing disrepair claims with a claim for specific performance of repairs, where the financial limit remains unaltered at £1,000, but with the current proposal for the personal injury limit to be raised to £5,000[20]).

4. The encouragement to use standardised directions to ensure consistency and facilitate the production of orders (CPR r.29.1(2))

The proliferation of different forms of directions up and down the country **4–08** was identified by Jackson LJ as a source of unnecessary cost. If the same form of order is used in all courts, then the parties can use them as a starting point when discussing proposed directions as they will not be confronted by 'local' variations, there will be consistency of orders produced, less risk that a direction will be overlooked or that a direction will be phrased ambiguously (not to be underestimated given the potential sanction for non-compliance) and the final order will be easier for the court to generate. Accordingly he recommended that:

> "... a menu of standard paragraphs for case management directions should be prepared for each type of case of common occurrence and made available to all district judges both in hard copy and online. These standard directions should then be used by district judges as their starting point in formulating initial case management directions."[21]

CPR r.29.1(2) was introduced to achieve this by linking to a raft of standard orders. However, the uptake appears to have been distinctly lukewarm. The directions are under review, but in the meantime, some courts are insisting that draft directions are filed adopting the standard template orders and others are not. It is hard to see how practitioners can be faulted by the court if they use the standard orders under CPR r.29.1(2) as the provision does state that these *'should'* be taken as the starting point.

---

[20] Spending Review and Autumn Statement 2015, 25 November 2015
[21] Ch.39 para.5.3.

5. *More targeted disclosure provisions (CPR r.31.5(3–8))*

4–09   In the 7th Implementation Lecture,[22] Jackson LJ referred to the costs of the disclosure process in these terms:

> *"Even in medium sized actions where all the documents are in paper form, disclosure can be a major exercise which generates disproportionate costs."*

The resultant attempt to curb the costs of this phase of litigation can be found at CPR r.31.5. This introduces the 'disclosure report' (Form N263), which is designed to facilitate discussion between the parties as to the appropriate disclosure order prior to the first case management conference and to inform the court, in general terms, of the types of documents involved, by whom and where they are held, how electronic documents are stored, the costs of 'standard disclosure' and what disclosure order is suggested. CPR r.31.5(7) then sets out a menu of possible disclosure options. It is no surprise that other than a catch-all provision, 'standard disclosure' is listed as the last of the disclosure options. The pre-amble to the menu stresses that the court will decide which option to order 'having regard to the overriding objective and the need to limit disclosure to that which is necessary to deal with the case justly'. The reference to the overriding objective plainly imposes the requirement for proportionality.

CPR rules 31.5(1) and (2) combine to exclude personal injury claims from the new provisions. Standard disclosure remains the 'norm' in these claims, but with a residual discretion to the court to order otherwise (which it should exercise where appropriate – e.g. by limiting to the issue of limitation, liability, quantum etc. as appropriate.)

The 7th Implementation Lecture left little doubt as to the importance of the new disclosure provisions:

> *"The order made at the first CMC concerning disclosure will have a profound impact on the future course of the case and also upon the final costs of the litigation. Therefore this issue merits careful thought and analysis when the parties initially and the court ultimately are making their selection from the menu of possible disclosure orders."*

Notwithstanding the exhortation to select from the menu after careful thought and analysis, anecdotal evidence suggests that 'standard disclosure' is the type most generally suggested in the N263, perhaps unsurprisingly, as the requirement to cost this form of disclosure and it being the default disclosure option in the standard orders under CPR r.29.1(2), steer parties towards it. Jackson LJ recognised this when reverting to the topic in his 'Disclosure' lecture in October 2016[23] and answering with a resounding 'no' the question he posed himself of whether everyone was using the new rules properly. He added, by way of comment:

---

[22] 7th Implementation Lecture: Controlling the Costs of Disclosure, 24 November 2011.

[23] 'Disclosure' Lecture at the Law Society's Commercial Litigation Conference, 10 October 2016.

"Parties frequently agree standard disclosure, seemingly without considering whether other options may be preferable, and the courts accept their agreements. It would be to the public benefit if all involved in the disclosure process gave more attention to the full range of options before simply proposing or agreeing to standard disclosure."

In the same lecture he made reference to a 'disclosure working group' that has been established Chaired by Gloster LJ and suggested that this group may want to consider 'whether what is needed is a culture change rather than a rule change'.

Even if standard disclosure is to remain more routinely used than had been envisaged under the reforms, the definition of standard disclosure that appears at CPR r.31.6 merits repetition as it is far narrower than many appear to think:

"31.6 Standard disclosure requires a party to disclose only —
(a) the documents on which he relies; and
(b) the documents which —
   (i)   adversely affect his own case;
   (ii)   adversely affect another party's case; or
   (iii)   support another party's case; and
(c) the documents which he is required to disclose by a relevant practice direction"

Tales of trial judges inundated with bundles based on 'standard disclosure' from which they are taken to only a few pages may be apocryphal, but do not be surprised if some judges add to an order for standard disclosure "as defined by CPR r.31.6".

6.   More prescriptive powers in respect of witness statements (CPR r.32.2(3)).

The court has always had the power to control evidence under CPR r.32.1.   **4–10** However, the specific reference in CPR r.32.2(3) to the ability of the court to give directions identifying and limiting the issues upon which factual evidence is to be given, identifying specific witnesses and limiting the length and format of statements, gives the court the ability to case manage factual evidence in a proportionate way. The identity of witnesses and the facts to which their evidence will be directed should be readily available from Section F of the Directions Questionnaire. Notwithstanding this, draft directions and orders still routinely make no attempt to limit evidence whether by number of witnesses or length of statements. Given that proportionate trial time estimates require strict control of evidence it appears inevitable that this case management provision will, and should, be used increasingly. Even if the number of witnesses listed in Directions Questionnaires appears reasonable and proportionate, expect the court still to impose a limit as this prevents further witnesses, whose evidence may only emerge later or whose names have been left out of Section F, being relied upon without a further order of the court.

An early illustration of the use of this provision was in *MacLennan v Morgan Sindall (Infrastructure) Plc*.[24] The court was concerned with a significant claim for loss of earnings in a severe brain injury claim. This element of loss raised four broad issues upon which the claimant wished to call 43 witnesses. The defendant sought an order under CPR r.32.2(3) limiting the number to eight. In the end the court made an order restricting the number of witnesses to 28 and identifying those issues with which the witnesses would deal.

7. The provision of more information about any expert evidence proposed (CPR r.35.4).

4–11   It is curious that almost four years after the introduction of CPR r.35.4, any party still completes a directions questionnaire and attends a subsequent case management conference, indicating that expert evidence is required without providing details of the expert, the issues that the expert will address and the likely cost of the expert. Curious because:

- This information is a pre-requisite to the court giving permission for expert evidence. CPR r.35.4(2) makes the provision of this information mandatory (qualified to the extent that the name is required where reasonably practicable) when applying for permission to rely upon expert evidence in any type of claim.
- Notwithstanding the failure to provide this information, some parties still feel able to complete the costs budget providing details of what the reasonable and proportionate expenditure on the expert phase will be – inserting figures for the expert – at a stage when the expert has not even been identified and the extent of that expert's remit not determined.

There is a real risk that if this information is not available, the court will simply not give permission. This means that in those cases that are costs managed, they will be costs managed without provision for permission for that/those expert(s) whom the party in default seeks to rely upon, with inevitable implications on the expert phase of the budget. If the party in default sees the way the wind is blowing and does not pursue the application for permission at the case management conference, but, instead, seeks to rely on a subsequent free standing application, it is likely to confront difficulties as the rectification of a previous failure is unlikely to be viewed as a 'significant development' for the purpose of budget variation under CPR r.3 PD E 7.6. Even if the court were minded to entertain the subsequent application and permit the expert evidence, this would mean consequential recasting of the directions and variations of costs budgets at considerable expense. It is not difficult to envisage what the costs order in respect of that additional expenditure would be!

If the intention behind failing to provide the name of the expert witness is to enable 'expert shopping' (meaning in this context to avoid having to

---

[24] *MacLennan v Morgan Sindall (Infrastructure) Plc* [2013] EWHC 4044 (QB) Green J.

disclose the unfavourable report of a named expert before having any prospect of being permitted to move on to another expert), then it should be
noted that even when courts do permit expert evidence when they are not
able to name the expert at the time of the order, they are drafting orders to
prevent this. A common order in such circumstances is to permit reliance on
the expert evidence from an unnamed expert in a specific discipline provided
that, as well as service of the report by a set date, *"the name of the expert is
provided in writing to all parties and the courts by 4pm [y days] and that thereafter
this order is read as though that name appears in it"*. In other words reliance
upon the report is conditional upon naming the expert within a limited time
period and the order will then expressly be read to provide for permission for
the named expert only.

8. The option to hear the oral evidence of experts concurrently (CPR r.35 PD 11).

CPR r.35 PD 11 provides the court with the option of taking expert evidence   **4–12**
concurrently and sets out, subject to judicial discretion to alter the process,
the procedure to adopt. In reality though, the process is inevitably case and
judge specific.

There was a pilot run in the Manchester 'Construction and Technology'
and 'Mercantile' Courts. The feedback from that was limited, inevitably due
to the small number of cases involved prior to the pilot report. Subsequently
the Civil Justice Council has produced a report[25], which, at page 10, illustrates
the breadth of case type in which concurrent expert evidence has been used.
Interestingly, one area where the report recommended further work was in
respect of the costs savings achieved by concurrent expert evidence, as of
those providing evidence to the Council a relatively low percentage were of
the view that there was necessarily any saving, although the same evidence
revealed that time at trial was saved by adopting this process. The report made
recommendations for amendment to CPR r.35 PD 11 and the minutes of the
October 2016 Civil Procedure Rules Committee meeting reveal that these are
to be considered. Jackson LJ in a lecture in June 2016 concluded with the hope
that the use of concurrent expert evidence will increase as the benefits become
more widely appreciated[26].

There has yet to emerge any authority that sheds light on the potentially
challenging issue of ensuring that the parties feel they have had a sufficient
opportunity to advance the expert evidence that they wish in this format (a
point highlighted in the Civil Justice Council report[27]). Albeit in a different
scenario (that of experts and site inspections), the case of *Hatton v Connew*[28]
is a timely reminder of the need for the court to take expert evidence in an
appropriate fashion which is fair to the parties.

---

[25] Concurrent Expert Evidence and 'Hot-Tubbing' in English Litigation since the 'Jackson Reforms' 25 July 2016.
[26] Concurrent Expert Evidence – A Gift from Australia, 29 June 2016.
[27] Concurrent Expert Evidence and 'Hot-Tubbing' in English Litigation since the 'Jackson Reforms' 25 July 2016 page 50.
[28] *Hatton v Connew* [2013] EWCA Civ 1560.

9.   *Increasing the incentive for claimants to make realistic settlement proposals (CPR r. 36.17(4)(d)).*

4–13   Giving the lead judgment in *Fox v Foundation Piling Ltd*,[29] Jackson LJ high-lighted one of the major reasons that cases that ought to resolve without the expense of a trial failed so to do:

> *"A not uncommon scenario is that both parties turn out to have been over–optimistic in their Part 36 offers. The claimant recovers more than the defendant has -previously offered to pay, but less than the claimant has previously offered to accept."*[30]

Therefore, it was not a surprise that CPR Part 36 was amended to increase the incentive for the parties to adopt more realistic valuations to encourage earlier settlement. That amendment comes in the form of CPR r.36.17(4)(d)). If a claimant makes a relevant Part 36 offer, then in addition to the 'established' consequences (an entitlement to indemnity costs and increased interest on both the substantive award and the costs), there will be an award of an additional amount, unless the court thinks it unjust to make such an award. The additional amount is 10% of the damages awarded up to £500,000 and that sum plus 5% of the damages awarded that are over £500,000, with a cap on the additional amount of £75,000.

The re-written CPR r.36 from April 2015 also contains an incentive at CPR r.36.23 for an offeree to accept an offer where the offeror has fallen foul of the provisions of CPR r.3.14 by failing to file a costs budget – this is to avoid the situation where the 'risk' to the offeree is limited solely to future court fees[31].

Part 36 is considered in more detail in **Chapter 5**.

10.   *The introduction of costs management (CPR r.3.12–3.18 and CPR r.3 PD E).*

4–14   In the Final Report, Jackson LJ described costs management in these terms:

> *"(i) The parties prepare and exchange litigation budgets or (as the case proceeds amended budgets).*
> *(ii) The court states the extent to which those budgets are approved.*
> *(iii) So far as possible, the court manages the case so that it proceeds within the approved budgets.*
> *(iv) At the end of the litigation, the recoverable costs of the winning party are assessed in accordance with the approved budget."*[32]

In essence these four characteristics form the basis of the regime introduced at CPR rules 3.12–3.18 and at r.3 PD E. However, the implementation and regulation of costs management has proven, and is proving, more challenging than the simple assertion of the regime's principles. To facilitate the understanding

---

[29] *Fox v Foundation Piling Ltd* [2011] EWCA Civ 790.
[30] para.46.
[31] See **Q67** below for further consideration of this.
[32] *Review of Civil Litigation Costs: Final Report*, December 2009, Ch.40 para.1.4.

and practical application of the regime, it is simplest to approach it under the following five headings:

A. Which cases are subject to costs management?
B. What procedural requirements are imposed on the parties in respect of costs management?
C. How does the court 'costs manage'?
D. Variation of budgets.
E. The effect of a costs management order on subsequent assessment.

A. Which cases are subject to costs management?

Although costs management is less than four years old, there has already been **4–15** substantial revision of the rules regulating which types of cases are covered by the regime. The current provisions relate to those cases issued after 22 April 2014 but incorporate some further amendments from April 2016 in respect of those who are children, as defined by CPR r.21, at the time of the making of the claim and those with a limited life expectancy (five years or less). In summary, the regime applies to:

- All CPR Part 7 where the amount claimed or the limit in the statement of value is less than £10,000,000 (CPR r.3.12 (1)(a) and (b)) save i) where the party was a child at the time that the claim was made (note that this exclusion covers those parties who cease to be a child during the proceedings unless the court orders otherwise), ii) where the claimant has a limited or severely impaired life expectancy (CPR r.3 PD E 2(b)) and the court disapplies costs management iii) where the court orders otherwise (CPR r.3.12(1)(e)) iv) where proceedings are subject to fixed or scale costs.
- Any other proceedings (including applications) where the court so orders (CPR r. 3.12(1A)). CPR r.3 PD E 2–5 'Other cases' sets out both the procedure that will apply where costs management is proposed by either the court of its own motion or the parties in cases not otherwise within the scheme and the types of case that are particularly suitable (the types of case are set out in CPR r.3 PD E 5(a)–(f)).

If the initial form of CPR r.3.15 was deemed less than prescriptive as to when the court should costs manage, the current version leaves little room for doubt. The court will make a costs management order in cases where a costs budget has been filed and served unless it can be satisfied that the litigation can be conducted justly and at proportionate costs in accordance with the overriding objective without such an order being made. Given that the court cannot make this assessment until it has seen the budgets, it is hard to imagine why the court will not always be making costs management orders, because either the budgets are plainly disproportionate, immediately triggering court concern, or they are obviously proportionate, in which case, to ensure that costs stay that way, and as it will take no time to do, it seems prudent that the court would make a costs management order in the terms of those parts of the Precedent H that it is permitted to budget. Whilst there remains an 'opt out' for the court in CPR r.3.12(1)(e), this is surely a provision to be used sparingly, otherwise it risks undermining the regime and may result in both forum shopping (for those keen to avoid budgeting) and the suggestion of 'local practice directions'. (See **Q3** below in respect of recent developments in some Chancery claims that would otherwise fall within the costs management regime)

In *Wright v Rowland*[33] the court declined to costs manage certain phases of the defendants' budgets because there were disputes between the parties as to the complexity of the claim, whether there was a reputational issue and whether the defendants should have separate representation. The court was concerned that these disputes would only be resolved at trial, and that therefore the prospective budgeting exercise raised the risk that the defendants' costs might be set too high or too low, depending upon which party's submissions it adopted when budgeting. Those phases were left for detailed assessment. However, such an approach is likely to be a rare occurrence as, in most cases, the court will be able to record the basis of its analysis of the CPR r.44.3(5) factors upon which a budget is set (i.e. its preliminary conclusion on complexity, whether there were reputational issues etc.), recognising that if, subsequently, it becomes clear that those conclusions are not sustainable and, with hindsight were not sustainable at the time of the costs management hearing, parties may apply to vary under CPR r.3 PDE.7.6 (in respect of those costs not yet incurred) and/or rely on 'good reason' in seeking to depart from the budget at an assessment under CPR r.3.18 (in respect of those costs that were already incurred at the time of any CPR r.3 PDE 7.6 application and, in respect of all other budgeted costs).

The level of prescription imposed by CPR r.3.15 saw the one area of potential disagreement between Jackson LJ and Dyson MR in their respective *'Confronting costs management'* lectures in May 2015. Jackson LJ envisaged the possibility of courts not case managing if they lacked the resources to do so other than at the risk of delay and disruption to the particular case before them and other cases generally. Dyson MR perceived a risk that the *'lack of resources'* card might be 'played' in many cases with costs management becoming the exception and not the 'norm'. What is clear is that agreements between the parties to avoid the costs management regime will need to be well reasoned to survive the rigorous consideration that they merit.

Litigants in person are exempted from the obligation to file and exchange costs budgets (CPR r.3 P DE 7.8), although they must be served with the budget of any other represented party and clearly are entitled to make representations about the budget at any costs management hearing. (See **Q2** below considering whether the court may order litigants in person to file and exchange budgets).

---

[33] *Wright v Rowland* [2016] EWHC 2206 (Comm).

B. What procedural requirements are imposed on the parties in respect of costs management?

In general terms the parties (other than litigants in person) in receipt of a notice **4–16** of provisional allocation to the multi-track (CPR r.26.3(1)) where the statement of the value of the claim is less than £50,000 must exchange and file a budget in Precedent H with their Directions Questionnaires. In all other multi-track cases Precedent H must be exchanged and filed twenty one days before the first case management conference or, if the case is one not automatically subject to costs management under CPR r.3.12, the budget must be exchanged and filed by any date specified by the court. Failure to comply results in the automatic sanction under CPR r.3.14, namely that the defaulting party is treated as having filed a budget comprising only applicable court fees. The effect of this for any party subject to a costs management order on this basis is that only future court fees may be budgeted, but costs incurred at the time of the order are still recoverable, either because they have been agreed or because, absent agreement, as a costs management order only relates to budgeted costs, which are "the costs to be incurred" (CPR r.3.15). For those thinking that post *Denton*, the likelihood of relief from this sanction is high, the case of *Jamadar v Bradford Teaching Hospitals NHS Foundations Trust*[34] should come as a stark reminder of the danger of non-compliance (see para.**4–05** above).

As of April 2016 parties who have exchanged costs budgets (so not litigants in person) must file an agreed budget discussion report (Precedent R) no later than seven days before the CCMC (CPR r.3.13(2)). This must set out the figures agreed for each phase, the figures not agreed for each phase and a brief summary of the grounds of dispute (CPR r.3 PD E 6A). (See **Q35** for consideration of the detail required in Precedent R).

The budget must be in the form of Precedent H attached to CPR r.3 PD E. Where the total costs do not exceed £25,000 or where the statement of value in the Claim Form is less than £50,000, then only page 1 of the Precedent H should be completed. There have been two cases already that seek to test the prescription of this requirement. In *The Bank of Ireland v Philip Pank Partnership*[35] the claimant failed to include the full wording of the statement of truth, although the budget was signed and dated by the legal representative. The court found that this omission did not render the budget a nullity and as such, the claimant had complied with the requirement to file and exchange its budget. Instead the Precedent H was simply subject to an irregularity. In the second case, *Americhem Europe Limited v Rakem Limited*,[36] the same judge found that the failure to have a budget signed by a senior legal representative (it was signed by a costs draftsman) also did not render a budget a nullity, again amounting to no more than an irregularity. The judge, having noted that this was the second occasion when he had to deal with a mere irregularity

---

[34] *Jamadar v Bradford Teaching Hospitals NHS Foundation Trust* [2016] EWCA Civ 1001.
[35] *The Bank of Ireland v Philip Pank Partnership* [2014] EWHC 284 (TCC) Stuart-Smith J.
[36] *Americhem Europe Linited v Rakem Limited* [2014] EWHC 1881 (TCC) Stuart-Smith J.

in budget form, took the opportunity to cite from the judgment of Leggatt J in *Summit Navigation Ltd v Genrali Romania Asigurare*[37] as follows:

> "*But, as the Master of the Rolls emphasised . . . it is not the aim of the reforms to turn rules and compliance into 'trip wires' . . .*"

If the court makes a costs management order, then CPR r.3 PD E 7.7 requires a party to re-file and re-serve the budget in the form approved by the court. In fact, some courts are budgeting either electronically using the first page of the budget in a self-calculating form so that the budget recalculates as the hearing progresses or manually using the first page of the budget and recalculating at the end. In those cases, to reduce costs and ensure absolute clarity of the outcome of the costs management exercise, the courts are simply attaching the first page of each budget as costs managed to the directions order and dispensing with the requirement at 3 PD E 7.7, saving the time and resource of re-filing and re-serving.

4–17   The preparation of the Precedent H itself is assisted by a guidance note on what work to insert in which phases within the form. Whilst the guidance was updated in July 2015 and has been updated again in April 2016, it remains brief, some would say too brief. Note that CPR r.3 PD E 6(b) now expressly requires the guidance to be followed. However, in general terms, it does identify the allocation of work amongst the phases of Precedent H. All costs incurred, even those pre-action, which are attributable to a phase of the budget should be inserted in the 'incurred' columns in the specific phase and all work to be incurred should be inserted in the 'estimated' columns in the specific phases.

One obvious lacuna in the guidance relates to work that has already commenced post-issue, such as on an interim application, which by definition is not contingent, but which does not fit neatly into any of the phases, e.g. applications for interim payments, security for costs, etc. Remembering that the budget should inform the other parties and the court, there is a danger that the exercise becomes one of form over substance. However, the difficulty of where to include this work has become harder from April 2016. This is because before this date this type of work was often included as a contingency (even though that is not strictly correct), which enabled the court to see the sum already incurred on the application and the estimated sum to be incurred. Courts often took the view that so long as this work was clearly identified, and the budget attributed incurred and estimated expenditure transparently, it did not really matter that this was included as a contingency even though it is already a reality. That option no longer exists, as the amendments to the Precedent H in April 2016 understandably removed the incurred costs column from the contingency phase. This leaves the conundrum of whether to insert this work somewhere in Precedent H and, if so, where (this is considered further in **Q27** and **Q28** below).

The guidance also contains the occasional oddity:

---

[37] *Summit Navigation Ltd v Genrali Romania Asigurare* [2014] EWHC 398 (Comm) Leggatt J.

- Under the Case Management Conference ("CMC") phase the suggestion is that any subsequent CMC should not be included in this phase. This begs two obvious questions—why have an 'estimated' column for this phase and where does any budget for a subsequent CMC ordered by the court fit in the budget? Anecdotally, it seems that some courts are ignoring the guidance and budgeting for the cost of a later CMC in the 'estimated' column of Precedent H for this phase. Certainly this provides ready clarity when the budget comes to be examined against expenditure later. It also avoids the problem of where else to budget a future CMC as the guidance is silent upon this. As it is a certainty (as the court will have ordered it), it cannot be a contingency.
- Why is specific disclosure excluded from the disclosure phase when it is one of the types of disclosure order mentioned in the menu of orders at CPR r.31.5(7)? The answer, presumably, is that the original guidance form pre-dated the change to CPR r.31.5(7) and this has been overlooked on subsequent revisions. Whatever the reason it is unhelpful when the court is encouraging parties to move away from the default position of standard disclosure. As Jackson LJ saw disclosure as one of the most expensive phases of litigation and continues to encourage the proper use of the range of disclosure orders by parties and courts alike[38], it makes no sense that if the guidance is followed when the court makes an order under CPR r.31.5(7)(b), it does not budget the costs. If, as with non-party disclosure, it is deemed a contingent cost, this too appears illogical. This is because CPR r.31.5(7)(b) envisages a request for specific disclosure being made with disclosure of a party's own list. Accordingly, the time between case management order and compliance with the disclosure order is minimal. The notion that at the CMC this might be only a contingency is not credible. However, even if it is a contingency the court must budget it, so uncertainty over the proportionate expenditure cannot be the reason for it being excluded from the phase. As the court has to budget it anyway, why not do it within the phase within which it most naturally arises – namely disclosure? Another option is to regard specific disclosure as not reasonably to fall within the budget and so it falls to be dealt with under CPR r.3 PD E 7.9. However, it is hard to argue that something is reasonably not included when it is what the court is ordering to take place! The final option is to treat any subsequent request for specific disclosure as a 'significant development in the litigation' justifying a budget variation under CPR r.3 PD E 7.6. Again, it is difficult to see the occurrence of something the court has ordered as a 'significant development' when the guidance refers to costs under CPR r.7.6 as those 'which are not anticipated.' What makes the guidance even more confusing is that it suggests that work considering the scope of disclosure by other parties and undertaking investigations having reviewed that disclosure (which may well

---

[38] 'Disclosure' Lecture at the Law Society's Commercial Litigation Conference, 10 October 2016.

involve consideration of whether specific disclosure is required) should be included in this phase.

- Why is mediation (which is a form of ADR) specifically excluded from the ADR/Settlement phase and is to be included as a contingency? One answer may be so that the court can readily identify the costs attributable for this discrete form of ADR. However, if that is the case, this would sit more happily as a named phase rather than as a contingency.
- Why does the guidance note still refer to a 'Settlement' phase when Precedent H refers to 'Settlement/ADR?' This is a legacy of the pilot costs management budget forms.
- The PTR phase refers to "preparation of updated costs budgets and reviewing opponent's budget". However, budgets only need to be updated once set by the court in the event of 'significant developments in the litigation' under CPR r.3 PD E 7.6 and not as a matter of routine.

C. How does the court 'costs manage'?

4–18   The only provisions in respect of the form of the budgeting exercise itself are in CPR r.3.12, 3.15 and 3 PD E 7.3, 7.4 and 7.10. These provide that:

- The court cannot budget costs already incurred[39]. Having said that the court cannot budget costs already incurred, CPR r.3 PD E 7.4 seems to countenance a situation where costs incurred between the date of the budget and the date of the costs management hearing may be budgeted if the costs are being approved by the court. However, both CPR rules 3.12 and 3.15 use the words 'costs to be incurred'. As the rule takes precedence over the practice direction, it seemed clear that only future costs could be budgeted. However, the Court of Appeal in *SARPD Oil International Ltd v Addax Energy SA*[40] concluded, in the context of considering the relevance of an approved budget when setting the amount of security for costs, that the absence of the word 'agreed' from CPR r.3 PD E 7.4, meant that there was no restriction preventing the court making costs management orders in respect of incurred costs where the costs were said to be agreed. Anecdotally this caused many a sleepless night for those who had agreed budgeted costs prior to this decision, understanding this to be in respect of estimated costs only. Certainly the words 'to be incurred' in both CPR rules 3.12(2) and 3.15(1) are hard to reconcile with any sense of retrospection. To the relief of those seeking both clarity and proportionality of process (as the Court of Appeal had also suggested that the CCMC was the opportunity to contest 'incurred costs' – see **Q49**) the Civil Procedure Rules Committee ("CPRC") has reacted to amend the relevant rules to make it clear that budgeted costs under a costs management order are those that have not been incurred at the time of the costs management

---

[39] See **Q27** for further consideration of this.
[40] *SARPD Oil International Ltd v Addax Energy SA* [2016] EWCA Civ 120.

conference.[41] Accordingly from 6 April 2017 the short lived consequences of *SARPD Oil* will reverberate no more. However, from that date the court will have the additional option under CPR r.3.15(2)(c), by way of a costs management order, of 'recording the extent (if any) to which incurred costs are agreed'. In addition a new CPR r.3.15(4) now codifies that the court may make recitals by recording comments about incurred costs. Whilst this is nothing new, the fact that these 'are to be taken into account in any subsequent assessment proceedings' is an addition (and one repeated at CPR r.3.18(c)).

- The amendment at CPR r.3.13(1)(b) means that there is no longer any risk of significant delay between the preparation of the budget and the costs management hearing, save where the claim form statement of value is less than £50,000 (and the delay there should be shorter, because one would expect the budgets to be lower and therefore the hearing to require a lesser time estimate). However, if there is delay in listing in those cases parties may consider filing and exchanging updated budgets and making an application to be heard at the costs management for permission to rely on the updated budgets at that hearing. However, in this situation the court is likely to expect to see the same figure in the grand total on p.1 as in the earlier budget – for all that has changed is the passage of time means that some costs that were estimated in the future have now been incurred and so the incurred costs have gone up, but by the same amount. as the originally 'estimated' costs have reduced, unless during that 'delay period' the assumptions upon which the budget was originally prepared have altered. In all cases the parties must discuss their respective budgets and must file an agreed budget discussion report seven days before the CCMC.

- Whilst the court can only make a costs management order recording the extent of any agreement on incurred costs, these costs are still relevant to the wider costs management process. CPR r.3 PD E 7.4 provides that the court may record its comments on incurred costs and, more importantly, will take these into account when considering the reasonableness and proportionality of all subsequent costs. This means that when determining the sum to budget for costs 'to be incurred' for a phase, the court's decision will be informed by the amount already spent e.g. if the court concludes that the reasonable and proportionate sum for the disclosure phase is £8,000 and £6,000 has already been incurred, the budget for the phase will be £2,000. The treatment of incurred costs has arisen in a number of cases[42], has proved challenging, has resulted in a variety of approaches being adopted by the court and is considered in more detail in the Q&A section of this chapter.[43] In addition, the new CPR r.3.18(c)

---

[41] The Civil Procedure (Amendment) Rules 2017 SI 2017/95.

[42] e.g. in *CIP Properties (AIPT) v Galliford Try Infrastructure Ltd (Costs No.2)[2015] EWHC 481(TCC)* and *Yeo v Times Newspapers Ltd* [2015] EWHC 209 (QB).

[43] See Qs **44–47** for further consideration of this.

makes it clear that any comments recorded under CPR r.3 PD E 7.4 will be taken into account on any subsequent standard basis assessment.

- When undertaking the budgeting exercise, the court is only charged with setting a total sum which is reasonable and proportionate for each phase of the proceedings. The court is expressly not required to do a detailed assessment and, whilst it 'may have regard to the constituent elements of each total figure', it is not compelled to do so. In other words, the court simply sets one figure per phase for the future costs of that phase.

- The parties may agree budgets or discrete phases of the budgets. If they do this, then the court either makes a costs management order in respect of these costs recording the extent of the agreement or elects not to make a costs management order. Some see this as a curious provision. Whilst parties are to be encouraged to co-operate and narrow issues, the apparent inability of the court to interfere with agreement of what it may see as disproportionate costs seems an odd fetter in the pursuit of proportionality. If the court manages the case on a different basis from that upon which the parties have based their agreement of budget, then the court will expect the parties to revisit the budgets (as the basis upon which agreement has been reached has been altered). If, however, the proportionate case management directions are in line with those upon which agreement of budgets was reached, then the court either makes a costs management order on the basis of the agreement or makes no costs management order. Remember that costs (and costs liabilities to another party) are those of the client. Any agreement of all or part of a budget requires client approval, which is why access to the client during, or very specific instructions from the client before, a costs management hearing is essential.

In other words the precise mechanics of costs management are not prescribed. However, it is imperative that the exercise itself does not become disproportionate. The adoption of the broad brush of setting one total sum per phase as required under CPR r.3 PD E 7.3 combined with the avoidance of arguments that are of the type routinely raised at the assessment stage, seems to meet this requirement, both in respect of the proportionality of the exercise for the parties and for the court in allocating its resources between cases. That this was the intention was confirmed by Jackson LJ in his '*Confronting Costs Management*' lecture in May 2015 when he said this:

> "*At the conclusion of the exercise the court should approve a single total figure for each phase of the proceedings. The party is then free to spend that sum as it sees fit. The court should not specify rates or numbers of hours. That adds to the length of CCMCs and is unnecessary micro-management.*"[44]

The introduction of CPR r.3 PD E 7.10 from April 2016 reinforces this and should toll the death knell for the arguments of those keen that the court

---

[44] *Confronting costs management*, May 2015, para. 3.4.

should set an hourly rate and multiply it by an amount of time (despite the fact that CPR r.3 PD E 7.3 already disavowed this process).

Unfortunately, for a period this laudable intention of keeping the budgeting process proportionate and steering well clear of the micro management of a detailed assessment sat unhappily with the apparent 'call to arms' from the Court of Appeal in *SARPD Oil International v Addax Energy SA*[45] that:

> *"Parties coming to the first CMC to debate their respective costs budgets therefore know that that is the appropriate occasion on which to contest the costs items in those budgets, both in relation to the incurred costs elements in their respective budgets and in relation to the estimated costs elements."*

Anecdotally, it appears that first instance courts undertaking costs management, by reliance on CPR r.3 PD E 7.3 and 7.10 and by use of CPR r.44.3(5), have been resisting any attempts by parties to rely on the passage cited above in seeking to turn the budgeting exercise into a 'quasi' detailed assessment. As stated above it appears that amendments to the CPR will make it clear that the court cannot make a costs management order in respect of incurred costs unless they are agreed, otherwise its function in respect of those is limited to making comments and using these sums to inform the reasonable and proportionate sums to be budgeted for estimated costs, (the budgeted costs).

D. Variation of budgets

There is an apparent tension between CPR r.3.15(3), which requires the court to control the parties' budgets once a costs management order has been made, and CPR r.3 PD E 7.6, which suggests that where there is a significant development in the litigation that necessitates a variation to the budget, the parties should seek to agree this between themselves and only involve the court if agreement is not possible.   **4–19**

What is clear is that the budget may only be varied if there is a significant development in the litigation. Perhaps the dissipation of the tension lies here. It is hard to imagine a 'significant development' that does not require consequential case management. If further case management directions are proportionate, then inevitably, budgets will have to be re-visited and it is no surprise that the parties are encouraged to agree these. Of course, the court may take the view, informed by the revised budgets, that the directions sought are disproportionate and refuse them and the budget variation that accompanied them. The meaning of significant development is considered at **Q68** below.

CPR r.3 PD E 7.6 envisages both downward and upward budget revision. Examples of the former may be where a claimant discontinues part of a claim or where a defendant withdraws part of a defence and of the latter where a final prognosis in a personal injury claim provides a bleaker outlook than expected with a significant increase in future loss and the evidence in support of this. Clearly all of these are significant developments, affect the

---

[45] *SARPD Oil International Ltd v Addax Energy SA* [2016] EWCA Civ 120.

proportionality assessment under CPR r.44.3(5) and respectively are likely to result in lesser or increased costs being expended (see consideration of the decision in *Churchill v Boot*[46] at **Q68** below). A failure to seek a variation in respect of additional costs means that at least one party may have to rely upon 'good reason' to depart from the budget at any subsequent standard basis assessment (the paying party when the variation ought to have resulted in lesser expenditure and the receiving party when the variation has resulted in increased expenditure, unless appropriate concessions are made). A cross application of *Mitchell* suggests that an oversight is unlikely to be a 'good reason'. If a party fails to vary downwards when it should there is no obvious 'sanction' (treating any downward variation as an inevitability of reduced work rather than as a sanction). However, plainly if costs have to be assessed simply because a party has failed to vary downwards or make an appropriate concession when it ought to have done, that raises issues in respect of the costs of the assessment under CPR r.47.20(3).

If there was any doubt that the court may only permit variation in respect of costs 'to be incurred' (and it is hard to see why there should have been any doubt given the wording of CPR r.3 PDE 7.6 expressly refers to 'future costs'), this was dispelled in *Yeo v Times Newspapers Ltd*[47].

CPR r.3 PD E 7.9 makes it clear that discrete applications that were reasonably not included in the budget shall be treated as additional to the budgets. In such cases, the court will make an award of costs and, if that is for one party to pay the costs of another, undertake a summary assessment and order payment in the usual way (subject to any consideration of qualified one way costs shifting or indemnity issues deferring an immediate entitlement to be paid costs) with this having no impact on the budget. If the order is for 'costs in case', then these costs fall outside the budget, and are additional to it, at any subsequent assessment once an award of the costs of the case is made.

E. The effect of a costs management order on subsequent assessment

4–20 CPR r.3.18 clearly sets out that on a standard basis assessment, the court will not depart from the last approved or agreed budget for each phase without 'good reason'.

This provision applies to summary and detailed assessments. On a straightforward reading of this rule unless there is 'good reason', the budgeted costs will be assessed as budgeted and any assessment will focus on the non-budgeted costs. However, an argument has emerged that this provision may not be as transparent as it appears. This argument is considered below and, in more detail, at **Q76** below. Even if the rule does mean no more and no less than what it says at face value (and that is how we understand it,) it still begs the question 'What constitutes 'good reason''? There is no guidance to help answer this question in the rules.

---

[46] *Churchill v Boot* [2016] EWHC 1322 9QB.)
[47] *Yeo v Times Newspapers Ltd* [2015] EWHC 2132 (QB) para. 47.

One of the few reported authorities so far on CPR r.3.18 and departure from a budget in general terms and not in a specific situation (for an example of the latter see **Q32** below), presents more questions than answers. In *Simpson v MGN Ltd*[48] it was argued that where a party had exceeded its budget and there was no good reason for this, the inevitability was that under CPR r.3.18(b) the costs over and above the budget would not be recoverable. However, the court concluded that neither CPR r.3.18 nor CPR r.3 PDE prescribed an automatic sanction in this circumstance. Instead, the court adopted what it described as a just and proportionate sanction which involved *'an assessment which makes every assumption against the party which has failed to submit an amended budget, and properly compensates the defendant for the additional costs involved'*. It is arguable that whether or not CPR r.3.18(a) and (b) include a sanction is of academic interest only, as, on the simple construction referred to above, they combine to preclude departure from the agreed/approved budget for any phase in the absence of good reason. By contrast in *Sony Communications International AB v SSH Communications Security Corporation*[49], the court expressly concluded that CPR r.3.18 means exactly what is says – namely that there can only be departure from a budget with 'good reason'. The consideration of 'good reason' in *Simpson* is considered at **Qs 81** and **83** below and *Sony Communications* is explored further at **Q76**.

However, as indicated above, there seems to be a concerted challenge to this 'simple construction' in any event. The argument concludes with the proposition that the budget is only either a cap or some kind of 'draw down fund' and. as such, at the end of the claim there should be a traditional item by item assessment with the upshot that the receiving party recovers the lower of the budget or the item by item sum assessed for each phase. This is considered in detail in **Q76** below. For the moment, to remain with the decision in *Simpson*, there is no doubt that, at first blush, some support for this argument appears to emerge from that case, in particular from the comment of Warby J. That:

> *"It is clear from CPR 3.18(b) that if a figure has been agreed or approved for a particular phase of proceedings the amount recoverable by the receiving party in respect of that phase will be capped at that figure, unless there is good reason to depart upwards. (If the receiving party has incurred costs less than budgeted there will be good reason to depart downwards)."*

However, there is an equally clear analysis of this part of the judgment in *Simpson* that a) makes sense, when the cited passage is read with the rest of paragraph in which it arises, b) requires no additional words to be added to the quoted text to support an argument and c) permits CPR r.3.18 to say no more nor no less than it actually says with the result that, unsurprisingly given the clear wording of CPR r.3.18, there is no departure from the last agreed or

---

[48] *Simpson v MGN Ltd* [2015] EWHC 126 (QB).
[49] *Sony Communications International AB v SSH Communications Security Corporation* [2016] EWHC 2985 (Pat).

approved budget, upwards or downwards, for any phase absent 'good reason'. This analysis is that:

- The passage cited is selective. It is interesting to note that the paragraph from which the extract is taken begins by stating that *"It is clear that if costs management is to work conclusions reached upon reviewing costs budgets must be adhered to, and not second-guessed at a later stage."* In other words supporting entirely the certainty of outcome intended by costs management and dismissing the notion that the budgeted costs are subject to some subsequent re-determination.

- The challenge requires the court to have said *'If the receiving party has incurred less than budgeted <u>after an assessment</u>'*. It did not. As such the court appears, in fact, to have been making no more than the obvious point that breach of the indemnity principle would be a 'good reason' to depart from the budget. Accordingly, rather than *'costs being less than budgeted costs'* representing authority to embark upon an assessment of these costs, the court was simply making the trite observation that if, under the terms of the fee retainer, the amount for which the client is liable to his solicitor is less than the budgeted costs, then it would be a breach of the indemnity principle to recover costs beyond the extent of that liability and that would be 'good reason' to depart downwards from the budget. This interpretation sits entirely happily with the point made in the cited passage in the previous bullet point. On this construction *'incurred costs less than budgeted'* does not equate to *'incurred costs less than budgeted after an assessment'*. Precedent bill AB enables easy identification of where the indemnity principle would be breached without departure from the last approved/agreed budget, and the amount by which there should be departure for this 'good reason' (see page 9 of Precedent AB).

- Accordingly, rather than supporting an item by item assessment, *Simpson* does precisely the opposite and supports a simple construction of the words used in CPR r.3.18. That this is so is reinforced by the court expressly limiting its conclusions to the CPR PD3E para.7.6 consideration before it and adding that CPR r.3.18 is aimed *'at ensuring that once the court has reached a decision on what it is reasonable for a party to spend on a given phase that conclusion should be final in the absence of some good reason.'*

It seems that further court intervention on this topic is imminent (and may have occurred by the time of publication of this edition).[50] In the meantime, as stated, a more detailed analysis of the argument, which extends beyond *Simpson*, may be found at **Q76** below.

---

[50] The appeal in the case of *Merrix v Heart of England NHS Foundation Trust* [2016] EWHC EWHC B28, QB was to be heard on 16 February 2017, a matter of days before this edition went to press and at which point the outcome was not known. In any event it seems unlikely that the debate will end there.

In any event the provision at CPR r.3.18 does not apply to costs assessed on the indemnity basis. There was initially some suggestion within the pilot schemes that the budgets still formed the starting point for an assessment on the indemnity basis (see *Elvanite Full Circle Ltd v Amec Earth & Environmental (UK) Ltd*,[51] which advanced this proposition and *Kellie v Wheatley & Lloyd Architects Ltd*[52] which disagreed with that approach). This is not the position as proportionality has no place in an indemnity basis assessment and budgets have been produced and set by specific reference to proportionality. Any doubt was resolved by the Court of Appeal in *Denton v T H White*.[53] When referring to the consequence of an indemnity based costs order, the Master of the Rolls described it as follows:

> *"If the offending party ultimately loses, then its conduct may be a good reason to order it to pay indemnity costs. Such an order would free the winning party from the operation of CPR rule 3.18 in relation to its costs budget."*[54]

The intention is surely plain – that assessments, whether of a summary or detailed nature, will be both less time-consuming and more proportionate, because the court will be concerned only with determining the reasonableness of those costs that have not been budgeted and the overall proportionality cross check under CPR r.44.3(2)(a). An illustration of the ease of summary assessment where a budget has been set can be found in *Slick Seating Systems v Adams*,[55] where the trial judge concluded that the sum sought was within the budget for each phase, assessed in that sum and commented that detailed assessment had been rendered 'otiose'. Inevitably if the argument that the budget is no more than a cap or a fund prevails, the intention will be scuppered. On that basis even proponents of costs management will need to take stock as, if a traditional 'item by item' assessment is required in any event, it becomes hard/impossible to justify as purposeful and proportionate a process that adds significant cost, but neither provides the certainty of outcome to enable litigants to make informed decisions nor saves the time and cost (for parties and the court) of subsequent assessments.

The fact that an order for indemnity costs sees 'escape' from the constraints of the budget is not a reason for an increase in applications for such orders. The principles surrounding when the court will make an order for indemnity costs have not altered (save by the identification in *Denton* of a specific type of conduct that might merit such an award).

4–21

However, an indemnity costs award arising under CPR r.36.17(4)(b) presents unique challenges. A claimant is entitled to indemnity basis costs from "the date on which the relevant period expired" (relevant period is defined in CPR r.36.3(g)). However, this means that for some part of the litigation costs

---

[51] *Elvanite Full Circle Ltd v Amec Earth & Environmental (UK) Ltd* [2013] EWHC 1643 (TCC) Coulson J.
[52] *Kellie v Wheatley & Lloyd Architects Ltd* [2014] EWHC 2886 (TCC) HHJ Keyser QC.
[53] *Denton v T H White* [2014] EWCA Civ 906.
[54] para.43 majority judgment.
[55] *Slick Seating Systems v Adams* [2013] EWHC 1642 (QB) HHJ Simon Brown QC.

are constrained by the budget (absent 'good reason') and, for another part, the budget becomes irrelevant. However, the chance of the date when this transition takes place falling neatly at the end of a phase of Precedent H so it is clear which parts of the budget remain wholly relevant is slim (not non-existent, e.g. if the relevant period expired just before trial it may be possible to identify the phases clearly).

What happens in this situation where only part of the phase falls to be assessed on the standard basis? Sadly the answer is not clear. It is arguable that as the court is not looking at a phase exclusively on the standard basis, then CPR r.3.18 has no application or if it does, then this is a 'good reason' to depart from the budget. However, this potentially presents a windfall to the receiving party beyond the ordinary benefit of an indemnity costs order. Even if this is the position, the court is still required to undertake an assessment in part on the standard basis and in part on the indemnity basis and the proportionality cross-check pursuant to CPR r.44.3(2)(a) continues to apply to the standard basis costs. Does this mean that bills where there is a relevant CPR r.36 offer will need to be split between dates as well as, within the new format bill, phases matching the Precedent H? Certainly the new Precedent Q of the Costs Precedents provides no assistance with the division of phases between those on a standard and those on an indemnity basis. At the moment questions abound and there are no clear answers.

Those accepting a CPR Pt 36 offer, but then seeking an order for costs on the indemnity basis (in order to escape from the confines of a budget), should take note of the decision in *Courtwell Properties Ltd v Greencore PF (UK) Ltd*,[56] in which Akenhead J stated:

> "In cases where the parties have settled through the Part 36 procedure or otherwise but leave the judge to decide costs, particularly where indemnity costs are claimed, parties must act in a proportionate way. There can be few if any cases in which there should in effect be a trial of all or some of the settled issues in the case. Where the indemnity cost application depends on evidence which is likely to involve material conflicts of evidence, the applicant party needs to think long and hard about whether it is appropriate to pursue the application."[57]

Case and costs management in harmony

4–22   Having identified the key case management amendments and the costs management provisions, the practical link between the two becomes obvious. By requiring the court to costs manage by phases (which broadly equate to the procedural steps on the way to trial), the court is able to tailor the directions to the reasonable and proportionate cost of the respective phases. This should result in the court:

---

[56] *Courtwell Properties Ltd v Greencore PF (UK) Ltd* [2014] EWHC 184 (TCC) Akenhead J.
[57] para.42.

- Selecting the appropriate form of disclosure from the options at CPR r.31.5(7), which includes the possibility of dispensing with disclosure altogether.
- Controlling the number of witnesses, the issues they may address and the length of their statements (CPR r.32.2(3)).
- Controlling the extent of expert evidence by number, by reliance on jointly instructed experts, by specific identification of the issues upon which they may report and by the use of concurrent evidence at trial.
- Conducting ongoing case and costs management preventing claims changing fundamentally in nature without court intervention. Any variation in the budget is linked to 'significant developments in the litigation'. It is hard to imagine any such developments that do not require further court case management directions. At such a stage the ongoing control of the parties' budgets required by CPR r.3.15 and the requirement at CPR r.3.17 for the court to take account of the costs in each procedural step, combine so that the court must determine the extent, if at all, to which it is prepared to permit the claim to change course.
- Limiting the trial length. In a sense one should start here, for the assessment of proportionality dictates the trial length and all other directions must then be crafted to ensure that the trial can be completed within that period. Inevitably this informs the court's decisions on the matters listed above.
- Conducting a summary rather than detailed assessment at the conclusion of the trial. In some cases the 'costs of the costs' are disproportionate. One way to avoid this is for the court to undertake more assessments on a summary basis.

What is clear from the consideration of case and costs management above is that this presents new challenges to both the judiciary and court users (albeit that the exact nature of some of those challenges requires procedural rule and/or jurisprudential clarification as arguments are advanced to 'test' the parameters of the rules as they stand). All must now be astute to ensure that rules, practice directions and orders are followed and to 'cut the cloth' proportionately. For the court this may mean deciding cases on more limited evidence than might previously have been available. For the professions this, inevitably, places a far greater emphasis on compliance with timetables and the management of client expectations. For the parties they have to co-operate with timescales and temper their expectation of a case being dealt with justly to what outcome can be achieved at a proportionate cost.

Questions and answers

A. The scope of the costs management scheme

Q1. How prescriptive is the wording of CPR r.3.12(1) and (1A)? In particular can the court costs manage cases that fall within the definition of

those outside the scheme and when may the court exclude cases from the regime under CPR r.3.12(1)(e)?

4–23   The wording of CPR 3.12(1) and (1A) allows the court flexibility, both of an inclusionary and exclusionary nature.

Under CPR r.3.12(1A) it may bring into the costs management regime other proceedings. Although a case involving consideration of the provisions in force from 1 April 2013 until 22 April 2014, Coulson J considered the question of extension of the regime in *CIP Properties (AIPT) Ltd v Galliford Try Infrastructure Ltd*.[58] In this case the claim was put in the region of £18,000,000 – so in excess of both the £2,000,000 cut off in place until 22 April 2014 and the £10,000,000 cut off since that date. He concluded that the provision at CPR r.3.12(1A), and in particular the reference to 'any other proceedings', did indeed extend to multi-track claims worth £10,000,000 or more, stating:

> "I take the view that the exercise of the court's discretion under CPR 3.12(1) is unfettered. There is nothing in the CPR to suggest otherwise. This discretion extends to all cases where the claim is for more than £2 million (old regime) and £10 million (new regime). . .There is no presumption against ordering budgets in claims over £2 million or £10 million, and no additional burden of proof on the party seeking the order."[59]

Coulson J recognised that to have concluded otherwise would have left the court's hands tied and the system open to abuse by claimants wishing to avoid the costs management regime simply valuing their claims at £1 more than the cut off.

The fact that the regime is sufficiently flexible to permit costs management in cases not strictly within the provisions is, in any event, borne out by the express provision in CPR r.3 PD E 2. This allows the court, whether on the application of a party or of its own initiative, to costs manage in those cases where the parties are not required to file budgets under CPR rules 3.12 and 3.13. CPR r.3 PD E 5 sets out examples of cases strictly outside the regime where it may be particularly appropriate to costs manage. The fact that the £10 million limit is not a bar is reinforced by the inclusion in CPR r.3 PD E 5 of personal injury and clinical negligence cases where the value exceeds that sum.

The reverse position is envisaged by CPR r.3.12(1)(e), which permits the court to disapply the regime in multi-track Part 7 claims that would otherwise fall within the provisions.

If the court does not do so prior to the deadline for filing and exchanging budgets then the court must make a decision not to costs budget based on CPR r.3.15(2) – namely that it is satisfied that the litigation can be conducted justly and at proportionate cost in accordance with the overriding objective without a costs management order.

---

[58] *CIP Properties (AIPT) Ltd v Galliford Try Infrastructure Ltd* [2014] EWHC 3546 (TCC) Coulson J.
[59] para.27.

Cases where the court disapplies the regime before the filing and exchange of budgets ought to be rare (save for example where temporary exclusions are given, such as that which was given to clinical negligence before the Queen's Bench Masters). The reason for this is that it is hard to see how the court can reconcile the obligation imposed on it by the overriding objective and, more specifically by CPR r.3.17 (to take into account the costs of each procedural step) without any information about costs.

If the parties wish to persuade the court that a case is not suitable for costs management then they should apply before the expiry of the time for filing and exchanging budgets both to disapply the regime and, in the alternative, for an extension of time to file and exchange budgets until a date after the determination of the application in the event that the primary application is refused. If they do this and the court dismisses the application to disapply the costs management provisions, then the parties are dealing with an application to extend time and not an application for relief from the sanction under CPR r.3.14 (see consideration of *Hallam Estates v Baker*[60] in **Q21** below).

In *Sharp (and the other claimants detailed in the GLO Register) v Blank*[61], the court had to grapple with whether or not a claim fell within the costs management regime. The situation was where a claimant indicated on the Claim Form that the claim had a value of over £25,000 (and so complied with CPR r.16.3(2)(b)(iii)), gave no value in the 'amount claimed' box on the Claim Form, but it subsequently transpired the claim had a value in excess of £10 million. On the face of the rules, the court concluded this type of case was strictly caught by the costs management provisions, even though it was known by the time of the case management hearing that the claim value exceeded £10 million. Nugee J concluded that it might be useful for CPR r.16.3 to require confirmation of whether or not a claim exceeds £10 million, which would avoid this situation arising, but then used *'unless the court otherwise orders'* in CPR r.3.13 to dispense with budgets in the particular case.

Q2. Can the court order a litigant in person to file and serve a Precedent H?

In *Campbell v Campbell*[62] the Chief Chancery Master decided that a litigant in person could opt to file a budget or the court could order him to do so. He reached this conclusion on the basis that:

4–24

- CPR r.3.12(2) sets out the objective of the costs management, it is in general terms and gives no indication that litigants in person will not benefit from the regime
- The words *'unless the court orders'* otherwise' in CPR r.3.13(1) amount to

---

[60] *Hallam Estates v Baker* [2014] EWCA Civ 661.
[61] *Sharp(and the other claimants in the GLO Register) v Blank* [2015] EWHC 2685 (Ch).
[62] *Campbell v Campbell* [2016] EWHC 2237 (Ch).

an enabling provision under which a litigant in person, otherwise not required to file and exchange a budget, could be ordered to do so.

- Litigants in person fall within those to whom CPR r.3.15(2) applies when it provides for the court to manage costs to be incurred *'by any party'*.
- CPR r.3 PDE permits the court to order filing and exchange of costs budgets even in those cases not otherwise falling within CPR rules 3.12 and 3.13.
- There is nothing in the remainder of CPR r.3 PDE that precludes a litigant in person filing and exchanging a budget. In particular, the reference in 3 PDE 7.8 to a litigant in person not being *'required to prepare a budget'* does not mean that a litigant in person may never be required to serve a budget.

Notwithstanding this decision, there is certainly a procedural argument that may lead to a different conclusion. This is that:

- CPR r.3.13(1) does not provide this enabling provision. An alternative interpretation is that the words *'unless the court otherwise orders'* actually permit the court to disapply the requirement on all non-litigant in person parties to file and exchange budgets or to vary the time within which they must do so. In other words this rule simply requires all non-litigant in person parties in cases falling within the regime (as set out in CPR r.3.12) to file and exchange budgets *'unless the court orders otherwise'* and prescribes the time when they are to do so, *'unless the court orders otherwise'*.
- Whilst litigants in person are not listed amongst the exceptions in CPR r.3.12(1), as there cannot be costs management without a party filing and exchanging a budget, the effect of CPR r.3.13(1) is plainly to except them from the costs management regime.
- Accordingly neither of the more general provisions relating to costs managing the costs of the parties or any party in CPR rules 3.12(2) and 3.15(1) apply.
- CPR r.3.12(1A) does not assist as it is not the proceedings that are excepted from the costs management regime, but a particular party.
- CPR r.3 PDE 2 only assists in cases either where all parties are litigants in person as it only provides a discretion in cases where the parties, as opposed to a party or any party, are not required to file and exchange costs budgets under CPR rules 3.12 and 3.13 or where the case is excepted from the regime under CPR r.3.12.

The last point best illustrates the unsatisfactory nature of this argument (as why should the court a) be precluded from ordering a litigant in person to file and exchange a budget where the other party is represented, but could impose the regime if all parties are litigants in person or b) be permitted to exercise its discretion in any case where costs management does not automatically apply, but not in cases within the regime under CPR r.3.12?). Whilst Higher court authority would clarify the position once and for all, subject to the practical difficulty set out below, we suspect that the court will, in appropriate cases, wish to have the ability to order litigants in person to file and serve costs budgets to enable it to consider costs managing part of the costs and so will prefer a procedural interpretation that permits this. An appropriate case might well be one such as confronted the court in *Campbell*. In what is likely to become an increasingly frequent situation, the litigant in person was assisted by counsel under a direct access instruction. In such situations one can well understand the desire of the court to exercise some budgetary control of the direct access costs and to impose the costs management regime.

As stated above, there is a practical difficulty supporting the exclusion of litigants in person from the costs management regime. It stems from the fact that budgets are not set by rate multiplied by time (see para.**4–18** and **Q50 below**). Instead the court sets a sum per phase that is reasonable and proportionate under CPR rules 44.4(3) and 44.3(5). However, this will necessarily not equate to what a litigant in person will recover because such a party is limited to £19 per hour, his actual financial loss or a combination of both and in any case that cannot exceed 2/3rd of that which would have been allowed if that party were legally represented. The costs management exercise is expressly not a detailed assessment and does not involve CPR r.46.5 (express provisions for litigant in person costs). Accordingly, when dealing with litigant in person costs there seems an inevitability that any budget set by reference to CPR rules 44.4(3) and 44.3(5) must be revisited under 'good reason' in CPR r.3.18 as the budget will not have taken account of the constraints imposed by CPR r.46.5. Accordingly, in many cases the time and cost involved in budgeting litigant in person costs seems destined to be wasted. However, this simply means that the court must be selective if it determines that it has the jurisdiction to order a litigant in person to file and serve a budget as to those cases in which it decides to do so. Examples of cases where it may be appropriate are those where:

- It is clear that the litigant in person proposes to incur direct access fees and other fees for legal services and expert assistance.
- The detail provided will inform the court to enable it to case manage proportionately.

A final point is that if the court does order a litigant in person to file and exchange a budget then, unless it also makes a further specific order to the contrary, CPR r.3.13(2) still applies, leading to the curious position of that party not having to file a Precedent R (budget discussion report) in respect of any represented party's budget, but any represented party having to file Precedent R in respect of the litigant in person's budget.

Q3. Do the costs management provisions at CPR r.3.12–3.18 apply to cases in the Chancery Division?

4-25   Yes, in principle, they do in respect of those claims that fall within CPR r.3.12. The Chancery Guide (Last amended November 2016) contains a chapter on case and costs management (Chapter 17) that applies save in respect of claims in the Patents Court, claims in either of the Shorter Trials or the Flexible Trials pilot schemes (CPR r.51 PDN) and claims in the Financial List (r.51 PDM). **Q13** below considers separately why parties might want the court to consider costs managing within the Shorter Trials Scheme as para.2.56 of CPR r.51 PDN, which excludes the provision of CPR r.3.12, expressly permits the parties to agree to costs management. Remember also that CPR r.3.12 excludes CPR r.8 claims from automatically coming within the costs management regime and, as many Chancery claims will fall within CPR r.8, that will, inevitably, reduce the incidence of costs management in these cases.

However, recently there have been two reported developments that may limit the application of the costs management regime in Chancery cases further. These are as follows:

- The appearance on the Chancery Bar Association website of an informal note (expressly stated not to be a Practice Note) from the Senior Chancery Master dated 1 November 2016 detailing how the Chancery Division in London approaches the subject of costs management. The upshot of this is that parties are invited to consider jointly whether they want the court to exercise its costs management powers. Even if there is agreement that the parties do not want the court to exercise its powers, parties must still serve and file Precedent H. This, then, enables the court to make an informed decision under CPR r.3.15(2) as to whether it is satisfied that the litigation can be conducted justly at reasonable and proportionate cost in accordance with the overriding objective. Extending the provision at CPR r.3 PD E 6(c), the note permits parties who agree to exclude costs management to file and serve only page 1 of Precedent H even where the practice direction strictly requires the full form (although any CPR aficionado will have spotted that the note incorrectly suggests that one of the permitted instances in the rules for page 1 only is where the costs are 'less than £25,000'. In fact the exception is where the costs <u>do not exceed £25,000</u>). The agreement of the parties is not determinative and the informal note lists a number of factors that the court will consider, whilst stressing that the decision is case specific – the agreement of the parties, the type and size of the claim, the costs contained in the budgets and the extent to which there is equality of arms. A case is unlikely to be taken out of the costs management regime where one of the parties is a litigant in person or where a represented party objects.
- The suggestion that a similar approach is adopted by Chancery District Registries. There appears to be a six month pilot running in Leeds which permits parties, when filing their directions questionnaires, to express a wish to limit the extent of costs budgeting. They must still file a budget (but again adopting only page 1 of Precedent H). The pilot provides that if the

court considers the budgets to be reasonable and proportionate an order may be made dispensing with costs management under CPR r.3.15(2).

Some obvious points arise:

1. Those practising in the Queen's Bench Division and the County Court may pause to wonder why similar possibilities for exception from the regime do not apply to their cases.
2. Under the pilot, if the court considers the budgets to be reasonable and proportionate then why not make a costs management order, as that will avoid the possibility of the costs escalating to figures that are not reasonable and proportionate by the time a claim is concluded (and experience from the costs capping regime suggests that costs that did not satisfy the requirements for a costs capping order at the time of an interim application did not necessarily stay at that level)? The cost of preparing a budget (albeit in a reduced format) has been incurred and the court has invested time in examining it. The additional time and expense in taking that a step further to provide certainty going forward by making a costs management order seems, in context, relatively minor and almost as quick as making an order to dispense with costs management. The budgeting exercise could be done as a paper one at the same time as the court approves the agreed directions, with a right to apply under CPR r.3.3(5) if a party is dissatisfied (although dissatisfaction seems unlikely unless parties envisage exceeding the estimated costs, in which case a costs management order is necessary anyway).
3. The pilot is silent on service/exchange of the abridged Precedents H. Clearly that stage must take place for parties to satisfy themselves on an informed basis that it is in the interests of their clients to forego costs management.
4. The pilot only applies where the parties also file agreed case management directions. However, the dispensation from costs management is solely linked to whether the budgets are reasonable and proportionate – indeed the wording suggests that the court will only consider whether the agreed directions can be approved after it has decided whether or not to dispense with costs management (see – "*The court will also <u>then</u> consider whether the agreed directions can be approved*") [our emphasis]. What happens if the court does not approve the agreed directions upon which the budgets are agreed and, presumably, upon which the budgets were predicated to be proportionate, but has decided that the budgets are reasonable and proportionate? In other words, as case and costs management go hand in hand, should one actually read the pilot to say that the court will only make an order dispensing with costs management if, having considered them together, the court is satisfied that the agreed directions and the costs budgets are all reasonable and proportionate. Certainly CPR r.3.17 requires the court to consider available budgets when making any case

management decision. If the court does not approve the directions as reasonable and proportionate, it is difficult to see how it can determine that the discretion to dispense with costs management arises and so, presumably, in such a situation such an order will not be made. In these cases, where the costs exceed £25,000 or the stated value of the claim is £50,000 or more, will the court then order full Precedents H?

5. Does CPR r.44 PD 3 apply to these short form Precedents H? It is certainly arguable that these budgets have not been filed in accordance with CPR r.3 PD E, but under a pilot or an 'informal note' (this is particularly true in respect of those forms that under r.3 PD E 6(c) should be full budgets, but under the pilot are page 1 only). If the pilot and 'informal note' are treated as the court ordering 'otherwise' under CPR r.3 PD E 6(a), then the budgets do fall within CPR r.44 PD 3.

Q4. Can parties agree to dispense with costs management?

4–26   Whilst it is open to parties to agree to dispense with costs management, they will still need to persuade the court to do so (even under the 'Informal Note' and 'Pilot' referred to in **Q3** above). As a general rule expect the court to approach such an agreement with caution. In *Agents Mutual Limited v Gasgoine Halman*[63], notwithstanding a consent order made in the Chancery Division dispensing with costs management, this was found not to have effect in the Competition Appeals Tribunal ("the Tribunal"). The judge also found that even if there were an agreement in the tribunal to dispense with costs management that would not be determinative, but merely a factor to consider.

If parties wish to seek dispensation from costs management, then to avoid preparing, filing and exchanging Precedent H they must apply to dispense with/defer costs management before the date prescribed for compliance or find themselves caught by the provisions of CPR r.3.14. For the reason given in **Q1** above in relation to the court's obligation under CPR rules 1 and 3.17, it is difficult to see any situation where the court would dispense with Precedents H. Once Precedents H are filed and exchanged, then the parties will have to satisfy the court under CPR r.3.15(2) (see **Q1** above). If successful in persuading the court at this stage, the parties should remember that CPR r.44 PD 3 then applies in respect of the costs budgets that were filed.

Q5. Does costs management apply to the disposal stage of a claim after the entry of a default judgment for damages to be decided by the court?

4–27   Strictly a disposal hearing is defined in CPR r.26 PD 12.4 as a hearing that will not exceed 30 minutes and at which the court will not take oral evidence. Such claims are not allocated to track (unless they are within the small claims limit and are allocated to that track – see CPR r.PD 12.3(2)). Accordingly, claims listed for disposal are not allocated to the multi-track and they do not fall within the costs management regime under CPR r.3.12.

---

[63] *Agents Mutual Limited v Gasgoine Halman* [2016] CAT 20.

However, parties often refer to a disposal hearing when, in fact, they mean a trial on quantum where the final hearing will exceed 30 minutes and at which oral evidence will be given. These cases should be allocated. If they are allocated to the multi-track, then, as CPR r.7 multi-track cases, the costs management provisions apply. In such cases there may not be any requirement to file directions questionnaires under CPR r.26.3. Instead the file may be referred to the District Judge on entry of the judgment for damages to be decided to give directions. Prior to the introduction of costs management, the District Judge might have ordered the filing of directions questionnaires, listed the claim for case management conference or given directions as a paper exercise. The likelihood now is that the last of those options is unlikely to occur in cases where allocation is to the multi-track. Accordingly, parties should be astute to when a Precedent H is triggered under the provisions of CPR r.3.13 in these cases. **Q14** below provides more detailed consideration of relevant time limits, but this does not cover the situation where the statement of value of the claim is for less than £50,000, but there is no requirement to file a directions questionnaire as neither CPR r.3.13 (1)(a) nor (b) appear to envisage this situation. It seems that if the court still requires a directions questionnaire by express order then CPR r.3.13(1)(a) will apply in this situation, but if it does not, then there is no direct provision, but if the court orders a case management hearing without expressly ordering a Precedent H, it would still be prudent to comply with CPR r.3.13(1)(b) (see *Jamadar* at **4–05** above). If the statement of value of the claim is for £50,000 or more, then CPR r.3.13(1)(b) certainly applies.

Q6. Do the provisions apply to a claim brought under CPR r.8, where the court has expressly listed a case management conference?

No, unless the court has also expressly made an order requiring the parties to file and exchange costs budgets. As set out in the text above the costs management provisions from April 2014 do not apply to CPR r.8 claims (see CPR r.3.12(1)). Whilst the court retains a discretion under CPR r.3.12(1A) and CPR r.3 PD E 2 to bring claims that would not otherwise be subject to costs management into the regime, this would require an express order.

4–28

The court may convene a directions hearing before giving directions in CPR r.8 claims (see CPR r.8 PD 6.4). If no order for costs budgets has been made, the description of the hearing as a 'case management conference' rather than as a directions hearing carries no significance other than to distinguish the hearing from a final one.

Q7. Do Landlord and Tenant Act 1954 lease renewal claims automatically fall within the costs management regime?

It is important to remember that Landlord and Tenant Act 1954 ("the statute") claims are split into two distinct types. The first is those where the claim is unopposed and the second is where the claim is opposed. We shall look at each separately.

4–29

An unopposed claim is defined by CPR r.56.3.2(b) as being where the grant of a new tenancy is not opposed (although there may be disagreement as to the precise terms). CPR r.56.3(3) provides that where the claim is an unopposed one, then r.8 procedure must be adopted. Under CPR r.3.12 such a claim does not automatically fall within the costs management regime.

An opposed claim is defined by CPR r.56.3(2)(c) as one where a new tenancy is opposed under s.24 of the statute or where the claim is for termination of the tenancy under s.29 of the statute. CPR r.56.3(4) provides that where the claim is an opposed one, then CPR r.7 procedure must be adopted. The question then is whether or not the claim is allocated to the multi-track. The likelihood is that it will be, as, even if it is allocated to the fast track, District Judges cannot hear these claims (see CPR r.2 BPD 11.1(a)). If it is allocated to the multi-track then as a CPR r.7 claim in that track it is within the regime unless it is one of the exceptions. The only one of relevance is CPR r.3.12(1)(b) as this is a non-monetary claim. However, non-monetary claims only come within the exception from the regime if the claim form contains a statement of value of £10 million or more. As this is unlikely, then it appears that most opposed renewals do automatically fall within the costs management regime. Amongst other issues, this immediately creates the potential for tension between CPR r.3 PD E 6(a) that requires the Precedent H to extend to cover the whole proceedings and CPR r.56 PD 3.16, which provides that unless the circumstances of the case render it unreasonable to do so, any grounds of opposition shall be tried as a preliminary issue – suggesting that initially Precedent H should be limited to the costs of the preliminary issue. In these circumstances it may be prudent to seek a specific direction that Precedent H may be so limited before the date for filing and exchanging Precedent H expires. The risk is that the court finds such an application unnecessary, but the wasted costs will be significantly less than those lost if the sanction in CPR r.3.14 is applied.

Q8. Must parties file and exchange Precedents H in possession claims under CPR r.55 which the court concludes are genuinely disputed on grounds which appear substantial, which the court then allocates to the multi-track and lists for a CMC?

4–30 No. Possession claims are issued under CPR r.55 and CPR r.55.3(5), 55 PD 1.5 and CPR r.4 PD provide that claim form N5 (Claim form for possession of property) must be used. Accordingly the claim is not a CPR r.7 claim and its allocation to multi-track does not automatically bring it within the costs management regime. However, the court may still exercise its discretion under CPR r.3 PDE 2(a) ordering parties to file and exchange budgets, but this will be by a specific order to that effect.

Q9. Are claims where the claimant has a limited or severely impaired life expectation (defined as five years or less of life remaining) excluded from the costs management regime without the need for any court order to that effect?

No. These claims do not fall within the exceptions expressly set out in CPR r.3.12(1). However, CPR r.3 PDE 2(b) states that in such claims the court will ordinarily disapply costs management. This suggests that the court is required to specify that the regime will not apply and practitioners should not simply assume that it will not apply. If there is no specific order in a case disapplying the provisions of Section II of CPR r.3, parties would be well advised either to raise this with the court before any date under CPR r.3.13(1) expires or comply by filing and exchanging budgets in accordance with that provision.

4–31

Q10. What should parties do when the notice of provisional allocation under CPR r.26.3 is to the multi-track, but one or more parties believe that the appropriate allocation is to the fast track?
The risk of ignoring the consequence of the provisional allocation to multi-track in claims where the statement of value of the claim is less than £50,000 and simply filing a directions questionnaire with proposed directions seeking allocation to the fast track but without a Precedent H, or, in claims with a stated value on the Claim Form of £50,000 or more, failing to file one 21 days before the CCMC, is that if the court concludes that the provisional allocation was appropriate, then there is a breach of CPR r.3.13 and the consequences of CPR r.3.14 apply. A more prudent approach is to file a consent application (if all parties agree that the provisional allocation is inappropriate) or an on notice application (if all parties do not agree that the provisional allocation is inappropriate) prior to the date for filing and exchanging costs budgets, seeking an extension of the time for so doing until a date to be fixed after determination of the appropriate track at an allocation hearing. This avoids the potentially wasted expense of producing a Precedent H if subsequently the court allocates other than to the multi-track, but means that the argument is one of extension of time for compliance under CPR r.3.13 and not relief from the sanction of 3.14 if the court maintains the provisional allocation to multi-track.

4–32

However, one of the major criticisms of the costs management regime is that there is a significant delay between the listing and hearing of a CCMC. If there is an argument on appropriate allocation the court will need to convene an allocation hearing and then, if it decides to allocate to the multi-track, at that juncture list a CCMC. The scope for delay is obvious. One way to ameliorate this without pre-determining what the decision of the court may be on allocation is to suggest that the court lists a short allocation hearing as soon as possible and, in the same request, ask it to list a separate full CCMC as soon as possible after the allocation hearing (allowing time for Precedents H to be filed and exchanged, if the outcome of the allocation hearing renders them relevant, after the allocation hearing but before the CCMC). If the allocation hearing results in allocation to the fast-track, then the CCMC may be vacated. If the allocation hearing results in allocation to the multi-track, there will only be a short delay between this decision and the CCMC. This may be easier to arrange in some courts than others (as quite often the time can be backed or there is always box work so the vacation of a CCMC does not result in a disproportionate waste of court time). Certainly some courts are already adopting this approach in this situation.

Q11. Does the fact that a party has a contractual right to indemnity costs against the other party mean costs management is not applicable or pointless because the claimant has a contractual right to claim costs under *Gomba Holdings (UK) Ltd v Minories Finance Ltd (No.2)*?[64]

4–33   Whilst the position of the contractual costs of a mortgagee may be some-what different from those parties holding contractual rights to costs in other situations, this question seems directed to those cases where, in one form or another, there is a contractual right to costs on an indemnity basis between the parties in favour of one party, which is known about at the time that costs management would ordinarily arise.

The position is really a matter for the court. Whilst there is merit in avoiding the time and expense of budgeting by not costs managing the costs of the party who will rely upon the contractual obligation, the court still has a duty to case manage proportionately. Knowing what that party sees as the proportionate expenditure for the directions it advances will assist the court in determining the proportionate procedural approach to adopt. By so doing the court may, incidentally, reduce the costs due under the contract, as the directions proposed may not be proportionate and the effect of a different procedural route to trial may well limit what is reasonably incurred and reasonable in amount under the contractual entitlement.

Q12. Can the court costs manage detailed assessment proceedings?

4–34   Some see it as curious that claims worth £25,001 are subject to the full rigour of the costs management regime and yet detailed assessments, where the costs claimed may run into many millions and the 'costs of the costs' proceedings are substantial, fall outside the provisions. We say 'fall outside' as Precedent H specifically excludes the costs of detailed assessment (although this does not seem to stop some parties erroneously including these costs as a contingency).

However, there seems to be no reason why the court cannot exercise its power under CPR r.3.12(1A) to costs manage detailed assessment proceedings where that is appropriate. CPR r.47.1 clearly implies that the substantive proceedings are over by the time of assessment and CPR r.47.6 expressly refers to detailed assessments as 'proceedings'—both suggesting that detailed assessments are 'proceedings' in their own right (an interpretation supported by *Crosbie v Munroe*[65]) and capable of consideration under CPR r.3.12(1A).

The difficulty with costs management of detailed assessment proceedings is when and how it is undertaken. This raises many of the same arguments as to the inability of the court to costs manage 'incurred costs' (and particularly

---

[64] *Gomba Holdings (UK) Ltd v Minories Finance Ltd (No.2)* [1993] Ch 171.
[65] *Crosbie v Munroe* [2003] EWCA Civ 350.

pre-action costs) other than by recording agreement in substantive proceedings. Does the court decide to budget whenever it makes an order for detailed assessment so that costs are managed from the inception of the process even though this will require a significant time and costs investment when most costs are settled without there even being a request for a detailed assessment hearing under CPR r.47.14? In addition, at that stage it may not be known whether or not the assessment will fall within the Provisional Assessment provisions of CPR r.47.15, with capped costs of £1,500 in which case costs management is plainly inappropriate. However, if an early decision to costs manage is not made, there is a real danger in most cases, that by the time the court does step in all that remains is the assessment hearing itself and significant costs have already been incurred in settlement skirmishes, preparation of the bill, drafting of the Points of Dispute and any Replies to them. This is against a backdrop of repeated concern expressed by the judiciary about the 'costs of the costs'.

Inevitably, the consideration above leads to the conclusion that costs management is an option in detailed assessment proceedings, but that its suitability is entirely case specific. It will require robust costs and case management by the costs judge or costs officer and an early identification of those cases where costs management is purposeful – which essentially means that it is, in context, a proportionate exercise. In practice, complex assessment proceedings are already the subject of robust case management, with the resolution of preliminary issues often leading to settlement.

Q13. The Shorter Trial Pilot Scheme available for certain claims issued after 1 October 2015 under CPR r.51 PD N disapplies CPR r.3.12 and the costs management regime unless the parties agree otherwise (CPR r.51 PD N 2.58). Why might parties wish to opt in?

Ignoring the larger debate raised by this question of the merits of the costs management regime generally (and for those interested in this, Jackson LJ set out seven benefits in his *'Confronting costs management'* lecture in May 2015[66]), there may be case specific reasons for departure from the general rule in the Shorter Trial Scheme pilot. Certainly the scheme is designed to avoid protracted disputes and ensure proportionate directions (e.g. as to disclosure, witness statements, experts, interim applications, trial, summary assessment and appeals), by robust prescribed case management and determination at various stages on paper, where appropriate. These address some of the perceived 'ills' that costs management is designed to prevent and the general rule avoids the expense of the costs management exercise. However, there may still be valid reasons that parties opt for costs management. The three most significant seem to be:

4–35

- The clients may wish this to ensure that the shorter trial scheme provides 'up front' certainty as to potential costs exposure.

---

[66] *'Confronting costs management'* May 2015 paras 2.2–2.12.

- Linked to this, reinforcing the lack of certainty, is that no costs management exposes all the costs to the CPR r.44.3(2)(a) proportionality cross check on summary assessment after the costs have been incurred. This may result in the receiving party recovering a lesser amount than expected as proportionality 'trumps' both reasonable and necessary expenditure. In other words, whilst work may have been reasonably or necessarily incurred under a specific direction, if the total, when judged retrospectively against the relevant factors at CPR r.44.3(5), is deemed disproportionate, the costs will be reduced to that sum which is determined to be proportionate.
- CPR r.51 PD N 2.57 and 2.58 require parties to file and exchange costs schedules containing 'sufficient detail of the costs incurred in relation to each applicable phase identified by Precedent H to the costs budgeting regime. . .'. In other words the parties must record time by phase in any event so that they can produce this detail at the conclusion of the claim. As such the only real saving is the initial costs of budgeting and the costs of managing expenditure under the budget. In some cases this saving may not seem proportionate when viewed against the uncertainty referred to in the two points above.

B. The time for filing and exchanging Precedent H

Q14. In respect of those cases where the value of the claim is less than £50,000 and a party fails to file and exchange Precedent H by the date set out in the CPR r.26.3(1) notice, but does file and exchange it by the extended date given in the further notice under CPR r. 26.3(7A), does CPR r.3.14 apply?

4–36   Until the April 2016 amendments to the provisions of CPR r.3.13, this situation posed a procedural trap for the unwary in all multi-track claims within the costs management regime. However, that trap has now gone because:

- In those cases where the stated value on the claim form is £50,000 or more the time for filing and exchange of Precedents H is no longer linked to the time for filing directions questionnaires.
- In those claims where the statement of value of the claim is less than £50,000, the trigger for filing and exchanging budgets is the filing of the directions questionnaire and so any extension of time for filing the directions questionnaire provides an automatic extension of time for filing of the Precedent H.

Q15. Can the parties agree to extend the times prescribed in CPR r.3.13 for the filing and exchange of Precedents H by using CPR r.3.8(4)?

4–37   It is essential to look at the two 'triggers' for filing and exchanging Precedents H separately as follows:

- In respect of claims where the statement of value of the claim is less than £50,000 the position is not straightforward and produces a different outcome depending upon whether it is the notice under CPR r.26.3(1) or that under CPR r.26.3(7A) that the parties wish to vary.

  i) **CPR r.26.3(1) notice** – CPR r.26.3(6A) states categorically that the time for compliance with a notice under CPR r.26.3(1) may not be varied by agreement between the parties. CPR r.3.8(4) only applies where a party is required to do something within a time specified by a rule and that rule imposes a sanction for failure to comply. In this situation there has been non-compliance with CPR r.26.3(1) and the sanction is imposed by CPR r.26.3(7A). Is the rule CPR r.26.3 and are 3(1) and 3(7A) sub-rules within it? The answer seems to be yes. Although there is no definition of 'rule' in the CPR, when it refers to a rule it seems to do so to, for example, all of CPR r.26.3. However, does the provision permitting agreement under CPR r.3.8(4) take precedence over the bar to agreement in CPR r.26.3(6A)? The answer is that specific rules take precedence over general rules. CPR r.26.3(6A) is a specific rule and CPR r.3.8(4) is a general rule. As such it would seem that the period cannot be extended by agreement and that CPR r.3.8(4) does not apply to the time for compliance with CPR r.26.3(1).

  ii) **CPR r.26.3(7A) notice** – CPR r.26.3 contains no bar to an extension of the time provided under CPR r.26.3(7A) and, therefore, it seems to fall squarely within the provisions of CPR r.3.8(3) and (4) and the parties may agree to an extension. However, parties so doing would be well advised to notify the court as otherwise the court may well respond to any subsequently filed directions questionnaires and Precedents H with a letter saying that the claim, defence and any counterclaim have been struck out.

- In respect of claims where the statement of value of the claim is £50,000 or more where the trigger for filing and exchanging is 21 days before the first CCMC, no sanction applies and so CPR r.3.8(3) and (4) do not apply. The parties' ability to agree a variation is governed by the more general 'agreement to vary' provisions at CPR r.2.11. However, this is qualified by CPR r.29.5. Whilst it is arguable that at this stage the claim may not have been formally allocated (as opposed to provisionally allocated), the reality is that court approval will be required if the variation that the parties agree impacts upon the date fixed for the CCMC (CPR r.29.5(1)(a)). Parties should also be astute to the fact that the ability to agree a variation for Precedents H is also constrained by the provision at CPR r.3.13(2) to file a 'budget discussion report' seven days before the CCMC.

Q16. Does filing by e-mail satisfy the requirement in r.3.13 to file a budget?
CPR r.5.5, and by direct reference, CPR r.5 BPD permit filing of documents at court by email provided this is of a file type permitted under the list of specified documents in the guidance referred to at 5 BPD 1.2(a).

4–38

Accordingly, in principle, a party may file Precedent H by email. However, there are some qualifications in the practice direction. CPR r.5 BPD 2.2 deals with the High Court and 2.3 deals with the County Court. The court may refuse to accept a document if a party fails to comply with the provisions in those sub rules. CPR r.5 BPD 3, 4 and 5 impose further technical specifications and other provisions with which a party must be familiar. Given the sanction in CPR r.3.14 for late filing it is important to note 5 BPD 4.2 and 4.3 which provide:

> "*4.2 Where an e-mail, including any attachment, is sent pursuant to this practice direction and the e-mail is recorded by HMCTS e-mail software as received in court at or after 4.00pm and before or at 11.59pm-*
> *(a) the date of receipt of the e-mail will be deemed to be the next day the court office is open;*
> *. . .*
> *(c) any document attached to that email will be treated as filed on that date.*
> *4.3 It remains the responsibility of the party sending an application or other document to the court pursuant to this practice direction to ensure that it is received or filed within the applicable time limits, taking into account the operation of this practice direction."*

In addition CPR r.5 BPD does not apply to those cases:

- In the 'Electronic Working Pilot Scheme' running for two years from November 2015. These cases are covered by the provisions of CPR r.51 PDL.
- Started under Money Claims online if the claim has not been sent to a County Court hearing centre.

Q17. Does CPR r.3.14 apply to any failure to file a costs budget?

4–39 A strict interpretation of CPR r.3.14 reveals that it applies to failure to comply with any requirement to file a budget and not just to the preliminary requirement to do so under CPR r.3.13 – '*Unless the court otherwise orders, any party which fails to file a budget despite being required to do so. . .*'. Accordingly, any order of the court requiring the filing of a costs budget carries the sanction of CPR r.3.14. The practical outcome where this occurs before any costs management order has been made is simple – the defaulting party is limited in the terms of CPR r.3.14. However, what if the failure arises after a costs management order has been made e.g. where the court orders amended budgets to determine the effect on proportionality of any proposed further direction or after there is a discontinuance or admission of part of the claim and the costs will reduce?

This presents a number of options and to date there is no guidance on this. The options are:

- The sanction applies only to all costs from the date of the breach – so any budgets set are varied to reduce them from the date of breach to future court fees only. However, this may be a complicated exercise when the breach arises in mid stage of many of the phases and there will need to be agreement or assessment of how much of the permitted budget had been spent at the time of default. This increases the likelihood of detailed assessment – defeating one objective of costs management. In addition this has the effect of 'varying' a previous order, as applying the sanction to future costs, means that any budget the court may have already set for those phases is reduced.
- The sanction applies only to the costs directly linked to the significant variation in the litigation. This is simple if the development would ordinarily lead to increased budgets. The defaulting party's budget is only increased by any further and additional court fees. However, this approach does not work where the significant development should result in a reduction in costs – not only because there are unlikely to be any further court fees, but, more importantly, because the purpose of the amended budgets was to enable the court to revise budgets downwards in the light of the development that alters the reasonableness and proportionality assessment going forward anyway. Accordingly the failure to file the budget leads to no sanction as the outcome should be the same as if the party had filed a reduced budget removing these costs anyway (albeit that the court is deprived of the clear information to make this decision).
- The sanction applies retrospectively and the previously set budgets are void, This sanction would appear to breach the provisions of 3.12 and 3.15 that costs management can only be of costs 'to be incurred'.

On balance the first option appears both the most logical and the one that seems to fit the closest with the costs management mechanism, but Higher Court authority appears inevitable at some stage.

C. The content of Precedent H

Q18. Does the budget have to be on Precedent H or can parties produce their own forms provided that they recognisably contain the same information?
CPR r.3PD E 6 is clear: a budget must be in the form of Precedent H annexed **4–40** to CPR r.3PD E. This degree of prescription contrasts with the more flexible language adopted by the CPR when 'suggesting' the use of a particular Form e.g. in CPR r.44 PD 9.5(3) *'The statement of costs should follow as closely as possible Form N260.'* This interpretation is supported by the fact that CPR r.3 PD E 6 refers expressly to Page 1 of Precedent H when considering budgets not exceeding £25,000 or where the statement of value is below £50,000. Note also that the same PD provision requires the Precedent H to be in landscape format and an easily legible typeface. A final and more general point on this

topic, is that experience shows that even when use of a particular form is recommended, but not mandatory, problems often arise for those who devise and use their own version. Unless there is a very good reason, counsel of caution is to adopt the recommended version of a form – this avoids the risk of omitting an essential piece of information.

Q19. Which version of Precedent H should be used and is a budget discussion report required in a claim with a statement of value that exceeds £50,000 and which falls within the costs management regime, which was issued before 6 April 2016, but, following various extensions of time for filing and serving statements of case and subsequent stays, has only just been listed for a CCMC?

4-41   The Civil Procedure (Amendment) Rules 2016/234 implementing the 83rd update to the CPR make it clear that the revised provisions of CPR r.3.13(1) concerning the timing of filing and exchanging budgets and the addition of CPR r.3.13(2) requiring Precedents R only apply to proceedings which were commenced on or after 6 April 2016. The Practice Direction transitional arrangements similarly provided that the April 2016 new format of Precedent H was to be used in proceedings which were commenced on or after 6 April 2016. However, subsequently the 86th Update introduced the latest form of Precedent H from 3 October 2016. The Practice Direction Amendments for the 86th update did not provide for any transitional arrangements on this (perhaps because the amendments are not substantial – see **Q20** below). Therefore the answer is that the latest version of Precedent H should be used (the October 2016 version), but that no budget discussion report is strictly required. Having said this it seems unlikely that the court will criticise parties for adopting the provisions of CPR r.3.13(2) as to do so may narrow budgetary issues between the parties and, in any event, ought to enable the court better to prepare for the CCMC.

Q20. Given that the format of Precedent H was amended substantially in April 2016 why was it altered again in the 86th CPR amendment in October 2016?

4-42   The revision of Precedent H in October 2016 was simply to correct omissions and inconsistencies of wording. No alterations of substance were made. Principally the revision of the form was to:

- Substitute 'estimated' for 'future' in the breakdown of experts' fees section to ensure consistency of description throughout the form (although even then a late amendment had to made to the first published revised form as initially the total of the 'estimated' costs was still referred to as 'future' costs).
- Include a designated space for insertion of the date of the signature in the statement of truth section on page 1 of the form.

One might be forgiven for describing the amendments as being ones of style over substance!

Note that there is no transitional provision for use of this version of Precedent H. Its implementation date was 3 October 2016. As a result the new Precedent H should be used whenever that form is to be filed/exchanged after 2 October 2016.

Q21. Should a party file its Precedent H on the basis of the way in which it thinks the claim should progress, e.g. if it thinks a split trial is appropriate should the budget be completed on that basis?

CPR r.3 PD E 6(a) is clear on this. The court may direct that budgets are limited initially to part of the proceedings and subsequently extended to cover the whole of proceedings. Accordingly, unless the court has so directed, the budget must cover the whole proceedings. This means that any party which proposes to seek costs management of part only of the proceedings has two options. The first is to file and exchange a budget of the whole proceedings and then seek a direction before the case management conference that budgets are filed and exchanged on the additional alternative basis. The second is to apply before the time expires for budgets to be filed and exchanged under CPR r.3.13 for an extension of time to file budgets and for a direction that budgets should be limited initially to a discrete part of the proceedings. **4–43**

The advantage of the first approach is that the party has complied with CPR r.3.13 and does not face sanction under CPR r.3.14. The disadvantage is that if the court agrees that the claim proceeds with budgeting of part only, then the parties may have incurred the cost of preparing two budgets instead of one.

The advantage of the second approach is that if the court agrees with it, then one or both parties may have saved the cost of preparing two budgets at this stage. The disadvantage is that whilst a prospective application will be treated as one for an extension of time and not as one involving relief from sanctions (see *Hallam Estates v Baker*[67]), in this age of robust case management, it is a brave course to adopt. However, there is no doubt that it is better than filing and exchanging a full budget and raising the possibility of limited costs management only at the case management hearing when the court will then have difficulties deciding whether that is proportionate (without knowing the cost of so doing) and costs managing if it agrees (e.g. the court accepts that it is just and proportionate that there should be a preliminary trial on liability, but the budgets are not readily divisible between costs on liability and costs on quantum).

Interestingly, the Precedent H guidance suggests that the trial of a preliminary issue may be dealt with as a contingency in the budget. In practical terms it is hard to see how this could be done in an informative way, as to do so would have the court budgeting one figure under one contingency phase for all the work to be incurred to the end of the preliminary point, rather than

---

[67] *Hallam Estates v Baker* [2014] EWCA Civ 661.

by the identified phases in Precedent H. As such it would be difficult, if not impossible, for the court to determine the proportionality by phases to enable it to manage the steps to be incurred in the preliminary issue proportionately.

Some courts may want to see three budgets to enable a decision to be made as to whether it is just and proportionate to order a split trial as follows:

1) A budget for the whole proceedings without a split trial.
2) A budget for the costs of the preliminary issue.
3) A budget for the costs of the remainder of the proceedings if a split trial is ordered, but the preliminary issue does not dispose of the proceedings.

Q22. Will the introduction of 'J-Codes'[68] or other forms of time recording all work against the discrete phases lead to Precedent H being completed to include all costs – including those of a solicitor/client nature?

4–44   No. The court has no role in budgeting solicitor and client costs – those remain a matter of contractual retainer. J-Codes and other time recording against phase systems will simply enable representatives to record time against the specific phases of the Precedent H and should simplify both the production of Precedent H and the management of any budget set by a costs management order. So far as the court is concerned the use of this method of time recording should enable easier comparison of the budgeted costs and the sum spent on each phase budgeted if there is a challenge on any subsequent assessment in respect of a breach of the indemnity principle in connection with any budgeted costs. It also enables ready comparison of time recorded as against the non-budgeted incurred costs set out in the bill at later assessments. This is relevant as the court may have set budgeted costs for a phase predicated by the incurred costs. If it transpires that the incurred costs were understated in the budget, then that might be a 'good reason' to depart from the budgeted costs (e.g. by specific reference to incurred costs of £4,000 for a phase, the court has budgeted the estimated costs at £3,000. Had the court known that in fact the incurred costs were £6,000 it might have only budgeted the estimated costs at £1,000).

This type of time recording should also make it easier for a party to identify the costs attributable to any free standing application that falls outside a budget under CPR r.3 PD E 7.9.

The voluntary pilot in the SCCO from 1 October 2015, with, the intention that this will become compulsory from October 2017 (subject to the Civil Procedure Rules Committee confirming a date at its May 2017 meeting), and the use of Precedent Bill AB, should provide further information.

Q23. Do the costs allocated to contingencies count when determining whether or not a budget exceeds £25,000 and, in consequence,

---

[68] For more information on J-Codes, see Jackson Review Drafting Group, *Civil Litigation J-Code Set Overview and Guidelines*, 4 August 2014.

in determining whether only page 1 of the Precedent H needs to be completed?

As the budget is in Precedent H and that includes contingencies and, as any **4-45** contingencies that the court includes in the costs management order it makes plainly form part of the budget, it follows that the sums included by parties as contingencies in Precedent H count towards the total budget and even if, absent these, the budget would be less than £25,000, the full Precedent H must be completed.

Q24. Should applications to enforce compliance with case management decisions be included in the contingency section of Precedent H?

The instinctive answer is that such applications should not be in the budget **4-46** at all. The reason is simple. The court makes orders with which the parties are required to comply. To include as a contingency an application to enforce compliance means, following para.6 of the Guidance Notes on Precedent H, that a party believes that such an application is more likely than not. In other words, anyone including such a contingency is, in effect, saying to the court that, on the balance of probabilities, its orders will be breached. One might expect the court to respond that an order of the court is an order of the court with which there should be compliance and it is not prepared to countenance non-compliance. However, in *Group Seven Limited v Nasir*[69] the court indicated that it *'would be prepared to allow. . .sums for contingencies to reflect the possibility that there will be procedural difficulties which might be attributable to a lack of cooperation from some of the defendants'*. It should be noted, though, that this comment was made against a backdrop of alleged procedural difficulties and delay that had already been encountered. In essence, therefore, the court could, quite properly apply the para.6 test and conclude that future problems were more likely than not. In most cases this is unlikely to be the case and an anticipatory budget for applications to address breach of orders will be exception and not the 'norm'.

On a practical level there is a sound reason not to include the possibility of these applications as a contingency. It is that the parties (and therefore the court) does not know how many applications may be required, making it challenging to budget a reasonable and proportionate sum – opening up the possibility, uncertainty and expense of interim applications to vary or arguments on assessment on 'good reason'. This difficulty is avoided if these applications are not included as contingencies and instead, if and when they arise, are dealt with under CPR r.3 PD E 7.9 as freestanding applications outside and additional to the budget.

Q25. How detailed should be the assumptions upon which the budget is based?

The length of assumptions accompanying Precedent H is an acknowledged **4-47**

---

[69] *Group Seven Limited v Nasir* [2016] EWHC 620 (Ch).

area of contention. The minutes of the July 2015 meeting of the Civil Procedure Rules Committee revealed that '*An attempt should be made to limit the amount of detail provided by way of schedules of assumptions*'. The result is a clearer steer to proportionality in the revised Precedent H guidelines, which parties are obliged to follow pursuant to CPR r.3 PDE 6(b). The amount of detail falling within those guidelines depends upon the case.

What is clear is that attached breakdowns of costs that rendered the Precedent H far more akin to a bill for a prospective detailed assessment are clearly contrary to requirements and are things of the past. The guidelines have made it clear that the purpose of the assumptions is so that other parties and the court can readily understand the case plan upon which the budget is predicated, e.g. how many witnesses, what type of disclosure, how many experts and whether party or jointly instructed and the length of trial. Remember that the court is also likely to have both the directions questionnaire and draft directions from all parties, which should also provide clear indications as to the assumptions under which the parties propose to progress the claim.

Q26. Do parties who are required to file and exchange budgets using only page 1 of Precedent H (i.e. claims where the costs do not exceed £25,000 or the value of the claim as stated on the claim form is less than £50,000) need to provide assumptions upon which the budget is based? If assumptions are required in these cases where should they be inserted in Precedent H? If not required, how will the court know the basis upon which the budget is predicated?

4–48   Section 8b of the Guidance Notes on Precedent H is clear. Written assumptions are not normally required by the court in these cases. It is for this reason that the short form Precedent H does not provide any room for the insertion of assumptions. However, there appears to be a tension between CPR r.3 PDE 6(c), which makes it mandatory in this situation for parties to use p1 only, and the insertion of the word 'normally' in the Guidance Notes, which suggests that parties may be asked to provide the assumptions in cases 'out of the norm'. Perhaps the tension is eased by an interpretation that recognises that the PD requirement is one imposed on the parties, but the Guidance Note refers to a requirement imposed by the court. Whilst there is no specific reference in Section 11 of CPR r.3 to the court having jurisdiction to make an order that a party must file a 'full' budget, where the PD only requires use of page one, there is certainly an argument that the court could make such an order under either CPR r.3.1(2)(ll) or (m) which provide that the court may:

> "(ll) *order any party to file and exchange a costs budget;*
> (m) *take any other step or make any other order for the purpose of managing the case and furthering the overriding objective. . ."*

If the court does make such an order where, then, should the assumptions be inserted? Assuming that the order of the court does not require a 'full' budget, but simply that assumptions are provided there is no reason why the court cannot order that these are filed and exchanged as a separate document. Parties should still be astute to Section 8a of the Guidance Note indicating the detail required.

If no assumptions are ordered the court should still have a clear idea of the basis upon which budgets are based from the information provided in parties' directions questionnaires, the draft directions filed and CPR r.35.4 information relating to permission for any expert evidence.

Q27. If work has already been undertaken on an interim application at the time that Precedent H must be prepared, should this work be reflected in the budget, and, if so, where?

As well as prescribing the form of the budget CPR r.3 PD E 6 now imposes **4–49** an obligation on parties to follow the Precedent H Guidance Notes in all respects. These provide what type of work should appear under which phase in a budget. However, as considered in para.**4–17** above these notes contain curiosities. There are also some omissions and this question highlights one of them. Although one might consider that it is challenging to describe as a contingency something that has already happened (i.e. a decision has already been made to make an application and costs have been incurred consequent upon that decision), it seems that the Guidance Note leads to that conclusion. This is because paragraph 6 of the Guidance Notes says this:

> *"The 'contingent cost' sections of this form should be used for anticipated costs which do not fall within the main categories set out in this form. Examples might be the trial of preliminary issues, a mediation, applications to amend, applications for disclosure against third parties or (in libel cases) applications re meaning. Only include costs which are more likely than not to be incurred. Costs which are not anticipated but which become necessary later are dealt with in paragraph 7.6 of PDE3"*

Application of this guidance leads to the following conclusions:

- Costs associated with the application are anticipated (indeed some have been incurred).
- Costs associated with the application are more likely than not to be incurred (again, some have already been incurred and more will be).
- This application does not fall into another section of Precedent H.

This appears to lead, inexorably, to the conclusion that this application sits firmly within the contingent cost sections of Precedent H.

The only alternative is that the application comes within CPR r.3 PD E 7.9 – namely that it is an interim application which is not reasonably included in the budget and so the costs will be dealt with outside of and additional to the budget. Many have viewed 7.9 as referring to applications that were made after the budget has been prepared and which were neither anticipated nor more likely than not to occur at that time. For this provision to assist *"'If interim applications are made which reasonably, were not included in a budget. . ."'* would have to be interpreted to extend to non-inclusion on the basis that there is nowhere for them to appear in the budget.

Assuming that such an application does fall within the contingent cost sections, then as of April 2016 a further problem arises. Until the April 2016 amendment to Precedent H there was an incurred column in the contingent cost sections. This is no longer the case and the contingent cost sections permit entry of detail only in respect of estimated costs. Where should the 'incurred costs' appear? There is no ready answer to this. However, it is essential that the court has the 'incurred' and 'estimated' information separately so that it a) may use the 'incurred' information under CPR r.3 PD E 7.4 to inform what 'estimated costs' it budgets and b) knows what the 'estimated costs' are, to ensure that it does not inadvertently budget the entire phase (both incurred and estimated). One solution, and it is accepted that this does not sit happily with CPR r.6.2(a) or (b), is to put both incurred and estimated costs in the estimated costs section of the phase <u>but</u> in the assumptions under the phase explain this and provide the breakdown between incurred and estimated. At least this way the court has all the information that it needs to budget the phase properly (although the court must then be astute to ensure that the costs management order expressly records the budgeted estimated costs and records somewhere the incurred costs which informed this decision, so that it is clear later, particularly on any subsequent assessment, what was budgeted and what was incurred and not budgeted). However, we stress that adopting this approach means that Precedent H is not compliant with CPR r.3 PDE 6.3(a) and (b). Accordingly, a prudent party may consider that an application pursuant to the *'otherwise order'* provision in PD E 6.3(a) is necessary to avoid any possible sanction (e.g. CPR r.3.14) for non-compliance. Albeit in a different context the question of sanction is considered below at **Q28.**

Q28. The guidance notes for completion of Precedent H are brief and it is not always clear where certain items of work should be included. Is there any sanction for inserting items in what the court may regard as the wrong phase of the budget?

4–50 The decisions in *Bank of Ireland v Philip Pank Partnership*[70] and *Americhem Europe Ltd v Rakem Ltd*[71] suggest that the court may treat insertion of items in the wrong place in the budget as irregularities rather than things that render the budget a nullity.

Obviously parties should follow the Precedent H guidance but where it is not clear there is a real danger that the process of completing the Precedent H becomes one of form rather than substance. The document should inform

---

[70] *Bank of Ireland v Philip Pank Partnership* [2014] EWHC 284 (TCC) Stuart-Smith J.
[71] *Americhem Europe Ltd v Rakem Ltd* [2014] EWHC 1881 (TCC) Stuart-Smith J.

the parties and the court to enable the parties to reach agreement or raise any issues of contention and to enable the court to case and costs manage properly. If it is not clear where to insert specific work and the cost incurred and to be incurred on that (such as the scenario in **Q27** above) surely to be purposeful the key is to ensure that wherever it is included it, and the costs attributable to it, are clearly identified, even if, as set out in **Q27** above, that means being creative. At least by so doing the expenditure is in the budget and the costs attributable to it are set out separately – assisting the court under CPR r.3 PD E 7.4, as what has already been spent informs what costs should be budgeted going forward. We repeat that a prudent party may wish to seek court permission to do this in advance of the date for filing and exchange to avoid any possibility of a sanction being imposed.

Q29. Is it better for a party to over-estimate costs in the budget filed and exchanged, on the basis that it is then likely to see a higher budget set and less likely to need to go back to the court asking for the budget to be varied under CPR r.3 PD E 7.6? Conversely, if a party recognises that it is likely to be the paying party is underestimation better, trying to persuade the court to reduce the budgets of all parties to that level to limit the potential liability for costs or limit the work that can be undertaken, making the outcome of the claim less certain as a result?

The simple answer to the related questions above is that the parties must complete Precedent H in a fashion that enables them to sign the statement of truth set out in CPR r.22 PD 2.2A. As is clearly set out in CPR r.22 PD 5 and, by cross reference, CPR r.32.14, the consequence of verifying the budget by statement of truth knowing that the Precedent H does not give a fair and accurate statement of incurred and estimated costs that it would be reasonable and proportionate for the client to incur, is possible proceedings for contempt of court. Representatives should be extremely wary of adopting 'tactical budgets'- whether high or low. They ought also to be aware that as the court will form its own view of what is reasonable and proportionate, it will recognise budgets that are artificially high or low for whatever reasons. 4–51

Q30. If a defendant brings an additional claim against a party other than the claimant, does the defendant need to produce two budgets – one for the defence of the claim and one for the pursuit of the additional claim – or will one total budget suffice?

There is no clear guidance on this. However, the situation did arise and was considered by Coulson J in *CIP Properties (AIPT) Ltd v Galliford Try Infrastructure Ltd*[72] (see **Q1** above). In that case one of four additional parties suggested that the defendant should provide separate costs budgets for the defence of the claim and for the discrete claims against each additional party. The response of 4–52

---

[72] *CIP Properties (AIPT) Ltd v Galliford Try Infrastructure Ltd* [2014] EWHC 3546 (TCC) Coulson J.

the defendant was that the costs overlapped, with some costs being common costs, and that to do separate budgets would be "unworkable, impractical and expensive". Coulson J concluded that as it was a case where it would be difficult to identify what of the overall costs would be spent on the defence and what on the additional claims, it would be unfair and disproportionate to order separate budgets. He cited with approval the judgment of Master Kaye QC in *Lotus Cars Ltd v Mechanica Solutions Inc.*[73] In multi-party litigation the Master had concluded that:

> "... *where the management of cases is to be treated as common and is dealt with accordingly, there is no sensible reason why the costs budgeting should always be considered separately and some good reasons why it should not*".

What seems clear is that each case is likely to be fact specific, but that where the issues overlap inextricably then the court is unlikely to order separate budgets.

Q31. If a number of defendants are represented by the same solicitors, should separate budgets be prepared for each such defendant?

4–53   The answer to this depends upon the nature of the retainer and the claim/s that is/are being brought. If these defendants have filed one common defence, then it seems both reasonable and proportionate that they should file and exchange one budget as their interests obviously coincide. Any costs incurred are in respect of all these defendants and so it is unnecessary to separate them out as any subsequent order for costs in their favour would be made in respect of them all. However, there are some claims where the same firm, but a different fee earner, represents different defendants. This is where there is no conflict of interest between these defendants, but the claims against them stand or fall on their own. A classic illustration of this is in historic industrial disease claims. The claim against each defendant is free standing, but there may be no conflict between different defendants. In such cases then clearly there should be separate budgets for each defendant as the court will need to make costs management orders identifying the agreed or approved budget for each defendant.

Q32. Should the costs of surveillance evidence be included in a budget? If not, if surveillance evidence is subsequently obtained, should applications be made under CPR r.3 PD E 7.6 to amend the budgets?

4–54   In *Purser v Hibbs*[74] the court concluded that, contrary to the note at 3.15.3 of the 2015 *White Book*, a defendant should be allowed to recover the costs of surveillance evidence, notwithstanding that those costs had not been included in the costs budget on the basis there was 'good reason' for those costs not to have been included in the budget at all. The court referred to

---

[73] *Lotus Cars Ltd v Mechanica Solutions Inc* [2014] EWHC 76 (QB) Master Kaye QC.
[74] *Purser v Hibbs* unreported 19 May 2015 QBD HHJ Moloney QC.

the absence of any reference to this type of evidence in either Precedent H or the guidance upon it. The rationale for the decision was that alerting a fraudulent claimant to the possibility of covert surveillance evidence would discourage judicious use of such evidence and the court did not wish to do so. As a result when the evidence showed the claimant to be exaggerating injuries there was 'good reason' to allow recovery in excess of the budget figure. In fact, the court had already decided to award these costs on the indemnity basis, rendering their lack of inclusion in the budget of academic interest only for, as a result, the requirement for 'good reason' under CPR r.3.18 did not arise on subsequent assessment anyway as it only applies to a standard basis assessment. Accordingly the defendant would not have been constrained by the budgeted figures (see para.4–20 above). It is also arguable that the guidance and the Precedent H do cover this situation without requiring express reference, as this type of evidence falls within both disclosure and witness statement evidence.

In any event *Purser* only deals with half the story (this is not intended to be a criticism, because it only had to do so). The reason for this is that the court in *Purser* was determining the award of costs after the claimant accepted the defendant's CPR r.36 offer on receipt of the surveillance evidence, but outside the relevant period for acceptance. As the parties could not agree the incidence of costs, the court had to determine them under what is now CPR rules 36.13(4) and (5). However, what of the situation where surveillance evidence is served, but the claim continues? Clearly the case/costs managing judge cannot budget retrospectively, but the admission of the evidence is surely a significant development in the litigation pursuant to CPR r.3 PD E 7.6.and as a result that provision requires parties to revise budgets. At this stage there is no 'secrecy' requirement – the evidence has been served. In that situation one would expect both parties to apply for a prospective variation of budgets (regardless of the obligation to do so under CPR r.3 PD E 7.6), because they want prospective approval of additional costs, rather than find themselves arguing 'good reason' under CPR r.3.18 at a later date. The claimant's solicitor will want to view the evidence and take instructions, parties will want to put the evidence to experts, ask questions and review answers, counsels' views may be sought, the evidence may impact on any settlement work and it is likely to affect the trial time estimate. Accordingly service of surveillance evidence should be accompanied (by the defendant) and swiftly followed (by the claimant) by service of revised budgets, an attempt to agree these, and, failing that, by applications to the court for variation of the budgets set. If revision is not sought it seems unlikely that the court will conclude that the costs related to surveillance after disclosure of it either fall outside the budget or that there is a 'good reason' to depart from the original budget at any subsequent assessment on the standard basis as there seems no logical explanation for why parties would not seek prospective variation.

How does the court approach this evidence and any costs budget variation going forward, assuming, if the evidence is served outside the time set for disclosure and witness statement evidence, that the court permits the 'late' evidence by any appropriate grants of relief from sanction or retrospective extensions of time and the parties seek budget variation? This involves consideration of CPR r.1.1 (to manage cases justly and at proportionate cost), CPR r.3.17 (taking into account the cost of any procedural step), CPR r.3.15(3) (if a costs management order has been made the court will thereafter control the parties' budgets) and CPR r.3 PD E 7.6 (the court may approve, vary or disapprove the proposed variations to the budget). When undertaking this exercise the court will be astute to the fact that any previous determination of the relevant proportionality factors under CPR r.44.3(5) may require revision because this evidence may engage 44.3(5)(c) and (e) – a timely reminder that proportionality is a flexible concept and may vary during the lifetime of a claim. The court will then determine, against the proportionality factors, the extent to which it is just and proportionate to permit the evidence and, if so, the reasonable and proportionate costs that should be added to the relevant phases of the budgets.

D. Preparation for the CCMC

Q33. Some courts are asking parties to produce a composite summary enabling comparison of the parties' budgets. Is there a specified precedent form for this? If not, what format should be used for that summary?

4–55 Some courts do like to see a one page summary of the respective budgets in all cases (the Chancery Guide at para.17.13 requires one and sets out the content required). Others are happy simply to look at the respective pages 1 of the Precedents H for comparison, or only order such a summary in specific cases (e.g. where there are a large number of parties). As a result a summary should not be filed routinely unless one is expressly requested by the court. Where a summary is ordered there is no prescribed precedent form. There is also no prescribed form of order and so parties should ensure that they comply with any specific requirements for a summary in any order requesting one. If the order is simply something to the effect that:

> *"'The claimant/defendant must file and serve a one page summary of the Precedent H of all parties to enable the Court to compare budget totals for each phase'"*,

and is silent as to format, then provision of this information in a tabular form such as that below may be thought suitable. Contingencies have not been included as the parties' contingencies may not be the same and so there is no useful comparison to be made. If they are and there is, then these can be added (also adding to what the contingency relates). Columns can be added for each additional party. A total column is included as the court may find this informative when considering the proportionality of a particular case management direction for any given phase.

Phase	Claimant	Defendant	Total
Pre-action costs			
Issue/statements of case			
CMC			
Disclosure			
Witness statements			
Expert reports			
PTR			
Trial preparation			
Trial			
Settlement			

(See **Q34** below for consideration of other requirements imposed by some courts before the CCMC)

Q34. A number of courts are issuing detailed directions when listing a CCMC. Are these necessary and should they be standardised?

This was a topic considered by Jackson LJ in his May 2015 *Confronting costs*   **4–56**
management lecture[75]. He concluded that it ought to be possible to create a standard order, distilling the best from those orders that have emerged from the (then) 2 3/4 years' experience acquired by the judiciary. What is essential is that any order is proportionate to the needs of the specific case. In many cases a light touch only will be needed e.g. those judges who budget and create case management orders electronically will require the Precedents H and draft directions in electronic and alterable form (and self-calculating in respect of the budgets). Even when there is a 'standard order' only those parts of it pertinent to the individual case should be used. The danger of a tick box form is that there is a temptation to tick all the boxes in every case. If concerns over the costs of the costs management process are to be addressed, directions must be targeted proportionately and this demands that whilst the form of any orders used should be standardised, it should not be mandatory to issue the orders.

Q35. How detailed should be the summary in Precedent R of the reasons why a phase of the budget is not agreed?

The answer comes by way of a combination of the procedural provisions at CPR   **4–57**
r.3 PDE 6A(c), 7.3 and 7.10. The first of the three provisions mentioned could not be clearer. Precedent R 'must set out a brief summary of the grounds of dispute' (our emphasis). The reference made to CPR r.7.3 is simply a reminder that the court is expressly not undertaking a detailed assessment and CPR

---

[75] *Confronting costs management*, May 2015, para 8.1.

r.7.10 stresses that the court is not descending to the detail of setting hourly rates (and therefore is not prescribing time). Accordingly this document must not be viewed as Points of Dispute. The document is intended to allow both the party whose budget is being commented upon and the court to understand, at a glance, which phases are contentious and why. Whilst Precedent R is in Excel format (and so the boxes will expand), it may be informative that the spreadsheet is published on only one page.

There have been a few cases where parties have used Precedent R to reply to the other party's Precedent R! Those documents have received short shrift. There is no provision in the rules permitting the filing of any formal document in reply.[76]

Q36. Should the discussions that the parties have when attempting to agree the costs budgets be without prejudice?

4–58   As noted in **Q35** above, CPR r.3.13(2) requires the parties (other than a litigant in person) to file an agreed 'budget discussion report' (Precedent R) at least seven days before the CCMC, setting out an 'open position'. However, as with any discussions, there is nothing to prevent both 'open' and 'without prejudice' proposals being made in an attempt to reach agreement over budgets or certain phases within the budgets.

Q37. Is there a sanction if a party fails to agree a budget discussion report (Precedent R) or fails to file this?

4–59   The wording of CPR r.3.13(2) is curious. It does not specify that a party must serve Precedent R on all other parties, but this is surely implicit in the requirement that the form filed is 'agreed'. Obviously it cannot be agreed unless the party agreeing it has had the opportunity to see it to consider it! One practical problem that this raises is that there is, therefore, no provision for the time by which it is to be served – the only time constraint is that by which it must be filed (no later than seven days before the first CCMC).

Of course this begs the question: what is an agreed budget discussion report? Presumably, the party whose budget is the subject of the form simply notes the content and either accepts proposals in respect of certain phases so that an amended final version may be filed or confirms that the form accurately reflects the measure of agreement and disagreement.

What can be done if one party either does not serve Precedent R or does so allowing insufficient time for the other party to consider it with a view to agreeing it less than seven days before the first CCMC? There is no automatic sanction applied to CPR r.3.13(2) and there has been no authority on this subject. Whilst it might be thought that an obvious sanction linked to the breach is for the court to refuse to permit the party in breach to 'challenge'

---

[76] Note that the 88th amendment to the CPR refers to an amended Precedent R. At the time of going to print this revised form was not available. It is assumed it has been altered in the light of the changes made to defining 'budgeted costs' and incurred costs.

the budget, this sits entirely unhappily with the court's obligation to manage the costs to be incurred under CPR r.3.12(2) and CPR r.3.15(1), its more general obligation to consider the costs of any case management decision under CPR r.3.17 and the obligation under the overriding objective to deal with cases at proportionate cost. Another possible sanction that is unlikely to be imposed, for the same reason, is to accept the compliant party's Precedent H comments on the defaulting party's budget. More likely, therefore, is the imposition of some form of delay sanction in the form of an order that the defaulting party pays all or part of the costs of the CCMC or that, if it subsequently recovers costs, then the costs associated with the production of budgets under CPR r.3 PD E 7.2 are disallowed. There is some logic to the second of these options, particularly where there is a complete failure to comply with CPR r.3.13(2), as the likelihood is that the CCMC will take more time as neither the court nor the other party/parties will know in advance which, if any, phases are agreed.

Another option might be to apply to the court for an 'unless order'. However, the time between making this and the CCMC will, necessarily, be brief and it may not be possible for the court to deal with this before the CCMC (either in terms of not dealing with it or there being enough time for any extended compliance. Again the issue arises as to the appropriate sanction.

The final option is for the CCMC to be adjourned to afford time for compliance with an adverse costs order against the defaulting party. However, a decision to adjourn is a case management one and compensating one party in costs overlooks CPR r.1.1(2)(e) as this will waste court time that has been allocated to this case. Given the demands on court time one must expect the court to be loath to adjourn an, often long awaited, CCMC.

The same difficulties emerge where a party serves its Precedent R in good time, but the other party neither engages in any discussions nor indicates any response and so the party serving the Precedent R has no idea if it is 'agreed'. In those circumstances it seems the best course is to ensure that the form is still filed no later than seven days before the CCMC, but indicating that it is not agreed with an explanation for why that is the case. The same options (and difficulties) arise in connection with any sanction for non-compliance.

E. Approval and agreement of budgets

Q38. If one party puts in an absurdly low budget is it advisable for the other party to agree it or will this suggest an acceptance that any costs above that level are not reasonable and proportionate and so prejudice its own budget which is significantly higher?

Yes it is advisable to agree it. This will not prevent submissions being made to the court, both in Precedent R and orally, that such a budget is artificially low, that it has been agreed because that is in the other party's best interest to limit potential exposure to 'between the parties' costs in the event of a subsequent adverse costs order, but that budget has no relevance whatsoever to what the reasonable and proportionate costs of the other party may be. Courts will be

4–60

astute to the possibility of tactical budgeting (whether high or low). Indeed this is one reason why a budget comparison summary (see **Q33** above) is not only unhelpful, but can present an utterly misleading picture when viewed in isolation, in some cases.

Q39. The Precedent H guidance notes have been amended to include a specific reference to CPR rules 44.3 (5) and 44.4(3) and state that when deciding the reasonable and proportionate costs the court will include in its consideration *"where and the circumstances in which the work was done as opposed to where the case is heard"*. What is the significance of these amendments?

4–61   The reference to the two CPR provisions is because these are, respectively, the procedural provisions that define whether costs are proportionate and whether costs are reasonable and CPR r.3 PD E 7.3 requires the court to set budgets by reference to reasonableness and proportionality. Although they have been put in chronological order, as they follow a reference to reasonable and proportionate costs it may have made this link easier to understand if they had been inverted so it was clear that CPR r.44.3(5) referred to proportionality and CPR r.44.4(3) to reasonableness.

The words at the end are an extension of CPR r.44.4(3)(g). However, the tenses used do not sit happily with the task of budget setting, which is about prospective costs, and seem to resonate more with a retrospective assessment of costs. However, as these words appear in the guidance notes for completion of a form for use in prospective costs budgeting they should be interpreted purposively. Doing so, it seems likely that these words have been inserted to deal with the possibility of forum shopping – where representatives are based in one location, but issue proceedings out of another, where, for example, guideline hourly rates are higher or lower, resulting in a budget that is artificially high or low. However, as budgets are not set by reference to hourly rate and as the court is astute to tactical budgeting arguments[77], forum shopping should not result in any benefit in any event. Linked to this, it is worth remembering that amendments inserted at CPR r.29 PD 2.6A already compel parties in claims in specialist lists to justify in detail why these should be heard in London and not in regional specialist courts where the dispute arises in a region outside London.

In passing, it is worth noting those who seek to argue that CPR r.3.18 does not exclude a traditional item by item assessment of those costs budgeted will need to surmount the hurdle that on a standard basis assessment costs allowed are those which are reasonable and proportionate, but as the budget has been set by reference to both of these any attempt to revisit them may be seen as an attempt to ask the assessing court to adopt an appellate function, which it does not have (see **Q76** below for further consideration of this).

---

[77] See, for example, *CIP Properties (AIPT) Ltd v Galliford Try* [2015] EWHC 481 (TCC) para.24.

Q40. Does the introduction of costs management mean that the court is rarely likely to dispense with a case/costs management conference and deal with directions and budgets as a paper exercise?

Clearly having a case/costs management hearing introduces delay and   **4–62** expense to cases (although as parties and courts become accustomed to the discipline these should lessen). If the court is able to undertake this work as a paperwork exercise that would be the preferable course (indeed Jackson LJ in the final report was at pains to stress that only case management hearings that had a purpose should be listed). However, unless the case management directions and budgets are agreed and the court is prepared to approve both, then it is difficult to envisage how a hearing can be dispensed with at this stage. Even the optional provisional paper budget scheme introduced for certain work in the Manchester Civil Justice Centre envisages an oral hearing, if any party wishes, after the provisional setting of the budget. It is hoped that as the regime settles in and the experience of practitioners and judges alike grows, then an increasing number of budgets and proposed directions will lend themselves to a paper determination. In the meantime, parties should seek to narrow as many issues as possible and the insertion of 'budget discussion reports' at CPR r.3.13(2) will assist in this process and enable the judge to 'target' preparation in advance of the CCMC. If there is early and significant agreement the parties should inform the court of this as soon as possible as that will reduce the required hearing time for a case management conference and that may both expedite the listing of the hearing (as a shorter time estimate ought to lead to earlier court availability) and reduce the cost of the hearing. It is fair to observe that the amendment to CPR r.3.13 means that in many cases Precedents H will be filed and exchanged later and this means that CCMC time estimates will have to be set on a 'worst case assumption', allowing sufficient time for both case and costs management and the chances of the court dealing with the matter as a paper exercise are reduced.

Parties should remember, in any event, that they are under a duty to endeavour to agree appropriate directions anyway (CPR r.29.4).

Where it is not possible to dispense with a hearing, the parties should, at least, consider whether a telephone case/costs management hearing is feasible (subject to the court being prepared to accommodate this). In many cases there is an argument to be made that a hearing by telephone is more proportionate (e.g. where the advocates are not local to the hearing centre). However, whilst CPR r.23 APD.6.2(c) suggests that a case management conference will be by telephone unless the court orders otherwise, this is in respect of hearings up to an hour long. Many case/costs management hearings are listed for longer than this.

Q41. Does the court give the directions first and subsequently costs manage?

As costs management and case management go hand in hand, the two cannot   **4–63** be separated. If the case management directions are set without reference to the costs, with the budgeting exercise conducted afterwards, then all the court is doing when costs managing is pricing directions that have been given. The consequence is that if the court subsequently determines that a particular direction cannot be budgeted proportionately, there is nothing it can do as the direction has already been given. In contrast, if the two are done hand in hand the proportionate expenditure informs the appropriate direction. In this respect it is curious that the Chancery Guide suggests that normally directions are dealt with first and costs management afterwards, but with the directions only <u>likely</u> to be informed by the budgets. In simple terms, the danger of setting the directions and then costing them is that the directions ordered are those that the court determines are needed in the particular case. However, CPR r.44.3(2)(a) makes it clear that proportionality trumps need and the overriding objective 'to deal with a case at proportionate cost' applies to any case management decision. The court should be giving directions that see the case dealt with proportionately and that assessment can only be made by dealing with the directions and the relevant phase of the budget simultaneously. This was a theme to which Jackson LJ returned in *'Confronting costs management*[78]' concluding that the proportionate cost for a phase inevitably determined the proportionate case management direction for that phase[79]. This approach is one that the Court of Appeal implicitly approved in *Jamadar v Bradford Teaching Hospitals NHS Foundation Trust*[80] when highlighting that case and costs management should take place simultaneously. This might mean that the court's preliminary view of the proportionate direction needs to be revised if the cost associated with it is not proportionate e.g. a more limited disclosure order may have to be adopted to ensure proportionality of spend on that phase.

Q42. Should costs lawyers attend CCMCs?

4–64 This must be for the client to decide. In principle there is no reason why a costs lawyer/costs draftsman should not attend provided that this person has rights of audience. Anecdotally it seems that some CCMCs are attended by counsel/solicitor and a costs lawyer/draftsman. Views differ, but, provided only one of the advocates addresses the court on each point, there appears to be nothing wrong with this approach. Indeed there has long been a history of costs counsel and a costs lawyer/draftsman attending detailed assessment with the former addressing the court on substantive points of principle and then handing over to the costs lawyer/draftsman for the minutiae of assessing actual sums. This begs the question of whether a costs lawyer/draftsman is necessary at the CCMC as the court will not be undertaking anything approaching an assessment and the appropriate person to attend is the one

---

[78] *Confronting costs management*, May 2015, paras 7.4–7.6.
[79] An illustration of this is given by Jackson LJ in his Law Society Disclosure Lecture on 10 October 2016 when he said:*"Since the court should be doing case and costs management together, it can a) adjust the level of disclosure to fit with the budgets and/or b) set the budgets to take account of the level of disclosure ordered."*
[80] *Jamadar v Bradford Teaching Hospitals NHS Foundation Trust* [2016] EWCA Civ 1001.

best able to address the court on proportionality and how this translates into the reasonable and proportionate directions and budget for each phase.

Q43. The Court of Appeal has suggested that costs already incurred at the time of the costs management order can be the subject of a costs management order by agreement. Is this correct?

This issue arose in *SARPD Oil Ltd v Addax Energy S.A*[81]. This case is consid- **4–65** ered in some detail in **4–18** above and **Q49** below. The judgment presented a number of challenging issues, which the Civil Procedure Rules Committee considered over a number of months. The outcome of its deliberations is that amendments will be made to the CPR[82] that will leave no doubt that budgeted cost are those that have not been incurred at the time of the costs management order, but that the court will be able to make a costs management order recording the extent of any agreement on incurred costs.

Q44. The court seems to have adopted a number of approaches to dealing with incurred costs. Is it possible to discern clear guidance on the treatment of these costs in the budgeting exercise?

There is no doubt that the treatment of incurred costs is difficult and that **4–66** the court has adopted different approaches to try to address this. The difficulty is that the court cannot budget 'incurred costs', (although under amendments from 6 April 2017 it may make a costs management order recording the extent, if any, to which incurred costs are agreed), but is required to take these into account when considering the reasonableness and proportionality of all subsequent costs. This presents a number of problems, the most obvious of which are:

- What if the incurred costs already exceed the sum that the court considers a reasonable and proportionate sum for the entire claim?
- What if the incurred costs on a certain phase which is incomplete exceed the sum that the court considers a reasonable and proportionate sum for the entire phase?
- What if the court sets the budget for a phase by determining the reasonable and proportionate sum for that phase, deducts from it the amount that has been incurred and budgets the difference for the 'costs to be incurred', but at assessment the assessing judge allows less than the full amount of the incurred costs?

These specific problems are addressed in more detail in the answers to **Qs 45, 46** and **47**, below. However, they have caused the court to grapple with how best to treat incurred costs against the backdrop of case specific situations.

In *Yeo v Times Newspapers Ltd* the court considered the position when it

---

[81] *SARPD Oil Ltd v Addax Energy S.A* [2016] EWCA Civ 120.
[82] The Civil Procedure (Amendment) Rules 2017 SI 2017/95.

was presented with substantial costs incurred prior to the costs management hearing. It set out CPR r.3 PD E 7.4 and concluded that comments on those costs 'briefly recorded at the time the budget is approved' would greatly assist the parties and the court at the conclusion. Reports suggest that this claim has concluded and the parties have agreed the amount the losing party is to pay for costs without need for an assessment.

The problem was more acute in *CIP Properties (AIPT) Ltd v Galliford Try Infrastructure Ltd*. The court was confronted by a budget that it considered 'unreliable', that had been 'deliberately manipulated' and which revealed both the incurred and estimated costs to be disproportionate. Challenged by the extent of the incurred costs, but to ensure that the overall costs were limited to those that he determined to be reasonable and proportionate, Coulson J. adopted a mechanism that enabled him to control all the costs whilst recognising the problem of the assessing judge taking a different view to his in respect of incurred costs. His solution was to limit the recoverable incurred costs per phase, but to devise an off-setting calculator so that if the assessing judge allowed more than that sum, then an equivalent amount should be deducted from the estimated spend budgeted. In other words, regardless of how ultimately the costs are divided between those incurred and those budgeted, the claimant will be limited to the overall sum permitted by this mechanism. This raises a number of issues e.g. can the costs managing judge prospectively limit recoverable costs on a subsequent assessment of non-budgeted costs (para.98 plainly refers to 'assessed costs'), the extent to which, if at all, the costs managing judge may off-set incurred costs in one phase against budgeted costs in another phase (para.97(a) expressly offsets incurred costs on the pre-action phase against future costs generally), the extent to which the court can effectively set a budget for a phase to include both incurred and estimated costs by adopting the set off formula used by the court when CPR r.3.12 and CPR r.3.15 are clear that budgets are in respect of 'costs to be incurred' and whether the effect of setting a total sum (para.98) precludes arguments under 'good reason' or the exercise by the assessing judge of discretion on 'good reason' for the budgeted sums to be increased on assessment (the effect of which anyway would seem simply to be a £ for £ off-set against incurred sums). This approach has subsequently been adopted in *GSK Project Management Ltd v QPR Holdings Ltd*.

The simple answer to the question is that 'guidance' on the treatment of incurred costs comes from CPR r.3 PD E 7.4. However, it is clear from the above that the court is still grappling with the question of how to implement this fairly on a practical level., Further authority seems inevitable. In the meantime the answers to the subsequent three questions attempt to address some of the issues that arise.

Q45. Are incurred costs relevant to the overall costs at the budgeting stage or only relevant on a phase by phase basis?

4–67   This picks up on the previous answer. CPR r.3 PD E 7.4 refers to incurred costs without reference to specific phases. Although the judgment does not overtly say so, it may be that it is the absence of an express link between 7.4 and individual phases that was relied upon by the court in *CIP Properties (AIPT) Ltd v Galliford Try* (see above) to justify off-setting of the incurred expenditure on one phase against the 'to be incurred' budget on another phase (e.g. the off-set at paragraph 97(a) of any pre-action costs subsequently assessed above £680,000 against the prospective budgeted figures in other phases – albeit without specifying any particular phase). Difficulties with adopting this approach have been mentioned above. However, this narrower question highlights what appear to be insurmountable procedural hurdles to the adoption of a general off-set. These are that:

- Costs management orders are made in respect of budgets which are set by what is reasonable and proportionate for individual phases. Accordingly a formula that may operate, albeit retrospectively, to reduce what has been determined as the reasonable and proportionate sum for a specific phase to a sum less than that by an off-set of incurred costs from another phase, means that in those instances where the off-set operates, the court has not set the budget as required under CPR r.3 PD E 7.3.
- At assessment on the standard basis, by a combination of CPR rules 44.3(1) and (2)(a), the receiving party may only recover those costs which are reasonable and proportionate. CPR r.3.18 is clear that the court looks at whether there should be a departure from the budget by reference to the last agreed/approved sums for each phase. As the agreed/approved sums for those phases budgeted have been expressly determined by reference to the same criteria (under CPR r.3 PD E 7.3), how can it be a 'good reason' under CPR r.3.18 (or, indeed, correct under CPR r.44.3) to reduce budgeted costs on one phase by an off-set from another phase.

Although it did not arise in *CIP Properties (AIPT) Ltd v Galliford Try*, it is conceivable that this situation could arise in reverse adopting this formula. This would happen where a party actually recovers less at subsequent assessment for incurred costs than the court had assumed it would when ordering the general inter phase off-set. The same problems arise, albeit in reverse. The budget for a particular phase would be retrospectively varied to a sum over that which was reasonable and proportionate for that phase or the court would have to assess the sum for the budgeted costs for that phase in excess of the reasonable and proportionate sum.

As stated above, depending upon how the court articulates its decision and with properly drafted recitals reflecting this in the costs management order, there is a possibility of applying a later off-set between incurred and budgeted costs within a phase, resulting in either an addition or a deduction to the budgeted sum for 'good reason', if the assessing judge is so minded., However, for the reasons set out above these options are not available when the off-set is between different phases.

However, this does not mean that overall incurred costs have no relevance.

Clearly when the court undertakes its initial determination of overall reasonableness and proportionality, to inform the reasonable and proportionate case management directions and budgets for the discrete phases, the total 'incurred costs' will determine how much of the overall figure remains.

Q46. What happens if the total incurred costs means that even with the most proportionate case management possible it is not possible to budget costs 'to be incurred' at a level that, when added to those 'incurred costs', comes within the court's overall assessment of reasonableness and proportionality?

4–68   As discussed in response to the previous two questions this is a real, rather than merely theoretical problem. There are a number of possible outcomes as follows:

- The court declines to make a costs management order (as was the decision of Coulson J. in *Willis v MRJ Rundell and Associates Ltd*[83]). Whilst this leaves all of a budget exposed to the subsequent proportionality cross-check at any subsequent assessment under CPR r.44.3(2)(a), it does mean that the court has lost one of the vital tools out of its robust case management armoury. In reality, even with robust case management and the provisions of CPR r.44 PD 3 (which deals with the relevance of filed budgets in cases where no costs management order is made), the costs incurred by the end are likely to be even higher than those in the budget and it will be more challenging to manage the case in accordance with the overriding objective. The one occasion where this may be less challenging is if the case managing judge is also to be the assessing judge on any subsequent assessment (an option for the District Bench). As trenchant comments and recitals to the case management order justifying the fact no costs management order has been made and giving a view of what the case managing judge determined to be the overall proportionate figure, coupled with the fact both parties know that the same judge will conduct any subsequent detailed assessment, may encourage greater cost control going forward, recognising the inevitability of outcome on assessment of increased expenditure. This may also avoid the need for an assessment as the parties will know what is likely to happen at any subsequent assessment when the assessing judge undertakes the CPR r.44.3(2)(a) proportionality cross check at the end (a figure not dissimilar to that indicated at the case management conference).
- The court adopts the approach of Warby J. in *Yeo v Times Newspapers Ltd*[84] and records as recitals comments on 'incurred costs'. He adopted this route adding, by way of explanation, that to do so "'. . .is likely to help the

---

[83] *Willis v MRJ Rundell and Associates Ltd* [2013] EWHC 2923 (TCC).
[84] *Yeo v Times Newspapers Ltd* [2015] EWHC 209 (QB).

parties reach agreement without detailed assessment later on if these reasons are briefly recorded at the time the budget is approved".'

- The court adopts the approach of Coulson J as set out above. In *GSK Project Management Ltd v QPR Holdings Ltd*[85] this is precisely what the court did. As noted above this approach does raise interesting challenges. It is right to record that the problems of 'incurred costs' in *CIP* presented far more of a challenge on costs management than they did in *Yeo*. In *CIP* the 'incurred costs' totalled £4,226,768.16. At the end of the costs management exercise, adopting his off-set formula across the phases, the total that the court decided would ultimately be recoverable was £4,280,000. As the pre-action phase spend was over £1.3 million and as the total sum Coulson J 'allowed' overall in those phases where there was an incurred sum was always less than the incurred sum, the extent of his difficulty in costs management is obvious.

- Another way is a variation of the *CIP* approach, but one that may be seen to sit more comfortably within the existing rules. It extends the recitals approach advocated in *Yeo*. Under this approach the court first indicates and recites its view of overall reasonableness and proportionality of each party's costs. The court then case and costs manages by phases. In those phases where the 'incurred costs' already equal/exceed what the court decides is the reasonable and proportionate sum for that phase, nothing is budgeted and the court recites its finding on the reasonable and proportionate overall sum for the phase. In those phases where the 'incurred costs' do not equal or exceed the overall reasonable and proportionate figure for that phase, the court budgets the difference and recites its view on the overall reasonable and proportionate sum for that phase. This does leave matters to the assessing judge and, as such, is less prescriptive than the *CIP* approach, but provides a formula that sits happily with the budgeting by phase requirement, does not remove the assessing judge's discretion on arguments on 'good reason', provides clarity of intended outcome from the costs managing judge to the assessing judge and provides a mechanism to ensure that the overall costs are ultimately proportionate. Remember that the assessing judge will apply CPR r.44.3(2)(a) as a cross-check at the end of any assessment. Whilst this cannot apply to budgeted costs, as they have already been set by reference to proportionality, all costs incurred (and, therefore, not budgeted) at the time of the costs management order are subject to the cross check. Armed with this clear order and forewarned of the likely outcome of any assessment it will be a brave party, or one armed with genuine 'good reason' on any particular phase, who accepts the challenge of an assessment.

Q47. If there has been a significant front loading of the costs so that by the time of the costs management hearing the costs already spent exceed

---

[85] *GKN Project Management Ltd v QPR Holdings Ltd* [2015] EWHC 2274 (TCC).

what the court regards as the proportionate expenditure on the claim, can the court set a budget going forward of nil?

4-69 No. As set out above, the reason for this is that the budget is not set as an overall sum. It is set by phase under CPR r.3 PD E 7.3. Accordingly, even if the court concludes that the incurred sum to date exceeds that which is proportionate to have dealt with the entire claim, it must look at the budget on a phase by phase basis. This may mean that the budget for certain phases may be set at nil if the court thinks the incurred sum under that phase already equals or exceeds the reasonable and proportionate cost for the entire phase. This is because CPR r.3 PD E.7.4 requires the court to take costs already incurred 'into account when considering the reasonableness and proportionality of all subsequent costs'. However, there will be other phases, such as PTR, trial preparation and trial, where plainly there will be no incurred costs at the CCMC stage and it would be wrong, as the budget is set by reference to the reasonable and proportionate costs for each phase, for the court to budget these phases at nil.

Of course, as noted in the answers to **Qs 44–46** above, the court may also record its comments on the costs incurred before the date of any budget to assist the court at any later assessment when it considers the non budgeted costs.

Q48. What can be done to avoid the potential injustice of the court setting a phase budget by basing this on an overall view of the reasonable and proportionate sum for that phase, deducting the incurred costs and budgeting the difference, only for the assessing judge then to reduce the incurred costs undermining the basis upon which the budget was set?

4-70 This has already been identified above as a real risk of setting budgets by reference to the overall reasonableness and proportionality of a phase. However, the final suggested approach in the answer to **Q46** (above) may provide the solution. If the court adopts that approach, then it will be clear to the assessing judge the basis upon which the budget was set, both within the context of overall reasonableness and proportionality and on a phase basis. Of course, the assessing judge is not bound by the costs managing judge's recitals, but if the assessing judge allows less for the incurred costs than the costs managing judge included when setting the budget this may open the door for the receiving party to argue that there is a 'good reason' under CPR r.3.18 to depart from the budget for that phase. The 'good reason' being that the budget sum was calculated on the basis that £w had already been spent of the overall reasonable and proportionate sum for that phase of £x and so the budget for the phase is £x-w, but as the assessing judge has only allowed £w-y for the incurred costs, to achieve the outcome the costs managing judge envisaged requires the budget for that phase to be £x-w+y. This preserves the discretion of the assessing judge, which it is arguable that the *CIP* approach does not.

Q49. Should parties coming to the first CCMC to debate their respective budgets do so on the basis that it is the appropriate occasion on which

to contest the costs in the budgets (both incurred and estimated) as per para.44 of *SARPD Oil International Ltd v Addax Energy SA* [86]?

No. We boldly stated in the previous edition when considering the first   4–71
instance decision in *SARPD Oil*, that the costs management exercise is concerned with budgeting costs prospectively. It followed, inevitably, that our view was that whilst the court must take account of incurred costs under CPR r.3 PD E 7.4 when considering the reasonableness and proportionality of the budget, the CCMC was not the forum to contest those incurred costs. The Court of Appeal decision in *SARPD Oil* followed hot on the heels of the previous edition, immediately stated to the contrary! However, the Civil Procedure Rules Committee has agreed amendments to the CPR[87] which will make it clear that the costs management exercise is largely a prospective one (with a glance over the shoulder to incurred costs, either to record any agreement to them or to inform budgeted costs under CPR r.3 PD E 7.4) and is not the venue for challenges to incurred costs (see para.4–18 above).

Q50. Should the court set hourly rates as part of the budgeting exercise?
Curiously, there still appears to be a divergence of approach on this topic.   4–72
Curiously, because the straightforward answer is that the court is not required to set hourly rate when costs managing because CPR r.3 PD E 7.3 specifically states that the court sets 'total figures for each phase of the proceedings'. This provision has been reinforced by CPR r.3 PD E 7.10 (which is considered below in **Q51**). There are those who still favour the setting of hourly rates and suggest that the court can only set a total figure by reference to an hourly rate. However, hourly rate in isolation is worthless. It is only relevant if it is multiplied by an amount of time. However, hours multiplied by time smacks of what is 'needed', which brings us back to CPR r.3 PD E 7.3 as the court is not charged with setting a budget to allow necessary work – instead it is charged with setting a budget for each phase that is reasonable and proportionate.

There are a number of other reasons why setting the budget by reference to an hourly rate is inappropriate for those still attracted to this approach despite the clear and reinforced provisions of CPR r.3 PD E. These reasons are:

- It is too prescriptive. It is for the legal representatives and the client to determine how to spend the sum budgeted for a phase. If the budget is set by a specific hourly rate, then the court is effectively saying that that particular fee earner must do that amount of work. This is micro-management taken to an extreme. Setting a total figure enables the representatives and, more importantly, the client, to decide who does what work and what work is contracted out to counsel.
- If the budget is set by reference to hourly rate it opens doors for arguments at assessment as to whether, in fact, a fee earner commanding that

[86] *SARPD Oil International Ltd v Addax Energy SA* [2016] EWCA Civ 120
[87] Civil Procedure (Amendment) Rules 2017 SI 2017/95.

rate actually undertook the phase work in question. If the answer is no, then that may be 'good reason' to depart from the budget. These arguments do not arise if the budget is simply a total sum for the phase.

- If an hourly rate is set and at the end of the case, on assessment a different hourly rate is set for the non budgeted work (as the hourly rate set for the budget cannot be determinative in respect of the non budgeted costs as the court has no power to budget them under CPR rules 3.12 and 3.15), then immediately that opens the door to one or other party to argue 'good reason' to depart from the budget, submitting that the budget was set on the 'wrong' hourly rate.

- Setting rate and then determining the time by which to multiply it has all the hallmarks of a detailed assessment, which CPR r.3 PD E 7.3 specifically cautions the court against undertaking when costs managing.

- The amount of court time taken to determine rate and then the time by which to multiply it renders the budgeting exercise disproportionate – both for the parties and for the court.

- There is a very real risk that parties/representatives will 'forum shop' in cases with no requirement to proceed in a particular court venue.

In summary, CPR r.3 PD E 7.3 and 7.10 do not require the court to set hourly rates – indeed 7.10 makes it perfectly plain that the position is quite the reverse – it is expressly not the role of the costs manager to fix or set hourly rates. The emphasis is on a far simpler, less time-consuming and more proportionate process. One aim of costs management is to reduce the incidence of, and time taken on, subsequent assessments of costs. Setting a rate within the budget seems designed to encourage more contested assessments and to defeat this aim.

Q51. If the court does not set the budget by reference to hourly rates and time, then why does Precedent H require this information and, linked to this, what does *"the underlying detail in the budget for each phase used by the party to calculate the totals claimed is provided for reference purposes only to assist the court in fixing a budget"* in CPR r.3 PD E 7.10 mean?

4–73 This is a very fair point. Whilst this text has always maintained that CPR r.3 PD E 7.3 was clear that the court does not set hourly rate and this has been bolstered by CPR r.3 PD E 7.10, why does Precedent H require a breakdown, which simply serves to reinforce the 'old' approach to costs – set a rate and multiply it by an amount of time? It is arguable that a form that makes those completing it focus on reasonableness and proportionality in the round is more likely to achieve the desired effect. On that basis Precedent H could be reduced to just the first page in all cases as some have suggested.

However, that is not the position, and CPR r.3 PD E 7.10 considers the 'underlying detail'. This suggests that some courts may be assisted by this detail. An example of this may be where the parties' budgets are poles apart, but their proposed directions are similar and the court is endeavouring to discern a reason for this. In other words there may be cases where some of the detail assists, but at the end of the day the court will not set rates, will not prescribe the amount of time to be taken, but will simply budget a reasonable and proportionate sum and leave it to the parties to manage the budgets. A review of CPR r.3 PD E 7.3 suggests that this was always an option for the court. However, given the apparent inconsistency of approach, notwithstanding that provision, the iteration in CPR r.3 PD E 7.10, that the court does not set rate is a welcome one and should reduce some CCMC hearing times significantly.

Q52. How can the court set the budget without assessing prospectively the work that is required and the appropriate hourly rate(s) at which that work should be done?

The court is not charged when setting a budget with 'assessing', giving the word its customary meaning in a costs context. The court is also not charged with determining what work is required. What the court is charged with doing, is determining the just and proportionate case management directions and whether the budgeted costs for a phase of these directions 'fall within the range of reasonable and proportionate costs'. This inevitably involves a decision based on the definition of proportionality at CPR r.44.3(5). It is against the backdrop of this definition that the court determines whether the sum sought for a phase is reasonable and proportionate and, if it is not, whether there is a more suitable case management direction and what total sum should be substituted. When looked at in these stark terms, it is clear why a detailed analysis of hourly rate and time does not inform the outcome. The court simply determines the work to be done by reference to reasonable and proportionate expenditure (with the latter having the final say under CPR r.44.3(2)(a)). It is for that reason that case and costs management have to go hand in hand, so that the directions ordered only permit work that can be undertaken at proportionate cost.

Q53. If the court is budgeting only be reference to a global sum and not taking account of the respective hourly rates, surely this means that a party who has agreed a lower hourly rate retainer will be able to do more work than one with a higher hourly rate? If so this appears unfair.

Yes – a party with a lower hourly rate retainer is, in theory, able to undertake more work than one with a higher hourly rate. However, there are relevant factors that militate against the apparent unfair consequence:

- The court determines the appropriate proportionate case management directions. These inevitably define the extent of work that may be undertaken, e.g. limits on the number of factual witnesses, the amount of disclosure, the length of trial, etc.
- If the budget is set globally, then it is for a party to determine how to spend that money. Remember, costs are the client's and the budget is

4–74

4–75

the client's to spend – see **Chapter 9** below. The budget 'set' by the court will have to be explained to the client. Professional obligations on legal representatives may dictate that the way that sum is spent necessitates that the case plan is re-visited (e.g. does the client wish the work to be done by a lower level fee earner or is the client happy to have the higher level fee earner for less time or for the same amount of time, but in the knowledge that some of that cost will, inevitably be irrecoverable from the other party? Does the client want a less expensive expert/counsel or lesser input from the expert/counsel?). In certain instances this may mean that the client seeks alternative representation. What this does highlight is the importance of the retainer, both at the outset and on any variation, in defining precisely what work will be done for what remuneration. There is no doubt that the introduction of budgets reiterates the ongoing importance of managing client expectation, particularly in terms of any restraints that the case and costs management orders impose on a client's instructions. This is considered in the Q&A section of **Chapter 3**.

However, at the end of the day it is for each client to negotiate the retainer with the legal representatives. If one negotiates a lower rate than another, then any consequences based on the differential rate stem from the choice of retainer and not from any costs management order.

Q54. If the court does set the hourly rate in the budget what happens if, at assessment, the assessing court sets a different hourly rate for the non budgeted work?

4–76   This should not happen as CPR r.3 PD E 7.10 is clear that this is not the role of the costs managing judge. Accordingly any attempt by one party to persuade the costs managing judge to do so should be resisted. See the answer to **Q50** above. If rates are set then this may open the door to arguments that there is 'good reason' to depart from the budget. The possible consequences are that the length of summary assessments may be increased, that this persuades the trial judge to order a detailed assessment instead of assessing summarily in a fraction of the time and at a fraction of the cost and that there is an increased incentive for a paying party to take its chances on a detailed assessment. All fly in the face of a desire to make decisions about 'the costs of the costs' simpler and proportionate.

Q55. What, if anything, can the court do when the parties agree budgets or phases of the budgets in sums that the court thinks are disproportionate?

4–77   This is one of the curiosities of the costs management regime. CPR r.3.15 clearly envisages that the parties may agree all or part of the budgets and that if they do so, the court is left with the options of making no costs management order at all or making a costs management order recording the extent of the agreement (and approving a budget in respect of those phases not agreed).

However, CPR r.3.12(2) makes it clear that the function of the court is to manage both the steps and the costs to be incurred. Accordingly, if the court takes the view that the case management approach of the parties upon which the budget agreement is based is not proportionate, then the court must give proportionate directions. This is reinforced by the duty on the court imposed by CPR r.3.17 to take account of the cost of any procedural step and by the overriding objective.

It is unlikely that an agreed budget will remain so if the assumptions upon which the agreement was reached are altered, e.g. if the disclosure phase is agreed on the basis of an order for standard disclosure, but the court permits only a more limited form of disclosure, is a party really likely to maintain the agreement? This means that representatives at court must have ready access to the client during the case management hearing (if the client is not present) so that further instructions may be taken. Of course, if the parties have agreed what the court perceives to be proportionate case management directions, but have simply agreed figures more than the court thinks are proportionate, then there genuinely is nothing that the court can do to interfere with the agreement.

Q56. How important is the breakdown between disbursements and solicitors' fees in an approved/agreed budget?

Whilst the format of Precedent H requires a division between profit costs and various types of disbursement, CPR r.3 PD E.7.3 simply requires the court to set the budget for phases by way of total figures. Accordingly, many courts are not breaking down the sum budgeted for a specific phase between profit costs, counsel, experts and other disbursements, and for good reason. The rationale for this is that it is for the solicitor and the client to agree how the sum for a phase is to be spent. Solicitors may model this in many ways for the client to choose, e.g. where the proposed budget has been reduced by the court, the client may agree to place less reliance than had been envisaged on counsel or the same amount of reliance, but with the solicitors then using a less expensive fee earner.

4–78

Another difficulty of the court being too prescriptive about how the total sum for a phase is spent, is that it reduces the flexibility for the solicitor and client, e.g. if the budget for the pre-trial review is based on a division between solicitor and counsel on the assumption that counsel will attend the PTR and, in fact, the solicitor and the client agree that the solicitor will conduct that hearing, is that then 'good reason' to depart from the budget that was based on counsel attending? As one aim of costs budgeting is to reduce the number of assessments, this is better achieved by the court setting one figure for each phase and leaving the solicitor and client to decide how to spend that sum. Remember that the court is not sanctioning, for example, use of counsel or a fee earner with a set hourly rate at a specific stage: it is instead simply determining what is the reasonable and proportionate' sum of costs for each phase.

Having said all the above, there is no doubt that the breakdown in the Precedent H may inform the court of the case plan upon which the filed budget is predicated and so influence the decision as to what is the reasonable and proportionate overall sum for a phase.

Q57. Should parties re-file budgets after the CCMC when a costs management order has been made under CPR r.3.15?

4–79 Whilst the answer is simple, as CPR r.PD E 7.7 imposes an obligation upon the parties to do precisely this, it is worth stressing that if the court has made a costs management order that makes it plain from the face of the order, or any attached pages 1 of the budgets, which phases of the Precedent H have been budgeted, and in what amount, the court should be asked, if it does not automatically so do, to dispense with the requirements of CPR r.3 PD E 7.7 as they are superfluous and disproportionate in that situation. The purpose of this provision is to ensure that there is a clear record of what phases have been budgeted and in what amount. If this information is readily available on the court file and to the parties without them going to the expense of compliance with CPR r.3 PD E 7.7 so much the better.

F. Post costs management order general issues

Q58. Can the parties agree to vary their budgets from that recorded by the court in a costs management order, where there has been no 'significant development' in the litigation, but both are unhappy with the amount budgeted by the court?

4–80 No. Once a costs management order has been made by the court, it may only be varied where there are significant developments. The fact that all parties may be unhappy with the costs management order made is not a significant development. The remedy of the parties in such a situation would be to seek to appeal the costs management order. This is reinforced by CPR r.3.15(3) which places an obligation upon the court having set a budget to control the parties' budgets thereafter.

Q59. Once a budget has been set, should solicitors be monitoring the budgets?

4–81 Although the answer to this question is so obvious it ought not to need answering, it leads to a slightly different and more important issue. The answer to the basic question is yes. However, merely monitoring the budget is insufficient in isolation. The more important issue arises if one substitutes the word 'managing' in place of 'monitoring'. Simply watching as the budget for a phase dissipates is largely purposeless, it simply identifies when the money has been spent regardless of whether there has been compliance with the phase direction. What is needed is a planned expenditure within the budget. This requires consideration immediately after the CCMC of how the directed phase work is to be undertaken within the budgets set for the phases (assuming that the client is not prepared to fund additional work over and above the budget in the knowledge that it will be irrecoverable 'between the parties').

This must be followed by management to ensure that the directed phase work is completed within budget as planned. Accordingly, it comes as no surprise that some firms are/are considering engaging project managers accustomed to delivering work within budgetary constraint.

Q60. Upon taking over instructions for a client from another firm it is clear that the 'incurred costs' for the pre-action phase in the Precedent H filed and exchanged by that firm are considerably lower than the amount of costs that the client paid that firm for work done during that period. Whilst estimating future costs may be somewhat speculative, is there any explanation for why the incurred costs in Precedent H differ from 'actual costs' incurred?

Yes, there is an explanation, although whether it applies to a particular budget is fact specific both as to the terms of the solicitor and client retainer and as to whether the costs incurred are reasonable and proportionate. The explanation is that the Precedent H is meant to be prepared as a fair and accurate statement of incurred and estimated costs which it would be reasonable and proportionate for the client to incur. This is the wording of the statement of truth under CPR r.22 PD 2.2A that appears on the Precedent H. In other words, regardless of the costs actually incurred by the client at the time of the preparation of Precedent H, only those that are reasonable and proportionate should be included. Of course, this does not preclude the actual billed/incurred costs and those appearing in the Precedent H coinciding, but that should only occur if the representative signing the statement of truth on that form are satisfied that those costs are reasonable and proportionate. **4–82**

Q61. To which sum do the percentages in CPR r.3 PD E 7.2 apply – the total sum in the Precedent H after the budget has been set or just those parts of the Precedent H that the court has budgeted?

There appears to be some debate about this, with anecdotal evidence that some take the view that the percentage is to be applied to the 'Grand Total' sum in the bottom right hand box of page 1 of the Precedent H after the budget has been set and others taking the stance that the percentage applies only to the budgeted costs to be incurred in those phases of the Form H that have been costs managed. CPR r.3 PD E 7.2 states: **4–83**

> *"i) that the costs of initially preparing Precedent H are the greater of £1,000 or 1% of the approved and agreed budget;*
> *ii) all other recoverable costs associated with the budgeting and costs management process shall not exceed 2% of the approved or agreed budget."*

The definition of budget in the Glossary to the CPR does not help as it can be read in a way that suits either interpretation. It is this:

> *"Budget – An estimate of the reasonable and proportionate costs (including disbursements) which a party intends to incur in the proceedings"*

'in the proceedings' suggest overall, but'intends to incur' suggests in the future. However, and of greater significance, is that there is no definition in the glossary of what is an 'approved or agreed budget'.

Those arguing for the former interpretation can point to the fact that throughout CPR r.3.12–3.18, and the accompanying CPR PD E, the budget is described as being in the format of Precedent H. As such, reference to the budget is to the entire Precedent H. Whilst this point has some resonance, it seems to overlook the fact that CPR r.3 PD E 7.2 refers to the percentage as being set by reference to the 'approved or agreed budget' and not 'the budget'. The amendment to CPR r.3.15(2) with effect from 6 April 2017 blurs the issue. The court can now make costs management orders in respect of agreed or approved 'budgeted costs' (to be incurred), but can also record the extent of any agreement to incurred costs. In other words if the percentage is limited to those costs approved or agreed a party whose incurred costs have been agreed receives a higher sum than a party whose incurred costs are not agreed! On the other hand if the percentage applies to all the costs in Precedent H, then what is the purpose of including the words 'approved or agreed'?

It may be that this is something that the Civil Procedure Rules Committee proposes to address. Until then there are three valid reasons why an interpretation limiting the percentage to approved or agreed sums may be preferred: the first two are by specific reference to the rules and the third is one of common sense:

i) CPR r.3.18 expressly uses the words 'approved or agreed budget' and it is clear that in doing so it refers only to those parts of the Precedent H in respect of which the court has made a costs management order for budgeted costs, suggesting that there is a difference between the respective definitions of 'budget' and 'last approved or agreed budget'.

ii) If the words 'approved or agreed budget' automatically apply to the entire Precedent H total after the costs management exercise then, for the purpose of continuity under CPR r.3.18, the court has costs managed incurred costs (and in the absence of agreement to incurred costs it cannot do so) and the CPR r.3.18 provisions would apply to all the costs in the Precedent H and so any subsequent assessment would be on 'good reason' alone.

iii) There would be nothing that the court could do, save to try to rely on the 'exceptional circumstances' provision in CPR r.3 PD E 7.2 as one permitting a lower figure, to prevent a party over-estimating 'incurred' costs within the Precedent H to ensure that whatever happened on those parts costs managed, the percentage still came to an inappropriately high sum, even if, at a subsequent assessment of the 'incurred' costs, most were assessed to be irrecoverable as unreasonable and/or disproportionate. It seems utterly illogical that in rules designed to ensure both reasonableness and proportionality of costs, the percentage should be set by reference to a figure, over much of which the court has no control (and, indeed, in respect of which it may have made recitals recording unfavourable views!).

Q62. What if a client still wants the legal representatives to incur costs that the court has not allowed within the budget?
Remember that the costs management exercise is concerned with recoverable   **4–84**
costs 'between the parties' only. The basis of retainer remains a contractual issue between the solicitor and the client – see **Chapter 9**. To that extent, provided that the retainer permits it and the expenditure is agreed, the client is not constrained in what costs are actually incurred by the budget set by the court. So, for example, the client may still choose to engage counsel whose brief fees will mean that the client inevitably exceeds the budgeted sum for the trial phase. This is entirely the prerogative of the client provided he/she realises that there will be a shortfall between expenditure incurred and recovery of costs even if he/she is awarded the costs – see **Q63** and the reference to CPR r.46.9(3)(c) below.

However, clearly the case management directions that the court has given do impose an inevitable constraint. For example, if the court has limited a party to a set number of named expert witnesses, then there is no purpose in the client insisting upon the instruction of further experts as their evidence cannot be relied upon in court.

In summary, as Jackson LJ stated in his *Preface and Guide to the Civil Justice Reforms* in the *White Book* 2014:

> "*Within the confines of the directed procedure any party is free to waste its own money if it wishes to do so.*"

Q63. Does the statement of truth on the budget prevent a solicitor recovering more than the budget from the client?
No, subject to the appropriate wording of any specific solicitor and client fee   **4–85**
retainer (the qualification is because in County Court proceedings, s.74(3) of the Solicitors Act 1974 limits costs to those which could have been recovered from another party in the absence of any agreement to the contrary).

CPR r.22 PD 2.2A makes it clear that the budget is concerned with reasonable and proportionate costs. Proportionality has no place in solicitor/client assessments (which are effectively on the indemnity basis).

However, plainly a solicitor should inform the client of the budgeted sum so that the client is aware of the limit on those costs that may be recovered from another party in the event a costs order is made in the client's favour. This should enable the client to give informed instructions after the budget has been set. CPR r.46.9(3)(c) makes clear that on any assessment of solicitor and client costs, costs are assumed to be unreasonably incurred if they are of an unusual nature or amount and the solicitor did not tell the client that as a result they might be irrecoverable.

Q64. What is the position if a Part 7 claim commences as a fast track claim, but subsequently it becomes apparent that the claim is undervalued and needs to be re-tracked to the multi-track, but it is not within one of the costs management exceptions in CPR r.3.12(1)?

4–86 This is not an uncommon scenario – particularly in personal injury proceedings where the prognosis is uncertain at the time of allocation. Whilst the court is not constrained by a statement of value or allocation as to what sum it may award (see CPR r.16.3(7)), plainly the claimant must apply to amend the statement of value and to seek re-allocation. In any event, the increase in value is likely to result in a need to be linked with an application for further substantive directions (e.g. change of trial time estimate/trial window/further expert evidence, etc.).

As the costs management provisions apply to all multi-track CPR r.7 claims (subject to the exceptions detailed in CPR r.3.12(1)), then the effect of any re-allocation is to bring the claim within the costs management provisions. As such, it would be prudent for the claimant to attach a Precedent H to the application (and if the application is by consent for the defendant to do likewise). In any event, expect the court to order Precedents H to be filed and exchanged when listing the application or before it considers any consent order if the parties have not already provided them. This is not only because the court wishes to consider costs managing, but also because of the provisions of CPR r.3.17. Re-allocation is a case management decision and the court will need to know the cost consequence of any decision it takes.

If the application comes very late in the claim and the only variations to the existing case management directions are the amendment to statement of value, re-allocation and fresh trial window, it may be appropriate to include in the application a request that the court exercises its power under CPR r.3.12(1)(c) not to costs manage. This would be on the basis that the cost of the exercise may, in context, be disproportionate as the costs and steps to be incurred at that stage are limited. Of course this argument is something of a double-edged sword, as the court may take the view that as such, the costs management exercise will not occupy much court time and can be dealt with promptly and proportionately and as preparation for trial and trial are usually two of the most expensive phases of the budget (if not the most expensive), the exercise is still worthwhile and necessary. In the case of *Hegglin v Person(s) Unknown, Google Inc.*[88] the court was confronted with an application to cap costs ten days before the commencement of the trial. Edis J declined to do so, based on the late stage of the proceedings and the procedural threshold for making such orders, but, instead, exercised costs management powers under CPR r.3.15 to budget the trial and some outstanding work on an expert's report (see **Q89** below).

---

[88] *Hegglin v Person(s) Unknown, Google Inc.* [2014] EWHC 3793 (QB) Edis J.

Q65. Is a party who was acting in person at the costs management conference (and so has no budget), but who subsequently instructs solicitors, required to exchange and file a Precedent H?

Strictly the answer is that there is no procedural provision that requires the party to serve and file a budget in this situation. However, in practice the position is not quite as simple as this initial answer suggests as there are a number of potential triggers for a Precedent H in this situation. These are as follows: **4–87**

- Whilst the court file is unlikely to be referred to a judge simply because a party has become represented and a Notice of Acting is filed, experience suggests that frequently solicitors coming on record make applications for directions at the same time. If the file is referred to the judge to consider listing of any such application it is likely that the court will take the opportunity to order the filing and service of a Precedent H, triggering the possibility of costs management. Remember that under CPR r.3.16 a hearing may be convened by the court solely for purpose of costs management.
- It is arguable that the instruction of solicitors by a party previously unrepresented is a significant development in the litigation for any other party who is subject to a costs management order already (e.g. representation may shorten the trial or any application made by the new representatives, if successful, would have an effect on the budget previously set). This would engage CPR r.3 PD E.7.6 for the budgeted party and it is hard to see that if the court had to be involved in respect of any variation of budgets it would not also wish to budget the costs of the party who had previously been a litigant in person.
- Any other party who was subject to a budget might apply to the court to make a costs management order in respect of the previously unrepresented party's costs under CPR r.3.16 (see above). This seems likely as otherwise any budgeted party may feel prejudiced by having to conduct litigation within the parameters of a budget, whilst the previously unrepresented party would not be so constrained.
- The represented party may want a budget set so that the 'recoverable costs' are known at this stage and that party may then make decisions about the litigation fully informed about the costs consequences i.e knowing what, if anything, will be the shortfall between recoverable and solicitor/client costs if a costs order is secured.

Q66. Is a further Precedent H required with a pre-trial checklist ("PTCL") as CPR r.29 imposes no such requirement and yet the wording of the Precedent H guidance still suggests this is work included at the PTR stage?

CPR r.29 PD 8.1(1) requires a PTCL to be in Form N170. Form N170 no longer refers to a budget at Section F. Instead it refers to an estimate of costs. However, guidance at the beginning of the N170 suggests that in cases not costs managed an estimate of costs is required. However, it is clear from the   **4–88** wording used (reference to costs estimates and reference to these being provided in accordance with the provisions of the CPR) that the guidance is an unhappy and unwelcome failure to take account of the revised CPR. The only provisions relating to budgets are to be found at CPR r.3.1(7)(ll), 3.12–3.18, 3.20, 3 PD E, 3 PD F and CPR r.44 PD 3. These do not contain any requirement for an estimate at the time of PTCL (and neither does CPR r.29—other than by cross reference to Form N170 in the PD as referred to above).

The only requirement to file a further budget actually arises in costs managed cases where a party seeks revision of the budget and cannot agree that revision and so applies to the court.

Whether because of the confusion in the wording of Form N170, because the parties have not understood the significance of CPR r.3 PD E 7.6 or because of the reference in the Precedent H guidance on the PTR phase, most Precedents H filed under CPR r.3.13 contain within the assumptions in the PTR phase 'Updating of the budgets'. This is wrong as there is no automatic right to update. The only provision is CPR r.3 PD E 7.6 which permits revision only in specific circumstances. Expect the court to examine the PTR phase closely and reduce it where it contains the assumption set out above as work updating the budget is not time routinely reasonable and proportionate. There is also a danger that including this will make the court concerned as to what else has been included in the budget that ought not to have been and lead to a far closer scrutiny of all of the assumptions.

As an aside there appears little reason for the reference to 'an estimate of costs' in cases not costs managed in Form N170. By this stage directions will have been given and so the estimate is unlikely to inform the route the claim takes to trial. In addition the provisions of CPR r.44 PD.3 do not apply as the estimate is not 'a budget in accordance with' CPR r.3 PDE. It is also not clear what form the estimate should take as one is not prescribed. This version of Form N170 is well into its third year. It is clearly ripe for an update.

Q67. What is the purpose of the reference in CPR r.36.23 to CPR r.36.17(4)(b)?

4–89 CPR r.36.23 provides a limited 'automatic' relief from the sanction of CPR r.3.14 if an offeror pursuant to CPR r.36 is subject to the constraints imposed by CPR r.3.14. In the three situations set out in CPR r.36.23 (namely under CPR r.36.13(5)(b), 36.17(3)(a) and 36.17(4)(b)), the offeror may still be able to recover 50% of the costs assessed for those costs otherwise subject to the sanction and any other recoverable costs (i.e. those that were incurred at the time of the failure to file Precedent H). The rationale is clear. It is to provide the offeree with an incentive to accept the offer (the incentive being some adverse costs risk if the offer is a good one).

However, why does CPR r.36.23 expressly refer to CPR r.17(4)(b) because that provision is one specifically awarding the claimant costs on the indemnity basis? Having secured such an award of costs one might think that the sanction under CPR r.3.14 falls away anyway, because the constraints imposed on recoverable costs as a result of an approved or agreed budget by CPR r.3.18 expressly only apply to costs awards 'between the parties' on the standard basis (see **4–20** above and **Q76** below). Accordingly one might assume that any budget set on the basis of what is deemed under CPR r.3.14 to be in the budget (namely future court fees) ceases to be relevant on an indemnity basis award of costs. On this interpretation the provision seems designed to cover the period from the date the budget is set at future court fees only until the date from which the indemnity basis costs order runs. However, if that is the intention why link the provision to CPR r.36.17(4)(b) expressly, which already offers a solution for the particular period covered by that provision and not to CPR r.36.17(1) more generally?

Another construction is that CPR r.36.23 is a 'freestanding' procedural sanction designed to constrain the effect of an award of indemnity costs where there has been a breach of CPR r.3.13, so that the award of indemnity costs under CPR r.36.17(4)(b) does not provide an unqualified escape route for a claimant. In other words, it is a specific rule, the 50% is not expressed to be 50% of what would have been budgeted and therefore CPR r.3.18 is not engaged at all. This would mean that CPR r.36.23 provides a benefit where the offeror comes before the court under either CPR r.36.13(5)(b) or 36.17(3)(a), but a sanction if the offeror is a claimant coming before the court under CPR r.36.17(4)(b). However, this would mean that a claimant whose costs are constrained under CPR r.3.14 who secures an indemnity basis costs award outside the CPR r.36 regime is in a better situation than one who secures the award under CPR r.36.17(4)(b) – a curious outcome when CPR r.36 is designed to promote settlement.

On balance, given that CPR r.36.23 does not refer to the 50% being linked to what would have been budgeted, instead being an assessed sum outside of the budget, and because it expressly refers to a specific rule for indemnity costs that the rule makers would have realised gives 'relief' from CPR r.3.14 without the need for any further provision, the arguments for the latter of these two constructions appear more compelling. However, with an increasing number of 'costs managed' cases coming to fruition and with this provision having been in place for approaching two years, it cannot be long before some authorities emerge from the Higher Courts to provide guidance on the purpose of this discrete provision.

A final option is that the reference to CPR r.36.17(4)(b) in 36.23 is one made in error. However, it must be assumed that this is not so and that it reflects the intention of the rule makers. Unless and until it is removed it raises the issues set out above.

G. Variation of budgets and freestanding costs orders

Q68. What is a significant development for the purposes of CPR r.3 PD E 7.6?

There is no formal definition of 'significant development'. No doubt the **4–90** reason for this is that the interpretation has to be sufficiently flexible to enable the court to consider the position in the specific context of the case before it. Much has been made of the decision in *Churchill v Boot*[89] in which Picken J. refused permission to appeal the decision of the QB Master not to permit variation of the claimant's budget in circumstances where the claimant argued that each of:

- the doubling in the size of the claim;
- the adjournment of the trial; and
- there being further disclosure,

amounted to a 'significant development'. However, in fact, this decision simply confirms the 'case specific' approach to be adopted. The court concluded that:

- a doubling of the size of the claim does 'not necessarily' amount to a significant development (and in any event this was something that could have been anticipated at the time of costs management);
- whilst adjournment of a trial <u>could</u> amount to a significant development, it did not in this case; and
- the issue of further disclosure was something apparent <u>before</u> the costs management order.

In other words, these were not significant developments in this case as they were known about and/or should have been considered at the time of the costs management order. Some examples of developments that the court may consider significant are given in **4–19** above.

Q69. Is there a potential tension between CPR r.3.15(3) and CPR r.3 PD E 7.6?

4–91   CPR r.3 PD E 7.6 provides that if there is a significant development in the case any party may seek to vary budgets set. It also provides that in such circumstances the parties need only involve the court if they cannot agree the budget variation. This seems to sit unhappily with CPR r.3.15(3), which imposes on the court the obligation to control the parties' budgets once it has made a costs management order. How can it do so if the parties may vary the budget by agreement (and, it seems, without any requirement that the agreed varied budget is even filed at the court)? The answer, perhaps, lies in the first sentence of CPR r.3 PD E 7.6. The parties may only revise budgets if 'significant developments in the litigation warrant such revisions'. It is hard to think of such developments that will not require consequential case management directions. As already stated, as soon as the court is concerned with case management CPR r.3.17 applies and the court must determine whether the procedural step is worth the candle. This may mean that

---

[89] *Churchill v Boot* [2016] EWHC 1322 (QB).

if court determines that the costs the parties have agreed as a consequence of the further directions necessitated by the 'significant developments' are disproportionate, then the directions will not be given. This leaves the parties with the options of proceeding on the basis of the case that was originally budgeted or revisiting the varied budget to try to reach a figure at which the court will determine the significant developments can be dealt with at a proportionate cost.

Q70. Can a party make repeated agreed variations or, in default of agreement, applications to the court to vary a budget?

Yes, if that is appropriate. Under CPR r.3 PD E 7.6 a party shall revise its budget **4–92** in respect of future costs if significant developments in the litigation warrant this. Accordingly, provided that there are a number of significant developments, then there is no reason why there should not be repeated attempts to agree variations to the budget or, if agreement is not forthcoming, repeated applications to vary. What a party may not do is to make repeated applications to vary in respect of the same alleged significant developments. If there is no agreement and an application is made, but the court finds that there is, in fact, no significant development or the court finds that there is a significant development but either that this does not justify revision of the budget or not to the level that the party wishes, any dissatisfied party may appeal the decision of the court in the usual way under CPR r.52 (recognising that it will be rare indeed for an appellate court to interfere with a discretionary case management decision).

Q71. If an appeal is launched against a decision on an interim application that falls within a discrete phase (e.g. against an order in respect of permission for expert evidence) does CPR r.3 PD E 7.6 apply and should budgets be revised with a view to agreement or an application to vary?

Precedent H itself makes it clear that the costs of any appeals are excluded. **4–93** Accordingly, unless the appellate court decides to costs manage the appeal under the provisions of CPR r.3.12(1A) and so orders, there is no requirement either to file and exchange budgets for the appeal itself or to seek revision of the existing budget in the substantive proceedings simply to budget the appeal. However, where the substantive appeal requiring determination raises issue of proportionality (e.g. should an additional expert have been permitted) the appellate court may require revised budgets to enable it to determine the issue. In any event, if the consequence of the appeal, whether allowed or dismissed, is to have an effect on the budgets set for the substantive litigation, then variation of those existing budgets does arise e.g. the appeal results in permission for another expert, for strike out of, or judgment on, part only of the claim. This latter point raises the issue of whether the appellate court undertakes any budget revision required or refers this back to the first instance case managing court. If the appeal allowed is one such as in respect of additional expert evidence, the appellate court has had the revised budgets to enable it to determine the issue of proportionality, then it is likely to be proportionate for it to undertake the revision. If the appeal is one such as summary judgment in part, that does not require consideration of the costs consequences and which, in any event, completely alters the complexion of the case (and, inevitably in consequence, the budget set), then adjourning the revision to the case managing judge, seems more appropriate.

Q72. It seems that some parties are not applying to vary budgets, but instead prefer to wait to argue 'good reason' to depart from the budget at any subsequent assessment. Is this because it is easier to depart from a budget retrospectively when the work may be easier to justify than to vary prospectively when the work may be seen to be speculative?

4–94   As noted under **Q69** above, a party is obliged to try to agree a budget variation or, in default of agreement, apply to the court for variation where there is a significant development in the litigation. CPR r.3 PD E 7.6 is prescriptive – *"'Each party shall revise its budget in respect of future costs upwards or downwards. . ."'* Accordingly any party choosing to ignore this and seek to argue 'good reason' at any subsequent assessment does so contrary to mandatory requirements in the CPR. Whilst it is for the court in each individual case to determine whether the 'good reason' requirement for departure from a budget under CPR r.3.18 is met, it is difficult to imagine that a deliberate decision to defer could ever constitute 'good reason'.

It is also challenging to imagine a significant development in the litigation that does not require court intervention by way of further case management decision. As the court is under an obligation pursuant to CPR r.1.1, CPR r.3.15(3) and 3.17 to control costs and ensure that case management decisions are made against a backdrop of whether or not a step is proportionate, it should not be possible for directions that result in or follow a significant development in the litigation to be determined without consideration of the budgetary implications at that juncture. It follows from this that any application for any additional case management directions that will result in or follow a significant development in the litigation, after a budget has been set, should be accompanied by a revised budget setting out the implications on the budget set, if the additional direction/s is/are granted. Any respondent to such an application, whether opposing it or not, should also file and submit any revised budget. This is true even if the parties have agreed the budget revision as the court will still want to know potential cost implications of any decision, to inform it when determining under the provisions set out above, whether to make the order sought.

The suggestion that work (and, more precisely, the costs associated with it) may be easier to justify with the benefit of hindsight, also risks overlooking the provisions of CPR r.44 3(2)(a) – namely that considerations of proportionality trump both reasonable and necessary work. Accordingly, unless the application of CPR r.44.3(5) leads to a different conclusion than it did when the budget was set, the fact that more work might have been necessary or reasonable is irrelevant.

Q73. If a costs management order has been made in a case but not long afterwards a party makes a potentially determinative application for summary judgment ("SJ"), should the parties apply promptly for the budgets to be revised? Suppose that they do, but the hearing for SJ is likely to come on before the application to revise costs budgets can be heard, what should they do? Could the potential respondent to the SJ application not justifiably seek, in such circumstances, an order that the costs thrown away by this change of tack by the applicant be paid by it in any event?

These questions raise two issues. The first relates to contingencies and the second to the relationship between budgets and CPR r.3 PD E 7.9. Dealing with those in turn: **4-95**

1) Depending upon the temporal proximity the position may be different for the applicant and the respondent to the application.
   - **The applicant** This seems to be an example of when something (the application) was more likely than not to occur at the time of the budget, and so ought to have been included as a contingency. If it ought to have been in the budget as a contingency, it raises the interesting question of whether the failure to include it means that the applicant to the application can neither seek budgetary variation because it is not, for that party, a significant development in the litigation (as it knew at budget setting time it was going to issue the application imminently) nor, if successful on the application, seek a freestanding order for costs of the application outside the budget (considered in more general terms below) as it is not an interim application made that, reasonably, was not included in the budget. The fact that the application itself may fall within a fixed costs regime (e.g. a CPR r.24 application) offers no assistance either, as it is only if the proceedings (as opposed to the application) are subject to fixed costs that there is an exclusion from costs management under CPR r.3.12(1)(c).
   - **The respondent** Obviously the respondent's budget did not include in it anything for the application, as it was not in a position to determine whether it was more likely than not to occur. As a result CPR r.3 PD E 7.9 applies (see below) to any costs to which the respondent may become entitled, as it reasonably did not include this in the budget.
2) If the application was not 'more likely than not to occur' at budget setting time and so was reasonably not included in either budget, then CPR r.3 PD E 7.9 applies. As such costs of the application will be dealt with at the end of the application and fall outside the budget. In other words, any costs awarded to a party will be in addition to, and freestanding of, any costs under the budget.

Q74. If a costs management order was made based on the Precedent H in use before 6 April 2016 and a party seeks variation of the budget set, which version of Precedent H should be completed and submitted to the other parties and the court?

4–96 The amended Precedent H introduced under the 83rd CPR Update was for use in claims issued on or after 6 April 2016. It has subsequently been revised again in the 86th CPR Update (see **Qs 19** and **20** above). The revised form was introduced as of 3 October 2016 and there is no transitional provision, meaning it should be used in all cases immediately. This suggests that the form in use at the time that the varied budget is prepared to submit to the other party/parties for agreement should be used (it is hoped that the court would surely regard it as disproportionate for a party to redo the budget onto the one in place from 3 October 2016, where the variation had been prepared and submitted to the other party/ies for possible agreement prior to 3 October 2016, no agreement had been forthcoming and the application was then made after 2 October but where the varied budget sums remained the same).

Q75. What sort of applications fall within the provisions of CPR r.3 PD E 7.9? How does this link with the provisions for contingencies in the budget and budget variation?

4–97 CPR r.3 PD E 7.9 (considered above)) and the Precedent H guidance give very clear steers in respect of those costs that will fall outside the budget. CPR r.3 PD E 7.9 refers to interim applications 'which reasonably were not included in a budget'. The guidance provides some distinction between those costs and ones that fall within CPR r.3 PD E 7.6 (significant developments requiring variation), defining the latter as those "costs which are not anticipated but which become necessary later". These comments link to the definition of contingent costs in the Precedent H guidance. The definition is that these are "costs which are more likely than not to be incurred". The result is this:

- If something is more likely than not to occur at the time of the costs management order, but is not certain and so does not fit into another phase under estimated costs, it should be included as a contingency. Parties need to be astute to whether or not a budgeted contingency becomes a reality as otherwise they may overlook that some of the contingencies never came to fruition for the purpose of 'good reason' to depart from the budget (as the fact that a contingency for which budgetary provision was made did not occur, must surely be a 'good reason' for departing from the budget).
- If the cost relates to an application that was not reasonably included in the budget at the time of the costs management order, it falls within CPR r.3 PD E 7.9 e.g. an application to enforce compliance with directions, and that cost is outside the budget and the costs of that application fall to be

determined and then assessed as part of the determination of the application, which is entirely free standing and independent of the budget.

- If something representing a significant development in the litigation arises (other than an application which is either more likely than not to occur at the time of costs management or which it was reasonable not to include in the budget), then the costs fall to be dealt with under CPR r.3 PD E 7.6 as a revision to the budgets.

H. The relevance of a budget at a subsequent assessment

Q76. What is the effect of a costs management order at an assessment of costs on the standard basis?
One might think this is obvious as CPR r.3.18 is expressed in utterly unam-   **4–98**
biguous language as follows:

> *"3.18 In any case where a costs management order has been made, when assessing costs on the standard basis, the court will -*
> *(a) have regard to the receiving party's last approved or agreed budget for each phase of the proceedings: and*
> *(b) not depart from such approved or agreed budget unless satisfied that there is good reason to do so."*

Indeed, in the past we have not lingered long on this topic as the position seemed clear. However, it appears this confidence was misplaced for, as mentioned in para.**4–20** above, there is a concerted challenge to the apparent clarity of CPR r.3.18. In essence the argument is that:

- CPR r.47 obliges the court to carry out a detailed assessment (and that applies to incurred and budgeted costs).
- At a detailed assessment the court will make an individual 'line by line' assessment of the reasonable costs and then decide issues of proportionality.
- Nowhere in CPR r.44 or 47 is there any provision that the paying party has to show a good reason to seek a departure from any approved or agreed budget. Indeed, budgets are just one of a non-exclusive list of factors in CPR r.44.4(3), which requires the court to consider all the circumstances when assessing costs. It is neither afforded primacy in the list, nor said to be determinative.
- The instruction to the court not to undertake a detailed assessment at the time of budgeting (in CPR r.3 PD E 7.3) and the express requirement that the court should not fix hourly rates at the time of budgeting (in CPR r.3 PD E 7.10) clearly evidence that these are matters for later and that the budgeting exercise is not intended as a substitute for detailed assessment.
- The budget is no more than a 'cap' on costs (in other words a sum that must not be exceeded) or a fund against which a party may draw down and the requirement for 'good reason' in CPR r.3.18(b) only applies where the receiving party seeks to recover more than the budget for a phase. If, after

assessment on an item by item assessment, the sum for a phase is within the sum budgeted then it is the lesser sum that is recovered. Support for the argument that a budget is no more than a cap and that 'good reason' in CPR r.3.18 only applies to an upwards departure, can be found in the decision in *Simpson v MGN Ltd*, in particular from the comment that:

> "*It is clear from CPR 3.18(b) that if a figure has been agreed or approved for a particular phase of proceedings the amount recoverable by the receiving party in respect of that phase will be capped at that figure, unless there is good reason to depart upwards. (If the receiving party has incurred costs less than budgeted there will be good reason to depart downwards.)*" (para.19.)

- Unless the reasonable amount is determined first the court cannot fulfil its function under CPR r.44.3(2)(a) to step back and determine if the reasonably assessed sum is proportionate.
- The decisions of Moore-Bick LJ in both *Henry v News Group Newspapers Ltd*[90] and *Troy Foods v Manaton*[91] are clear that approval of a budget does not demonstrate *"without further consideration, that the costs incurred by the receiving party are reasonable or proportionate simply because they fall within the scope of the approved budget."* (*Troy* para.8)

These arguments received a large measure of approval in the first instance decision of *Merrix v Heart of England NHS Foundation Trust*[92] in which the District Judge concluded that a budget is a fund within a range of reasonable and proportionate costs and not a fixed sum and that the powers and discretion of a costs judge on detailed assessment are not fettered by the costs budgeting regime, save that budgeted figures should not be <u>exceeded</u> unless 'good reason' can be shown (effectively inserting the word 'upwards' after 'depart' in CPR r.3.18(b)).

The decision in *Merrix* is not binding and there are compelling arguments, which we prefer, (some not addressed in that case – presumably because they were not argued) that lead to a completely opposite conclusion – namely that CPR r.3.18 means precisely what it says, that there shall be not departure from the last agreed or approved budget without good reason. These arguments are that:

- CPR r.3.18 is absolutely transparent in its meaning and requires no insertion of any words to make sense. This view is reinforced if one reverts to the intention expressed equally unambiguously by Jackson LJ in his final report at Page 401 under the general description of 'The essential elements of costs management' that *"'at the end of the litigation the reasonable costs of the winning party are assessed in accordance with the approved budget'"* (see **4–14** above).

---

[90] *Henry v News Group Newspapers Ltd* [2013] EWCA Civ 19.
[91] *Troy Foods v Manaton* [2013] EWCA Civ 615.
[92] *Merrix v Heart of England NHS Foundation Trust* [2016] EWHC B28(QB).

- CPR r.44.4(2), which is set out in the judgment in *Merrix*, appears not to have been the topic of submission and is, therefore, not analysed in the judgment. This is an important omission, as the rule is of direct relevance to the situation where a costs management order has been made. This is because CPR r.44.4(2) – under the general heading of CPR Pt 44 'Factors to be taken into account when deciding the amount of costs' – states that *"in particular, the court will give effect to any orders which have already been made."* A costs management order is an order that has already been made, with a procedurally prescribed consequence on the decision on the amount of recoverable costs and, as such, the court must give effect to it. Accordingly, the assertion that there is nothing in the costs provisions of the CPR that fetters the powers and discretion of an assessing judge where a costs management order has been made appears to be flawed: any decision to depart from budgeted costs in the absence of a good reason to do so is contrary to the express requirement at CPR r.44.4(2).

- Any attempt to revisit reasonableness and proportionality, other than under the guise of 'good reason', overlooks that the budgeted costs have already been subject to a judicial determination of reasonableness and proportionality (see the wording of CPR r.3 PDE 7.3 and paragraph 3 of the Guidance Notes on Precedent H – which expressly refers to CPR r.44.4(3) and 44.3(5)). Accordingly, there has already been judicial determination of the reasonableness and proportionality of the budgeted costs and the assessing judge has no jurisdiction to exercise an appellate function (note this is not the same thing as revisiting the budget under 'good reason' as the rules specifically convey this jurisdiction on to the assessing judge in the same way that CPR PD3E para.7.6 expressly reserves the jurisdiction for the court to vary budgeted costs provided it does so prospectively).

- The fact that CPR r.3 PD E 7.3 expressly warns the court against undertaking a detailed assessment in advance, is not a preservation of an unfettered right to a detailed assessment in respect of the same costs later. Instead it simply means that the court is not to approach the budgeting exercise as though it has been asked to undertake a traditional detailed assessment. In other words it is simply an explanation of the process of budgeting and not any attempt to reserve a position for subsequent detailed assessment. That this is so, is surely supported by the fact that the court may elect, as is both permissible and, in suitable cases, proportionate, to undertake a summary assessment of costs in budgeted cases (see for example *Sony Communications International AB v SSH Communications Security Corporation*, in which it was accepted that the winning party would only recover less than the budget for a phase if it had actually spent less on the phase – amounting to nothing more than an articulation, and the application, of the indemnity principle [considered further below]). CPR r.3 PD E 7.3 is silent as to summary assessment. As such, if the argument as to preservation of the right to revisit budgeted costs is founded on the words of CPR r.3 PD E 7.3, then strictly that right only arises on a detailed but not summary assessment. To create such a distinction seems nonsensical and introduces a distinction between the two forms of assessment that does not exist in CPR r.3.18.

- The fact that CPR r.44.4(3)(h) is one of eight factors to which the court must have regard in a non-exhaustive list does not mean it is not determinative. It is a reminder to the court and the parties that this is a relevant factor in respect of those costs within the bill that have been cost managed. The relevance to be attached to that factor is set by a combination of CPR rules 3.18 and 44.4(2).

- Jackson LJ specifically rejected the notion that a costs budget is a costs cap in his final report when describing the Law Society submission that "'budgeting is not costs capping'" as, helpful (page 413). Indeed, if a budget is no more than a costs cap, one cannot help but wonder why the costs management rules are found in Section II (Costs Management) and not in Section III (Costs Capping) of CPR Pt 3. CPR PD3E para.7.3 clearly states that the budget for a phase is a specific figure. If one accepts that CPR r.3.18 and CPR r.44.4(2) are determinative, it matters not how one seeks to define budgeted costs as there can be no departure from the sum specified on any phase in the absence of a good reason. If the budget is simply a cap or a fund to be reviewed, why is there a requirement to revise downwards in CPR PD3E para 7.6? An alternative construction of the conclusions reached in *Simpson v MGN Ltd*, which sits happily with this view is set out above at **4–20**.

- There is no difficulty with undertaking the CPR r.44.3(2)(a) proportionality cross check (see **Chapter 3 Q11**).

- The judgment of Moore-Bick LJ in *Henry* was under a pilot scheme with a different stated objective than the current regime (CPR 51 PD 1.3 as was), with a 'broad' range at costs management and with a different proportionality approach (having no equivalent of CPR r.44.3(5) or CPR r.44.3(2) (a)). The current regime does provide for the court to determine both reasonableness and proportionality of the budget at costs management with express reference to these specific costs provisions. It should also be remembered that in *Henry* the court was actually concerned with a party who had exceeded the budget and not complied with the provisions of the scheme itself and this was the focus of the decision. In respect of the reverse situation, what the court said in para.16 may, if one accepts that reasonableness and proportionality have already been determined, be seen as no more than an iteration of the indemnity principle, namely that 'if the costs incurred in respect of any stage fall short of the budget, to award no more than has been incurred does not involve a departure from the budget'. In fact it is suggested that it does represent a departure as the budget is for a specific sum, but plainly one for good reason – namely that a receiving party cannot recover more costs from a paying party than it is obliged to pay under its retainer with its solicitors.

- Not only is the decision in *Troy* not binding, as the court recognised in *Merrix*, but the pilot scheme under CPR r.PD 51G, under which it was budgeted, was less prescriptive as to how a budget was to be set. Whilst CPR r.51 PD G, para.1.3 contained a reference to 'reasonable and proportionate' costs, that was in the context of incurred costs, which could not be budgeted. CPR r.51 PD G, para.4.2 stated the purpose of costs management to be *"'to control the costs of litigation in accordance with the overriding objective'"*. It is important to remember that the then the overriding objective did not include the words 'and at proportionate cost'. Accordingly, there was certainly scope under the pilot to argue that the costs budgeting process had not involved a prospective evaluation of reasonable and proportionate costs and that, therefore, the comments of Moore-Bick LJ that there should be further consideration of these twin requirements was unsurprising. It is also worth remembering that in *Troy* the court was concerned with a budget that Moore-Bick LJ described as having been set by the first instance judge *"on the basis that he would approve any figure for a particular element of the claim, provided it was not so unreasonable as to render it obviously excessive or, as he put it, 'grossly disproportionate'"*. This does not bear analogy with a budget set by express reference under CPR PD3E para.7.3 to both reasonableness and proportionality. (See **Chapter 3 Q10** for a more detailed consideration of *Troy*).
- If CPR r.3.18 is not given its clear meaning, then a core reason for costs management disappears – the certainty that it provides to clients in respect of recoverable costs (both for and against them) that enables them, the ultimate court users, to make informed decisions knowing the costs risks involved.
- The then Master of the Rolls in *Denton v T H White*[93] seemed under no doubt as to the effect of a costs management order when considering the benefit of an indemnity costs order, making a clear link between the budget set and the effect of CPR r.3.18 *"If the offending party ultimately loses, then its conduct may be a good reason to order it to pay indemnity costs. Such an order would free the winning party from the operation of CPR rule 3.18 in relation to its costs budget."*
- Case and costs management are inextricably linked. Dealing with a case in a way that is just and proportionate, means that, when considering the appropriate directions that determine the procedural path a claim takes, the decision is inseparably linked to the reasonable and proportionate budget for each phase (see *Jamadar v Bradford Teaching Hospitals NHS Trust* para.38). To permit wholesale revision of the budget downwards in the absence of good reason retrospectively, having required the parties to adopt the procedural route ordered, recognising the reasonable and proportionate sum that this would cost, might be said to be illogical, unfair and, arguably, in breach of the overriding objective.

---

[93] *Denton v T H White* [2014] EWCA Civ 906.

Merrix is the subject of an appeal listed to be heard just before this edition goes to print, but at the time of print the judgment is not available. However, whatever the outcome whether the debate will end there is a moot point. In the meantime, in *Sony Communications International AB v SSH Communications Security Corporation*[94], a case in which the parties elected to submit to the costs management regime, the court recorded that *"'The parties have agreed that as the Cost Budgets were drawn up and accepted on the basis that the costs identified therein were reasonable and proportionate, there is no need for a detailed assessment and they have asked me to make a summary assessment on the basis of the relevant Cost Budget.'"* This seems to articulate one of the intended consequences of costs management and the reason for it. In addition, when reviewing *Henry*, the court concluded, amongst other matters, that the budget was not a cap and that there could be departure from the budget for a phase, but only if there was 'good reason'. In other words, giving effect to the clear meaning of CPR r.3.18.

What is certain is that until there is clarity, at the risk of both disproportionate costs and allocation of court time, it is likely that the competing arguments will continue to be advanced on detailed assessments of budgeted cases on a case by case basis.

It has to be said that if the arguments against applying CPR r.3.18 precisely as it is drafted prevail, then this seems to undermine the very purpose and the proportionality of the costs management regime. What is the point of the investment of time and costs into budgeting if, in fact, all it achieves is to provide a maximum figure unless there is 'good reason' to exceed that (and whether that maximum figure is called a cap or the extent of a fund seems a debate without a purpose)? If it does not provide the certainty to enable informed risk analysis and decision making, if an 'old fashioned' item by item detailed assessment can 'trump' a costs management order in any event and if the 'costs of the costs' are not reduced, rather than enabling the court to manage the costs to be incurred, costs budgeting simply adds a further tier of case management and cost consequential upon that for no real discernible benefit.

Q77. Is the budget 'without prejudice' to any subsequent assessment?

4–99   See **Q76** above which considers the competing arguments as to the effect of a costs management order.

There is no provision in the rules for applying a 'without prejudice' qualification beyond 'good reason' to a costs management order, it is not part of the costs management regime and seems, simply to add time and costs to the case management process for no purpose – other than possibly assisting the court to identify the proportionate case management directions that should be given (by virtue of setting the budget in the normal way), but in a thoroughly disproportionate way if the budget is qualified other than by CPR r.3.18.

---

[94] *Sony Communications International AB v SSH Communications Security Corporation* [2016] EWHC 2985 (Pat).

Adopting this approach seems to deprive the parties of the certainty that CPR r.3.18 provides, involves everyone in an exercise that may well prove futile and seems to act as a clear encouragement to pursue costs issues further at assessment. Accordingly, such an approach seems contrary to the specific costs management provisions and the overriding objective.

Anecdotally, it appears some parties are trying to agree budgets subject to reserving the right to argue about the hourly rate at a subsequent assessment. As budgets are either agreed or are not agreed, parties advancing this position should expect to be given fairly short shrift by the court. They are likely to find themselves deciding between maintaining the agreement on the budget, but without the qualification, or electing to have the court approve the budget.

Q78. Can you explain how an award of costs on the standard basis differs from an award of costs on the indemnity basis in circumstances where a costs budget is in place?

The difference stems from the respective definitions of standard basis and indemnity basis costs in CPR r.44.3. Under the former costs will only be allowed if costs are reasonably incurred and reasonable and proportionate in amount. Under the latter costs will be allowed if they are reasonably incurred and reasonable in amount. In other words there is no consideration of the proportionality of the costs under an award of indemnity basis costs. As costs budgets are set under CPR r.3 PD E 7.3 on the basis of setting a figure within the range of reasonable and proportionate costs, it immediately becomes apparent that a budget cannot be relevant on an indemnity basis assessment as it has been set taking account of something that does not arise under the indemnity basis. This is why CPR r.3.18 expressly only applies to standard basis assessments. Accordingly on a standard basis assessment CPR r.3.18 applies and there may only be departure from those costs budgeted if there is 'good reason', whilst on an indemnity basis assessment CPR r.3.18 does not apply, the budget does not operate as any constraint on recovery of costs and the court simply allows those costs reasonably incurred and reasonable in amount, with the benefit of any doubt going to the receiving party (which is also not something that the court applies on budgeting). It is obvious that the potential differential between costs on the standard basis and those on the indemnity basis in budgeted cases may, where the costs incurred exceed the budgeted sum, be significant.

4–100

Q79. If an award of indemnity costs is made and CPR r.3.18 does not apply, does the budget still form the starting point for the assessment of costs?

No – see para.4–20 above. The starting point is that CPR r.3.18 only applies on standard basis assessments. In effect this provides the explanation for the short answer given. However, to provide greater clarity there are three obvious justifications linked to the same underlying principle. These are:

4–101

- The statement of truth on the Precedent H makes it clear that the form should only include 'incurred and estimated costs which it is reasonable and proportionate' for that party to incur. However, on an indemnity basis assessment proportionality has no part to play and, so, using a budget based on a Precedent H, which was prepared taking account of proportionality, as the starting point for an assessment which takes no account of it is immediately and obviously flawed.
- Under CPR r.3 PD E 7.3, any budget set by the court will be one within the range of 'reasonable and proportionate costs'. Accordingly the budgeted figures have been set taking account of proportionality which has no place on an indemnity basis assessment.
- On an indemnity basis assessment the benefit of any doubt as to whether costs were reasonably incurred or reasonable in amount is given to the receiving party. This is not something that has been applied at the budgeting stage.

If there remained any doubt, the comments of Dyson MR cited in para.4–20 should dispel it.

Q80. What effect will a 'costs sanction' for unreasonable conduct, as suggested by the Court of Appeal in *Denton v T H White*,[95] have on a costs budget?

4–102   At para.42 of the majority judgment the Court of Appeal said this:

> *"The court will be more ready in the future to penalise opportunism . . . Heavy costs sanctions should, therefore, be imposed on parties who behave unreasonably in refusing to agree extensions of time or unreasonably oppose applications for relief from sanctions. An order to pay the costs of the application under rule 3.9 may not always be sufficient. The court can, in an appropriate case, also record in its order that the opposition to the relief application was unreasonable conduct to be taken into account under CPR rule 44.11 when costs are dealt with at the end of the case. If the offending party ultimately wins, the court may make a substantial reduction in its costs recovery on grounds of conduct under rule 44.11. If the offending party ultimately loses, then its conduct may be a good reason to order it to pay indemnity costs. Such an order would free the winning party from the operation of CPR rule 3.18 in relation to its costs budget."*

Accordingly, it is clear that the 'costs sanction' envisaged may be relevant to budgets set in two scenarios:

1)   If the offending party subsequently becomes the receiving party on an assessment, then the unreasonable opposition may be a 'good reason' to depart from the budget relying upon the provisions at CPR r.44.11(1)(b) and 44.11(2)(a).
2)   If the offending party subsequently becomes the paying party, then an

---

[95] *Denton v T H White* [2014] EWCA Civ 906.

award of costs on the indemnity basis may follow and, as has already been stated, this means that the provisions of CPR r.3.18 do not apply (as that rule is limited to where the court is assessing on the standard basis).

In both situations the effect may be substantial – in the first limiting and in the second increasing costs recovery.

Q81. What guidance is there on what may constitute 'good reason' under CPR r.3.18 to enable a departure from a budget at assessment?
At the moment there have been limited no reported authorities on the current provisions in respect of what might constitute good reason. However, as is clear from the text of this chapter, Moore-Bick LJ in *Henry v News Group Newspapers Ltd*,[96] a case within the defamation pilot scheme, clearly envisaged that 'good reason' was intended to present a high hurdle and that the court would not lightly permit departures from the budget. Although in a different context (CPR r.3.9), the Court of Appeal has already reinforced the view that the 'good reason' definition bar is set high.

4–103

Some 'good reason' departures from the budget are obvious, e.g. where a budgeted contingency does not arise or where a claim is resolved before a specific phase has commenced. Beyond these, counsel of caution must be to seek prospective variation under CPR r.3 PD E 7.6 whenever it is appropriate, rather than to run the gauntlet of arguing 'good reason' at assessment.

Whilst awarding costs on the indemnity basis, and so there was no practical effect of considering departure from the budget (as CPR r.3.18 only applies to standard basis assessments), in *Barkhuysen v Hamilton* the court accepted that conduct of litigation, increasing costs beyond the budgeted amount by the generation of work beyond that contemplated within the budget, was 'good reason' under CPR r.3.18, as, indeed, was a change of trial venue. Although *Simpson v MGN Ltd*[97] saw a departure from the budget, this case provided no guidance on 'good reason' as the court found that there was no 'good reason' – see **4–20** above and **Q83** below.

Q82. Can a trial judge ordering a detailed assessment of the costs of a party subject to a costs management order, give guidance to the assessing judge on what may be 'good reason' to depart from the budget set.?
This issue was mentioned in passing in *Capital for Enterprise Fund A LP and another v Bibby Financial Services Ltd (HHJ Pelling QC unreported, 18 November 2015)*. The judge concluded that even if, which he doubted, the trial judge had jurisdiction to indicate that it would be appropriate for there to be a departure from a budget, such power should only be used in exceptional circumstances. This immediately creates an inconsistency if an assessing judge is not assisted by any indication that the trial judge, but if the trial judge

4–104

---

[96] *Henry v News Group Newspapers Ltd* [2013] EWCA Civ 19.
[97] *Simpson v MGN Ltd* [2015] EWHC 126 (QB).

conducts a summary assessment then information from the trial relevant to departure for 'good reason' under r.3.18 will be before the court. It is arguable that the court in *Capital for Enterprise Fund ALP* took too narrow a view of its function. If it could have used 'trial information' to assist it on a summary assessment, why should that not be before the assessing judge on a detailed assessment: it is the same information and surely carries the same relevance whoever assesses the costs? This view is supported by established authority that trial judges should assist assessing judges with relevant information (e.g. in the context of the application of the conduct provisions under CPR r.44.2 [trial judge] and 44.4 [assessing judge] – see for example *Northstar Systems Limited v Fielding*[98] and *Drew v Whitbread Plc*[99]) and there appears no discernible reason why the position should be any different in this situation.

Q83. Does CPR r.3.18(b) prescribe an automatic sanction where the receiving party has failed to amend its budget prospectively and can show no 'good reason' for this failure or, as is suggested in *Simpson v MGN Ltd* (see 4.20 and Q81 above), is it for the court, applying the overriding objective, to determine what the just and proportionate sanction should be?

4–105   This depends entirely upon the construction of the wording at CPR r.3.18(b). In *Simpson* the court concluded that this provision did not provide a sanction and so, even where there was no 'good reason' to depart from the last approved or agreed budget, that did not mean that the receiving party was automatically precluded from recovering in excess of the budgeted sum. An alternative view was expressed in *Sony Communications International Ab v SSH Communications Security Corporation*[100].

This alternative view is considered at **4–20** above. This is that the inclusion of the words *'unless satisfied that there is good reason to do so'* in CPR r.3.18(b) provide a sanction, which is that absent 'good reason' there is no departure from the budget. We prefer this interpretation. It also seems better to meet two of the objectives of costs management, namely:

- Increased certainty of costs exposure between the parties at the earliest possible juncture so that they make informed decisions about pursuit of a claim or a defence and settlement.
- Increased certainty of costs outcome, resulting in fewer detailed assessments (occupying both court time and resulting in increased expenditure for the parties).

The lesser the clarity as to where the bar to departure from agreed or approved budgets is positioned, the greater both of uncertainty of outcome and of the costs incurred in locating its position.

---

[98] *Northstar Systems Limited v Fielding* [2006] EWCA Civ 1660 para.34.
[99] *Drew v Whitbread Plc* [2010] EWCA Civ 53.
[100] *Sony Communications International AB v SSH Communications Security Corporation* [2016] EWHC 2985 (Pat).

What does seem certain, is that as more costs managed cases come to assessment, further authority on both the interpretation of the effect of the rule itself and what constitutes 'good reason' is likely to emerge. (See **Q76** above on the need for such authority).

Q84. Can the budgeted sum exceed the sum due from that party to the solicitor under the contractual retainer, and, if so, is this a permitted breach of the indemnity principle?

The budgeted sum may exceed the sum provided for within the retainer.   **4–106** However, the fact that the court makes a costs management order does not mean that those costs are recoverable from another party regardless of the indemnity principle. Indeed the amendment to the statement of truth on Precedent H was, in part at least, to address the problem where specific fee retainers made completion of the budget difficult (e.g. in-house lawyers, fixed fee cases, etc.).

Breach of the indemnity principle would be a 'good reason' under CPR r.3.18 to depart from the budget (see comments on *Henry* and *Simpson* at, respectively, **Q76** and **4–20** above). However, this may prove a more challenging exercise than it seems at first sight. Imagine the case where the fee retainer is a fixed fee for all work or a Damages Based Agreement where there is simply 'the payment' which cannot be calculated until the end of the claim. How does the solicitor apportion between the phases of Precedent H in those situations? Client retainers may need to be drafted in creative fashion to enable this apportionment and to meet any challenge under 'good reason', e.g. that apportionment of the overall fixed fee/the payment is a matter for the solicitor provided that the work that has been agreed to be done under the retainer is undertaken. It is likely that as these cases work through the system, the court will be confronted with the challenges that they present and authority will emerge.

I. Case management

Q85. Does the decision of the Court of Appeal in *Denton v T H White*[101] mean that relief from sanction will be granted provided that there is no prejudice to any other party that cannot be compensated by a costs order and that a trial date can still be met?

No, not necessarily. All cases will be fact specific. The Court of Appeal has set   **4–107** out a clear three-stage approach to applications under CPR r.3.9 and it is the application of that which will determine the outcome of each specific request for relief. As such that may mean that in some cases the fact that there is no prejudice to the other party and a trial date can be met will, in all the circumstances, result in relief and in others it will not.

Whilst *Denton* clearly provides those seeking relief with a greater prospect of success than *Mitchell*, it is clear from the phraseology adopted by the court

---

[101] *Denton v T H White* [2014] EWCA Civ 906.

in *Denton* that there is not to be a return to the approach of pre-1 April 2013 as set out in the quote from the judgment in the text. Instead, as is stated in the judgment of the majority, what is required:

> *"is a more nuanced approach . . Anything less will inevitably lead to the court slipping back to the old culture of non-compliance which the Jackson reforms were designed to eliminate"*[102].

It is also important to remember that whilst *Denton* may have clarified and amplified the judgment in *Mitchell*, much of what that latter case determined remains pertinent and the actual facts of *Mitchell*, and the conclusion reached on those facts, still represents a far more robust approach to non-compliance than prior to 1 April 2013. If there was any doubt about that it is dispelled by the decision of the Court of Appeal in *Jamadar v Bradford Teaching Hospitals NHS Foundation Trust*[103] (see **4-05** above).

The fact that a lack of prejudice is not determinative (rather than simply a circumstance to take into account under stage 3 of *Denton*) was confirmed by the Court of Appeal in *R (on the application of Idira v The Secretary of State for the Home Department*[104] when it stressed:

> *"At para.43 in Denton, this court said that parties should not "adopt an unco-operative attitude in unreasonably refusing to agree extensions of time and in unreasonably opposing applications for relief from sanctions". It added: "it is unacceptable for a party to try to take advantage of a minor inadvertent error. . .". I would emphasise the words "unreasonably" and "minor inadvertent". A party is not required to agree to an extension of time in every case where the extension will not disrupt the time-table for the appeal or will not cause him to suffer prejudice. If the position were otherwise, the court would lose control of the management of the litigation."*

Similarly the fact that refusal to grant relief will cause significant prejudice to the party in default does not mean that relief should be granted. In *Sinclair v Dorsey & Whitney*[105] a professional negligence claim said to be valued at £30 million was struck out for breach of an unless order to provide security for costs. An application for relief was dismissed on application of the *Denton* 3 stage test. The fact of prejudice (in terms of the lost opportunity to pursue such a claim) was insufficient when considered in all the circumstances and giving particular weight to the two factors in CPR r.3.9.

Q86. Does the decision in *British Gas Trading Ltd v Oak Cash and Carry Ltd*[106] impact on the likelihood of relief from sanction being granted under CPR r.3.9?

---

[102] para.38.
[103] *Jamadar v Bradford Teaching Hospitals NHS Trust* [2016] EWCA Civ 1001.
[104] *R (on the application of Idira) v The Secretary of State for the Home Office* [2015] EWCA Civ 1187.
[105] *Sinclair v Dorsey Whitney* unreported QBD 20 November 2015.
[106] *British Gas Trading Ltd v Oak Cash and Carry Ltd* [2016] EWCA Civ 153.

In this case the defence was struck out because the defendant failed to file **4–108** its pre-trial checklist by the date specified in the case management order and then failed to comply with an 'unless order' requiring filing by a later date and providing for strike out unless there was compliance. The claimant applied for judgment in default of defence and the entry of this triggered an application for relief by the defendant almost five weeks after the strike out. Relief was granted at first instance. This decision was overturned on appeal and the defendant appealed to the Court of Appeal, which dismissed the appeal. The importance of the Court of Appeal's decision is that it clarified that at the first stage of the *Denton* test for relief, the court should recognise that the breach of the 'unless order' is not a free-standing brief and should look at both the original breach which led to the 'unless order' and the breach of the 'unless order' when considering whether the breach is serious or significant. Having clarified this, Jackson LJ drew the inevitable conclusion that breach of an 'unless order' was a pointer towards both seriousness and significance because:

- It evidences breach of more than one obligation to do the same specific task; and
- The importance of compliance has been highlighted to the defaulting party by the very fact that an 'unless order' has been made.

To answer the question, the effect of the decision is that parties applying for relief from sanction after the breach of an 'unless order' start from the position that there is a pointer towards the breach being treated as serious or significant that does not exist where the breach is of what the court described as an 'ordinary (i.e not an'unless) order'.

Q87. Does the emphasis on proportionality impact on the situation where a claim falls within fast track financial limits, but the number of witnesses is such that the time needed for trial exceeds one day?
Indeed it does. Many of these cases would have been allocated to the multi- **4–109** track based on the trial time estimate prior to 1 April 2013. Since that date, allocation must be viewed against the revised overriding objective and the court must determine whether allocation to the multi-track is proportionate. It will do so by reference to the revised overriding objective and the CPR r.44.3(5) factors. The mere fact that the number of witnesses that the parties wish to call would mean that the trial will exceed one day is not determinative in isolation. If there is that number of witnesses because of the complexity of the claim or because there are issues of public importance or reputation, then that may justify allocation to the multi-track as proportionate. If no such factors exist, then the court is likely to allocate to the fast track. This will be in conjunction with effective case management using the powers that the court has under CPR r.32.2(3) to control the extent of witness evidence permitted and its powers under CPR r.39.4 to timetable the trial to ensure that the trial does not exceed one day. In such a case parties may expect the

trial timetable to limit the time allocated for opening the case (if permitted), cross examination, closing submissions and judicial consideration, judgment delivery, award of costs and summary assessment under any award. In other words, parties may have to select their 'best' evidence and their 'best' cross examination points. As Jackson LJ stated in the Final Report:

> "*The essence of proportionality is that the ends do not necessarily justify the means.*"[107]

Remember that not only will allocation to the multi-track incur the parties in further expenditure, but also that CPR r.1.1(2)(e) expressly includes in the definition of "dealing with a case justly and at proportionate cost" the allocation of court resources and the express requirement to take account of the resource needs of other cases. Allocation to multi-track simply to accommodate a longer trial time erodes the judicial time available for other cases.

Q88. Do the case management rules apply as much to litigants in person as to represented parties?

4–110   Prior to 1 October 2015 the answer was yes, with the exception of the costs management provisions (as litigants in person are not required to prepare Precedents H under CPR r.3 PD E 7.8 – but see **Q2** above). However, from 1 October 2015 CPR r.3.1A has added a discrete provision relating to case management and the taking of evidence in claims involving litigants in person. The rule applies where at least one party is unrepresented (3.1A(1)) and requires the court to have regard to the fact that at least one party is unrepresented when exercising any case management function. This includes the court adapting the standard directions under CPR r.29.1(2) (**4–08** above) and adopting any procedure that it considers appropriate to further the overriding objective. When taking evidence the court may ascertain from an unrepresented party matters about which a particular witness may be able to give evidence and upon which that witness should be cross examined and may put to that witness or cause to be put to that witness such questions as appear to the court to be proper. What this means in practice remains to be seen. However, it seems likely that in terms of case management, properly interpreted, any alterations to usual procedure'/directions in any particular case by the application of this rule will apply equally to represented and unrepresented parties in that particular claim.

Q89. Will cost capping under CPR 3 Section III be ordered more rarely?

4–111   It seemed that costs capping had run its course. In his May 2015 '*Confronting costs management*' lecture there is a record of one question put to Jackson LJ that evening. It was: "*Is there now any place for costs capping?*". His answer was unequivocal: "*No. In my view the costs capping rules should be repealed*". Reports of the Civil Procedure Rules Committee meeting in July 2015 suggested that

---

[107] Ch.3.para 5.3.

this was to happen. However, they were granted an 11th hour reprieve and remain.

However, it is difficult to see how costs capping has a future in those cases where the costs management regime applies (see *Hegglin v Person(s) Unknown, Google Inc.*[108]). By definition, a costs management order ensures that the costs budgeted are proportionate, as that is the basis upon which they have been set under CPR r.3 PD E 7.3. As the court in the costs capping regime can only apply a cap to future costs, then where costs management is available a party will never be able to satisfy the requirement of CPR r.3.19(5)(b), that without a cap there is a substantial risk that costs will be disproportionately incurred, because if they can do so, the court is inexorably drawn back to the requirement in CPR r.3.15(1) that it must costs manage where budgets have been filed and exchanged unless it is satisfied that the litigation can be conducted justly and at proportionate cost in accordance with the overriding objective.

It would be nonsensical to look at costs capping in those cases where the court exercises its discretion under CPR r.3.12(1)(e) to exclude cases that would otherwise fall within the costs management regime. This would fly in the face of the decision not to costs manage in the first place.

The relevance of costs capping in cases where the court chooses not to make a costs management order or which fall outside the regime is, at first blush, unaltered by costs management. However, in cases outside the regime where the court is concerned at the level of costs and the likelihood of these being adequately controlled by case management and subsequent assessment, the court may choose to exercise its discretion under CPR r.3.12(1A) to costs manage, rather than to costs cap. As the budget to be filed and served in an application for costs capping will be in the format of Precedent H (see CPR r.3 PD F 2) and as the court will have to assess the quantum of the costs for the purpose of imposing a cap anyway (CPR r.3 PD F 4.1), it may determine that costs management is preferable to costs capping. This also avoids the difficulty presented by the 'exceptional circumstances' threshold set for costs capping. As a result it may be that a party seeking a costs cap may wish to link the application to one for costs management under CPR r.3 PD E 2(a).

Obviously, if the court is to consider costs management as an alternative to costs capping it will require Precedents H from all parties and will need to exercise its discretion under CPR r.3.20(3)(a) to ensure that it has these when dealing with a multi-party claim.

A point of interest arises in respect of the subsequent relevance of budgets where a claim is not subject to the costs management regime, but where, in the course of an unsuccessful application for costs capping, Precedents H are filed and served. Are these budgets of relevance at any subsequent assessment of costs? Strictly under CPR r.44 PD 3.1 only budgets filed under 3 PD E are relevant when considering the provisions relating to a 20% or more difference between budget and eventual costs claimed. As the budget in a costs capping

---

[108] *Hegglin v Person(s) Unknown, Google Inc.* [2014] EWHC 3793 (QB) Edis J.

application has been filed under CPR r.3 PD F it seems that these provisions do not apply. It does seem curious that the provisions of CPR r.44 PD 3 have been limited and do not apply to all budgets filed under any rule, practice direction or court order.

The question is limited to CPR 3 Section III. Amendments have been made to CPR r.46 to introduce the discrete costs capping regime in Judicial Review cases at Section VI.

CHAPTER 5

Part 36 and Other Settlement Offers Including ADR and Costs Consequences

Introduction

This chapter deals both with Part 36 offers and with other methods of achieving settlement; and is divided into two sections, the first dealing with Part 36 and the second with methods of settlement other than Part 36.

5–01

Section 1 Part 36

Background to Part 36

Part 36 has undergone significant changes in recent years following two Court of Appeal decisions: *Crouch v Kings Healthcare NHS Trust*[1] and *Trustees of Stokes Pension Fund v Western Power Distribution (South West) Plc*.[2] The Civil Procedure (Amendment No.8) Rules 2014,[3] which came into force on 6 April 2015, contain an entirely new version of Part 36 in Sch.1. There are also consequential amendments to other Parts. The intention of the new Part 36 is to align the rules with the case law developed since the Part was last amended.

5–02

Transitional provisions

The new Part 36 applies in its entirety only in relation to Part 36 offers made on or after 6 April 2015, save that CPR r.36.3 (definitions), CPR r.36.11 (acceptance of a Part 36 offer), CPR r.36.12 (acceptance of a Part 36 offer in a split trial case) and 36.16 (restriction on disclosure of a Part 36 offer) also apply in relation to any Part 36 offer where the offer is made before 6 April 2015, but a trial of any part of the claim or any issue arising in it starts on or after 6 April 2015.[4]

5–03

CPR Part 36 after 5 April 2015

Section I of Part 36 contains a self-contained procedural code about offers to settle made pursuant to the procedure set out in that Part. Section I contains general rules about Part 36 offers. Section II contains rules about offers to settle where the parties have followed the Pre-Action Protocol for Low Value Personal Injury Claims in Road Traffic Accidents ("the RTA Protocol") or the Pre-Action Protocol for Low Value Personal Injury (Employers' Liability and Public Liability) claims ("the EL/PL Protocol") and have started proceedings under Part 8 in accordance with Practice Direction 8B.[5]

5–04

---

[1] *Crouch v Kings Healthcare NHS Trust* [2004] EWCA Civ 1332; [2005] 1 W.L.R. 2015.
[2] *Trustees of Stokes Pension Fund v Western Power Distribution (South West) Plc* [2005] EWCA Civ 854; [2005] 1 W.L.R. 3595.
[3] SI 2014 No.3299.
[4] Civil Procedure (Amendment No.8) Rules 2014, rr.18(1) and (2).
[5] r.36.1.

Under Section I, any party to an action may make an offer to settle in whatever way that party chooses, but if the offer is not made in accordance with CPR r.36.5 (form and content of a Part 36 offer) it will not have the consequences specified in Section I.[6] Where an offer does not comply with the requirements set out in CPR r.36.2, it is not a Part 36 offer.[7]

A Part 36 offer may be made in respect of the whole or part of any issue that arises in a claim, counterclaim or other additional claim, or an appeal or cross-appeal from a decision made at a trial.[8] Counterclaims and other additional claims are treated as claims, and references to a claimant or a defendant include a party bringing or defending an additional claim.[9]

In proceedings following a road traffic accident, the defendant, who alleged contributory negligence, made an offer, under the previous regime, to settle that issue on the basis of a 25% reduction, three weeks before the trial was due to start. The claimant accepted the defendant's offer one week before trial. Neither the offer nor the acceptance made any mention about the costs of the contributory negligence issue. The judge at first instance found that the defendant was in fact the claimant for the purposes of the contributory negligence issue, and ordered the claimant to pay the defendant's costs in relation to it. On the claimant's appeal, it was held that the defendant's offer amounted to an offer solely in relation to liability. It fell within old CPR r.36.2(5) (which provided that "An offeror may make a Part 36 offer solely in relation to liability"—this provision has been omitted from the new rule, presumably because it was superfluous), and the fact that the context was contributory negligence did not affect that. The defendant's offer was, and was intended to be, a Part 36 offer and the claimant's entitlement to costs arose under old CPR r.36.10(1) (now CPR r.36.13). In the light of the settlement at 75% to 25% liability split, it was wholly artificial to describe the claimant as anything other than the winner.[10]

The definition section of Part 36 makes it clear that a trial means any trial in a case whether it is a trial of all the issues or a trial of liability, quantum or some other issue in the case. A trial is in progress from the time when it starts until the time when judgment is given or handed down. A case is decided when all issues in the case have been determined, whether at one or more trials.[11] CPR r.36.3 also defines the relevant period, as to which see paragraph 5–06 below.

Part 36 offers in appeal proceedings

5–05   Except where a Part 36 offer is made in appeal proceedings, it has effect only in relation to the costs of the proceedings in respect of which it is made and

---

[6] r.36.2.
[7] See *Thewlis v Groupama Insurance Co Ltd* [2012] EWHC 3 (TCC); [2012] BLR 259. Rule 44.2 requires the court to consider an offer to settle which is not an offer to which costs consequences under Part 36 apply.
[8] r.36.2(3).
[9] rr.20.2 and 20.3.
[10] *Onay v Brown* [2009] EWCA Civ 775; [2010] 1 Costs LR 29 CA.
[11] r.36.3.

not in respect of any appeal in those proceedings. Composite first instance and appeal offers to settle are not permissible and separate offers must be made. If a Part 36 offer is made in appeal proceedings the references in the rules to, e.g. claimant/-defendant are replaced by corresponding terms, e.g. appellant/respondent[12].

In personal injury proceedings, the claimant at first instance had been awarded damages which failed to beat two Part 36 offers made by the defendant. The claimant was held liable for the costs incurred from the date of expiry of the first offer. On appeal, the total damages award was increased to an amount in excess of the first Part 36 offer, although less than the second. The Court of Appeal revised the first instance costs decision ordering the claimant to pay the costs from the date of expiry of the second Part 36 offer. With regard to the costs of the appeal, the Court held that the claimant had already been penalised in costs for having failed to accept the defendant's offers and the second offer had not been open for acceptance after May of 2014. It had therefore been necessary for the claimant to pursue the appeal in order to improve his position. The claimant was awarded his costs subject to two exceptions relating to specific categories of costs.[13]

Form and content of a Part 36 offer

A Part 36 offer must:

5–06

(a) be in writing;
(b) make clear that it is made pursuant to Part 36[14];
(c) specify a period of not less than 21 days within which the defendant will be liable for the claimant's costs, where a Part 36 offer is accepted in accordance with CPR r.36.13 or, where Section IIIA of Part 45 applies, in accordance with CPR r.36.20 if the offer is accepted;
(d) state whether it relates to the whole of the claim or part of it or to an issue that arises in it and if so, to which part or issue; and
(e) state whether it takes into account any counterclaim.[15]

Where a defendant had made what purported to be a claimant's Part 36 offer in respect of the defendant's counterclaim, "the proceedings in respect of which" it was made included the claim and the proposed counterclaim, but were not restricted only to the counterclaim. A Part 36 offer may be made before the commencement of proceedings (under old CPR r.36.3(2), now CPR r.36.7) so the fact that the defendant's counterclaim had not been formulated or pleaded did not of itself matter.[16]

---

[12] r.36.4(1) and (2).
[13] *Pawar v JSD Haulage Limited* [2016] EWCA Civ. 551.
[14] This is a change from the earlier version of the rule which required the offer to "state on its face if it was intended to have the consequences of Section I of Part 36".
[15] r.36.5(1).
[16] *AF v BG* [2009] EWCA Civ 757. Contrast *Van Oord UK Ltd v Allseas UK Ltd* [2015] EWHC 3385, [2016] 1 Costs L.O. 1, Coulson J, **Q13** below.

A Part 36 offer may be made at any time including before the commencement of proceedings. Such an offer is made when it is served on the offeree.[17] The period of 21 days specified in (c) above or such longer period as the parties agree in the case of an offer made not less than 21 days before trial, is known as "the relevant period". Where an offer is made less than 21 days before a trial, the relevant period is the period up to the end of the trial.[18] A Part 36 offer may be made using Form N242A. If the other party is legally represented the notice must be served on the legal representative.[19]

Where a claimant had accepted a Part 36 offer made jointly by all defendants in relation to part of the proceedings and the offer expressly stated that it did not concern the counterclaim, a defendant sought summary judgment on its counterclaim arguing that the offer covered all allegations of wrongdoing on which the claimant's defence to the counterclaim was founded. The court concluded that the acceptance of the defendants' offer did not prevent the claimants from relying in their defence to the counterclaim on facts alleged as part of the settled claim.[20]

Withdrawing or changing the terms of a Part 36 offer generally

5–07   A Part 36 offer may only be withdrawn or its terms changed if the offeree has not previously served notice of acceptance. The offeror may withdraw the offer or change its terms by serving written notice of the withdrawal or change of terms on the offeree.[21] CPR r.36.10 makes provision about when permission is required to withdraw or change the terms of an offer before the expiry of the relevant period. Subject to that, notice of withdrawal or change of terms takes effect when it is served on the offeree.[22]

Provided that the offeree has not previously served notice of acceptance, after expiry of the relevant period the offeror may withdraw the offer or change its terms without the permission of the court, or the offer may be automatically withdrawn in accordance with its terms. Where the offeror changes the terms of the offer to make it more advantageous to the offeree, the improved offer will be treated not as the withdrawal of the original offer, but as the making of a new Part 36 offer on the improved terms, and provided that the new offer is not made less than 21 days before the start of the trial, the relevant period will be 21 days or such longer period (if any) identified in the written notice of change of terms.[23]

CPR r.36.9(4)(b) provides that an offer may be automatically withdrawn after the expiry of the relevant period in accordance with its terms. This is both the effect and apparent intention of the rule – a Part 36 offer can now include within it a provision by which the offer is automatically withdrawn

---

[17] r.36.7.
[18] rr.36.3(g) and 36.5(2).
[19] r.36.7 and see Practice Direction 36, para.1.1.
[20] *Marathon Asset Management LLP v Seddon* [2016] EWHC 2615 (Comm), Leggatt J.
[21] See r.36.17(7) as to the costs consequences following judgment of an offer which is withdrawn.
[22] r.36.9(1), (2) and (3).
[23] r.36.9(4) and (5).

(and therefore time limited) – though it must still usually be open for a minimum of 21 days and CPR r.36.9(4)(b) cannot be used until that relevant period has passed. This alters the position under the previous version of Part 36, as confirmed in *C v D*.[24]

Where, under the previous version of Part 36, the offer did not specify a period of not less than 21 days, or any period, in compliance with CPR r.36.2(2)(c) (now CPR r.36.5(1)(c)), the offer was not a Part 36 offer. It was not part of the mandatory requirements of the rule, once the period had been specified, to state expressly that that was the period "within which the defendant will be liable for the claimant's costs if the offer is accepted". But the solicitors' letter did not specify any period for the purposes of the rule and that was fatal[25]. The offeror had not sought the more extreme consequences of a successful claimant's offer, namely indemnity costs or interest at an enhanced rate. It was difficult to see how the court could award additional interest unless the offer complied with Part 36 and in the absence of a true Part 36 offer any claim for indemnity costs would have to be justified on the relevant general principles. The impact of the offer on costs was properly to be considered not as if it had complied with Part 36 when it had not, but as part of the court's general discretion as to costs under Part 44[26].

A claimant in libel proceedings made a Part 36 offer which was not accepted and was withdrawn after 21 days. At trial the claimant beat her own Part 36 offer and sought indemnity costs on the grounds of the defendant's failure to beat the Part 36 offer and on the basis of the defendant's unreasonable conduct during the proceedings. The court decided that the procedural matters carried little weight and did not amount to unreasonable conduct sufficient to justify an award of costs on the indemnity basis. In considering that the withdrawn Part 36 offer had not been beaten, the judge decided that to award indemnity costs on that basis would involve the introduction of such an award for behaviour which was not necessarily unreasonable[27].

A building contractor sued a householder for work done. The householder counterclaimed for losses alleging poor workmanship. The defendant made a Part 36 offer, inclusive of interest, and subsequently made increased offers. The claimant made counter-offers, but the parties did not reach agreement. The defendant withdrew all the offers, except the original one. At trial before the District Judge the claimant recovered some £300 more than the defendant's original Part 36 offer. The defendant appealed against the costs order, arguing that the judgment was not materially more advantageous to the claimant than the original Part 36 offer. On appeal the Court of Appeal held that the provisions of Part 36 state clearly how an offer may be made, how it may be varied and how it may be accepted. Unlike ordinary common

---

[24] *C v D* [2011] EWCA Civ 646; [2012] 1 W.L.R. 1962; [2011] 5 Costs L.R. 773

[25] *Onay v Brown* [2009] EWCA Civ 775 and *C v D* [2011] EWCA Civ 646.

[26] *Carillion JM Ltd v PHI Group Ltd, Carillion JM Ltd v Robert West Consulting Ltd*, [2012] EWCA Civ 588; [2012] 4 Costs L.O. 523.

[27] *Gulati v MGN Limited* [2015] EWHC 1805 (Ch.) Mann J. Mann J's judgment on damages was upheld on appeal: [2015] EWCA Civ 1291; [2016] 2 W.L.R. 1217.

law principles they do not provide for an offer to lapse or become incapable of acceptance on being rejected by the other party. Once made, a Part 36 offer remains open for acceptance until the start of the trial or its withdrawal in the manner set out in previous CPR r.36.3(7) (now CPR r.36.9(4)). Where a party makes several offers in different terms, a later offer does not revoke or vary an earlier offer, and all of them may be capable of acceptance at any one time.[28]

Following a collision at sea, the claimant offered to settle liability 60/40 in favour of the claimant. The offer was said to be made in accordance with CPR Part 61.4(10)–(12) and/or Part 36. The offer was subsequently withdrawn two months before trial, when the claimant offered to settle on a two thirds/one third basis. At trial, liability was apportioned 60/40 in favour of the claimant. In relation to costs, the court decided that there was a line of authority starting before the CPR but continuing after it, indicating that where an offer had been withdrawn which should have been accepted, it would not be unjust to award the offeror all of its costs, because, had the offer been accepted, no further costs would have been incurred thereafter (see *Bristol and West Building Society v Evans Bullock & Co*[29]). The mere fact that an offer had been withdrawn did not necessarily deprive the offer of effect on the question of costs. The defendant should have accepted the offer when it was available, or should have appreciated the costs risk and taken protective steps by making a realistic Part 36 offer itself. The fact that the offer was withdrawn two months before trial did not make it unjust to order that the claimant should get all their costs from 21 days after the offer was made. Prior to that the defendant should pay 60% of the claimant's costs, and the claimant should pay 40% of the defendant's costs.[30]

Withdrawing or changing the terms of a Part 36 offer before the expiry of the relevant period

5–08   Where the offeree has not previously served notice of acceptance and the offeror serves notice of withdrawal of the offer or changes in its terms to be less advantageous to the offeree before the expiry of the relevant period, if the offeree has not served notice of acceptance of the original offer by the expiry of the relevant period, the offeror's notice has effect on the expiry of that period; if the offeree serves notice of acceptance of the original offer before the expiry of the relevant period, that acceptance has effect unless the offeror applies to the court for permission to withdraw the offer or to change its terms within seven days of the offeree's notice of acceptance, or, if earlier, before the first day of trial. If such an application is made, the court may give permission for the original offer to be withdrawn or its terms changed if satisfied that

---

[28] *Gibbon v Manchester City Council LG Blower Specialist Bricklayer Ltd v Reeves* [2010] EWCA Civ 726; [2010] 1 W.L.R. 2081; [2010] 5 Costs L.R. 828.

[29] *Bristol and West Building Society v Evans Bullock & Co* Unreported February 5, 1996 CA.

[30] *Owners and/or Bareboat Charterers and/or Sub Bareboat Charterers of the Ship Samco Europe v Owners of the Ship MSC Prestige* [2011] EWHC 1656 (Admlty) Teare J.

there has been a change of circumstances since the making of the original offer and that it is in the interests of justice to give permission.[31]

Where the offeror seeks permission of the court to withdraw a Part 36 offer or to change its terms to be less advantageous to the offeree before expiry of the relevant period, the permission of the court must, unless the parties agree otherwise, be sought by making a Part 23 application which must be dealt with by a judge other than the trial judge or at a trial or other hearing provided that it is not to the trial judge.[32]

Acceptance of a Part 36 offer

Acceptance of a Part 36 offer is effected by serving written notice of acceptance on the offeror. Except where the permission of the court is required (see below) or in a split trial case, a Part 36 offer may be accepted at any time unless it has already been withdrawn, whether or not the offeree has -subsequently made a different offer.[33]   5–09

A claimant who was already in breach of an unless order requiring him to serve certain documents purported to accept a Part 36 offer. On appeal it was held that a claim that had been struck out (under the unless order) was at an end, therefore the claimant could not have accepted the Part 36 offer once he was in breach of the order, as his claim had, in substance, been brought to an end.[34]

Acceptance of a Part 36 offer made by one or more but not all defendants

The court's permission is required to accept a Part 36 offer where: 5–10

- an offer is made by one or more but not all defendants (subject to the exceptions set out below);
- a defendant in personal injury claims who has made a Part 36 offer has stated that it is intended to include any deductible amounts, the relevant period has expired and further deductible amounts have been paid to the claimant since the date of the offer;
- an apportionment is required under CPR r.41.3A in proceedings under the Fatal Accidents Act 1976 and Law Reform (Miscellaneous Provisions) Act 1934; or
- a trial is in progress.

Where the court gives permission, unless all the parties have agreed the costs, the court must make an order dealing with costs and may order that the costs consequences set out in CPR r.36.13 (costs consequences of acceptance of a Part 36 offer) apply.[35]

---

[31] r.36.10.
[32] Practice Direction 36, para.2.
[33] r.36.11(1) and (2).
[34] *Joyce v West Bus Coach Services Ltd* [2012] EWHC 404 (QB), [2012] 3 Costs L.R. 540, Kenneth Parker J.
[35] r.36.11(3) and (4).

5–11   In the case of Part 36 offers made by one or more, but not all, of a number of defendants, if they have been sued jointly or in the alternative, the claimant may accept the offer, if the claimant discontinues the claim against those defendants who have not made the offer, and those defendants give written consent to the acceptance of the offer. If the claimant alleges that the defendants have a several liability, the claimant may accept the offer, and continue with the claims against the other defendants if entitled to do so. In any other case the claimant must apply to the court for an order permitting acceptance of the Part 36 offer.[36]

Acceptance of a Part 36 offer in a split-trial case

5–12   Where there has been a trial but not all the issues in the case have been determined,[37] a Part 36 offer, which relates only to parts of the claim or issues that have already been decided, can no longer be accepted. Subject to that proviso, and unless the parties agree, any other Part 36 offer cannot be accepted earlier than seven clear days after judgment is given or handed down in that trial.[38]

Costs consequences of acceptance of a Part 36 offer

5–13   Subject to the exceptions set out below, where a Part 36 offer is accepted within the relevant period, the claimant will be entitled to the costs of the proceedings (including their recoverable pre-action costs) up to the date on which notice of acceptance was served on the offeror[39].

Where a defendant's Part 36 offer relates to part only of the claim and the claimant abandons the balance of the claim at the time of serving notice of acceptance within the relevant period, the claimant will only be entitled to the costs of that part of the claim unless the court orders otherwise.[40]

Where a Part 36 offer which was made less than 21 days before the start of the trial is accepted; or, which relates to the whole of the claim and is accepted after expiry of the relevant period; or, subject to the previous paragraph, a Part 36 offer which does not relate to the whole of the claim is accepted at any time; the liability for costs must be determined by the court unless the parties have agreed the costs.[41] Where the offer has been accepted after expiry of the relevant period but the parties are unable to agree the liability for costs, the court must, unless it considers it unjust to do so, order that the claimant be awarded costs up to the date on which the relevant period expired and that the offeree pay the offeror's costs for the period from the date of expiry of the relevant period to the date of acceptance. In considering whether it would be unjust to make the orders specified, the court must take into account all the circumstances of the case including the matters listed in CPR r.36.17(5) (**see**

---

[36] r.36.15(1)–(4).
[37] Within the meaning of r.36.3 (e).
[38] r.36.12 and also see r.36.3.
[39] r.36.13(1).
[40] r.36.13(2).
[41] r.36.13(4).

paragraph 5–15 below, costs consequences following judgment). The claimant's costs include any costs incurred in dealing with the defendant's counterclaim if the Part 36 offer states that it takes it into account.[42]

Despite the variation in wording between old CPR r.36.10(5) and the new CPR r.36.13(5) and in particular the new reference to whether it is "unjust" to disapply the normal costs consequences, the new Rule has not materially changed the proper approach to be taken by the court when deciding how to deal with costs where there has been a late acceptance of a Part 36 offer. The appropriate test is whether, bearing in mind the factors listed under CPR r.36.17(5), the usual costs rules should be departed from because it would be unjust to apply it in the particular circumstances of the case. In the particular case, the claimant was found to have grossly exaggerated her damages claim and the court ordered that the costs payable by the claimant to the defendant should include the defendant's reasonable costs of collecting the surveillance evidence, even though this had not been included in the defendant's approved budget. The court did not agree with the note at paragraph 3.15.3 of the 2015 White Book, which suggested that some allowance should be made in budgets for surveillance (see **Chapter 4 Q32** for further consideration of this topic).[43]

In a claim for disputed commission, the defendants offered the claimants £25,000 plus their reasonable costs. The claimants did not accept the offer. The claimants ultimately made a Part 36 offer to settle for £18,000. The defendants deliberately accepted it one minute after the expiry of the 21 day relevant period. As a result, the claim settled but the automatic costs consequences under CPR r.36.10(1) (now CPR r.36.13(1)) were avoided. The parties could not agree with costs and the defendants argued that the claimants should have accepted their earlier higher offer which had been made 15 months earlier. The judge found that the defendants had elected to accept the offer rather than reminding the claimants of their earlier offer which had never been withdrawn. A decisive factor was that the value of the claim net of the counterclaim was uncertain because of the defendant's unwillingness to disclose the strengths and weaknesses of their case. It was accordingly not unjust to apply the presumption that the defendant should pay the claimant's costs. The first instance decision was upheld on appeal.[44]

In a clinical negligence action, the claimant accepted the defendant's Part 36 offer eight months after it had expired. The defendants argued that an order that the claimant should be awarded costs until the expiry of the offer and to pay the defendant's costs from that date until the date of acceptance

---

[42] r.36.13(5) to (7). In a County Court decision by a District Judge, the court ordered a claimant who had exaggerated his claim to pay costs on the indemnity basis. The Court found that the claim would have been resolved by the end of June 2012 had the claimant not exaggerated his claim. Accordingly, the usual costs consequences of previous r.36.10(5) (now r.36.13(5)), did not apply. The claimant was awarded costs on the standard basis up to the 30 June 2012 but was ordered to pay the defendant's costs thereafter on the indemnity basis. The claimant was also ordered to meet the entire costs of gathering the surveillance evidence and the costs of the application. *Worthington v 03918424 Limited* [2015] 16 June, unreported.
[43] *Purser v Hibbs* [2015] EWHC 1792 (QB) HHJ Moloney QC.
[44] *Dutton v Minards* [2015] EWCA Civ. 984, [2015] 6 Costs LR 1047.

would be unjust, since the claimant had failed in relation to the vast majority of his pleaded case, namely causation. The court held that there was nothing unjust in making the normal order under Part 36. The difficulty with the defendant's arguments was that it had the means and opportunity to protect itself in respect of the costs that it was going to have to incur in relation to causation, yet it had chosen, when making its offer, to frame it as a settlement of the whole claim. When its offer was not accepted it had not made any revised offer excluding causation. The court found that the claimant had acted unreasonably in rejecting the offer and pursuing the action to within two weeks of trial. Accordingly, for the period when the claimant had to pay the defendant's costs, the costs would be on the indemnity basis.[45]

Unaccepted offers

Restriction on disclosure of a Part 36 offer

5-14 A Part 36 offer is treated as being *"without prejudice except as to costs"*. The fact that such an offer has been made must not be communicated to the trial judge until the case has been decided. This restriction does not apply where:

- the defence of tender before claim has been raised;
- the proceedings have been stayed following the acceptance of a Part 36 offer;
- the offeror and offeree agree in writing that it should not apply; or
- although the case has not been decided, any part of it or issue in it has been decided, and the Part 36 offer relates only to parts or issues which have been decided.

Where a part or issue has been decided, the trial judge may be told whether or not there are Part 36 offers other than those relating to the parts or issues which have been decided, but must not be told any of the terms of the other offers unless any of the above exceptions apply to them.[46]

Costs consequences following judgment

5-15 Save where Section IIIA of Part 45 applies,[47] where, upon judgment being entered, (i) a claimant fails to obtain a judgment more advantageous than the defendant's Part 36 offer, or (ii) judgment against the defendant is at least as advantageous to the claimant as the proposals contained in the claimant's Part 36 offer, the court must, unless it consider it unjust to do so, where (i) applies: order that the defendant is entitled to costs (including any recoverable pre-action costs) from the date on which the relevant period expired, and

---

[45] *ABC (A Protected Party) v Barts Health NHS Trust* [2016] EWHC 500 (QB); [2016] 2 Costs LR 271, HHJ McKenna.
[46] r.36.16(1)–(4). For cases which led to the revision of this Rule, see *Experience Hendrix LLC v Times Newspapers Ltd* [2008] EWHC 458 (Ch) Warren J; *Beasley v Alexander* [2012] EWHC 2715 (QB) Sir Raymond Jack; *Ted Baker Plc v Axa Insurance UK Plc* [2012] EWHC 1779 (Comm) Eder J.
[47] See r.36.21.

interest on those costs.[48] The provision does not apply to a soft tissue injury claim to which CPR r.36.21 applies.

Where (ii) applies the court must, unless it considers it unjust to do so, order that the claimant is entitled to:

(a) interest on the whole or part of any sum of money (excluding interest) awarded, at a rate not exceeding 10% above base rate for some or all of the period starting with the date on which the relevant period expired;

(b) costs (including any recoverable pre-action costs) on the indemnity basis from the date on which the relevant period expired;

(c) interest on those costs at a rate not exceeding 10% above base rate; and

(d) provided that the case has been decided and there has not been a previous order under this provision, an additional amount, which may not exceed £75,000, calculated by applying the prescribed percentage set out in the rule to an amount which is:
   (i) the sum awarded to the claimant by the court; or
   (ii) where there is no monetary award, the sum awarded to the claimant by the court in respect of costs.[49]

The prescribed percentage where the amount awarded by the court is up to £500,000 is 10% of the amount awarded. Where the amount awarded by the court is above £500,000, the prescribed percentage is 10% of the first £500,000 and (subject to the limit of £75,000) 5% of any amount above that figure.[50]

Neither of these consequences apply to a Part 36 offer which has been withdrawn, which has been changed so that its terms are less advantageous to the offeree – where the offeree has beaten the less advantageous offer, or made less than 21 days before trial unless the court has abridged the relevant period.[51]

In considering whether it would be unjust to make the orders referred to above, the court must take into account all the circumstances of the case including:

(a) the terms of any Part 36 offer;

(b) the stage in the proceedings when any Part 36 offer was made, including in particular how long before the trial started the offer was made;

(c) the information available to the parties at the time when the Part 36 offer was made;

(d) the conduct of the parties with regard to the giving of or refusal to give information for the purposes of enabling the offer to be made or evaluated; and

(e) whether the offer was a genuine attempt to settle the proceedings[52].

---

[48] In relation to any money claim or any money element of a claim, "more advantageous" means better in money terms by any amount however small and "at least as advantageous" is to be construed accordingly – r.36.17(1)–(3).
[49] r.36.17(3) and (4).
[50] r.36.17(4).
[51] r.36.17(7) and (8).
[52] r.36.17(5).

Where the court awards interest under these provisions and also awards interest on the same sum and for the same period under any other power, the total rate of interest must not exceed 10% above base rate[53].

The correct approach in determining whether a judgment award is more advantageous than a Part 36 offer is:

> "*to ensure that the offer or the Judgment sum is adjusted by eliminating from the comparison the effect of interest that accrues after the date when the relevant offer could have been accepted*"[54].

In a construction dispute, the claimant Jockey Club made a Part 36 offer to settle liability on the basis that the defendant should pay 95% of damages to be assessed. The defendant did not respond to this offer and the claimant amended its particulars of claim to set out the quantified costs of the repairs. The court directed a split trial. The defendant subsequently conceded liability and preliminary liability issues were settled by consent in the claimant's favour. The Club, accordingly, claimed its costs on the indemnity basis as it had beaten its own Part 36 offer. The court held that there was no possibility of contributory negligence so that a decision that the defendant should pay 95% of the damages was not one which was open to the court. It was, however, not necessary for a Part 36 offer to reflect an outcome that would be possible at trial. The court accepted that the claimant's offer was a genuine attempt to settle and whilst the 5% discount was very modest it was not derisory. Accordingly, the offer had to be given effect unless it would be unjust. It would be unjust to order indemnity costs from 21 days after the offer given that the defendant has just learned of a major increase in the claim but the claimant was entitled to costs on the indemnity basis from the earliest date after which the defendant should have been equipped to assess the claim on liability. On the facts this was four months after the offer.[55]

In proceedings where the defendant were in breach of their duty, but the claimant failed on primary causation, the defendants claimed costs, approximately one third of which were incurred in expert's fees on technical tax points which were lost. The defendants relied on their Part 36 offer made prior to trial which had not been accepted by the claimants. The court held that the general principles for determining an order for costs were subject to the operation of CPR Part 36, in particular CPR r.36.17. The starting point was that the defendants had been successful and were entitled to their costs. However, those costs did not reflect success on the issues for which they had been incurred. The defendants were awarded 50% of their costs for the period before the Part 36 offer expired and the whole of their costs from the date of the offer expiring. The offer ought to have been accepted and the trial avoided.[56]

---

[53] r.36.17(6).

[54] *Purrunsing v A'Court & Co. (a firm)* [2016] EWHC 1528 (Ch), HHJ Pelling QC. See also *Blackman v Entrepose UK* [2004] EWCA Civ 1109.

[55] *Jockey Club Racecourse Limited v Willmott Dixon Construction Limited* [2016] EWHC 167 (TCC), Edwards-Stuart J.

[56] *Altus Group (UK) Limited v Baker Tilly Tax and Advisory Services LLP* [2015] EWHC 411 (Ch) 2015 2 Costs LR 267, HHJ Keyser QC.

Solicitors sued under a non-contentious business, contingency fee agreement and the defendants were ordered to pay the full amount of the claim plus contractual interest. They were further required to pay under CPR r.36.17(4)(d) an additional amount of 10% of the judgment. Three issues arose:

(i)   whether an additional amount was payable in respect of the contractual interest award;

(ii)   the rate of interest payable on costs incurred prior to judgment; and

(iii)   the amount to be paid on account of costs.

The parties agreed that the interest rate prior to judgment was 4% above base rate from the date on which the work was done or the liability for the disbursement was incurred or 9 March 2015 whichever was the later. Payment on account of 80% of the approved costs budget was ordered to be paid. With regard to the additional amount, the sum awarded by way of interest was a contractual entitlement. As such it was part of a *"specific sum"* awarded to the claimant as was thus part of the sum in respect of which the additional amount was to be calculated.[57]

Under CPR Part 36, as it was in force prior to 6 April 2015, costs did not fall to be taken into account in determining whether, for the purposes of CPR r.36.14(1)(b), a judgment against a defendant was at least as advantageous to the claimant as proposals contained in its Part 36 offer. If *"Judgment"* in CPR r.36.14(1) were to include a decision on costs, it would be necessary for the court to undertake the exercise of determining what the incidence and basis of costs would be in the absence of a Part 36 offer. It would first have to exercise its discretion under Part 44 on the basis of all the circumstances of the case before considering the effect of Part 36. Such a potentially elaborate and otiose exercise could not have been intended. The justice of the case indicated that the defendant should pay the claimant's costs from a given date but without the other Part 36 consequences. The claimant's Part 36 offer was, in commercial terms and taking into account its costs consequences, too ambitious. Had it been accepted the defendant would have paid more than it would if the court had given judgment on liability and costs at the date of the expiry of the offer. There was also criticism of the claimant's conduct. On the other hand, the defendant could have protected itself by making a counter-offer which protected its costs position.[58]

In a claim for damages for an accident at work, the defendant accepted liability and made a Part 36 offer for "£18,500 net of CRU and inclusive of interim payments in the sum of £18,500". The defendant also stated that the offer was made "without regard to any liability for recoverable benefits". The claimant obtained judgment for £29,550 made up of £4,000 general damages and the balance for loss of earnings. A CRU certificate was issued for £16,262.

---

[57] *Bolt Burdon Solicitors v Tariq* [2016] EWHC 1507 (QB); [2016] 4WLR 112 Spencer J.

[58] *Transocean Drilling UK Limited v Providence Resources Plc* [2016] EWHC 2611 (Comm), Popplewell J.

This was subsequently revised down to £6,760 because some of the benefits paid were not attributable to the accident. At first instance the Recorder decided that the claimant's had failed to beat the defendant's Part 36 offer. On appeal, the court held there was no contradiction between the concept of the offer being made "net of CRU" and it's being made "without regard to any liability for recoverable benefits". The natural meaning of "net of CRU" was "remaining after all necessary deductions of benefits".

The words "without any liability for recoverable amounts" did not mean that the court was to have no regard to the amount of recoverable benefit when deciding whether the claimant had obtained a judgment more advantageous than the offer. The offer was for £18,500 leaving aside any liability in respect of recoverable benefits once such liability had crystallised. The real measure of whether, after the CRUs revised certificate was issued, the claimant had bettered the offer, was whether the total payment he actually received was more or less than the amount of the offer. On that basis the claimant had beaten the Part 36 offer[59].

The Court of Appeal has dealt with a case where the claimant had failed to beat the defendant newspaper's Part 36 offer at trial. At first instance the judge found that the newspaper's wrongdoing was far more extensive than it was prepared to admit and concluded that, since the newspaper had made limited admissions and had denied any liability until shortly before the trial, the claimant had some justification for proceeding. The claimant could not recover his costs from the defendant but the judge did not order him to pay the defendant's costs using his powers under CPR r.36.17. On appeal by the defendant the court found that the trial judge had correctly decided that, where a claimant rejected a Part 36 offer because it reasonably wished to have the facts investigated at trial, that did not normally make it unjust for the normal costs consequences to follow; there had to be some further element: implicitly unjustness. The onus was on the person who had failed to beat the offer to show that it would be unjust for the normal consequences to apply. The appeal was dismissed.[60]

A defendant accepting a claimant's Part 36 offer outside the 21 day period but before the offer had been withdrawn was not entitled to an order under CPR r.36.14 (now CPR r.36.17) as the issue of liability had been compromised and judgment had not been entered. The appropriate regime was under CPR r.36.10 (now CPR r.36.13) and CPR r.36.11 (now CPR r.36.14).[61]

The court has considered the correct application of CPR r.36.17(4) (formerly CPR r.36.14(3)) (It was agreed between the parties, following judgment at the end of a split trial on liability in favour of the claimant, that the judgment the claimant was awarded was more advantageous than the offer that he had made and which had been rejected. It was also agreed that Part 36 is

---

[59] *Crooks v Hendricks Lovell Limited* [2016] EWCA Civ.8; [2016] 1 Costs L.O. 103.

[60] *Yentob v MGN Ltd* [2015] EWCA Civ 1292; [2015] 6 Costs L.R. 1103.

[61] *Jolly v Harsco Infrastructure Services Ltd* [2012] EWHC 3086 (QB); [2013] 1 Costs L.R. 115 Cranston J.

to be read as a self-contained code and not to be confused with contractual notions or general costs discretion under Part 44 or non-Part 36 offers such as Calderbank type offers. The cases which support that proposition are *Gibbon v Manchester City Council*[62]; *Fox v Foundation Piling Limited*[63]; and *Coward v Phaestos*[64]. The claimant had made an offer to settle of 80% of the damages to be awarded in the split trial case. The defendant did not accept the offer within the relevant period so that CPR r.36.17 (formerly CPR r.35.14) applied. The judge in his draft costs order awarded indemnity costs to run throughout. He also ordered interest on those costs but at a lower rate than the maximum, from the end of the relevant period. The judge expressly made no order under CPR r.36.17(4)(a) (interest on the whole of or any part of any money awarded) or under CPR r.36.17(4)(d) (an additional amount not exceeding £75,000). Counsel for the claimant argued that the judge did not have the power to take that course given that Part 36 was not only a complete code but was "as it were a menu all of whose courses must be delivered". It was argued that the judge was not free to choose between the relevant features of sub-rule (4) or to find that to apply one would be unjust and to apply another would not. The judge held, reading the plain language of the Rule, that he was required to consider each stage of the sub-paragraph and ask whether the application of the particular sub-paragraph to this case with its own particular circumstances would be unjust. Having heard the argument, the judge amended his draft order so that the provision that the defendant should pay the claimant's costs relating to the issue of liability on the indemnity basis should be restricted expressly to the costs incurred or recoverable after the expiry of the relevant period.[65]

The provisions of CPR r.36.17(4) apply equally in provisional assessment proceedings where a successful claimant's Part 36 offer has been made. This is in spite of the wording of CPR r.47.15(5) imposing a cap on the recoverable costs[66]. For a discussion of this topic see **Chapter 8 Qs 18 and 19**.

The court is willing to impose sanctions on a defendant who seeks to avoid his liabilities and abuse the court's process. The defendant had sought an adjournment on the grounds that the Malaysian receiver needed time to decide whether or not to defend the summary judgment proceedings. The judge found that it could not be right that, if a defendant decided to petition for his own bankruptcy, at a time when he did not have to, the court must forget about the defendant and focus instead on the receiver. That would allow any defendant to avoid or delay proceedings. Further, an adjournment would serve no purpose from the Malaysian receiver's point of view. The judge also found that there was no real prospect of a successful defence and no other compelling reason for a trial. The judge awarded:

---

[62] [2010] 1 WLR 2081.
[63] [2011] EWCA Civ.790.
[64] [2014] EWCA Civ.1256; [2014] 6 Costs L.O. 843.
[65] *RXDX v Northampton Borough Council* [2015] EWHC 2938 (QB); [2015] 5 Costs L.R. 897, Sir Colin Mackay.
[66] *Lowin v W Portsmouth & Co Ltd* [2016] EWHC 2301 (QB), Laing J.

- The capital sums invested by the claimants through the defendant, together with interest at a rate *"in the region of 20 per cent"*, being the sort of return expected on the claimants' investment.
- The claimants' costs on the indemnity basis, given that the defendant's conduct in these proceedings had been *"nothing short of abusive"* and he had failed to beat the claimants' Part 36 offer.
- An additional amount under r.36.17(4)(d). Although the judge had jurisdiction to award up to £75,000, he considered a more *"modest"* sum appropriate, bearing in mind that the Part 36 offer was in relation to a simple application for summary judgment, rather than, say, a lengthy trial, and that the interest rate already awarded was high.[67]

Where a claimant who had made a Part 36 offer under the Rules prior to 6 April 2015 and obtained judgment for almost three times the amount of the offer, the court held that it was not appropriate to reduce the costs award, because, although the claimant had not succeeded on every single issue, it had been overwhelmingly successful on the points which mattered most in terms of financial recovery. The defendant was ordered to pay costs on the standard basis up to the date upon which the court considered it was in a position to take an informed view of the quantum of the claim. Thereafter the defendant was ordered to pay costs on the indemnity basis together with enhanced interest for the same period at the rate of 8%.[68]

5–16   The High Court has clarified that the additional amount which can be awarded under CPR r.36.17(4)(d) should be calculated as a percentage of the basic monetary award but should not be applied to any award of interest. The court awarded a Liquidator £360,000, plus statutory interest at 3% above base rate. The defendant was also ordered to pay all the costs on the indemnity basis. The court expressed the view that this was a case that should never have been defended. The Liquidator had beaten its own Part 36 offer of £325,000 inclusive of interest and the judge also awarded an enhanced rate of interest of 10% above base rate on the sum awarded from the end of the relevant period until the date of judgment, interest at 10% above base rate on the costs and the additional amount allowed under CPR r.36.17(4)(d).

This decision illustrates the potential advantages for claimants of making a Part 36 offer and also clarifies that where the claim includes a money claim, the additional amount is calculated as a percentage of the basic monetary award exclusive of interest.[69]

The additional amount was not allowed in a case where, having made a Part 36 offer just before trial, the claimant beat her offer and sought payment of the additional amount under CPR r.36.17(4)(d). The court declined to make such an order, because she had raised a matter of fundamental importance to

---

[67] *Bataillon v Shone [2015] EWHC 3177 (QB) HHJ Waksman QC.*
[68] *Thai Airways International Public Company Limited v KI Holdings Co. Limited* [2015] EWHC 1476 (Comm), [2015] 3 Costs L.R. 545, Leggatt J. The subsequent appeal was dismissed by the Court of Appeal.
[69] *Watchorn v Jupiter Industries Ltd* [2014] EWHC 3003 (Ch), [2015] 3 Costs L.O. 337 HHJ Purle QC.

her case only in the course of opening, and other important information was disclosed only on the eve of the trial.[70]

The Court of Appeal has dealt with the tension between the provisions of CPR Part 45 IIIA (CPR r.45.29B) and Part 36 (CPR r.36.21) where a claimant obtains judgment at least as advantageous as her Part 36 offer. The particular appeals were dealt with under the rules as they were before 6 April 2015, but the Master of the Rolls made it clear that the underlying provisions remain the same.

The question for the court was whether CPR r.36.17(4) (formerly 36.14(3)) Costs consequences following judgment, applies where a claimant makes a successful Part 36 offer, or whether the recoverable costs are limited to the fixed costs set out in Table 6 of CPR r.45.29C.

CPR r.45.29B provides: *"the only costs allowed are—(a) the fixed costs in rule 45.29C; (b) disbursements in accordance with rule 45.29I"*. CPR r.36.21 was introduced to prescribe the costs consequences following judgment in section IIIA cases. While it modified some aspects of CPR r.36.17 in fixed costs cases, it left CPR r.36.17(4) unmodified.

In the two appeals before the court one, *Broadhurst*, had been limited to the fixed costs in Table 6 whilst in the other, *Smith*, the Judge had not limited the costs to Table 6.

The court was referred to the Explanatory Memorandum to the 2013 Amendment Rules:

"... If a defendant refuses a claimant's offer to settle and the court subsequently awards the claimant damages which are greater than or equal to the sum they were prepared to accept in the settlement, the claimant will not be limited to receiving his fixed costs, but will be entitled to costs assessed on the indemnity basis in accordance with rule [36.17] ."

The Master of the Rolls giving judgment with which the other members of the court agreed said:

"23 rule 45.29B does not stand alone. The need to take account of Part 36 offers in section IIIA cases was recognised by the draftsman of the rules. Indeed, rule 36.14A [36.17] is headed "costs consequences following judgment where section IIIA of Part 45 applies". Rule 45.29F (8) provides that, where a Part 36 offer is accepted in a section IIIA case, "rule 36.10A [36.20] will apply instead of this rule". And rule 45.29F(9) provides that, where in such a case upon judgment being entered the claimant fails to obtain a judgment more advantageous than the claimant's Part 36 offer, "rule 36.14A [36.21] will apply instead of this rule". Rule 45.29F does not, however, make provision as to what should happen where the claimant makes a successful Part 36 offer.
25 The effect of rules 36.14 [36.17] and 36.14A [36.21] when read together is that, where a claimant makes a successful Part 36 offer, he is entitled to costs

---

[70] *Feltham v Bouskell* [2013] EWHC 3086 (Ch), [2014] 1 Costs L.O. 29, Charles Hollander QC.

assessed on the indemnity basis. Thus, rule 36.14 [36.17] is modified only to the extent stated by 36.14A [36.21]. Since rule 36.14(3) [36.17(4)] has not been modified by rule 36.14A [36.21], it continues to have full force and effect. The tension between rule 45.29B and rule 36.14A [36.21] must, therefore, be resolved in favour of rule 36.14A [36.21].

31 Where a claimant makes a successful Part 36 offer in a section IIIA case, he will be awarded fixed costs to the last staging point provided by rule 45.29C and Table 6B. He will then be awarded costs to be assessed on the indemnity basis in addition from the date that the offer became effective. This does not require any apportionment. It will, however, lead to a generous outcome for the claimant."[71]

The provisions of CPR r.36.17(4) apply equally in provisional assessment proceedings where a successful claimant's Part 36 offer has been made. This is in spite of the wording of CPR r.47.15(5) imposing a cap on the recoverable costs[72]. For a discussion of this topic see **Chapter 8 Qs 18 and 19**.

More advantageous

5–17   Sub-paragraph 72(vii) of the judgment in *Multiplex Construction (UK) Ltd v Cleveland Bridge UK Ltd*[73] (dealing with the effect of *Carver v BAA*) should be disregarded. *Carver* had effectively been reversed by the rule change in previous CPR r.36.14(1A) (now CPR r.36.17(2)) – a change that was recommended by Lord Justice Jackson in his *Review of Civil Litigation Costs: Final Report*. The judge making a Costs Order under CPR r.44.2 is exercising a broad discretion, not just deciding who the winner on each issue was, but taking into account the conduct of the parties and all the circumstances of the case. The judge is the best person to exercise that discretion having been immersed in the trial details.[74]

In a successful claim for dilapidations, it was common ground that there was no offer under CPR Part 36 which had any automatic costs consequences. The defendant had however made a Part 36 offer by letter dated 23 December 2011 in the sum of £1,000,000. When interest was added to the sums awarded of £900,000 and £20,320.40 up to 13 January 2012, the last date for acceptance of the Part 36 offer, the sum awarded to the claimant exceeded the defendant's Part 36 offer by £3,637.90, which represented a very small percentage of the sum offered.

The court noted that previous CPR r.36.14, had been amended on 1 October 2011, by the insertion of CPR r.36.14(1A) (now CPR r.36.17(2)). The claimant had not failed to obtain a judgment more advantageous than the defendant's Part 36 offer and therefore CPR r.36.14 (CPR r.36.17) did not apply. Ramsey J stated:

"The Part 36 Offer made in this case could be said, in principle, to come within the wording of CPR 44.2(4)(c). It is an admissible offer to settle and is not an

---

[71] *Broadhurst (1) Taylor (2) v Tan (1) Smith(2)* [2016] EWCA Civ 94.
[72] *Lowin v W Portsmouth & Co Ltd* [2016] EWHC 2301 (QB), Laing J.
[73] *Multiplex Construction (UK) Ltd v Cleveland Bridge UK Ltd* [2008] EWHC 2280 (TCC) Jackson J.
[74] *Dufoo v Tolaini* [2014] EWCA Civ 1536; [2014] 6 Costs L.R. 1106.

offer to which costs consequences under Part 36 apply. However I do not consider, even in a case such as this, where [the claimant] has only received a very small amount more than the sum which [the defendants] offered in its Part 36 Offer, the court should approach CPR 44.2(4)(c) on the basis that this could lead to an order that a claimant should pay the defendants' costs. In my judgment, to do so would be to seek to use the provisions of CPR 44.2(4)(c) to give a similar effect to a Part 36 Offer and thereby introduce the same uncertainty into Part 36 Offers which are near to but below the sum awarded, as led to the criticism of Carver and the subsequent amendment introduced in CPR 36.14(1A) [now r.36.17].

In my judgment the principle in sub-paragraph (vii) of [72] in Multiplex, derived as it was from Carver, is no longer a principle which applies to Part 36 and should not be applied as a special 'near miss' rule through CPR 44.2(4)(c). If there is an unreasonable refusal to negotiate then that is a matter which comes within the circumstances which the court can take into account under CPR 44.2(4) and -sub-paragraph (a) in particular. I am doubtful that, on analysis, a 'near miss' offer can generally add anything to what otherwise would be conduct in the form of unreasonable refusal to negotiate . . ."[75]

The court considered issues of conduct by both parties and the relative success and failure on various issues. In the light of those circumstances the court assessed costs by reference to the factors in CPR r.44.2(4)(a) and (b). The claimant was awarded 80% of its costs.[76]

At a trial on quantum, the claimant succeeded in beating the defendant's Part 36 offer. The judge when considering what order for costs to make, took into account, as a matter of discretion, the Part 36 offer which had been beaten. Eder J made it clear that he was not introducing a 'near miss' rule for Part 36 offers by the back door.[77] In the judge's view the circumstances indicated that the claimant had insisted unreasonably on a higher figure than that offer, the claim had been much exaggerated and delays regarding disclosure and evidence had caused the defendant real difficulties in taking appropriate precautions to protect its position.[78]

The claimant appealed. The Court of Appeal found that the judge had erred in his approach to the Part 36 offer and in mischaracterising S's conduct as unreasonable. He had effectively characterised S's pursuit of a business interruption claim in excess of £600,000 after receipt of the Part 36 letter as misconduct. In doing so, he had converted what was not an offer to compromise the business interruption claim at £600,000 into just such an offer. It could not be misconduct simply to pursue a claim greater than the amount accepted by the defendant; something more was required to render pursuit of the claim unreasonable. The matters discussed by the judge did not justify

5–18

---

[75] paras 26 and 36.
[76] *Hammersmatch Properties (Welwyn) Ltd v Saint-Cobain Ceramics & Plastics Ltd* [2013] EWHC 2227 (TCC), [2013] 5 Costs L.R. 758, Ramsey J.
[77] See *Hammersmatch Properties (Welwyn) Ltd v Saint-Cobain Ceramics & Plastics Ltd* [2013] EWHC 2227 (TCC), [2013] 5 Costs L.R. 758 Ramsey J.
[78] *Sugar Hut Group Ltd v A J Insurance* [2014] EWHC 3775 (Comm).

the characterisation of S's conduct as unreasonable. The main judgment had not described the claim or any part of it as exaggerated. Significant parts of the business interruption claim had failed, but that did not mean that it had been exaggerated.

At first instance the claimant had been awarded 70% of its costs up to 21 days after the defendant's offer and was also ordered to pay the defendant's costs of the assessment of damages. The claimant had therefore been penalised twice for the same shortcoming. There was no basis on which it was appropriate to deprive the claimant of its costs after the offer, still less to require it to pay the defendant's costs. Its failure to succeed on all its claim was adequately reflected in the deduction of 30% of their costs (para.31)[79].

There are numerous reported cases where offers which did not comply with CPR r.36.5 have been held not to be Part 36 offers. In these circumstances however, the court is not precluded from considering the fact that an offer has been made as part of the circumstances which it is required to take into account when considering what order for costs to make.[80] The court has held that Part 36 should be construed as designed to protect defendants from claims being pursued, on the basis that a claimant might be able to persuade a defendant to pay more than the legal entitlement, or to pay the legal entitlement more quickly than would otherwise be the case, where the costs of contesting the entitlement would not be worth incurring. Part 36 is not intended to reward in costs, claimants who pursue their claims on such a basis.[81]

Where an offer was expressed to relate to an additional claim which the defendants had set out in draft Amended Particulars of Claim, that claim was not yet part of the claim for the purposes of CPR r.36.5(1)(d) therefore the offer was not a Part 36 offer and the normal costs consequences did not apply. Although the claimant argued that it was possible to make a Part 36 offer before the commencement of proceedings and the references to the whole or part of a claim should be taken to include references to a claim that had not yet been brought but which was brought after the offer was made, the judge held that Part 36 is a highly prescriptive and self-contained code and it would not be right to add in further provisions on the basis that it would have an analogous effect to an existing express provision.[82]

In a case where the claimant had achieved judgment against the defendant which was more advantageous than the proposal set out in its Part 36 offer, the defendants argued that it would be "unjust" to apply the previous CPR r.36.14(3)(b) and (c) (now CPR r.36.17(4)(b) and (c)). It was argued that the claimant had only succeeded as a result of material that had come to light since the Part 36 offer had been made. The argument was rejected by the Court of Appeal on the basis that the defendants were experienced litigators

---

[79] *Sugar Hut Group Ltd v A J Insurance* [2016] EWCA Civ 46.
[80] For example, *Rowles–Davies v Call 24-7 Ltd* [2010] EWHC 1695 (Ch) Bernard Livesey QC; *Carillion J M Ltd v PHI Group Ltd* [2012] EWCA Civ 588; [2012] CP Rep 37.
[81] *D Pride & Partners v Institute for Animal Health* [2009] EWHC 1617 (QB); [2009] 5 Costs LR 803, Tugendhat J.
[82] *Hertel v Saunders* [2015] EWHC 2848 (Ch), [2015] 5 Costs L.R. 825, Morgan J.

in the field and must have appreciated that there was a very serious risk that there would be a significant recovery above the interim payment which had already been made. The defendants had enough information to evaluate the Part 36 offer which they had rejected.[83]

It is for the offeree to satisfy the court that it is unjust for the court to make the normal order. The court must take into account all the circumstances of the case including the matters set out in previous CPR r.36.17(5). They are not the only matters to be considered. Anything which is relevant must be considered as well, including uncertainty as to the developing condition and prognosis of a claimant under a disability.[84] There is no limit to the circumstances which could make it unjust that the ordinary consequences under CPR r.36.17 should follow. Where an action had been about restoration of reputation and the conduct of the defendant's disciplinary -procedures the court ordered the costs to lie where they fell.[85]

Where a claimant obtained judgment materially in excess of the figure proposed by way of settlement in the claimant's Part 36 offer, which had been rejected by the defendant company, the claimant applied to add the husband and wife directors as defendants in order to obtain an order for costs against them under s.51 of the Senior Courts Act 1981. A third party costs order was made. The question then arose as to the appropriate rate of interest on the claimant's costs in respect of the Part 36 offer. The court held that previous CPR r.36.17 dealt with the position which applied when judgment was entered. The relevant judgment was that against the defendant company and interest at 6% above base rate was awarded from the date of the refused Part 36 offer until the date of judgment. In respect of the costs of the s.51 proceedings, which were governed by CPR r.44.2(6)(g) the court awarded interest at 1% above base rate.[86]

Where a claimant made an offer to accept a specific sum including interest, in sterling, and subsequently obtained judgment in US dollars, the Commercial Court declined to allow the successful claimant the Part 36 enhancements, for the period between expiry of the "*relevant period*" and the date of judgment, since the difference in the value of the judgment was a direct consequence of the fall in sterling following the referendum vote to leave the EU. The judge stated it would be "*adventitious and inconsistent with the principle of risk allocation which underlies Part 36*" to penalise the defendant for not accepting the offer.[87]

In personal injury proceedings, the court, having found in favour of the claimant, ordered that the costs should be on the standard basis, save that the costs attributable to dealing with the evidence of the defendant's expert witnesses should be assessed on the indemnity basis.[88] The defendant con-

5–19

---

[83] *Bent v Highways and Utilities Construction & Allianz Insurance* [2011] EWCA Civ 1539, [2012] 2 Costs L.O. 127.
[84] *SG (a child) v Hewitt* [2012] EWCA Civ 1053, [2013] 1 All E.R. 1118; [2012] 5 Costs L.R. 937.
[85] *Smith v Trafford Housing Trust* [2012] EWHC 3320 (Ch) Briggs J.
[86] *Chantrey Vellacott v The Convergence Group plc* [2007] EWHC 1774 (Ch) Rimer J.
[87] *Novus Aviation Limited v Alubaf Arab International Bank BSC (c)* [2016] EWHC 1937 (Comm), Leggatt J.
[88] Such an order would be extremely difficult to assess, and would probably not result in any significant difference in the amount of costs awarded.

tended that it had made a written offer on costs, with a better outcome than the claimant had obtained. The court held that it was not possible to conduct a preliminary assessment of costs to establish arithmetically whether the defendant's offer was better on a pound for pound basis than the outcome achieved by the claimant. The justice of the case required the defendant to pay the claimant's costs of the oral hearing, together with the costs of the subsequent dispute as to costs of that hearing on the standard basis.[89]

Costs in the case and Part 36

5–20   In a libel action brought by three claimants against three defendants in respect of emails sent in January and July 2012, the claimants each accepted offers of settlement which had been made by the third defendant. At the same time, the claimants gave notice of discontinuance of their claims against the first and second defendants.

The court had to determine the appropriate final orders in respect of damages and costs to give effect to the settlements and the discontinuance. The main issues were: whether such costs orders as were made against the claimants should be on the standard or the indemnity basis; whether the claimants should be jointly and severally liable for costs ordered in favour of the third defendant; and whether—and if so to what extent—costs and damages due to the claimants should be set off against costs due to the third defendant. There was also an issue in respect of the effect of an order for costs in the case in respect of the third defendant's strike out application.

The court explained:

> "The 'general effect' of an order for costs in the case is that 'the party in whose favour the court makes an order for costs at the end of the proceedings is entitled to that party's costs of the part of the proceedings to which the order relates': PD44 paragraph 4.2. Here, that general rule cannot be very readily applied; at the end of the proceedings the court has made orders for costs in favour of each party, save for [one].
>
> The action has concluded by settlement via Part 36 and without prejudice save as to costs offers. All the claimants have obtained judgment for damages. [Two of the claimants] have recovered substantial damages, sums which on [the third defendant's] case are the maximum they could possibly have obtained. Yet it is said that they are the losers because their recovery is but a fraction of what they claimed. Views could differ about that conclusion, in this case and in others. It is easy to see that if [that] criterion were adopted there could often be lengthy -argument as to which party has in reality 'won'.
>
> A simpler and better criterion is to hand for a case like this, which is to have regard to when in the proceedings the relevant costs were incurred and which party has obtained an order for costs in relation to that phase of the proceedings. As a starting point I would suggest that acceptance of a Part 36 Offer, which will

---

[89] *Williams v Jervis* [2009] EWHC 1838 (QB) Roderick Evans J.

ordinarily lead to an order for the costs up to the relevant date, should also carry with it any costs incurred within that period which are the subject of an order for costs in the case. Equally, if an offer is accepted 'out of time' and an order is made, in the ordinary way, for the offeree to pay costs since the expiry of the relevant period that order should carry with it any costs incurred in that period which are the subject of an order for costs in the case."[90]

What the judge found to be highly unreasonable conduct by claimants following their acceptance of the settlement offers justified awarding the defendant costs on the indemnity basis from the expiry of the offers' acceptance period. The claimants were jointly and severally liable for those costs incurred by continuing their common case after the offers. The court ordered the third defendant to pay the two claimants' costs of the strike out application.[91]

Cases in which the offeror's costs have been limited to court fees

Where, because of failure to file a costs budget on time or otherwise, the offeror is limited to applicable court fees, "costs"[92] means, in respect of the costs subject to any such limitation, 50% of the costs assessed without reference to the limitation together with any other recoverable costs (see **Chapter 4 Q67** for further consideration of this).[93]

5–21

RTA Protocol and EL/PL Protocol offers to settle

Section II of Part 36 applies to an offer to settle where the parties have followed the RTA Protocol or the EL/PL Protocol, and started proceedings under Part 8, in accordance with Practice Direction 8B (the Stage 3 procedure). Parties may make an offer to settle in whatever way they choose, but any offer which is not made in accordance with Section II will not have any costs consequences.[94]

5–22

A Protocol offer under Section II must be set out in the Court Proceedings Pack (Form B) Form, and contain the final total amount of the offer from both parties. The offer is deemed to be made on the first business day after the Court Proceedings Pack is sent to the defendant.[95]

A Protocol offer is treated as exclusive of all interest, and has costs consequences only in relation to the fixed costs of the Stage 3 procedure (as provided for in CPR r.45.18), not in relation to the costs of any appeal from the final decision in those proceedings. The amount of a Protocol offer must not be communicated to the court until the claim is determined. Any other offer to settle must not be communicated to the court at all.[96]

---

[90] paras 89–91.
[91] *Ontulmus v Collett* [2014] EWHC 4117 (QB) Warby J.
[92] In rr.36.13(5)(b), 36.17(3)(a) and 36.17(4)(b).
[93] r.36.23. The purpose of r.36.23 is to put the receiving party at some risk if an offer is accepted late (r.36.13(5)(b)) or the offer prevails at trial (rr.36.17(3)(a) and 36.17(4)(b)) while not allowing the paying party to escape entirely the consequences of the default.
[94] r.36.24.
[95] rr.36.25, 36.26.
[96] rr.36.27, 36.28.

Costs consequences following judgment

5–23 CPR r.36.29 applies where on any determination by the court, the claimant obtains judgment against the defendant for an amount of damages that is:

(a) less than or equal to the amount of the defendant's Protocol offer;

(b) more than the defendant's Protocol offer, but less than the claimant's Protocol offer; or

(c) equal to or more than the claimant's Protocol offer.

Where (a) applies, the court must order the claimant to pay the fixed costs in CPR r.45.26, and interest on those fixed costs from the first business day after the deemed date of the Protocol offer under CPR r.36.26. Where (b) applies, the court must order the defendant to pay the fixed costs in CPR r.45.20.

Where (c) applies, the court must order the defendant to pay interest on the whole of the damages awarded at a rate not exceeding 10% above base rate for some or all of the period, starting with the date specified in CPR r.36.26, the fixed costs in CPR r.45.20, interest on those fixed costs at a rate not exceeding 10% above base rate, and an additional amount calculated in accordance with CPR r.36.17(4)(d).[97]

Deduction of benefits

5–24 For the purposes of (a) above, the amount of the judgment is less than the Protocol offer where the judgment is less than the offer once deductible amounts identified in the judgment are deducted.[98]

Costs of detailed assessment proceedings

5–25 CPR r.47.20(4) clarifies that the provisions of Part 36 apply to the costs of detailed assessment proceedings with certain modifications. Where an offer to settle is made whether under Part 36 or otherwise, it should specify whether or not it is intended to be inclusive of the costs of preparation of the bill, interest and VAT. Unless the offer makes it clear that the position is otherwise, it will be treated as being inclusive of all those matters.[99]

In proceedings for detailed assessment, the paying party wrote to the receiving party, setting out what they described as Part 36 offers, which were stated to be open for 21 days, and offered a proportion or fixed sum in respect of the receiving party's costs. The offers were rejected, and the paying party made a further offer in respect of a third receiving party, if the other receiving

---

[97] r.36.29(1)–(4).

[98] r.36.30.

[99] Practice Direction 47 para.19. The County Court at Nottingham has allowed an appeal by the defendant, who claimed that Part 36 costs consequences could not be applied to an offer that purported to be a Part 36 offer, but which was exclusive of interest. The offer arose in the context of detailed assessment proceedings. The district judge's order for payment to the claimant of an additional 10% plus interest, for having beaten their Part 36 offer, was set aside. r.36.5(4) provides that a Part 36 offer to pay or accept a sum of money will be treated as inclusive of interest. The practice direction supporting r.47.20 provides that, unless an offer specifies otherwise, it is intended to be inclusive of the cost of preparation of the bill, interest and VAT. *Potter v Sally Montague Hair and SPA* (unreported), 7 October 2016, (County Court at Nottingham).

parties were willing to accept the Part 36 offers. These offers were accepted, but the costs hearing still took place because the paying party contended they were entitled to costs in respect of the period from the expiry of the 21 days referred to in the original offers, until the point when the offers had been accepted. The court made no order for the costs in respect of that period. The court held, on the facts, that the earlier offer was not a Part 36 offer, because it specifically excluded the offerors from recovering all of their costs, and it could not, by its very terms, comply with CPR r.36.10(1) (now CPR r.36.13(1)).

The subsequent offer was indistinguishable from that in *C v D*,[100] and the subsequent offer should be treated as a Part 36 offer, particularly since all the parties treated the offers as having been made under Part 36. The overriding objective, and common sense, suggested that an offer which was expressed to be a Part 36 offer, and which otherwise appeared to comply with Part 36, had to be given substantially the same effect as a Part 36 offer. The offer which was accepted was significantly better than the original offer, and the allocation of liability for costs for the period between the expiry of the 21 days and acceptance was a matter for the judge's discretion, without the presumption in favour of the paying party inherent in CPR r.36.10(4) and (5) (now CPR r.36.13(4) and (5)). The right order to make was that each party should bear its own costs from the expiry of the 21 days.[101]

Section 2 Settlement other than under Part 36.

In Chapter 36 of his Final Report Jackson LJ wrote:

5–26

> "*4.2 I recommend that:*
> (i) *There should be a serious campaign (a) to ensure that all litigation lawyers and judges are properly informed about the benefits which ADR can bring and (b) to alert the public and small businesses to the benefits of ADR.*
> (ii) *An authoritative handbook should be prepared, explaining clearly and concisely what ADR is and giving details of all reputable providers of mediation. This should be the standard handbook for use at all JSB seminars and CPD training sessions concerning mediation.*"

There is growing pressure from the judiciary and court users for greater use of ADR. The Jackson ADR Handbook is now in its second edition, written by three distinguished authors[102] under the banner of the Judicial College, the Civil Justice Council and the Civil Mediation Council.

The book deals with the general principles of Alternative Dispute Resolution (ADR) as well as the range of ADR options. These include: Offer and Acceptance (offers other than under Part 36); Negotiation; Mediation; Early Neutral Evaluation; Expert Evaluation; Adjudication; and Arbitration.

---

[100] *C v D* [2011] EWCA Civ 646.
[101] *Howell v Lees-Millais* [2011] EWCA Civ 786.
[102] Susan Blake, Julie Browne and Stuart Sime.

All of these processes may be used in connection with the resolution of costs disputes.

The Court of Appeal has firmly endorsed the advice given in the ADR Handbook to the effect that, as a general rule, silence in the face of an invitation to participate in ADR is itself unreasonable, regardless of whether a refusal to engage in ADR might have been justified. There might be rare cases where ADR is so obviously inappropriate that to characterise silence as unreasonable would be pure formalism, or where the failure to respond was a result of a mistake, in which case the onus would be on the recipient of the invitation to make that explanation good. The court stated that the reasons for extending the guidelines set out in *Halsey v Milton Keynes General NHS Trust*[103], were: first, because an investigation of the reasons for refusing to mediate advanced for the first time at a costs hearing, perhaps months or years later, posed forensic difficulties for the court concerning whether those reasons were genuine. Second, a failure to provide reasons for refusal was destructive of the objective of encouraging parties to consider and discuss ADR. Any difficulties or reasonable objection to a particular ADR proposal should be discussed so that the parties could narrow their differences. Third, it would also serve the policy of proportionality. The court held it would be perverse not to regard silence in the face of repeated requests for mediation as anything other than a refusal. A finding of unreasonable conduct by a refusal to mediate did not produce an automatic result in terms of a costs penalty. The judge has a broad discretion.[104]

A defendant police commissioner who successfully defended proceedings was found to have refused to engage in the alternative dispute resolution process without adequate justification. The court found that the claimants could have obtained some level of damages. There were issues of fact to be resolved from which both parties ran the risk of adverse findings. The defence was not so strong as to have justified a refusal to engage in ADR. The commissioner did not make any offers to settle before ADR was suggested and ADR would not have delayed the trial of the action. The commissioner was awarded two thirds of his costs.[105]

When the court exercises its discretion under CPR r.44.2, it has to have regard to all the circumstances including the conduct of the parties both before and during the proceedings. "Conduct" includes a refusal to agree to ADR. The factors to be taken into account include: the nature of the dispute; the merits of the case; the extent to which other settlement methods have been attempted; whether the costs of ADR are disproportionately high; whether any delay in setting or attending the ADR would be prejudicial; and whether ADR has a reasonable prospect of success.[106]

---

[103] [2004] EWCA Civ 576, [2004] 1 W.L.R. 3002.
[104] *PGF II SA v OMFS Co 1 Ltd* [2013] EWCA Civ 1288, [2014] 1 W.L.R. 1386; [2014] 1 All E.R. 970; [2014];[2013] 6 Costs L.R. 973.
[105] *Laporte v Commissioner of Police of the Metropolis* [2015] EWHC 371 (QB), [2015] 3 Costs L.R. 471. Turner J.
[106] See *Halsey v Milton Keynes General NHS Trust* [2004] EWCA Civ 576; [2004] 1 WLR 3002.

The Advantages of ADR

The advantages of ADR include: lower costs (provided that the ADR process is 5–27 entered into sufficiently early); the speed of resolution of the issues; the choice of forum and process; the flexibility of process (the parties may agree how they wish to proceed; a wider range of issues/outcomes may be considered; and shared future interests may be protected. In mediation, the parties may choose the mediator and the process is entirely confidential. In litigation there will usually be a winner and a loser with damages and costs being paid by one party to another. In ADR the parties may have been unable to agree on the contentious issues but may wish to maintain a potentially lucrative business relationship.

Offers other than Part 36 offers

It is open to either party in litigation to make offers which do not comply 5–28 with the requirements of Part 36. These may be open offers or offers without prejudice save as to costs. The latter are generally known as Calderbank offers, which arose in the Family Division where there was no provision for payment into court, but the parties could be at risk as to costs, particularly in respect of financial arrangements.

In deciding what order to make about costs the court is required to have regard to all the circumstances including the conduct of all the parties, whether a party has succeeded on part of its case and if not wholly successful, the extent to which that party has succeeded and any admissible offer to settle which is drawn to the court's attention and which is not an offer to which the costs consequences of Part 36 apply.[107] The question of who was the successful party or the unsuccessful party to an action can be determined by who ultimately wrote the cheque at the end.[108]

In professional negligence proceedings against a firm of solicitors, the firm made an offer which was not a Part 36 offer, on the basis that the Financial Services Compensation Scheme would meet 90% of the liability and the solicitors would pay the shortfall. The claimant bank subsequently made a Part 36 offer but, shortly before trial, purported to accept the original offer made by the solicitors. The court held that since the solicitors' offer was not a Part 36 offer, the impact on it of any counter-offer had to be addressed by reference to common law principles. On that basis, the subsequent Part 36 offer was a counter-offer with the result that the solicitors' offer was rejected and no longer available for acceptance. The matter, accordingly, had to proceed to trial.[109]

In litigation concerning an easement, the defendants offered to settle but did not deal with the question of costs, nor did they respond to enquiries about this. The offer was time limited and it lapsed. Shortly before trial the

---

[107] r.44.2(4), Practice Direction 44, paras 4.1–4.2.
[108] *Day v Day* (Costs) [2006] EWCA Civ 415; [2006] CP Rep 35.
[109] *DB UK Bank Limited (t/a DB Mortgages) v Jacobs Solicitors* [2016] EWHC 1614 (Ch.), Andrew Hochhauser QC.

defendants made an identical offer which the claimant did accept. The question of costs then came before the judge at first instance who ordered the defendants to pay the claimant's costs up to the date of the expiry of the first offer and the claimant to pay the defendant's costs thereafter. On appeal, the court held that the justice of the case meant that the appropriate order was no order for costs after the date of expiry of the first offer. There was no good reason for the claimant not to have accepted the first offer, equally there was no good reason for the defendants to have withdrawn it rather than letting it stand. Taking into account all the circumstances including the conduct of both parties, the costs order was partially overturned.[110]

Fraud and dishonesty in making offers

5–29   Where parties in family proceedings had entered into a consent order compromising the wife's financial claims, it subsequently came to light that the husband had failed to disclose arrangements being made to float a software company in which he had a substantial shareholding. The judge at first instance found that the husband's evidence had been dishonest but did not set aside the consent order as the initial public offering had not taken place and was not likely to do so in the future. This decision was upheld by the Court of Appeal but overturned by the Supreme Court. The Supreme Court endorsed the broad approach to dishonesty that *"fraud unravels all"*. The court emphasised the fundamental principle that parties have a duty to provide full and frank financial disclosure to one another and the court in financial remedy proceedings. The court and the parties must have all relevant information before them to enable an informed decision to be made about what constitutes a fair financial outcome.[111] This principle will clearly apply in all negotiated settlements.

Negotiation

5–30   Negotiation needs no explanation. It is the method by which the majority of civil cases are still settled. Negotiation may be between the parties themselves; between their lawyers; between experts, reporting back to the lawyers/clients; or any combination of the above.

Mediation

5–31   Mediation is conducted by an independent third party (who is normally an accredited mediator) who is independent of the parties and whose function it is to try to bring the parties together so that a settlement or compromise may be achieved. It is a confidential process, which can usually be arranged to take place within a reasonably short timescale. Lord Justice Jackson, in Chapter 36 of his Final Report, stated[112]:

---

[110] *Patience v Tanner* [2016] EWCA Civ. 158; [2016] 2 Costs LR 311.
[111] *Sharland v Sharland* [2015] UKSC 60, [2016] A.C. 871; [2015] 3 W.L.R. 1070; [2016] 1 All E.R. 671.
[112] Para.3.2.

"Mediation is not, of course, a universal panacea. The process can be expensive and can on occasions result in failure. The thesis of this chapter is not that media- tion should be undertaken in every case, but that mediation has a significantly greater role to play in the civil justice system than is currently recognised."

There are several types of mediation, the most usual being facilitative and evaluative. In facilitative mediation the mediator tries to help the parties reach a position with which they can live. There is often a matter of pride which prevents a party from compromising for fear of appearing weak. The cloak of confidentiality helps in this regard.

Evaluative mediation requires a rather more robust approach by the media- tor. The writer has found that although one starts out on the facilitative track one finds that one ends up going down the evaluative route. Each party ulti- mately asks: *"What do you think would happen on assessment?"* or *"What do you think it is worth"*.

Many mediation agreements contain a clause to the effect that if the parties fail to agree, the mediator may be asked to give a non-binding opinion as to the final outcome.

The main benefits are that a neutral third party may be able to help each side see the strengths and weaknesses of its case. A skilled mediator may help parties step outside the adversarial framework and entrenched positions so the mediation may work even where a negotiation has failed. A skilled media- tor may make possible offers and concessions look more acceptable. A robust and experienced mediator can help to find a way forward even in a relatively intractable dispute. The structure of a mediation allows a lawyer and a client time to review offers and options in a way which may not be possible in nego- tiation. Mediation can be used to allow a party to make a statement about something of particular personal importance. Experience suggests that media- tion generally achieves good success rates and party satisfaction.

The Mediator needs to be selected with care as regards expertise, experience etc. to ensure the parties have confidence in the process. The most obvious advantages of mediation are that, provided the parties are able to agree the process, a mediation can be set up quickly rather than having to wait nine to 12 months for a court hearing. The parties may choose their Mediator. Parties are not permitted to choose the judge where a matter proceeds to litigation. The process is confidential, whereas in the absence of a specific Order, all hear- ings in courts are in public.

The Court of Appeal has addressed the question of ADR in greater detail.[113] The court indicated that the burden was on the unsuccessful party to show why there should be a departure from the general rule on costs, in the form of an order to deprive the successful party of some or all of his costs on the grounds that he refused to agree to ADR. A fundamental principle was that such a departure was not justified unless it had been shown that the success-

---

[113] *Halsey v Milton Keynes General NHS Trust* [2004] EWCA Civ 576; [2004] C.P. Rep.34.

ful party had acted unreasonably in refusing to agree to ADR. In deciding whether a party had acted unreasonably the court should bear in mind the advantages of ADR over the court process and have regard to all the circumstances of the particular case. The factors that could be relevant include:

(i)   the nature of the dispute;
(ii)   the merits of the case;
(iii) the extent to which other settlement methods have been attempted;
(iv)   whether the costs of ADR are disproportionately high;
(v)   whether any delay in setting up and attending the ADR would have been prejudicial;
(vi)   whether the ADR had a reasonable prospect of success.

Where failure to mediate was due to the attitudes taken on either side it was not open to one party to claim that the failure should be taken into account in the order as to costs. A party who agreed to mediation but then took an unreasonable position in the mediation was in the same position as a party who unreasonably refused to mediate. That was something which the court should take into account in its costs order.[114]

Where a party reasonably considered that it had a strong case and where a party was faced with an unfounded claim and wished to contest it rather than buy it off, the court should be slow to characterise that as unreasonable conduct. The fact that a party reasonably believed that it had a watertight case might well be sufficient justification for refusal to mediate.[115]

The court has to look beyond the polarised positions of the parties. A skilled mediator might be able to find middle ground by analysing the parties' position and making each reflect on its own and the other's position. By bringing other commercial arrangements or disputes into the discussion or by finding future business opportunities, a mediator might find solutions that the parties had not considered. On the facts of the particular case, the defendant's refusal to mediate had deprived the parties of the opportunity of resolving the case without a hearing, as had the claimant's failure to accept the defendant's offer. The fair and just outcome was that neither party's conduct should modify the general rule on costs. The claimant was accordingly ordered to pay the whole of the defendant's costs on the standard basis.[116]

In *Garritt-Critchley v Ronnan*[117] the defendants accepted the claimant's Part 36 offer just before judgment was about to be given following a four day trial. The judge did not criticise the late acceptance of the Part 36 offer but penalised the defendants in costs because he considered that they had been wrong in consistently refusing to mediate. The defendants had refused to mediate

---

[114] *Carleton (Earl of Malmesbury) v Strutt & Parker (A Partnership)* [2007] EWHC 424 (QB). 118 Con. L.R. 68, Jack J.
[115] See *Halsey* (above) and *Daniels v Commissioner of Police of the Metropolis* [2005] EWCA Civ 1312; [2006] CP Rep.9.
[116] *Northrop Grumman Mission Systems Europe Limited v BAE Systems (AL Diriyah C41) Limited* [2014] EWHC 3148 (TCC); [2015] 3 All E.R. 782; [2014] T.C.L.R. 8; [2014] 6 Costs L.O. 879, Ramsey J.
[117] *Garritt-Critchley v Ronnan* [2014] EWHC 1774, [2015] 3 Costs L.R. 453 .

because they were confident of their position and believed that the parties were too far apart. The judge stated that the claim involved a question of fact which was a classic case for mediation and parties did not know whether they were too far apart until they sat down and explored settlement. Mediation also costs less than trial[118]. If the defendants had accepted the claimant's last offer of mediation, the difference in costs might have been almost £100,000. The judge applied *Halsey*, which held that in deciding whether a party had acted unreasonably in refusing ADR, the court should bear in mind the advantages of ADR over the court process and have regard to all the circumstances of the particular case.[119]

A defendant in person who unsuccessfully opposed a grant of probate in favour of the claimants, having lost at trial, argued that he should not have to pay the claimant's costs as they had initially refused to mediate. The court held that a successful party's unreasonable refusal to mediate might warrant a reduction in the amount of costs. In the instant case, however, the claimants had subsequently changed their attitude to mediation, but it did not take place because the defendant was not ready to take part. There was, therefore, no reason why the defendant should not face the usual order as to costs. The order was made on the standard basis since, although the defendant should not have challenged the will, the case did not cross the threshold for ordering costs on the indemnity basis. An order for payment on account was also made. Another issue was whether the claimant's counsel was entitled to a separate brief fee in respect of the defendant's late application to amend his defence to include a claim for forgery. The court did not specifically disallow the claim for a separate brief fee, but directed the Costs Judge to pay particular attention to the matter and to consider whether there would be any element of double recovery.[120]

Where a defendant had agreed to a mediation but then failed to attend the mediation itself without giving any reason, the court took the view that this was a very serious matter both because of the expenditure incurred and more importantly because the defendant had shown himself unwilling to engage in a serious attempt to resolve the litigation. In the view of the court this was serious misconduct that the court could take into account in an application where that party asked for relief on the basis that it was just to make the order sought. In the particular case, the defendant was seeking an order for security for costs under CPR r.25.13(2)(c). The application was refused and the court noted that the defendant's misconduct would itself have been sufficient justification for dismissing the application.[121]

In a building dispute the claimant made a Part 36 offer to settle, and also suggested mediation. At trial the judge awarded damages which were less than

---

[118] Unless the mediation fails.
[119] In *Reid v Buckinghamshire Healthcare NHS Trust* [2015] EWHC B21 Master O'Hare in the SCCO ordered the losing defendant to pay the costs of detailed assessment from the date they unreasonably refused an offer of mediation.
[120] *Murray v Bernard* [2015] EWHC 2395 (Ch.), [2015] 5 Costs L.O. 567, Mann J.
[121] *Gresport Finance Limited v Battaglia* [2015] EWHC 2709 (Ch.), Chief Master Marsh. This decision is persuasive only.

the claimant had claimed, and less than their Part 36 offer. The judge made no order for costs up to the expiry of the period for acceptance of the Part 36 Offer, and ordered the claimant to pay the defendant's costs thereafter. The Court of Appeal held that the judge had erred fundamentally in his appreciation of the significance of the claimant's Part 36 offer. There was nothing in Part 36 which stated that an offeror was to be prejudiced as to costs because she expressed her willingness to accept less than her formal claim. An order for no order as to costs did substantial justice between the parties. The claimant was the winner but only just. On an issues-based approach she had failed on three issues, but succeeded on one issue which had taken a substantial amount of time. The defendants' rejection of offers to enter into settlement negotiations or mediation was unreasonable, and conduct which ought to be taken into account.[122]

While mediation is not compulsory, it is now well established that the courts may robustly encourage parties to embark on it and an unreasonable failure to do so places a party at risk of being penalised in costs. This decision is a reminder that refusing mediation is a high risk strategy, and lawyers and their clients should consider their position carefully.

In holiday litigation, 205 claimants who had suffered misfortune, ranging from poor quality through minor illness to serious illness, sought their costs from the defendant holiday company. On assessment, the Master (using the Lownds test) found the overall base costs to be disproportionate and applied the test of necessity. The defendants appealed on the basis that the necessity test had not been applied with sufficient rigour. The defendants argued, among other things, that the quality only claimant should either recover no costs at all or be restricted to the costs of using the ABTA Scheme. The judge on appeal found that if, at the detailed assessment stage, a defendant wished to rely on the availability of an industry-specific ADR Scheme (i.e. the ABTA Scheme), which was referred to in the relevant contract but was not binding and did not expressly oust the court's jurisdiction, the defendant had to make that clear in its pre-action protocol response, the defendant had not done so. It did not admit liability and robustly contested the claims. Furthermore, the company had not responded to the claimants' offer of ADR. The appeal was dismissed[123].

Mediation in the Commercial Court

5–32   The Commercial Court normally strongly encourages the parties to attempt to resolve their dispute by ADR. The parties are required to co-operate with each other by exchanging the names of three mediators, who are available to conduct the mediation by the date fixed by the court. If the parties cannot

---

[122] *Rolf v De Guerin* [2011] EWCA Civ 78 [2011] 5 Costs L.R. 892.
[123] *TUI UK Limited v Tickell* [2016] EWHC 2741 (QB), Elisabeth Laing J. In *Briggs v First Choice Holidays and Flights Ltd* (unreported), 23 September 2016, (Senior Courts Costs Office) An Interim Costs Certificate refused where group litigation costs not reasonable and proportionate. The Master found that some of the claimants should have pursued their claims via industry-specific mediation.

agree, the court will give directions. In the event that the mediation fails the parties are required to explain why the mediation failed.

Early Neutral Evaluation

Early Neutral Evaluation (ENE) is carried out by an independent person, who is normally experienced in the particular field of the issue under dispute. That person may be appointed by one or all parties.

5–33

The Technology and Construction Court Guide and the Commercial Court Guide both deal with ENE.[124] ENE may be carried out by the court with the consent of the parties. In *Seals v Williams*[125] Norris J concluded that the wide jurisdiction provided by CPR r.3.1(2)(m), to the effect that the court can make any order to manage cases and further the overriding objective, provided the power to order ENE. This did not therefore require the consent of the parties. Following this, CPR r.3.1(2)(m) was amended to read:

> "*Except where these rules provide otherwise, the court may . . . (m) take any other step or make any other order for the purpose of managing the case and furthering the overriding objective, including hearing an early neutral evaluation with the aim of helping parties to settle the case*".

This Rule is not limited to Chancery proceedings but is of general application. It is expected that its use in appropriate cases in the Chancery Division, the Queen's Bench Division and the County Court is likely to become increasingly common. To date there is no dedicated ENE Practice Direction. General guidance (excluding the need for party consent) can be obtained from the TCC and Admiralty and Commercial Court Guides.

ENE is intended to be an advisory and evaluative process. ENE can take place within the court system in which case it is usually carried out by a judge. There is no requirement for proceedings to be in progress, any party may appoint an independent third party to carry out an ENE. It is of course preferable and more conducive to settlement if all the parties can agree to the appointment.

Expert Evaluation

Expert evaluation may take different forms. This may be an evaluation similar to Early Neutral Evaluation or a Determination. As the name implies one or more neutral experts are appointed by the parties to evaluate or determine the issues between the parties. The evaluation/determination may be agreed to be binding between the parties or merely advisory, leaving the parties to proceed further if they so decide. Expert evaluation/determination is most commonly employed in cases of a technical nature (e.g. costs). The way in which matters proceed will be governed primarily by the terms of the contract by which the

5–34

---

[124] See Technology and Construction Court Guide paragraphs 7.5.1–7.5.4; the Admiralty and Commercial Court Guide, parasgraphs G2.1-G2.5.
[125] [2015] EWHC 1829 (Ch), Morris J.

expert is appointed. The parties will usually agree that the determination will be final and binding and this is usually recorded in the contract.

Adjudication

5–35   Adjudication usually takes place in a specialist commercial field where the parties prefer a system adapted to the needs of their industry or business. It is most frequently used in construction disputes. It is used to resolve specific issues and is usually agreed by the parties to a contract as a means of resolving disputes which may arise by a process agreed to be binding on the parties.

Construction industry adjudication is a creature of statute which requires all construction contracts to have a provision for adjudication.[126] The statutory requirement is for adjudication by an independent third person who produces a decision on the dispute which is binding on an interim basis until finally determined as appropriate by the court, arbitration, or agreement. The adjudicator is required to give a decision within a limited time. The decision is enforceable through the courts and appeal is only possible on the grounds of lack of jurisdiction or breach of the rules of natural justice.

In a construction dispute, the defendant made an open offer in the sum found by the adjudicator. The claimant believed it was entitled to more than the adjudicator had found and brought court proceedings. The claimant did not accept the offer and it was withdrawn. The claimant company applied for judgment on the basis that the offer was a formal admission of liability under CPR r.14.1. The court held that the open offer contained a package of terms that the claimant could accept or reject. It would run contrary to the basis of the offer if the claimant could accept part of it as being an admission of liability but then reject other terms. The court had to encourage the making of offers which was in accordance with the overriding objective. If a party were able partially to accept an offer and to reject other parts which ensured that the litigation continued, the purpose of making offers would not be met. The defendant's offer letter did not refer to CPR r.14.1, nor did it admit the truth of the claimant's case. It did not in any way admit that any of the defendant's points were bad. To be a formal admission under CPR r.14.1, it needed to be clear and unequivocal. The alleged admission was neither. The claimant had had to seek clarification and had been told that there was no admission in respect of early payment discounts. If there had been any admission at all, it was in respect of the sums identified by the adjudicator which was the opposite of the claimant's case.[127]

Arbitration

5–36   Arbitration is effectively a trial process outside the court system. Arbitrations may be domestic or international. They may be conducted under the Arbitration Act 1996 or under the rules of any of the numerous arbitration

---

[126] Housing Grants Construction and Regeneration Act 1996 ss.108 and 108A.
[127] *Dorchester Group Limited (T/A Dorchester Collection) v Kier Construction Limited* [2015] EWHC 3051 (TCC), Coulson J.

providers. In many commercial contracts there are clauses providing terms for arbitration should a dispute arise. Arbitrators may be appointed by -agreement between the parties or, if no agreement is possible, by the President of the relevant professional body. If the arbitration requires three arbitrators, each side usually nominates one arbitrator and the third will be appointed by a neutral person e.g. the President of the professional body.

The agreement to arbitrate may be made before or after the relevant dispute has arisen. There is a strong public policy in favour of upholding arbitration agreements, which is supported by the idea that an arbitration clause in a contract is separable from the rest of the substantive contract[128] and so continues to apply even if the substantive contract is avoided. Where court proceedings are commenced in breach of an arbitration agreement, the defendant may apply to the court to stay those proceedings.[129]

It is worth looking at some of the provisions of the Arbitration Act 1996: s.1, s.4, s.61, and s.63. It is clear from the extracts below that the terms of any arbitration agreement are very much in the hands of the parties. Apart from the mandatory provisions (which are basically common sense), the terms may be agreed in whatever form the parties wish. The Act provides certain long stop provisions, e.g. in s.61, the powers of the Tribunal where the parties have not agreed.

1. General principles.
The provisions of this Part are founded on the following principles, and shall be construed accordingly:

(a) the object of arbitration is to obtain the fair resolution of disputes by an impartial tribunal without unnecessary delay or expense;
(b) the parties should be free to agree how their disputes are resolved, subject only to such safeguards as are necessary in the public interest;
(c) in matters governed by this Part the court should not intervene except as provided by this Part.

4. Mandatory and non-mandatory provisions.

(1) The mandatory provisions of this Part are listed in Sch.1 and have effect notwithstanding any agreement to the contrary.
(2) The other provisions of this Part (the "non-mandatory provisions") allow the parties to make their own arrangements by agreement but provide rules which apply in the absence of such agreement.
(3) The parties may make such arrangements by agreeing to the application of institutional rules or providing any other means by which a matter may be decided.

---

[128] Arbitration Act 1996, Section 7.
[129] Arbitration Act 1996, Section 9.

(4) It is immaterial whether or not the law applicable to the parties' agreement is the law of England and Wales or, as the case may be, Northern Ireland.

(5) The choice of a law other than the law of England and Wales or Northern Ireland as the applicable law in respect of a matter provided for by a non-mandatory provision of this Part is equivalent to an agreement making provision about that matter.

For this purpose an applicable law determined in accordance with the parties' agreement, or which is objectively determined in the absence of any express or implied choice, shall be treated as chosen by the parties.

61. Award of costs.

(1) The tribunal may make an award allocating the costs of the arbitration as between the parties, subject to any agreement of the parties.

(2) Unless the parties otherwise agree, the tribunal shall award costs on the general principle that costs should follow the event except where it appears to the tribunal that in the circumstances this is not appropriate in relation to the whole or part of the costs.

63. The recoverable costs of the arbitration.

(1) The parties are free to agree what costs of the arbitration are recoverable.

(2) If or to the extent there is no such agreement, the following provisions apply.

(3) The tribunal may determine by award the recoverable costs of the arbitration on such basis as it thinks fit.

If it does so, it shall specify:

(a) the basis on which it has acted, and

(b) the items of recoverable costs and the amount referable to each.

(4) If the tribunal does not determine the recoverable costs of the arbitration, any party to the arbitral proceedings may apply to the court (upon notice to the other parties) which may:

(a) determine the recoverable costs of the arbitration on such basis as it thinks fit, or

(b) order that they shall be determined by such means and upon such terms as it may specify.

(5) Unless the tribunal or the court determines otherwise:

(a)   the recoverable costs of the arbitration shall be determined on the basis that there shall be allowed a reasonable amount in respect of all costs reasonably incurred, and

(b)   any doubt as to whether costs were reasonably incurred or were reasonable in amount shall be resolved in favour of the paying party.

(6)   The above provisions have effect subject to section 64 (recoverable fees and expenses of arbitrators).

(7)   Nothing in this section affects any right of the arbitrators, any expert, legal adviser or assessor appointed by the tribunal, or any arbitral institution, to payment of their fees and expenses.

There are no budgeting requirements in arbitration, unless the parties agree. This is unlikely to happen, although commercial clients are bound to want to keep strict control of expenditure. There should be no problems of the sort generated by *Mitchell v NGN Ltd*[130] and *Denton v White*[131].

Questions and answers

Section 1 Part 36

A. Circumstances in which Part 36 offers can be made (CPR r.36.2).

Q1. Is there anything in CPR Part 36 or the Privy Council Rules which prevents a Part 36 offer being made in costs proceedings before the Privy Council? (CPR r.2.1).
CPR r.2.1 states that the rules apply to all proceedings in the County Court, the High Court and the Civil Division of the Court of Appeal. There is no mention of the Privy Council. The Judicial Committee (Appellate Jurisdiction) Rules 2009 set out the procedure before the Judicial Committee but make no mention of Part 36 or anything equivalent to it. A party wishing to make an offer may make a Calderbank type offer. CPR r.43(1) of the 2009 Rules provides "the Judicial Committee may make such orders as it considers just in respect of the costs of any appeal, application for permission to appeal or other application to or proceeding before the Judicial Committee". Practice Direction 8 dealing with Costs states:

5–37

> "*To the extent that the Judicial Committee (Appellate Jurisdiction) Rules and Practice Directions do not cover the situation, the rules and Practice Directions relating to Parts 44 to 47 of the Civil Procedure Rules are applied by analogy at the discretion of the Costs Judge, with appropriate modifications for appeals from foreign jurisdictions. The legal principles applied are those also applicable to assessments between parties in the High Court and Court of Appeal in England and Wales.*"

---

[130] *Andrew Mitchell MP v News Group Newspapers Limited* [2013] EWCA Civ 1537.
[131] *Denton v T H White Ltd* [2014] EWCA Civ 906 [2014] CP Rep 40.

B. Content requirements for Part 36 offers (CPR r.36.5).

Q2. Can a valid Part 36 offer include settlement terms which (if accepted), impose conditions; require a defendant to do something other than pay money; or provide for interest to run after the end of the relevant period? (CPR r.2.1; CPR r.36.2(2), (CPR r.36.5(4)).

5–38   CPR r.36.2(2) states *"Nothing in this Section prevents a party making an offer to settle in whatever way that party chooses, but if the offer is not made in accordance with Rule 36.5, it will not have the consequences specified in this Section."* CPR r.36.5 sets out the form and content of a Part 36 offer. Provided therefore that CPR r.36(5) is complied with, the terms of an offer may be in whatever terms the offeror chooses.

Q3. There are numerous questions on the effect of Part 36.5:
i) Must a valid defendant's Part 36 offer include an offer to pay the claimant's costs?
ii) Can an offeror now legitimately state in his Part 36 offer that the offer is only open for a limited period of time? Does a Part 36 offer automatically expire after the 21 day period or does it only expire if it is withdrawn or if explicitly states it expires after a certain amount of time?
iii) Is a Part 36 offer valid if it includes non-monetary terms e.g. the defendant will provide an indemnity to the claimant in respect of any direct claim by a third party which arises out of current proceedings?
iv) Can a Part 36 offer be made in relation to liability rather than an offer to pay a settlement sum? For example, offering to agree that liability is a 50/50 basis in relation to motor claims?
v) Is it possible to make two offers in a single Part 36 offer? E.g., the defendant pays £8500 immediately, or £10,000 in instalments?
vi) Can a valid Part 36 offer be made in a small claim?

5–39   All these questions concern the operation of CPR r.36.2(2): a party may make an offer to settle in whatever way that party chooses and CPR r.36.5: form and content of a Part 36 offer. The rules are intended to promote offers to settle rather than restrict them.

Answering each question briefly:

i) Not necessarily, terms as to costs are inconsistent with the scheme of Pt 36: see *Mitchell v James* [2002] EWCA Civ 997; [2004] 1 W.L.R. 158; [2003] 2 All E.R. 1064, CA. The offeror may be offering to drop its claim/counterclaim and for both parties to walk away. There are numerous instances of the court deciding that no order for costs is appropriate.

ii) Yes, after expiry of the relevant period. Provided the offeree has not previously served notice of acceptance, the offeror may withdraw the offer or change its terms without the permission of the court; or the offer may be automatically withdrawn in accordance with its terms. See CPR r.36.9.

iii) Yes, provided it complies with CPR r.36.5.

iv) Yes, provided it complies with CPR r.36.5. See *Owners and/or Bareboat Charterers and/or Sub Bareboat Charterers of the Ship Samco Europe v Owners of the Ship MSC Prestige* [2011] EWHC 1656 (Admlty) Teare J. paragraph 5–07 above.

v) A defendant's offer that includes an offer to pay all or part of the sum at a date later than 14 days following the date of acceptance will not be treated as a Part 36 offer unless the offeree accepts the offer. (CPR r.36.6(2)); save for two exceptions relating to personal injury claims, a Part 36 offer by a defendant to pay a sum of money in settlement of a claim must be an offer to pay a single sum of money. (CPR r.36.6(1)). These restrictions are not mentioned in relation to claimants' offers. Again such an offer may be permissible provided it complies with CPR r.36.5.

vi) No, r.27.2(1)(g) provides that Part 36 does not apply to small claims.

Q4. If a defendant makes a Part 36 offer which does not take into account its counterclaim and the offer is then accepted, what happens to the counterclaim? (CPR r.36.5).

CPR r.36.2(3)(a) now clarifies that Part 36 offers can be made in respect of counterclaims and other additional claims. When making an offer in a case concerning a counterclaim or other additional claim, it is important to make clear whether it is intended to be a claimant's or a defendant's offer. A counterclaiming defendant may wish to make a claimant's offer i.e where the offer is to accept some payment on the counterclaim; or a defendant's offer i.e. where the offer is to pay some money on the claim. Such an offer may take the other adverse claim into account: see CPR rules.36.5 (1)(d) to (e).[132]

"Counterclaim" is defined by the CPR glossary as 'a claim brought by a defendant in response to the claimant's claim which is included in the same proceedings as the claimant's claim'. A counterclaim is treated for certain purposes as if it were a claim (CPR r.20.3). CPR r.36.2(3) provides that a Part 36 offer may be made in respect of the whole, or part of, any issue that arises in a claim, counterclaim or other additional claim, and state whether it takes into account any counterclaim CPR r.36.5(1)(c)). CPR r.36.14(3) provides that if a Part 36 offer which relates to part only of the claim is accepted, the claim will be stayed as to that part upon the terms of the offer. The question which has to be decided is whether the counterclaim is 'part only of the claim' or is a claim in its own right. Whilst the rules provide for a Part 36 offer to take into account the existence of a counterclaim if so desired, there is no requirement to do so and it is accordingly arguable that a counterclaim is a claim in its own right and would continue notwithstanding any Part 36 offer accepted in respect of the claim. The options for a party making a Part 36 offer, where a counterclaim exists, appear to be: either to ensure that the offer takes into account the counterclaim or to make an offer without prejudice save as to costs, i.e. a Calderbank offer.

Where a defendant had made what purported to be a claimant's Part 36

5–40

---

[132] See also *Van Oord UK Ltd v Allseas UK Ltd* [2015] EWHC 3385 (TCC), [2016] 1 Costs L O 1, Coulson J.

offer in respect of the defendant's counterclaim, *"the proceedings in respect of which"* it was made included the claim and the proposed counterclaim, but were not restricted only to the counterclaim. A Part 36 offer may be made before the commencement of proceedings under CPR r.36.7 so the fact that the defendant's counterclaim had not been formulated or pleaded did not of itself matter.[133]

Q5. Where there's more than one claimant, in his Part 36 offer must the defendant apportion the settlement sum he offers between each claimant? I'm trying to find out if there is a case or any legislation that states that Part 36 offers to more than one claimant need to be apportioned between the offerees? For example, if a Part 36 offer of £50,000 is made to two claimants, do you have to specify that it's 50/50 for each, or, say, 70% for one and 30% for the other. (CPR r.36.5).

5–41   CPR r.36.5 states that a part 36 offer must *"(d) state whether it relates to the whole of the claim or to part of it or to an issue that arises in it and if so to which part or issue; and*

(e) state whether it takes into account any counterclaim." If there is more than one claimant the offeror may make a blanket offer leaving the claimants to sort out the apportionment, or make it clear how the offer is intended to be apportioned. CPR r.36.2 makes it clear that an offer to settle may be made in whatever way the party chooses, provided it complies with CPR r.36.5.

Q6. In a case where there is no counterclaim and the claimant makes a Part 36 offer, does that offer need to state whether it takes into account any counterclaim given that there is no counterclaim in existence? (CPR r.36.5(1)(e)).

5–42   If the offeree were to argue that the Part 36 offer was invalid in that it failed to indicate whether it took into account any counterclaim, this would be, to say the least, a pedantic argument since there is no counterclaim in existence. In *C v D*[134] the Court of Appeal held that where an offer has been made which has been presented as a Part 36 offer and otherwise complied with the required form, the courts would not readily interpret it in a way which would prevent it from being a Part 36 offer.

Q7. If one of two defendants with joint and several liability makes a Part 36 offer, what are that defendant's costs implication assuming that before the offer he would have been jointly and severally liable for all of the plaintiff's costs? (CPR r.36.5).

5–43   CPR r.36.15 deals with acceptance of a Part 36 offer made by one or more but not all defendants. The Rule goes on to provide that if the defendants are sued jointly or in the alternative, the claimant may accept the offer: if the claimant

---

[133] *AF v BG* [2009] EWCA Civ 757.
[134] [2011] EWCA Civ 646; [2012] 1 WLR 1962; [2012] 1 All ER 302; [2011] 5 Costs LR 773.

discontinues the claim against the defendant who has not made the offer and that defendant gives written consent to the acceptance of the offer. If the claimant alleges that the defendants have a several liability, the claimant may accept the offer and continue with the claim against the other defendant if entitled to do so. Otherwise, the claimant must apply to the court for permission to accept the Part 36 offer.

C. Time when a Part 36 offer may be made (CPR r.36.7).

Q8. What is the position when a Part 36 offer is made pre-action and accepted after the issue of proceedings, but before the proceedings have been served on the defendant, where service has been reserved for up to four months? (CPR r.36.7.)
CPR r.36.7 permits a Part 36 offer to be made at any time including before the   **5–44** commencement of proceedings. If the offer is not made in accordance with CPR r.36.5, it will not have the consequences specified in Section I of Part 36. If the offer is not a valid Part 36 offer CPR r.44.2 requires the court to consider any offer to settle, that does not have the costs consequences set out in Section I, in deciding what order to make about costs.

CPR r.7.2(1) provides that proceedings are started when the court issues a claim form at the request of the claimant. The fact that the proceedings have not been served or that service has been reserved for a period is immaterial. The purpose of Part 36 is to enable and encourage parties to settle cases at an early stage, without the need for a trial.

Q9. Will a Part 36 offer still have effect if it is made during a stay of proceedings which were for reasons other than to allow for settlement of the case? (CPR r.36.7).
The Rules appear to be quite clear. CPR r.36.7(1) provides *"A Part 36 offer may*   **5–45** *be made at any time . . ."* and CPR r.36.11(2) provides that a Part 36 offer may be accepted at any time (whether or not the offeree has subsequently made a different offer), unless it has already been withdrawn. Depending upon the terms of the stay, it may be necessary to apply to the court for permission to proceed.

D. Part 36 and asking for clarification (CPR r.36.8).

Q10. Where there is a Part 36 offer, what is the position where the offeree seeks clarification of the offer? Should I ask my opponent to clarify his badly drafted unclear Part 36 offer? (CPR r.36.8).
Under CPR r.36.8 the offeree may, within seven days of an offer being made,   **5–46** request the offeror to clarify it. If the offeror does not give the clarification requested within seven days of receiving the request, the offeree may, unless the trial has started, apply for an order that the offeror do so. If the court makes an order, it must specify the date when the Part 36 offer is to be treated

as having been made. Where there had been a settlement agreement of the substantive claim, one party asserted that the other was in repudiatory breach and terminated the agreement. The party against whom breach was alleged, claimed damages from the other. The defendant (later appellant) made a Part 36 offer of £200,000. The offer stated that it did "not take into account any counterclaim". The claimant (later respondent) requested clarification as to whether it was intended to bring a counterclaim and the defendant stated that he did not intend to. The claimant sought further information about the valuation of the claim but that was not provided.

The claimant refused the offer and issued proceedings, and the defendant filed a defence and added a counterclaim. The claimant then served a Part 36 offer which offered to accept £185,000 and stated that it "took account of the entire claim and counterclaim". The defendant accepted that offer outside the 21 day period to avoid an automatic costs order.

The defendant sought an order that the claimant pay his costs from 21 days after the first Part 36 offer. The claimant sought an order that the defendant pay her costs up to the date of his acceptance. At first instance the Master held that she could not regard the offers as being on similar terms, as the claimant was proposing to settle the claim and counterclaim, thereby bringing finality, whereas an acceptance of the defendant's offer would not necessarily have done so. In light of the fact that the first Part 36 offer did not state whether it took into account any counterclaim, as required by CPR r.36.2, (now CPR r.36.5) she declined to 'order otherwise' pursuant to CPR r.36.10(4) (now CPR r.36.13(4)) and ordered that the defendant pay the claimant's costs of the claim.

On appeal the court held that the Master had taken account of the clarification but had concluded that it did not modify it and she was entitled to that view as a matter of law. However, in construing the first Part 36 offer, the subsequent clarification had to be taken into account. The Master had failed to adopt that approach and should have seen that, had the respondent (claimant) accepted the first Part 36 offer, the appellant (defendant) would have been bound. The Master had wrongly construed the first Part 36 offer as excluding any counterclaim without having regard to the whole of the correspondence. The first Part 36 offer had been modified in correspondence so as to encompass any counterclaim.

The counterclaim that had later been brought was not in fact a discrete claim but no more than a claim for a declaration as to the repudiation of the settlement agreement and therefore no more than a mirror image of the defence. The fact of the later counterclaim did not therefore alter the court's conclusion. Even if the first Part 36 offer had been capable of comparison with the second, the respondent had not initially acted unreasonably in refusing it. She had made reasonable requests for information that the appellant had not thought were relevant. The purpose of the Part 36 regime was to encourage early settlement and allow the offeror costs if their offer was not accepted within 21 days. The appellant's letter and first Part 36 offer clearly explained the valuation of the respondent's claim. It was reasonable for the respondent to seek further clarification. However, she had misunderstood the valuation. There was no doubt that that misunderstanding had been corrected by the appellant and the respondent had received all the information needed to understand the official valuation shortly after the original offer.

The further information that the respondent requested was not relevant and it was not unreasonable of the appellant not to provide it. The respondent's questions had been answered by the letter accompanying the first Part 36 offer and she could have made an informed decision on that basis. It was not unreasonable conduct for the appellant to refuse to give further information and his actions were not unreasonable or obstructive. It would be unjust for the appellant to pay costs past the 21 day period following the first Part 36 offer.[135]

Whilst Part 36 requires an offer to state whether it includes a counterclaim or not, provided the position is clear or is made clear by way of clarification, it therefore appears the court will give effect to the offer.

E. Withdrawing or changing terms of Part 36 offers (CPR rules 36.9, 36.10).

Q11. If an offeree serves a notice of acceptance during the relevant period, when does that acceptance take effect, given that the offeror may apply for permission to withdraw or vary its offer within seven days of the notice of acceptance (or, if earlier, before the first day of trial)?
If the offeror's application is unsuccessful, it is not clear when the notice of   5–47
acceptance will be treated as having been accepted. (CPR rules 36.9; 36.10).

Q12. Where a claimant made a pre-action Part 36 offer which was rejected and now that proceedings have been issued wishes to make a Part 36 offer that is more advantageous to the defendant, what is the position with regard to the original offer? If the claimant equals or beats the offer at trial when are indemnity costs likely to be awarded from: the earlier offer date or the one which supersedes it? (CPR r.36.9(5)).
CPR r.36.9 provides that a Part 36 offer can only be withdrawn or its terms   5–48
changed if the offeree has not previously served notice of acceptance. Changing the terms of an offer is done by serving written notice of the change of terms on the offeree. The offer must specify a period not less than 21 days within which the defendant will be liable for the claimant's costs if the offer is accepted but that provision does not apply if the offer is made less than 21 days before the start of a trial.

CPR r.36.9(5) provides:

"Where the offeror changes the terms of a Part 36 offer to make it more advantageous to the offeree (a) such improved offer shall be treated, not as the withdrawal of the original offer; but as the making of a new Part 36 offer on the improved

---

[135] *Bailes v Bloom* [2015] EWHC (QB) 23 November Simler J, unreported.

223

terms; and (b) subject to Rule 36.5(2) the period specified under Rule 36.5(1) (c) shall be 21 days or such longer period (if any) identified in the written notice referred to in paragraph (2)."

Under CPR r.36.17(4)(b), if the judgment against the defendant is at least as advantageous to the claimant as the proposals contained in the Part 36 offer, the court must, unless it considers it unjust to do so, order that the claimant is entitled to costs on the indemnity basis from the date on which the relevant period expired. The relevant period for the purpose of this question would seem to be that attaching to the changed offer.

5–49 A Part 36 offer can only be withdrawn or its terms changed if the offeree has not previously served notice of acceptance CPR r.36.9(1)). If the offeree serves notice of acceptance before the expiry of the relevant period, that acceptance has effect unless the offeror applies to the court for permission to withdraw the offer or to change its terms within seven days of the offeree's notice of acceptance; or, if earlier, before the first day of trial. Where the offeror makes such an application, the court may give -permission for the original offer to be withdrawn or its terms changed if satisfied there has been a change of circumstances since the making of the original offer and that it is in the interests of justice to give permission (CPR r.36.10).

As to when the acceptance takes effect if the offeror's application is unsuccessful, the answer may be fact sensitive but the starting point must be the date of the notice of acceptance. This has the slightly odd result that the case will then be deemed to be settled and stayed from a date before the hearing of the offeror's application.

Q13. What is the position where a Part 36 offer is withdrawn at the same time as the claimant purports to accept it? (CPR rules 36.9, 36.10).

5–50 The rules governing the withdrawal of offers are CPR rules 36.9 and 36.10. The following decision still holds good. An NHS Trust made a Part 36 offer to a claimant which stated that if it was accepted within 21 days, the Trust would be responsible for the claimant's costs. The offer pointed out that it could be withdrawn before the expiration of that period with permission of the court. Before the expiration of the relevant period the Trust obtained permission to withdraw its offer but did so without serving any notice or evidence on the claimant who had accepted the offer on the day it was withdrawn. Leggatt J held that an application should not be made without notice unless that would enable the respondent to take steps to defeat the purpose of the application or there had been no time to give notice before the urgent assistance of the court was required. It was wrong in principle for the Trust to make its application for permission without notice to the claimant and for the court to entertain the application. It was all the more wrong to conceal from the claimant the grounds on which the order had been made. The making of orders which determined questions of substantive rights between the parties without notice could only be justified if that party had the right to apply to set aside the order.

The test to be applied, when considering whether to grant a party permission to withdraw a Part 36 offer, was whether there had been a sufficient change of circumstances to make it just to do so.[136] The only new circumstances which could make it just were circumstances which the Trust was able and willing to make known to the claimant at the time of serving notice of withdrawal.[137]

Under CPR r.36.10(3), where the offeree serves notice of acceptance of the offer before the expiry of the relevant period and the offeror applies to court for permission to withdraw or change its terms within seven days of the offeree's notice (or, if earlier, before the first day of trial), the court will only give permission if satisfied that there has been a change of circumstances and that it is in the interests of justice.

F. Part 36 offer acceptance requirements (CPR rules 36.11, 36.12)/Disclosure of Part 36 offer (CPR r.36.16).

Q14. Where there has been a split trial or a trial of preliminary issues, what is the position with regard to Part 36 offers which may have been made? (CPR r.36.12).

Where there has been a trial but all the issues in the case have not been determined,[138] any Part 36 offer, which relates only to parts of the claim or issues that have already been decided, can no longer be accepted. Subject to that proviso, and unless the parties agree, any other Part 36 offer cannot be accepted earlier than seven clear days after judgment is given or handed down in that trial.[139]

5–51

Where an offer, which relates to the whole of the claim, is accepted after the expiry of the relevant period, the court must, unless it considers it unjust to do so, order that the claimant be awarded costs up to the date on which the relevant period expired, and, that the offeree pay the offeror's costs for the period from the date of the expiry of the relevant period to the date of acceptance. In considering whether it would be unjust to make such orders the court must take into account all the circumstances of the case including the matters set out in CPR r.36.17(5) (see Costs consequences following judgment above). The claimant's costs include any costs incurred in dealing with the defendant's counterclaim if the Part 36 offer states that it takes the counterclaim into account.[140] CPR r.36.16 deals with restrictions on disclosure in such cases.

It is open to the court to depart from the normal costs rule in CPR r.36.13(5). Where a young boy had suffered frontal lobe damage in a road traffic -accident, it was material that the inherent uncertainty in prognosis would have resolved well before the limitation period expired so that the child did not need to

---

[136] *Cumper v Pothecary* [1941] 2 KB 58.
[137] *Evans v Royal Wolverhampton Hospitals NHS Foundation Trust* [2014] EWHC 3185 (QB), [2015] 1 W.L.R. 4659; [2015] 1 All E.R. 1091;[2014] 6 Costs L.O. 899; Leggatt J.
[138] Within the meaning of r.36.3(e).
[139] r.36.12 and also see r.36.3.
[140] r.36.13(5)–(7). For cases which led to the revision of this rule, see *Fitzpatrick Contractors Ltd v Tyco Fire & Integrated Solutions (UK) Ltd* [2009] EWHC 274 (TCC) Coulson J; *Thompson v Bruce* [2011] EWHC 1730 (QB) John Leighton Williams QC; *Kunaka v Barclays Bank Plc* [2010] EWCA Civ 1035; *Sutherland v Turnball* [2010] EWHC 2699 (QB) Stadlen J.

commence proceedings before the position was clear. The defendant had made a pre-action Part 36 offer in full and final -settlement; the claimant accepted the offer after the date of its expiry. The court approved the settlement, but at first instance it was held that the defendant should be entitled to its costs from the date of acceptance. The Court of Appeal held that the judge's conclusion did not give weight to the particular features of the claimant's case, the consequence of omitting to give weight to the matters that were in the claimant's favour was that the normal rule dominated when it should not have done. In the circumstances it was unjust to make the normal costs order, and the claimant was awarded his costs throughout.[141]

There was previously no general rule that in the case of a split trial the court should ordinarily reserve the costs until the end of the case. Mr Justice Eder stated that there was an urgent need for the rule to be reviewed and possibly reformulated in order to address the question of split trials. In the particular case, due to the substantial level of costs, costs were reserved.[142] In response to these concerns, with effect from 6 April 2015, paras (3)(d) and (4) were added to the rule. There is now no restriction on telling the trial judge at the end of a preliminary trial (a) about the terms of any Part 36 offers relating only to issues that have been decided (CPR r.36.16(3)(d)); and (b) about the existence (but not the terms) of any other Part 36 offers (CPR r.36.16(4)).

In a different case, the judge decided that success on the preliminary issue did not mean that the claimant would ultimately establish any claim in contract at all, and the incidence of costs should therefore be the same as if it had been tried as part of that claim. The judge did not think that this was a reason for departing from the general rule. The defendants had asked for a preliminary issue. They did so because it was thought to be helpful to the parties, and to the court, for the question of proper law to be determined as a discrete issue. The judge agreed, but the corollary of this was that the question did not arise as part and parcel of the trial but was tried separately. That necessarily involved a separate hearing with separate preparation and the incurring of separate costs on that issue. It is in general a salutary principle that those who lose discrete aspects of complex litigation should pay for the discrete applications or hearings which they lose, and should do so when they lose them rather than leaving the costs to be swept up at trial.[143]

G. Costs consequences of acceptance of a Part 36 offer (CPR r.36.13).

Q15. What is the procedure for recovering costs in an action that settles without proceedings as a result of the acceptance of a pre-action Part 36 offer? (CPR r.36.13).

5–52   Under CPR r.36.13, where a Part 36 offer is accepted within the relevant

---

[141] *SG v Hewitt* [2012] EWCA Civ 1053.
[142] *Ted Baker Plc v Axa Insurance UK Plc* [2012] EWHC 1779 (Comm) Eder J.
[143] *Merck KGaA v Merck Sharp & Dohme Corp* [2014] EWHC 3920 (Ch) Nugee J.

period, the claimant is entitled to the costs of the proceedings, including their recoverable pre-action costs, up to the date on which notice of acceptance was served on the offeror. Rule 44.9(1)(b) states that where a right to costs arises under CPR r.36.13(1) or (2), a costs order will be deemed to have been made on a standard basis; but CPR r.44.9 (2) states that paragraph 1(b) does not apply where a Part 36 offer is accepted before the commencement of proceedings. If the costs cannot be agreed, there is no doubt about the claimant's right to costs including the pre-commencement costs and the appropriate procedure is to issue costs only proceedings in accordance with CPR r.46.14. When the order for costs to be assessed is made, the normal procedure for detailed assessment under Part 47 applies. As to interest, CPR r.36.5(4) provides that a Part 36 offer which offers to pay or offers to accept a sum of money will be treated as inclusive of all interest until the relevant period expires. CPR r.36.14(5)(b) provides that any stay arising on the acceptance of a Part 36 offer will not affect the power of the court to deal with any question of costs (including interest on costs) relating to the proceedings.

Q16. I act for a proposed claimant in a dispute where legal proceedings have yet to be issued. The proposed defendant has served a Part 36 offer by form N242A which states that the defendant will be liable for the claimant's costs in accordance with Part 36.13. Part 36.13 states the claimant will be entitled to the Costs of proceedings including their recoverable pre-action costs. Does this mean my client can only recover pre action costs as part of the costs of any proceedings? If this is so, can we agree that the pre-action costs are recoverable and if so, if the amount cannot be agreed can we issue costs only proceedings pursuant to Part 8A to have the court adjudicate upon costs? (CPR r.36.13).

Part 8 Costs Only proceedings are the way forward. CPR r.36.13 depends on 5–53 there being extant proceedings. With that in mind, if parties make a pre-issue settlement, they might consider making it a term of the settlement that the usual CPR Part 36 consequences will follow. Alternatively, a party could make an offer to settle outside the terms of Part 36, offering to pay the other party's reasonable costs. It may be possible to bring costs-only proceedings under CPR r.46.14. **See also the Q&A above.**

In a road traffic case where a Part 36 offer had been made and accepted before proceedings had been issued, the claimant contended that a deemed order for costs would have arisen providing a sufficient basis for commencing a detailed assessment. The court held that an order for costs:

"...cannot exist in a vacuum divorced from any substantive proceedings, and accordingly an order for costs cannot be deemed to have been made under rule [44.9(1)(b)] if a Part 36 offer is made and accepted before any proceedings have been commenced."

The court stated:

> *"18. On the face of it, the procedure in rule [46.14 (Costs Only Proceedings)] is apt to refer to cases that fall within Part [36.13(1)] as well as to those" that do not . . .it provides for Section II of Part 45 to take precedence in cases to which it applies: see rule [46.14(5) and (6)]. In my view the mechanism provided by rule [46.14] is intended to apply both to cases settled through the operation of Part 36 and to those settled without recourse to it."*

The court commented that it was not easy to see why a claimant who proceeds under CPR r.46.14 should be subject to a more restrictive costs regime, than one who started proceedings under Part 7 to recover his costs:

> *"The whole purpose of introducing Section II of Part 45 was to impose a somewhat rough and ready system in a limited class of cases. . ."*

If the claimants' argument was correct, the acceptance of a Part 36 offer would always result in an order for costs on the standard basis in low value road traffic accident cases which would undermine the fixed costs regime and provide a powerful incentive for defendants not to make Part 36 offers in such cases. The court concluded that, subject to any agreement between the parties to the contrary, neither could recover more or less by way of costs than is provided for.[144]

Q17. If a defendant accepts a claimant's Part 36 offer after proceedings have been issued, is a consent order to dispose of the proceedings necessary?
I understand that generally speaking, there is no need for there to be a consent order if a settlement results from acceptance of a Part 36 offer. Am I right? If so, are there any significant exceptions from this general proposition? (CPR r.36.13(1)).

5–54   No. Under CPR PD 36A 3.1 a copy of the acceptance must be filed at court. CPR r.36.14(1) provides that the claim will be stayed.

In the event that a defendant accepts a claimant's Part 36 offer, r.44.9(1)(b) provides that where a right to costs arises under CPR r.36.13(1) or (2), a costs order will be deemed to have been made on the standard basis. This provision does not apply where the Part 36 offer is accepted before the commencement of proceedings. The existence of the deemed order for costs enables the claimant to commence detailed assessment proceedings under Part 47.

Q18. CPR r.36.2 provides that a Part 36 offer may be made in a counterclaim or additional claim, and it includes a reminder that CPR r.20.2 and CPR r.20.3 provide that counterclaims and other additional claims are treated as claims. With that in mind, if a defendant makes a Part 36 offer in relation to its counterclaim, which is accepted within the relevant period ("RP"), does that mean that the defendant is automatically

---

[144] *Solomon v Cromwell Group Plc* [2011] EWCA Civ 1584; [2012] 1 W.L.R. 1048; [2012]. C.P. Rep. 14.

"entitled to the costs of the proceedings" (that is, the costs relating to both the original claim and the counterclaim) under CPR r.36.13(1)? (CPR r.36.13(7)).

There have been numerous questions covering more or less the same ground. **5–55** This question is directed at a situation where the offer is made by a defendant. All that changed when Part 36 was reformed was that the rules made explicit what was already implicit: a defendant can make an offer on their counterclaim because it is treated as being a claim under CPR Part 20. The answer to the question is that the defendant recovers the costs of their counterclaim, no more and no less.

To try to help with the evident confusion among practitioners, the CPRC drafted some guidance notes to Form N242A.

Note 5 reads as follows:

> "*In summary, Part 36 provides that: 'A party making a claimant's offer is offering to accept something to settle their own claim, counterclaim, additional claim, appeal, cross-appeal or costs assessment proceedings on terms that their opponent pays their costs.'*
>
> *A party making a defendant's offer is offering something to settle their opponent's claim, counterclaim, additional claim, appeal, cross-appeal or costs assessment proceedings and to accept a liability to pay costs.*"

Coulson J in the TCC dealt with this situation.[145] A defendant contractor was sued by a sub-contractor for £10 million damages and interest on the basis of disruption and prolongation. The defendant counterclaimed in relation to interim payments made in relation to the claims. The judgment resulted in the claimant having to repay the defendant almost £2.8 million.

The defendant had made and beaten a Part 36 offer and the question arose whether this was a claimant's Part 36 offer attracting the enhancements in CPR r.36.17(4).

The court held that the offer was a defendant's Part 36 offer. Although the Court of Appeal in *AF v BG* (**see Q4 above**) had held that the offer was a claimant's offer, that case could be distinguished. The defendant's offer did not say expressly that it was a claimants' offer; it did not offer to accept an amount of money in settlement of claim and counterclaim (instead, it offered to pay an amount to the claimants); it offered to pay the claimants' costs; further, it did not spell out the enhanced consequences of non-acceptance. Instead, the offer had all the hallmarks of a defendant's Part 36 offer. It offered to pay a sum in settlement of the litigation (taking into account the counterclaim). The defendant stated that the claimants could retain the sums already paid. The defendant offered to pay the claimants' costs up to the date of acceptance, for a maximum period of 21 days after the date of the offer. And when the offer letter stated that "for the avoidance of any doubt" the defendant would seek an order that the claimants pay its costs from the date of the

---

[145] *Van Oord UK Ltd v Allseas UK Ltd* [2015] EWHC 3385 (TCC), [2016] 1 Costs L.O. 1, Coulson J.

expiry of the offer if the claimants failed to do better than the offer at trial that was classically in accordance with a defendant's Part 36 offer. No separate, stand-alone counterclaim had been asserted by the defendant at the time of the offer, and no sum was set out in the offer as representing the liquidated amount of any such counterclaim. The court made an award of costs on the indemnity basis since the claim should not have been pursued.

The CPR do not give a great deal of guidance in relation to Part 36 offers where there is a counterclaim. Nothing in s.1 of Part 36 prevents a party making an offer to settle in whatever way that party chooses, but if the offer is not made in accordance with CPR r.36.5, it will not have the consequences specified in the Section. A Part 36 offer may be made in respect of the whole, or part of, or any issue that arises in – (a) a claim, counterclaim or other additional claim (CPR r.36.2(2)(3)). A Part 36 offer must (a) be in writing; (b) make clear that it is made pursuant to Part 36; (c) specify a period not less than 21 days within which the defendant will be liable for the claimant's costs in accordance with CPR r.36.13 (costs consequences of acceptance of a Part 36 offer) or CPR r.36.20 (costs consequences of acceptance of a Part 36 offer where Section IIIA of Part 45 applies); (d) state whether it relates to the whole of the claim or to part of it or to an issue that arises in it and if so to which part or issue; and (e) state whether it takes into account any counterclaim (CPR r.36.5(1)). Subject to certain exceptions (**explained in paragraph 5–15 above**), where a Part 36 offer is accepted within the relevant period, the claimant will be entitled to the costs of the proceedings (including their recoverable pre-action costs) up to the date on which notice of acceptance was served on the offeror (CPR r.36.13(1)). The claimant's costs include any costs incurred in dealing with the defendant's counterclaim if the Part 36 offer states that it takes it into account (CPR r.36.13(7)).

The topic of offers in claim and counterclaim has also been examined by the Court of Appeal. A landlord sued a tenant for rent arrears and the parties agreed that approximately £6,000 in arrears were due. The landlord also claimed for physical damage to the property and consequential loss of rent both of which claims were disputed. The tenant counterclaimed for breach of the covenant of quiet enjoyment and for the landlord's failure to address the property's state of disrepair which far outweighed any sum claimed by the landlord. The landlord made what purported to be a Part 36 offer offering to withdraw the claim for the rent arrears if the tenant also discontinued the disrepair claim with each party paying its own costs. The offer specified a relevant period under CPR r.36.5(1)(c) of 21 days, but did not state that the tenant would be liable for the landlord's costs if the offer was accepted.

At trial the landlord was awarded the rent arrears and interest amounting to £16,000. The tenant was awarded damages for discomfort and inconvenience in the sum of about £7,000. The tenant was ordered to pay the costs of the landlord's claim on the standard basis until the date of the offer and on the indemnity basis with 8% interest after expiry of the relevant period. On appeal to the Court of Appeal, the court held that Part 36 had been carefully drafted and meant what it said. It is open to a party to make an offer in whatever way the party chose but an offer not made in accordance with CPR r.36.2 would not have Part 36 consequences. The court held that the landlord's offer had not complied with CPR r.36.2(2)(c) which was a mandatory requirement that the offer specified a period within which the defendant would be liable for the claimant's costs. The offer had only specified the relevant period. Notwithstanding the fact that it was the tenant's counterclaim which determined the issue, the landlord and the tenant had been claimant and defendant respectively for the purposes of the rule. Accordingly, Part 36 did not apply, the correct approach was under CPR r.44.2 under which the unsuccessful party would generally pay the successful party's costs. The court did not encourage issue-based costs orders and an appellate court would normally be slow to intervene with costs orders made by judges who were best placed to have a feel for the case. In the instant case, the judge at first instance had taken a mistaken starting point. Where much time had been taken by a party unsuccessfully taking numerous points, the court could give less weight to the fact that on balance that party had been ultimately successful. The case had not only been about the amount of equitable set-off versus the rent arrears. The landlord had sued for substantial damages and had failed on many issues. The judge had insufficiently considered the parties' conduct and partial successes. The tenant had substantiated his allegation as to the state of the property and had been entitled to vindicate his claim even if the damages awarded were small. The landlord's offer had been very realistic and the tenant should have considered it more. The tenant had however received no response to his many requests for mediation. No dispute was too intractable for mediation and silence towards an invitation to engage an alternative dispute resolution was in itself unreasonable.[146] The tenant had won more issues than the landlord even if the latter had succeeded financially. A fair and balanced approach was to make no order as to costs. The fact that the landlord had incurred costs of £85,000 and the tenant of £100,000 made a stronger case as was possible that there should be some form of limitation on the costs recoverable in such cases.[147]

Q19. Are costs recoverable if a claimant's Part 36 offer is accepted in circumstances where the claimant's costs budget has not been filed on time? (CPR r.36.13).

This question was originally raised after the decision in *Mitchell* but before the Court of Appeal decision in *Denton*. Given the more measured approach of the court in *Denton*, it would seem that if the Part 36 offer has been accepted within the relevant period, the claimant will be entitled to the costs of the proceedings up to the date on which notice of acceptance was served on the offeror (CPR r.36.13(1)). If the acceptance of the offer is after the expiry of the relevant period and the parties are unable to agree the liability for costs, liability for

5–56

---

[146] See *PGF II SA v OMFS Co. 1 Ltd* [2013] EWCA Civ.1288; [2014] 1 WLR 1386.
[147] *N J Rickard Ltd v Holloway* [2015] EWCA Civ 3 November, unreported.

costs must be determined by the court (CPR r.36.13(4)). The outcome may, however, depend on how late the budget was – if, indeed, it has been filed – and all the circumstances because the canny defendant might argue that the offer was only made because it knew it had only a very limited costs liability after the date the budget fell due and CPR r.3.14 applied. On the other hand the consequences of the court requiring the claimant to apply for relief from sanction and then refusing such relief would merely be to generate further satellite litigation, an outcome which the court in *Denton* was at pains to avoid. CPR r.36.23 somewhat ameliorates the draconian effect of CPR r.3.14. The purpose of CPR r.36.23 is to put the receiving party at some risk if an offer is accepted late (CPR r.36.13(5)(b)) or the offer prevails at trial (CPR rules 36.17(3) (a) and 36.17(4)(b)) while not allowing the paying party to escape entirely the consequences of the default. (For further discussion see **Chapter 4 Q67.**)

H. Other effects of acceptance of a Part 36 offer (CPR r.36.14).

Q20. In a claim by a claimant (C) against two separate defendants (D1 and D2), where separate allegations are advanced against each defendant, if C makes a Part 36 offer to settle the whole of his claim which is addressed to both D1 and D2 as "the offeree", and only D1 accepts the offer, is the claim against D2 stayed, even though D2 did not accept the offer? (CPR r.36.14).

5–57   The answer will depend on the exact wording of the offer. CPR r.36.14 is clear:

> "*(1)   If a Part 36 Offer is accepted the claim will be stayed.*
> (2)   *In the case of acceptance of a Part 36 Offer which relates to the whole claim the stay will be upon the terms of the offer.*"

Since the offer to settle in this question was an offer in respect of the whole claim, which has been accepted, it must follow that the whole claim is stayed. Had the offer been differently worded, CPR r.36.14(3) would apply "*if a Part 36 Offer which relates to part only of the claim is accepted the claim will be stayed as to that part upon the terms of the offer.*"

CPR r.36.15 deals with acceptance of a Part 36 offer made by one but not all defendants. The rule does not cover the circumstances described in this question.

Q21. Where a defendant has failed to comply with a Part 36 offer that has been accepted, is it possible for the claimant to disclose the Part 36 offer to the court when seeking judgment on the Part 36? (CPR r.36.14).

5–58   If the defendant has made a Part 36 offer which is accepted, there would be no difficulty in producing this to the court, should the need arise. If the defendant's default is in respect of costs, the notice of acceptance is a deemed order under CPR r.44.9 and a costs order will be deemed to have been made on the standard basis.

The court has no discretion under CPR Part 3 to extend the 14 day time limit for payment of a Part 36 sum under CPR r.36.14(6). The claimant had accepted the defendants' Part 36 offer some months after the expiry of the relevant period but the defendants did not pay the sum in accordance with CPR r.36.14(6). When the claimant sought an order for payment, the defendants applied to extend the time for payment pending determination of the party's costs claims. The court found that the time limit could only be disapplied by the parties' written agreement. Furthermore the court had no power under Part 3 to order payment of the sum into court as security for the defendants' costs. The court ordered the defendants to pay the sum and the claimant to make a payment on account of the defendants' costs (from the expiry of the relevant period until the date of acceptance).[148]

Q22. May a defendant who is a protected party acting by her litigation friend make a joint Part 36 offer with three other defendants? Is it possible to avoid the obligation under CPR r.36.14(6) to pay out within 14 days? (CPR r.36.14(6)).

A defendant who is a protected party may, provided the litigation friend has   5.59
been properly advised, make a joint offer with other defendants. Whether this is a wise thing to do depends upon the circumstances of the case and the interrelationship of the defendants, since if the offer is accepted and the other defendants default on payment, the protected party could find herself liable for the whole of the offer and the costs. Any acceptance of the protected party's Part 36 offer would require court approval under CPR r.21.10.

The court has no discretion to extend the 14 day time limit for payment of a Part 36 sum under CPR r.36.14(6). The time limit can only be disapplied by the party's written agreement. See *Titmus v General Motors UK Limited*.[149]

I. Part 36 offers in multi party disputes (CPR r.36.15).

Q23. Can a Part 20 defendant make a Part 36 offer? We have a case where the claimant is suing the first defendant (D1), the claimant is also suing the second defendant (D2), and D1 is suing D2, who they brought in as a Part 20 defendant. D2 wishes to make a Part 36 offer, but is it possible for one Part 36 offer to encompass both claims?

How can you best use Part 36 in multi-party disputes? We act for Party A in an action against Party B. Party B has issued Part 20 proceedings against Party C. Our client wishes to resolve the claim by making a Part 36 offer to settle the entire action, including the Part 20 proceedings, on terms that my client will accept a small sum in settlement from Party B, and that Party B will discontinue against the Part 20 defendant (who is a LiP, and therefore has no costs consequences). There is a connection between Party A and Party B. (CPR r.36.2(1), CPR r.36.5, 36.15).

It is open to anyone who is a party to make an offer; and there is no restriction   5–60

---

[148] *Titmus v General Motors UK Limited* [2016] EWHC 2021 (QB), Laing J.
[149] [2016] EWHC 2021 (QB) Laing J.

on the terms of the offer provided it complies with CPR r.36.5 (see below). In the first question both C and D1 are suing D2, so there seems no reason why one offer should not encompass both claims.

In the second question there is apparently no lis between claimant and Party C. The offer that claimant wishes to make appears to be *"If you B will pay me a modest amount and discontinue against C, the matter can end there."* Party C will obviously not object if proceedings are discontinued against him. The offer would therefore be between claimant and B, (it would be sensible to inform C of the offer being made to B).

CPR r.36 2(1) states: *"Nothing in this Section prevents a party making an offer to settle in whatever way that party chooses, but if the offer is not made in accordance with rule 36.5, it will not have the consequences specified in this Section."* CPR r.36.5 sets out the form and content of a Part 36 offer necessary to comply with the rule. If the offer does not comply with CPR r.36.5, CPR r.44.2 requires the court to consider an offer to settle that does not have the costs consequences set out in Part 36 in deciding what order to make about costs.

J. Calculating whether judgment more advantageous than Part 36 offer (CPR r.36.17).

Q24. Can an admissions payment improve the value of Part 36 offer? (CPR r.36.17).

5–61   In proceedings where the defendant made a Part 36 offer totalling £35,000 and subsequently made an admission of part of the claim amounting to £17,504 at trial, the defendant argued that the total value of the Part 36 offer was in fact £52,504 (£35,000 plus £17,504). That argument was rejected at first instance. On appeal the Court of Appeal held that the true analysis of the relationship between the Part 36 offer and the admission payment was first, the Part 36 offer was an offer to settle the entirety of the landlord's claim for £35,000, no more and no less. There was nothing in the correspondence concerning the admission payment referring to the Part 36 offer. Second, the admission payment was plainly made on the basis that it was a payment on account following admission against the landlord's entire claim. Third, the admission payment was liable to be taken into account as a part payment in advance of the £35,000 that would have been due and payable to the claimant if the Part 36 offer had been accepted. Accordingly, the defendant had obtained a judgment more advantageous than the value of the Part 36 offer.[150]

Q25. When considering whether a claimant has failed to obtain a judgment more advantageous than a defendant's Part 36 offer how do you deal with any interest element that the judge awards the claimant at trial? Assuming that the defendant's offer was inclusive of interest until the expiry of the relevant period do you compare that figure with the

---

[150] *Littlestone v MacLeish* [2016] EWCA Civ. 127.

principal sum that the judge awards at trial plus any interest awarded too up to the date of judgment? Or can you argue that for the purposes of working out whether the judgment is more advantageous you should only take into account the principal sum awarded and interest up to the date of expiry of the Part 36 offer? (CPR r.36.17).

CPR r.36.5(4) provides that a Part 36 offer which offers to pay or offers to accept a sum of money will be treated as inclusive of all interest until the date on which the relevant period expires; or, if the offer is made less than 21 days before the start of the trial, a date 21 days after the date the offer was made. When the judge gives judgment, any interest awarded in the judgment is part of that judgment. There appears to be no basis upon which, when considering whether or not the judgment is more advantageous, one should only take into account the principal sum awarded and ignore the interest element.   5–62

K. Part 36 and costs consequences (CPR rules 36.17, 36.20, 36.21).

Q26. Where a defendant has made a Part 36 offer for settlement of the claimant's costs, and the claimant has rejected that offer but fails to beat/ meet it at trial: a) is there a cap on how much the claimant has to pay to the defendant? b) is the cost consequence awarded as a percentage of the settlement offer or as a percentage of the value of the claim?

The matter is covered by CPR r.36.17(3) and CPR r.47.20, to which reference should be made. There is no cap, as such, on the amount that the claimant has to pay the defendant. The amount is determined by the tests of reasonableness and proportionality. The costs consequences bear no relation to a percentage of the offer or a percentage of the claim. Recent authorities make It clear that there is no "near miss" principle in Part 36. CPR r.36.17(2) provides: *"For the purposes of [r.36.17(1)], in relation to any money claim or money element of a claim, "more advantageous" means better in money terms by any amount, however small, and "at least as advantageous" shall be construed accordingly."*   5–63

Q27. In a case where the claimant makes a Part 36 offer less than 21 days before trial, would the claimant still recover the additional 10% damages if he/she obtains a judgment at least as advantageous as the offer? (CPR r.36.17).

Under CPR r.36.17(1)(b), where judgment against the defendant is at least as advantageous to the claimant as the proposals contained in a claimant's Part 36 offer, the court must (subject to what appears below) unless it considers it unjust to do so, order that the claimant is entitled to various items and interest on costs including the additional amount. CPR r.37.16(7)(c) however, provides that that provision does not apply to a Part 36 offer made less than 21 days before trial, unless the court has abridged the relevant period. There is no indication in this case that the relevant period has been abridged and accordingly the additional amount is not payable.   5–64

There does not appear to be any authority as to the circumstances in which the court would abridge the relevant period, although in *PGF II SA, PGF II (Lime) SA v Royal and Sun Alliance Insurance Plc, London and Edinburgh Insurance Company Limited* [151]the court, in refusing to abridge the relevant period since the offer related only to a very small part of the overall costs of the litigation, stated *"The position might have been different if there had been a Part 36 offer which would resolve the whole dispute between the claimant and the defendants"*.

Q28. Can you explain how an award of costs on the standard basis (e.g. under CPR r.36.17(3)(a)) differs from an award of costs on the indemnity basis (e.g. under CPR r.36.17(4)(b)) in circumstances where a costs budget is in place? The definition of 'standard basis' and 'indemnity basis' appear to be hard to reconcile with the concept of costs budgets, because there should be no doubts about reasonableness to resolve in anyone's favour if the costs are within the court-approved costs budget. (CPR r.36.17(4).

5–65 See **Chapter 4 Qs. 78 and 79** on this topic.

Q29. Is it appropriate to award a lower additional amount under CPR r.36.17(4)(d) than the prescribed amount because the proceedings were determined early, for example, as a result of summary judgment being given, rather than going to full trial?

5–66 Defendants will not always be penalised. Where a claimant's Part 36 offer which had been refused, but not bettered at trial, expired days before the trial commenced and the defendants had not received its witness statements until the final day of the expiry of the offer, the High Court ruled that making a defendant who rejected a Part 36 offer pay an additional 10% of the sum awarded for costs, pursuant to CPR r.36.17(4)(d), would introduce a 'penal' element and be unjust. The ruling was made after an injunction had been granted to the claimant restraining the defendant from joining another company before the end of his 12 month notice period.[152]

Q30. How do the Court of Appeal decision in *AJ Insurance v Sugar Hut, Hammersmatch Properties (Welwyn) Ltd v Saint Gobain Ceramics and Plastics Ltd and another*, tie together with the Court of Appeal decision in *Coward v Phaestos*? It's not clear to me why a party who makes a Part 36 offer should be deprived of the benefits of CPR r.44.2, as interpreted by the Court of Appeal in *Coward v Phaestos*.

5–67 The answer is that Part 36 is a self-contained code. There is no overlap with Part 44. Part 36 is to be read as a self-contained code and not to be confused with contractual notions or general costs discretion under Part 44 or non-Part 36 offers such as Calderbank type offers.[153] See also **Q40** below.

---

[151] [2010] EWHC 1981 (TCC).

[152] *Elsevier Ltd v Munro* [2014] EWHC 2728 (QB), [2014] 5 Costs L.O. 797 Warby J. See also *Feltham v Bouskell* [2013] EWHC 3086 (Ch) Charles Hollander QC; and see: *Bataillon and another v Shone* [2015] EWHC 3177 (QB) HHJ Waksman QC. **Paragraph 5–54** above.

[153] *RXDX v Northampton Borough Council* [2015] EWHC 2938 (QB); [2015] 5 Costs L.R. 897, Sir Colin Mackay.

Q31. Do you agree that it may be difficult to decide who has obtained the more advantageous result in a detailed assessment? Also, does CPR r.36.17(4)) about enhancing claimants' recovery by 10% apply in detailed assessments? (CPR r.36.17).

Where a Part 36 offer has been made in detailed assessment proceedings, it will be for a specified amount. When the bill is totalled at the end of the detailed assessment there should be no difficulty in ascertaining whether or not the offer has been beaten. The power of the court under CPR r.36.17(4) to award interest not exceeding 10% above base rate on the sum awarded; to award indemnity costs; to award interest on those costs at a rate not exceeding 10% above base rate; and, an additional amount in accordance with CPR r.36.17(4)(d) is certainly exercisable. In detailed assessment proceedings, the receiving party made a Part 36 offer to settle for £152,500. At the detailed assessment the bill was allowed at £173,693 which was more advantageous to the receiving party than the Part 36 offer. The Costs Judge declined to award the 10% additional amount stating that in circumstances where there had been a significant reduction in the claimant's bill, it would be unjust to reward the claimant with the additional amount prescribed by CPR r.36.17(4). On appeal, the court found that the Costs Judge was in error in relying on the degree of reduction on assessment. That approach penalised the appellant for making a reasonable Part 36 offer. It was the terms of the Part 36 offer not the level of the sums claimed in the bill of costs which were to be considered. Accordingly, the appellant was entitled to the additional award.[154]

5–68

L. Part 36 and IPEC, Part 45, Section IV

Q32. How does the cap on damages in the IPEC apply where there is also a claim for costs? (CPR r.36.17(4)).

In the Intellectual Property Enterprise Court (IPEC) the cap on the maximum value permitted for a claim for damages on an account of profits is £500,000. A claimant in IPEC proceedings obtained judgment for an amount well in excess of its rejected Part 36 offer. The question was whether the 'additional amount' payable by the defendant under CPR r.36.17(4) should be treated as further damages (subject to the £500,000 cap) or whether it was a separate payment unaffected by the cap. The court held that it appeared to be clear from the note to CPR r.36.14 in the *White Book* and the authorities there mentioned that the 'additional amount' had nothing to do with compensating a claimant for any wrong committed by the defendant in the substantive dispute. It was solely intended to serve as an incentive to encourage claimants to make and defendants to accept appropriate Part 36 offers.[155]

5–69

---

[154] *Cashman v Mid-Essex Hospital Services NHS Trust* [2015] EWHC 1312 (QB) 2015 3 Costs LO 411, Slade J.
[155] *OOO Abbott v Design and Display Ltd* [2014] EWHC 3234 (IPEC) HHJ Hacon; upheld on appeal [2016] EWCA Civ 95.

M. Genuine attempt to settle (CPR r.36.17(5)).

Q33. We represent a client in a case where we feel that the client is bound to succeed. We are considering making a claimant Part 36 offer to settle at 100% liability plus costs. This would save the defendant the time and cost of preparing for trial and the trial itself. Will this succeed? What is a genuine effort to settle under Part 36? (CPR r.36.17).

5–70 CPR r.36.17(5)(e) was added to deal with the problem of claimants making very high settlement offers (often as much as 95% of the value of the claim) not in a genuine attempt to settle the claim but to place the defendant at risk of indemnity costs pursuant to CPR r.36.17(4). "A genuine attempt to settle proceedings" is not defined further in the rules. The question will always be fact sensitive and will arise only when the court is considering whether or not it would be unjust to make the normal order.

In the light of the decision below caution is advisable with what you propose.

Prior to a trial, one of the issues in which was the claimant's age (i.e. whether the claimant was a child), the claimant made what purported to be a Part 36 offer stating that the defendant should accept the claimant's age and agree to pay the claimant's costs. The claimant was successful at trial and the issue arose as to whether the indemnity costs and interest on costs consequences set out in CPR r.36.17(4) should apply in view of the terms of the offer made. The defendant argued that the offer made by the claimant was not a genuine offer to settle as understood by CPR r.36.17(5)(e) and that it would be unjust to make the order sought. The defendant's counsel relied on *AB v CD*[156] and also *East West Corporation v DKBS*[157] arguing that there was no give and take involved in the offer made. It was a total capitulation offer. It did not assist the claimant to contend that the Part 36 offer was genuine because had the defendant accepted it, it would have gained by saving the costs of the hearing. There was no obvious answer to the matter in issue in the present case and the court's jurisdiction in disputed age cases was inquisitorial not adversarial.[158] The court held that the claimant's offer was not a give and take offer, as the claimant was offering to take "nothing short of what he was claiming in the proceedings". It was not a settlement offer in any real sense but a "tactical ploy". It did not constitute a concession on the claimant's part but, had the defendant accepted the offer, the defendant would have saved costs. Accordingly, the claimant failed to obtain an order for enhanced interest, indemnity costs, enhanced interest on those costs and an additional amount under CPR r.36.17(4). Instead the defendant was ordered to pay costs on the standard basis.[159]

---

[156] [2011] EWHC 602 (Ch.), Henderson J at 22.
[157] [2002] All ER (D) 361, Thomas J.
[158] See *R (CJ) v Cardiff* [2011] EWCA Civ.1590.
[159] *R (MVN) v London Borough of Greenwich* [2015] EWHC 2663 Admin, Picken J.

N. Part 36 and set off (CPR r.36.22).

Q34. Where a claimant accepts a defendant's Part 36 offer after the expiry of the relevant period, can the defendant's costs for the period after the end of the RP to the date of acceptance be offset against the amount of the Part 36 offer? (CPR r.36.22).

Where a Part 36 offer which relates to the whole of the claim is accepted after expiry of the relevant period, the liability for costs must be determined by the court unless the parties have agreed the costs (CPR r.36.13(4)). The court's powers as to set off as to costs are at CPR r.44.12.

Where a party entitled to costs is also liable to pay costs, the court may assess the costs which that party is liable to pay and either set off the amount assessed against the amount the party is entitled to be paid and direct that party to pay any balance; or delay the issue of a certificate for the costs to which the party is entitled until the party has paid the amount which that party is liable to pay. And see *Lockley v National Blood Transfusion Service*[160]. Where, by operation of CPR r.36.14(6)(a), a claimant is entitled to be paid the offered sum within 14 days, he is entitled to such payment without set off against an unquantified costs liability (*Cave v Bulley Davey*[161]).

5–71

O. Relief from sanctions where Part 36 offer may be affected (CPR r.3.9).

Q35. My firm needs to serve an expert's report out of time. The defendants are objecting to relief from sanctions. How does this affect potential Part 36 offers? (CPR r.3.9).

It depends on the particular facts of your case but this decision may help. The claimant applied to serve its expert report late, accepting that it was out of time and that the default was serious and without good reason. The issue for the court was whether it was appropriate to grant the claimant relief from sanctions. The defendant submitted that there would be prejudice if relief were granted as the date for making a Part 36 offer giving rise to costs consequences had passed. The defendant had already seen the expert report in draft and it was reasonable to suppose that it would be similar to the final version of the report. Therefore if the defendant was influenced by the report to make a Part 36 offer, it would most probably have done so before service of the final report. The court found that there was minimal prejudice to the defendants and granted relief from sanctions on very strict terms including that the claimant could not recover from the defendant any of its costs relating to the expert's report.[162]

5–72

---

[160] [1992] 1 W.L.R. 492, CA.
[161] [2013] EWHC 4246 (QB), 15 July 2013, unreported. (HHJ Seymour QC).
[162] *Art and Antiques Limited v Magwell Solicitors* [2015] EWHC 2143 (Ch) Klein J.

P. Part 36 and detailed assessments (CPR rules 44.2 and 47.20).

Q36. If we make a successful Part 36 offer will we recover all our costs? (CPR r.44.2). Please explain the decision in *Webb v Liverpool Womens' NHS Foundation Trust* [2015] EWHC 449 (QB).

5–73   The existence of a Part 36 offer does not, in principle, insulate the offeror from a proportionate costs order. The fact that there has been a Part 36 offer does not mean that the court is unable to make an issue based or proportionate costs order. Part 36 is a self-contained regime and the rule itself makes no reference to such orders. Nevertheless, insofar as such an order is necessary to avoid injustice, it is permissible for the court to make it.

In *Webb*, the claimant, who had suffered injuries at birth, sued the NHS Trust for failing to perform a caesarean section and secondly for managing the delivery inappropriately. The trial judge upheld the first allegation but rejected the second. The claimant was awarded damages on a full recovery basis. She had earlier made a Part 36 offer to settle for 65% of the damages claimed. The judgment was more advantageous to her than the offer. She accordingly sought all her costs on the indemnity basis. At first instance, the judge had made an issue based costs order and reduced the costs accordingly. On appeal to the Court of Appeal, the court held that the judge could not properly have deprived the claimant of her costs relating to the second allegation incurred before the effective date. The two allegations had been part of one event i.e. the claimant's birth. It was not unreasonable for her to pursue the second allegation. It was not unusual for a claimant to succeed on some but not all allegations in personal injury cases. There was no reason to deprive the claimant of any part of her costs. In deciding what order for costs to make the only discretion was that conferred under Part 36. The discretion under CPR r.36.17 (formerly CPR r.36.14) related both to the assessment of costs and to the determination of what costs were to be assessed. It was not unjust for the claimant to be awarded all her costs. The judge below had not taken into account the fact that the trust could have avoided all the trial costs[163].

Q37. When the question of costs is being decided is it possible for a party to refer to without prejudice correspondence in order to establish that the other party did not respond to Part 36 offers? (CPR r.44.2).

5–74   A defendant who had been found liable for misusing the claimants' confidential information made two Part 36 offers during the course of an inquiry as to damages. The claimants did not respond to either offer and made no counter-offer. When the court was dealing with the costs of the inquiry the defendant criticised the claimants' conduct and served a witness statement which referred to an exchange of without prejudice correspondence between solicitors attempting to settle the question of costs. The claimants

---

[163] *Webb v Liverpool Women's NHS Foundation Trust* [2016] EWCA Civ 365; [2016] 1 W.L.R. 3899; [2016] 2 Costs L.R. 411.

sought an order to strike out those passages which referred to the without prejudice correspondence.

The court stated that there was a strong public policy justification for denying the ability to rely on without prejudice correspondence at any stage in the proceedings including costs assessment. Where a without prejudice offer was made the recipient was free to make a without prejudice response. The response might be to make a counter-offer, ask for more information, reject the offer or simply ignore it. All these responses were protected by privilege. The fact that the claimants were seeking costs on the indemnity basis did not amount to a waiver of privilege but was based on criticism of the defendant's conduct.[164]

Q38. Where a Part 36 offer is accepted in a small claim that has not yet been allocated to the small claims track, is it the case that the fixed costs regime will generally apply?
Is the claimant entitled to its costs if it accepts a pre-action Part 36 offer where the case would be allocated to the small claims track if it went to court? (CPR r.46.13).
CPR r.46.13(3) is a new provision following the Jackson Reforms and the decision of the Court of Appeal in *O'Beirne v Hudson*[165]. The Rule provides that where the court is assessing costs, on the standard basis, of a claim which concluded without being allocated to a track, it may restrict those costs to the costs that would have been allowed on the track to which the claim would have been allocated if allocation had taken place. The position is further explained in para.8.2 of Practice Direction 46. The Court of Appeal has since decided that in relation to CPR r.46.13(2) (Allocation and Re-Allocation), the court has power to backdate the reallocation for costs purposes if the court is satisfied that there were good reasons for doing so.[166]

5–75

Where a mother and two children were passengers in a car and claimed damages, following an accident, and instructed the same solicitor, a District Judge decided that it was appropriate for all three claims to be issued on the fast track (the claims of the children were small claims). Liability had been denied and the claims had left the portal. Costs were provisionally assessed rather than being fixed costs.[167]

Q. Part 36 offers made after issue but before service

Q39. We have a matter which settled following acceptance of a Part 36 offer after the issue of proceedings but prior to service. Proceedings were never served, and the time for service has now expired. We take the view that we can commence detailed assessment proceedings without Part 8

---

[164] *Vestergaard Frandsen v Bestnet Europe Ltd* [2014] EWHC 4047 (Ch) Iain Purvis QC.
[165] [2010] EWCA Civ. 52; [2010] 1 WLR 1717; [2010] CP Rep. 23.
[166] *Conlon v Royal Sun Alliance Insurance Plc* [2015] EWCA Civ. 92.
[167] *Dilip v Paynes Dairies Ltd. Case No: A53YJ800 Leicester County Court.*

proceedings, despite the fact that proceedings were never served. We refer to CPR r.46.14(1)(c) which says that Part 8 proceedings are required if no proceedings have been "started". Do you agree, or do you believe that we would need to issue Part 8 proceedings for an Order for costs before commencing assessment? (CPR r.46.14).

5–76 Rule 7.2 states: "(1) Proceedings are started when the court issues a claim form at the request of the claimant." In your case proceedings have started and so you may proceed to assessment without having to commence Part 8 proceedings.

Q40. What is the requirement for open offers in detailed assessment proceedings meant to achieve and how they will co-exist with Part 36 offers? (PD47 para 8.3).

5–77 Practice Direction 47 para.8.3 sets the matter out clearly:

> *"The paying party must state in an open letter accompanying the points of dispute what sum, if any, that party offers to pay in settlement of the total costs claimed. The paying party may also make an offer under Part 36."*

Lord Justice Jackson's objective in inserting this requirement was to ensure that the parties were not in fact arguing over an insignificant amount of money. It is clearly open to the paying party to make an open offer of 0%. This would presumably only be done if there were an arguable point of principle which might well result in the receiving party recovering nothing. There is no requirement that the open offer and any Part 36 offer should be in the same terms.

If a paying party fails to make an open offer as required by the Practice Direction, it would clearly be within the power of the costs judge to strike out the points of dispute or if that were felt to be too draconian, to rely only on the written points of dispute and not permit any further oral argument.

The Court of Appeal expressly considered provisions of the CPR which contain mandatory language, but where no sanction is provided for any failure to comply in *Altomart v Salford Estates (No.2) Ltd*.[168] The court accepted the proposition that there might be implied sanctions which were capable of engaging CPR r.3.9 and equally there might be cases not analogous with CPR r.3.9 and where it was a matter for the court to determine the consequence of non-compliance. It is clear that the open offer does not form part of the Points of Dispute (it merely accompanies that document) and therefore it is difficult to see how any argument suggesting that the Points of Dispute should be struck out would find favour (indeed there is a risk it would be seen as an attempt to turn the rules into 'tripwires' and invoke possible costs sanctions). Perhaps a more measured approach would be to identify the failure to comply to the paying party promptly, suggesting a short period for rectification, and, in default of compliance reserve the position to the question of costs of the assessment, if relevant, under 'conduct' within CPR r.47.20(3)(a).

---

[168] *Altomart v Salford Estates (No.2) Ltd* [2014] EWCA Civ 1408.

Section 2 Settlement other than under Part 36

R. Calderbank offers

Q41. How are Calderbank offers treated in relation to costs? (Rule 44.2(4)).
Our opponent, the claimant, has sent us a letter headed *"Without prejudice   5–78 save as to costs"*, offering on that basis to accept 98% of the amount claimed. (I'm not sure whether he's also demanding costs..) There has been controversy in recent years about whether a Part 36 offer in such terms would be a valid one because it's debatable whether it's a true offer: but what do you think the position would be in the law and practice of Calderbank offers?

With regard to Calderbank offers, the situation is obviously going to be fact sensitive. Bear in mind that under CPR r.44.2(4)(c) the court is required to take into account any admissible offer to settle made by a party which is drawn to the court's attention, and which is not an offer to which costs consequences under Part 36 apply.

The Court of Appeal has made it clear that the effect of a Calderbank offer is not to be assessed by analogy with the terms of CPR r.36.17(2) which defines a 'more advantageous' judgment as one that is 'better in money terms by any amount, however small' than the relevant offer. Parts 36 and 44 of the CPR are separate regimes with separate purposes. Part 36 is a self-contained procedural code which specifies particular consequences in the event that such offers are not accepted. Those consequences include features which go far beyond that which might be ordered by way of costs under Part 44. Whilst Part 36 is highly prescriptive and highly restrictive of the exercise of any discretion by the court, Part 44 confers on the court a discretion in almost the widest possible terms. It contains no rules as to the way in which the court has to have regard to offers and there is no equivalent to the *'more advantageous'* test in Part 36.[169]

S. ADR and Mediation

Q42. Does anyone/any kind of company (for example) have to use ADR because the law says so? If so we would be grateful if you would direct us to that law or illuminate what kind of people MUST use ADR.
In short: Yes. The Alternative Dispute Resolution for Consumer Disputes   5–79 (Competent Authorities and Information) Regulations 2015 (2015 No. 542) which came into force for the purposes of Parts 1 to 3 on 7 April 2015 and for the purposes of Parts 4 & 5 on 9 July 2015, as amended by The Alternative Dispute Resolution for Consumer Disputes (Amendment) Regulations 2015 (2015 No 1392) together implement the provisions of Directive 2013/11/EU of the European Parliament and of the Council of 21 May 2013 on alternative dispute resolution for consumer disputes. Regulation 2(3) of the amending

---

[169] *Coward v Phaestos Ltd* [2014] EWCA Civ 1256.

regulations substitutes a new coming into force date for Parts 4 and 5, the effect of which is to postpone the commencement of the trader information requirements until 1 October 2015.

"Consumer" and "trader"

"Consumer" means an individual acting for purposes which are wholly or mainly outside that individual's trade, business, craft or profession.

"Trader" means a person acting for purposes relating to that person's trade, business, craft or profession, whether acting personally or through another person acting in the trader's name or on the trader's behalf.[170]

This includes those providing legal services.

Schedule 1 lists the Competent Authorities: the Financial Conduct Authority; the Financial Ombudsman Service; the Legal Services Board; and the Office for Legal Complaints. Others may be added from time to time.

Consumer information by traders

The Regulations provide:

"19.—(1) Where, under an enactment, rules of a trade association, or term of a contract, a trader is obliged to use an alternative dispute resolution procedure provided by an ADR entity or EU listed body the trader must provide the name and website address of the ADR entity or EU listed body— (a) on the trader's website, if the trader has a website; and (b) in the general terms and conditions of sales contracts or service contracts of the trader, where such general terms and conditions exist. (2) Where a trader has exhausted its internal complaint handling procedure when considering a complaint from a consumer relating to a sales contract or a service contract, the trader must inform the consumer, on a durable medium— (a) that the trader cannot settle the complaint with the consumer; (b) of the name and website address of an ADR entity or EU listed body that would be competent to deal with the complaint; and (c) whether the trader is obliged, or prepared, to submit to an alternative dispute resolution procedure operated by an ADR entity or EU listed body. (3) The trader information requirements set out in paragraphs (1) and (2) apply in addition to any information requirements applicable to traders regarding out-of-court redress procedures contained in any other enactment.

Consumer information by online traders and online marketplaces regarding the ODR platform.

19A.—(1) Where under an enactment, rules of a trade association, or term of a contract, an online trader is obliged to use an alternative dispute resolution procedure provided by an ADR entity or EU listed body, the trader must— (a) provide a link to the ODR platform in any offer made to a consumer by email; and (b) inform consumers of— 5 (i) the existence of the ODR platform; and (ii) the possibility of using the ODR platform for resolving disputes. (2) The information in (1)(b) must also be included in the general terms and conditions of online sales

---

[170] Regulation 3, The Alternative Dispute Resolution for Consumer Disputes (Competent Authorities and Information) Regulations 2015 (2015 No. 542).

contracts and online service contracts of the trader, where such general terms and conditions exist. (3) An online trader must on its website— (i) provide a link to the ODR platform; and (ii) state the online trader's email address. (4) An online marketplace must provide a link to the ODR platform on its website. (5) The online trader requirements set out in paragraphs (1) to (3) apply in addition to the trader information requirements set out in regulation 19. (6) The online trader and online marketplace requirements in paragraphs (1) to (4) apply in addition to any information requirements regarding out-of-court redress procedures contained in any other enactment. (7) In this regulation— 'online marketplace' has the meaning given in Article 4(f) of the Regulation (EU) No 524/2013 of the European Parliament and of the Council of 21 May 2013 on online dispute resolution for consumer disputes and amending Regulation (EC) No 2006/2004 and Directive 2009/22/EC; 'online sales contract' means a sales contract where the trader, or the trader's intermediary, has offered goods on a website or by other electronic means and the consumer has ordered such goods on that website or by other electronic means; 'online service contract' means a service contract where the trader, or the trader's intermediary, has offered services on a website or by other electronic means and the consumer has ordered such services on that website or by other electronic means; 'online trader' means a trader who intends to enter into online sales contracts or online service contracts with consumers."

The Law Society in its advice dated 12 January 2016 advises:

"The Law Society has changed its advice for firms on compliance with UK regulations which transpose the EU Directive on consumer alternative dispute resolution (ADR Directive).
This is in response to the unexpected withdrawal of the Legal Ombudsman's (LeO) application to the Legal Services Board (LSB) to become certified as an ADR approved body for the purposes of the ADR Directive. Although the Legal Ombudsman has withdrawn its application, solicitors must still comply with the government regulations. New requirements will apply from 1 October 2015 in relation to the information solicitors are required to provide to clients at the end of a solicitor's internal complaints process.
In order to be as comprehensive as possible, this advice provides:
1. a description of the requirements
2. suggested text to be included in letters at the end of first-tier complaints, from 1 October 2015
3. information on further changes that are likely to be made
4. web links to further information
5. frequently asked questions (FAQs)"[171]

In short, from 1 October 2015, solicitors must: continue to provide information on the Legal Ombudsman as the statutory complaints scheme for solicitors, and provide information on an additional ADR entity certified

---

[171] The full advice can be found at: www.lawsociety.org.uk/support-services/advice/articles/changes-to-client-care-information-and-leo-time-limit/. See also: www.tradingstandards.uk/advice/AlternativeDisputeResolution.cfm.

under the EU Consumer ADR Directive[172.] Solicitors will be under no obligation to use such a scheme and information need only be provided at the end of the complaints process. Given the clear indications from the courts that unreasonably refusing ADR is likely to have costs consequences, it is in the interests of those providing legal services to have an appropriate procedure in place and to utilise it.

All this may change, in time, given the vote to leave the EU.

T. Mediation and unreasonable refusal

Q43. Can you give examples when it is reasonable to refuse to mediate? Are parties using the court's sanctioning of parties for unreasonable refusal to mediate tactically particularly in detailed assessments? To avoid such costs orders and keep the idea and costs of mediation sensible, is it sensible to agree to mediate but make it clear that both sides should bear their own costs.

5–80 See the text at paragraph 5–31 above. It is normal in a mediation for the parties to agree to split the cost of the Mediator's fee, room hire etc and for each side to bear its own costs..

Q44. When we suggest mediation on behalf of clients we are often met with a variety of reasons why there should be no mediation. Have you any suggestions?

5–81 Parties can be reluctant to mediate for various reasons. The following are some common misconceptions and ideas to address them[173]:

Mediating is a sign of weakness. Mediation is, in fact, usually a sign of strength; the strength of knowing what the lawyer and the client want to achieve, and pursuing that objective through a negotiated outcome. The key to negotiating from a position of strength is the ability to identify what the client and the opponent really need to achieve. The CPR including the Pre-Action Protocols and the Practice Direction – Pre-Action Conduct require parties to consider mediation before commencing proceedings. Failure to comply with this can lead to costs sanctions. Referring to this may help to focus the parties' minds.

In *Jane Laporte v Commissioner of Police of the Metropolis*[174], a police commissioner was found to have failed, without adequate justification, to have engaged in the alternative dispute resolution process, despite successfully defending the proceedings and, after taking into account the factors listed in *Halsey*, that was to be reflected in the costs order made.

Lawyers and clients can negotiate directly so mediation is unnecessary. There can be barriers to effective communication when negotiations are direct (between lawyers or between clients). The intervention of a neutral third

---

[172] The Department for Business, Innovation and Skills has confirmed that the following ADR entities are currently available to deal with disputes in the legal services sector: Ombudsman Services, ProMediate and Small Claims Mediation.
[173] With acknowledgements to The Practical Law Company.
[174] [2015] EWHC 371 (QB) Turner J.

party can change the dynamics and help to overcome these barriers. The mediator can use several techniques to manage the negotiating process, free up communications, encourage a problem-solving approach or brainstorming of options, and overcome deadlock. Parties tend to be unwilling to disclose information about their view of the case to an opposing party during direct negotiations.

Direct negotiations have failed so mediation will not succeed. Direct negotiations may become positional, with each party assuming entrenched and unrealistic positions and becoming increasingly defensive. A mediator can focus each party on a problem-solving approach, directing energy away from threats, attacks, or challenges to the credibility or good faith of a party in the dispute, towards a focus on the issues to be resolved and the potential implications of a failure to settle the problem.

The mediator is just a messenger. A mediator's task is considerably more sophisticated. It includes coaching, developing strategies and reality testing. The mediator is an active participant in the mediation process, and will use a range of techniques to engage people in the process and encourage them to consider a range of settlement options.

You cannot mediate until full disclosure is provided. Lawyers especially tend to argue that early mediation, before the disclosure process has been completed, is not appropriate. In practice, mediation simply requires knowledge of enough information (about the facts and the relevant law) for the lawyer to be able to advise the client on:

- the strengths and weaknesses of the case;
- the alternatives to settlement; and
- any options for settlement of the dispute.

The earlier that mediation takes place and an agreement is reached, the lower the costs will be.

Mediation will be a waste of time and money if the case does not settle at mediation. Even a failed mediation can help to narrow the issues and increase the likelihood that the case will settle without the need for trial. The parties will certainly have a better understanding of each other's positions and perspectives, and the potential barriers to settlement. A failed mediation can also generate options and opportunities that can be discussed after the mediation. In practice, a large proportion of cases that do not settle during a mediation settle shortly afterwards.

Mediation only delays the progress of litigation. Agreeing to attempt mediation does not stop court proceedings unless the parties agree and the court stays the proceedings. Awareness of the implications of failing to reach settlement during the mediation (for example, in terms of the costs and management time that would be incurred going to trial) can help to focus the parties' minds, and encourage them to engage positively in the mediation process.

Q45. There must be drawbacks to mediation – what are they?

5–82   There are possible drawbacks to mediation. A successful conclusion may depend, to a certain extent, on the abilities of the mediator. Costs may be increased if the mediation fails. The mediator may need to handle the parties with some skill and firmness if a party tries to misuse the process, for example to obtain an unjustified offer in a weak case. Mediation may simply not work if the parties are deeply antagonistic. One can reach a point where each side complains that the other is "not engaging". Sometimes this is true and it becomes clear that one or possibly both parties have come to the mediation with the view that they are willing to negotiate provided that the other side will agree to everything they seek. Trying to get it through to them that a successful settlement may involve some pain on both sides is sometimes very difficult. The process may be more difficult where one or both parties are not represented or not fully advised in advance. Some mediators say that the presence of lawyers can prevent settlement, because the lawyers are programmed to litigate not to compromise. The situation is even worse when the parties are lawyers arguing about their own costs. There are no winners or losers in mediation and it can be difficult to get this altered mind-set across to the parties and their lawyers.

U. Options when all issues resolved except costs

Q46. Can you please advise on the available options where the parties to an ongoing case have essentially agreed on every issue other than costs. It is at an early stage (just post CCMC). Both sides are saying that the other should pay their costs. Both parties are alleging that the other's conduct has been in breach of the pre-action protocol. Because of the circumstances it is uncertain which party (if any) will be deemed to have "won" the case. What are the options available to the parties? It doesn't seem correct that the main case should proceed as everything other than costs is essentially agreed. I see from the practice note that costs only proceedings are not available where it is not decided as to who is paying who's costs. So, for example, could the parties make an application to end the current proceedings and just deal with costs, or go straight to assessment?

5–83   Where proceedings are already in existence, costs only proceedings are not available. Where the parties have agreed the substantive issues between them, there appears to be no reason why an application should not be made to the court to decide the one remaining issue namely which party should be liable for the costs. It is not possible to go straight to assessment since there is no authority to assess i.e. there is no judgment or order under which the costs can be assessed. The question asks what the options available to the parties are and these, of course, include mediation and expert evaluation. The prospects for a successful mediation seem good given that the parties have managed to agree all the other issues.

Q47. We have a matter in which our client has successfully sued for profes-sional negligence. The opponent made a Part 36 offer which was accepted and the damages settled. The issue remaining is our costs. The Part 36 offer included an offer to pay reasonable expenses. Having assessed our costs schedule the opponent has made a Part 36 offer significantly less than our costs. How does one challenge the offer made by the opponent for costs? This is a matter in which we do not want this to go to court for a detailed assessment but would certainly want a better offer than is cur-rently being made.

It is not possible to *"challenge the offer made by the opponent"* since it is entirely   5–84
up to the opponent what offer they are prepared to make. The options include a counter offer and one would normally allow the matter to proceed to detailed assessment where the Costs Judge would deal with the costs of the assessment as well as the assessment itself. Given that the questioner does not wish to go for a detailed assessment, expert evaluation and/or mediation are the obvious answers.

Q48. Are you aware of any cases where a refusal to mediate a small claims track claim has resulted in the court making an adverse costs award against the refusing party? It is settled that refusal to accept an offer which is not beaten at trial is not "unreasonable behaviour" for the pur-poses of CPR Part 27 and will not lead to adverse costs consequences, but it is unclear what effect, if any, refusal to mediate might have on the usual "no costs" rule.

There do not appear to be any reported cases on this point. The reason for this   5–85
may well be that the Small Claims Track was originally intended to be lawyer free and to have a (virtually) no costs regime. If the parties go to mediation there will inevitably be a charge for the mediator and possibly room hire, even if no lawyers are instructed. The only possible justification seems to be the saving of court time if the matter goes to mediation, but that rather defeats the objective of the small claims track.

V. Assessing costs in arbitration

Q49. What is the proper approach to assessing costs in an Arbitration?

The form of words used in s.61 of the 1996 Act is derived from the Rules of   5–86
the Supreme Court which were in force between 1986 and 1998. RSC Order 62 r.3(3) states:

> *"If the Court in the exercise of its discretion sees fit to make any order as to the costs of any proceedings, the Court shall order costs to follow the event, except where it appears to the Court that in the circumstances of the case some other order should be made as to the whole or any part of the costs."*

Section 63(5) of the Act states that the successful party shall be allowed a

-reasonable amount in respect of all costs reasonably incurred. Again the wording is very similar to RSC Order 62, Rule 12 (in force between 1986 and 1998) which reads:

> "*(i) On the taxation of costs on the standard basis there shall be allowed a reasonable amount in respect of all costs reasonably incurred and any doubt which the taxing officer may have as to whether the costs were reasonably incurred or were reasonable in amount shall be resolved in favour of the paying party and in these rules the term 'the standard basis' in relation to the taxation of costs shall be construed accordingly.*"

It is clear that the Parliamentary Draftsman was ensuring consistency between the Rules and the 1996 Act.

As to the correct approach to deciding whether costs have been reasonably incurred and are reasonable in amount, RSC Order 62 Appendix 2 (in force between 1986 and 1998), paragraph 1 provides:

> "*Amount of Costs*
> *1-(1) The amount of costs to be allowed shall . . . be in the discretion of the taxing officer.*
> *2. In the exercise of his discretion the taxing officer shall have regard to all the relevant circumstances, and in particular to:*
> *(a) the complexity of the item or of the cause or matter in which it arises and the difficulty or novelty of the questions involved;*
> *(b) the skill, specialised knowledge and responsibility required of, and time and labour expended by, the solicitor or counsel;*
> *(c) the number and importance of the documents (however brief) prepared or perused;*
> *(d) the place and circumstances in which the business involved is transacted;*
> *(e) the importance of the cause or matter to the client;*
> *(f) where money or property is involved its amount or value;*
> *(g) any other fees and allowances payable to the solicitor or counsel in respect of other items in the same cause or matter but only where work done in relation to those items has reduced the work which would otherwise have been necessary in relation to the item in question.*"

Under Appendix 2 to RSC Order 62, the taxing officer is required to have regard to "*all the relevant circumstances*" and in particular to the seven -headings set out above. Conduct of the parties should be considered as part of "the relevant circumstances", when assessing the reasonableness of costs. Reasonableness, rather than proportionality, is the proper test to apply in assessing the costs of an arbitration under the 1996 Act.

If the arbitration is not proceeding under the 1996 Act it will depend entirely on the rules of the arbitral body which has been chosen and the terms of the arbitration agreement itself.

CHAPTER 6

Qualified One-Way Costs Shifting

Introduction

The introduction of a system of one-way costs shifting (QOCS) in personal injury litigation was the subject of close and detailed scrutiny and debate during Lord Justice Jackson's review. Amongst its primary attractions was that it was seen to provide a possible solution to the problem and costs of the 'indefensible' regime of After the Event Insurance (ATE) in such cases,[1] particularly given that claimants were perceived as being successful in the -majority of personal injury claims.   6–01

In clinical negligence claims where the success rate of claimants was lower, the relatively higher costs of ATE premiums in such cases provided a counter-balancing justification for the consideration of one way costs shifting.

Accordingly, the firm recommendation was made that a system of one-way costs shifting should be introduced in all such cases with the specific aim of reducing the costs of personal injury litigation, in particular by removing the need for ATE. One way costs shifting was part of a package, therefore, along with the restrictions in recoverability of ATE introduced by s.46 of LASPO.

Jackson LJ, however, was alive to the need to deter frivolous or fraudulent claims and to encourage acceptance of reasonable offers, aims which would be undermined by wholesale protection to claimants from the risk of adverse costs orders no matter what. Accordingly, the proposed system of one-way costs shifting was to be qualified to address these requirements, hence QOCS.

To avoid undue complexity and impracticality, QOCS was to be introduced for all personal injury claims, rather than merely being restricted to low value claims or claims run on Conditional Fee Agreements. In fact, the definition in CPR r.44.13(1) makes clear that QOCS applies (at least in part) not merely to a 'pure' personal injury claim, but to any proceedings which include such a claim, though CPR r.44.12(2)(b) then allows an order for costs against a claimant to be enforced, with the leave of the court, where 'a claim is made for the benefit of the claimant other than a claim to which this section applies.

When introduced, the only absolute exception to QOCS was for cases where a claimant had entered into a pre-commencement funding arrangement (considered below).

Jackson LJ's proposal was for a system which provided a *"broadly similar degree of protection against adverse costs"* to that which applied to publicly funded litigants through what was then s.11 of the Access to Justice Act 1999.[2]   6–02

The proposal involved a broad test, based on the test applicable in such

---

[1] Final Report, pp.184 and 188.
[2] Now s.26 of LASPO – see Final Report, p.189.

cases, whereby the costs ordered against a claimant in such cases would not exceed:

> "... the amount, if any, which is a reasonable one for him to pay having regard to all the circumstances including (a) the financial resources of all parties to the proceedings; and (b) their conduct in connection with the dispute to which the proceedings relate."

The proposal would firstly have allowed the courts to address concerns in relation to frivolous and fraudulent claims. Secondly, it would have ensured that QOCS could be limited where the claimant's means were such that it would be unjust not to require the claimant to pay costs. It would also have allowed for the possibility of a 'football pools' type application, whereby a defendant who was not allowed to enforce a costs order might, in limited circumstances, reapply to do so where the claimant finances subsequently and substantially improved.

Whilst Jackson LJ's general proposal for a system of qualified one-way costs shifting was adopted, his proposed test was not and a more rigid approach, which does not include any limitation by reference to the claimant's financial resources, was introduced.

In order to address Jackson LJ's second concern, that of incentivising claimants to make Part 36 offers despite QOCS protection, Jackson LJ proposed the 10% increase in general damages which did come into effect, in relation to cases where there was no pre-commencement funding arrangement,[3] as a result of the Court of Appeal's second bite of the cherry in *Simmons v Castle*.[4]

The new rules

6–03   The new rules are set out in CPR 44 Part II and CPR 44 PD 12.1.

The scope of the new rules

6–04   The rules apply to all proceedings which include a claim for damages for personal injuries or under the Fatal Accidents Act 1976 or claims under the Law Reform (Miscellaneous Provisions) Act 1934 (CPR r.44.13(1)) (this includes claims arising out of clinical negligence (see the broad definition of 'claim for personal injuries' in CPR r.2.3). Pre-action disclosure applications are excluded (CPR r.44.13(1)).

Although there will often be little doubt as to whether a claim includes a claim for damages for personal injuries, there will be the occasional situation where the issue is in doubt. The matter arose in *Howe v Motor Insurer' Bureau*[5] in relation to claims under the unidentified driver scheme. After very careful consideration, Mr Justice Stewart concluded that such a claim – which is a rare event since the untraced drivers agreement contains its own inter-

---

[3] As defined in r.48.2.
[4] *Simmons v Castle* [2012] EWCA Civ 1288; [2013] 1 WLR 1239.
[5] [2016] EWHC 884 (QB), [2016] 1 WLR 2751.

nal resolution procedure – was not a claim for damages for personal injury because the claim was made under express secondary legislation and independently of any need to establish a civil wrong. The need to establish such a wrong was an essential part of a civil claim and absent the same, the claim fell outside QOCS. The Court of Appeal will be hearing an appeal from that decision in the early part of 2017.

QOCS does not apply to proceedings 'ancillary' to personal injury claims – that is to say claims such as Civil Liability (Contribution) Act 1978 claims by a defendant to a personal injury action against a third party alleging that that third party was responsible for the claimant's injuries, even where such claims are brought as Part 20 claims within the claimant's personal injury action. 'Proceedings', in CPR r.44.13, is intended to refer to the claimant's claim for damages for personal injury.[6]

There is no exception for appeals (arising from claims within the scope of CPR r.44.13). The previous edition of this book therefore boldly asserted that QOCS therefore applies to such appeals. The point was, in fact, argued in *Parker v Butler*[7] where Mr Justice Edis reached the same conclusion. Whilst there is robust authority[8] that where costs are concerned generally, first instance proceedings and appeals are different proceedings, Edis J concluded that this was clearly not the intention behind the operation of QOCS. An appeal in a personal injury claim remains a proceeding which includes a claim for damages for personal injuries and QOCS applies. There has been no further appeal against the decision in *Parker*.

An interesting potential variant on the point arises in the context of approval hearings involving children and patients. Clearly, where such approval is sought in the context of ongoing substantive proceedings the approval is likely to be seen as part of the substantive personal injury proceedings and QOCS would apply. The same would probably apply to any appeal arising out of the approval hearing (for example a costs point), though the point is not wholly addressed by the reasoning in *Parker*. More arguable is the position where the substantive matter was concluded without the issue of proceedings. In such a situation, approval is sought pursuant to CPR r.21.10(2) and CPR r.21.10(2)(b) provides that, in that situation, *'the sole purpose of the proceedings is to obtain the approval of the court. . .'*. It appears arguable that, in this situation, the proceedings for approval and, in particular, any appeal from them might not therefore be a *'claim for damages for personal injuries'* and QOCS might not apply to them.

This would appear to be entirely against the purpose of the introduction of QOCS and appears to be a result of the almost impossible task of ensuring that there is no apparent conflict between each and every aspect of the CPR when the rules are amended, rather than reflecting any intention that

---

[6] *Wagenaar v Weekend Travel Ltd* [2014] EWCA Civ 1105, at 34–46.

[7] [2016] EWHC 1251 (QB), [2016] 3 Costs LR 435.

[8] See *Hawksford Trustees Jersey Ltd v Stella Global UK Ltd* [2012] EWCA Civ 987, [2012] 1 WLR 3581.

approval hearings – which are intended to protect the most vulnerable – and appeals therefrom should be excluded from QOCS.

Importantly, there is no restriction on the application of QOCS by reference to the date on which proceedings were brought. Although the new rules only came into effect on 1 April 2013, they apply from that date to all costs orders in all claims involving a claim for damages for personal injury (subject to one exception below), whether or not proceedings were issued prior to 1 April 2013.

This has the somewhat unexpected, but apparently intended, effect that not only did defendants who were involved in litigated personal injury claims which had been issued prior to 1 April 2013 find that the risks the claimant faced in the claim had shifted mid litigation[9], but that even in claims which had concluded prior to 1 April 2013 and where the defendant had obtained a costs order in its favour, its ability to enforce that costs order was now restricted by virtue of QOCS.

This effect was tolerably clear from the face of the rules, but has been affirmed by the Court of Appeal's decision in *Wagenaar*, where Vos LJ considered that the rules were clearly intended to operate 'retrospectively' in this way.[10]

6–05   There is a single operative transitional provision – CPR r.44.17 – which provides that QOCS does not apply where the claimant has entered into a pre-commencement funding arrangement as defined in CPR r.48.2.

That definition broadly covers Conditional Fee Agreements (but not any other kind of retainer) or ATE policies entered into before 1 April 2013 in relation to the matter that is the subject of the proceedings in which the cost order is made.[11]

Accordingly, where a claimant has entered into either a CFA or has taken out ATE in respect of the claim before 1 April 2013, QOCS is not available at all. There may be cases where the claimant has taken out one, but not the other (for example has entered into a CFA pre-April 2013 but did not take out ATE, perhaps because none could be found before the deadline). In such cases, it may seem harsh that the claimant is denied QOCS protection when QOCS was intended, primarily, to be a quid pro quo for not taking out ATE and the claimant has not taken ATE. However, such apparent injustices in individual cases are arguably an inevitable consequence of broad based -procedural reform.

---

[9] Although from the claimant's perspective this may often have been theoretical since many such claimants in pre-April 2013 issued cases will have been insulated against adverse costs orders by virtue of After the Event Insurance.

[10] *Wagenaar v Weekend Travel Ltd* [2014] EWCA Civ 1105, at 29–30.

[11] There are technical complexities to the definitions which are addressed in the section on funding arrangements. Note that the taking out of a post 31 March 2013 ATE policy does not affect the availability of QOCS, even where part of that ATE premium may remain recoverable in principle between the parties in a clinical negligence claim pursuant to the Recovery of Costs Insurance Premiums in Clinical Negligence Proceedings Regulations 2013. Note also that by virtue of the definitions in r.48.2, where the case is in one of the categories where there is a LASPO 'exemption', allowing for continued between the parties recoverability of success fees and ATE premium, then QOCS will not apply. The only such category which involves claims which will also satisfy the definition of being 'personal Injury claims' is a mesothelioma claim. Accordingly a mesothelioma claimant who funds their case by way of CFA (with a success fee) or ATE policy (even if taken out after April 2013) will not have the benefit of QOCS.

Indeed, it appears that QOCS will be lost even where the claimant has not entered into a pre-commencement funding arrangement, but has erroneously told the defendant that he has, at least if the defendant relies on that representation. Such was the effect of His Honour Judge Lopez's judgment in *Price v Egbert H Taylor & Co. Ltd*[12]. In that case, the judge ruled that the claimant was estopped from denying that he had a pre-April 2013 CFA with success fee in place, even where the evidence appeared to be that he did not. QOCS was lost.

The Court of Appeal is due to hear an appeal in *Price* in January 2017 and the outcome is likely to be known shortly after publication. The broad justice of the judge's decision seems obvious, but it is likely to be set against the need for a clear, simple and certain operation of the rules and the injustice to a claimant of being denied QOCS in this situation – though the strong suspicion must be that it is the claimant's solicitor and not the claimant himself who is likely to suffer any adverse consequences.

In addition to arguments such as that in *Price* there may be scope for arguments as to what the position would be if the claimant had entered into a pre-April 2013 CFA, for example, but chose to 'abandon' that arrangement pre-issue (whether because of a change of solicitors or otherwise) and to enter into a new funding arrangement. CPR r.44.17 provides that QOCS is unavailable 'where the claimant has entered into' such an arrangement and would, therefore, appear to exclude the ability to gain QOCS protection by later abandoning that arrangement. The factual question upon which the availability of QOCS is predicated appears to be simply whether or not such an arrangement has ever been entered into in connection with the case, and not whether or not that is the operative arrangement at the time any application of QOCS is being considered.

6–06

This approach seems to have been adopted by Master Haworth in the SCCO in the case of *Landau v The Big Bus Company*[13] where, in a situation where the claimant (acting in person by this point) had entered into a pre-commencement funding arrangement in relation to matters at first instance, but not in relation to an appeal from the first instance judgment, the court held that QOCS was not available in respect of the costs of the appeal, firstly because the appeal related to the same 'matter' which was the subject of the proceedings (and therefore the first instance CFA was a pre-commencement funding arrangement per CPR r.48.2(1)(i)(aa)) and secondly that, in any event, the appeal was part of the same 'proceedings' for the purposes of CPR r.44.17. This is consistent with the later decision of Mr Justice Eady in *Parker v Butler*, noted above.

However, in *Casseldine*[14], Regional Costs Judge Phillips took a more purposive approach. In that case, the claimant had entered into a pre-April 2013 CFA with success fee and had taken out an ATE policy. However, those solici-

---

[12] Birmingham County Court, 16 January 2016, unreported.
[13] *Landau v The Big Bus Company*, unreported, 31 October 2014.
[14] *Casseldine v Diocese of Llandaff Board for Social Responsibility* (Cardiff County Court, unreported, 3 July 2015).

tors had terminated the CFA pre-issue. The claimant found new solicitors who took the case on a post-April 2013 CFA. The claim was dismissed at trial. In considering whether QOCS applied, the judge took into account that, because it was the claimant's solicitor that had ended the agreement (and, under the terms of that agreement, the solicitor had no right to payment of base costs or success fee), there were no circumstances whereby the claimant could, in the issued claim, have sought to recover any additional liability under the pre-April 2013 arrangements from the defendant. Accordingly, applying the rules purposively, it would be unfair to deny the claimant QOCS protection.

Whether that analysis is correct is likely to require a decision of a higher court. As noted above, with *Price v Egbert H Taylor & Co. Ltd*, there is an apparent tension in these cases between the desire to achieve what the court considers to be a just outcome in the individual case, and ensuring that the rules are applied in a clear, transparent and predictable fashion. The more the courts introduce exceptions which are outside the specific rule based exceptions, the more difficult it is to predict in a given case when QOCS will or will not apply. This risks increasing the need for claimants to then consider seeking some alternative or additional form of costs protection, which would risk undermining (in part at least) the purpose of the reform.

In any event, the *Casseldine* type situation is likely to be a relatively rare one and whether a similar reasoning would apply in circumstances where a claimant and her solicitor simply abandoned existing arrangements before then entering into new, post LASPO, arrangements between the same parties in order to obtain QOCS protection (particularly if this was done at a time when the claimant or the solicitor had just appreciated that the case was likely to be lost) appears very much open to argument.

The effect of the new rules

6–07   QOCS does not prevent the making of a costs order against a personal injury claimant. Any question of whether to make such an order falls to be decided on 'usual' principles by reference to CPR r.44.2.

By the same token, it is a mistake for claimants to regard QOCS as a guarantee of an award of costs in their favour in a successful case. The court's discretion under CPR r.44.2 remains entirely untrammelled and unaffected by QOCS and regardless of the impact of QOCS, a claimant may still find their costs being disallowed or reduced in a case where they have won if their conduct or other circumstances warrant it.

The effect of QOCS is limited to the defendant's ability to enforce any costs order that has been made.

In practice, however, it can be anticipated that the presence of QOCS, as with the presence of adverse costs protection for publicly funded litigants, will, in certain circumstances, have an effect on the frequency with which defendants seek adverse costs orders where the option might be open to them to do so. This is particularly so given the absence of a 'football pools' or 'lottery win' provision allowing the defendant to return to seek enforcement of an order is an otherwise impecunious claimant's resources drastically improve. As noted, financial resources (present or future) are (probably) immaterial to any question of the application of QOCS.

Because the QOCS rules operate on enforcement of orders, where a claim comes within the scope of CPR 44 Part II any issue of the enforcement of any costs order (including interim orders) against a claimant is deferred until after the conclusion of the proceedings, including after any agreement or assessment of costs (CPR r.44.14(2)). Note, this does not mean that the assessment or agreement itself is deferred, merely the enforcement. Quite the opposite. These still take place at the usual time and must be concluded before any issue of enforcement, and therefore whether QOCS prevents enforcement, falls to be considered. However, again in practice it is to be anticipated that in many cases parties will wish to deal with any question of whether QOCS applies and, if so, to what extent, before spending time and money on the assessment of costs that might never be payable.

Where there are interim awards of costs, which may well take place at a time when the application of QOCS is yet to be decided, a defendant would be well advised in most cases to pursue an order for interim costs and the summary assessment of any such costs as if QOCS did not apply. To assume QOCS does not apply, and to allow the opportunity to obtain such an order to pass would be to risk losing an entitlement to costs which might be of benefit either (i) to set off against any damages or interest awarded to the claimant if the claim succeeds, even if QOCS applies and/or (ii) to seek against the claimant in the event QOCS is disapplied for some reason.

If such an order is obtained, a claimant might wish to consider obtaining a stay of enforcement of the order in light of the default provision that payment is due within 14 days (CPR r.44.7). However, this is probably unnecessary, since the QOCS rules themselves operate as an effective stay preventing enforcement save in the express terms set out in the rules and therefore it would be an unwise defendant that sought to enforce – by way of seeking immediate payment – an interim costs order in usual circumstances.

The wording of CPR r.44.14(2) also supports the argument that the assessment of costs is not to be regarded as 'proceedings' within the meaning of that word for the purposes of QOCS. Detailed assessment is an ancillary part of the substantive proceedings, not a discrete proceeding in its own right.

The basic operation of the rules, where QOCS applies, may be summarised as follows:

6–08

(i)   Any adverse costs order may be enforced in full to the extent that it does not exceed the damages and interest awarded to the claimant (CPR r.44.14(1)).

(ii)   Where the claimant's claim has been struck out on the basis that it: (i) discloses no reasonable grounds; or (ii) was an abuse of process; or (iii) the conduct of the claimant or someone acting on his behalf (and with the claimant's knowledge of their conduct) was likely to obstruct the just disposal of the proceedings, then the costs order may be enforced in full (CPR r.44.15(1)). In such a situation, of course, the claimant will not have been awarded any damages, so this provision simply allows full enforcement of any costs orders made in the defendant's favour in the proceedings, as if QOCS did not exist.

(iii)   Where the claimant's claim is found, on the balance of probabilities, to have been 'fundamentally dishonest', then the order for costs may be enforced to its full extent with the permission of the court (CPR r.44.16(1)). This, of course, covers a number of possibilities. The claim may have failed, but not been struck out per CPR r.44.15, in which case the defendant will need permission to enforce the costs order at all. The claim may have succeeded and some damages may have been awarded, but the claim may still be found to have been fundamentally dishonest, in which case the defendant can enforce without permission to the extent of the damages and interest awarded, but requires permission to enforce any further. This latter position is considerably less likely following the introduction of s.57 of the Criminal Justice & Courts Act 2015, with effect from the 13 April 2015 (and only applying to claims issued on or after that date). This requires the court to dismiss any claim in its entirety where the claimant has been fundamentally dishonest in relation to it or a related claim, even though the primary claim has succeeded in whole or part. The only qualification is that the court has a discretion not to do so if it considers that to do so would cause substantial injustice.

Accordingly, in respect of post April 2015 claims, where the claimant has been fundamentally dishonest, the claim as a whole is likely to be dismissed and the claimant is likely to be denied QOCS protection in whole or part. There may still be a benefit to defendants in seeking to strike out such claims as being abusive or on the basis that the claimant's conduct is obstructing just disposal, since this will give rise to an automatic disapplication of QOCS in its entirety, removing any question of judicial discretion.

(iv) Where the claim is brought in whole or part for the benefit of a person other than the claimant or a dependant in a Fatal Accidents Act case, or where the claim is only in part a personal injury claim, the defendant may enforce the order up to the full extent with the permission of the court (CPR r.44.16) – see further below. Again, in such cases, the defendant will be entitled to enforce in part without permission if damages have been awarded, but needs permission to go beyond the level of damages and interest (if any).

Each of these provisions warrants a little further examination. In relation to the basic operation of QOCS by restriction on enforcement (CPR r.44.14), perhaps the single most interesting question is what is meant by 'enforcement'. The defendant's right to 'enforce' a costs order in its favour is restricted.

It is restricted to the limit of damages and interest awarded to the claimant. There is no mention of the claimant's costs.

However, the very section of the CPR which precedes QOCS deals with the ability of a party to 'set off' one costs order against another. Is a set off enforcement? If it is not, then it would appear that the QOCS rules do not prevent a defendant setting off its costs against any costs awarded to the claimant, in addition to enforcing the costs order to the extent of damages awarded (subject, of course, to the total limit of the costs awarded to the defendant).

If, however, a set off of costs against costs does amount to enforcement, then the defendant's rights are limited to those under CPR r.44.14.

The issue remains undecided, at least in the specific context of QOCS. In *Vava*,[15] Andrew Smith J declined to allow a set off of one costs order against another in circumstances where parties had entered into a QOCS type contractual arrangement (but where QOCS did not in fact apply). He did so on the grounds that it would be 'unfair' in the circumstances to do so.

6–09

Existing authority in the not dissimilar area of costs protection for publicly funded litigants indicates that an order for set off of costs is not to be regarded as enforcement of the order because it does not place the claimant under any obligation to pay, but merely reduces the amount that they can recover.[16] This would appear to support an argument that a defendant can firstly seek to set off costs awarded to it against those awarded to a claimant and, if thereafter, there remains a net liability to the defendant, seek to set this against damages and interest under CPR r.44.14, rather than being limited to the CPR r.44.14 set off. The issue will no doubt be the subject of specific argument and authority in due course in the QOCS context.

CPR r.44.15 requires relatively little further discussion. The categories of strike out referred to therein mirror those in CPR r.3.4(2)(a) and (b) and issues as to when such a strike out is appropriate are beyond the scope of this section. The only real gloss to note is that where the strike out is on the basis that the conduct of the proceedings was such as to be likely to obstruct the just disposal of the proceedings, in order to disapply QOCS it is necessary, in addition, that the court concludes that such conduct was that of the claimant himself or that he knew of the relevant conduct on the part of the person so acting on his behalf. A defendant seeking a strike out on this basis in a personal injury claim should take care to ensure that this additional aspect is specifically addressed in any judgment given on the strike out (and ideally recited in the order).

However, the case of *Brahilika*[17] illustrates that the court <u>may</u> be prepared to apply a relatively wide interpretation of the conduct likely to obstruct the just disposal of proceedings. In that case, the relevant conduct was the failure of the claimant to attend trial, due to being on holiday (it not being known whether the holiday was booked before or after the trial date was fixed).

---

[15] *Vava v Anglo American South Africa Ltd* [2013] EWHC 2326 (QB); [2013] 5 Costs LR 805.
[16] *R (Burkett) v London Borough of Hammersmith & Fulham* [2004] EWCA Civ 1342, at 50.
[17] Unreported, Romford County Court, 30 July 2015.

6–10   CPR r.44.16 and the introduction of a test of 'fundamental dishonesty' had given rise to much debate, which has been added to by the introduction of s.57 of the Criminal Justice and Courts Act 2015 (discussed further at 6–08 above and 6–11 below).

What does 'fundamentally dishonest' mean? It is relatively early days, but some guidance is available. 'Dishonesty' is a concept the courts are extremely familiar with and there is clear judicial guidance as to the issues a court must consider in deciding in a personal injury context whether a claimant has been dishonest.[18] More contentious is the 'fundamentally' aspect, which has troubled parliamentarians in recent debates in relation to the use of the term in s.57 of the new Act.

6–11   There have been a number of first instance cases where the issue has arisen. Whilst such cases – as with *Brahilika* above – do not contain any binding statement of principle, they are useful to illustrate the approach the courts have been adopting, particularly in the relatively early days of the application and interpretation of these rules. One of the most thoroughly argued earlier cases was that of *Gosling*,[19] which was a classic case of a successful, but dishonestly exaggerated, claim, though with an added complication that the claimant succeeded only against one defendant and discontinued against a second. In that case, the judge held that a claim was not fundamentally dishonest merely because the claimant had been dishonest in respect of some collateral matter or some minor, self-contained head of damage, but that where the dishonesty went to the root of a substantial part of the claim the test was made out.

The case appears to confirm, though only at first instance level, a number of propositions. Firstly, that CPR r.44.16(1) may apply where the dishonesty does not infect the entire claim, but goes only to a substantial part of it—the classic exaggerated claim case. Secondly, where the test in CPR r.44.16(1) is made out, the court is not bound to allow the defendant to enforce the costs order to its full extent, but is then given a discretion to decide to what extent to allow such enforcement.

Both propositions appear logical interpretations of the rule, though there will no doubt be further argument on these and related topics. *Gosling* was held to be a correct analysis of the meaning and scope of fundamental dishonesty by HHJ Hodge QC in *Meadows*[20] and a District Judge's failure to follow it was criticised in allowing an appeal in *Rouse*[21].

The first proposition – that a claim may be seen as being fundamentally dishonest as a whole even where the dishonestly only relates to part of the claim – is, of course, supported by the approach taken in s.57 of the 2015 Act, requiring the dismissal of the entire claim even where there are elements of that claim in respect of which the claimant has not been dishonest (see s.57(3)). It is also consistent with the Court of Appeal's approach to the

---

[18] See, for example, *Brighton & Hove Bus v Brooks* [2011] EWHC 2504.
[19] *Gosling v Hailo & Screwfix Direct*, unreported, 29 April 2014 CC (Cambridge).
[20] *Meadows v La Tasca Restaurants Ltd*, Manchester County Court, 16 June 2016, unreported.
[21] HHJ Gosnell, *Rouse v Aviva Insurance Ltd*, Bradford County Court, 15 January 2016, unreported.

issue of fraud in personal injury claims, as seen in *Hayward v Zurich Insurance Company PLC*[22] where, despite the fortuitous outcome for the appellant, it is clear from the judgments that the court regarded the whole claim as being fraudulent, despite the fact that there was no doubt that the appellant had been injured and his dishonesty related to the claim that the injury was continuing and had not resolved.

The case of *Diamanttek Ltd v James*[23] appears to be consistent with this analysis. In that case, the judge cited *Gosling*, without disagreement, but approached the matter (necessarily) from a slightly different perspective to conclude that a claim could still be 'fundamentally dishonest' where a claimant had 'not told the truth' about a key aspect, even where the judge has also concluded that the judge was not himself a 'dishonest person'. The case may, perhaps, best be seen as one where the appellate judge is wrestling with a slightly unfortunate use of terminology at first instance and not one which derogates in any way from the analysis contained in *Gosling*.

The issue of fundamental dishonesty has probably given rise to more cases on the issue of QOCS than any other. However, the majority of these tend to concern first instance decisions as to whether, on the facts, the claim was a fundamentally dishonest one and they add little to the arguments of principle. They are not reviewed here, but are readily available online and may be of assistance to anyone making or facing such an application.

CPR rule 44 PD 12 contains clear guidance in relation to arguments under CPR r.44.16(1) and in particular that where parties settle proceedings the court will not, 'save in exceptional circumstances' order that issues relating to fundamental dishonesty be tried (12.4(b)) and that such issues will normally be determined at trial (12.4(a)). The logic is obvious and needs little explanation, but the point should not be overlooked by defendants. Settlement of a claim will usually be an effective bar to taking this point.

A claimant cannot, however, escape such scrutiny (at least in relation to fundamental dishonesty) by discontinuing the claim (CPR r.44 PD 12.4(c)) – and see the discussion of the same in *Rouse* (above).

It must be noted, however, that CPR r.44 PD 12.4(c) only applies to allow the court to consider matters despite a notice of discontinuance where the issue raised by the defendant is one of fundamental dishonesty. Where the claimant has served such a notice and the defendant, for example, seeks to contend that the claim, whilst not dishonest, was one that disclosed no reasonable grounds for being brought, for example, and would therefore have been struck out allowing for the automatic disapplication of QOCS under CPR r.44.15(1)(a), the defendant will face the burden of having to satisfy the court as to why the notice of discontinuance should be set aside pursuant to CPR r.38.4 to allow the defendant to then apply to strike the claim out. As *Magon*[24]

---

[22] [2015] EWCA Civ 327.
[23] Coventry County Court, unreported, the decision was of a Circuit Judge (His Honour Judge Gregory) on appeal but has wrongly been reported in some quarters as being a decision of the Court of Appeal.
[24] *Magon v Royal Sun Alliance,*Central London County Court, 26 February 2016, unreported.

illustrates, the defendant may find such an application difficult and the court will usually expect to see that there has been some kind of abuse of process warranting such a course. Such an application will be particularly difficult if, as in *Magon*, it is brought after the 28-day time limit for doing so under CPR r.38.4.

CPR r.44.16(2) has attracted less debate. However, its impact should not be overlooked.

6–12   CPR r.44.16 applies in two types of claims. The one which has received less attention is the second (CPR r.44.16(2)(b)), namely where a claim is made *"for the benefit of the claimant other than a claim to which this section applies"*. This is intended to cover claims where the beneficiary of the claim is the claimant, but the claimant's claim is only partially a personal injury claim (the classic example being a housing disrepair claim where there may be a claim for personal injuries as part of a wider claim).

By virtue of CPR r.44.16(2) the mere fact that procedurally, the claim as a whole is deemed a personal injury claim, because it includes a claim for damages for personal injury, does not appear to prevent the court disapplying QOCS, to the extent just[25]. Commonly, this is likely to be used so that the court can allow full enforcement of adverse costs orders in relation to that part of the claim which was not a personal injury claim, and is likely to be used in cases where the personal injury claim is viewed as being the more modest or less complex part of the claim. An example might be a professional negligence claim which included an ancillary claim for damages for personal injury.

More contentious is CPR r.44.16(2)(a), which allows the court to disapply QOCS where the claim in whole or part is for the financial benefit of a third party.

The Rule itself gives only limited guidance as to the circumstances where it will apply. The Practice Direction is more specific and provides examples of where the claim is *"made for the financial benefit of a person other than the claimant"*, including credit hire claims and subrogated claims (PD 12.2).

6–13   Whilst this seems to be the clear intention of the rulemakers, there is likely to be argument in the future as to whether or not claims, such as credit hire or subrogated claims are properly claims brought for the financial benefit of another party, a wording which appears to cut across the traditional and well established legal status of claims by such parties where the involvement of the third party is seen as being *res inter alios acta* (that is to say something which is

---

[25] The precise ambit and operation of the interestingly worded r.44.12(2)(b) is unclear. As noted, r.44.13 provides that QOCS applies where a claim 'includes' a personal injury claim. Rule 44.12(2)(b) might be thought to be intended to address those situations where there is only a modest personal injury element 'tacked on' to a large claim, allowing the court, at its discretion, to allow 'normal' costs enforcement in relation to the non-personal injury element. However, the wording is a little ambiguous and it is noted that the preceding subsection, r.44.12(2)(a) expressly refers to an exception where 'the proceedings include a claim [for the financial benefit of another]', yet r.44.12(2)(b) does not say 'where the proceedings include a claim other than a personal injury claim'. This may be slightly lax drafting or it may be arguable that r.44.12(2)(b) has a narrower operation and is only aimed at making clear that if a claimant brings two, distinct, claims (but perhaps arising from the same facts), the fact that QOCS is available for one does not necessarily mean it will be available for the other. The discussion set out above assumed the former.

considered not to be the court's business when considering the claim between the parties), particularly in the context of costs, save in particular and unusual circumstances.[26]

The fact that the 'examples' are given in the Practice Direction rather than forming part of the rule might be said to provide greater scope for such arguments.

The clear intention of CPR r.44.16(2) is that where QOCS is disapplied in this situation, it is not the claimant that should suffer. CPR r.44.16(3) contains a clear point to the making of a costs order directly against the third party in such a circumstance, subject to consideration of the usual rules for such orders under CPR r.46.2. Whilst such a third party costs order would not remove the order against the claimant, it is to be anticipated that in such cases the court's likely approach would be to decline to allow enforcement (beyond damages and interest) against the claimant, but to make a third party costs order for the relevant sum or percentage or issues against the third party for whose benefit that part of the claim was brought, and CPR r.44 PD 12.5 clearly points in this direction, indicating that it will be 'exceptional' that (further) enforcement will be allowed against the claimant.

Whether the working of CPR r.44.16(3) (and CPR r.44 PD 12.5) is intended to and does in any way relax the established common law as to the circumstances in which a third party costs order is available is a moot point and will no doubt be argued in due course.

A wider use of QOCS

The Ministry of Justice published detailed proposals for the extension of a version of QOCS to defamation and privacy claims, such proposals being put out to consultation which closed in November 2013. Although the original intention was for QOCS to be introduced in this area with effect from April 2014, no implementation date has yet been given and it is not clear if, when or if so in what final form QOCS will be introduced in this area.   **6–14**

Given the uncertainty, the proposals are not considered in any detail here, save to note that the proposals were for a rather different model of QOCS, whereby QOCS would be available to both claimants and defendants and organisations and parties with significant financial resources would be excluded from the scheme, with full costs protection only being available to those who would suffer 'severe financial hardship' if forced to pay adverse costs. Whether that model remains and is implemented in due course remains to be seen.

The Civil Justice Council's Working Group on the impact of the Jackson reforms also considered arguments for and against the extension of QOCS to other categories of cases which are said to be characterised by an asymmetric relationship between the parties, such as actions against the police and

---

[26] See the classic case of *TGA Chapman v Christopher* [1998] 1 WLR 12 in the context of subrogated claims.

professional negligence claims against solicitors arising out of personal injury claims. Nuisance claims are also under consideration.

In its final report[27] the Working Group described the arguments in favour of extension to claims against the police as being 'strong if not compelling' and noted that principled arguments to the contrary did not appear to have been made out. It noted that claims against the police might give rise to particular issues about how to apply QOCS in 'mixed claims' and that this issue merited further consideration both in the context of police claims and personal injury claims as a whole, as to which see above. This concern did not undermine what can only be seen as a whole hearted recommendation for extension of QOCS to actions against the police. The MOJ has yet to provide a formal response.

The Working Group was more equivocal on the issue of extending QOCS to professional negligence claims arising out of personal injury claims, describing the arguments for such extension as being a 'fair case' and noting a number of concerns about the practical effect of such extension, not least the risk of creating an expanded 'secondary market' in the pursuit of such claims. The subject also gave rise to a need to consider wider issues such as the available alternative forms of funding for such claims. Again, the ultimate decision remains one for the MOJ.

There have been other calls for the wider extension of QOCS, most notably from Ramsey J,[28] including to actions against the police. The delays and difficulties with the privacy and publication extension and the lack of response to the work undertaken by the CJC Working Group suggest that it may be some considerable time before any such extension might materialise. It is reasonably to be anticipated that if and when the LASPO exemptions for privacy and publication claims and mesothelioma claims are removed that QOCS will be extended to those areas. In the mesothelioma case, this can reasonably be anticipated to be a simple extension of the existing QOCS provisions (subject to the Government taking the operation to revise those provisions at the same time). In respect of privacy and publication claims, there is far greater scope for a different scheme to be introduced, not least in light of the complex and competing political -pressures surrounding reform in that area.

Questions and answers

A. *The circumstances in which QOCS applies*

Q1. How will QOCS apply where a claim comprises both a personal injury and a non-personal injury element?

6–15   This will have to be the subject of judicial guidance in due course. The rule expressly allows the court to disapply QOCS to the extent that it considers

---

[27] https://www.judiciary.gov.uk/wp-content/uploads/2011/03/cjc-qocs-2016-report.pdf
[28] In his speech to the Compass Law Commercial Litigation Conference: http://www.litigationfutures.com/news/extension-qocs-key-true-jackson-says-ramsey [Accessed 29 January, 2015].

just where this situation arises (CPR r.44.16) and the Practice Direction envisages that where this arises the court will normally order the claimant to pay costs notwithstanding that they exceed the level of damages and interest awarded (i.e. will allow enforcement beyond the limit in CPR r.44.14, which is what CPR r.44.16 expressly envisages). There is, however a degree of tension and some lack of clarity in the rules as to precisely how this will operate.

In practice, it is likely that the court will seek to identify the true nature of the claim. Where the personal injury claim was dominant and the 'additional claim' a modest ancillary part which is unlikely to have significantly increased the costs then the court may decide not to allow any enforcement beyond CPR r.44.14. Where the 'additional claim' was dominant, and the court may be reasonably satisfied that the defendant would have had to incur broadly the same level of costs to meet that claim alone, then the court may allow full enforcement. Perhaps more commonly, the court may seek to identify, by percentage, date or in some other way, the 'additional claim' and allow enforcement in that regard accordingly.

Given that the claimant in this scenario will already probably have suffered some costs deduction against damages (CPR r.44.14) and given that the quantum of costs may have been assessed (CPR r.44.13(3)) the court may simply make an order that enforcement of a certain sum above the level of damages is just. The Court of Appeal is unlikely to be keen to interfere with a broad exercise of discretion here unless the outcome is manifestly unjust.

Q2. Is QOCS excluded where the claimant has Before The Event Insurance?

No. Provided the claim is within CPR r.44.14, and provided that the claim-   6–16
ant has not entered into a CFA or ATE prior to 1 April 2013 in relation to the claim, then the method of funding is irrelevant. QOCS is available.

This applies even where the claim was commenced prior to 1 April 2013 – and even where the costs order was made prior to 1 April 2013 but has not yet been enforce. It is the presence of a funding model which contains provision for recoverable additional liabilities which leads to the loss of availability of QOCS. Whether the claimant is otherwise indemnified for the costs liability is irrelevant.

Q3. Does QOCS apply to costs incurred prior to 1 April 2013?

Yes. Provided the claim is within CPR r.44.13 and provided the claimant has   6–17
not entered into a pre-commencement funding arrangement (CPR r.48.2), then QOCS applies and the defendant's ability to enforce a costs order is restricted accordingly. Although there is scope for argument beyond that raised in *Wagenaar*, the Court of Appeal's decision in that case disposed of the primary argument that COCS could not operate retrospectively in this way.

Q4. Is QOCS excluded where the claimant has entered into a pre-commencement funding arrangement, even if the claimant then is

advised not to pursue the claim by the initially instructed solicitor but later does so under a post April 2013 funding arrangement with a -different firm?

6–18   In the first edition of this supplement, it was stated that these issues needed to be resolved, but that the wording of CPR r.48.2 and CPR r.44.17 suggested that the answer to this is 'yes'. In *Casseldine* (above), the regional costs judge concluded to the contrary on the facts of the case before him.

Authoritative resolution of this point will only be possible at a high appellate level. As was acknowledged in *Casseldine*, the strict wording of the provisions points to the conclusion that the fact that there has been a pre-commencement funding arrangement in respect of that claim, even if as a matter of fact that arrangement no longer operates and as a matter of fact there will not and could not have been any claim for additional liabilities if the claim succeeded, will mean that QOCS is not available.

This undoubtedly seems harsh. Whether the correct answer is that this is simply an unfortunate consequence of the introduction of a broad brush provision where there will be individual harsh decisions which are necessary as part of a wider desire to ensure consistency, simplicity and to avoid satellite litigation (as with the Court of Appeal's reasoning in *Wagenaar*) or whether the correct approach is the more purposive one remains a matter of argument in respect of which there is no binding authority.

Q5. Can a personal injury claimant who had a pre-action CFA (entered into before 1 April 2013) with a 100% success fee, and who wishes to proceed with the claim with the benefits of QOCS protection, terminate the existing CFA, on the basis that the law firm will waive its success fee, and enter into a new post-Jackson CFA? Would the claimant then be able to benefit from QOCS, even though the pre-action base costs are covered under a CFA entered into before 1 April 2013? Alternatively, could the client and or the solicitor agree to end the existing CFA, but enter into a new, post LASPO CFA, with any success fee payable by the client only, but with the CFA expressly covering all work done since first instruction and thereby benefit from QOCS?

6–19   This is a variant of the *Casseldine* type situation discussed above. On a strict interpretation of CPR r.44.17, the claimant 'has' entered into a pre-commencement funding arrangement in respect of the claim and QOCS is not available. However, *Casseldine* is an illustration of the scope for a wider, more purposive, approach to be adopted. In particular, if the abandonment of the success fee and the use of a post LASPO CFA take place before the issue of proceedings and if the abandonment of the success fee (or at least the ability to claim it on a between the parties basis) the ending of the earlier CFA is done in some irrevocable way, such that the court could conclude that there was no possibility of the defendant being required to pay the success fee (or any ATE premium) then the point would be arguable. However, such cases perhaps serve to illustrate the difficulties with adopting a purposive approach.

Ultimately, until such matters receive higher judicial attention, it is not possible to provide a definitive answer to this question. Given that in any case which reached the stage of a letter before action (at the latest) the defendant should have been notified of the existence of a CFA with a success fee in the case then there must be a substantial risk that the defendant will be alive to the point and will seek to challenge the application of QOCS if the claim is defeated.

Moreover, in light of *Price*, above, if such a course of action has been followed and if the case is one where the defendant has previously been notified that the case was funded by a CFA with a success fee, it is likely to be important to expressly inform that defendant that this is no longer the case if the claimant is not to risk losing QOCS despite having abandoned the recoverable success fee.

Q6. Will qualified one way costs shifting apply where a personal injury claimant entered into a CFA pre Jackson reforms but did not enter into an after the event insurance policy until after the introduction of QOCS?
No. Whilst the broad intention behind the introduction of QOCS was to act   **6–20** as a quid pro quo for the loss of between the parties recoverability of ATE premiums, the transitional provision at CPR r.44.17 expressly provides that QOCS does not apply to proceedings where the claimant has entered into a pre commencement funding arrangement. These are defined in CPR r.48.2. They include a CFA with a success fee. Accordingly where either or both of a CFA with a success fee or an ATE policy have been entered into prior to the 1 April 2013, QOCS will not be available.

Q7. Does QOCS apply to just personal injury? We have a commercial litigation matter for breach of contract so nothing to do with personal injury.
Yes, at present QOCS only applies to personal injury – see CPR r.44.13(1). The   **6–21** main body of the text identifies some areas where QOCS might be introduced, whether in the same form as at present or in a revised form. It is not presently anticipated that general commercial litigation will be one of these areas.

Q8. Does QOCS apply to claims for damages for clinical negligence?
Yes – see the definition of a claim for personal injuries at CPR r.2.3(1).   **6–22**

Q9. Where a claimant is currently subject to an 'old style' CFA (pre-April 2013 where QOCS would not apply) but the client seeks the protection of QOCS, would the previous presence of the old style CFA prevent the claimant ever obtaining the benefit of QOCS under the workings of CPR r.44.17 If the claimant was to continue as a litigant in person would she then obtain the benefit of QOCS?
On the strict wording of the transitional provision, CPR r.44.17 provides that   **6–23** the fact of the pre-April 2013 CFA (assuming it had a success fee) would mean

that QOCS is not available. However, cases such as *Casseldine* (above) suggest that a more purposive approach might mean that if the claimant in some way conclusively abandoned her pre-April 2013 funding arrangements she may benefit from QOCS after all. *Casseldine* is a first instance County Court decision and care should be exercised before placing relying on the reasoning therein.

Q10. In *Howe v Motor Insurers' Bureau* [2016] EWHC 884 (QB), the High Court concluded that a claim for compensation from the MIB (motor insurers' bureau) under the untraced drivers agreement was not a *"claim for damages for personal injury"* as required for QOCS to be applicable. The court acknowledged that this was an unusual situation because claims before a court in respect of the untraced drivers agreement are rare because it contains its own internal procedure. Will the position be the same if C sues an RTA insurer direct?

6–24   The precise answer to this will not be known unless and until the point is argued. *Howe* is, any event, on appeal to the Court of Appeal, so even the outcome in the MIN untraced drivers situation remains uncertain. However, on close consideration of the judgment in *Howe*, it would appear that a fundamental distinction may be drawn between that situation (where there was no need to establish a wrong) and the situation described, where the insurer is only directly liable where the claimant has a cause of action against the insured. However, the point is open to argument.

B. QOCS and discontinuance

Q11. The claimant has incurred costs unnecessarily in an unmeritous claim. They have now served a notice of discontinuance and, as QOCS applies, they are not liable for the defendant's costs (unless an exception applies). In the above circumstances, is it possible for the defendant to apply for a wasted costs order even though a notice of discontinuance has been filed by the claimant?

6–25   This question covers a number of issues.

Firstly, the assumption that the claimant is not liable, in principle, for the defendant's costs is wrong. CPR r.38.6 is not disapplied merely because QOCS applies. As discussed above, the defendant is entitled in principle to the same costs order whether QOCS applies or not. QOCS only addresses the enforcement of that order. Of course, as with publicly funded claims, it may be the case that the difficulties with enforcement mean that, save where the costs order is automatic (which, of course, it is under CPR r.38.6(1) unless the court orders otherwise), there will be cases where the defendant chooses not to spend money arguing for a costs order which serves little practical benefit. However, in the example given, the defendant will by default have a costs order in its favour.

As to exceptions, CPR r.44 PD 12.4(c) must not be overlooked. A claimant cannot (automatically) escape the risk of a finding of fundamental dishonesty by discontinuing the claim.

An interesting issue arises where the claim is one which was arguably abusive or in relation to which it could be argued that there were no reasonable grounds for bringing the claim, but the claimant has beaten the defendant to the point by discontinuing the claim before an application could be heard to have the proceedings struck out. CPR r.44 PD 12.4(c) does not address this. Under CPR r.38.4 it would be possible to apply to have the notice of discontinuance set aside in order for the court to hear an application to strike out which, if successful, would allow for full enforcement of the costs order without permission. It earlier editions of this supplement it was stated that is was likely that the court would only permit this in exceptional circumstances – perhaps where a claimant has been repeatedly warned as to the abusive nature of the claim, but has persisted, but then responds to a formal application to strike out by discontinuing. That now appear to accord with the practice adopted in such limited cases as are reported – see in particular *Magon v RSA* above.

Accordingly, the defendant is not left entirely without remedy in this situation (though in practice, whether even an enforceable costs order is of any value against an impecunious claimant is a question which must be considered), but faces a significant burden and must also act quickly if it wishes to raise matters, such as those under CPR r.44.15, to allow effective enforcement of a costs order in a discontinued case.

This approach, which was noted in the previous edition, appears similar to that following in *Kite*[29]. In that case, the judge concluded that in the rather unusual circumstances of that case – where a claimant had obtained judgment in default, which was set aside and the defendant applied for a strike out on the basis that there were no reasonable ground for bringing the claim – an attempt by the claimant to avoid the strike out and therefore the risk of an automatic loss of QOCS, by discontinuing his claim, was prevented by the court readily setting aside the notice of discontinuance so that it could deal with the strike out application. Although only a first instance decision, the outcome appears logical and the ability of the court to set aside such a notice whether under CPR r.38.4, which expressly provides for this, or under CPR Part 3 (relied on by the judge in *Kite*) is clear. Discontinuance is unlikely to be an effective remedy to prevent the loss of QOCS where the court considers that it is simply a tactical ploy to avoid an otherwise likely application of CPR r.44.15 or 44.16.[30] The outcomes in *Kite* and *Magon* were to opposite effect – in one case the defendant's application succeeding and in the other failing.

---

[29] *Kite v Phoenix Pub Group*, unreported.
[30] The case of *Akhtar & Khan v Ball* (unreported, HHJ Gregory, 10 July 2015) raises further interesting issues. In that case, not only was QOCS disapplied, but the defendant mounted a counterclaim, which was successful to the sum of £3,000 in exemplary damages, relying on *Kuddus v Chief Constable of Leicestershire* [2001] UKHL 29, where the claimant's claims were held to have been entirely fraudulent (and therefore fundamentally dishonest). Although unusual, this does suggest that a dishonest claimant may not merely be exposed to the loss of QOCS and now the dismissal of the claim, but also a risk of paying damages – and of course any risk of contempt or criminal proceedings.

However, the principled approach is the same. The difference in outcome arises from the different facts.

As to the possibility of seeking a wasted costs order, the ability to make such an application is not ousted by the fact of the discontinuance. However, as is the case with publicly funded claimants (see the guidance in *Symphony Group PLC v Hodgson*[31]) the court will be very astute to guard against the risk that the wasted costs application is motivated by an inability to recover costs against the claimant, rather than being a properly founded application for wasted costs against a solicitor. Wasted costs orders will not be made against a solicitor merely because they acted for a claimant in respect of a claim which is doomed to fail. The courts will assume, unless it can be established to the contrary, that the solicitor will have properly advised the client and will have been acting on instructions.

Q12. I need to discontinue proceedings against a number of defendants in an action. Obviously, when I file a notice of discontinuance, there will be a deemed order for costs against the claimant unless the court orders – otherwise (CPR r.38.6(1)). However, my understandings of QOCS (from rules 44.14, 44.15 and 44.16) is that an order for costs may only be enforced if the claim has been struck out (no court permission needed) or if it is fundamentally dishonest (court permission needed). We do not have sufficient time to obtain written consent from each and every defendant in a consent order but in any event consider that we would be QOCS protected even by serving a Notice of Discontinuance.

6–26   This is largely answered in the previous answer. A costs order will be deemed to be made against the claimant unless the court orders otherwise, pursuant to CPR r.38.6. Assuming the claim is within CPR r.44.13 and no other exception applies, then QOCS protection will be available. However, if the claim is one which might be said to have been brought in a 'fundamentally dishonest' fashion, the defendants will still be able to ask the court to grant permission to enforce some or all of the costs order.

There is also a risk that the defendants might be able to persuade the court to set aside the notice of discontinuance and ask the court instead to strike the claim out, to avail themselves of the exceptions under CPR r.44.15. Some discussion of the circumstances in which the same may be allowed and consideration of such case law as there is available to date is set out above.

C. QOCS and settlement offers

Q13. In respect of CPR r.44.14 (1) relating to QOCS, can an order for costs be made up to the extent of any damages when a Calderbank offer has been made, or does this rule only apply when a Part 36 offer has been made (i.e. this rule does not apply to Calderbank offers)?

---

[31] *Symphony Group PLC v Hodgson* [1993] 3 WLR 830, 842.

CPR r.44.14 (1) is unrelated to Part 36 (or indeed Calderbank offers). In any   6–27
situation where the defendant has a costs order in its favour – whether this be
an interim costs order due, say, to a disclosure application, a final costs order
because of a claimant's failure to beat a Part 36 or Calderbank offer or indeed
a costs order in favour of a defendant on detailed assessment, the order may
been enforced, without the court's permission, to its full extent save where
that full extent exceeds the aggregate amount the claimant was awarded by
way of damages and interest.

In this regard, the often used comment that, from a defendant's perspective, 'Part 36 trumps QOCS' must be approached with some circumspection.
Whilst it is correct that a Part 36 offer – or indeed a Calderbank offer – if effective, may lead to a costs order in the defendant's favour for part of the proceeding, that costs order itself is still subject to QOCS and therefore – absent
any of the QOCS exceptions being made out – can only be enforced to the
extent of damages and interest awarded to a claimant. Of course, Part 36 (or,
where appropriate, the use of Calderbank offers) remain powerful tools for
defendants in light of their ability to (i) deny a claimant their own costs after
a particular date and (ii) obtain an adverse costs order which has the potential
to diminish or extinguish the value of the claimant's claim. However, it would
be an error to operate on the basis that the successful use of a Part 36 offer
meant that the QOCS provisions did not apply.

D. QOCS and set off

**Q14. A claimant loses a personal injury claim and a costs order is made in
the usual way but the judge also finds fundamental dishonesty and thus
allows enforcement of the costs order totalling £7,210.00. The claimant
appeals against the finding of fundamental dishonesty, but not the loss
of the claim, and wins and so the finding of fundamental dishonesty is
quashed and the claimant is awarded costs of the appeal of £12,500.00.
The original order against the claimant in respect of the costs of losing the
personal injury claim remains in place but is now unenforceable. Could
the defendant, successful in the primary claim, set-off the £7,210.00 owed
to it, under the common law doctrine of set-off?**

The question of set off of costs against costs, whether under CPR r.44.12 or at   6–28
common law, is one of the unanswered questions about QOCS. It is discussed
in some detail above. There are some cogent arguments as to why such set off
should be allowed, particularly since QOCS only prevents enforcement and
a set off has not traditionally been seen as a form of enforcement. However,
equally QOCS might be thought to be an all-inclusive code of the circumstances in which a claimant may be 'liable' in whatever form for adverse costs.
The point is likely to be the subject of appellate consideration in due course.

E. QOCS and costs management

Q15. Do parties still have to costs budget where QOCS applies and, if so, is the agreeing of budgets in such cases likely to be more difficult?

6–29 In answer to the first part of the question, the answer is a simple 'yes', assuming the case is within CPR r.3.12. QOCS relates to enforcement only. Until a case is concluded, a defendant will not know whether or not the case is one where there might be good grounds to seek a disapplication of QOCS. In any event, the defendant may be in a position to enforce a costs order against damages without needing to seek to disapply QOCS. There are a wide range of situations where the defendant may be entitled to, and able to enforce, some or all of its costs. In any and all of these situations, the defendant will need to be able to quantify its costs and, if it has failed to file a costs budget, is likely to find those costs (at least post the date on which a budget should have been supplied) limited to court fees only pursuant to CPR r.3.18 or to suffer some other form of costs penalty or reduction.

As to agreeing budgets in such cases, there is no reason in principle why the budget should be more or less difficult to agree. QOCS also applies, for example, in publicly funded claims, where a not dissimilar form of costs protection exists. In both types of case, the budgeting rules apply without amendment. In practice, there will be concerns in such cases that defendants will be inclined to underestimate their own costs (because they are unlikely to be recovering them in many cases, or recovering them in full even in cases where some success is achieved), with a view to painting the claimant's budgeted costs as disproportionate by comparison. Also, that in such cases the perceived greater likelihood that the claimant will be recovering costs at the end of the case may make the defendant more inclined to take every opportunity to limit those costs, and therefore to take a more aggressive approach at the budgeting stage.

Anecdotally, it appears to be the case that the most regularly contested CCMCs relate to personal injury claims, including clinical negligence and there appears to be a greater willingness to agree budgets between the parties in commercial claims. Whether this has anything particularly to do with QOCS or is merely a reflection of the fact that personal injury has long been the hotbed of satellite costs litigation is a moot point.

F. QOCS – the future

Q16. Will QOCS be extended to other areas in due course?

6–30 This seems highly likely. If the mesothelioma exemption from the ending of between the parties recoverability of additional liabilities is ended, then QOCS for such cases is likely to be introduced at the same time, on the current lines. The extension of QOCS to publication and privacy claims was anticipated. However, the process is slow and it seems highly likely that in that area at least any model of QOCS introduced will differ significantly from the model in CPR 44 Part III. Other areas, in particular claims against the police, may benefit from a QOCS extension and in those cases at least it is likely that the QOCS regime will follow the current model. The extension to claims against the police, addressed in detail by the CJC Working Group (above) would appear to be the most compelling and also, perhaps, the simplest to introduce since it would slip relatively simply into the existing model (though such introduction might provide an opportunity to review some of the existing provisions).

CHAPTER 7

Fixed Costs; Indemnity Costs; Litigants in Person

Background

Part 45 of the Civil Procedure Rules deals with fixed costs and is divided into sections. The topics dealt with are as follows:

7-01

Section I	Fixed Costs in the normally accepted sense, i.e. costs which are payable in a given set of circumstances.
Section II	Road Traffic Accidents—fixed recoverable costs.
Section III	Pre-Action Protocol for Low Value Personal Injury Claims in Road Traffic Accidents and Low Value Personal Injury (Employers' Liability and Public Liability) Claims.
Section IIIA	Claims Which No Longer Continue Under the RTA and EL/PL Pre-Action Protocols-Fixed Recoverable Costs.
Section IV	Scale Costs for Claims in the IPEC.
Section V	Fixed Costs: HM Revenue & Customs.
Section VI	Fast Track Trial Costs.
Section VII	Costs Limits in Aarhus Convention claims.

Section I

Section I of Part 45 sets out the amounts which are to be allowed in respect of solicitors charges in cases to which it applies unless the court otherwise orders.[1] Any appropriate court fee will be allowed in addition to the costs set out in Section I. The fixed costs provisions apply where the only claim is a claim for a specified sum of money exceeding £25 and certain circumstances apply.[2] Section I also applies where (i) the only claim is a claim where the court gave a fixed date for the hearing when it issued the claim and judgment is given for the delivery of goods, and the value of the claim exceeds £25; (ii) the claim is for the recovery of land, including a possession claim under Part 55, whether or not the claim includes a claim for a sum of money and the defendant gives up possession, pays the amount claimed, if any, and the fixed commencement costs stated in the claim form; (iii) the claim is for the recovery of land, including a possession claim under Part 55, where one of the grounds for possession is arrears of rent, for which the court gave a fixed

---

[1] r.45.1(1) and see PD 45, paras 1.1–1.3.
[2] The provisions apply where: (i) judgment in default is obtained under r.12.4(1); (ii) judgment on admission is obtained under r.14.4(3); (iii) judgment on admission on part of the claim is obtained under r.14.5(6); (iv) summary judgment is given under Ptart 24; (v) the Court has made an order to strike out a defence under r.3.4(2)(a) as disclosing no reasonable grounds for defending the claim; or (vi) r.45.4 applies (defendant only liable for fixed commencement costs plus the relevant amount set out in Table 2).

date for the hearing when it issued the claim and judgment is given for the possession of land (whether or not the order for possession is suspended on terms) and the defendant:

(a) has neither delivered a defence, or counterclaim, nor otherwise denied liability; or

(b) has delivered a defence which is limited to specifying his proposals for the payment of arrears of rent;

(iv) the claim is a possession claim under Section II of Part 55 (accelerated possession claims of land let on an assured shorthold tenancy) and a possession order is made where the defendant has neither delivered a defence, or counterclaim, nor otherwise denied liability; (v) the claim is a demotion claim under Section III of Part 65 or a demotion claim is made in the same claim form in which a claim for possession is made under Part 55 and that demotion claim is successful; or (vi) a judgment creditor has taken steps under Parts 70 to 73 to enforce a judgment or order.

The provisions of CPR r.45.3 operate to apply the costs fixed by Section I of Part 45 when the defendant is liable only for fixed commencement costs, unless the court otherwise orders. The court refused to exercise its discretion to allow more than the fixed costs, on the particular facts of the case, stating, among other reasons:

> "...this Court has recognised the importance of a summary and prompt procedure to secure enforcement of adjudicators' decisions properly reached".
>
> "A party which makes a 'without prejudice save as to costs' offer is not entitled in some way to have it responded to or to assume that threatened proceedings against it will or might be withheld. It would be different if the without prejudice correspondence had revealed some agreement by which the claimant undertook, at least temporarily, not to issue proceedings ... It would not be fair to limit a successful claimant which complied with the steps called for in the rule and the [TCC] Guide".

The claimant was justified in issuing proceedings and the Part 24, summary judgment, application following a threatened defence and an unqualified admission on the part of the defendant after issue.[3]

Where the claimant has claimed fixed commencement costs under CPR r.45.2; and judgment is entered in a claim (to which CPR r.45.1(2)(a) or (b) applies) in the circumstances specified in Table 2, the amount to be included in the judgment for the claimant's legal representative's charges is the total of the fixed commencement costs; and the relevant amount shown in Table 2 depending on the particular type of judgment.[4]

---

[3] *Amber Construction Services Ltd v London Interspace HG Ltd* [2007] EWHC 3042 (TCC); [2008] 5 Costs L.R. 715; [2008] B.L.R. 74, Akenhead J.

[4] r.45.4.

The remainder of Part 45 Section I contains rules covering: the amount of fixed commencement costs in a claim for the recovery of land or a demotion; costs on entry of judgment in a claim for the recovery of land or a demotion claim; miscellaneous fixed costs; and fixed enforcement costs[5].

Section II

Section II of Part 45 sets out the costs allowable in proceedings relating to certain road traffic accidents. The provisions apply to road traffic accident disputes,[6] where the accident giving rise to the dispute occurred on or after 6 October 2003. The fixed costs provisions are intended to meet the case where the parties have been able to agree damages within certain limits but have been unable to agree the amount of costs. The agreed damages include damages in respect of personal injury, damage to property or both. The total value of the agreed damages must not exceed £10,000 or be within the small claims limit.[7] The provisions of this section do not apply where the claimant is a litigant in person, or where Sections III or IIIA of Part 45 apply[8]

Except where an application to exceed the fixed recoverable costs is made the only costs which are to be allowed are fixed recoverable costs calculated in accordance with CPR r.45.11; and disbursements allowed in accordance with CPR r.45.12[9]. CPR r.45.11 sets out how the fixed costs are to be calculated.

The court will only entertain a claim for costs greater than the fixed recoverable costs if it considers that there are exceptional circumstances making it appropriate to do so. Failure to achieve an amount 20% greater than the amount of the fixed recoverable costs, will result in an order that the defendant pay to the claimant the lesser of the fixed recoverable costs; and the assessed costs[10].

Section III

Section III: Pre-Action Protocols for Low Value Personal Injury Claims in Road Traffic Accidents and Low Value Personal Injury (Employers' Liability and Public Liability) Claims is in two distinct parts.

The RTA Protocol Scheme

The provisions of the RTA Protocol apply to a claim for damages exceeding £1,000, but not exceeding £10,000, arising from a road traffic accident occurring on or after 30 April, 2010, and before 31 July 2013, or a claim for damages not exceeding £25,000 arising from a road traffic accident occurring on or after 31 July 2013. Claims which fall within the scope of the scheme must follow the process, although a claimant is entitled to settle directly with an insurer/defendant without using the process. The process may be adopted by

7–02

---

[5] r 45.5–45.8.
[6] "Road traffic accident", "motor vehicle" and "road" are defined in r.45.9(4).
[7] r.45.9(2), r.26.8(2) sets out how the financial value of a claim is assessed for the purposes of allocation to track.
[8] r.45.9(3).
[9] r 45.10.
[10] r.45.13, 45.14.

agreement for claims arising from an accident prior to the implementation date, but the claimant's solicitor will only be allowed the fixed recoverable costs applicable to the new process.

The rules and practice directions are unusual, in that they relate to work done in accordance with the RTA and EL/PL Protocols, rather than (except in relation to Stage 3) to proceedings in court. The case will no longer continue under the Protocol if there is fraud at any stage, and under Stage 1 if there is no admission of liability or there is an allegation of contributory negligence; under Stage 2 if damages cannot be agreed. Stage 3 applies where quantum cannot be agreed; application is then made to the court to determine the quantum.

The pre-action protocol for low value personal injury claims in road traffic accidents has been amended as from 24 March 2016. Paragraph 1.1(A1)(a) and (b) reads as follows:-

> *"(A1)"Accredited medical expert" means a medical expert who*
> (a) *prepares a fixed cost medical report pursuant to paragraph 7.8A(1) before 1ˢᵗ June 2016 and, on the date that they are instructed, the expert is registered with MedCo as a provider of reports for soft tissue injury claims; or*
> (b) *prepares a fixed cost medical report pursuant to paragraph 7.8A(1) on or after 1ˢᵗ June 2016 and, on the date that they are instructed, the expert is accredited by MedCo to provide reports for soft tissue injury claims;"*

Changes have been made to the RTA Protocol, principally for the purpose of introducing a new regime in respect of the costs allowed for medical reports in claims to which the Protocol applies and which fall within the definition of "soft tissue injury claim" in paragraph 1.1(16A) of the Protocol. A "fixed cost medical report" is defined as a report in a soft tissue injury claim which is from a medical expert who, save in exceptional circumstances:

> *"(a) has not provided treatment to the claimant, (b) is not associated with any person who has provided treatment and (c) does not propose or recommend that they or an associate provide treatment"* (Protocol paragraph 1.1(10A)).

A low value RTA claim proceeding within the protocol did not automatically exit the protocol when the personal injury element of the claim was settled. The protocol was carefully designed to whittle down the disputes between the parties as the case passed through the various stages. CPR r.8.1(3) could not be used to subvert the protocol process. Where a district judge, faced with a claim where the only outstanding issue was the claim for car hire charges, decided that the claim was not suitable to continue under the Stage 3 procedure but should continue under CPR Part 7, the Court of Appeal held that the district judge had not been entitled to make that order. The cost which the district judge's order caused the parties to incur were totally disproportionate to the sum at stake (the amount in dispute being £462).[11]

---

[11] *Phillips v Willis* [2016] EWCA Civ. 401.

The Pre-action Protocol for Low Value Personal Injury (Employers' Liability and Public Liability) Claims

This protocol deals with low value personal injury employers' liability and public liability claims. An employers' liability claim is a claim by an employee against the employer for damages arising from a bodily injury sustained by the employee in the course of employment, or a disease that the claimant is alleged to have contracted as a consequence of the employer's breach of its duty of care in the course of the employee's employment, other than a physical or psychological injury caused by an accident or other single event. A public liability claim is a claim for damages for personal injuries arising out of a breach of duty of care made against a person other than the claimant's employer, or the claimant's employer in respect of matters arising other than in the course of the claimant's employment, but it does not include a claim for damages arising from a disease that the claimant is alleged to have contracted as a consequence of breach of a duty of care, other than a physical or psychological injury caused by an accident or other single event.[12]

7–03

The protocol sets out the behaviour which the court expects of the parties prior to the start of proceedings where a claimant claims damages not exceeding £25,000 in an EL or PL claim.[13] The EL/PL Protocol applies where either the claim arises from an accident occurring on or after 31 July 2013, or in a disease claim no letter of claim has been sent to the defendant before that date. The claim must include damages in respect of personal injury and must not exceed the upper limit of £25,000 on a full liability basis, including pecuniary losses but excluding interest. The claim must not be one in which the small claims track would be the normal track (i.e. the claim must be for more than £1,000). The protocol ceases to apply to a claim where at any stage the claimant notifies the defendant that the claim has now been re-valued at more than the upper limit.[14] The protocol does not apply to a claim:

(i) where the claimant or defendant acts as personal representative of a deceased person;

(ii) where the claimant or defendant is a protected party[15];

(iii) in a public liability claim—the defendant is an individual;

(iv) where the claimant is bankrupt;

(v) where the defendant is insolvent and there is no identifiable insurer;

(vi) in the case of a disease claim, where there is more than one employer defendant;

(vii) for personal injury arising from an accident or alleged breach of duty occurring outside England and Wales;

---

[12] EL/PL Protocol 1.1.
[13] EL/PL Protocol 2.1. The Civil Procedure Rules 1998 enable the court to impose costs sanctions where this Protocol is not followed.
[14] EL/PL Protocol 4.-4.2.
[15] As defined in r.21.1(2).

(viii)   for damages in relation to harm, abuse or neglect of or by children or vulnerable adults;
(ix)   which includes a claim for clinical negligence;
(x)   for mesothelioma; or
(xi)   for damages arising out of a road traffic accident.

The fixed costs in CPR r.45.18 apply in relation to a claimant only where a claimant has a legal representative.[16]

The Protocol procedure for both RTA and EL/PL is highly prescriptive and any further commentary would in effect be a mere repetition of the rules.

Section IIIA

7–04   With effect from 31 July 2013, Section IIIA applies where a claim is started under either the RTA or EL/PL Protocol, but no longer continues under the relevant protocol or the stage 3 procedure. This section does not apply to a disease claim which is started under the EL/PL Protocol.[17]

The Court of Appeal has decided the question whether a disposal hearing, listed for the quantification of damages payable after judgment under CPR r.26 PD12.2(1)(a) is or is not a trial within the meaning of CPR r.45.29E(4)(c). The issue turned on the special definition of *"trial"* for the purposes of EL/PL Protocol cases in CPR r.45.29E(4)(c). An identical definition applies in cases started under the RTA Protocol. Many EL/PL Protocol cases are dealt with at disposal hearings and if such a hearing constitutes listing for trial, the fixed costs recoverable are at a higher rate than would otherwise be the case where there is a settlement between the date of listing and the date fixed for the disposal hearing.

Lord Justice Briggs, who gave the leading judgment, stated:

> "6. *The issue with which this appeal is concerned is not fact sensitive. It is common ground that whenever an EL/PL Protocol case is listed for a disposal hearing after Judgment for damages to be assessed, under Part 26 PD12.2(1)(a), and is then settled before the date listed for that disposal hearing, then either the first or the third column in Table 6D Part B must be applicable so as to determine the fixed costs. The second column will not be applicable, since there will not have been a 'date of allocation under Part 26', because listing for disposal is an alternative to allocation to a track. . ."*

In the particular case, a customer visiting a garage was injured when a spanner was dropped on his hand. The claimant's solicitors entered his claim through the portal in September 2013. The defendant garage did not respond and the claim was withdrawn from the portal in October. Liability was, however, admitted in correspondence in November by the defendant's insurers. Although

---

[16] EL/PL Protocol 4.3, 4.4.
[17] r.45.29A. Nothing in Section IIIA prevents the Court from making an order under r.45.24 (Failure to comply or electing not to continue with the relevant Protocol-costs consequences).

medical evidence and details of special damages were submitted to the insurer, nothing was agreed and proceedings were issued in April 2014. The defendant failed to acknowledge service and default judgment was obtained in May 2014. The case was transferred from the County Court Money Claims Centre to the County Court at Birkenhead for assessment of damages. The matter was listed for a disposal hearing in September 2014.

The case then settled and a Tomlin Order was filed with the Court in July 2014, recording the terms of settlement. There was no agreement as to costs and the claimant's bill was provisionally assessed by the District Judge in December 2014. The defendant requested an oral review confined to the issue of which column, within Table 6D Part B, applied.

Having rehearsed the arguments, Briggs LJ stated:

"12. In my judgement, listing a case for a disposal hearing following Judgment pursuant to Part 26 PD12, is listing for trial, for the purposes of triggering column 3 in Table 6D Part B where a case which originated in the EL/PL Protocol settled after listing. My reasons follow.

"13. First listing a case for "disposal" means exactly what it says. The purpose of doing so is, so far as possible, finally to dispose of the case at first instance. A default or other judgment for damages to be assessed leaves that assessment outstanding, as the last stage in the final disposal of the proceedings. For that purpose, it matters not whether the judgment has been obtained by default (as here) or on an application for summary judgment on liability, judgment on admissions, or after a liability only trial: see generally Part 26 PD12(2)."

14. The fact that it may be impossible to tell, prior to the disposal hearing itself, whether it will prove to be final in that sense, or merely the occasion for giving Directions, cannot be conclusive against listing of a disposal hearing triggering column 3 of Table 6D Part B because that table is concerned with settlement prior to trial. If the possibility of a disposal hearing being used for the giving only of Directions were to be admitted, then it is hard to see how listing could ever be a trigger for the application of column 3 following a settlement. Even the hearing date of a full trial may turn into a hearing for Directions if it proves impossible or unjust to do otherwise than permit an adjournment.

15. Secondly, the fact that a disposal hearing might prove to be uncontested is, again, neither here nor there. It is common ground that, even after a Judgment in default, the Defendant may attend and oppose the Claimant's case as to quantification of damages at the disposal hearing. Again, if the possibility that such a hearing might prove to be uncontested were sufficient to prevent its listing being a trigger for the application of column 3, then that possibility exists at all kinds of final hearing, including traditional trials.

16. Thirdly, as DJ Campbell emphasised, listing for a disposal hearing is the trigger for the Claimant (and any other party which wishes to take an active part at that hearing) to prepare and serve the requisite evidence. . .

17. Fourthly, there is a useful pre-history to the formulation 'final contested hearing' in Part 45.29E(4)(c). Part 45.15 deals with the success fee percentages *applicable in road traffic accident claims. By Part 45.15(6)(b), as it was before April 2013, a reference to 'trial' was a reference to the final contested hearing. This rule was introduced in 2004. <u>Lamont v Burton</u> [2007] 1 WLR 2814 was about a road traffic accident claim which had concluded at a disposal hearing. It was taken for granted in this court (rather than determined after argument) that the disposal hearing had been a trial for the purposes of Part 45.15. I consider it very likely that, when it adopted the same definition of trial in 2013 for the purposes of fixed costs in the EL / PL Protocol cases, the Rule Committee had the analysis in <u>Lamont v Burton</u> well in mind."*

The appeal was dismissed[18].

The Court of Appeal has considered, in respect of claims started under the RTA protocol, whether the fixed costs regime continues to apply to a case which no longer continues under the RTA protocol but is allocated to the multi-track after being issued under Part 7. Lord Justice Briggs gave the leading judgment. He pointed out that the court was required not merely to interpret the relevant provisions of Section IIIA of CPR Part 45 together with the relevant provisions of the RTA protocol but also to consider whether they suffer from an obvious drafting mistake which could be put right so as to bring them into compatibility with the intention of the Civil Procedure Rule Committee. The EL/PL protocol has a very similar fixed costs regime and although the appeals before the court concern cases within the RTA protocol, it is expected that their outcome will affect the interpretation and application of the similar and overlapping provisions in Part 45 about the EL/PL protocol. The judge reviewed the provisions of the fixed costs regime including Table 6B. Briggs LJ stated:

"14. ... The formulation of the detailed tabular provisions for the recovery of fixed costs in relation to claims started but no longer continuing under the relevant protocols was developed upon an assumption that, if Part 7 proceedings were issued, they would in due course be allocated to the fast track, if not determined at a disposal hearing following judgment for damages to be assessed ...

15. ... claims for an amount for more than £25,000, or claims likely to require a trial lasting longer than one day or the deployment of multiple expert witnesses, are normally allocated to the multi-track. Plainly, they involve the expenditure of costs on a scale which will be higher, and often much higher, than the requisite for the determination of claims in the fast track ..."

Briggs LJ gave three examples of cases likely to be allocated to the multi-track rather than the fast-track:

(i) Where a claim originally thought to be worth no more than £25,000 is revalued at a substantially higher level;

---

[18] *Bird v Acorn Group Limited* [2016] EWCA Civ 1096.

(ii) Because of the exclusion of vehicle related damages from the valuation of a claim for the application of the RTA Protocol, where the aggregate of the non-vehicle related damages is below £25,000 but the claim then ceases to continue within the Portal because liability is in issue, the Part 7 claim may then be well in excess of £25,000;

(iii) Where a claim is properly started in the RTA protocol but is met by an allegation that the claim has been dishonestly fabricated. Such proceedings are inherently likely to be pursued and defended on the basis that no stone is left unturned and therefore at very substantial cost.

There is a problem because there is nothing in Part 45.29 which expressly limits the fixed costs regime applicable to cases started but no longer continuing under the relevant protocol to fast track cases, or which excludes the fixed costs regime when a case is allocated to the multi-track. CPR r.45.29J provides for relief in exceptional circumstances, but only by permitting the court to conduct an immediate summary assessment or make an order for detailed assessment neither of which appear apposite at the case management stage when allocation takes place. CPR r.45.29J appears to offer a measure of relief only at the end of a trial or other resolution of the proceedings.

In *Qader*, the judges at first instance and on appeal were persuaded that Part 45.29 clearly provided that fixed costs should apply notwithstanding allocation to the multi-track. In the conjoined appeal of *Khan v McGee*, the District Judge allocated the case to the multi-track but took the view that this disapplied the fixed costs regime and directed filing of costs budgets and adjourned the case to a CCMC. Briggs LJ concluded:

> "35. *After more hesitation than my Lords I have come to the conclusion that section IIIA of Part 45 should be read as if the fixed costs regime which it prescribes for cases which start within the RTA protocol but then no longer continue under it is automatically disapplied in any case allocated to the multi-track, without the requirement for the claimant to have recourse to Part 45.29J, by demonstrating exceptional circumstances. . . .".*

Briggs LJ then set out his reasoning at some length and went into the history of the making of the fixed costs scheme continuing:

> "54. *In the present case the Rule Committee's apparent failure to implement the continuing intention of the Government, in response to stakeholder concerns, to exclude multi-track cases from the fixed costs regime being enacted for cases leaving the RTA and EL/PL protocols seems to me to satisfy all three of Lord Nicholls' preconditions [see Inco Europe Limited v. First Choice Distribution[19]]. The intended purpose of the fixed costs regime in this context was that it should apply as widely as possible (and therefore to cases allocated to the fast track, and to cases sent for quantification of*

---

[19] [2000] 1 WLR 586 at 592.

> *damages at disposal hearings), but not to cases where there had been a judicial determination that they should continue in the multi-track. The intended restriction on the ambit of the fixed costs regime is clear, and the only reason for that restriction not being enacted in section 3A of Part 45 appears to be inadvertence, rather than a deliberate decision by the rule committee to take a different course . . .*
>
> . . .
>
> 56. *The best way to give effect to that intention seems to me to add this phrase to Part 45.29B, after the reference to 45.29J:*
>   *". . . and for so long as the claim is not allocated to the multi-track . . ."*[20]

The wording has been corrected, as recommended by Briggs LJ, by the Civil Procedure (Amendment) Rules 2017 paragraph 8.[21]

In respect of applications for pre-action disclosure (PAD) in claims which started but no longer continue under the EL/PL Protocol the Court of Appeal had to decide whether the fixed costs regime under Section IIIA of Part 45 applied to such application. Part 46, Section 1 makes specific provision (distinct from the general rules about costs) for the costs of PAD applications both in the High Court and the County Court departing from the ordinary general rule under CPR r.44.2, namely: that the unsuccessful party pays. Lord Justice Briggs, who again gave the leading judgment stated:

> *"30. In my judgment the fixed costs regime plainly applies to the costs of a PAD application made by a claimant who is pursuing a claim for damages for personal injuries which began with the issue of a CNF in the portal pursuant to the EL/ PL Protocol but which at the time of the PAD application, is no longer continuing under that protocol . . .*
>
> *31. The starting point is that the plain object and intent of the fixed costs regime in relation to claims of this kind is that, from the moment of entry into the portal pursuant to the EL/PL Protocol (and, for that matter, the RTA Protocol as well) recovery of the costs of pursuing or defending that claim at all subsequent stages is intended to be limited to the fixed rates of recoverable costs, subject only to a very small category of clearly stated exceptions. To recognise implied exceptions in relation to such claim related activity and expenditure would be destructive of the clear purpose of the fixed costs regime which is to pursue the elusive objective of proportionality in the conduct of the small or relatively modest types of claim to which that regime currently applies.*
>
> *32. That conclusion is, in my view, expressly prescribed by the clear words of Part 45.29A(1) and 45.29D. In particular, paragraph D provides that the fixed costs and disbursements prescribed by the regime (in paragraph 29E and I respectively) are "the only costs allowed". Although this is subject to paragraphs F, H and J they are each part of the fixed costs regime, even though they permit different or enlarged recovery in certain precisely defined circumstances.*

---

[20] *Qader v Esure Services Limited and Khan v. McGee* [2016] EWCA Civ 1109.
[21] SI 2017/95.

. . .

35. For those reasons it seems to me entirely apposite for a PAD application to fall within the description of interim applications in Part 45.29H, as being "an interim application . . . in a case to which this section applies. . . ."

It had become apparent during the submissions that insurance backed defendants were frequently failing in their protocol disclosure obligations, unless a PAD application was made. Counsel for the appellant argued that including the costs of such applications within the fixed costs regime would largely deprive such applications of their value as a spur to proper compliance. In respect of this submission, Briggs LJ stated:

"39. But in my judgment the answer to this submission lies not in subjecting the fixed costs regime to an implied exemption for PAD applications which exposed recalcitrant defendants to an altogether higher but variable level of recoverable costs liability, to be determined by assessment. Rather the answer lies in the availability of an application under Part 45.29J, if exceptional circumstances can be shown or, for the future, in recognition by the Rule Committee that the fixed costs regime needs to be kept under review, and defects in it remedied by adjustment of the fixed allowances where they can be shown to be justified."[22]

The remainder of Part 45 IIIA deals, among other things, with: the application of fixed costs and disbursements – RTA Protocol; the amount of fixed costs – RTA Protocol; the application of fixed costs and disbursements – EL/PL Protocol; and the amount of fixed costs – EL/PL Protocol[23]. The Part also deals with: disbursements; claims for an amount of costs exceeding fixed recoverable costs; and failure to achieve costs greater than fixed recoverable costs. If it considers that there are exceptional circumstances making it appropriate to do so, the court will consider a claim for an amount of costs (excluding disbursements) which is greater than the fixed recoverable costs referred to in rules 45.29B to 45.29H. Failure to achieve an amount 20% greater than the amount of the fixed recoverable costs, will result in an order for the party who made the claim to be paid the lesser of the fixed recoverable costs; and the assessed costs[24].

An RTA claim proceeding under CPR Part 45 IIIA was listed for trial and on the day the parties were granted further time for negotiation and the matter settled, the claimant being awarded damages and costs. A recorder refused to award the fixed trial advocacy fee on the basis that the case had settled before the final contested hearing had commenced. On appeal, Coulson J. held that the case had not settled prior to the date of trial and the costs should have been dealt with under Section C of Table 6B. It did not strain the language of the rule to conclude that the case was disposed of at trial albeit by way of settlement rather than judgment. There were sound policy reasons for concluding that

---

[22] *Sharp v Leeds City Council* [2017] EWCA Civ. 33.
[23] r 45.29–45.29E.
[24] r.45.29I-45.29K.

the interests of justice would be better served if the advocate were not penalised financially for negotiating a settlement at the door of the court.[25]

In the two appeals before the court one, *Broadhurst,* had been limited to the fixed costs in Table 6 whilst in the other, *Smith,* the Judge had not limited the costs to Table 6.

The court was referred to the Explanatory Memorandum to the 2013 Amendment Rules:

> "... *If a defendant refuses a claimant's offer to settle and the court subsequently awards the claimant damages which are greater than or equal to the sum they were prepared to accept in the settlement, the claimant will not be limited to receiving his fixed costs, but will be entitled to costs assessed on the indemnity basis in accordance with rule [36.17]."*

The Master of the Rolls giving judgment with which the other members of the court agreed said:

> "23 *rule 45.29B does not stand alone. The need to take account of Part 36 offers in section IIIA cases was recognised by the draftsman of the rules. Indeed, rule 36.14A [36.17] is headed "costs consequences following judgment where section IIIA of Part 45 applies". Rule 45.29F (8) provides that, where a Part 36 offer is accepted in a section IIIA case, "rule 36.10A [36.20] will apply instead of this rule". And rule 45.29F(9) provides that, where in such a case upon judgment being entered the claimant fails to obtain a judgment more advantageous than the claimant's Part 36 offer, "rule 36.14A [36.21] will apply instead of this rule". Rule 45.29F does not, however, make provision as to what should happen where the claimant makes a successful Part 36 offer.*
>
> 25 *The effect of rules 36.14 [36.17] and 36.14A [36.21] when read together is that, where a claimant makes a successful Part 36 offer, he is entitled to costs assessed on the indemnity basis. Thus, rule 36.14 [36.17] is modified only to the extent stated by 36.14A [36.21]. Since rule 36.14(3) [36.17(4)] has not been modified by rule 36.14A [36.21], it continues to have full force and effect. The tension between rule 45.29B and rule 36.14A [36.21] must, therefore, be resolved in favour of rule 36.14A [36.21].*
>
> 31 *Where a claimant makes a successful Part 36 offer in a section IIIA case, he will be awarded fixed costs to the last staging point provided by rule 45.29C and Table 6B. He will then be awarded costs to be assessed on the indemnity basis in addition from the date that the offer became effective. This does not require any apportionment. It will, however, lead to a generous outcome for the claimant."*[26]

Section IV

Section IV of Pt 45 sets out the scale costs for claims in the IPEC. The provisions do not apply where the court considers that a party has behaved in a manner which amounts to an abuse of the court's process or the claim

---

[25] *Mendes v Hochtief (UK) Construction Limited* [2016] EWHC 976 (QB), Coulson J.
[26] *Broadhurst (1) Taylor (2) v Tan (1) Smith(2)* [2016] EWCA Civ 94.

concerns the infringement or revocation of a patent or registered design, the validity of which has been certified by a court in earlier proceedings.[27]

The court will make a summary assessment of the costs of the party in whose favour any order for costs is made. CPR rules 44.2(8), 44.6(b) and Pt 47 do not apply to Section IV.[28] The court will reserve the costs of an application to the conclusion of the trial when they will be subject to summary assessment.

Save where a party has behaved unreasonably the court will not order a party to pay total costs of more than £50,000 on the final determination of a claim in relation to liability; and £25,000 on an inquiry as to damages or account of profits. The amounts above apply after the court has applied the provision on set off in accordance with CPR r.44.12(a). The maximum amount of scale costs that the court will award for each stage of the claim is set out in Practice Direction 45. The amount of the scale costs awarded by the court will depend on the nature and complexity of the claim. Subject to assessment, the following may be recovered in addition to the amount of the scale costs set out in Practice Direction 45: court fees; costs relating to the enforcement of any court order; and wasted costs. Where appropriate, VAT may be recovered in addition to the amount of the scale costs and any reference in Section IV to scale costs is a reference to those costs net of any such VAT[29].

Where a party has behaved unreasonably the court may make an order for costs at the conclusion of the hearing. Where the court makes a summary assessment of costs it will do so in accordance with Section IV of Part 45.[30]

The Intellectual Property Enterprise Court could only depart from the overall caps on costs and scale costs in truly exceptional circumstances. It was, however, possible not to apply scale costs for one or more of earlier stages of the claim provided the total award remained within the overall cap. Under CPR r.45.30(2), the overall IPEC cap could only be lifted where the court considered that a party had behaved in a manner which amounted to an abuse of process; or the claim concerned a registered right whose validity had been certified in earlier proceedings.[31] The court has an overriding discretion under CPR r.44.2 to award costs outside the cap in a truly exceptional case. In the instant case, the claimant's conduct had not been ideal but was not close to an abuse and was not truly exceptional. The overall cap of £50,000 was not disturbed. The general discretion to lift one or more of the caps on stage costs could be exercised in less than truly exceptional circumstances if the result was that the overall cap on total costs was left undisturbed. The defendants were awarded an extra £5,000 above the IPEC application cap.[32]

In patent infringement proceedings, the court found in favour of the

---

[27] r.45.30(1) and (2).
[28] r.45.30(3).
[29] r.45.31
[30] r.45.32 and r.63.26.
[31] See *FH Brundle v Perry* [2014] EWHC 979 (IPEC).
[32] *Skyscape Cloud Services Limited v. Sky Plc* [2016] EWHC, 8 June (IPEC), HHJ Hacon.

defendants in respect of the claimant's claim for misrepresentation and the defendants' counterclaim for royalties.

The claimants' claim of unjustified threats of patent infringement proceedings remained undecided. The defendants sought their costs in relation to the decided issues. The claimants argued that the assessment should be adjourned until the remaining allegations had beendealt with. The court held that the word "*claim*" in CPR r.45.31(1)(a) referred to a single set of proceedings. Accordingly, the court could not assess costs until all the issues including the threat allegation had been resolved.[33]

Section V

Section V of Part 45 sets out the amounts which are to be allowed in respect of HMRC charges in specified cases, unless the court orders otherwise.[34] Part 8 applies where the only claim is a claim conducted by an HMRC officer in the County Court for recovery of a debt, and the Commissioners obtain judgment on the claim. Any appropriate court fee will be allowed in addition to the costs set out in Tables 9 and 10 and the claim may include a claim for fixed commencement costs.[35]

Table 9 sets out the fixed costs on commencement of the County Court claim conducted by an HMRC officer, the amount claimed in the claim form is used to determine which band in Table 9 apples. Table 10 sets out fixed costs on entry of judgment in a County Court claim conducted by an HMRC officer. The total to be included in the judgment for HMRC charges is the total of the fixed commencement costs, and the amount in Table 10 relevant to the value of the claim. In cases where the only claim is for a specified sum of money, and the defendant pays the money claimed within 14 days after service of the particulars of claim, together with the fixed commencement costs stated in the claim form, the defendant will not be liable for any further costs unless the court orders otherwise.[36]

Section VI

7–05 Section VI of Part 45 governs the amount of fast track trial costs and their application. "Fast track trial costs" means the cost of a party's advocate for preparing for and appearing at the trial. It does not include any other disbursements, or any VAT payable on the advocate's fees. The "trial" includes a hearing where the court decides an amount of money or the value of goods. "Trial" does not include the hearing of an application for summary judgment, or the court's approval of a settlement or other compromise by, or on behalf of, a child or protected party.[37]

---

[33] *Global Flood Defence Systems Limited (1) UK Flood Barriers Limited (2) v Johann van den Noort Beheer BV (1) Johann Heinrich Reindert van den Noort (2) Flood Control International Limited (3)* [2016] EWHC 189 (IPEC) HHJ Hacon.
[34] r.45.33. "HMRC charges" are claimed as "legal representative's costs" on relevant Court forms and means the fixed costs set out in Tables 9 and 10 of Section V.
[35] r.45.33(3)–(6).
[36] r.45.34, 35 and 36 and Tables 9 and 10.
[37] Under r.21.10; r.45.37(1) and (2) and Practice Direction 45, paras 4.1–4.3.

Section VII Prior to 28 February 2017

Section VII of Part 45 limits the amount of costs recoverable in Aarhus Convention claims.[38] The Civil Procedure (Amendment) Rules 2017[39] introduced an entirely new version of Section VII. The amendments in relation to Section VII and in respect of orders to limit the recoverable costs of an appeal in an Aarhus Convention claim under CPR r.52.19A (see below), apply in relation to Aarhus Convention claims commenced on or after 28 February 2017.

> "45.41(2) . . . *An Aarhus Convention claim means a claim brought by one or more members of the public*
>
> (i) *By judicial review or review under statute which challenges the legality of any decision act or omission of a body exercising public functions and which is within the scope of Article 9(1) or 9(2) of the UNECE Convention on Access to Information, Public Participation in Decision Making and Access to Justice in Environmental Matters done at Aarhus Denmark on the 25th June 1998; or*
>
> (ii) *By judicial review which challenges the legality of any such decision act or omission and which is within the scope of Article 9(3) of the Aarhus Convention.*"

Section VII does not apply to appeals other than appeals brought under s.289(1) of the Town and Country Planning Act 1990 or s.65(1) of the Planning (Listed Buildings and Conservation Areas) Act 1990 which are, for the purposes of Section VII, to be treated as reviews under statute.[40]

Where a claimant, who is a member of the public, has stated in the claim form that the claim is an Aarhus Convention claim, and filed and served with the claim form a schedule of the claimant's financial resources which takes into account any financial support which any person has provided or is likely to provide to the claimant and which is verified by a statement of truth, CPR r.45.43 to CPR r.45.55[41] do not apply, provided that the claimant has stated in the claim form that, although the claim is an Aarhus Convention claim, the claimant does not wish those Rules to apply. If there is more than one claimant, CPR r.45.43 to CRP r.45.45 do not apply in relation to costs payable by or to any claimant who has not filed and served a schedule of the claimant's financial resources etc. as set out above or has stated that the claimant does not wish those Rules to apply or is not a member of the public.[42]

Limit on costs recoverable from a party in an Aarhus Convention claim

A claimant or defendant in an Aarhus Convention claim may not be ordered to pay costs exceeding, in the case of a claimant, £5,000 where the claimant

---

[38] An Aarhus Convention claim means a claim for judicial review of a decision, act or omission all or part of which is subject to the provisions of the UNECE Convention on Access to Information Public Participation in Decision Making and Access to Justice in Environmental Matters done at Aarhus, Denmark on 25 June 1998, including a claim which proceeds on the basis that the decision, act or omission or part of it is so subject – r.45.41(2).

[39] SI 2017/95.

[40] CPR r.45.41. CPR r.52.19A makes provision in relation to costs of an appeal.

[41] CPR r.45.43. Limit on costs recoverable from a party in an Aarhus Convention claim. CPR r.45.44. Varying the limit on costs recoverable from a party in an Aarhus Convention claim. CPR r.45.45. Challenging whether the claim is an Aarhus Convention claim.

[42] CPR r.45.42.

is claiming only as an individual or not as or on behalf of a business or other legal person; or £10,000 in all other cases. In the case of a defendant the amount is £35,000.

Where there are multiple claimants or multiple defendants, the amount set out above (subject to any direction by the court) apply in relation to each claimant or defendant individually and may not be exceeded irrespective of the number of receiving parties. These provisions are subject to cases where CPR r.45.43 to CPR r.45.45 do not apply to a claimant (under CPR r.45.42) or to cases in which the court varies the limit on costs recoverable (under CPR r.45.44).[43]

Varying the limit on costs recoverable from a party in an Aarhus Convention claim

The court has the power to vary the amounts set out above and may remove altogether the limits on maximum costs liability. The court may do this only if it is satisfied that to do so would not make the costs of the proceedings pro-hibitively expensive for the claimant; and where the variation would reduce the claimant's maximum liability or increase that of a defendant without the variation, the costs of the proceedings would be prohibitively expensive for the claimant.

CPR r.45.44 sets out when proceedings are to be considered prohibitively expensive as follows: if the likely costs of the proceedings (including any court fees payable by the claimant) either exceed the financial resources of the claimant; or are objectively unreasonable having regard to:

(i)   the situation of the parties;
(ii)   whether the claimant has a reasonable prospect of success;
(iii) the importance of what is at stake for the claimant;
(iv)   the importance of what is at stake for the environment;
(v)   the complexity of the relevant law and procedure; and
(vi)   whether the claim is frivolous.

When the court is considering the financial resources of the claimant, it has to have regard to any financial support which any person has provided or is likely to provide to the claimant.[44]

Challenging whether the claim is an Aarhus Convention claim

Where a claimant has stated in the claim form that the claim is an Aarhus Convention claim and complied with CPR r.45.42(1) (and subject to the exceptions in CPR r.45.42(2) and (3)), CPR r.45.3 (Limit on recoverable costs) will apply unless the defendant has denied in the acknowledgement of service that the claim is an Aarhus Convention claim and has set out the

---

[43] CPR r.45.43.
[44] CPR Rule 45.44. Rule 39.2(3)(c) makes provision for a hearing to be in private if it involves confidential information (including information relating to personal financial matters) and publicity would damage that confidentiality.

grounds for such a denial and the court is determined that the claim is not an Aarhus Convention claim. Where the defendant denies the claim is an Aarhus Convention claim, the issue must be determined at the earliest opportunity. If the court holds that the claim is not an Aarhus Convention claim it will normally make no order for costs in relation to those proceedings; if it holds that it is such a claim, it will normally order the defendant to pay the claimant's costs of those proceedings on the standard basis and that order may be enforced even if this would increase the costs payable by the defendant beyond the amount stated in CPR r.45.43(3) or any variation of it.[45]

Orders to limit the recoverable costs of an appeal in Aarhus Convention claims

A new CPR r.52.19A has been added to Part 52 which provides that in an appeal against a decision made in an Aarhus Convention claim to which CPR r.45.43 to 45.45 apply, the Court must consider whether the costs of proceedings will be prohibitively expensive for a party who was a claimant; and if they think it will be, make an order limiting the recoverable costs to the extent necessary to prevent this. When considering the financial resources of a party, the court must have regard to any financial support which any person has provided or is likely to provide to that party.[46]

Section VII Prior to 28 February 2017

Lord Justice Jackson: Review of Fixed Costs

1. In the Supreme Court in *Coventry v Lawrence*[47] Lord Neuberger commented:

    [36]. . .it would be wrong for this court not to express its grave concern about the base costs in this case, and express the hope that those responsible for civil justice in England and Wales are considering what further steps can be taken to ensure better access to justice.

2. Sir Rupert Jackson recommended that there should be a fixed costs regime for the whole of the fast-track and at the lower end of the multi-track. Professor Paul Fenn carried out a great deal of work during the course of the Jackson Review and produced a matrix for fixed costs across the fast track based on a considerable amount of data which had been made available to him by the ABI and others. The matrix was published in the final report having been accepted both by Jackson LJ and his assessors. The fixed costs in relation to Low Value Personal Injury Claims in Road Traffic Accidents ("the RTA protocol") or for Low Value Personal Injury (Employers' Liability and Public Liability) Claims ("the EL/PL protocol") have been reduced significantly below the earlier figures which had been

---

[45] CPR Rule 45.45.
[46] CPR Rule 52.19A.
[47] [2014] UKSC 46; [2015] AC 106.

the result of industry–wide agreement. The new figures appear to have been arrived at following the prohibition of referral fees by reducing the previous figures by the perceived amount of referral fees. This has done nothing to reduce arguments about hourly rates since solicitors now argue that instead of paying referral fees, they have to pay the same or larger amounts in marketing costs.

3. On 28 January 2016 Lord Justice Jackson delivered a speech[48] about extending fixed costs to the whole of the Fast Track and the lower end of the Multi Track up to claims for £250,000.

4. He suggested that his ideas should include clinical negligence actions. He set out a grid with four different value bands and ten stages based on the stages in Precedent H. His scheme was essentially a variation of the ABC/123 scheme in use in New Zealand.

5. On 11 November 2016 Lord Justice Jackson was commissioned to undertake a review of fixed recoverable costs. The review was commissioned by Lord Thomas, the Lord Chief Justice, and Sir Terence Etherton, the Master of the Rolls. The review's recommendations will help to inform a Government public consultation on reforms to extend fixed recoverable costs to further areas of civil litigation.

6. The terms of reference for the review are:

   1. To develop proposals for extending the present civil fixed recoverable costs regime in England and Wales so as to make the costs of going to court more certain, transparent and proportionate for litigants.

   2. To consider the types and areas of litigation in which such costs should be extended, and the value of claims to which such a regime should apply.

   3. To report to the Lord Chief Justice and the Master of the Rolls by 31 July 2017.

7. On 30 January 2017 the Government launched an open consultation on fixed recoverable costs for clinical negligence claims, seeking views on proposals for a mandatory system of fixed recoverable costs for lower value clinical negligence claims in England and Wales.[49]

"The proposed fixed recoverable costs scheme aims to improve the efficiency and cost-effectiveness of clinical negligence claims by supporting:

- *quicker and more cost effective resolution for all parties;*
- *greater opportunities for early learning of lessons from harmful incidents to inform safer clinical practice;*
- *access to justice for those claimants bringing clinical negligence claims of a low monetary value, but complex nature;*

---

[48] https://www.judiciary.gov.uk/wp-content/uploads/2016/01/fixedcostslecture-1.pdf
[49] Between £1,000 and £25,000.

- *patients' access to justice by streamlining the system and incentivising earlier resolution of such claims"*.[50]

The consultation closes on 1 May 2017.

When considering whether to make an order for costs on the indemnity basis the trial judge has a wide discretion but it is critical that there be some conduct or circumstance that takes a case out of the norm. Such factors include the high-risk situation where a claim is speculative, weak, opportunistic or thin, and where a claimant commenced and pursued large-scale and expensive litigation in circumstances calculated to exert unfair and commercial pressure on a defendant to renegotiate what had become a commercially unattractive contract. The fact that one party lost resoundingly, does not automatically mean that the other should be awarded costs on the indemnity basis. On the facts, an order for costs on the indemnity basis was not made although it had not been unreasonable for the successful party to seek such an order.[51] The provisions of Section VII do not apply where the claimant has not stated in the claim form that the claim is an Aarhus Convention claim, or has stated that it is not an Aarhus Convention claim, or, although it is such a claim, the claimant does not wish those rules to apply.[52] If the claimant has stated in the claim form that the claim is an Aarhus Convention claim, the limits on costs apply unless the defendant has in the acknowledgment of service denied that the claim is an Aarhus Convention claim and has set out the grounds for that denial and the court has determined that the claim is not an Aarhus Convention claim. In such a case, the court is required to determine the issue at the earliest opportunity. If the court holds that the claim is not an Aarhus Convention claim it will normally make no order for costs in relation to those proceedings. If it holds that the claim is an Aarhus Convention claim, it will normally order the defendant to pay the claimant's costs of those proceedings on the indemnity basis and the order may be enforced notwithstanding that this would increase the costs payable by the defendant beyond the amount to which such Convention claims are limited.[53] Subject to the above, a party to an Aarhus Convention claim may not be ordered to pay costs exceeding £5,000 where the claimant is claiming only as an individual and not as or on behalf of a business or other legal person, or £10,000 in all other cases.[54] Where a defendant is ordered to pay costs the amount recoverable is limited to £35,000.[55]

The Environmental Protective Costs Orders regime in Part 45, Section VII applies to Aarhus Convention cases (where members of the public challenge decisions on environmental matters taken by public authorities)[56]. Similarly,

---

[50] https://www.gov.uk/government/consultations/fixed-recoverable-costs-for-clinical-negligence-claims
[51] *Obrascon Huarte Lain SA v Government of Gibraltar* [2014] EWHC 5 June (TCC) Akenhead J.
[52] r.45.42.
[53] r.45.44.
[54] r.45.43, PD 45, para.5.1.
[55] r.45.43, PD 45, para.5.2.
[56] *R (HS2 Action Alliance and Another) v Secretary of State for Transport and Another* [2015] EWCA Civ. 203; [2015] 2 Costs L R 411.

"Environment" is to be given a broad meaning. A decision granting authorisation to carry out surveys, both non-intrusive and intrusive, related to the environment, especially when that was given a broad meaning. Accordingly, the claim benefited from the protection of the Convention.[57] The availability of protective costs orders for environmental cases falling within the Aarhus Convention had been deliberately limited to judicial review claims and did not extend to statutory appeals or applications. Accordingly, it was not appropriate for the court to exercise its discretion to grant cross-protection in respect of an application to quash planning permission under the Town & Country Planning Act 1990 s.288, as this would side-step the limitation deliberately enacted in the CPR to give effect to a convention which had not been directly incorporated into domestic law. Legislative action was necessary to remedy CPR r.45.41's non-compliance with the Convention (it applies only in relation to judicial review proceedings).[58]

Several individuals and a Parish Council failed in judicial proceedings in respect of planning permission granted by the Borough Council. The Borough Council sought costs of £15,000 and argued that the individual claimants should pay the costs in the amount of £5,000 and the Parish Council in the amount of £10,000. The administrative court held that where a claimant is ordered to pay costs in an Aarhus Convention claim, the amount ordered must not exceed £5,000 where the claimant claimed only as an individual; and otherwise must not exceed £10,000. The individual claimants fell into the first category and the Parish Council into the second. It was accordingly appropriate to consider the liability of the two sets of claimants separately and to award costs against each up to the maximum of the respective costs cap[59].

The Ministry of Justice launched a consultation on its proposals to adjust the costs protection for environmental claims under the Aarhus Convention on 17 September 2015. This was mainly in response to a number of cases that challenged whether the pre-2013 CPR r.45 costs protection for environmental legal challenges complied with the Aarhus Convention, in particular, whether it was prohibitively expensive as follows: *R (Edwards) v Environment Agency* [2010] UKSC 57 and (No 2) [2013] UKSC 78; and *European Commission v United Kingdom* [2014] EUECJ C-530/11. The judgments also clarified that, in meeting the requirement not to be prohibitively expensive, the CCO regime under CPR r.45 from 2013 for Aarhus Convention claims could be made significantly more flexible.

The consultation closed on the 10 December 2015. On 17 November 2016, the Ministry of Justice (MoJ) published the response to the consultation The *Edwards* principles are that the costs of proceedings must not subjectively be prohibitively expensive (exceed the financial resources of the claimant) and must not appear objectively to be unreasonable.

---

[57] *R. (Dowley) v Secretary of State for Communities and Local Government.* [2016] EWHC 2618 (Admin) Patterson J.
[58] *Secretary of State for Communities & Local Government v Venn* [2014] EWCA Civ 1539.
[59] *R (Botley Parish Action Group) v Eastleigh Borough Council* [2014] EWHC 4388 (Admin), Collins J.

The government reforms include:

- Extending the CCO regime for Aarhus Convention claims beyond judicial review to include environmental reviews under statute that engage EU law. Importantly, this should include applications under s.288 of the Town and Country Planning Act 1990 questioning the validity of planning decisions.
- Introducing a hybrid costs capping regime, which allows caps to be varied up or down, if appropriate, and requires the claimant to provide financial information from the start.

The 2017 Amendment Rules are the result.

Lord Justice Jackson: Review of Fixed Costs

1. In the Supreme Court in *Coventry v Lawrence*[60] Lord Neuberger commented:

> *[36]. . .it would be wrong for this court not to express its grave concern about the base costs in this case, and express the hope that those responsible for civil justice in England and Wales are considering what further steps can be taken to ensure better access to justice.*

2. Sir Rupert Jackson recommended that there should be a fixed costs regime for the whole of the fast-track and at the lower end of the multi-track. Professor Paul Fenn carried out a great deal of work during the course of the Jackson Review and produced a matrix for fixed costs across the fast track based on a considerable amount of data which had been made available to him by the ABI and others. The matrix was published in the final report having been accepted both by Jackson LJ and his assessors. The fixed costs in relation to Low Value Personal Injury Claims in Road Traffic Accidents ("the RTA protocol") or for Low Value Personal Injury (Employers' Liability and Public Liability) Claims ("the EL/PL protocol") have been reduced significantly below the earlier figures which had been the result of industry--wide agreement. The new figures appear to have been arrived at following the prohibition of referral fees by reducing the previous figures by the perceived amount of referral fees. This has done nothing to reduce arguments about hourly rates since solicitors now argue that instead of paying referral fees, they have to pay the same or larger amounts in marketing costs.

3. On 28 January 2016 Lord Justice Jackson delivered a speech[61] about extending fixed costs to the whole of the Fast Track and the lower end of the Multi Track up to claims for £250,000.

4. He suggested that his ideas should include clinical negligence actions. He set out a grid with four different value bands and ten stages based on the

---

[60] [2014] UKSC 46; [2015] AC 106).
[61] https://www.judiciary.gov.uk/wp-content/uploads/2016/01/fixedcostslecture-1.pdf

stages in Precedent H. His scheme was essentially a variation of the ABC/123 scheme in use in New Zealand.

5.   On 11 November 2016 Lord Justice Jackson was commissioned to undertake a review of fixed recoverable costs. The review was commissioned by Lord Thomas, the Lord Chief Justice, and Sir Terence Etherton, the Master of the Rolls. The review's recommendations will help to inform a Government public consultation on reforms to extend fixed recoverable costs to further areas of civil litigation.

6.   The terms of reference for the review are:

1.   To develop proposals for extending the present civil fixed recoverable costs regime in England and Wales so as to make the costs of going to court more certain, transparent and proportionate for litigants.
2.   To consider the types and areas of litigation in which such costs should be extended, and the value of claims to which such a regime should apply.
3.   To report to the Lord Chief Justice and the Master of the Rolls by the 31 July 2017.

7.   On 30 January 2017 the Government launched an open consultation on fixed recoverable costs for clinical negligence claims, seeking views on proposals for a mandatory system of fixed recoverable costs for lower value clinical negligence claims in England and Wales.[62]

"The proposed fixed recoverable costs scheme aims to improve the efficiency and cost-effectiveness of clinical negligence claims by supporting:

- *quicker and more cost effective resolution for all parties*
- *greater opportunities for early learning of lessons from harmful incidents to inform safer clinical practice*
- *access to justice for those claimants bringing clinical negligence claims of a low monetary value, but complex nature*
- *patients' access to justice by streamlining the system and incentivising earlier resolution of such claims"*[63]

The consultation closes on 1 May 2017.

Costs on the indemnity basis

The basis of assessment

7–06   Where the court assesses costs, whether by summary or detailed assessment, it will (subject to any statutory provisions relating to, e.g. legal aid costs) assess those costs on either the standard basis or the indemnity basis. In either

---

[62] Between £1,000 and £25,000.
[63] https://www.gov.uk/government/consultations/fixed-recoverable-costs-for-clinical-negligence-claims

case the court will not allow costs which have been unreasonably incurred or which are unreasonable in amount. Where the court is assessing costs on the standard basis it will in addition only allow costs which are proportionate to the matters in issue and will resolve any doubt which it may have as to whether costs were reasonably incurred or reasonable and proportionate in amount in favour of the paying party. Where the amount of costs is to be assessed on the indemnity basis there is no proportionality requirement but the court will resolve any doubt which it may have as to whether the costs were reasonably incurred or were reasonable in amount in favour of the receiving party.[64] Where the court makes an order about costs without indicating the basis upon which costs are to be assessed or purports to make an order on a basis other than the standard or indemnity basis the costs will be assessed on the standard basis.[65]

When the court may order costs on the indemnity basis

The court awarding costs on the indemnity basis should be satisfied that there   7–07
is something in the conduct of the action or the circumstances of the case which takes the case out of the norm in a way which justifies an order for indemnity costs.[66] Following *Excelsior Commercial & Industrial Holdings* it is appropriate to award costs on the indemnity basis where the conduct of a party has taken the situation away from the norm. It is not always necessary to show deliberate misconduct, in some cases unreasonable conduct to a high degree would suffice. The claimant's refusal of two reasonable offers to settle would have been enough in itself to warrant an order on the indemnity basis.[67]

The power to award costs on the indemnity basis may extend to the manner in which a party's expert had prepared and given evidence. In the particular case the defendant was ordered to pay the claimant's costs of having to recall its own expert, on the indemnity basis.[68] In another case involving an expert who was "inexperienced and overenthusiastic" the claimants, having put forward a figure at which they were prepared to settle, refused to settle at that figure when the defendants offered it. No explanation for the refusal was given. Akenhead J awarded costs on the indemnity basis against the claimants. Because of the claimants' unwillingness to accept the amount offered by the defendants in settlement, an enormous amount of time, costs and court resources had been wasted, and the defendants were entitled to costs on the indemnity basis.[69]

The Court of Appeal has held that there should be no general principle applicable to all applications under CPR r.31.22 (concerning subsequent use

---

[64] r.44.3(1)–(3).
[65] r.44.3(4).
[66] *Excelsior Commercial & Industrial Holdings Ltd v Salisbury Hammer Aspden & Johnson* [2002] EWCA Civ 879; [2002] C.P. Rep. 67.
[67] *Franks v Sinclair (Costs)* [2006] EWHC 3656 (Ch); [2007] W.T.L.R. 785, David Richards J.
[68] *Siegel v Pummell* [2015] EWHC 195, [2015] 3 Costs L.O. 357 Wilkie J.
[69] *Igloo Regeneration (General Partner) Ltd v Powell Williams Partnership (Costs)* [2013] EWHC 1859 (TCC), Akenhead J.

of disclosed documents) to the effect that indemnity costs would be awarded against the applicant. There are many different kinds of such applications and the general rules as to costs ought to be applicable to them as to any other application before the courts. On the facts of the case the judge at first instance had ample grounds for awarding indemnity costs in the circumstances. The applicant's application was one which was extraneous to the existing proceedings. It required a huge amount of effort from the respondent in terms of liaison, checking and legal consideration. The respondent had been fully entitled to resist the application in the public interest. These factors took the case outside the norm. An order for costs on the indemnity basis was justified.[70]

When considering whether to make an order for costs on the indemnity basis the trial judge has a wide discretion but it is critical that there be some conduct or circumstance that takes a case out of the norm. Such factors include the high-risk situation where a claim is speculative, weak, opportunistic or thin, and where a claimant commenced and pursued large-scale and expensive litigation in circumstances calculated to exert unfair and commercial pressure on a defendant to renegotiate what had become a commercially unattractive contract. The fact that one party lost resoundingly, does not automatically mean that the other should be awarded costs on the indemnity basis. On the facts, an order for costs on the indemnity basis was not made although it had not been unreasonable for the successful party to seek such an order.[71]

Litigants in person

7–08   Prior to 1975, litigants in person who were successful in proceedings could recover only their out of pocket expenses.[72] The Litigants in Person Fees and Expenses Act 1975 and the Rules of Court made subsequently, enable litigants in person to recover some payment for the time which they expend in conducting litigation. CPR r.46.5 is so worded that it is possible for a litigant in person to recover payment for legal advice as well as payment for time spent in conducting the litigation. There is an absolute cap on the amount recoverable by the litigant in person, namely two-thirds of the amount which would have been allowed if he had been legally represented, plus disbursements reasonably expended. The Court of Appeal has decided that in principle a litigant in person is entitled to his time for researching his case at the rate fixed by statute, subject to a cap of two thirds of what he would have recovered if he had been legally represented.[73]

In certain specified proceedings, where any costs of a litigant in person are ordered to be paid by another party to the proceedings or in any other way, there may be allowed on the assessment or other determination of the costs sums in respect of any work done and any expenses and losses incurred by the

---

[70] *Tchenguiz v Serious Fraud Office* [2014] EWCA Civ 1471.
[71] *Obrascon Huarte Lain SA v Government of Gibraltar* [2014] EWHC 5 June (TCC) Akenhead J.
[72] *Buckland v Watts* [1970] 1 QB 27 CA.
[73] *R v Legal Services Commission Ex p. Wulfshon* [2002] EWCA Civ.

litigant in or in connection with the proceedings to which the order relates.[74] This provision applies to civil proceedings as follows:

(a)   in the County Court, in the Senior Courts or in the Supreme Court on appeal from the High Court or the Court of Appeal;

(b)   before the Lands Tribunal for Northern Ireland;

(ba)   before the First-tier Tribunal or the Upper Tribunal; or

(c)   in or before any other court or tribunal specified in an order made under s.1 of the Litigants in Person (Costs and Expenses) Act 1975 by the Lord Chancellor.[75]

A litigant in person who does not fall within the provisions of the 1975 Act   **7–09** may claim only out of pocket expenses, although these may include fees and expenses charged by a solicitor to a litigant to equip him to argue a case in person.[76] There is no provision for the costs of litigants in person in criminal proceedings. Proceedings before the VAT Tribunal are also excluded. The Court of Appeal has held that the power to award costs for tribunal hearings is confined to sums recoverable at common law.[77]

The official receiver, acting without a solicitor in disqualification proceedings, is a litigant in person, and is not limited to disbursements merely because he is salaried. Where costs over and above disbursements have been incurred these are pecuniary in nature and amount to pecuniary loss. The costs will be assessed in accordance with CPR r.46.5.[78]

The court has no power to award costs to a litigant in person in respect of assistance given by a non-legally qualified acquaintance. "Legal services" refer to services that are legal and provided by or under the supervision of a lawyer. Any payment made by the litigant to the assistant is not recoverable because it is not a disbursement which would have been made by a legal representative. The assistance being given was not expert assistance within CPR r.46.5(3)(c).[79]

Tugendhat J commented in *Mole v Hunter*[80], that reform of the Rules was unnecessary to deal with the effect that litigants in person were increasingly having on the courts. In his view, reform was unnecessary because the court already had sufficient power to manage cases effectively where one or more parties were litigants in person. In this way it could, to a certain extent, ameliorate the procedural problems that litigants experienced. Notwithstanding

---

[74] Litigants in Person (Costs and Expenses) Act 1975 s.1(1).

[75] The scope of the Act has been extended to the Employment Appeal Tribunal by the Litigants in Person (Costs and Expenses) Order 1980 (SI 1980/1159) and to Magistrates' Courts in England and Wales in relation to civil proceedings before these Courts by the Litigants in Person (Magistrates' Courts) Order 2001 (SI 2001/3438).

[76] *Buckland v Watts* [1970] 1 Q.B. 27; [1969] 3 W.L.R. 92; (1969) 113 S.J. 384; *Malloch v Aberdeen Corp* [1973] 1 W.L.R. 71; [1973] 1 All E.R. 304; 1973 S.L.T. (Notes) 5. See also *Commissioners of Customs and Excise v Ross* [1992] All E.R. 65; [1990] S.T.C. 353.

[77] *Nader (t/a Tryus) v Customs and Excise Commissioners* [1998] S.T.C. 806, CA, and see *Customs and Excise Commissionersv Ross* (1990) 2 All E.R. 65; [1990] S.T.C. 353, Simon Brown J.

[78] *Re Minotaur Data Systems Ltd* [1999] 1 W.L.R. 1129; [1999] 3 All E.R. 122; [1999] B.C.C. 571, CA. (Magistrates' Courts) Order 2001 (SI 2001/3438).

[79] *Uhbi (t/a United Building and Plumbing Contractors) v Kajla* [2002] All E.R. (D) 265, CA.

[80] [2014] EWHC 658 (QB).

this view, a new CPR r.3.1A (unrepresented parties) has been introduced which imposes a positive obligation on the court to take certain steps where at least one party is unrepresented. These include: adopting a formal procedure appropriate to furthering the Overriding Objective; and, where necessary, questioning witnesses. The new rule, in making explicit the court's power to adapt its procedure to deal with a case justly and at proportionate cost for litigants in person, provides useful clarity.

The Court of Appeal refused to entertain an application under CPR r.52.9A (now CPR r.52n.19) (Orders to limit the recoverable costs of an appeal), as the application had not been made as soon as practicable, as was required under CPR r.52.9A(4). The fact that the defendant applicant was a litigant in person, and was ignorant of his rights, did not mean it was not practicable for him to make the application. There were not, nor ought there to be, special rules for litigants in person. The applicant's original claim should never have been brought, nor ought he to have appealed the Employment Tribunal's rejection of it. The fact that the other party had appealed the decision of the EAT would not have come as a surprise to the applicant. It would be unjust not to make an order for costs of the appeal against the applicant.[81]

A dispute arose between co-executors to a will. The court made an order under s.50 of the Administration of Justice Act 1985 removing the claimant as a co-executor. The first defendant had acted in person and which did not comply with the CPR, was struck out under CPR r.3.4(2)(b) as an abuse of the court's process or as otherwise likely to obstruct the just disposal of the proceedings. The counterclaimant had also failed to comply with a court order designed to rectify deficiencies in the form of the counterclaim. The question arose whether the court should take a different approach to assessing costs in respect of the first defendant on that basis. Whilst the Chief Chancery Master accepted that the court had a wide discretion, it could not adopt a differential approach to applying the rules as to costs depending upon whether a litigant was legally represented or not.[82]

McKenzie Friends

7–10   On 12 July 2010 the Master of the Rolls and President of the Family Division handed down a Practice Note,[83] which applies to civil and family proceedings in the Court of Appeal (Civil Division), the High Court, County Courts and the Family Proceedings Court in the Magistrates' Courts. The Note is issued as guidance, not as a Practice Direction, and sets out to remind courts and litigants of the principles set out in the authorities.

Litigants have the right to have reasonable assistance from a lay person (McKenzie Friends), but McKenzie Friends have no independent right to

---

[81] *JJ Food Service Ltd v Zulhayir* [2013] EWCA Civ 1304.
[82] *Jones v Longley* [2015] EWHC 3362 (Ch.) 20 November, Chief Master Matthews.
[83] Practice Note (Sen Cts: McKenzie Friends: Civil and Family Courts) [2010] 1 W.L.R. 1881; [2010] 4 All E.R. 272; [2010] 2 F.L.R. 962.

provide assistance. They have no right to act as advocates or to carry out the conduct of litigation.

McKenzie Friends may:

(i)   provide moral support for litigants;

(ii)   take notes;

(iii) help with case papers; and

(iv) quietly give advice on any aspect of the conduct of the case.

A McKenzie Friend may not: (a) act as a litigant's agent in relation to the proceedings; (b) manage litigants' cases outside court, for example by signing court documents; or (c) address the court, make oral submissions or examine witnesses. The Practice Note points out that while litigants ordinarily have a right to receive reasonable assistance from McKenzie Friends, the court retains the power to refuse to permit such assistance. It may do so where it is satisfied that, in that case, the interests of justice and fairness do not require the litigant to receive such assistance[84].

The following factors should not be taken to justify the court refusing to permit a litigant receiving such assistance: (i) the case or application is simple or straightforward, or is for instance a directions or case management hearing; (ii) the litigant appears capable of conducting the case without assistance; (iii) the litigant is unrepresented through choice; (iv) the other party is not represented; (v) the proposed McKenzie Friend belongs to an organisation that promotes a particular cause; and (vi) the proceedings are confidential and the court papers contain sensitive information relating to a family's affairs.

A litigant may be denied assistance of a McKenzie Friend because its provision **7–11** might undermine or has undermined the efficient administration of justice. Such circumstances might include:

(i)   the assistance is being provided for an improper purpose;

(ii)   the assistance is unreasonable in nature or degree;

(iii) the McKenzie Friend is subject to a civil proceedings orders or a civil restraint order; (iv) the McKenzie Friend is using the litigant as a puppet;

(v)   the McKenzie Friend is directly or indirectly conducting the litigation; and

(vi) the court is not satisfied that the McKenzie Friend fully understands the duty of confidentiality.

The Note points out that McKenzie Friends do not have a right of audience or a right to conduct litigation, and it is a criminal offence to exercise rights of audience or to conduct litigation unless properly qualified and authorised to do so. The court may grant such rights to a McKenzie Friend on a case by

---

[84] In *Ravenscroft v Canal & River Trust* [2016] EWHC 2282 (Ch) Chief Master Marsh permitted an almost illiterate party to appoint a McKenzie friend to act as his advocate in circumstances where his near illiteracy and emotional involvement with the issues meant that he was unlikely to be able to adequately represent himself.

case basis, but the courts should be slow to grant any application from a litigant for a right of audience or a right to conduct litigation to any lay person, including a McKenzie Friend. The court should only be prepared to grant such rights where there is good reason to do so, taking into account all the circumstances of the case. Such grants should not be extended to lay persons automatically or without due consideration. They should not be granted for mere convenience.

Litigants may enter into lawful agreements to pay fees to McKenzie Friends for the provision of reasonable assistance in court, or out of court by, e.g. carrying out clerical or mechanical activities such as photocopying documents, preparing bundles, delivering documents to opposing parties or the court, or the provision of legal advice in connection with court proceedings. Such fees cannot lawfully be recovered from the opposing party. Even where the court has granted a McKenzie Friend the right to conduct litigation, fees said to be incurred by a McKenzie Friend are, in principle, recoverable from the litigant for whom the work was carried out, but cannot lawfully be recovered from the opposing party. Where a McKenzie Friend is granted a right of audience, the fees incurred by the McKenzie Friend are, in principle, recoverable from the litigant on whose behalf the right is exercised, and are also recoverable, in principle, from the opposing party as a recoverable disbursement.

The court has power to deny a litigant, a McKenzie friend, if to allow it would undermine the administration of justice, especially where the assistance was for an improper purpose or the McKenzie friend was subject to a civil proceedings order. Such an order was made following a Crown Court recorder's findings that the respondent had attempted to deceive the court and had wasted public funds.[85]

Since the Guidance, which summarised the case law as it stood in 2010, was introduced there has been a significant increase in the number of both LIPs and McKenzie Friends. The Judicial Executive Board issued a consultation paper: Reforming the Courts' approach to McKenzie Friends. The consultation closed on 9 June 2016. A formal response is awaited.

Questions and answers

A. Fixed Costs

Q1. What indications are there about fixed costs for the future? Are there any arguments for fixed fees?

7–12   See **Chapter 1** as to the Review of Fixed Costs being conducted by Lord Justice Jackson. On 30 January 2017 the Government launched an open consultation on fixed recoverable costs for clinical negligence claims, seeking views on

---

[85] *Attorney-General v Carruthers* [2016] EWHC 26 April (DC), Simon LJ, Cox J.

proposals for a mandatory system of fixed recoverable costs for lower value clinical negligence claims in England and Wales.[86]

"The proposed fixed recoverable costs scheme aims to improve the efficiency and cost-effectiveness of clinical negligence claims by supporting:

- *quicker and more cost effective resolution for all parties;*
- *greater opportunities for early learning of lessons from harmful incidents to inform safer clinical practice;*
- *access to justice for those claimants bringing clinical negligence claims of a low monetary value, but complex nature;*
- *patients' access to justice by streamlining the system and incentivising earlier resolution of such claims"*[87]

The consultation closes on 1 May 2017

Q2. What guidance can be given about retainer arrangements to emphasise the importance of the advice to a client about these and ensuring that retainer arrangements are still clear and enforceable where a legal representative is asked to represent a client in litigation which will inevitably involve the application of fixed costs?

CPR r.45.1 states that Section I sets out the amounts which, "unless the court orders otherwise", will be allowed in respect of legal representatives' charges. The provisions of CPR r.45.3 operate to apply the costs fixed by Section I of Pt 45 unless the court otherwise orders. On the particular facts of the case the court refused to exercise its discretion to allow more than the fixed costs, stating, among other reasons:

7–13

"this court has recognised the importance of a summary and prompt procedure to secure enforcement of adjudicators' decisions properly reached .A party which makes a 'without prejudice save as to costs' offer is not entitled in some way to have it responded to or to assume that threatened proceedings against it will or might be withheld. It would be different if the without prejudice correspondence had revealed some agreement by which the claimant undertook, at least temporarily, not to issue proceedings . . . It would not be fair to limit a successful claimant which complied with the steps called for in the rule and the [TCC] Guide".

The claimant was justified in issuing proceedings and the Pt.24 application following a threatened defence and an unqualified admission on the part of the defendant after issue. See *Amber Construction Services Ltd v London Interspace HG Ltd* [2007] EWHC 3042 (TCC); [2008] B.L.R. 74, Akenhead J. The situation must be clearly explained to the client. A solicitor may agree that any charges will be limited to the amount recoverable from a paying party

---

[86] Between £1,000 and £25,000.
[87] https://www.gov.uk/government/consultations/fixed-recoverable-costs-for-clinical-negligence-claims

(i.e. the limit of fixed costs). If the legal representative intends to charge the client an amount which is likely to exceed the fixed recoverable costs, this must be explained to the client in clear terms. Chapter 1 of the SRA Code of Conduct, which came into effect on 6 October 201, sets out the general outcomes including that clients are in a position to make informed decisions about their matter. "Indicative behaviour" sets out how solicitors might go about this by, for example, agreeing an appropriate level of service with the client. The Solicitors Regulation Authority states that the new code allows greater flexibility according to the needs of the client and the type of work that the solicitor undertakes, but there is also greater emphasis on the needs of the individual client, particularly those who are vulnerable.

Chapter 1 of the Code does not specify the information that must be given to clients or the form it should take. This is because solicitors are required to focus on the principles and achieving the right outcomes for clients. The SRA Handbook points out:

> "Providing clear information at the outset and as the matter progresses is a benefit not only to clients but also to [the solicitor's firm]. Some of the most common causes of complaints are lack of clear information about costs, failure to follow instructions, delay and failure to keep clients informed. It is important to monitor complaints to [the solicitor's firm] as these can indicate failure to provide good client care as well as other problems within the firm."

Solicitors should only enter into fee agreements with their clients that are legal and which the solicitor considers are suitable for the client's needs and take account of the client's best interest. Clients must receive the best possible information both at the time of engagement and, when appropriate, as their matter progresses about the likely overall cost of their matter and must be informed of their right to challenge or complain about a bill and the circumstances in which they may be likely to pay interest on an unpaid bill.

Retainer is the name given to the contract which exists between a solicitor and the client. Where there is no retainer the relationship of solicitor and client does not exist and the solicitor is not entitled to render a bill. The contract between the solicitor and the client may be on any terms which are mutually agreeable provided that the terms do not infringe the restrictions laid down in Part III of the Solicitors Act 1974 or the statutory requirements relating to conditional fee agreements or damages-based agreements.

B. Fixed costs and multi-party situations (where fixed costs may not apply equally)

Q3. Where a claim is made against more than one defendant, one of whom admits the debt and judgment is obtained under CPR r.14.4(3), while the other defendant does not respond and judgment in default is obtained under CPR r.12.4(1), is the claimant entitled to two sets of fixed costs

given that there are two defendants and judgment has been obtained on two different bases? (CPR r.45.1).

Section I of Part 45 deals with fixed costs. CPR r.45.1(2) states *"this section applies where (a) the only claim is a claim for a specified sum of money where the value of the claim exceeds £25 and [judgment is obtained under one of a number of provisions]"*. From the wording of the Rule it would appear that only one set of costs is recoverable. There has been a single claim against two defendants and judgment has been obtained against each defendant. The defendants are presumably jointly and severally liable but the judgment debt would be recovered only once and logic dictates that only one set of costs is recoverable. There does not appear to be any authority on the point.

C. Getting the court to order more than fixed costs

Q4. Can you/how do you get more than fixed costs? Can you give some guidance/authorities regarding when the court will order otherwise than fixed costs under CPR r.45 in a case where the fixed costs provisions should otherwise apply?
Is it possible for costs be assessed when requesting default judgment or are only fixed costs allowed pursuant to CPR r.45?
CPR rules 45.13, 45.14, 45.29J and 45.29K contain the relevant provisions. Fixed costs apply unless a party can persuade the court that there are exceptional circumstances. The court will only entertain a claim for costs greater than the fixed recoverable costs if it considers that there are exceptional circumstances making it appropriate to do so. Failure to achieve an amount 20% greater than the amount of the fixed recoverable costs, will result in an order that the defendant pay to the claimant the lesser of the fixed recoverable costs; and the assessed costs. CPR rules 45.29J and 45.29K contain broadly similar provisions. The most likely reason for being able to persuade the court is that the opponent's conduct has been such as to require the receiving party to do far more work (remember the 20% requirement) than was ever envisaged when the rule was drafted.

7–15

D. Relationship between fixed costs and assessed costs and between fixed costs and Part 36 costs

Q5. What is the relationship between fixed costs and assessed costs and fixed costs and Part 36? IE what happens if they overlap?
Ideally there should be no overlap between assessed costs, fixed costs and Part 36 costs. See *Broadhurst v Tan* [2016] EWCA Civ 94 discussed at paragraph 5–16 above .

7–16

Rule 44.6 deals with assessed costs:

"(1) Where the court orders a party to pay costs to another party (other than fixed costs) it may either—

> (a) *make a summary assessment of the costs; or*
>
> (b) *order detailed assessment of the costs by a costs officer,*
>
> *unless any rule, practice direction or other enactment provides otherwise.*
>
> *(Practice Direction 44—General rules about costs sets out the factors which will affect the court's decision under paragraph (1).)*
>
> *(2) A party may recover the fixed costs specified in Part 45 in accordance with that Part.*
>
> *Rule 44.1(1) defines fixed costs: ""fixed costs" means costs the amounts of which are fixed by these rules whether or not the court has a discretion to allow some other or no amount, and include—*
>
> > (i) *the amounts which are to be allowed in respect of legal representatives' charges in the circumstances set out in Section I of Part 45;*
> >
> > (ii) *fixed recoverable costs calculated in accordance with rule 45.11;*
> >
> > (iii) *the additional costs allowed by rule 45.18;*
> >
> > (iv) *fixed costs determined under rule 45.21;*
> >
> > (v) *costs fixed by rules 45.37 and 45.38."*

Part 36 is a self contained code:

> *"36.1 (1) This Part contains a self-contained procedural code about offers to settle made pursuant to the procedure set out in this Part ("Part 36 offers").*
>
> *(2) Section I of this Part contains general rules about Part 36 offers.*
>
> *(3) Section II of this Part contains rules about offers to settle where the parties have followed the Pre-Action Protocol for Low Value Personal Injury Claims in Road Traffic Accidents ("the RTA Protocol") or the Pre-Action Protocol for Low Value Personal Injury (Employers' Liability and Public Liability) Claims ("the EL/PL Protocol") and have started proceedings under Part 8 in accordance with Practice Direction 8B."*

It is not clear from the question exactly what circumstances are envisaged.

Q6. In proceedings in the Intellectual Property Enterprise Court where costs are awarded against a party for unreasonable behaviour does the stage costs cap in Part 45 apply?

7–17   A claimant who had behaved unreasonably in proceedings in the IPEC was ordered to pay the defendant's costs of the claimant's failed application for permission to re-amend its particulars of claim under CPR r.63.26(2). The court held that CPR r.45.31 imposed the overall cap on total costs. The Rule allowed for an exception to the overall cap where costs were awarded for unreasonable behaviour in the course of an application. The wording of CPR rules 45.31 and 45.32 were too clear to permit the conclusion that costs awarded against an unreasonable party were free of the stage caps on costs, accordingly the caps applied. The court would exercise its discretion on costs to lift a stage cap only in truly exceptional circumstances if the result was that the overall cap on total costs was left undisturbed. The defendants between them were entitled to their costs of the claimant's application up to a maximum of £3,000 permitted under the stage caps of Part 45.[88]

Q7. Does CPR r.46.5 apply to Litigants in person on the small claims track? What costs can a Litigant in person recover in the small claims court?
Costs on the small claims track are governed by Part 27. Essentially the costs   7–18
are limited to the fixed costs attributable to issuing the claim plus certain
exceptional items set out in CPR r.27.14(2); "The court may not order a party
to pay a sum to another party in respect of that other party's costs, fees and
expenses, including those relating to an appeal, except:

(a) the fixed costs attributable to issuing the claim which:
     (i) are payable under Part 45; or
     (ii) would be payable under Part 45 if that Part applied to the claim;
(b) in proceedings which included a claim for an injunction or an order
     for specific performance a sum not exceeding the amount specified in
     Practice Direction 27 for legal advice and assistance relating to that
     claim;
(c) any court fees paid by that other party;
(d) expenses which a party or witness has reasonably incurred in travelling
     to and from a hearing or in staying away from home for the purposes of
     attending a hearing;
3)   (e) a sum not exceeding the amount specified in Practice Direction 27
          for any loss of earnings or loss of leave by a party or witness due to
          attending a hearing or to staying away from home for the purpose of
          attending a hearing;
(f) a sum not exceeding the amount specified in Practice Direction 27 for an
     expert's fees;
(g) such further costs as the court may assess by the summary procedure and
     order to be paid by a party who has behaved unreasonably;
(h) the Stage 1 and, where relevant, the Stage 2 fixed costs in r.45.18 where:
     (i)   the claim was within the scope of the Pre-Action Protocol for Low
           Value Personal Injury Claims in Road Traffic Accidents ("the RTA
           Protocol") or the Pre-action Protocol for Low Value Personal Injury
           (Employers' Liability and Public Liability) Claims ("the EL/PL
           Protocol");
     (ii) the claimant reasonably believed that the claim was valued at more
           than the small claims track limit in accordance with paragraph
           4.1(4) of the relevant Protocol; and
     (iii) the defendant admitted liability under the process set out in the
           relevant Protocol; but
     (iv) the defendant did not pay those Stage 1 and, where relevant, Stage
           2 fixed costs; and

---

[88] *Akhtar v Bhopal Productions (UK) Ltd* [2015] EWHC 154 (IPEC), HHJ Hacon.

(i)   in an appeal, the cost of any approved transcript reasonably incurred."

CPR rules 46.11 and 46.13 make provision in relation to orders for costs made before a claim has been allocated to the small claims track. Once a claim is allocated to a particular track, those special rules shall apply to the period before, as well as after, allocation except where the court or a practice direction provides otherwise. Any costs orders made before a claim is allocated will not be affected by allocation.

Q8. Following the decision in *Chaplair v Kumari*, it is clear that a landlord can recover costs of proceedings under a leasehold indemnity in its favour irrespective of whether the claim would fall within the fixed costs regimes of the small and fast tracks. What is the position in relation to residential possession claims under CPR Part 55, to which the fixed costs regime under CPR Part 45 applies?

7–19   The position in *Chaplair v Kumari* was as follows: A claim brought by a landlord for recovery of unpaid rent and service charges was allocated, by consent, to the small claims track. The claim was successful. In the lease there was a contractual right to recover the costs of proceedings. At first instance the District Judge awarded costs to the landlord but held that there was no power to award costs other than CPR r.27.14 fixed costs. On appeal to the Circuit Judge, the appeal was successful and the defendant appealed to the Court of Appeal. The court refused to grant permission on that particular issue as the law on the point was well established: where there was a contractual right to costs, the court should normally exercise its costs discretion to reflect those rights; CPR r.27.14 should be read as being subject to CPR r.44.5 which gives effect to the general principle set out above and which was not excluded from Part 27 by CPR r.27.2. The rule-making power cannot, in any event, set aside or overrule a contractual entitlement which would be necessary for CPR r.27.14 to have an exclusionary effect.[89]

So far as possession claims under Part 55 are concerned the White Book states (at 55.7.8):

> *"Fixed costs apply to certain types of possession claims—unless the court orders otherwise. CPR r.45.1 provides that fixed costs apply where—*
> * *The defendant gives up possession and pays the amount claimed (if any) and the fixed commencement costs;*
> * *One of the grounds for possession is arrears of rent, the court gave a fixed date for hearing, a possession order is made (whether suspended or not) and the defendant has either failed to deliver a defence or the defence is limited to specifying proposals for payment of arrears; and*
> * *The claim is brought under the accelerated procedure (Pt 55 Section 2) against*

---

[89] *Chaplair Limited v Kumari* [2015] EWCA Civ. 798.

> *an assured shorthold tenant, a possession order is made and the defendant*
> *has neither delivered a defence nor otherwise denied liability*
> * *The claim is a demotion claim or a demotion claim is made in the same*
>   *claim form in which a possession claim is made and the demotion claim is*
>   *successful."*

It is certainly arguable that, provided the "indemnity" costs provision in the Landlord and Tenant agreement is properly drafted, CPR r.44.5 should apply. It might in fact be easier to persuade the court to "order otherwise" rather than get into a discussion about whether the contractual terms should take precedence.

E. Costs on the Indemnity Basis

Q9. Is the indemnity basis applicable in cases where there is an abuse of process or where a party has been guilty of unreasonable conduct?

The Companies Court, in applying the decision in *Excelsior Commercial and Industrial Holdings Ltd*[90] ordered the claimant to pay the costs of an unfair prejudice petition on the indemnity basis where the petition had been an abuse of process and should never have been brought, and where the claimant had no basis for defending the company's claim for breach of duty as a director and employee. The costs of both actions had been increased significantly by virtue of the claimant's highly aggressive tactics in the conduct of the litigation. Overall the case constituted a departure from the norm, which made it just to order costs to be paid on the indemnity basis.[91]

7–20

A different court ordered an unsuccessful claimant to pay costs on the indemnity basis and to pay interest on the costs from one year before the commencement date of the trial because of the claimants' unreasonable conduct in that the case had changed constantly throughout the course of the proceedings and the claimant had produced wholly unacceptable volumes of documentation.[92]

In another example, where claimants had sued their former financial advisor, the defendant, before serving its defence, applied for summary judgment. Four months later the application was withdrawn. The court had to decide the question of costs. There was nothing sufficiently unusual about the case to justify departing from the general rule that the unsuccessful party should be ordered to pay the successful party's costs. The court went on to make an order on the indemnity basis because the defendant was not justified in seeking summary judgment before filing the defence. The application

---

[90] *Excelsior Commercial & Industrial Holdings Ltd v Salisbury Hammer Aspden & Johnson* [2002] EWCA Civ 879; [2002] C.P. Rep. 67.
[91] *Re Flex Associates Ltd* [2010] EWHC 3690 (Ch) David Donaldson QC.
[92] *ABCI (formerly Arab Business Consortium International Finance & Investment Co) v Banque Franco-Tunisienne (Costs)* [2002] EWHC 567 (Comm) HH Judge Chambers QC.

constituted conduct which was sufficiently 'out of the norm' within the meaning in *Excelsior* and other authorities.[93]

Q10. What is the position of litigation funders in relation to orders for costs, particularly orders for costs on the indemnity basis?

7–21 Where claimants funded by third party litigation funders lost the claim, the litigation funders were ordered to pay the costs of the defendant on the indemnity basis up to the limit of their investment. Christopher Clarke LJ stated:

> *"Justice requires that when the case fails so comprehensively, not merely on the facts but because it was wholly bad in law, the funder should, subject to the Arkin cap, bear the costs order to be paid by the person whom or which he has unsuccessfully supported, assessed on the scale which the Court thinks it just for that person to pay in the light of all the circumstances, including but not limited to that person's behaviour and that of those whom that person engaged."*

The judge stated that the funder should, absent special circumstances, follow the fortunes of those from whom he himself hoped to derive a small fortune. To do otherwise would be unfair to the defendants and their personnel. To make an order for indemnity costs would not be to penalise but to recompense. Christopher Clarke LJ further stated:

> *"If it serves to cause funders and their advisors to take rigorous steps short of champerty, i.e. behaviour likely to interfere with the due administration of justice—particularly in the form of rigorous analysis of law, facts and witnesses, consideration of proportionality and review at appropriate intervals—to reduce the occurrence of the sort of circumstances that cause me to order indemnity costs in this case, that is an advantage and in the public interest".*[94]

The Funders appealed, some arguing that they should not have been ordered to pay costs on the indemnity basis, others arguing that they should not have been ordered to pay costs at all, The Court of Appeal held that it was appropriate that the commercial funders, who had funded a hopeless action, should pay the successful defendants' costs on the indemnity basis even though they themselves were not guilty of any discreditable conduct or conduct which could be criticised. An argument arose as to whether additional security ordered to be paid should count towards the Arkin cap. The Court specifically declined to revisit the Arkin cap or to comment on it (paragraph 28) but dealt with the argument in this way:

> *"39.   In order to resolve these arguments it is simply necessary to return to first principles. As emphasised in Dymocks, the rationale for imposing a costs liability upon a non-party funder is that he has funded proceedings substantially for*

---

[93] *The Libyan Investment Authority v Goldman Sachs International* [2014] EWHC 3364 (Ch) Rose J.
[94] *Excalibur Ventures LLC v Texas Keystone Inc (Defendants and Costs Claimants) and Psari Holdings Ltd (Costs Defendants)* [2014] EWHC 3436 (Comm) Christopher Clarke LJ.

his own financial benefit and has thereby become "a real party" to the litiga-
tion. It is ordinarily just that he should be liable for costs if the claim fails. The
pragmatic solution reached in Arkin, and accepted by the funding community,
is that the funder who finances part of a claimant's costs of litigation should be
potentially liable for the costs of the opponent party to the extent of the funding
provided, i.e. invest one in the pursuit of the common enterprise and bear the
risk of liability in that same amount in the event of failure, in which event
by definition the initial investment is already lost. I see no basis upon which
a funder who advances money to enable security for costs to be provided by a
litigant should be treated any differently from a funder who advances money
to enable that litigant to meet the fees of its own lawyers or expert witnesses.
Both the provision of security for costs, if ordered by the court, and the payment
of the litigant's own lawyers and experts, are costs of pursuing the litigation
which, if not met, will result in the litigation being unable to proceed. I do not
understand why contribution to different categories of the costs of pursuing the
litigation should attract different regimes. All the sums advanced are used in
pursuit of the common enterprise and for the benefit of all of the funders."[95]

Q11. The rules suggest that costs management does not affect indemnity
costs. However there is now a confusion about this since Coulson J's deci-
sion in *Elvanite Full Circle Ltd v Amec Earth and Environmental UK Ltd*[96]
suggests otherwise.
On the facts of the case the judge decided not to make an order on the indem-　7–22
nity basis but went on to consider whether, if the defendant had been entitled
to indemnity costs, the costs management order was irrelevant and whether
it was possible for the defendant to recover more than the sums in the costs
management order. Having acknowledged that a costs management order is
expressed to be relevant only to an assessment of costs on the standard basis,
he continued:

"However as a matter of logical analysis, it seems to me that the costs manage-
ment order should also be the starting point of an assessment of costs on an
indemnity basis even if the 'good reasons' to depart from it are likely to be more
numerous and extensive if the indemnity basis is applied . . .

If [the budget] is an accurate estimate of all the costs that will be incurred then
it seems to me that it should be the relevant starting point for an assessment of
costs on an indemnity basis as well as for an assessment on the standard basis
. . .

There is concern that, if an order for indemnity costs allows the receiving party

---

[95] Excalibur Ventures Llc (Claimant) V (1) Texas Keystone Inc (2) Gulf Keystone Petroleum Ltd (3) Gulf Keystone Petroleum International Ltd (4) Gulf Keystone Petroleum (Uk) Ltd (Defendants): (1) Texas Keystone Inc (2) Gulf Keystone Petroleum Ltd (3) Gulf Keystone Petroleum International Ltd (4) Gulf Keystone Petroleum (Uk) Ltd (Claimants/Costs Respondents) V Psari Holdings Ltd & 8 Ors (Costs Defendants) & (1) Psari Holdings Ltd & 6 Ors (Costs Defendants/Appellants) & Association Of Litigation Funders Of England & Wales (Intervener) (2016). [2016] EWCA Civ 1144.
[96] *Elvanite Full Circle Ltd v Amec Earth and Environmental UK Ltd* [2013] EWHC 1643 (TCC), [2013] 4. Costs L.R. 612, Coulson J.

> to ignore the costs management order, then that will encourage successful parties to argue for indemnity costs every time . . .A paying party will have fought the trial assuming that, even if it loses, its opponent will be unlikely to recover more than the amount recorded in the costs management order, unless there is good reason for any departure. That is the certainty that the new regime provides. Even if the paying party has to pay costs on an indemnity basis that does not seem to me automatically to justify an abandonment of that certainty and the encouragement of a costs free for all . . . .
>
> In any given case it might be said that an award of indemnity costs—which does not require any assessment of proportionality—might be a 'good reason' to depart from the costs budget approved by the Court . . . I can well see that, in particular factual circumstances, an award of indemnity costs might be a good reason to permit such a departure. But that would be fact specific and it would not detract from the principle of at least starting the costs assessment by reference to the approved budget."[97]

It is probable that the Court of Appeal in *Denton* has overtaken this decision which was a decision under a pilot scheme which did not require the Precedent H to assert that it was in any way an attempt at proportionate costs. (See **Chapter 4** at para **4–20** and **Qs 78 and 79** for further consideration of this topic)

Q12. What is the position if the losing party has won on certain issues and lost on others?

7–23 Claimants who had been unsuccessful at trial were liable to pay all the costs of the successful defendant, to be assessed on the standard basis, where the evidence showed that the no-loss defence and the limitation defence run by the defendant were not discrete issues and where they had made no identifiable difference to the costs incurred by either party.[98]

In a County Court decision by a district judge, the court ordered a claimant who had exaggerated his claim to pay costs on the indemnity basis. The court found that the claim would have been resolved by the end of June 2012 had the claimant not exaggerated his claim.

Accordingly, the usual costs consequences of previous CPR r.36.10(5) (now CPR r.36.13(5)),[99] did not apply. The claimant was awarded costs on the standard basis up to the 30 June 2012 but was ordered to pay the defendant's costs there-after on the indemnity basis. The claimant was also ordered to meet the entire costs of gathering the surveillance evidence and the costs of the application.[100]

---

[97] paras 28–31.
[98] *Kellie and another v Wheatley & Lloyd Architects Ltd* [2014] EWHC 2886 (TCC); [2014] 5 Costs L.R. 854; HHJ Keyser QC.
[99] The wording has altered slightly.
[100] *Worthington v 03918424 Limited* [2015] 16 June Manchester DR unreported.

F. Litigants in Person

Q13. What is the position of a solicitor or barrister acting on his or her own behalf?

It is a question of fact whether a solicitor in sole practice is acting for himself   7–24
as a true litigant in person or, is, instead, represented by himself in the firm
name. It was relevant that the underlying litigation concerned a claim for
professional fees with allegations of negligence and breach of duty since those
were matters arising out of the solicitor's practice as a solicitor and not out of
the course of his private life.[101]

In proceedings where the claimant was a solicitor who had, at the same
time, practised as a costs draftsman until July 1999, the court had to decide
whether or not she was a litigant in person before 26 April 1999 and also
whether she was a litigant in person after that date under the CPR. The question depended upon the criteria used to define the term "practising solicitor".
Prior to 26 April 1999, the court found that the claimant was undoubtedly a
practising solicitor from a regulatory point of view under the Solicitors Act
and the Rules of Practice, but she was not a practising solicitor who was able
to charge for her time for the purposes of RSC Ord.62 r.18(6) and the rule in
London Scottish Benefits Society v Chorley.[102] The court therefore held that she
was only entitled to recover costs for that period as a litigant in person. With
regard to the period after 26 April 1999, it was accepted by the claimant that
if a court found that she was not a practising solicitor for the purposes of RSC
Ord.62 r.18 then she was unable to take advantage of PD 46, para.3.2. The
court held that this provision was designed to do no more than preserve the
rule in *London Scottish Benefits Society*. The criteria remained the same.[103]

Where the Bar Standards Board brought proceedings against a non-prac-
tising barrister before the Disciplinary Tribunal of the Council of the Inns
of Court, the barrister successfully defended the proceedings in person. The
Administrative Court expressed the view that the principle in *London Scottish
Benefit Society* that a solicitor litigant acting in person was entitled to costs
incurred in the expenditure of his own professional skill had been overturned
by CPR r.46.5(6) (formerly CPR r.48.6(6)). Neither a solicitor nor a barrister acting in person could include in his proof of financial loss under CPR
r.46.5(4)(a) the cost of the provision of his own professional skill. Since a
barrister was not a solicitor coming within the exception in PD 46(3) there
was no means by which a barrister could avoid that conclusion and claim
costs unless she employed someone else on her behalf. The Civil Procedure
Rules did not apply however and were not even persuasive authority. If the
Bar Standards Board wished to avoid having to pay the costs of a barrister's
time and that barrister had successfully defended proceedings it was open to

---

[101] *Hatton v Kendrick* [2002] EWCA Civ 1783; [2003] C.P. Rep. 32, CA.
[102] *London Scottish Benefits Society v Chorley* [1884] 13 Q.B.D. 872.
[103] *Joseph v Boyd & Hutchinson* [2003] EWHC 413 (Ch); [2003] 3 Costs L.R. 358, Patten J.

it to provide in its rules that the CPR should apply but it had not done so. The correct basis of assessing the cost was in accordance with the Board's own rules, namely to award such costs as the Tribunal thought fit. There was no basis for saying that the expenditure of a barrister's own time and skills should not be compensated where that -barrister was successful.[104]

Q14. If a litigant in person instructs a barrister under the Direct Access scheme can the litigant recover any costs?
Are there any rules relating to recovery of costs, where the party is a litigant in person, but uses a barrister through direct access? Has a barrister been used throughout whole claim, not just for hearings?

7–25   The Direct Access Scheme is a useful device for reducing costs, particularly in cases of a technical nature where a solicitor would otherwise be no more than a conduit between, e.g. a specialist tax practitioner and a specialist tax barrister. The scheme has however produced a difficulty in that a tax payer being advised by members of the Institute of Taxation and by counsel under the Direct Access Scheme appealed from a decision of the Commissioners and thence to the Court of Appeal where the tax payer was successful. Although it was conceded that the tax payer was entitled to his costs, there was considerable argument as to the extent of those costs. The Court of Appeal found that the tax payer had been acting as a litigant in person (although he had in fact taken no active part in the proceedings), that counsel's fee was recoverable since it was a disbursement which would have been made had solicitors been instructed but that the fees of the tax advisers were not recoverable save to the extent that they may have been acting in an expert capacity.[105]

Services provided by a lawyer qualified in another jurisdiction did not constitute *"legal services"* for the purposes of CPR r.46.5(3)(b). There was no material difference between the position of a lawyer qualified in another jurisdiction and the specialist tax advisers in *Agassi v Robinson (Inspector of Taxes) (Costs)*[106]. The service provider had valuable knowledge and expertise but was not authorised to conduct litigation and was not subject to the wasted costs jurisdiction of the court.[107]

In construction litigation brought by the employer, the defendant contractor, who had acted with the assistance of claims consultants, was successful. The contractor claimed the costs incurred by the claims consultants. It was common ground between the parties that the contractor was acting as a litigant in person for the purposes of CPR r.46.5. The court held that *Agassi v Robinson* was not authority for a general proposition that costs of claims consultants or other consultants who gave advice and support in litigation

---

[104] *R (Bar Standards Board) v Disciplinary Tribunal of the Council of the Inns of Court and Sivanandan (Interested Party)* [2014] EWHC 1570 (Admin).
[105] *Agassi v Robinson (Inspector of Taxes)* [2005] EWCA Civ 1507; [2006] 1 W.L.R. 2126; [2006] 1 All E.R. 900; [2006] S.T.C. 580, CA.
[106] [2005] EWCA Civ. 1507; [2006] 1 WLR 2126.
[107] *Campbell v Campbell* [2016] EWHC 1828 (Ch.), David Foxton QC.

could never be recovered. The relevant question was whether, in the particular instance, the costs of a claims consultant were recoverable as a disbursement; the question was answered by establishing whether those costs would have been recoverable as a disbursement had it been made by a solicitor. It was necessary to recognise that a solicitor might well normally not carry out work himself but rely on a specialist, even though the work might be *"solicitor's work"*. There were distinct features of adjudication and adjudication enforcement proceedings that could and should be taken into account in considering what disbursements would be recoverable if made by solicitors and which were consequently recoverable by a litigant in person. Costs incurred by claims consultants assisting a litigant in person would usually be recoverable in adjudication enforcement proceedings, assuming that the same consultants had represented the party in the adjudication. The costs of the claims consultant were recoverable as disbursements[108].

From 6 January 2014 The Public Access Rules are Rules C119–C131 of the Code of Conduct in the Bar Standards Board Handbook. The Handbook contains rules and guidance on the conduct of barristers. The revised Code now forms Part two of the new BSB 'Handbook', which brings together all the BSB's regulations and guidance for barristers into one publication. For Public Access barristers, one of the key changes is that self-employed barristers are allowed to apply for an extension to their practising certificate in order to be able to conduct litigation. This means that, as long as Public Access barristers have the correct authorisation, their clients no longer have to act as a self-representing litigant or instruct a solicitor, should the case go to court.[109] See **Chapter 4 Q2** which considers LiPs and Direct Access in the context of costs management.

Q15. Is it possible for the court to make an order for costs on the indemnity basis against a litigant in person?

Section 51 of the Senior Courts Act 1981 gives the court full power to determine by whom and to what extent the costs are to be paid. In appropriate circumstances therefore, it is entirely open to the court to make an order for costs on the indemnity basis against a litigant in person. In family proceedings, the father made committal applications against two CAFCASS officers and the mother's solicitor. The judge found the application to be fundamentally flawed with no real prospect of success. The mother's solicitor had written to the father at an early stage on an open basis setting out the grounds of the defence all of which had succeeded. The court found that the father's very serious allegations had no evidential basis and the application having fatal procedural defects and no real prospect of success ought therefore to be regarded as an abuse of process. The mother's solicitor had

7–26

---

[108] *Octoesse LLP v Trak Special Projects Limited* [2016] EWHC 3180 (TCC), Jefford J; and see *NAP Anglia Limited v Sun-Land Development Co. Limited* (Costs) [2012] EWHC 51 (TCC).
[109] See: www.barstandardsboard.org.uk/regulatory-requirements/for-barristers/public-access/

incurred significant costs and the father was ordered to pay those costs on the indemnity basis.[110]

Q16. Is it possible for a firm of solicitors which is an LLP to be regarded as a litigant in person for the purpose of a costs assessment?

7–27 CPR r.46.5(6) states:

> *"For the purposes of this rule, a litigant in person includes:-*
> *(a) A company or other corporation which is acting without a legal representative; and any of the following who acts in person (except where any such person is represented by a firm in which that person is a partner):*
>
> > (i)   *A barrister*
> > (ii) *A solicitor*
> > (iii) *A solicitor's employee*
> > (iv) *A manager of a body recognised under section 9 of the Administration of Justice Act 1985; or*
> > (v)   *A person who for the purposes of the 2007 Act is an authorised person in relation to an activity which constitutes the conduct of litigation (within the meaning of that Act)."*

A defendant solicitor was ordered to pay the claimant's costs following his unsuccessful application for summary judgment. The claimant was a limited liability partnership of practising solicitors. They had represented themselves and instructed counsel (the court did not deal with the significance of the instruction of counsel). At first instance, the defendant asserted that the claimant partnership was a litigant in person and that the costs should accordingly be limited. The Costs Judge did not accept that argument and the defendant appealed. The judge held that as the claimant was *"a company or other corporation"* which was acting with a legal representative, it was not a litigant in person under CPR r.46.5(6)(a). The defendant argued that the claimant was a litigant in person under CPR r.46.5(6)(b)(v). The judge held that the rule had no sensible foundation if *"person"* included a corporation. The judge queried why the rule should exclude from the definition of litigant in person an ordinary solicitors' partnership acting by one of its own solicitors (which was the effect of the rule) while including an LLP also acting by one of its own solicitors. Companies and corporations were dealt with comprehensively in CPR r.46.5(6)(a) whereas CPR r.46.5(6)(b) dealt with several categories all of whom were natural persons. The Judge further pointed out that in the rules individuals were described as acting in person but a company was described as acting *"without a legal representative"*.[111]

Q17. To what extent will the court grant some leeway to a litigant in person who fails to comply with a rule practice direction or court order?

---

[110] *H v Dent and McKay and Harman* [2015] EWHC 2228 (Fam.), Roberts J.
[111] *EMW Law LLP v Halborg* [2015] EWHC 2005 (Ch), HHJ Purle QC.

This question was raised before the coming into force of CPR r.3.1A (Case   **7–28**
Management – Unrepresented Parties). Under that Rule, the court must, when
exercising any powers of case management, have regard to the fact that at
least one party is unrepresented and is required to *"adopt such procedure at any
hearing as it considers appropriate to further the overriding objective"*.

The answer to the question will always be fact sensitive and the cases
below give examples of the different approaches the court may take. Where
a defendant litigant in person failed to file an appeal bundle in breach of an
unless order as a result of which her appeal was struck out, the court refused
an application for relief from sanctions under CPR r.3.9, holding, in applying the *Denton* test, that the failure to file an appeal bundle was a significant
breach. The process of registering a foreign judgment (which was the subject
matter of the appeal) was meant to be swift and seamless but the process
had been awkward and delayed. The court was bound to treat the default as
serious and significant. In giving judgment, the court emphasised that not
all litigants in person should be treated the same. The court could take into
account the needs of a litigant in person who was impecunious or unable to
speak the language. In the instant case, the defendant was a sophisticated
person with sufficient access to resources to protect her interest. There was no
good reason for her breach. Although the court would not usually take into
account the underlying merits of the claim when making case management
decisions in considering all the circumstances under r.3.9, the court found
that it was entitled to take into account the merits of the underlying proceedings and to conclude that the defendant had no right to delay registration of
the foreign judgments further.[112]

In a case where proceedings had been brought against four defendants, one
of the defendants owned and controlled another defendant. Judgment was
entered against all four defendants. The litigant in person did not attend as a
result of ill health. She appealed, arguing that she and her company should
never have been parties to the proceedings and that her application to strike
out the claims had not been dealt with by the court at first instance. Two days
before the appeal was due to be heard, the litigant in person realised she only
had permission to appeal the judgment and costs order made against her in
her personal capacity and not against the company. She applied for permission to file an appeal notice on behalf of the company at the appeal hearing
itself. The Court of Appeal applied the three stage test in *Denton v White* and
found that the delay was serious and significant. The explanation was that
the litigant in person did not realise that she also needed to appeal separately on behalf of the company. The court held that the circumstances were
"truly exceptional" and it was just to extend the time. A judgment against the
company could, at least in theory, result in proceedings against the litigant
in person under the Disqualification of Directors' legislation. The facts relating to the company were exactly the same as those relating to the litigant

---

[112] *Akcine Bendore Bankas Snoras (in Bankruptcy) v Yampolskaya* [2015] EWHC 2136 (QB), Green J.

personally and the claimant was fully aware that both were, for the purposes of the litigation, to be regarded as one and the same.[113]

A litigant in person sought an adjournment of her trial for two weeks because she was dissatisfied with the specific disclosure provided by the defendant, and wished to argue that this affected her ability to prepare for trial, and that, as a litigant in person, she needed more time to consider the newly disclosed material and to amend her skeleton argument. The court refused her application holding that if it became apparent during the trial that further information was required this could be dealt with by the trial judge. An adjournment of the trial would have a very considerable impact. The defendant had already incurred substantial costs which would be lost or duplicated if the trial were adjourned and the adjournment would not be for two weeks but for several months, and given that the proceedings had commenced in 2007, it was in the interests of both parties that the issues be determined. The documents which had been disclosed were *"relatively peripheral"* to the case. The date of trial was put back by four days to give the litigant some further time in which to consider the new material and finalise their skeleton argument.[114]

In a case where only quantum was in dispute, the court directed that there should be a meeting of experts on a specified date. The meeting did not take place because the claimant litigant in person fell out with his expert and had not paid his fees. The defendant applied to extend the time for the meeting and obtained an order that unless the experts met by the new date, the claimant's expert evidence should be struck out. The claimant's application to set aside the order and vacate the trial date and for new directions on expert evidence was dismissed. The judge held that the claimant was responsible for the expert ceasing to act, given his criticism of the expert's opinion and the non-payment of his fees. Also, it was not appropriate for the claimant to indicate that he would look to the expert for any shortfall in the sums he sought to recover. The judge considered the *Denton* principles and decided that the non-compliance with the relevant order was serious and significant and was the claimant's fault. It was not fair, just or reasonable in all the circumstances for relief to be granted.[115]

Where a litigant in person made eleven applications, all of which were wholly without merit, the court granted an application for an extended civil restraint order against the litigant in person. The defendant complained that the courts had never looked at the merits of her case and that she was a litigant in person who did not understand the procedure. In giving judgment the judge stated:

"...if it is otherwise appropriate to make a civil restraint order, the fact that the litigant is a litigant in person who does not understand procedures and gets things

---

[113] *Kishenin v Bleach* [2015] EWCA Civ. 1184.
[114] *El-Demellawy v European Bank for Reconstruction and Development* [2015] EWHC 3291 (QB), Hickinbottom J.
[115] *Sargeant v UK Insurance Limited* [2015] EWHC 3304 (QB), Picken J. See also *Brand and Goldsmith v Berki* [2015] EWHC 3373 (QB), Jay J.

wrong is precisely supportive of making a civil restraint order rather than not making one. [The litigant in person] needs to understand that by making a civil restraint order. . . .she does not lose any rights at all. If she has an application or an appeal or a claim that has any merit the judge who hears or deals with an application for permission to launch such an application, appeal or claim will make an order permitting her to proceed. The civil restraint order is only a filter to preclude the making of unmeritorious applications".[116]

Q18. Is it possible for a company to be represented by a McKenzie friend?
Hildyard J found that a company may be represented by a McKenzie friend under rights of audience granted in exceptional circumstances. Although there was no direct authority on the point, the court could rely on its power to regulate its own proceedings and in circumstances where otherwise the body corporate would have no-one capable of speaking for it, to prevent a failure of the administration of justice. The judge relied on Sch.3 of the Legal Services Act 2007 and on the Courts and Legal Services Act 1990 both of which assumed and recognised that the courts had such jurisdiction even if it was not conferred expressly. The litigation concerned the attempt by the claimant bank to wrest a large group of companies in the Russian Federation from the control and ownership of the defendants. An application for disclosure by the defendants had been admirably argued on their behalf by their McKenzie friend.

7–29

The company referred to CPR r.39.6 (Representation at Trial of Companies or Other Corporations) which provides:

"A company or other corporation may be represented at trial by an employee if:
(a) The employee has been authorised by the company or corporation to appear at trial on its behalf; and
(b) The Court gives permission."

The judge stated in relation to a helpful note on the applicable framework for a McKenzie friend provided by counsel for the claimants:

"It suggests the conclusion that, given that CPR 39.6 does now allow an employee of a body corporate, duly authorised to do so by it, to appear at trial on its behalf with the permission of the Court, the Court does have the jurisdiction to allow a body corporate the assistance of a McKenzie friend, and in appropriate (and exceptional) circumstances to allow that McKenzie friend the right of audience on an ad hoc basis."[117]

Q19. Will the court order interim payments to enable litigants in person to obtain legal representation?
Defendant litigants in person who had left Russia and were in France (for their

7–30

---

[116] *KL Communications Limited v Wenfei Fu* [2015] EWHC 2026 (IPEC), Warren J.
[117] *Bank St. Petersburg PJSC v Arkhangelsky* [2015] EWHC 2997 (Ch), Hildyard J.

own safety) issued a counterclaim for $80 million. The eight week trial had already been adjourned twice.

The defendants argued that without legal representation a fair trial was not possible and would not be ECHR Art.6 compliant. They sought a further adjournment and an interim payment to enable them to instruct representatives.

The court found that it had to be satisfied that there were good case management reasons for making an interim payment and that if the matter went to trial the defendants would obtain judgment for a substantial sum.[118] In ordinary circumstances the notion that an Interim payment should be made to fund a party's legal costs was fanciful, but there was the extraordinary factor in the instant case of the allegation that there would otherwise be an unfair trial. The counterclaim was complex and would require expert evidence. The prospect of identifying a separate issue with sufficient cohesion to be safely heard within five days, and deciding before then that the defendants would obtain judgment, was remote in the extreme. It would not be consistent with the court's judicial obligations, nor would it be fair to the bank, to order an interim payment.

The jurisdiction to award costs before the determination of an issue was normally confined to cases where there was a "common fund", such as in trust, company or matrimonial proceedings. The court was unlikely to exercise it outside of those circumstances to make one party fund another in a substantial amount going beyond disbursements reasonably required for the trial, and the application for costs was refused.

A definition of a fair trial was impossible and unwise. It was not impossible to afford the defendants proper access to the legal process and proper adjudication of claims. It was relevant that the defendants had voluntarily chosen England as a jurisdiction when they must have known of their travel difficulties, and that they had always encouraged the court's expectation that they would attend the trial, either themselves via video link or through their McKenzie friend. (**See the question above**).[119]

---

[118] See *Revenue and Customs Commissioners v GKN Group* [2012] EWCA Civ 57, [2012] 1 W.L.R. 2375.
[119] *Bank St. Petersburg PJSC v Arkhangelsky* [2015] EWHC (Ch) 27 November, Hildyard J.

CHAPTER 8

Assessments of Costs and Payments on Account of Costs

Introduction

The overall intentions of the 2013 reforms in respect of the process for deter-   8–01
mination of 'between the parties' costs were to reduce the issues and lessen
the time, and therefore the cost, expended upon this stage of a claim, recognising that in many cases the 'costs of the costs' had become unreasonable and disproportionate. These aims were achieved by a combination of
changes—some introducing entirely new concepts and procedures and some
being simply variations of what already existed. They were:

- Costs management designed, in part, to reduce the costs in dispute at
  the conclusion of a claim and reduce for the need for/the scope of assess-
  ments. This has been considered in **Chapter 4**.
- The introduction of the further fixed costs schemes considered in **Chapter
  7**, removing any need for assessments.
- Improvements to the summary assessment regime.
- A more efficient detailed assessment hearing process.
- The introduction of provisional assessments.
- A change of approach to payments on account of costs.

It is the last four of these upon which we shall concentrate in this chapter.

Summary assessment

One of the options outlined by Jackson LJ in his preliminary report[1] was   8–02
to abolish summary assessments altogether. He rejected this, describing the
procedure as:

> "a valuable tool which has made a substantial contribution to civil procedure,
> not least by deterring frivolous applications and reducing the need for detailed
> assessment proceedings."

Instead, the process has been altered, but only slightly, and the emphasis on
proportionality is likely to lead to more summary assessments in place of
detailed assessments. The procedure for assessing costs by summary assessment is now found at CPR r.44.6 and CPR r.PD 9. It remains familiar.

The court is charged with considering a summary assessment whenever it
makes an order about costs that does not provide for fixed costs. The general

---

[1] Review of Civil Litigation Costs: Preliminary Report, May 2009.

rule is that a court will undertake a summary assessment at the end of a fast track trial and at the conclusion of any other hearing which has lasted not more than a day, unless there is good reason not to do so. There is a further steer to a summary assessment when appropriate at the end of a multi-track trial in CPR r.29 PD 10.5. There is an issue about whether or not only the judge who has conducted the trial/hearing and made the relevant award of costs order may undertake the summary assessment. In *Transformers and Rectifiers Limited v Needs Limited*[2] the court concluded:

> "I consider that, in appropriate circumstances, another judge may be able sum-
> marily to assess the costs arising out of a hearing conducted (or an order made)
> by another judge. I do not consider that there is any binding authority under the
> current version of the CPR to the contrary."

In fact CPR r.44.1, to which no reference was made, does provide that a summary assessment 'means the procedure whereby costs are assessed by the judge who has heard the case or application'. Despite the comment above, in *Transformers and Rectifiers Limited* the court was only expressly considering the position in a more limited context, namely after a disposal of an application 'on the papers'. This is considered in more detail in the question and answer section of this chapter below (see Q6 below).

The parties must file and serve statements of costs not less than two days before a fast track trial and 24 hours before the time fixed for any other hearing.

The slight changes to the process in 2013 were:

i) a new N260 statement of costs (updated again in June 2015 and still in need of either further amendment or clear guidance in the CPR that where the proportionality transitional arrangements apply (CPR r.44.3(7)) there must be two Forms N260 one for each proportionality period); and

ii) the requirement to serve a statement of costs in advance now applies to Detailed Assessment hearings and the summary assessment of the costs of those proceedings.

i. The new N260—statement of costs

8–03 One of the major criticisms of the previous version of the N260, particularly where the summary assessment was of the entire costs of a claim, as distinct from a discrete application, was the lack of information that it contained. The new N260 ensures that the assessing judge has more detail by introducing a breakdown of the time spent on documents. Rule 44 PD 9.5(3) is no more prescriptive than its predecessor and only requires that "the statement of costs should follow as closely as possible Form N260". However, given the increased emphasis on enforcing practice direction compliance in the overriding objective at CPR r.1.1(2)(f), it will be a bold practitioner who uses a 'homemade'

---

[2] *Transformers and Rectifiers Limited v Needs Limited [2015] EWHC 1687 (TCC).*

variation, as there is likely to be little sympathy, rather the prospect of some sanction, if the form used does not provide the information necessary in clear terms. Given what is said in i) above if the costs span the 'old' and 'new' proportionality provisions, parties should consider separate Forms N260 (one for each period).

ii. The requirement to serve a statement of costs in advance of detailed assessment hearings

Rule changes made by omission of previous provisions are often overlooked as they are harder to spot. The provision previously found at s.45.3 of the Costs Practice Direction is no more. Parties seeking the costs of a detailed assessment must comply with the provisions of CPR r.44 PD 9.5(4) and file and serve an N260 24 hours before the assessment.

8–04

The change of emphasis

A decision as to whether to undertake a summary assessment or to order a detailed assessment is a case management decision. The amended overriding objective applies to all case management decisions and requires the court to consider the proportionality of its decision. Notwithstanding the 'costs cap' in the provisional assessment regime (see below), there can be little argument that a summary assessment requires significantly less resource, both in costs and in court time, than a detailed assessment. Accordingly, there should be an increased number of summary assessments. The likelihood of this is enhanced by the fact that many of the multi-track cases that might previously have gone to a detailed assessment will have been subject to costs management orders and, absent 'good reason', the court will only be troubled by the non budgeted costs (see **Chapter 4** for further consideration of this) reducing the scope of, and the time needed for, a summary assessment.

8–05

Parties wishing to seek summary assessment at the end of trials/hearings that exceed one day should ensure that Forms N260 are available to the court and have been served so that this is a realistic option for the court if time permits (even if summary assessment does not take place, the N260 can, in appropriate cases then be referred to as the basis for a payment on account). Whilst there is sometimes resistance to a summary assessment where the costs are substantial, it is interesting that para.F14.2 of the Admiralty and Commercial Courts Guide envisages summary assessments of the costs of interim applications where the statement of costs of the receiving party is no more than £100,000, but requires parties to be prepared for the court to undertake such an assessment even where the costs exceed this sum. This increased emphasis on the court to undertake summary assessments is illustrated by the provision at CPR r.51 PDN 2.59, that, save in exceptional circumstances, the court will undertake such an assessment at the conclusion of cases proceeding under the Shorter Trial Pilot (which means summary assessment of cases where there has been up to a four day trial).

Detailed assessment hearing process

8–06   In chapter 45 of his Final Report, Jackson LJ set out a number of recommendations designed to produce a more efficient and proportionate detailed assessment process. One, provisional assessment, is considered separately below. The others were:

- A new format of user-friendly bill that is inexpensive to prepare and ultimately can be linked to the same time capturing system that can prepare client costs estimates and Forms H for costs budgeting.
- Shorter and more focused Points of Dispute and Replies.
- Compulsory offers.
- The cross application of CPR r.36 to detailed assessment proceedings generally and the requirement upon the paying party to make an open offer.
- Clarity on the date from which time runs to appeal decisions made in the detailed assessment.
- Paper assessments when only disbursements are in issue.

Save in respect of the first of these recommendations, in respect of which a voluntary pilot has been operating in the SCCO since 1 October 2015 (see CPR r.51 PDL) and which has now been extended until September 2017 with a view to establishing a mandatory form of bill of costs to apply to all work done after 1 October 2017, the remainder were introduced in April 2013 by the following provisions:

- CPR r.47 PD 8.2 requires Points of Dispute to be 'short and to the point'. If a Reply is served (and it remains optional) it must be limited to points of principle and concessions (CPR r.47 PD 12.1).
- Under CPR r.47 PD 8.3 the paying party must make an open offer to accompany the Points of Dispute.
- CPR r.47.20 expressly applies the provisions of CPR r.36 to detailed assessment proceedings (it is worth noting that any CPR r.47.20 offer does not need to be the same as the open offer).
- CPR r.47.14(7) makes it plain that where the assessment takes place at more than one hearing, the time for appealing does not run until the conclusion of the final hearing (presumably this also means that where there is only one hearing, but over many days, the time for appealing any decision, regardless of which day it was made upon, does not run until the conclusion of the assessment).
- CPR r.47 PD 5.7 contains provisions for limited bills and paper assessments where the only dispute between the parties concerns disbursements.

Apart from the implementation of the recommendations above, the introduction of provisional assessment and the requirement to file and serve a Form N260 24 hours before the assessment hearing (see above), the procedure for detailed assessments largely remains as it was prior to April 2013. However, there have been two subsequent significant procedural amendments to detailed assessment proceedings – one to address the difficulties posed on an assessment of costs in a case subject to a costs management order pending the introduction of a new form of bill to facilitate comparison between any budgeted sum and the sum claimed on assessment for a particular phase and to identify those costs outside CPR r.3.18 which remain for assessment on the basis of reasonableness and proportionality and the other to provide certainty as to the correct proportionality test to apply where the transitional proportionality provisions apply under CPR r.44.3(7) – see **Chapter 3** and in particular **Q1** for more detailed consideration of these arrangements. The specific provisions apply from 6 April 2016 and are as follows:

- CPR rules 47.6 and 47 PD 5.8(8) provide that where a costs management order has been made and the costs are to be assessed on the standard basis (so CPR r.3.18 applies see **Chapter 4**), the bill must be divided into separate parts so as to distinguish between the costs claimed for each phase of the last approved or agreed budget, and within each such part the bill must distinguish between the costs shown as incurred in the last agreed or approved budget and the costs shown as estimated. To make the comparison even easier CPR r.47.6(1)(c) requires the bill to be accompanied by a breakdown of the costs claimed for each phase of the proceedings. An amendment from October 2015 introducing CPR r.47 PD 5.2(f) and 13.2(m) already required the paying party to serve and file a breakdown of the costs claimed for each phase of the proceedings. CPR r.47 PD 5.1A refers to the new Precedent Q in the Schedule of Costs Precedents to CPR r.47 PD as a model form of such a breakdown. It is important to note that both the breakdown and the division of the bill are required (the latter does not replace the former).
- CPR r.47 PD 5.8(7) provides that in any cases commenced on or after 1 April 2013, where the bill is to be assessed on the standard basis and covers costs for work done both before and after that date, the bill must be divided into parts so as to distinguish between costs shown as incurred for work done before 1 April 2013 and costs shown as incurred for work done on or after 1 April 2013.

Provisional assessment

In his final report, Jackson LJ recommended the introduction of provisional assessment under a pilot scheme. The pilot took place in certain courts in respect of bills for £25,000 and under. In the April 2013 amendments, the scheme was extended to all courts and applies to any 'between the parties' bill where the costs claimed are £75,000 or less (see **Qs 11** and **12** for consideration of what is included in this sum).

A provisional assessment is one undertaken by the court on the basis of papers filed, without an oral hearing and any attendance by the parties. There is a limited opt-out provision found at CPR r.47.15(6), under which the court

8–07

may at any time consider the bill unsuitable for provisional assessment and may list for hearing with the procedure for a detailed assessment hearing then applying.

The procedure is set out at CPR rules 47.15 and 47 PD 14. It can be divided into four stages as follows:

i)   Pre-assessment.

ii)   The assessment.

iii) After the assessment excluding an oral hearing.

iv)   Oral hearings.

i) Pre-assessment

8–08   The title given to CPR r.47 relates exclusively to detailed assessment. There can be no doubt that a provisional assessment is a form of detailed assessment. As such it is not surprising that many of the procedural provisions relating to the request for an assessment borrow heavily from those for detailed assessment hearings. CPR rules 47 PD.13.2 and 14.3(b)–(e) prescribe the documents that must be filed with the request itself. However, there is some confusion as to what, if any, further documents must be filed and when. Some have taken CPR r.47 PD 14.2(2) disapplying CPR r.47 PD 13.11 to mean that the receiving party does not file further documents in support of the bill. Others point to CPR r.47.15(3) and (4) as requiring supporting documents. This is supported by the fact that CPR r.47 PD 13.12 applies to provisional assessments. This apparent conflict is considered at **Q14** below. What is clear is that the court retains the power to direct the filing of any further documents which the court considers that it needs to reach a decision (CPR r.47 PD 13.13). The confusion means that at the moment there appear to be conflicting practices around the country with some courts requiring all documents in support as if this were a normal detailed assessment hearing, some simply making requests for specific documents when needed and some requesting no documents at all. Note that, unlike the position for detailed assessment hearings, the receiving party must file any 'without prejudice save as to costs' and CPR r.36 offers (in a sealed envelope marked "Part 36 or similar offers", but which does not reveal which party/ies have made the offers). The rationale is obvious—parties are not present to draw the attention of the court to any relevant offers as they would be at the end of a detailed assessment.

ii) The assessment

8–09   Strictly there is no requirement either for the court to fix a date for a provisional assessment or to give notice of it as CPR r.47 PD 13.4 and 13.6 do not apply (which might explain the logic behind CPR r.47 PD 13.11 not applying, but 13.12 applying – see **8–08** above) and the parties are not permitted to attend the assessment. The only obligation on the court is to use its best endeavours to undertake the assessment within six weeks of receipt of the request. In practice in the SCCO and the County Court, non attended hearing dates are being allocated – in other words the judge has time specifically allocated in the list to deal with a provisional assessment even though no parties attend. Some come with a further order that should the court be able to undertake the assessment at an earlier date it will do so without notice to the parties. The rationale behind these orders is understandable. The Costs Judges and the District Bench simply cannot accommodate these assessments in addition to other work requirements and so discrete time is made available within lists. However, should lists go short and there not be other work, then the further order enables the court to undertake these assessments earlier than listed.

CPR r.47.15(4) is clear that the assessment is based on the information in the bill, the supporting papers and the contentions in Form G (the Points of Dispute and any Reply to it). Documents filed beyond those required by the rules (eg lengthy skeleton arguments) or by specific requests from the court may be ignored by the assessing judge. The rules specify what documents must be considered and there is no obligation on the assessing judge to look at further documents filed unbidden (particularly when the time set aside for the assessment will not have been based on consideration of unrequested paperwork).

iii) After the assessment

After the assessment the court will return the Form G (and the bill or any   8–10
other documents, if decisions have been recorded on these). Whilst CPR r.47 PD 14.4(2) suggests that the court's decisions will be on the Form G, the decisions may be on that, may be on the bill or on a separate document – for example where the court is giving a written judgment on a substantive point and there is insufficient room to do this on the bill or Form G. On this point parties would be well advised to allow sufficient space for the judicial decision – too often a lengthy Point and Reply are followed by an utterly inadequate box for the reasoned determination. Some judges are requesting that Form G is filed electronically in an alterable form to avoid the problems of deciphering handwriting and for there to be sufficient space for the decisions to be recorded

The parties must agree the amount at which the court has assessed the bill within 14 days and any party wishing to challenge any aspect of the provisional assessment must file and serve a written request for an oral hearing within 21 days. If no request for an oral hearing is filed and served within that period then, save in exceptional circumstances, the provisional assessment is binding.

Practice varies on how costs of the provisional assessment itself are assessed where there is no challenge to the assessment. Some courts make costs orders when conducting the provisional assessment on alternative bases depending on whether or not any offers prove to be relevant. This becomes more complicated when the bill, or part of it, is subject to the proportionality cross-check under CPR r.44.3(2)(a) after the court has determined what is the reasonably incurred and reasonable in amount sum. (see **Q16** below).

The costs of the assessment are subject to the provisions of CPR r.47.20 and the general rule is that the receiving party is entitled to the costs. CPR r.47.15(5) caps the maximum costs the court will award to either party (other than the costs of drafting the bill and excluding court fees and VAT) at £1,500 (subject to CPR r.47.20(4) – see **Q18** and *Lowin v W Portsmouth & Co Ltd*[3] below).

iv) Oral hearings

8–11   Any written request for an oral hearing must identify the item(s) challenged and provide a time estimate for the hearing of the challenge(s). On receipt of the notice the court will then fix a date for the hearing, giving notice of at least 14 days to the parties.

The party requesting the oral hearing will pay the costs of that hearing unless it achieves an adjustment in its favour of 20% or more of the sum provisionally assessed or the court orders otherwise. This potential costs penalty clearly is designed to preclude minor challenges. On a bill where the costs are limited to £75,000 anything other than a challenge to an item of substance is unlikely to result in a 20% adjustment. There is limited guidance in CPR r.47 PD 14.5 as to when the court may order otherwise, indicating that conduct and offers will be taken into account. As yet no authorities have emerged to supplement this guidance.(See **Q19** for consideration of the position where a CPR r.47.20 Part 36 offer is relevant)

It is worth reiterating that a request for an oral hearing, as opposed to an application for permission to appeal, is the correct procedure to challenge any decision made on a provisional assessment.

A final word

8–12   Those keen to ensure that they comply with all relevant rules in the light of the more robust compliance regime now in place may find it a relief that CPR r.47 PD 14.2(2) does not require compliance with CPR r.47 PD 13.9 as this provision does not seem to exist.

Payment on account

8–13   Prior to April 2013 where the court made an order that a party was to pay costs it could order a payment on account of those costs pending an assessment. There was no presumption that it would do so, as was made clear in *Blackmore v Cummins*.[4] The April 2013 reforms reversed this by the introduction of CPR r.44.2(8), which provides that where the court makes a costs order and provides for a detailed assessment of those costs, then it will order a reasonable sum on account of those costs, unless there is good reason not to do so. This provision has also changed, seeming to make a temporal link between the order for costs to be assessed and the payment on account. Many courts interpret this to mean that there can only be one payment on account, with

---

[3] *Lowin v W Portsmouth & Co Ltd* [2016] EWHC 2301 (QB).
[4] *Blackmore v Cummins* [2009] EWCA Civ 1276.

this being ordered at the time of the costs order and that any further interim sums can only be obtained under the procedure for an interim costs certificate *after* the receiving party has filed a request for a detailed assessment hearing. (This is dealt with in more detail in **Q31** below)

In pursuit of proportionality of process the court is likely to adopt a robust procedure when determining the amount of any payment on account. In *Kazakhstan Kagazy PLC v Zhunus* [5] Leggatt J was asked to list a 1/2 day hearing to determine the amount of any payment. In dealing with the matter without a hearing he concluded:

> "The third request made in the claimants' letter is that, if the court intends to make an order for a payment on account of costs, a half day hearing should be fixed for this purpose for which the claimants would wish to instruct a specialist costs counsel. Not only is this request contrary to the terms of the order agreed by the claimants for the matter to be dealt with on paper, but to incur the costs of a half day hearing to argue about the amount of a payment on account of the costs of a two day hearing would be utterly disproportionate and wasteful."

Questions and answers

A. Summary and detailed assessment

Q1. What is the position when form N260 is either served/filed late or not at all?

Rule 44 PD.9.6 maintains the previous position – namely that a failure to file and serve form N260 without reasonable excuse will be taken into account when the court determines what order to make about costs of the claim or hearing (as appropriate) and about the costs of any further hearings/assessments which the failure may necessitate (so the failure is relevant both to the award, as well as the amount, of assessed costs).

The leading pre-April 2013 authority on this provision is *MacDonald v Taree Holdings Ltd*.[6] The appellate court held that despite the use of the word 'must', the provision is not mandatory and the judge had been wrong to refuse the successful party's application for summary assessment of his costs on the grounds that he had not served a statement of costs upon the respondent 24 hours in advance. The court made a distinction between cases where there had and had not been factors aggravating the failure to serve a statement. If there were no aggravating features then a party should not be deprived of all his costs. The court should take the matter into account but its reaction should be proportionate. In these cases the court was presented with three options as follows:

8–14

---

[5] *Kazakhstan Kagazy PLC v Zhunus* [2015] EWHC 404 (Comm).
[6] *MacDonald v Taree Holdings Ltd* [2001] C.P.L.R.439; [2001] 1 Costs L.R.147, Neuberger J.

- Whether it would be appropriate to have a brief adjournment for the paying party to consider the statement and then to proceed to a summary assessment of the costs. In such a case the 'sanction' was that the judge should err in favour of awarding a lighter figure.
- Whether the matter should be stood over for a detailed assessment.
- Whether the matter should be adjourned for summary assessment at a later date or for summary assessment to be dealt with in writing.

8–15   Does this approach survive the April 2013 reforms? In *Webb v E-Serv*,[7] albeit in an entirely different context of considering the time period to renew a request for permission to appeal, Turner J held that the word 'must' did convey a mandatory requirement. If this applied to a failure to comply with the provisions of CPR r.44 PD 9.5 a party otherwise entitled to a costs order may not secure it as that provision makes the preparation, lodging and serving of a statement of costs a condition precedent to applying for costs (CPR r.44 PD 9.5 refers to the fact that a party intending to seek costs must prepare a written statement and CPR r.44 PD 9.5(4) states that this must be filed and served the prescribed amount of time before the hearing).

However, the outcome of two cases, one where no statement of costs had been filed or served and the other where the statement had been filed and served late, suggests that the court is still resisting complete disallowance of costs.

In *Wheeler v The Chief Constable of Gloucestershire Constabulary*,[8] neither party had filed a statement of costs in advance of an appeal. The upshot for the successful party was an order for costs to be the subject of a detailed assessment, but with the receiving party to pay the costs of those proceedings.

In contrast, in *Kingsley v Orban*,[9] where the successful party had filed and served a statement late and the first instance court had pressed on and assessed those costs without any concession to the late service, the appellate court looked at whether there were aggravating factors, determined there were not, but that the first instance court ought to have adjourned for a short period to allow the paying party time to consider the statement before proceeding to assess, and allowed the paying party to raise further points on appeal (all of which failed). However, it is worth mentioning that the judgment makes no reference to the decision in *Wheeler*, instead determining that there was no reason not to apply *MacDonald*.

8–16   A halfway house was adopted by Akenhead J in *Group M UK Ltd v Cabinet Office*,[10] where a statement of costs was served only three hours before the handing down of a judgment when costs would be considered and, even then, that N260 did not contain the breakdown of time spent on documents.

---

[7] *Webb v E-Serv* [2014] EWHC 49 (QB) Turner J.
[8] *Wheeler v The Chief Constable of Gloucestershire Constabulary* [2013] EWCA Civ 1791.
[9] *Kingsley v Orban* [2014] EWHC 2991 (Ch) Nugee J.
[10] *Group M UK Ltd v Cabinet Office* [2014] EWHC 3863 (TCC) Akenhead J.

Akenhead J applied the *Denton v T H White*[11] three stage test to the breaches, concluding that the breaches were serious, that there was good reason for them and that it would be wholly disproportionate to allow no costs and, instead, imposed a 'delay discount' of £2,240 as a sanction for what he described as a breach *"at the lower end of serious"*.

Reference is made at **8–03** above to some parties using 'homemade' versions of Form N260. A regular omission from these is a breakdown of the document time. Whilst there is no authority on this, it is conceivable that the court may regard the *Group M UK Ltd* 'sanction' approach as of application in such a situation – and disallow all or part of the document time (the sanction being directly linked and limited to the breach).

Inevitably decisions will be case-specific. For example, whilst it may be appropriate to adjourn some cases for a detailed assessment where there is failure to file and serve a statement, if this failure were to occur in respect of a discrete application where the costs would be minimal, the court may take the view that an adjournment for a subsequent summary or detailed assessment in such a case would, applying the overriding objective, be disproportionate (even if the receiving party had to pay the costs of the assessment, as court time would have to be allocated to this). In such a case the court may determine that the successful party forfeits the right to a costs order on the application.

Avoid the uncertainty and the risk – comply both with the form of the costs statement and the provisions for service and filing of it!

Q2. Does the introduction of the breakdown of time spent on documents on the Form N260 mean that the court will deal with challenges to this on an item by item basis or will the court make one overall assessment of time spent on documents?

Notwithstanding the additional information provided in the documents schedule to the costs statement, the process remains a summary assessment. As such it would be inappropriate to expect the court to resort to micro management. The schedule was not introduced to turn summary assessments into quasi detailed assessments. Indeed, in his Final Report Jackson LJ indicated that he thought the 'old' N260 was adequate in respect of interim applications. His concern was that:

8–17

> *"...in respect of summary assessments at the end of a trial or appeal, I consider that Form N260 provides insufficient information. The court is assessing not only costs related to the trial or appeal, but also the costs of the whole pre-trial process. In the short term, I recommend that a revised and more informative version of Form N260 be prepared for use in connection with summary assessments at the end of trial".*

Whilst we would expect the court to entertain submissions that the document time is unreasonable by reference to some examples from the schedule, the

---

[11] *Denton v T H White* [2014] EWCA Civ 906.

court is extremely unlikely to determine disputes over individual items in the schedule – rather it will use the schedule to inform the decision over the total document time that is reasonable or the total time for a particular task, e.g. drafting statements.

Q3. How does the proportionality cross-check at CPR r.44.3(2)(a) work in the summary assessment process that is already one undertaken with a broad brush?

8–18   In *Morgan v Spirit Group Ltd*,[12] when overturning the decision of a recorder, the Court of Appeal made the obvious point that the court must undertake either a summary or detailed assessment of the costs. The recorder had not done so. Instead, in a paragraph, the recorder had simply determined a proportionate figure and added something to that to allow for the existence of what he had, erroneously, described as 'a contingent fee agreement'. Summary though the assessment is intended to be, the court concluded that what had taken place here was not a summary assessment. So, summary though the procedure may be, it must still recognisably be an assessment.

These comments resonate loudly under the new regime, where the court is required to undertake an assessment of what is reasonably incurred and reasonable in amount for those items reasonably incurred and then step back and apply the proportionality cross-check under CPR r.44.3(2)(a). If the summary assessment is too summary, then the court will struggle to draw a distinction between the determination of what is reasonable and the determination of what is proportionate. The court must undertake the determinations of reasonableness and proportionality separately as to do otherwise makes the flawed assumption that the conclusions always elide. They do not. Whilst they will in some cases, they will not in others. There will be cases where the reasonable costs fall within what is proportionate (in which case the court need do no more than articulate that, having considered the factors at CPR r.44.3(5), the reasonably assessed costs are also proportionate), but there will also be cases where the reasonable costs are not proportionate (in which case the court then determines the figure that is proportionate and assesses the recoverable costs in that sum – see **Chapter 3** on proportionality for more detail as to how the court will undertake this exercise).

Q4. How can the court use the costs budgets at a summary assessment of the costs of the claim when the N260 is, inevitably, not divided into the same phases as the Precedent H to enable easy comparison?

8–19   It is certainly the case that the N260 does not match the budget phases, making ready comparison impossible. In his Final Report, Jackson LJ looked forward to the day when time capture recording systems would lead to "*a new software system should be developed, which will be capable of generating bills of costs at different levels of generality*". That day has become closer in the light

---

[12] *Morgan v Spirit Group Ltd* [2011] EWCA Civ 6.

of the inception of the voluntary pilot under CPR r.51 PDL in the SCCO and the introduction of CPR r.47.6(1)(c), 47 PD 5.8(8) and Precedent Q as a temporary fix in all other detailed assessments (see **8–06** above). In the meantime, the 'broad brush' of summary assessment will make it difficult to challenge the sums budgeted for phases that the court has costs managed. As a practical exercise, the budgeted sums will have to be deducted from the total sum claimed in the N260 to calculate what sum must relate to the non budgeted costs and only that sum is, unless there is a 'good reason' to depart from the budget for a specific phase/phases, 'live' at the assessment.

If there is a successful argument that there is a 'good reason' under CPR r.3.18 to depart from the budgeted sum for a phase, then the court will have to assess the sum for that phase, deduct the budgeted sum for that phase from the overall budgeted sum and add back what it has assessed.

A more challenging exercise, in a summary assessment where there is no requirement for a breakdown in Precedent Q, or similar format, will be to argue that the receiving party has overspent on a particular budgeted phase (and compensated for this by an equivalent under spend on another budgeted phase), where the overall sum in the N260 accordingly does not exceed the budgeted sums and the costs set out as incurred in the Precedent H at the time of the budget. Of course there is no reason why a party should not produce a breakdown of the budgeted costs on a summary assessment. Whilst this may involve a larger time and costs investment in producing the N260, there is certainly a compelling argument to assist recovery of this, namely that this makes it easier for the court to undertake a summary assessment and a summary assessment is more proportionate than deferring to a detailed assessment.

However, even when/if both a new form of bill/N260 are compulsory that enable direct comparison between sums budgeted and spent per phase, challenging issues will remain in any claim that has settled and it is found or accepted that not all budgeted work under a particular phase has been completed at the time of settlement (and this is surely a 'good reason' to depart from the budget). It will remain difficult to determine what deduction should be made. This is because the phase budget has rightly been set by reference to what is a reasonable and proportionate sum for that phase and not by an assessment of hourly rate multiplied by time (see CPR r.3 PD E 7.3, 7.10 and see **Chapter 4** on case and costs management above). Accordingly, as the budget figure has not been set by overall time multiplied by hourly rates, it is inappropriate simply to work out what work has been done on that phase by reference to such a calculation and to deduct it from the total for that phase. Instead, the court may have to adopt a broad brush and determine what is reasonable and proportionate as a lump sum for the work done on the phase up to settlement and deduct that from the total phase figure.

The preceding paragraphs have concentrated on problems linking budgets **8–20** to the documents required for assessments and on calculating partial expenditure on phases in settled claims. It would be wrong not to balance the scales by pointing to a couple of positives. One is considered below under payments on account. The other is the simplicity of the assessment where there is no 'good reason' to depart from the budget (or at least what we trust remains the simplicity – see **Chapter 4** and, in particular **Q76** for further consideration of this). A useful illustration of this is the case of *Slick Seating Systems v Adams*.[13] In this case the trial judge had also case and costs managed the case throughout. In fact he concluded that an award of indemnity costs was appropriate (and duly assessed those summarily), but his approach amply illustrates the benefits of costs management as he was able to avoid a detailed assessment (as would probably have been the outcome prior to the costs management regime) and undertake the simplest of summary assessments as follows:

> *"By running this case with a costs budget, I approved a budget of a grand total of £359,710.35 pence for doing this case through to trial. In my judgment that budget was proportionate to what was at stake: the £4.4million sum that I have just awarded. The claimants have laudably kept within that budget and have exercised due control over their activities and expenditure in an exemplary fashion. The statement of costs on 13.5.13 (which is today) is favourably compared with the costs estimate of 22.5.12. The form is signed by the partner of the solicitors and a member of the client company as well, Mr Beasley; the grand total is £351,267.35 pence. In my judgment that is a sum which is, looking at each of the phases, within the budget that was set and the claimants are to be commended with controlling the budget throughout this particular period.*
> *That will be the sum that I would award to be paid within 14 days without the need for detailed assessment, detailed assessment becoming otiose . . ."*

Even where there is an argument on 'good reason' it may still be possible to dispose of this at a summary assessment, avoiding the costs, time and delay of an assessment. Precisely this occurred in *Sony Communications International AB v SSH Communications Security Corporation*[14].

Q5. Albeit in a family context, does not the case of *SB v MB (Costs)*[15] suggest that summary assessment is confined to fast track trials and other hearings lasting a day or less?

8–21   In *SB v MB (Costs)* Hayden J declined to undertake a summary assessment as to do so was "likely to fall foul" of what was para.13.2 of the Costs Practice Direction. In fact, the relevant provisions he identified of what was 13.2 (namely that this was not a fast track trial and that the hearing had exceeded one day) are in the same terms as what now appears at CPR r.44 PD 9.2(a) and (b)). However, it is clear that the possibility of 'falling foul' of the Practice Direction was not determinative. Hayden J had already identified that there were elements of costs which would require consideration beyond the time

---

[13] *Slick Seating Systems v Adams* [2013] EWHC 1642 (QB); [2013] 4 Costs LR 576, HH Judge Simon Brown QC.
[14] *Sony Communications International AB v SSH Communications Security Corporation* [2016] EWHC 2985 (Pat).
[15] *SB v MB (Costs)* [2014] EWHC 3721 (Fam).

and information available to the court that day. As such there was no need for the court to consider the application of the 'general rule' at what is CPR r.44 PD 9.1 and was Costs PD 13.1 and the other steers referred to above illustrating that CPR r.44 PD 9.2 is not an inflexible strait jacket (e.g. CPR r.29 PD 10.5).

Q6. Does the decision in *Transformers and Rectifiers Limited v Needs Limited*[16] mean that summary assessments of the costs a) of applications, whether disposed of either at a hearing or on the papers and, b) after trials, may be conducted by a judge other than the one who dealt with the application/trial?

As set out at paragraph 8–02 above, CPR r.44.1 seems clear that if there is to be a summary assessment after a hearing or a trial, this can only be undertaken by the judge who conducted the hearing or trial. Strictly this definition does not seem to apply where an application is disposed of on the papers, as was, in fact the case in *Transformers and Rectifiers Limited*, This is because CPR r.23.8 makes it clear that the court may 'deal' with an application without a hearing. In this situation the less prescriptive provisions of CPR r.44 PD 9.7 apply. Applying these the court reached its conclusion by noting the substitution of the word *'may'* in the current version instead of the word *'must'* in the previous versions in the phrase *'may give directions as to a further hearing before the same judge'* and interpreted this as permissive of a summary assessment by another judge, stating that:

> *'"The provision at paragraph 9.7 of the PD is permissive: if time does not permit the summary assessment then and there, it may be heard later by the same judge. Equally, therefore, it may be heard by another judge"'*

If this interpretation is correct and any judge may deal with the summary assessment at a further hearing, then what purpose do the words *'by the same judge'* serve in CPR r.44 PD 9.7? The alternative construction, and one that makes use of the words *'by the same judge'* purposeful, is that where a summary assessment is appropriate, but not possible immediately upon disposal of an application, the word *'may'* is permissive of a choice, between either a summary assessment at a later date before the same judge or of a detailed assessment.

Q7. In the light of the voluntary 'new bill' pilot introduced in the SCCO what, if anything, should practitioners be doing in anticipation of the new bill format becoming compulsory?

In essence this question is not only about the format of the 'new bill' (now in its 2nd incarnation in the form of Precedent AB), but also about the way in which solicitors' time is recorded and whether the adoption of J-codes should be prescriptive. One reason that the 'compulsory pilot scheme' in the SCCO

8–22

8–23

---

[16] *Transformers and Rectifiers Limited v Needs Limited* [2015] EWHC 1687 (TCC).

has been put back reflects concern that it is premature because insufficient numbers of practitioners have been recording time adopting the J-codes, or in some other fashion which enables similar information to be produced as easily, to enable production of bills in the new format by the proposed start of that pilot. Given that:

- A primary purpose of the new bill is to enable ready comparison between costs claimed and costs budgeted (see page 12 of Precedent AA and page 9 of Precedent AB).
- Pending the compulsory introduction of a new bill, CPR r.47 PD 5.2(f) requires a breakdown of the costs claimed for each phase of the proceedings in claims in which a costs management order has been made.
- Costs management appears here to stay, although possibly in fewer cases if any fixed fee regime is introduced that incorporates some cases within the multi-track (see **Chapter 4**).
- CPR rules 47.6(1)(c) and 47 PD5.8(8) require a paying party to be able to divide the costs claimed between phases and, within phases, between incurred and budgeted sums (see **8–06** above),

the sooner that solicitors time is recorded using a system that readily provides the information that permits easy comparison between overall costs claimed, non-budgeted sums (incurred costs at the time of the costs management hearing) and budgeted sums (costs subject to a costs management order) by phases, the better. This should not be something new. In any claim subject to a costs management order since the inception of the regime almost four years ago, solicitors ought to have been recording time in a way that enables them to monitor expenditure against budget for those phases budgeted. However, as Jackson LJ advocates in his 'The New Form Bill of Costs' lecture to the Law Society's Civil Litigation Conference in April 2016, the introduction of a mandatory new form of bill at a specified date in the future with a sufficient time lag before implementation to enable solicitors to adopt some form of time recording that will readily provide the information and with work prior to the date being in the existing bill format and work after that date being in the new bill format, offers an easy solution. The pilot at CPR r.51 PDL envisages that the Civil Rules Procedure Committee will fix the date for mandatory imposition of the new bill format at its May 2017 meeting.

Another obvious advantage of time recording in such a specific manner means that the entire time recording process becomes a more transparent one in the event of any dispute over fees between solicitor and client.

Q8. Who is responsible for the costs of providing the breakdown required in a model form like Precedent Q?

8–24   As production of this information is now a requirement in cases where a costs management order has been made and the bill must be divided into parts matching the budgeted phases, then this forms part of the bill preparation item. As such, subject to the receiving party being awarded the costs of the assessment, then it should recover the reasonable and proportionate costs of preparation of the form. However, certainly to begin with, if time has not been recorded in a fashion that leads to easy allocation to a particular phase, what is reasonable and proportionate may be the source of some argument – (the same point applies to bill preparation time).

Q9. Does qualified one-way costs shifting ("QOCS") apply to the detailed assessment procedure?

To date there has been very little authority on QOCS. The question of what constituted proceedings for the purpose of CPR r.44.13 was considered in *Wagenaar v Weekend Travel Ltd (T/A Ski Weekend and Nawelle Serradj*.[17] There was no doubt that the claim between claimant and defendant was a personal injury claim, but the court construed "proceedings which include a claim for damages for personal injuries" narrowly and determined that an additional claim by the defendant for an indemnity from the third party was not 'proceedings' for the purpose of CPR r.44.13. However, the court was clear that where there is a single claim against one or more defendants which includes a claim specified in CPR r.44.13(1) (even if there are other components to the claim such as property damage), QOCS applies to the entire claim. In *Parker v Butler*[18] the court concluded that an appeal against the substantive decision to dismiss a personal injury claim was within the QOCS regime as the parties were the same and the relief sought was the same.

8–25

Applying *Wagenaar*, it might seem that if the detailed assessment is in respect of costs in a single claim against one or more defendants for one of the types of claim specified in CPR r.44.13(1), then QOCS protection applies to the costs of the assessment process. However, *Wagenaar* was not considering this situation and the judgment is confined to consideration of the substantive litigation between the parties. The wording of CPR r.44.14(2) appears to support the alternative view:

> *"44.14(2) Orders for costs made against a claimant may only be enforced after the proceedings have been concluded and the costs have been assessed or agreed."*

The use of the word 'and' suggests that the process of assessment or agreement of costs is in addition to, and separate from, the proceedings, which conclude at the end of the substantive dispute involving one of the types of claim in CPR r.44.13(1). On that basis we lean to the conclusion that QOCS protection does not apply to the costs of the detailed assessment process, but accept that there is no authority directly on point and that the counter view is clearly arguable. Our conclusion gains further support from

---

[17] *Wagenaar v Weekend Travel Ltd (T/A Ski Weekend and Nawelle Serradj)* [2014] EWCA Civ 110.
[18] *Parker v Butler* [2016] EWHC 1251 (QB).

- CPR r.47.20(7) which, albeit in the context of consideration of CPR Part 36, expressly provides that detailed assessment proceedings "are to be regarded as an independent claim"; and
- The acceptance in *Parker v Butler* that *'not every step in proceedings (broadly defined) which began with a claim for personal injuries is included in the definition of the word "proceedings" as used in CPR 44.13'* – although it is accepted that *Parker* decries attempts to exclude appeals from the QOCS regime, stating that this 'would do nothing to serve the purpose of the QOCS regime', and the same might be said of the separation of the substantive claim and the costs of the substantive claim.

This may be a moot point where it matters not by what route the claimant has to pay any costs of the detailed assessment (namely where the damages are such that QOCS protection would not prevent off-setting in full anyway against damages and it is only the route by which the court reaches this outcome that turns on the construction of 'proceedings'), but, where there is insufficient to off-set, this argument is pertinent. A definition of 'proceedings' for the purpose of CPR r.44.13–44.17 would provide welcome certainty.

See **Chapter 6** for a detailed consideration of QOCS.

Q10. Is there any sanction if a paying party fails to make an open offer under CPR r.47 PD 8.3?

8–26   On the face of it no sanction applies to this provision. However, the Court of Appeal expressly considered provisions of the CPR which contain mandatory language, but where no sanction is provided for any failure to comply in *Altomart v Salford Estates (No.2) Ltd.*[19] The court accepted the proposition that there might be implied sanctions which were capable of engaging CPR r.3.9 and equally there might be cases not analogous with CPR r.3.9 and where it was a matter for the court to determine the consequence of non-compliance.

Accordingly, it seems that if a paying party wishes to rely on an open offer made after the service of the Points of Dispute, where no such offer accompanied that document, then, by implication the court should approach this as analogous to an application for relief from sanction. The outcome of any applications made by 'receiving parties' for some sort of sanction are far less predictable. It is clear that the open offer does not form part of the Points of Dispute (it merely accompanies that document) and therefore it is difficult to see how any argument suggesting that the Points of Dispute should be struck out will find favour (indeed there is a risk it will be seen as an attempt to turn the rules into 'tripwires' and invoke possible costs sanctions). Perhaps a more measured approach is to identify the failure to comply to the paying party promptly, suggesting a short period for rectification, and, in default of compliance reserve the position to the question of costs of the assessment, if relevant, under 'conduct' within CPR r.47.20(3)(a).

---

[19] *Altomart v Salford Estates (No.2) Ltd* [2014] EWCA Civ 1408.

B. Provisional Assessment

Q11. Does the £75,000 limit for provisional assessment include or exclude VAT?

This is a purely procedural point. CPR r.47.15 and its PD provisions describe   8–27
the limit of £75,000 as being in respect of costs. The definition of 'costs' in CPR
44.1 does not include a reference to VAT (albeit that this is not an -exhaustive
list) – in fact, VAT is defined separately in the same rule. Accordingly, it seems
that the £75,000 limit does not include VAT and refers to the total profit costs
and disbursement sum. There is also a clear logic to this. Why should one bill
fall within the scheme and one not where the difference is the VAT and one
party is VAT registered and the other is not where the non VAT sums claimed
are equal? Notwithstanding this, some practitioners are not completing the
provisional assessment part of form N258 and are requesting detailed assessment hearings where the total sum only exceeds £75,000 because of the VAT.

**Q12. Does the £75,000 limit for provisional assessment include 'addi-
tional liabilities' (where the transitional provisions still permit recovery
of these between the parties)?**

Yes. The limit of £75,000 makes no reference to 'base' costs, referring instead   8–28
simply to 'costs'. The definition of 'costs' under the previous regime at what
was CPR r.43.2(1)(a) included 'additional liabilities.

**Q13. There seems to be a feeling that a paying party who does not serve
Replies to the Points of Dispute is at a disadvantage at a provisional assessment. Should receiving parties serve Replies in this situation as a matter
of course?**

Rule 47.13, which makes Replies optional, and CPR r.47 PD 12, which requires   8–29
Replies to be limited to points of principle and concessions, both apply to
provisional assessment by virtue of the provisions of CPR r.47 PD 14.2.
Accordingly, the court ought not to be penalising a party who complies with
these provisions. Indeed the reverse is true and the court ought to be astute
not to entertain Replies that contain 'general denials, specific denials or standard form responses'. Replies should not be filed as a matter of routine and
there should be no disadvantage to the receiving party as a result.

By the same token, paying parties should not serve 'extended' Points of
Dispute in an attempt to make up for the fact that there will be no opportunity for oral submissions. CPR 47 PD 8.2 is unambiguous – Points of Dispute
must be 'short and to the point'.

**Q14. What papers should a receiving *party file in support of a bill for a
provisional assessment?***

The challenge of what documents to file and when to do so is considered at   8–30
8–08 above. It may be that any uncertainty arises out of the use of different
terms in CPR r.47.15 – 'supporting documents' and 'supporting papers'. The

starting point must be CPR r.47.15 (3) and (4). The former provides that the court will undertake a provisional assessment on receipt of, amongst other things, the relevant supporting documents specified in PD 47 and the latter provides that the court will undertake the provisional assessment based on the information contained in the bill and supporting papers and contentions set out in Precedent G. Reference to 'supporting papers' leads to CPR r.47 PD 13.12, which does apply to provisional assessments under CPR r.47 PD 14.2(2), and which identifies 'papers to be filed in support of the bill'. This lists the following documents:

- Instructions and briefs to counsel arranged in chronological order together with all advices, opinions and drafts received and response to such instructions.
- Reports and opinions of medical and other experts.
- Any other relevant papers.
- A full set of any relevant statements of case.
- Correspondence, file notes and attendance notes.

In other words the 'papers to be filed in support of the bill' are exactly the same whether the bill proceeds by way of a provisional assessment or at a detailed assessment hearing.

The reference to relevant supporting documents in CPR r.47.15(3) is because the obligation on the receiving party requesting a provisional assessment extends further than simply filing the papers in support. The receiving party must also file the documents referred to in CPR r.47 PD 14.3, namely:

- A copy of the open letter from the paying party with the offer that accompanied the Points of Dispute under CPR r.47 PD 8.3 (experience suggests that in practice this is rarely, if ever, included).
- The documents referred to in CPR r.47 PD 13.2.
- An additional copy of the bill, including a statement of the costs claimed in respect of the detailed assessment drawn on the assumption that there will not be an oral hearing following the provisional assessment.
- The offers made (with those made 'without prejudice as to costs' or under Part 36 in a sealed envelope).
- A completed Form G.

Where there is a difference between supporting papers in provisional assessments and in respect of bills proceeding to a detailed assessment hearing is the timing for filing these. In the former the combination of CPR r.47.15(3) and CPR r.47 PD 14.4(1) suggests that all the documents, including the papers in support must be filed with the request for the assessment (an alternative construction of these provisions would seem to mean that the court need do nothing, and certainly not do a provisional assessment, unless and until it has received both the N258 and all the supporting documents). In the latter the time for filing the papers in support is governed by CPR r.47 PD 13.11.

Q15. Is there a sanction if the receiving party fails to file the required documents with the request for provisional assessment and can this be rectified? If so how?

What is the position if a receiving party fails to file the documents required by the rules or by specific order? One possible answer adopting the approach to CPR r.47.15(3) and CPR r.47 PD 14.4(1) in the way considered in the brackets in the final paragraph of **8–30** above, is that the court simply does not undertake the provisional assessment unless and until there is compliance. As the court does not now simply let matters sit in abeyance, the likelihood is that if the court did decide that receipt of all documents was a precondition of there being a provisional assessment, it would make an 'unless order' providing for a period within which the breach should be remedied and, in the absence of compliance, the bill would be assessed at nil.

    However, what seems to be happening is that the court is listing and undertaking the provisional assessment. What happens then if there has not been compliance? This was precisely the position that confronted the court in *Mehmi v Pincher*[20]. The Points of Dispute raised a dispute about the receiving party's liability to pay costs to his solicitor. In breach of CPR r.47 PD 13.2(i) the receiving party failed to file the requisite documentation in respect of his retainer agreement. The assessing judge provisionally assessed the costs at nil. The claimant requested an oral hearing and applied for relief from sanction under CPR r.3.9. These were listed together and the relief application was taken first. The court concluded that the decision was a sanction and so CPR r.3.9 applied, dismissed the application for relief and upheld the nil assessment as a result. On appeal the court concluded that the PD itself did not prescribe an explicit sanction for non-compliance and nor could one be implied. Instead, as part of the assessment of costs, the court had simply concluded that on the available evidence there was a breach of the indemnity principle and so assessed the costs at nil, rather than imposing that assessment outcome as a sanction for non-compliance. The appeal was allowed and the matter was remitted for the oral hearing, with an indication that CPR r.47 PD 13.13 could be used by the court to afford the receiving party another opportunity to file the missing documentation.

    In addition the court highlighted in the judgment a standard order in use in that court to address routine non-compliance with CPR r.47 PD 13.2(i). That order provided for:

- an adjournment of the provisional assessment to a later date;
- the use of CPR r.47 PD 13.13 to make an 'unless order' requiring

8–31

---

[20] *Mehmi v Pincher County Court* at Liverpool hearing 20 July 2015, unreported, HHJ Wood QC.

compliance, with default resulting in an assessment at nil and an adverse costs order; and,

- a prospective reduction of 50% of any costs of the provisional assessment to which the receiving party might subsequently become entitled if there was compliance with the 'unless order', presumably in recognition of, and as a sanction for, the original non-compliance with CPR r.47 PD13.2.

This decision raises three interesting procedural issues, as follows:

(1) Does the reference to *'any document'* in CPR r.47 PD 13.13 include documents that the receiving party ought to have filed anyway under the mandatory requirement at 13.2? In strict terms there can be no doubt that where there is a dispute about retainer, the actual retainer documents are understandably necessary to enable the court to reach its decision on this issue—falling within the wording of the provision. Similarly the rule refers to *'any'* and not *'any further'* document. However, it seems illogical that one element of a specific procedural provision makes the filing of identified documents mandatory, whilst another element affords an unfettered opportunity for the court to disregard this without any involvement of either party.

(2) CPR r.47 PD13.2 is mandatory—it uses the word 'must'. There is a body of post March 2013 authority in different contexts e.g. time for renewing a request for permission to appeal at an oral hearing (under what was CPR r.52.3(5))[21] and applying promptly to set aside judgment in default (CPR r.13.3(2))[22], suggesting that even though no sanction is prescribed, the word 'must' means that when considering any extension of the time permitted for compliance with CPR r.47 PD 13.2(i), the court should still consider the three stages set out in *Denton v T H White Ltd*[23]. Accordingly, either if the court of its own volition engages 47 PD13.13 to remedy a breach of the requirements of 13.2 (ignoring the question posed in (1) above and assuming that it can do so), or whether it requires the receiving party to apply retrospectively to extend the time period for compliance with 13.2, the ultimate decision requires a reasoned judgment.

(3) Is it proportionate to adjourn the provisional assessment to permit late compliance with the filing obligation? The court will have lost the time already set aside and will have to allocate a further provisional assessment listing. The alternative is that the court proceeds with the assessment and is likely to conclude that the retainer is not proved and assess the costs at nil and leaves it to the receiving party to decide whether to apply for an oral hearing and an extension of time within which to comply with CPR

---

[21] *Webb Resolutions Ltd v E-Surv Ltd* [2014] EWHC 49 (QB).
[22] *Mid East Sales Ltd v United Engineering & Trading Company (PVT) Ltd* [2014] EWHC 1457 (Comm).
[23] *Denton v T H White Ltd* [2014] EWCA Civ 906.

r.47.PD 13.2(i) – a route that may (as opposed to definitely will) lead to further court time being expended. It is right to record that the court in *Mehmi* did implicitly consider this in the broader context of managing a large court where the issue had been occupying significant resources and explicitly felt an adjournment preferable to the *'more cumbersome process of the inevitable oral review'*.

One unarguable certainty is that compliance with the documentary filing requirements avoids many 'interesting procedural issues'.

Q16. How does the court deal with the proportionality cross-check after a provisional assessment where the assessed bill is returned to the parties to do the arithmetic?

As time passes and cases fall within the new proportionality provisions of CPR r.44.3(2)(a) rather than the old *'Lownds'* provisions (see **Chapter 3—Proportionality**), this will become a pertinent issue. It is unlikely that the court will calculate the total of the bill immediately after assessing what is reasonably incurred and reasonable in amount (not only because CPR r.47 PD 14.4(2) places the responsibility for agreeing the total sum at the door of the parties, but also because of the time it may take to do this and in case it makes an arithmetical mistake).

8–32

As some cases with the new proportionality test have already started to work their way through the provisional assessment process, it seems clear that there are already two schools of thought. They are that:

i)   The court returns the bill, the Form G and any separate rulings to the parties to do the arithmetic, but adds an order as follows (or in similar terms):

"The proportionate sum pursuant to CPR 44.3(5) factors is £x. If the reasonably incurred and reasonable in amount costs exceed £x when the bill is recalculated then anything over £x is disproportionate and the bill is provisionally assessed at £x. If the reasonably incurred and reasonable in amount costs are less than £x when the bill is recalculated then those costs are proportionate and the bill is provisionally assessed in the recalculated sum."

This completes the provisional assessment and time for requesting an oral hearing is triggered by this order.

ii) The court requires the parties to confirm the recalculated sum after assessing what is reasonably incurred and reasonable in amount, together with any submissions on proportionality, and this is then referred back to the assessing judge to determine proportionality. Having done so the bill is then returned to the parties provisionally assessed in the recalculated sum, if it was proportionate, or, provisionally assessed in a lower figure (being the sum determined proportionate) if the recalculated sum was disproportionate. The provisional assessment is only completed for the purpose of the time for requesting an oral hearing at this stage.

There are attractions to both procedures. The advantages of the former are that it concludes the provisional assessment earlier, leads to quicker payment and involves less time and costs commitment by the parties and the court. It is also prevents problems if the assessment was undertaken by a part-time member of the judiciary who may not be available to do the subsequent proportionality element of the assessment if it is deferred.

The advantages of the latter approach are that the parties have the yardstick of the reasonably incurred and reasonable in amount sum when considering and making submissions on proportionality and the assessing judge has the same yardstick when assessing proportionality.

As the assessment of proportionality under CPR r.44.3(5) is an entirely free standing one, the time, costs and judicial continuity arguments seem the more compelling at first blush. However, this approach seems to overlook the wording of CPR r.44.3(2)(a), which only refers to the fact that the court *may* disallow or reduce reasonably incurred costs if they are disproportionate. Surely until the costs reasonably incurred and reasonable in amount have been calculated the parties are not in a position to make specific submissions and, therefore, the court is not in a position to reach a decision? An illustration of this is where the receiving party wishes to rely upon CPR r.44.3(5)(d) to argue that the conduct of the paying party generated specific additional work. Until it is clear what the court has allowed in respect of the reasonably incurred and reasonable in amount costs for that additional work, it is impossible to determine whether the argument is purposeful – for if the court allowed none of that work anyway, then it cannot sound in the proportionality argument.

If the court adopts the latter approach it is important to note that the provisional assessment is not complete as it is not carried out until the proportionality cross check has taken place. Accordingly the court should not be serving notice that the assessment has been carried out until it notifies the parties of the outcome of the proportionality determination under CPR r.44.3(2)(a). This means that the time to request an oral hearing under CPR r.45.15(7) does not run until receipt of that notice. If it were otherwise the parties would be out of time to request an oral hearing before they were aware of the final outcome of the provisional assessment.

Q17. Does the costs cap include or exclude success fees (where the transitional provisions still permit recovery of success fees between the parties)?

8–33 The costs cap may include both base costs and success fees. The qualification is that combined they cannot exceed £1,500. So, by way of examples:

- If the base costs are assessed at £750 and the success uplift is allowed at 100%, then both base costs and success fees are recoverable in full, as together they do not exceed the cap.
- If the base costs are assessed at £1,000 and the success uplift is allowed at 100%, then the base costs are recoverable in full, but only £500 of the success fee is recoverable.

- If the base costs are assessed at £1,500 and the success uplift is allowed at 100%, then the base costs are recoverable in full, but none of the success fee is recoverable.

Q18. Can the court make an award of indemnity costs under CPR r.36.17(4)(b) in provisional assessment proceedings and, if so, what, if any effect does this have on the costs cap of £1,500.

The starting point is that CPR r.36.17(4) is relevant in provisional assessments   **8–34** by virtue of CPR r.47 PD14.2, which applies CPR r.47.20 to these proceedings. There is no doubt that the result of these provisions is that the court must make an award of indemnity costs to the receiving party who has made an effective offer under CPR r.36.17(1)(b) in a provisional assessment unless the court considers it is unjust to do so (CPR r.36.17(4)). However, how does an order for indemnity costs interact with the cap on costs at CPR r.47.15(5)?

Hot on the heels of the decision in *Broadhurst v Tan*[24], which provided that an award of indemnity costs to a claimant under CPR r.36.17(4)(b) in a fixed costs regime case under CPR r.45 permits escape from that regime, came the case of *Lowin v W Portsmouth & Co Ltd*[25] and the answer to this question. In this case the court concluded that an effective CPR r.36 offer made by a receiving party meant that it was no longer constrained by the costs cap in CPR r.47.15(5). The court determined that as CPR r.47 PD 14.2(1) applies CPR r.47.20 and, therefore, by cross application CPR r.36 to provisional assessments, had the rule makers not intended the award of indemnity costs under CPR r.36.17(4)(b) to include the possibility that the receiving party would receive in excess of the cap, the rule would expressly say so. The case is binding authority.

However, we wonder whether this argument has run its course. This is because:

- It is arguable that CPR r.47.15(5) is the specific rule. If that is correct then this reverses the reasoning as there is then nothing in CPR r.47.15, 47.20 or 36.17(4) or the practice direction to CPR r.47 which provides that the £1,500 cap does not apply when there is an award of indemnity costs under CPR r.36.17(4). Accordingly, it is arguable that the effect of an indemnity costs order does not remove the claimant from the restraints of CPR r.47.15(5). Instead it could be construed to mean that when determining the claimant's recoverable costs the court does so applying the indemnity basis test at CPR r.44.4(1)(b), but with a maximum award of £1,500.
- There is a distinction between fixed costs (as in *Broadhurst*) and a cap (as in *Lowin*). In a fixed costs regime the award of indemnity costs under CPR r.36.17 is purposeless unless the claimant escapes the fixed costs regime as the end outcome is still the prescribed fixed cost sum. Under a

---

[24] *Broadhurst v Tan* [2016] EWCA Civ 94.
[25] *Lowin v W Portsmouth & Co Ltd* [2016] EWHC 2301 (QB).

cap there remains the possibility that an award of indemnity costs may make a difference e.g. if the reasonable and proportionate costs of a provisional assessment on the standard basis are less than £1,500, but with the removal of proportionality considerations the costs on the indemnity basis are higher than the costs that would have been awarded on the standard basis.

- As the court accepted in *Lowin*, the decision has the undesirable effect of reducing the incentives on parties to keep the costs of a provisional assessment as low as possible in recognition of the cap. In fact, as we consider in **Q19** below, the decision also has the potential to increase the incentive to challenge provisional assessments by way of oral hearing. This will increase both the costs of the provisional assessment process and the demand on court time under the CPR r.47.15 process.

Interesting (or not) as these arguments may be, *Lowin* is, as stated, binding and currently provides the answer. Where CPR r.36.17(1)(b) applies the court must award indemnity basis costs unless it considers it unjust to do so and an assessment of costs on that basis is not constrained by the maximum amount specified in CPR r.47.15(5).

(See **Chapters 5** and **7** for further consideration of fixed fees and CPR r.36 offers)

Q19. What happens in respect of the costs where at an oral hearing a party does not achieve an adjustment in its favour of 20% or more, but the adjustment made does make a CPR r.47.20 offer relevant?

8–35 This question is best answered by reference to specific examples. Example A is where the receiving party makes a Part 36 offer to accept £10,000. The bill is provisionally assessed at £9,500. The receiving party seeks an oral hearing at which the bill is increased to £10,100. In example B the paying party makes a Part 36 offer to pay the receiving party £10,000. The bill is provisionally assessed at £10,500. The paying party seeks an oral hearing at which the bill is reduced to £9,900. In neither example is there a relevant Part 36 offer by the other party. In both examples, the party requesting the oral hearing has not achieved an adjustment in its favour of 20% or more of the sum provisionally assessed (in example A the adjustment is 6.3% and in example B the adjustment is 5.7%). However, in both examples the figure assessed after the oral hearing means there is a relevant Part 36 offer.

It is important to note that the question raises the costs of the provisional assessment generally and not just the costs of the oral hearing. They raise separate issues and need to be considered individually.

C. The costs of the oral hearing

CPR r.47.15(10) provides a general rule that the party requesting the oral hearing pays the costs of and incidental to that hearing. There are two qualifications to this general rule. The first is that the party requesting the oral hearing sees an adjustment in its favour of 20% or more. In neither of our examples has this been achieved. The second is if the court orders otherwise.

Which CPR provision prevails – CPR r.47.15 or 47.20 (and by implication CPR r.36.17))? A year ago we said that as a specific rule trumps a general rule and as CPR r.47.15(10)(a) relates specifically to oral hearings as part of the provisional assessment process, that provision prevails. However, whilst the court in *Lowin v W Portsmouth & Co Ltd*[26] was not concerned with CPR r.47.15(10)(a), the rationale of its decision, that had the rules intended CPR r.47.20 (and therefore CPR r.36) not to apply to CPR r.47.15(5) they would have said so, similarly would appear to apply to CPR r.47.15(10)(a) (see **Q18** above). In other words because CPR r.47.20 applies to all of CPR r.47.15 (because CPR r.47 PD 14.2(a) provides this), then if it applies to CPR r.47.15(5) it must also apply to CPR r.47.15(10)(a). Accordingly in example A CPR r.36.17(1)(b) and (4) apply and in example B CPR r.36.17(1)(a) and (3) apply. This only leaves consideration under CPR r.36.17(3) and (4) of whether the court thinks it is unjust to apply the consequences of those rules.

Obviously if the application of *Lowin* is not correct and CPR r.36 does not prevail then the starting points would be that the costs of the oral hearing would be paid in example A by the receiving party and in example B by the paying party, subject to the court ordering otherwise under CPR r.47.15(10)(b). There is some guidance as to when it might do otherwise in CPR r.47 PD 14.5. This requires the court to take into account the conduct of the parties and any offers made when considering whether to depart from the general rule. Whilst it is a matter of discretion, this suggests that even if *Lowin* does not mean that CPR Part 36 prevails, any such offer will still be relevant to the oral hearing, but not as a CPR Part 36 offer, with the consequences attached to that, but simply as an offer under CPR r.47 PD 14.5. The court must then determine what, if any, departure from the general rule in CPR r.47.15(10) is appropriate.

As stated in answer to **Q18** above, the analysis that *Lowin* does apply may lead to the unhappy consequence that there is an increased incentive to seek an oral hearing, resulting in an increase in the costs of the CPR r.47.15 procedure and the use of court time.

The costs of the provisional assessment (excluding the oral hearing)

Rule 47.20 applies to the provisional assessment itself and when determining the costs of that procedure (excluding the costs of the oral hearing) the court simply looks at the end result. In our example A, the receiving party, has obtained an outcome more advantageous than its offer and so CPR r.36.17(1)(b) and (4) apply. In our example B, the receiving party, has failed to obtain an outcome more advantageous than the paying party's CPR Part 36 offer and so CPR r.36.17(1)(a) and (3)) apply.

---

[26] *Lowin v W Portsmouth & Co Ltd* [2016] EWHC 2301 (QB).

Q20 Does the costs cap at CPR r.47.15(5) include the additional amount under CPR r.36.17(4)(d) as applied by CPR r.47.20?

8–36   The 'additional amount' under CPR r.36.17(4)(d) is not defined in CPR r.36.17, CPR r.47.20 or elsewhere in the rules. Perhaps of more significance is that the phrase does not appear in the definition of costs in CPR r.44.1. In these circumstances it is certainly arguable that it is a sum outside the cap. This interpretation would make sense of the word 'additional' and also give effect to the purpose of CPR r.47.20, namely to encourage settlement by the threat to the paying party of a heightened liability if a reasonable proposal is not accepted. This view is supported by the decision in *OOO Abbott v Design and Display Ltd*,[27] where it was argued that the 'additional amount' counted towards the £500,000 cap in the Intellectual Property Enterprise Court. HHJ Hacon held that the 'additional amount' had nothing to do with compensation, but was solely to do with a procedure to serve as an incentive to encourage claimants to make appropriate offers. In other words 'additional amount' is not defined because it is simply that, an additional amount.

Q21. How does the £1,500 cap operate in respect of cases that are dealt with under the provisional assessment provisions, but where there are interim applications, e.g. to set aside a default costs certificate, for an interim costs certificate or for relief from sanction?

8–37   It is important to stress that the costs cap of £1,500 at CPR r.47.15(5) is the maximum amount that the court will award to any party as the costs of the assessment.

    If there is an application to set aside a default costs certificate, then it seems that cannot be an application made within the assessment, as by definition, at that time, there is a default costs certificate with the costs of the assessment proceedings dealt with under CPR r.47.11. As such, any application to set aside a default costs certificate appears to be a free standing application and the costs under any award of costs fall to be assessed (one would expect summarily) there and then as costs of that discrete application.

    Similarly, an application for relief from sanction – presumably in connection with the late service of a Reply to the Points of Dispute – seems to be a free standing application. It is not part of the assessment process set out in CPR r.47. As such it follows that any costs awarded on such an application would not be costs of the assessment and would be entirely separate from the cap. Indeed, in both this scenario and that relating to default costs certificates, it is conceivable that the costs of these applications will be awarded to a different party than the one which is awarded the costs of the assessment.

    It is arguable that there is no jurisdiction for the court to issue an interim costs certificate in a provisional assessment. This is because CPR r.47.16(1), which enables the court to issue such a certificate, relates to cases where the receiving party has filed a request for a detailed assessment hearing. The very

---

[27] *OOO Abbott v Design and Display Ltd* [2014] EWHC 3234 (IPEC) HHJ Hacon.

nature of the provisional assessment regime dispenses with hearings save where the court determines that the matter is unsuitable for the regime and lists a hearing or, after the assessment on paper, when a party requests an oral hearing. Having said this, CPR r.47 PD 14.2 applies CPR r.47.14(1) to the provisional assessment regime and the wording of that provision refers to a 'request for a detailed assessment hearing'. In reality, the point is unlikely to arise as CPR r.47 PD 14.4(1) provides that the court will use its best endeavours to undertake the provisional assessment within six weeks of receipt of the request. This is reinforced in para.10.2(e) of the SCCO Guide 2013, which states that any application for an interim costs certificate in a case proceeding to a provisional assessment will not be listed for hearing before the date fixed for the provisional assessment unless there is some good reason for an early listing.

Q22. Is the amount of the bill or the sum in which it is assessed in a provisional assessment likely to inform how much of the capped fee is awarded, e.g. does a bill of £70,000 justify an award of a higher proportion of the £1,500 than a bill of £20,000?

There is no straightforward answer to this. The cap is not set as a sliding scale. On a standard basis assessment it will depend entirely upon what the court determines is the reasonable and proportionate sum in any given case. Value alone does not determine this. There may be complex points of principle raised for determination within the assessment of a £20,000 bill that do not arise in a bill of £70,000. This links to the factors defining proportionality at CPR r.44.3(5) and factors relevant to the assessment of costs at CPR r.44.4(3).

8–38

Q23. Can the court make more than one award of costs for the provisional assessment and, if so, is the total amount apportioned between the parties limited to £1,500 or may there be separate awards to each party, each with a cap of £1,500?

CPR Pt 47.20 applies to the principle of the award of costs of the assessment proceedings. As such there is a general rule (47.20(1)(a)) that the receiving party will recover the costs of the assessment. However, this is immediately qualified to permit the court to make some other order in respect of all or part of the costs of the assessment (47.20(1)(b)). Rule 47.20(3) then lists specific considerations, amongst all the circumstances, that the court must take into account and CPR r.47.20(4) applies CPR r.36. It is clear from this that the court may decide to make more than one costs award in the assessment (perhaps taking into account when a CPR r.36 offer was made). However, when considering this the court must consider the terms of CPR r.44.2(6) and (7). This may lead to two awards of costs for separate and specific periods or one award, but of a specified percentage only.

8–39

If the court does make awards of costs to more than one party to the assessment, the wording of CPR r.47.15(5) seems clear—the maximum it will award to 'any party' is £1,500 (subject to any award of costs being on the indemnity basis – see **Q18** above). So, if there are two parties who both receive standard basis costs awards for certain specified periods of the assessment, it appears that each may recover up to £1,500. However, given the amount of work required in the provisional assessment process, it seems unlikely that a reasonable and proportionate amount would see the combined costs exceed £1,500 by much (save if it was a case where there is still a success fee recoverable between the parties).

Q24. Does the £1,500 cap on costs under CPR r.47.15 include costs incurred in 'Costs Only Proceedings' under CPR r.46.14?

8–40   It would seem not. The argument that the costs of the CPR r.46.14 process are not costs of the substantive claim and so, by definition, must be costs of the provisional assessment (relying on the judgment of Brooke LJ in *Crosbie v Munroe*[28]) and included within the £1,500 limit, was dealt a fatal blow by the Court of Appeal in *Tasleem v Beverley: Bartkauskaute v BartKauskiene.*[29] As Sharp LJ concluded:

> *"The bringing of Part 8 costs-only proceedings is not the commencement of, or part of, the detailed assessment proceedings, albeit it is a necessary preliminary to that process if there are no underlying proceedings in existence. This is because detailed assessment proceedings are distinct from the proceedings whether under Part 7 or Part 8 which have given rise to the costs order (see CPR rule 47.6(1))."*[30]

Accordingly, any costs awarded under CPR r.46.14 are entirely separate from the costs cap in CPR r.47.15. Of course, the outcome of the provisional assessment may inform what award of costs the court makes on the CPR r.46.14 proceedings – for example, the paying party may have made an offer before those proceedings in a sum that exceeds the receiving party's subsequent recovery on the assessment. For this reason it may be inappropriate for the court to decide who is entitled to the costs of the CPR r.46.14 proceedings until after the assessment of the costs of the substantive proceedings has taken place. An appropriate order may defer the award of costs until the conclusion of the detailed assessment (whether by provisional assessment or not) and, if that is by settlement, give liberty to either party to restore for this purpose. The court will then deal with the award and any consequent summary assessment.

This may seem an obvious conclusion as the simple fact is that Pt.47.15 states that it only applies to certain "detailed assessment proceedings" and Pt.46.14 proceedings are not detailed assessment proceedings (as is clearly apparent from the title 'Costs only Proceedings'). If further support was needed, it can be found in CPR r.44.1 where 'detailed assessment' is defined

[28] *Crosbie v Munroe* [2003] EWCA Civ 350.
[29] *Kauskiene* [2013] EWCA Civ 1805.
[30] para.18.

as a procedure for determining the amount of costs under Pt 47. 'Costs only Proceedings' may enable a party to start detailed assessment proceedings, but they do not determine the amount of costs—obvious until one remembers that in *Crosbie*, Brooke LJ had concluded that:

"... *assessment proceedings cover the whole period of negotiations about the amount of costs payable through the Part 8 proceedings to the ultimate disposal of those proceedings, whether by agreement or court order.*"[31]

However, the Court of Appeal in *Tasleem* specifically considered *Crosbie* and took the view that it served only to support its conclusions.

The costs of detailed assessments (whether provisional or at a hearing) and additional amounts

Q25. Under CPR r.36.17(4)(d) can a party recover the additional sum on a detailed assessment by operation of CPR r.47.20 if it has already received an additional amount in respect of the substantive award in the claim?
This question raises a semantic issue that arises when considering the subtle qualification that appears at the beginning of CPR r.36.17(4)(d) with the words *'Provided that the case has been finally decided and there has not been a previous order under this sub-paragraph'* and the wording of CPR r.47.20(7) which provides that:

    8–41

"*For the purposes of rule 36.17, detailed assessment proceedings are to be regarded as an independent claim*"

Is a case finally decided before the costs of that case have been resolved and, is 'a claim' the same thing as 'a case'? The plot thickens when CPR r.47.1 is considered. At first blush this seems to suggest that detailed assessment comes after a final decision. However, this rule talks of a final decision in *'the proceedings'*. Are proceedings the same as 'a claim' and/or 'a case'? None of these three descriptive terms are defined in CPR r.2 or in the Glossary at the end of the CPR. However, as the only purpose of CPR r.47.20(7) seems to be to distinguish detailed assessment proceedings from the substantive litigation, the scales appear to weigh in favour of answering 'yes' to the question posed. This interpretation and conclusion is supported by the fact that CPR r.47 PD 1.1 clearly identifies a final decision as being of all the substantive issues other than costs and sits happily with the conclusion we reached in answering **Q9** above, that detailed assessments are separate proceedings and not subject to the QOCS regime. This does raise the interesting question of whether the claimant is able to recover an additional amount on both the costs of the provisional assessment and the costs of any oral hearing see **Q18** above. The logical conclusion is that as both the provisional assessment and an oral hearing following it are both component parts of one set of detailed assessment proceedings, then only one CPR r.36.17(4)(d) award may be made. However, they are

---

[31] para.34.

clearly separate components (CPR r.47.15(7) refers to an oral hearing 'when a provisional assessment has been carried out' and there are clearly different starting points for the award of costs for each [47.20(1) and 47.15(10)]). As such it seems that the costs of each must be dealt with separately which would suggest that only one may attract the additional amount.

Q26. Is the determination of disbursements under the procedure set out at CPR r.47 PD 5.7 a provisional assessment?

8–42   No. This procedure is not included within either CPR r.47.15 or CPR r.47 PD 14. It is a free standing detailed assessment procedure. Its origins can be found in Jackson LJ's Review of Civil Litigation Costs: Final Report, December 2009[32]. Although in the report the procedure was discussed in terms of disbursement only disputes in fast track cases where the profit costs are subject to a fixed fee regime, CPR r.47 PD 5.7 contains no such restriction and the procedure is, therefore, available in appropriate multi-track cases as well.

   As the procedure is not akin to a provisional assessment and a paper disposal is expressly provided for, it seems that any challenge to the outcome must be by appeal in the usual way.

   One practical difficulty is the assessment of the costs of the assessment itself. Logically (and for reasons of proportionality) one would expect this also to be undertaken as a paper exercise with the parties filing statements of costs for summary assessment and offers in sealed envelopes. As the exercise is not a provisional assessment the fee cap in CPR r.47.15(5) does not apply, although it is difficult to imagine a situation where the court would allow more than that cap where the disputed disbursements do not exceed the provisional assessment costs limit of £75,000.

D. Payments on account

Q27. Is there any rule of thumb as to what proportion of the costs claimed the court will order as a reasonable sum by way of payment on account?

8–43   There never has been any genuine 'rule of thumb'. *Mars UK Ltd v Teknowledge Ltd (Costs)*[33] is often cited as authority for the proposition that two-thirds of the sum claimed is an appropriate amount. In fact, the route by which the payment on account was reached in that case is far from straightforward and does not endorse any specific percentage as a general rule.

   The decision is fact specific in each case. This is a point reiterated by Clarke LJ in *Excalibur Ventures LLC v Texas Keystone INC.*[34] when ordering 80% of the sum claimed on account stating:

> "*What is a reasonable amount will depend on the circumstances, the chief of which is that there will, by definition, have been no detailed assessment and thus*

---

[32] Review of Civil Litigation Costs: Final Report, December 2009 Chapter 45 para 5.2.
[33] *Mars UK Ltd v Teknowledge Ltd (Costs)* [1999] 2 Costs L.R. 44 Jacob J.
[34] *Excalibur Ventures LLC v Texas Keystone INC.* [2015] EWHC 566(Comm).

an element of uncertainty, the extent of which may differ widely from case to case as to what will be allowed on detailed assessment"

He went on to tender this approach to payments on account, which reinforces the case specific nature of the determination of amount:

"A reasonable sum would often be one that was an estimate of the likely level of recovery subject, as the costs claimants (sic) accept, to an appropriate margin to allow for error in the estimation. This can be done by taking the lowest figure in a likely range or making a deduction from a single estimated figure or perhaps from the lowest figure in the range if the range itself is not very broad".

In *Rallison v North West London Hospitals NHS*[35], a clinical negligence claim settled for £450,000 (where a much larger sum had been sought) and where the claimant sought a payment on account of costs of £574,000 and the defendant was offering £250,000, the court stressed that determination of the likely level of recovery at assessment necessarily involved consideration of proportionality of the costs claimed (other than, of course, in cases where the award of costs is on the indemnity basis as proportionality does not arise). The court awarded a payment of £306,763 on account.

However, the advent of costs budgets may assist and simplify the process by creating greater certainty over likely recovery on any subsequent assessment because part of the costs are budgeted as reasonable and proportionate already and absent 'good reason' under CPR r.3.18 will be the sums recovered on assessment for that part of the costs (however see **Chapter 4 Q76** for further discussion of the effect of CPR r.3.18 at assessment). In *Elvanite Full Circle Ltd v AMEC Earth & Environmental (UK) Ltd*,[36] Coulson J used the budget set as the basis for a determination of the reasonable sum to be paid on account stating, "the costs management order is likely to be the benchmark for the costs to be recovered", and based the payment on account on the conclusion that the receiving party's costs were unlikely to be much under the budgeted sum. Accordingly, it may be that in the absence of an indication that the budget is to be subject to some fundamental challenge under 'good reason to depart from the budget' under CPR r.3.18, a starting point will be the budgeted sum. Indeed, in *Thomas Pink Limited v Victoria's Secret UK Limited*,[37] Birss J concluded that the advent of costs budgets had altered the position. The budget was £678,000. The claimant sought £644,000 as a payment on account and the defendant proposed £350,000 (which the court accepted was 'the sort of figure one would have expected to have awarded'). However, having posed the question whether the costs budgeting rules have a significant impact on orders for payments on account, Birss J concluded that:

---

[35] *Rallison v North West London Hospitals NHS* [2015] EWHC 3255 (QB).
[36] *Elvanite Full Circle Ltd v AMEC Earth & Environmental (UK) Ltd* [2013] EWHC 1643 (TCC) Coulson J.
[37] *Thomas Pink Limited v Victoria's Secret UK Limited* [2014] EWHC 3258(Ch) Birss J.

"The sum sought by the claimants is essentially the budgeted sum at the time they asked for it. It seems to me that the impact of costs budgeting on the determination of a sum for a payment on account of costs is very significant although I am not persuaded that it is so significant that I should simply award the budgeted sum. Bearing in mind that unless there is good reason to depart from the budget, the budget will not be departed from, but also taking into account the vagaries of litigation and things that might occur and the fact that it is, at least, possible that the assessed costs will be less, although no good reason why that is so has been advanced before me, I will make an award of 90% of the sum in the claimant's budget (£644,829.10) rounded up to the nearest thousand."[38]

Q28. Does the court consider the proportionality of costs sought when ordering a payment on account?

8–44   Yes it does. See the answer to **Q27** above and in particular the decision in *Rallison v North West London Hospitals NHS*[39]. In fact this case was one to which the pre-1 April 2013 proportionality test applied (see **Chapter 3**). The fact that proportionality now trumps both necessary and reasonable costs under CPR r.44.3(2)(a) only serves to increase the importance that the court will attach to proportionality when considering payments on account in cases governed by that provision.

Q29 Must a party have filed a Form N260 (or equivalent statement of costs) if it wishes to seek a payment on account of costs?

8–45   *In Astonleigh Residential v Goldfarb*[40] *the court concluded that the CPR contained no requirement that a party seeking a payment on account had to have produced a statement of costs to inform the court's decision.* Of course, in most CPR r.7 multi-track claims the court will have the better detail of a costs management order to inform its decision (**see Q27 above**). It seems inevitable that in the absence of either a budget or a statement of costs, the court is likely to be conservative in determining the amount of any payment on account.

Q30. When may a departure from the general rule at CPR r.44.2(8) be justified?

8–46   There may be facts particular to a case that render a payment on account inappropriate. As an example, in *Rawlinson & Hunter Trustees SA v ITG Ltd*[41] the court was asked either to order an immediate detailed assessment of an interim costs order or, if it was not prepared to do so, to order a payment on account of costs. In fact it declined to do either for the same reasons – namely that the claimant might later secure a costs order against the defendant, may have difficulties in enforcing that and, if it had already paid costs would have lost the chance to set off what if owed against what it was due.

---

[38] para.60.
[39] *Rallison v North West London Hospitals NHS* [2015] EWHC 3255 (QB).
[40] *Astonleigh Residential v Goldfarb* [2014] EWHC 4100 (Ch).
[41] *Rawlinson & Hunter Trustees SA v ITG Ltd.*

Q31 Can a payment on account of costs be ordered under CPR r.44.2(8) other than at the hearing awarding the costs?

As stated in **8–13** above courts appear to take different views when considering this question. The wording of CPR r.44.2(8) suggests that the court considers this when it makes the award of costs and orders a detailed assessment. This suggests a clear temporal link restricting the court's jurisdiction to the time of the award of costs. There is a clear logic to this interpretation. It is the awarding judge who best understands the issues of the case enabling a determination of what payment on account is reasonable. This sits happily with the provision that only when there is more detail about the costs (in the form of a bill, Points of Dispute and, possibly, a Reply) can an interim costs certificate be requested. This suggests that detailed information about the case is a pre-requisite to interim payments of costs, whether by a payment on account or an interim certificate. A judge asked to determine a request for a payment on account who has not heard the arguments leading to the costs award and who does not have the documents available following a request for a detailed assessment hearing does not have that detailed information. The decision of the court in the recent case of *Ashman v Thomas*[42] does not undermine this analysis as it simply confirmed that until an order is perfected the court retains the power to alter it, which is in effect what occurred by the addition of an order for a payment on account. Indeed, the case confirmed the underlying logic of the analysis above as it was the judge who had made the costs award who altered the order before it was perfected.

    However, we stress that we are aware that the answer given does not reflect the practice of all courts. A rule change or Higher Court authority would assist, although the mandatory nature of CPR r.44.2(8) may abrogate the need for this as the awarding judge must always consider awarding a payment on account and so, if the receiving party then follows the detailed assessment process in a timely fashion, it can pursue any further sum sought by way of an interim costs certificate.

8–47

---

[42] *Ashman v Thomas* [2016 EWHC 1810 (Ch)

CHAPTER 9

The Effect of the Jackson Civil Justice Reforms on Solicitor–Client Costs

Introduction

The Legal Aid, Sentencing & Punishment of Offenders Act 2012 and 9–01
associated secondary legislation, together with the reforms to the Civil
Procedure Rules introduced in April 2013, have had a significant effect on
the conduct of litigation and on the scope of costs recovery between the
parties.

Apart from the imposition of a number of statutory caps on the levels of
success fees (in personal injury claims) and on the levels of the 'payments'
under Damages Based Agreements, and some relatively minor procedural
amendments aside, those changes do not directly address the question of
solicitor–client costs.

It is important to note that the fundamental legal principles underpinning
the ability of a solicitor to charge a client and the ability of a client to dispute
those charges are unaffected. The law in this regard emanates from a combination of statutory provision (primarily ss.56–75 of the Solicitors Act 1974)
and common law and it is doubtful that amendments to the CPR alone would
have the standing to alter those principles.

However, a number of the key changes undoubtedly have an indirect
impact on the question of costs as between the solicitor and the client, and
the solicitor therefore needs to be alert to this in order to avoid negative consequences. In some areas of reform, such as costs budgeting, it appears that
the attempt to control solicitors charging by the back door was intentional. In
others, for example in relation to proportionality, the effect was perhaps less
intentional, and the precise impact less obvious.

Those key changes will be considered in turn. It is beyond the scope of this
chapter to consider in detail the established legal principles relating to assessment of solicitor client costs, beyond by way of brief overview and consideration of how those principles have been, or may be, affected by those changes.
Risk management and law firm management are also outside the scope of this
book. However, by pointing out where issues arise as a result of the Jackson
reforms, this chapter aims to give readers a clear steer that they should consider them carefully and, if appropriate, seek further guidance. It is also a plea
for detailed guidance to be given.

One of the inadvertent consequences of the reforms is that they have
shone a bright spotlight on issues surrounding changes in funding, for
example concerning the reasonableness of a switch from public funding to
a case being funded with a Conditional Fee Agreement. A combination of

anecdotal evidence and a number of reported decisions[1] indicate that in the run up to 1 April 2013 there may have been a substantial number of cases where such changes took place. In such cases, where the claimant is awarded costs, opponents may have an incentive to challenge the circumstances of such changes in order to try and avoid payment of any additional liabilities or even to identify some technical defect which might allow it to avoid paying costs altogether. Whilst the basic test for the reasonableness of such a change appears to have been set as long ago as 2002[2], the particular combination of circumstances following the reforms is has led to the parameters of those principles being closely examined and tested. In many such cases, one of the key issues in dispute will be the quality of the advice provided to the client about the change in funding and the between the parties cases may well have a marked effect on and implications for more general issues about the quality of the advice to be given to clients about costs and funding options generally[3]. The matter is likely to reach the Court of Appeal, courtesy of the Surrey case, in 2017.

A brief overview

9–02   There is a fundamental distinction between costs on a solicitor–client basis and costs between the parties. The latter are payable as a result of any costs order or agreement between the parties and are subject to the very broad discretion conferred on the court by s.51 of the Senior Courts Act 1981 and any rules of procedure made thereunder.

However, costs on a solicitor–client basis are payable as a result of the contract between the solicitor and the client. Subject to specific statutory and procedural restrictions, the key determining factor therefore is the terms of the contract between the solicitor and client.

As with any other form of costs payable under a contract where the liability is a contractual one, the costs are payable on the indemnity basis, unless the contract otherwise provides (see CPR r.44.5 for the position in relation to costs payable under contracts generally).[4]

Accordingly, the starting point is that a solicitor–client costs dispute is a contractual dispute and is subject to any limitations within that contract.

However, as noted, there are numerous statutory, common law and procedural restrictions imposed which fundamentally change the character of the claim as between solicitor and client. These exist primarily as a combination of a recognition of the peculiar position of solicitors and the court's

---

[1] See for example *Hyde v Milton Keynes NHS Trust* [2015] EWHC B1 (Costs) – (appellate judgment [2016] EWHC 72 (QB), *Proctor v Raleys Solicitors (A Firm)* [2015] EWCA Civ 400, *McDaniel & Co* (a firm) [2014] EWHC 3826 and the combined cases in the judgment of Mr Justice Foskett in *Surrey v Barnet & Chase Farm Hospitals NHS Trust* [2016] EWHC 1598 (QB).
[2] See *Sarwar v Alam* [2002] 1 WLR 125.
[3] Including the question of whether and if so what extent concepts of 'informed consent' akin to those seen in the Supreme Court's decision in *Montgomery v Lanarkshire Health* Board [2015] UKSC 11 are relevant in a solicitor–client context.
[4] The introduction of the concept of indemnity basis assessment of costs between the parties only came much later, with the introduction of the concepts of 'standard' and 'indemnity' basis in 1986.

supervisory jurisdiction over them and a form of what would, in modern par-
lance, be termed 'consumer protection'.

These provisions may be analysed in three main categories.

Retainers

Firstly, provisions which govern the nature of the contract that a solicitor may   9–03
enter into with a client are primarily restrictive – that is to say they limit the
nature of the arrangements beyond what would be permitted in an ordinary
commercial context.

These arrangements, in turn, fall primarily into two main categories,
namely those relating to what is termed 'non-contentious business' and those
relating to contentious business. As to what is and is not contentious business,
there is a very circuitous definition of both at s.87 of the Solicitors Act 1974,
whereby contentious business is defined as business done "in or for the purposes of proceedings begun before a court or before an arbitrator. . . not being
business which falls within the definition of non-contentious business" and
non-contentious business is defined as *"any business done by a solicitor which
is not contentious business"*. The key point to note is that work which would
have been classed as non-contentious business will be classed as contentious
business provided that that work was done with a view to proceedings being
begun and -proceedings were in fact begun.[5]

If further guidance on this issue is required, the most comprehensive recent
consideration of the issues is to be found in Chief Master Hurst's judgment in
Tel-Ka Talk Ltd.[6]

The primary statutory provisions in this regard are s.57 of the Solicitors Act
1974, which, at s.57(2) sets out the very broad nature of the arrangements
that a solicitor may lawfully enter into with their clients in relation to non-
contentious business ("Non-Contentious Business Agreements", of 'NCBA's),
including what might be described as contingency, or outcome based arrangements, and specified the requirements for such arrangements, and s.59 which
sets out the ability of solicitors to enter into Contentious Business Agreements
(CBA's) with clients.

It is important to note that both Contentious and Non-Contentious Business
Agreements with clients are merely optional and that it is not necessary for
a solicitor–client retainer in respect of contentious business, for example, to
take the form of a CBA – though the exemption of non-contentious business
agreements from the effects of s.58 and s.58AA Courts & Legal Services Act
1990 is an important reason why such agreements should be considered in
appropriate circumstances.

The effectiveness (for the solicitor) of a non-contentious business agreement, when properly used can be seen from the case of *Bolt Burdon v Tariq*[7],

---

[5] See *Re Simpkin Marshall Ltd* [1959] Ch 229.
[6] *Tel-Ka Talk Ltd v HMRC* [2010] EWHC 90175 (Costs).
[7] [2016] EWHC 811 (QB)

one of the very few reported and appellate cases relating to the modern use of such arrangements. The damages based agreement type contingency fee arrangement entered into there was upheld by the court in full. The judgment is a useful reference point for anyone considering the use of such an agreement as to the sort of challenges that might be raised and the legal tests that apply[8].

In contrast to s.57, s.59 (in relation to Contentious Business Agreements) expressly provides that nothing in that section shall give validity to (inter alia) any agreement by which the solicitor retained stipulates for payment only in the event of success (a "conditional" fee), or by way of a percentage of recovery (a "contingent" fee).

This reflects the proposition that s.59 does not prohibit such arrangements but equally is not to be taken to permit them, in contrast to s.57 which does expressly permit, for example, payment by way of a percentage for non-contentious business.

9–04   The restriction on such arrangements comes not from the Solicitors Act 1974 therefore but from the common law prohibition on champertous arrangements, which could have been overridden by the statutory provision at s.59 of the 1974 Act, but expressly was not. That common law prohibition has, however, been relaxed by express statutory provisions in s.58 of the Courts & Legal Services Act 1990 (permitting Conditional Fee Agreements that comply with the requirements of ss.58 and 58A) and then more recently s.58AA of the same Act permitting Damages Based Agreements that comply with the requirements of that section.

It has been recognised judicially that such relaxation of the ability of solicitors to enter into such arrangements is a matter to be decided upon by Parliament and not a matter for incremental judicial expansion.[9]

Any conditional or contingency fee agreement relating to contentious business which does not comply with those requirements is unenforceable, either by operation of the express provisions of those sections or the common law.

Both s.58 and s.58AA contain provisions (s.58(5) and s.58AA(9)) making clear that the statute does not limit the right to enter into a conditional or contingency fee agreement for non-contentious business—save in respect of employment matters. Accordingly, the position remains that, as between solicitor and client, the nature of arrangements that may be lawfully entered into, and the formality requirements that must be complied with in relation to those arrangements, are substantially more restrictive where the subject matter of the retainer relates to what may be classed as contentious business rather than non-contentious business.

---

[8] A more salutary tale for the solicitor may be found in *Ejiofor v Legal Ombudsman* where Wynn Williams J upheld the Legal Ombudsman's decision that the solicitor refund the majority of a 20% contingency fee where the solicitor was found to have known that the risk of a substantive dispute was small and that the amount of work he would undertake was substantial. The contrasting judgments – albeit reflecting very different facts – also highlight the alternative remedies available to a client. The remedies under the Solicitors Act 1974 are not the only remedy.

[9] See Lord Neuberger MR (as he then was) in *Sibthorpe & Morris v LB Southwark* [2011] EWCA Civ 25; [2011] 1 WLR 2111 at 40–41.

If a solicitor enters into an unlawful and unenforceable retainer with his client, the likely effect is that the solicitor will not be entitled to payment of any fees for the work done, even if the solicitor's work was not done as the conducting solicitor, but is still seen as the provision of litigation services (see, for example, *Rees v Gateley Wareing (a firm)*[10]).[11]

A number of issues relating to the ability of solicitors to 'transfer' retainers, whether by assignment or otherwise, have arisen following the reforms. These commonly arise in a between the parties context, though since they are based on an attempt by opponents to take advantage of the indemnity principle at their heart is a contention that the retainer between one or other of the firms of solicitors involved and their client has 'failed' in some way. This issue is addressed is some detail in the chapter on funding and is not separately addressed here.

Entitlement to payment

9–05

The second category of provision relating to a solicitor's entitlement to payment from their client concerns the way in which a solicitor should bill that client in order to be able validly to claim fees from the client.

Again, the primary provisions are to be found in the Solicitors Act 1974 and again, the primary consequence is to impose a series of obligations and restrictions which differentiate the position from that of a normal contractual dispute.

Firstly, in relation to CBAs and NCBAs, the broad effect is that they determine the client's liability without right on the client's part to a full assessment. However, they are subject to an ability on the court's part to set aside the agreements if they are considered to be unfair or unreasonable[12]. Where such agreements provide for remuneration by hourly rate, the time spent on the case is capable of assessment.

The Act also provides the basic requirements for the form of a solicitor's bill of costs for both contentious and non-contentious business (s.69). A bill complying with s.69 (known as a 'statute' bill) is a fundamental requirement before a solicitor can bring an action to recover his costs. Errors in the form of a bill are not infrequently a flaw in such actions[13]. The statutory requirements have been amplified in case law such that it is now well established that a statute bill must be reasonably complete, must have a sufficient narrative[14] (though what is sufficient may be fact dependent and may not be a bar

---

[10] *Rees v Gateley Wareing (a firm)* [2014] EWCA Civ 1351.
[11] ss.57 & 61 respectively.
[12] For modern consideration of the Court's approach to these tests, see the Bolt Burdon case above.
[13] See, for example, *Vlamaki v Sookias & Sookias* [2015] EWHC 3334 (QB) in which it was held that a claim for assessment was premature since the solicitor's bills were not statute bills. Accordingly, the client's remedy was to seek an order under s.68 of the Solicitors Act 1974 for delivery of a final bill, and not to seek detailed assessment. That decision was followed by the Senior Costs Judge in *Rahimian & Scandia Care Ltd v Allan Janes LLP* [2016] EWHC B18 (costs). The two cases illustrate that the point may be deployed by either solicitor or client, but it is usually the client that will seek to make use of the point, to try and avoid the time limits under s.70 of the 1974 Act that would otherwise apply if the bills were statute bills.
[14] See *Garry v Gwillim* [2002] EWCA Civ 1500 at 59–60.

if the client is held to have sufficient knowledge of the relevant matters in any event) and should contain a satisfactory breakdown of the fees claimed.[15]

9–06   An exception to the latter exists in relation to contentious business where a solicitor may deliver a 'gross sum' statute bill (s.64), though if this option is chosen certain additional rights to request further detail and/or challenge the bill are conferred on the client.

The rendering of a statute bill, whether on an interim or final basis, is important because it is the delivery of the bill that triggers the client's right to assessment of the costs claimed in the bill. There are strict time limits which apply, whereby the client's right to such an assessment reduces from an absolute right (s.70(1)), to a discretion on the court's part, which may be subject of conditions (s.70(2)), to a situation where either the client may have to show 'special circumstances' to obtain an assessment or the court's power to order an assessment may be removed completely (s.70(3)).

However, it is important to note that where the fees are unpaid and the solicitor sues the client for the unpaid fees the client is likely to have a common law right to dispute the quantum of the claimed fees, and therefore obtain an effective assessment, regardless of the time limits in s.70.[16]

The necessary form of a statute bill aside, perhaps the key issue which arises in solicitor client disputes is that in order to be able to render a statute bill on anything other than a final basis (that is to say other than when the work has been fully completed) there either must be an express or implied agreement allowing the solicitor to render 'interim' statute bills,[17] or the court must be able to identify a 'natural break'[18] in the matter at which it was appropriate to render a statute bill. If neither of these apply, then any interim bill will be merely an 'on account' bill, at best and will neither give the solicitor a right to sue for payment, nor trigger the time limits for the client's rights to assessment.

Solicitor–client assessment and disputes

9–07   The third set of provisions relate to the procedure for resolving solicitor–client disputes. As already noted, s.70 of the Solicitors Act 1974 sets out a set of time limits which apply to a client's right to assessment, such time limits generally being triggered by the delivery of a statute bill.

The basic principle is that a client may apply (usually by way of Part 8 claim

---

[15] A recent appellate example of a solicitor being held to have fallen down in this regard is *Bloomsbury Law Solicitors v Macpherson* (QBD, 27 October 2016, unreported). A far starker example, where the solicitor's claim was held to be dishonest such that he was ordered to repay all sums paid was *Alpha Rocks Solicitors v Alade* [2016] 4 Costs LR 657. Although part of the latter case deals with issues relating to statute and non-statute bills, the case was so far outside the norm that it is useful only as an illustration of the existence of improper practices rather than as any guide to the matters which are addressed in this chapter.

[16] See *Turner & Co v O Palomo SA* [2000] 1 WLR 37. However, it is important to note in this context that a common law assessment is not precisely the same thing as an assessment pursuant to s.70 of the Solicitors Act 1974 and, in particular, that s.70(9) of the Act – which applies a robust presumption that the client will be awarded the costs of the assessment if the bill is reduced by 20% or more – does not apply. See in particular *Ahmud & Co v Macpherson* [2015] EWHC 2240(QB). In such a case, the client should rather follow the approach in more conventional litigation of seeking to make Part 36 offers in order to achieve a measure of adverse costs protection.

[17] There is substantial case law in this area. See *Re Romer & Haslam* [1893] 2 QB at 293 for the fundamental principle.

[18] For example, see *Re Hall & Barker* (1878) 9 Ch D 538.

or by defence to a claim by the solicitor) for an assessment of any bill or series of bills within these time limits and to satisfy any applicable test (such as special circumstances), though a solicitor is entitled to apply for an order for assessment of his own bill.

Where such an assessment is ordered, as a matter of discretion or right, prior to April 2013, old CPR r.48.8 applied. Until April 2013, CPR r.48.8 confirmed that any assessment was to be on the indemnity basis. However, it also went further. In addition to the two key general indemnity basis principles (that is to say: (i) the fact that a test of proportionality does not apply; and (ii) that where a doubt persists as to whether an item was reasonably incurred or reasonably in amount the benefit of the doubt will be given to the receiving party[19]), old CPR r.48.8 confirmed:

(i)   that where the costs were incurred with the express or implied approval of the client they shall be presumed to be reasonably incurred;

(ii)   that where the amount of the costs was expressly or impliedly approved by the client, the amount shall be presumed to be reasonable; but that

(iii) where they are of an unusual nature or amount and the solicitor did not tell the client that as a result they might not be recovered in full between the parties, they are presumed to have been unreasonably incurred.

This latter point (CPR r.48.8(2)) is an important point and may have a particular impact in the context of 'unusual' disbursements. It is a significant gloss on the general application of the indemnity basis.

Although CPR r.48.8 did not strictly apply on a 'common law' assessment,   9–08
the general practice of the courts appears to be to treat such an assessment in a similar fashion to a statutory assessment and in particular to approach the assessment on an indemnity basis.

Old CPR r.48.10 (there was no CPR r.48.9) and CPR r.48 PD 54.1 provided a set of more practical guidance as to the mechanics of the conduct of a solicitor–client assessment (these provisions survived the reforms largely unchanged and the April 2013 amendments are considered below).

The key remaining statutory provision to note at this point is s.70(9) of the Solicitors Act 1974. This applies a very specific provision for determining liability for costs of the solicitor–client assessment, known as the '20% rule'. Where the bill (or that part of the bill which has been referred for -assessment—see s.70(5)) is reduced by one-fifth (20%) or more, the solicitor pays the costs of the assessment.[20] Otherwise, the client pays the costs.

This is subject to the court being able to make a different order where it considers there are 'special circumstances', a situation which appears to have

---

[19] See now, r.44.4(2) and (3).
[20] Save where the assessment was requested by the solicitor and the paying party did not attend the assessment.

been open to greater argument in recent years, particularly where one or other party has made an effective offer.[21] The Court of Appeal has recently confirmed that where part or all of a bill is disallowed because of some problem with the solicitor's retainer with the client—rather, for example, than the more common reason that the costs claimed in that part were unreasonable—the 20% rule still applies to the whole bill. Accordingly, provided the client reduced the bill by more than 20%, whether that was because of the retainer problem or because the costs were unreasonable, the client would benefit from the presumption of being awarded his costs unless there were special circumstances which warranted another order[22].

Accordingly, it can be seen that both in terms of the nature of the retainer, the ability of the solicitor to bill the client and sue for its costs and the mechanism that is used to determine any such dispute, the position as between solicitor and client is, and has long been, heavily modified from that which generally applies as between 'trader' and 'customer'.

In conclusion in this section, the availability of alternative remedies through the Legal Ombudsman should not be ignored[23]. The ability of the Ombudsman to provide enforceable rulings in relation to fee disputes which are binding on the solicitor, provided the client agrees to the ruling,[24] in circumstances where the Ombudsman will take into account, but is not bound by the decisions a court might make in similar circumstances,[25] and to order the payment of compensation in addition where appropriate,[26] in what is usually a no costs environment,[27] and where the client's complaint, though subject to some basic time limits,[28] is subject to less complicated restrictions than under the Solicitors Act 1974, arguably provides a far more flexible and effective and, from a solicitor's perspective, potentially more dangerous source of redress for a client.

Effect of the Jackson reforms

9–09   This will be considered under a number of headings. Many of these headings

---

[21] See for example *Angel Airlines v Dean & Dean* [2008] EWHC 1513 (QB).

[22] *Wilsons Solicitors LLP v Bentine* [2015] EWCA Civ 1168. One issue left open by this case is whether the court should consider the 20% 'rule' by reference to each individual statute bill which has been assessed or whether it can and/or should consider the totality of the bills. In both the case dealt with in *Bentine*, the latter approach was adopted, though this seems to have been without demur by and/or at the request of the parties. This will often be eminently sensible where a number of statute bills are assessed as a result of a single application. The position is not helped by the fact that s.70(9) appears to have been drafted in anticipation of a single assessment in respect of a single bill – perhaps a historical legacy reflecting times when the idea of interim statute bills, rather than a single statute bill at the conclusion of the work, was far less common. Although the point is open to argument, it would seem difficult in principle to the court making a single costs order in respect of the assessment of a number of statute bills where those bills were the subject of a combined application. The 'costs of the assessment' would relate to the assessment of all of the bills. However, in light of the wording of the statute, there would seem to be a strong argument that any such order would have to properly reflect the outcome in respect of each individual bill and whether the solicitor or client was the 'winner' by reference to s.70(9).

[23] See the Ejio for case mentioned above.

[24] Scheme Rules 5.49.

[25] Scheme Rules 5.37(a).

[26] Scheme Rules 5.38(b).

[27] Scheme Rules 5.39.

[28] Scheme Rules 4.4 and 4.5.

relate to issues which have been considered in detail elsewhere and only their effect on the solicitor–client position will be considered here.

Changes to the procedural rules in relation to solicitor–client assessments

Old CPR r.48.8 and 48.10 no longer exist, but have been repeated in substantially identical terms in current CPR r.46.9 and 46.10, including the important provision, now at CPR r.46.9(3)(c) relating to the presumed unreasonableness of costs where they are of an unusual nature or amount and the client was not warned that they may not be recovered from the other party to litigation as a result. **9–10**

For reasons which are not entirely clear, there has been a slight amendment to the wording such that where the rule used to provide that they were presumed to be unreasonable if the client was not warned that he might not recover 'all of them', the rule now merely provides that they are presumed unreasonable if the client was not warned that the costs 'might not be recovered'. This would appear to be merely a tidying up of the wording and is not thought to have been intended to introduce any substantive change.

The Court of Appeal has recently confirmed that the provision under CPR r.39.2(3) to order that a hearing may be held in private applies equally to solicitor client assessments under the 1974 Act and the case illustrates and provides guidance as to the sort of circumstances in which such an order may be made[29]. It is highly unlikely that the courts will allow such orders to become commonplace in this context.

Costs budgeting

Costs budgeting is addressed elsewhere.[30] From a solicitor–client perspective, the most significant impact is likely to be that, where a costs management order is made reflecting either agreement between the parties or approval by the court after making revisions, there exists a clear restriction from that point onwards on the costs that the client is likely to be able to recover from the opponent if the litigation succeeds. **9–11**

It is important that the client is made aware of that restriction and its effect. In particular, where, as will commonly, though not always, be the case, the retainer between solicitor and client provides that the client's liability is not limited to costs recovered between the parties, it will be extremely important, though perhaps difficult to achieve in practice, that the client is made aware of the likely shortfall in costs and is provided with an opportunity to provide an informed agreement to costs which fall outside the approved budget being incurred.

The practical approach to this is likely to differ from case to case (or at least type of case to type of case). However, as a minimum, it should be expected

---

[29] *Dechert LLP v Eurasian natural Resources Corp* Ltd [2016] EWCA Civ 375, [2016] 2 Costs LO 327
[30] See Ch.4.

that at the outset the client will be told in clear, written, terms of the risk of a shortfall of costs even if the claim succeeds and costs are awarded, and of particular types of costs which will not or might not be recovered. The obvious example, post-April 2013, is a success fee. Save for a limited class of cases, it is inexcusable not to tell the client, in clear terms, that where a success fee will be charged that success fee will not, in any circumstances, be recoverable from the opponent, even if costs are otherwise awarded and will be payable by the client alone. The same point applies to the costs of setting up a particular form of funding, or of considering After The Event insurance. More fact dependent examples might include the possibility of instruction of a QC, or of particular experts, or of particular types of costs being incurred (perhaps if an unusually large disclosure exercise is being contemplated).

Equally, the common warning in the past, that as a rule of thumb a between the parties recovery of two thirds (or 70%) was likely is now both inaccurate and insufficient, particularly in light of recent decisions on the 'new' proportionality test on a between the parties basis. What the client needs to be made aware of is the risk of a substantial shortfall generally, of the risk of not recovering particular items of costs that might be incurred, and that the client has a choice, which he should be given reasonable information in order to make, as to whether such costs are to be incurred (whilst, where appropriate, being informed whether, and if so why, the solicitor considers that those costs are appropriate, desirable or necessary).

9–12   Reference has already been made to the presumptions which apply under what is now CPR r.46.9. A failure to make it clear to the client that a cost to be incurred is one which falls outside the budget (because, for example, it is not a recoverable cost or it is a cost not included on approval of the budget) may well result in that cost being seen as falling within CPR r.46.9(3) and/ or (b) or, in any event, may lead to the court being satisfied that it is unreasonable for the client to be held liable to pay that cost. By the same token, obtaining the client's express approval to the cost being incurred despite the probability of it being irrecoverable between the parties, because it is outside the approved budget, will give the solicitor the benefit of the s.46.(3)(a) and/ or (b) presumptions.

It is, of course, in any event good practice (and possible essential) to provide the client with clear and accurate costs estimates, see for example Solicitors Code of Conduct 2011, IB 1.14–1.19.

Despite initial suggestions to the contrary (see, for example, HH Judge Simon Brown QC[31]), when CPR r.3 Pt II was introduced, there was no requirement to obtain the client's signature or to record in any other way the client's approval or agreement that the costs in the Precedent H budget submitted to the court were reasonable or proportionate or in any other way were an appropriate sum to expend on the case. In addition, oddly, there is also no

---

[31] HH Judge Simon Brown QC, "Costs control Costs management & docketed judges: are you ready for the big bang next year?" (2012) 6 April & 13 NLJ 498–499.

requirement that the terms of any costs management order are served on the client. The provision on the pilot scheme in the Commercial courts under CPR r.51 PD 51G para.6, which provided that the client should be notified with seven days of the budgeting hearing of the budget set by the court was also not carried through to the wider reforms.

However, it was clearly an intention of the costs budgeting reforms that effective between the parties costs management, whilst not fixing the price between the solicitor and client,[32] would be in the interests of the clients.[33] In the absence of express provision in the rules on costs management, it seems that in practice this might be achieved by the courts, on any subsequent solicitor–client assessment, placing a high burden on solicitors who charge clients sums above the costs budget to show that the client received proper information in this regard and was given an informed choice as to whether to incur such costs, or at the very least was made aware when such costs were being incurred that they were unlikely to be recoverable between the parties.

Both caution and good practice suggest that where the costs budget which is prepared shows costs potentially claimable between the parties which are materially less than those the client is liable to pay, the client should be given clear prior information and explanation in relation to this. The party/party costs budget filed under CPR r.3.13 is the client's costs budget, not the solicitor's, and if the budget indicates any 'limitation' on the costs which might be claimed, let alone recovered or allowed, between the parties then the client should be informed of this.

9–13

One way to address this might be by producing a modified budget for the client, showing the additional sums the client may be liable to pay.

It is important to remember that between the parties costs are not generally intended to be a full indemnity for the client. There will almost invariably be an element of costs incurred which simply are not and never would be recoverable between the parties (a classic modern example being the costs of arranging or considering various forms of funding[34]). In addition, it will be rare that the costs awarded on a between the parties basis cover the full costs which might have been reasonably incurred on the clients instructions. The fact that the indemnity basis is the default basis for solicitor–client-assessments expressly recognises this.

Equally, and perhaps even more importantly in light of the 'new' proportionality test, no test of proportionality applies on a solicitor client basis.

It is, therefore, unrealistic to expect that costs budgets, subject to rigorous review on the standard between the parties basis, applying a test of proportionality, should be expected also to set the proper level of costs on a solicitor–client basis, or that such budgets should simply be used by solicitors as their

---

[32] See *Judiciary: Lord Justice Jackson's paper for the Civil Justice Council conference* (21 March 2014), paras. 5.2 and 5.7.
[33] See Final Report, p.415, para.7.3 for example.
[34] See *Motto v Trafigura* [2011] EWCA Civ 1150; [2012] 1 WLR 657.

costs estimates on a solicitor–client basis unless those solicitors wish to restrict unduly the costs they might reasonably charge their clients[35].

What the budgeting provisions do emphasise, however, is the fundamental importance of solicitors providing clients with clear and regular costs information both as to costs they may have to pay to their solicitor and costs they may recover from the other side if they are successful in their litigation (and which they may have to pay the other side if they lose) and, in particular, of explaining in clear terms how and why the costs the client may be liable to pay may differ from the costs to be allowed between the parties. A simple statement that *'if you are awarded costs against your opponent, the costs awarded are unlikely to cover our full costs'* is no longer sufficient. A great deal more detail is now required – an explanation of the test(s) of proportionality (and the substantial uncertainty that it creates), of what costs budgeting means, of the various tests on assessment, the meaning of the retainer and so on. The standard, pre-April 2013, retainer letter wording is no longer sufficient. The information provided needs to be tailored to the individual client and repeated at various intervals. With regard to the effect of costs budgeting, if the client is closely involved in the process and there is a process set up for what happens if the court does not allow costs, it is likely to make for less argument later.

Proportionality

9–14 This has been touched on above. The new test of proportionality, introduced by CPR r.44.3(5), was expressly intended to reverse the unsatisfactory test as clarified in *Lownds*[36] with a view to reducing the costs of litigation, at least where the assessment of costs is being carried out on a standard basis.

The precise effect of this new test is addressed elsewhere in this supplement. However, it seems clear that the new test, reinforced by the amendment to the overriding objective and in conjunction with the wider use of costs budgeting and of summary assessment, is a robust tool in the judicial armoury[37].

If 'new proportionality' is to serve its intended purpose, the ultimate outcome seems to be that there will be a reduction in between the parties costs[38]. Further, that this will, by the very nature of the test and its intended use as a 'backstop' following the initial consideration of whether the costs are reasonable, be a somewhat arbitrary test, the precise effect of which will be difficult to predict in any given case.

Its impact seems likely to be greater in cases of relatively modest value, though again this remains to be seen.

All of this means that there is likely to be a greater shortfall between the costs recovered between the parties and those for which the client is prima facie liable on a solicitor–client basis and that this shortfall will potentially be proportionately all the greater in the very cases where the successful client's

---

[35] For further discussion on this topic see **Chapter 3, Q16.**
[36] *Lownds v Home Office* [2002] 1 WLR 2450.
[37] See, for example, *BNM v MGN Limited* [2016] EWHC B13 (Costs) on appeal to the Court of Appeal
[38] See the notes in the chapter on proportionality as to how this new approach is taking effect in practice.

damages are lower. However, because of the uncertainty surrounding proportionality, the actual amount of reduction is hard to specify.

This serves to emphasise further the points in the preceding section as to the increased need for clear and regularly updated guidance to clients as to any potential shortfall. Even if this is just in broad terms and all that can be said is that there is likely to be a shortfall and no one can say for certain in what amount.

Whilst no test of proportionality applies on a solicitor–client assessment, a solicitor is obliged to discuss with a client, in a clear and accessible form, whether the potential outcome of a case is likely to justify the expense involved. Where a solicitor fails to provide clear information in this regard both at the start and during the case, and where the solicitor fails to warn the client, particularly in a low value claim, that there may be a substantial shortfall, it may reasonably be anticipated that the courts will take an increasingly hard line towards solicitor–client assessments of the shortfall costs.

The wider effect of 'Jackson'

The costs management reforms were intended to be part of a coherent package   9–15
of reforms aimed at not merely reducing the cost of litigation, but improving the process.

It is the express purpose of costs management that the court should manage not merely the costs to be 'incurred by the parties' (note, not merely 'recovered by' or 'allowed to' the parties), but also the steps to be taken.

In this regard, the reforms extend beyond the introduction of costs management and seek to give the courts more robust powers in relation to case management generally. These include explicit powers to restrict expert evidence by reference to specific issues (CPR r.35.4), to limit the issues to be addressed by witnesses and the length and format of statements (CPR r.32.2) and to take a more focused, and where appropriate, restricted approach to disclosure (CPR r.31.5).

Although these matters do not necessarily directly impact on solicitor–client costs, they can arguably control spend. It is clearly an issue of vital importance that clients are made aware that, to the extent that there was before, there is no longer any guarantee of a system whereby the client can simply engage in 'chequebook' litigation. Clearly a client must be informed on occasions that, although it is open to the client to take a Rolls Royce approach to an aspect of litigation, the cost of doing so is unlikely to be recovered between the parties (for example, the instruction of a QC where the court considers it disproportionate). In addition, the client should be made aware that, whilst the solicitor may consider that a particular approach to the litigation is appropriate (for example the instruction of experts in a particular field), the court may disagree and is exhorted by CPR r.3.12 to take both case and costs management together.

Equally, there will increasingly be occasions where the client must be told that, however much it is prepared to spend, the cost will be to no benefit. This is not a question of recoverability but of restrictions on the client's options because of case management decisions There is little point in the client engaging a number of costly experts if it is likely that the court will direct evidence from a single expert on limited issues only and the client must be warned of this increased risk before the cost in incurred.

Case and costs management is looked at in more detail in **Chapter 4.**

Fixed costs claims

9-16   An element of fixed costs, whether in relation to certain aspects of the costs (such as trial costs in Fast Track claims) or the whole of the profit costs (for example in low value RTA claims) is an increasing part of the CPR and is a feature seems likely to apply much more widely in future[39].

In principle, the ability of a solicitor to charge a client for work done is unaffected by the fact that the costs are fixed in whole or part on a between the parties basis. However, it is a clear and obvious point that, where the solicitor's retainer does not limit the costs payable by the client to those recovered between the parties, the client must be told in clear terms that the costs of the claim are, or might be, fixed and that, even if successful, there is likely to be a significant difference between the costs payable by the client and those recovered from the opponent. A failure to do so is likely to lead to an inability to recover any shortfall between the two.

It is important to remember that any arrangement whereby the costs to be charged to the client are limited to sums recovered between the parties is a species of Conditional Fee Agreement (a CFA 'lite'), on the basis that it is "an agreement . . . which provided for fees and expenses, or any part of them, to be payable only in specified circumstances",[40] even where it does not provide for a success fee, and therefore such an agreement must comply with s.58 of the Courts & Legal Services Act 1990 if it is to be enforceable.

Conversely, it should be remembered that between the parties cost are an entitlement of the client and are recovered in the client's name. In a fixed costs claim (and assuming that the indemnity principle is effectively disapplied),[41] where the costs recovered between the parties exceed the sums the client is liable to pay under the retainer, the balance belongs to the client, not the solicitor. Accordingly, where fixed costs are likely to apply, the retainer should usually provide that if fixed costs apply, the sum charged shall (as a minimum, whether or not also as a maximum) be set at the level of the applicable fixed costs.

Further details in relation to Fixed Costs generally may be found in **Chapter 7.**

---

[39] As to which, see the discussion on this topic in Chapter 7.
[40] Courts & Legal Services Act 1990 s.58(2).
[41] See *Butt v Nizami* [2006] EWHC 159 (QB); [2006] 1 WLR 3307, as approved in *Kilby v Gawith* [2008] EWCA Civ 812; [2009] 1 WLR 853.

Additional liabilities

Further details in relation to additional liabilities and funding options may be found in **Chapter 2**.

9–17

Save in limited circumstances addressed in other chapters, additional liabilities are no longer recoverable on a between the parties basis in relation to funding arrangements entered into on or after 1 April 2013.

In practice, particularly in the context of lower value personal injury litigation, prior to April 2013 it was rare for a client to be charged a success fee where that success fee was not recovered on a between the parties basis, save possibly where a small additional percentage was charged in respect of the delay in payment, as opposed to the risk of the claim winning or losing.

Whilst the charging of an unrecovered success fee to the client was more common in higher value and commercial litigation, it nevertheless remained relatively rare that such success fees ever became subject of a solicitor–client assessment.

The removal of between the parties recoverability is likely to see such success fees being challenged increasingly on a solicitor–client basis.

Rule 46.9 expressly includes a provision (CPR r.46.9(4)) stating that in such circumstances the success fee is to be assessed by reference to all the relevant factors as they reasonably appeared to the solicitor (or counsel) at the time the CFA was entered into or varied (i.e. the same test that applies on a between the parties assessment) though, as noted, on a solicitor–client assessment, the benefit of any residual doubt goes to the benefit of the solicitor.

Accordingly, it will be at least as important as before that the solicitor keeps an accurate risk assessment in order to support any claimed success fee. Indeed, arguably the importance is increased since it is to be reasonably anticipated that the courts may take a harsher line towards the charging of success fees, particularly in lower value claims, where the success fee is being paid by a client or from a client's damages rather than by an opponent.

Of course, in personal injury claims, success fees are subject to maximum limits by reference to percentages of certain types of damages (essentially general damages and past loss) recovered. Nevertheless, it should not be assumed that this 'cap' on the maximum success fee chargeable will necessarily mean that the success fee cannot be challenged as long as it does not exceed that cap.

9–18

For example, if the permitted classes of damages were £20,000 and the success fee, set at 100%, amounted to £5,000 (which is precisely 25% of the prescribed damages, and therefore the 'capped' maximum), it would still be open to the client to argue that the 100% success fee was too high and should be reduced on assessment.

It will therefore be important to ensure that the success fee is set at a reasonable level, that the reasons for doing so are properly recorded, and that the client is made fully aware that the success fee will not be recoverable between the parties but will fall to be paid by the client.

A specific issue in this regard arose in relation to low value personal injury claims involving children (and possibly protected parties), where, pursuant to CPR r.46.4, the general rule is that the court must order a detailed assessment of the costs payable by or out of any money belonging to a child or protected party.

In a number of cases it had been held on such assessments that it is 'unreasonable' to charge the child a success fee and to seek to deduct the same from the child's damages. The precise reasoning for this appears to be legally flawed – CFAs with success fees are a legitimate means of access to justice and the loss of recoverability between the parties was part of a package of reforms, including an increase in general damages, intended to offset (in part at least) the effect of lost recoverability.

9–19   This was a repetition of an early problem following the original introduction of CFAs in 1995, when success fees were not recoverable, which was cured by a specific provision when the CPR was introduced in 1999 (CPR r.48.9(5)), but which was removed in due course because it was thought unnecessary following the introduction of between the parties recoverability of success fees. The short point is that the court should be able to reduce the success fee because it was set at an unreasonable level, but otherwise should not disallow such fees.

The position was, in part, addressed by virtue of the amendment to CPR r.21.12 with effect from 1 April 2015. Rather than the more simplified approach taken under the original 1999 regime, the amendment to CPR r.21.12 imposes limitations on the sums a Litigation Friend is entitled to out of any money recovered on behalf of a protected person.

A different approach is adopted depending on whether or not the damages awarded or agreed exceed £25,000. If they do not, the Litigation Friend's ability to recover costs will be limited to the (reasonable) success fee or sum payable under a Damages Based Agreement. If the sum awarded or agreed exceeds £25,000, a new CPR r.21.12(7) will limit the Litigation Friend's ability to recover costs to a sum not exceeding 25% of general damages and past pecuniary loss. Whether such restrictions are necessary given the ability of the court to scrutinise the reasonableness of costs and expenses and whether these restrictions will have an inhibiting effect on the willingness of individuals to act as Litigation Friends, or solicitors to act for protected persons, remains to be seen.

The decisions of Regional Costs Judge Lumb in the cases of *A&M v Royal Mail Group*[42] may be seen as the courts seeking to explore the proper working of these new arrangements, both in terms of the new procedure and of how to approach the previously rarely asked question of how to assess the reasonableness of success fees which are to be paid out of the damages of child claimants. Two points to note emerge. The first is that the procedure provided for under CPR r.21 and the accompanying Practice Direction—including the provision of proper evidence of why the claimed success fee is said

---

[42] Unreported, Birmingham County Court, 27 August 2015 and 1 October 2015.

to be reasonable – is there to be followed and a failure to follow it may lead to losing the ability to claim the success fee. The second is that the courts cannot be expected to simply 'sign off' on claims for success fees at a high percentage, particularly in low value claims, or to allow a practice whereby a high percentage success fee is routinely applied simply because the client will then be 'protected' by the 25% LASPO 'cap'. The correctness or otherwise of the particular decision in A&M is less important than the message that claims for success fees on a solicitor–client basis, particularly from child or other protected party claimants, will require careful preparation and delicate handling.

There is at least one further problem with CPR r.21.12 and in particular the amendment introduced in 2015 by CPR r.21.12(1A). CPR r.21.12(1A) expressly provides that *'costs recoverable under this rule are limited to. . .costs incurred by or on behalf of a child'*. This is despite the fact that the rest of CPR r.21.12 clearly and expressly refers to the recovery of costs incurred on behalf of a 'child or protected party'. Why CPR r.21.12(1A) then seeks to exclude costs incurred on behalf of a protected party from the ambit of a rule that is otherwise clearly intended to allow such recovery is entirely unclear. On its face, the effect of CPR r.21.12(1A) is to exclude any ability on the court's part to permit a litigation friend (and therefore in practice a solicitor) from recovering 'shortfall' costs from a protected party's damages, even where the court is satisfied that it would otherwise be reasonable to allow this. No explanation is given for this drastic effect in the explanatory memorandum accompanying the statutory instrument or elsewhere[43]. Moreover, as noted, it is inconsistent with the remainder of the rule. However, CPR r.21.12(1A) is unambiguous in its own terms. It is assumed to be an error in drafting. Put simply, the words 'or protected party' appears to have been missed out. However, it may require either a redraft of the rule or the sort of expansive approach to construction of rules exhibited in *Qader*[44] to allow for this to be corrected. In the meantime, it introduces yet another uncertainty for practitioners acting on behalf of protected parties in high value claims.

The introduction of Damages Based Agreements will bring a relatively new aspect to solicitor–client assessments. Although such arrangements have always been possible in non-contentious business, they have been rarely used and whilst a relatively limited number of DBAs appear to have been entered into since April 2013, there is no reported decision yet of a solicitor–client costs dispute in relation to such an agreement[45]. The closest is the decision *in Bolt Burdon v Tariq*, concerning a challenge by the client to a Non Contentious Business Agreement which, in its operation, was similar in terms to a Damages

---

[43] Indeed, it appears to be contrary to the explanation given in the explanatory note to the Civil Procedure (Amendment No. 8) Rules 2014 (SI 2014/3299) and to the explanation of the policy objectives provided at paragraph 7.1(c) of the explanatory memorandum.

[44] *Qader v Esure Services Ltd* [2016] EWCA Civ 1109.

[45] DBAS, the regulations surrounding them and the reasons why they have been little used to date are considered in depth in the Funding Chapter, along with the Civil Justice Council Working Committee's Report and some of the possible future amendments to the rules and regulations surrounding DBAs.

Based Agreement. That agreement was upheld and the Court awarded the solicitor the full amount of the contingent fee.

In contrast with the position in employment cases, there are no specific regulatory requirements for advice to the client prior to the entering into of a DBA and accordingly, given the nature of DBAs, there is substantial scope for argument at the conclusion of the case as to whether the fee claimed was 'reasonable'. Cases will be heavily fact dependent, but where a DBA is used there is a clear requirement for very clear information to be given to the client as to the basis on which any DBA fee is set, for clear records to be kept of cogent reasons for setting the fee at the level chosen and, perhaps above all, for clear written information to be given to the client about the difference between the DBA payment being charged and the basis on which fees might be recovered between the parties if the case is won.

Reference has already been made to the Legal Ombudsman, which has already expressed its critical view as to the lack of clarity of CFAs and its concerns as to the risks of the same with DBAs.[46] Solicitors should not underestimate the need to make the key facts in relation to CFAs and DBAs clear in plain and, if necessary, repeated terms. The present reluctance to use DBAs in light of the poor drafting of the DBA Regulations 2013 should not obscure the fundamental need to ensure a consumer focused approach to the drafting of such agreements and related documentation where they are used.

The introduction of DBAs, the changes to CFAs and the loss of recoverability between the parties of After The Event insurance premiums, together with the likely changes in between the parties costs recovery, mean that the range of funding options available to a client and the permutations in any given case are greater than ever. Whilst the risks have always been present, they are greater than ever and the obligation to give a client proper advice in order to allow the client to make an informed choice as to the appropriate funding option should not be ignored.[47]

Questions and answers

Q1. Have the 'Jackson' reforms changed the basis on which I, as a solicitor, can charge my client?

9–20   No, save that in theory the scope of lawful arrangements has widened to include DBAs. That apart, the ways in which you can agree with your client to pay you remain the same, though the Jackson reforms have had a material effect on whether certain major elements of those costs, primarily the success fee, can be recovered from an opponent.

In personal injury claims, that loss of between the parties recoverability has

---

[46] See Complaints in focus: 'No win, no fee' agreements: http://www.legalombudsman.org.uk/publications/no-win-no-fee/ [Accessed 29 January, 2015].
[47] See *Truex v Kitchin* [2007] EWCA Civ 618 (solicitor's claims for costs disallowed for failure to advise as to the availability of legal aid) and *McDaniel & Co v Clarke* [2014] EWHC 3826 (QB) (solicitor's claim disallowed for failure to advice of availability of trade union funding) for two examples of the dangers.

resulted in a limit being imposed on the maximum amount of the success fee you can charge your client.

Those matters apart, it was beyond the scope of the reforms, for example, to change the indemnity basis for assessment of solicitor client costs and that was neither their intention, nor is it their effect. The basic principle that such costs are to be assessed on the indemnity basis remains, and the core CPR provisions in relation to such an assessment, now at CPR r.46.9, remain unchanged.

However, the anticipated reduction in between the parties costs, combined with the changes in funding methods, including the loss of recoverability of success fees, means that there is likely to be a greater number of cases, in particular in low value claims, where the solicitor seeks to charge a 'shortfall' to the client where, in the past, such a shortfall might not have been charged.

This is likely to bring a more regular and greater scrutiny to such claims, either by the courts or by the Legal Ombudsman.

Accordingly, whilst the basis on which you can charge your client remains largely the same and whist the basis on which such costs will be assessed has not changed, the practical effect is that, particularly in personal injury claims, it is likely to be far more common that the client will be asked to meet some of the costs out of their damages and both as a result of this and other changes it seems probable that claims for 'shortfall' costs will be more regularly disputed than before.

Q2. Can you advise the client of the full range of funding options but then say but we as a firm do not offer X, or Y or only offer X or Y on this basis?
Yes. This was a common situation with publicly funded cases (when public   **9–21** funding was more widely available).

A solicitor's duty is to consider, at the outset (i.e. at the time the client first seeks to instruct the firm) what forms of funding are reasonably available to the client and to advise the client accordingly. This includes advising the client that there may be other forms of funding available which the firm does not provide. This may include public funding or may, in certain circumstances, include other forms of funding such as CFAs or DBAs which the firm may not offer.

Section IB(1.16) of the Solicitors' Code of Conduct 2011 indicates that the solicitor should discuss with the client how the client will pay, including whether public funding may be available, whether the client has insurance that might cover the fees and whether the fees may be paid by someone else, such as a trade union. This should not be treated as an exhaustive list, nor indeed as a list that applies in full in every case. It is an indication only and, as with many examples in this context, is particularly suited to personal injury claims.

The ultimate requirement is to treat the client fairly and to ensure that the solicitor complies with the duty to act in their best interests, even if that might mean advising them of a form of funding which the firm does not offer which means that the client chooses to instruct a different firm.

Provided this is done, it is entirely proper to indicate that if the client wishes to instruct the firm the only terms which the firm is prepared to offer are the X or Y referred to.

Q3. My case is subject to costs management. Am I required to seek my client's approval to the budget and does the budget, if agreed or approved, limit the costs I can charge my client?

9–22   In answer to the first part of the question, no. There was some discussion of a requirement for the client to sign the budget, or the solicitor to confirm the client's agreement to the budget, but this did not make it into the final rules.

However, as a matter of practice, it is important that the client is aware of the likely costs of the claim and of how the costs which might be recovered from the opponent relate to the cost that the solicitor is likely to charge the client. It is also important that the client is made aware of how the likely costs of the claim might impact on the conduct of his claim. For example, if, as a result of the costs being seen to be disproportionate on a between the parties basis, the scope or extent of witness or expert evidence is likely to be restricted, the client needs to be made aware of the reasons for this and the options available to address it.

The client should be receiving regular costs estimates and updates on a solicitor–client basis anyway and differences between these and the between the parties budget should be highlighted so that the client has an informed choice as to whether or not to incur the additional costs.

As to the second part of the question, again the answer is 'no', unless the solicitor–client retainer is such that the costs chargeable to the client are limited to sums recovered between the parties. Even then, the final effect will not be known until the end of the case, when it is known whether the client has won, what costs order has been made, whether indemnity costs are awarded (CPR r.3.18) and whether, if the budget applies, the budget is to be departed from for any 'good reason' (CPR r.3.18). In any event, the budget only 'bites' on costs from the date of the budget (CPR r.3 PD 3 E para.7.4 – subject to clarification of the Court of Appeal's decision in SARPD[48]).

Q4. Do the revised rules on Part 36 apply in a solicitor–client assessment?

9–23   There is a lack of clarity in this regard. There is a primary statutory provision dealing with the incidence of costs at the conclusion of a statutory assessment of solicitor–client costs, namely s.70(9) of the Solicitors Act 1974.

This provision cannot be, and has not been, displaced by CPR Pt 36 and continues to apply. However, that provision is subject to s.70(1), whereby the court can depart from the otherwise mandated outcome if there are 'special circumstances' (as to which, see *Wilsons Solicitors LLP v Bentine*, supra). It seems

---

[48] *SARPD Oil International Ltd v Addax Energy SA* [2016 EWCA Civ 120, [2016] QP Rep 24, discussed in detail in **Chapter 4**.

to be increasingly accepted that the making of effective offers by the parties to the assessment is capable in principle, dependent upon the particular facts, of amounting to a special circumstances, and this would appear to fit with the ethos of both the CPR generally and the Jackson reforms in encouraging the making of offers to compromise disputes at an early and less costly stage.[49]

Accordingly, the making of a Part 36 offer may, on the facts of a case, be capable of amounting to a special circumstance, but the automatic provisions of CPR r.36.10 and CPR r.36.14 do not appear to apply because they conflict with s.70(9).

Whether a successful Part 36 offer therefore attracts any greater benefit than a Calderbank offer is open to argument. Given that the full rubric of Part 36 cannot apply, and Part 36 is intended to be a complete and self-contained code, it seems more likely that a successful Part 36 offer should be treated as an admissible offer under the court's general discretion under r.44.2(4)(c), assuming that the automatic consequences under s.70(9) do not apply.

In 'common law' assessments (i.e. those which are based on a common law right to dispute the reasonableness of a claim for unpaid fees, rather than assessments under s.70 of the Solicitors Act 1974) Part 36 would appear to apply and to be an important aspect of any such claim—see *Ahmud v MacPherson* (above).

Q5. Can we charge/recover for preparing the solicitor–client estimate?

It is assumed that this question refers to the costs of provision of costs infor-   **9–24**
mation to the client rather than the costs of preparing a Precedent H for the purposes of between the parties costs management, which are limited by CPR r.3 PD 3 E, para.7.2.

The (reasonable) costs of preparing such a between the parties Precedent H will, of course, form part of the costs payable by the client.

Time reasonably spent advising the client in relation to their own costs, whether by way of costs estimates, funding arrangements or the like should ordinarily form a part of the charges payable by the client. However, there will be a limit on the extent to which such time is recoverable. It is to be expected that solicitors have systems in place which allow them to properly record, monitor and analyse time spent and the cost of these is an overhead. The court will not expect that, save in exceptional cases, the solicitor will have to spend substantial time providing an initial estimate or updating that in due course.

Q6. It is still not clear how solicitors should go about doing estimates of costs for their clients and the extent to which Precedent H is sufficient/useful for this purpose. Can you express a view?

A solicitor must provide a clear explanation to a client of the solicitor's   **9–25**
fees and if and when they are likely to change (Solicitors Code of Conduct

---

[49] As an aside, similar principles developed under the CPR, such as penalising a party in costs for failing to negotiate also seem to be capable of being 'special circumstances' – see *Allen v Colman Coyle LLP* [2007] EWHC 90075 (Costs).

2011 IB 1.14). This information must be given in a clear and accessible form which is appropriate to the client's circumstances and needs (IB 1.19). It is particularly important that they receive the best possible information, both at the time of the engagement and as their matter progresses, about the likely overall cost of their matter (O1.13).

Taking these requirements and indicative behaviours collectively, best practice would require the provision of an estimate and costs benefit analysis at the start of any retainer, together with regular updates and revisions of the estimate, particularly when there are any material changes which might affect the likely costs or the costs benefit analysis.

Precedent H produced for the between the parties costs management process may be a useful tool in this process and it may well be that some solicitors develop a practice of using a Precedent H type model to provide costs estimates to their clients from the outset of cases, particularly following the introduction of J Codes. However, care must be taken to make the client aware of any differences between the amounts set out in the between the parties Precedent H and the sums that the client may be required to pay.

Where a budget is agreed or approved on a between the parties basis, the client should be made aware of any differences between the sums agreed or approved and those which were sought and as to the client's liability for such sums (if any).

Index

Abuse of process
indemnity costs, 7–20
Adjudication
alternative dispute resolution, 5–35
After the event insurance
appeals, 2–36
change of solicitor, 2–28
generally, 2–10—2–11
increased premiums, 2–33
insolvency of one of two claimants,
2–35
quantum report costs, 2–34
questions and answers, 2–32—2–36
staged premiums, 2–32
Allocation
case management, 4–07
Alternative dispute resolution
adjudication, 5–35
advantages, 5–27
arbitration, 5–36
arbitration costs assessments, 5–86
consumer disputes, 5–79
early neutral evaluation, 5–33
encouragement, 5–26
expert determination, 5–34
generally, 5–26
mediation
Commercial Court, 5–32
generally, 5–31—5–32
negotiation, 5–30
overview, 1–09
questions and answers, 5–79—5–82,
5–85—5–86
Arbitration
advantages, 5–27
consumer disputes, 5–79
costs assessments, 5–86
encouragement of ADR, 5–26
generally, 5–36
questions and answers, 5–79, 5–86
success fees, 2–56
third party funding, 2–47
Assessment of costs
see Costs assessments
Before the event insurance
qualified one-way costs shifting, 6–16

Bills of costs
new bill of costs pilot scheme, 1–16,
8–23
***Calderbank* letters**
generally, 5–28, 5–78
qualified one-way costs shifting, 6–27
Case management
see also **Costs management**
changes to existing CPR provisions
allocation of claims, 4–07
concurrent hearing of experts' oral
evidence, 4–12
costs management, 4–14—4–21
directions questionnaires, 4–06
disclosure provisions, 4–09
enforcing compliance with orders,
rules and PDs, 4–03—4–05
generally, 4–02
incentives for making settlement
proposals, 4–13
information about proposed expert
evidence, 4–11
standardised directions, 4–08
witness statements, 4–10
costs management, relationship with,
4–22
introduction, 4–01
proportionality, 3–09
qualified one-way costs shifting, 6–29
questions and answers
claim within fast-track limits but trial
exceeding one day, 4–109
costs capping, 4–111
litigants in person, 4–110
relief from sanctions, 4–107—4–108
Compliance
case management, 4–03—4–05
Conditional fee agreements
amendment, 2–23—2–25
assignment, 2–20—2–22
backdating, 2–23
changing from legal aid to CFA,
2–26—2–27
consumer regulations, 2–62
costs capped as percentage of damages,
2–31

costs of drafting and negotiating, 2–64
death of claimant, 2–30
generally, 2–02
implementation issues, 2–08—2–09
naming all defendants, 2–29
notification requirements, 2–07,
    2–37—2–45
personal injury claims additional
    requirements, 2–04—2–06
qualified one-way costs shifting,
    6–19—6–20, 6–23
questions and answers
    CFA terms, 2–29—2–31
    success fees, 2–48—2–57
    transfer and variation of funding,
        2–20—2–27
success fees
    arbitration, 2–56
    calculation, 2–48
    defamation claims, 2–55
    group claims where claimants added
        post-commencement, 2–51
    human rights, 2–57
    insolvency proceedings, 2–52—2–54
    interim hearings, success at, 2–49
    provisional assessment, 8–34
    questions and answers, 2–48—2–57
    solicitor's CFA pre-commencement/
        counsel's post-commencement,
        2–50
    terms, 2–29—2–31
    transfer, 2–20—2–22
    transitional provisions, 2–03
    variation, 2–23—2–25
Consent orders
    Part 36 offers, 5–54
Consumer contracts
    alternative dispute resolution, 5–79
    conditional fee agreements, 2–62
Costs assessments
    arbitration, 5–86
    costs management
        basis of assessment, 4–100
        budget without prejudice to
            assessment, 4–99
        budgeted sum exceeding sum due
            under retainer, 4–106
        costs sanctions for unreasonable
            conduct, 4–102
        effect of CMO, 4–20—4–21, 4–98
        "good reason" to depart from budget,
            4–103—4–105
        indemnity costs, 4–100—4–101

detailed assessment
    additional amount, 8–42
    costs of assessment, 8–42—8–43
    determination of disbursements, 8–43
    generally, 8–06
    Part 36 offers, 5–25, 5–68, 5–73, 5–77
    qualified one-way costs shifting,
        8–25
    questions and answers, 8–25—8–26,
        8–42—8–43
    sanctions on failure to make open
        offer, 8–26
introduction, 8–01
payments on account
    departure from general rule, 8–47
    generally, 8–13
    orders other than at hearing awarding
        costs, 8–48
    proportionality, 8–45
    questions and answers, 8–44—8–48
    reasonable sum, 8–44
    statements of costs, 8–46
proportionality, 3–10
provisional assessment
    additional liabilities, 8–28
    compliance, 8–12
    costs cap, 8–37—8–41
    costs of assessment, 8–36—8–41
    indemnity costs, 8–35
    introduction, 8–07
    oral hearings, 8–11, 8–36
    post-assessment procedure, 8–10
    pre-assessment, 8–08
    procedure, 8–09
    proportionality cross-check, 8–33
    questions and answers, 8–28—8–41
    replies to points of dispute, 8–29
    sanctions for failure to file documents,
        8–31—8–32
    success fees, 8–34
    supporting documents/papers, 8–30
    VAT, 8–27
questions and answers
    costs of detailed assessment and
        additional amounts, 8–42—8–43
    costs of provisional assessment,
        8–36—8–41
    payments on account, 8–44—8–48
    provisional assessment, 8–28—8–41
    summary and detailed assessment,
        8–14—8–26
solicitor and client costs, 9–07—9–08,
    9–10

summary assessment
  change of emphasis, 8–05
  costs budget, 8–19—8–20
  costs of providing breakdown, 8–24
  document time, 8–17
  fast track trials, 8–21
  generally, 8–02
  judges, 8–22
  N260 filed late or not filed,
    8–14—8–16
  new bill of costs pilot scheme, 8–23
  proportionality cross-check, 8–18
  questions and answers, 8–14—8–24
  service of statement of costs, 8–04
  statements of costs, 8–03, 8–14—8–16
Costs budgets
  see also **Costs management**
  solicitor and client costs
    client approval, 9–22
    generally, 9–11—9–13
    limitation on charges, 9–22
  summary assessment, 8–19—8–20
Costs capping orders
  case management, 4–111
  IPEC claims, 7–17
Costs estimates
  charging for costs of preparation, 9–24
  generally, 9–25
Costs management
  approval and agreement of budgets
    absurdly low budgets, 4–60
    contesting costs in budgets, 4–71
    costs lawyers attending CCMC, 4–64
    directions, 4–63
    disbursements and fees, division
      between, 4–78
    dispensing with CCMC hearings, 4–62
    disproportionate agreed sums, 4–77
    hourly rates, 4–72—4–76
    incurred costs, 4–65—4–71
    proportionality and reasonableness,
      4–61
    re-filing budgets after CMO made,
      4–79
  assessment
    basis of assessment, 4–100
    budget without prejudice to
      assessment, 4–99
    budgeted sum exceeding sum due
      under retainer, 4–85, 4–106
    costs sanctions for unreasonable
      conduct, 4–102
    effect of CMO, 4–20—4–21, 4–98

"good reason" to depart from budget,
    4–103—4–105
  indemnity costs, 4–100—4–101
assumptions, 4–47—4–48
budget discussion reports, 4–58—4–59
case management, relationship with,
  4–22
cases subject to costs management, 4–15
Chancery Division cases, 4–25
change of solicitor, 4–82
client instructions to incur costs not in
  budget, 4–84
composite summaries, 4–55
contesting costs in budgets, 4–71
contingencies, 4–45—4–46
costs lawyers attending CCMC, 4–64
costs sanctions for unreasonable
  conduct, 4–102
detailed assessment proceedings, 4–34
directions, 4–63
disbursements and fees, division
  between, 4–78
dispensation by agreement, 4–26
dispensing with CCMC hearings, 4–62
disposal stage after default judgment,
  4–27
disproportionate agreed sums, 4–77
effect of CMO on subsequent
  assessment, 4–20—4–21, 4–98
"good reason" to depart from budget,
  4–94, 4–103—4–105
grounds of dispute, 4–57
hourly rates, 4–72—4–76
how the court "costs manages", 4–18
incurred costs, 4–65—4–71
indemnity costs
  assessment, 4–100—4–101
  contractual right, 4–33
  relevance of CMOs, 7–22
interim applications
  summary judgment applications, 4–95
  variation of budgets, 4–97
  work undertaken, 4–49
introduction, 4–14
landlord and tenant claims, 4–29
life expectancy of claimant, 4–31
litigants in person, 4–24, 4–87
monitoring budgets, 4–81
multi-track
  provisional allocation, 4–32
  re-allocation from fast track, 4–86
overview, 1–11
Part 8 claims, 4–28

Part 36 offers, 4–89
possession claims, 4–30
Precedent H
  additional claims, 4–52
  assumptions, 4–47—4–48
  content, 4–40—4–54
  contingencies, 4–45—4–46
  email filing, 4–38
  extensions of time, 4–37
  failure to file, 4–39
  interim applications, work undertaken
    on, 4–49
  items in wrong place, 4–50
  J-Codes and other time recording
    systems, 4–44
  litigants in person, 4–24
  multiple defendants represented by
    same solicitors, 4–53
  overestimation vs underestimation,
    4–51
  prescribed form, 4–40
  split trials, 4–43
  surveillance evidence costs, 4–54
  time for filing and exchanging,
    4–36—4–39
  variation of budgets, 4–96
  versions, 4–41—4–42
pre-trial checklist, further budget with,
  4–88
procedural requirements imposed on
  parties, 4–16—4–17
proportionality, 4–61
qualified one-way costs shifting, 6–29
questions and answers
  approval and agreement of budgets,
    4–60—4–79
  content of Precedent H, 4–40—4–54
  post costs management order general
    issues, 4–80—4–89
  preparation for CCMC, 4–55—4–59
  relevance of budget at subsequent
    assessment, 4–98—4–106
  scope of costs management scheme,
    4–23—4–35
  time for filing and exchanging
    Precedent H, 4–36—4–39
  variation of budgets and freestanding
    costs orders, 4–90—4–97
reasonableness, 4–61
re-allocation from fast track to multi-
  track, 4–86
re-filing budgets after CMO made, 4–79
scope of scheme, 4–23—4–35

Shorter Trials Pilot Scheme, 4–35
solicitor recovering more than budget
  from client, 4–85, 4–106
split trials, 4–43
standard directions, 4–56
sum to which percentages apply, 4–83
surveillance evidence costs, 4–54
variation of budgets
  agreement between parties, 4–91
  appeals, 4–93
  generally, 4–19
  "good reason" argument at assessment
    stage, 4–94
  interim applications, 4–97
  parties unhappy with amount set by
    court, 4–80
  prospective vs retrospective variation,
    4–94
  repeated variations, 4–92
  significant developments, 4–90
  summary judgment applications, 4–95
  version of Precedent H, 4–96
  without prejudice budget discussions,
    4–58, 4–99
Counterclaims
Part 36 offers, 5–40, 5–42, 5–55
Damages-based agreements
between the parties costs recovery,
  2–16
change from CFA to DBA, 2–59
enforceability in non-employment
  matters, 2–60
future amendment, 2–18
generally, 2–13—2–15
hybrid DBAs, 2–58
immediate right to payment, 2–61
notice of funding, 2–39
overview, 1–13
problems, 2–17
questions and answers, 2–58—2–61
Defamation claims
success fees, 2–55
Detailed assessment
additional amount, 8–42
costs of assessment, 8–42—8–43
determination of disbursements, 8–43
generally, 8–06
Part 36 offers, 5–25, 5–68, 5–73, 5–77
qualified one-way costs shifting, 8–25
questions and answers, 8–25—8–26,
  8–42—8–43
sanctions on failure to make open offer,
  8–26

Directions questionnaires
case management, 4–06
Disbursements
approval and agreement of budgets,
4–78
detailed assessment, 8–43
Disclosure
case management, 4–09
Discontinuance
qualified one-way costs shifting,
6–25—6–26
Dishonesty
offers to settle, 5–29
Early neutral evaluation
alternative dispute resolution, 5–33
EL/PL Protocol
see **Pre-action protocols**
Expert determination
alternative dispute resolution, 5–34
Expert evidence
concurrent hearing of experts' oral
evidence, 4–12
information about proposed expert
evidence, 4–11
Fixed costs
background, 7–01
costs cap in IPEC claims, 7–17
costs orders for more than fixed costs,
7–15
EL/PL Protocol, 7–03—7–05
future developments, 7–12
generally, 7–01
litigants in person, 7–18
multi-party disputes, 7–14
overview, 1–15
possession claims, 7–19
questions and answers, 7–12—7–15
relationship with assessed costs and Part
36 costs, 7–16
retainer arrangements, 7–13
RTA Protocol, 7–02
solicitor and client costs, 9–16
Fraud
offers to settle, 5–29
Funding arrangements
after the event insurance
appeals, 2–36
change of solicitor, 2–28
generally, 2–10—2–11
increased premiums, 2–33
insolvency of one of two claimants,
2–35
quantum report costs, 2–34

questions and answers, 2–32—2–36
staged premiums, 2–32
conditional fee agreements
amendment, 2–23—2–25
assignment, 2–20—2–22
backdating, 2–23
changing from legal aid to CFA,
2–26—2–27
consumer regulations, 2–62
costs capped as percentage of
damages, 2–31
costs of drafting and negotiating, 2–64
death of claimant, 2–30
generally, 2–02
implementation issues, 2–08—2–09
naming all defendants, 2–29
notification requirements, 2–07,
2–37—2–45
personal injury claims additional
requirements, 2–04—2–06
questions and answers, 2–20—2–27,
2–29—2–31
success fees, 2–48—2–57
terms, 2–29—2–31
transfer, 2–20—2–22
transitional provisions, 2–03
variation, 2–23—2–25
damages-based agreements
between the parties costs recovery,
2–16
change from CFA to DBA, 2–59
enforceability in non-employment
matters, 2–60
future amendment, 2–18
generally, 2–13—2–15
hybrid DBAs, 2–58
immediate right to payment, 2–61
notice of funding, 2–39
problems, 2–17
questions and answers, 2–58—2–61
introduction, 2–01
proportionality, 2–63
questions and answers
after the event insurance, 2–32—2–36
CFA terms, 2–29—2–31
consumer regulations, 2–62
damages-based agreements,
2–58—2–61
funding costs, 2–64
issue and notification, 2–37—2–45
proportionality, 2–63
success fees, 2–48—2–57
third party funding, 2–46—2–47

transfer and variation of funding,
2–20—2–28
third party funding
arbitration, 2–47
generally, 2–19
notification to opponent, 2–46
questions and answers, 2–46—2–47
Group litigation
success fees, 2–51
Hourly fees
costs management, 4–72—4–76
Human rights
success fees, 2–57
Indemnity basis
abuse of process, 7–20
costs management
assessment, 4–100—4–101
contractual right to indemnity costs,
4–33
relevance of CMOs, 7–22
generally, 7–06—7–07
litigants in person, 7–26
losing party winning on some issues,
7–23
proportionality, 3–16
provisional assessment, 8–35
questions and answers, 7–20—7–23
third party funding, 7–21
unreasonable conduct, 7–20
Insolvency proceedings
success fees, 2–52—2–54
Intellectual Property Enterprise Court
fixed costs, 7–17
Part 36 offers, 5–69
Interest
Part 36 offers, 5–15—5–16, 5–23, 5–62
Interim applications
success fees, 2–49
summary judgment applications, 4–95
variation of budgets, 4–97
work undertaken, 4–49
Landlord and tenant claims
costs management, 4–29
Life expectancy
costs management, 4–31
Litigants in person
case management, 4–110
costs management, 4–24, 4–87
fixed costs, 7–18
generally, 7–08—7–09
indemnity costs, 7–26
interim payments to pay for
representation, 7–30

leeway where non-compliance, 7–28
LLP firms of solicitors, 7–27
McKenzie friends
companies, 7–29
generally, 7–10—7–11
public access, 7–25
qualified one-way costs shifting, 6–23
questions and answers, 7–24—7–30
solicitor/barrister acting on own behalf,
7–24
Litigation funding agreements
arbitration, 2–47
generally, 2–19
indemnity costs, 7–21
notification to opponent, 2–46
overview, 1–14
questions and answers, 2–46—2–47
McKenzie friends
companies, 7–29
generally, 7–10—7–11
Mediation
advantages, 5–27
Commercial Court, 5–32
consumer disputes, 5–79
disadvantages, 5–81—5–82
encouragement of ADR, 5–26
generally, 5–31
questions and answers, 5–79—5–82,
5–85
refusal to mediate, 5–80, 5–85
Motor Insurers' Bureau
qualified one-way costs shifting,
6–24
Multi-party disputes
fixed costs, 7–14
N260
see **Statements of costs**
Necessity
proportionality, 3–14
Negotiation
settlement, 5–30
Notices of discontinuance
qualified one-way costs shifting,
6–25—6–26
Offers to settle
see **Part 36 offers; Settlement**
Part 8 claims
costs management, 4–28
Part 36 offers
see also **Settlement**
acceptance
acceptance by some but not all
defendants, 5–57

acceptance while service reserved,
5–44
costs consequences, 5–13, 5–52—5–56
generally, 5–09
offers made by some but not all
defendants, 5–10—5–11, 5–43
split trials, 5–12, 5–51
when notice of acceptance treated as
accepted, 5–47
admissions payments, 5–61
appeal proceedings, 5–05
background to Part 36, 5–02
basis of assessment, 5–65
cap on costs, 5–63
change of terms
change before expiry of relevant
period, 5–08, 5–47
generally, 5–07, 5–50
clarification, 5–46
consent orders, 5–54
content, 5–06, 5–38—5–39
costs management, 4–89
counterclaims, 5–40, 5–42, 5–55
detailed assessment, 5–25, 5–68, 5–73,
5–77
expiry, 5–39
failure to comply with accepted offer,
5–58
form, 5–06, 5–38—5–39
genuine attempts to settle, 5–70
interest, 5–15—5–16, 5–23, 5–62
introduction, 5–01
IPEC damages cap, 5–69
liability only, 5–39
"more advantageous" judgment,
5–17—5–19, 5–61—5–62
multiple offers in one Part 36 offer, 5–39
multiple parties
acceptance by some but not all
defendants, 5–57
apportionment of settlement sum
between multiple claimants, 5–41
multi-party disputes, 5–60
offers made by some but not all
defendants, 5–43
non-monetary terms, 5–39
overview, 1–10
Part 36
background, 5–01
post-5/4/15 provisions, 5–04
transitional provisions, 5–03
Part 44, 5–67
Privy Council proceedings, 5–37

protected parties, 5–59
qualified one-way costs shifting, 6–27
questions and answers
acceptance by some but not all
defendants, 5–57
acceptance while service reserved,
5–44
additional amount where offer made
less than 21 days before trial, 5–64
admissions payments, 5–61
apportionment of settlement sum
between multiple claimants, 5–41
basis of assessment, 5–65
cap on costs, 5–63
clarification of offers, 5–46
consent orders, 5–54
content of offers, 5–38—5–39
costs budget not filed on time, 5–56
costs consequences of acceptance,
5–52—5–56
counterclaims, 5–40, 5–42, 5–55
detailed assessment, 5–68, 5–73, 5–77
effect of Part 36.5, 5–39
expiry of offers, 5–39
failure to comply with accepted offer,
5–58
genuine attempts to settle, 5–70
interest, 5–62
IPEC damages cap, 5–69
liability only, 5–39
"more advantageous" judgment,
5–61—5–62
multi-party disputes, 5–60
multiple offers in one Part 36 offer,
5–39
non-monetary terms, 5–39
offers made after issue but before
service, 5–76
offers made by some but not all
defendants, 5–43
offers made during stay of
proceedings, 5–45
open offers in detailed assessment,
5–77
Part 44, 5–67
Privy Council proceedings, 5–37
proceedings determined early, 5–66
protected parties, 5–59
second offer after rejection of earlier
offer, 5–48—5–49
service of expert reports out of time,
5–72
setting off costs, 5–71

small claims, 5–39, 5–75
split trials, 5–51
when notice of acceptance treated as
accepted, 5–47
withdrawal of offer at same time as
purported acceptance, 5–50
without prejudice communications,
reference to, 5–74
RTA Protocol and EL/PL Protocol
costs consequences following
judgment, 5–23
costs of detailed assessment
proceedings, 5–25
deduction of benefits, 5–24
introduction, 5–22
second offer after rejection of earlier
offer, 5–48—5–49
setting off costs, 5–71
small claims, 5–39, 5–75
solicitor and client costs, 9–23
split trials, 5–12, 5–51
stay of proceedings, offers made during,
5–45
summary judgment, 5–66
transitional provisions, 5–03
unaccepted offers
costs consequences following
judgment, 5–15—5–16
costs in the case, 5–20
"more advantageous" judgment,
5–17—5–19
offeror's costs limited to court fees,
5–21
restriction on disclosure of Part 36
offer, 5–14
withdrawal
generally, 5–07
withdrawal at same time as purported
acceptance, 5–50
withdrawal before expiry of relevant
period, 5–08, 5–47
without prejudice communications
reference to without prejudice
communications, 5–74
restriction on disclosure of Part 36
offer, 5–14
Payments on account
departure from general rule, 8–47
generally, 8–13
orders other than at hearing awarding
costs, 8–48
proportionality, 8–45
questions and answers, 8–44—8–48

reasonable sum, 8–44
statements of costs, 8–46
Personal injury claims
see also **Qualified one-way costs
shifting**
fixed costs
EL/PL Protocol, 7–03—7–05
questions and answers, 7–12—7–15
RTA Protocol, 7–02
Part 36 offers
costs consequences following
judgment, 5–23
costs of detailed assessment
proceedings, 5–25
deduction of benefits, 5–24
introduction, 5–22
Pilot schemes
costs management in Shorter Trials Pilot
Scheme, 4–35
new bill of costs scheme, 1–16, 8–23
Possession claims
costs management, 4–30
fixed costs, 7–19
Pre-action protocols
EL/PL Protocol
fixed costs, 7–03—7–05
Part 36 offers, 5–22—5–25
RTA Protocol
fixed costs, 7–02
Part 36 offers, 5–22—5–25
Precedent H
see **Costs management**
Privy Council
Part 36 offers, 5–37
Proportionality
advising clients, 3–20—3–23
application of principle, 3–15
changing determinations throughout
life of case, 3–17
concept, 3–02
conduct of parties
assessment stage, 3–10
case/costs management stage, 3–09
generally, 3–08
costs exceeding sums in dispute, 3–12
costs management, 4–61
cross-check at assessment, 3–18—3–19
effect on litigation, 3–05
funding arrangements, 2–63
indemnity costs, 3–16
introduction, 3–01
meaning, 3–03—3–04
necessity, 3–14

outcomes, 3–20—3–23
overview, 1–08
payments on account, 8–45
provisional assessment, 8–33
questions and answers
  extent of proportionality
    considerations, 3–15—3–17
  outcomes and solicitor/client
    relationship, 3–20—3–23
  practical implications at assessment,
    3–18—3–19
  proportionality test, 3–06—3–10
  reasonableness and necessity,
    3–11—3–14
reasonableness, 3–11—3–13
solicitor and client costs, 9–14
summary assessment, 8–18
sums claimed and sums recovered,
  3–07
transitional provisions, 3–06
when the issue arises, 3–03—3–04
Protected parties
  Part 36 offers, 5–59
Provisional assessment
  additional liabilities, 8–28
  compliance, 8–12
  costs cap, 8–37—8–41
  costs of assessment, 8–36—8–41
  indemnity costs, 8–35
  introduction, 8–07
  oral hearings, 8–11, 8–36
  post-assessment procedure, 8–10
  pre-assessment, 8–08
  procedure, 8–09
  proportionality cross-check, 8–33
  questions and answers, 8–27—8–48
  replies to points of dispute, 8–29
  sanctions for failure to file documents,
    8–31—8–32
  success fees, 8–34
  supporting documents/papers, 8–30
  VAT, 8–27
Qualified one-way costs shifting
  before the event insurance, 6–16
  claims with PI and non-PI element,
    6–15
  clinical negligence claims, 6–22
  costs incurred pre-commencement, 6–17
  costs management, 6–29
  detailed assessment, 8–25
  discontinuance of claims
    availability of QOCS protection, 6–26
    wasted costs orders, 6–25

effect of rules, 6–07—6–13
future developments, 6–30
introduction, 6–01—6–02
litigants in person, 6–23
MIB claims, 6–24
non-PI claims, 6–21
overview, 1–12
post-commencement funding
  arrangement with different solicitors,
  6–18
pre-commencement CFAs, 6–19—6–20,
  6–23
questions and answers
  circumstances in which QOCS applies,
    6–15—6–24
  costs management, 6–29
  future developments, 6–30
  QOCS in practice, 6–25—6–26
  set-off, 6–28
  settlement offers, 6–27
scope of rules, 6–04—6–06
set-off, 6–28
settlement offers, 6–27
wider use, 6–14, 6–30
Reasonableness
  costs management, 4–61
  proportionality, 3–11—3–13
Retainers
  budgeted sum exceeding sum due under
    retainer, 4–85, 4–106
  fixed costs, 7–13
  solicitor and client costs, 9–03—9–04
RTA Protocol
  see **Pre-action protocols**
Set-off
  Part 36 offers, 5–71
  qualified one-way costs shifting, 6–28
Settlement
  see also **Part 36 offers**
  alternative dispute resolution
    adjudication, 5–35
    advantages, 5–27
    arbitration, 5–36
    arbitration costs assessments, 5–86
    consumer disputes, 5–79
    early neutral evaluation, 5–33
    encouragement, 5–26
    expert determination, 5–34
    generally, 5–26
    mediation, 5–31—5–32
    negotiation, 5–30
    questions and answers, 5–79—5–82,
      5–85—5–86

Calderbank offers
  generally, 5–28, 5–78
  qualified one-way costs shifting,
    6–27
case management, 4–13
fraud and dishonesty in making offers,
  5–29
introduction, 5–01
negotiation, 5–30
offers to settle
  fraud and dishonesty, 5–29
  generally, 5–28
  questions and answers, 5–78
open offers, 5–28
options when all issues resolved except
  costs, 5–83—5–84
qualified one-way costs shifting, 6–27
questions and answers
  alternative dispute resolution,
    5–79—5–82, 5–85—5–86
  Calderbank offers, 5–78
  options when all issues resolved
    except costs, 5–83—5–84
Shorter Trials Pilot Scheme
costs management, 4–35
Small claims
Part 36 offers, 5–39, 5–75
Solicitor and client costs
advising clients on funding options,
  9–21
assessment, 9–07—9–08, 9–10
basis of charging clients, 9–20
costs budgets
  client approval, 9–22
  generally, 9–11—9–13
  limitation on charges, 9–22
costs estimates
  charging for costs of preparation, 9–24
  generally, 9–25
disputes, 9–07—9–08
effect of Jackson reforms
  additional liabilities, 9–17—9–19
  changes to assessment procedural
    rules, 9–10
  costs budgets, 9–11—9–13
  fixed costs, 9–16
  introduction, 9–09
  proportionality, 9–14
  wider effect of reforms, 9–15
entitlement to payment
  assessment and disputes, 9–07—9–08
  generally, 9–05—9–06
introduction, 9–01

overview, 9–02
Part 36 offers, 9–23
questions and answers, 9–20—9–25
retainers, 9–03—9–04
Split trials
costs management, 4–43
Part 36 offers, 5–12, 5–51
Standard directions
case management, 4–08
costs management, 4–56
Statements of costs
payments on account, 8–46
summary assessment
  filed late or not filed, 8–14—8–16
  generally, 8–03
  service, 8–04
Stay of proceedings
Part 36 offers, 5–45
Success fees
arbitration, 2–56
calculation, 2–48
defamation claims, 2–55
group claims where claimants added
  post-commencement, 2–51
human rights, 2–57
insolvency proceedings, 2–52—2–54
interim hearings, success at, 2–49
provisional assessment, 8–34
questions and answers, 2–48—2–57
solicitor's CFA pre-commencement/
  counsel's post-commencement,
  2–50
Summary assessment
change of emphasis, 8–05
costs budget, 8–19—8–20
costs of providing breakdown, 8–24
document time, 8–17
fast track trials, 8–21
generally, 8–02
judges, 8–22
new bill of costs pilot scheme, 8–23
proportionality cross-check, 8–18
questions and answers, 8–14—8–24
statements of costs
  filed late or not filed, 8–14—8–16
  generally, 8–03
  service, 8–04
Summary judgments
Part 36 offers, 5–66
Surveillance
costs management, 4–54
Third party funding
see **Litigation funding agreements**

Unreasonable conduct
 indemnity costs, 7–20
 refusal to mediate, 5–80, 5–85
Variation of budgets
 see **Costs management**
Without prejudice communications
 costs budget discussions, 4–58, 4–99
 offers to settle
  Calderbank offers, 5–28, 5–78

 fraud and dishonesty, 5–29
 generally, 5–28
Part 36 offers
 reference to without prejudice
  communications, 5–74
 restriction on disclosure of Part 36
  offer, 5–14
Witness statements
 case management, 4–10